MACRO PHOTOGRAPHY

THE UNIVERSE AT OUR FEET

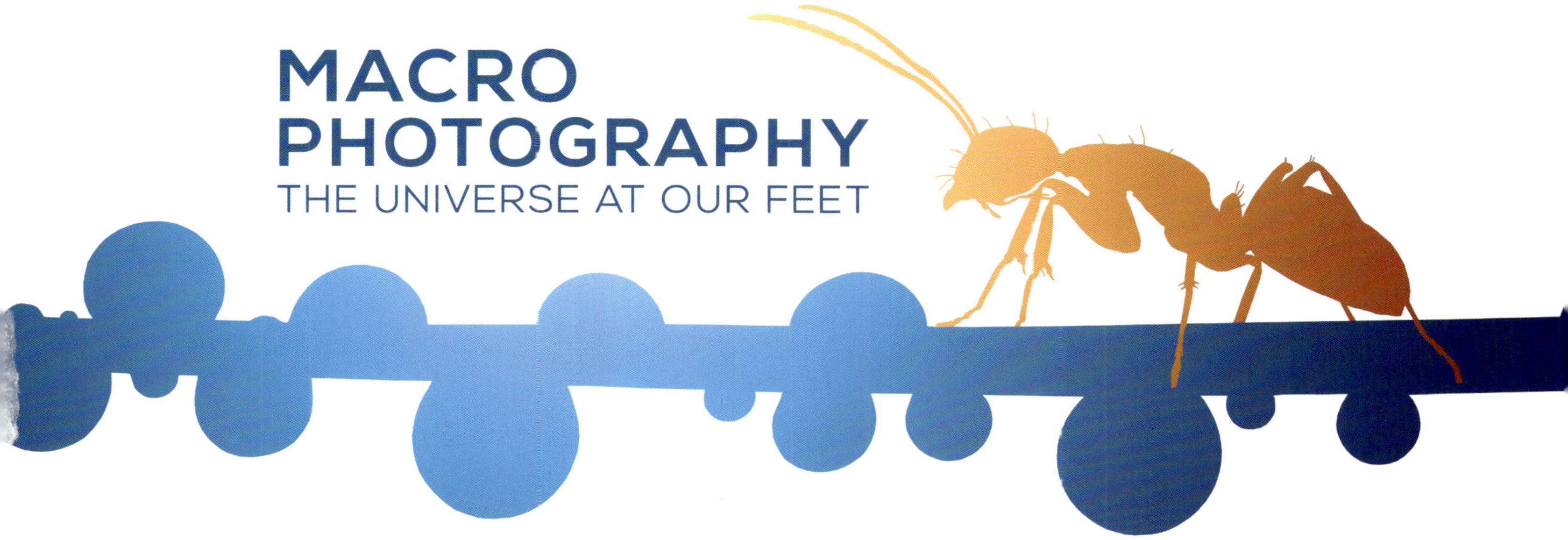

Don Komarechka

Acknowledgements

Thanks to everyone who helped fund the production of this book. This project was made possible by the crowd-funding efforts of thousands of people, including the overwhelming kindness of many strangers. Without constant encouragement and support from family and friends, this book would never have become a reality. My deepest thanks to all of you!

Macro Photography: The Universe at Our Feet

First Published in 2021 by Don Komarechka Photography. www.donkom.ca

ISBN 978-0-9868204-6-5 (hardcover)
Printed in Canada

To Danika,

Always stay curious!

Contents

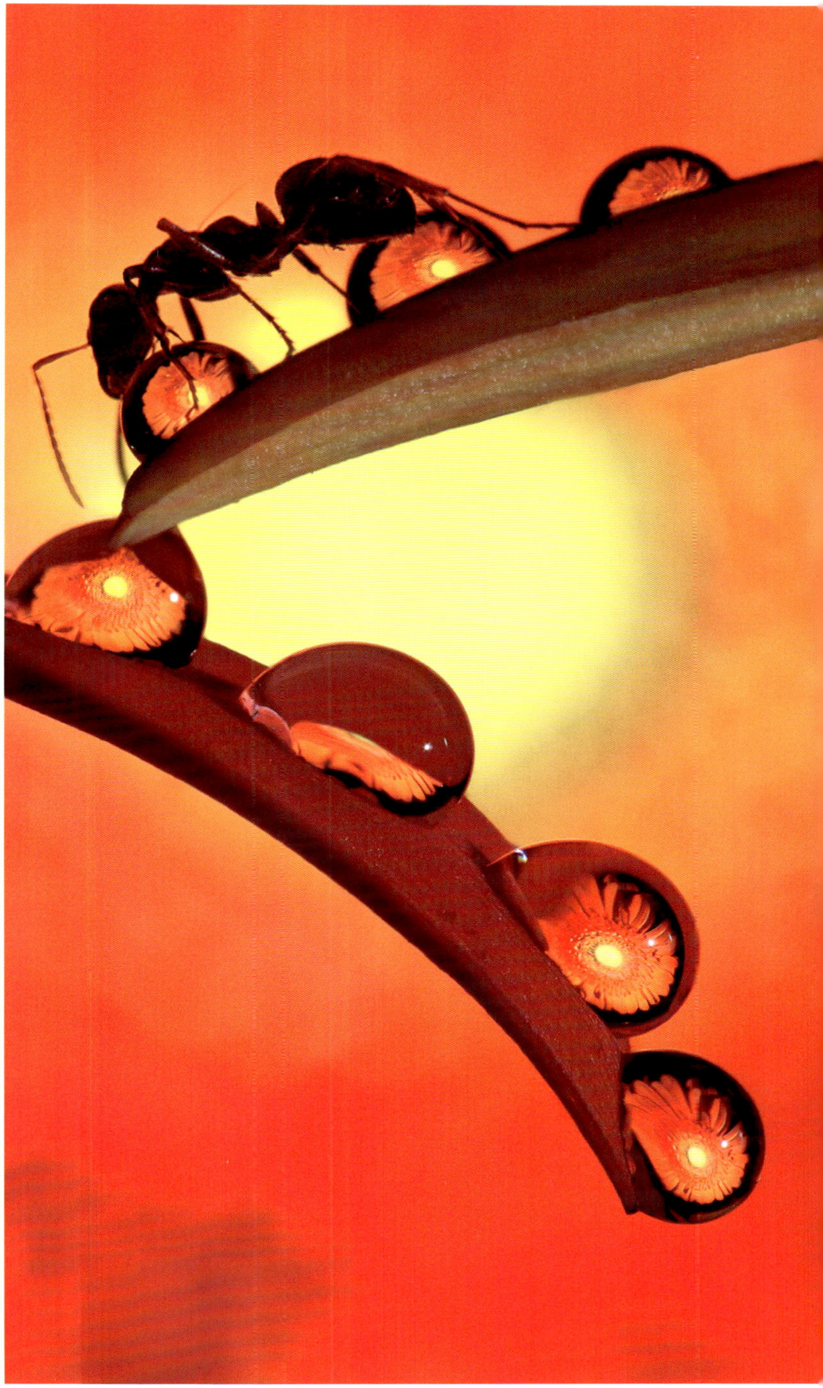

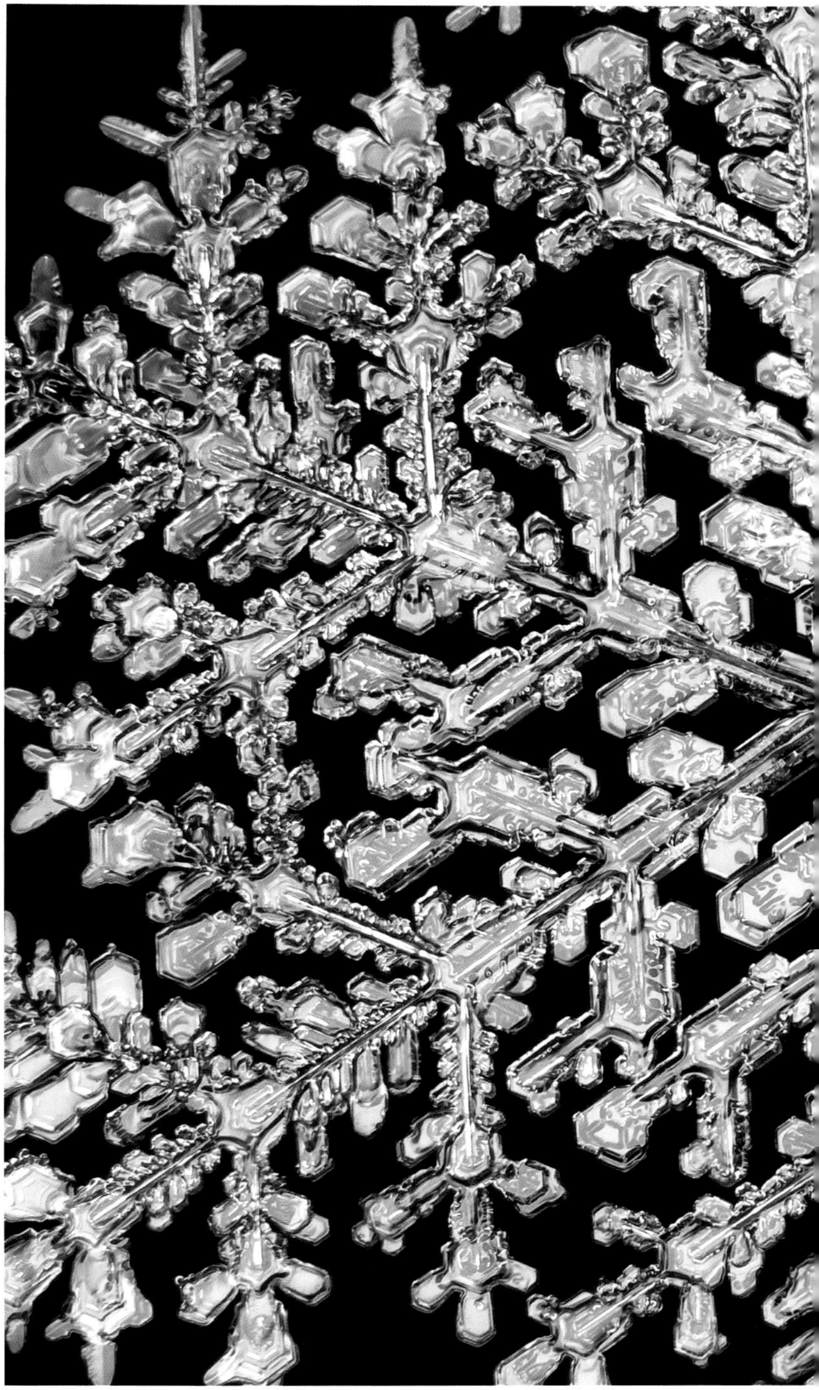

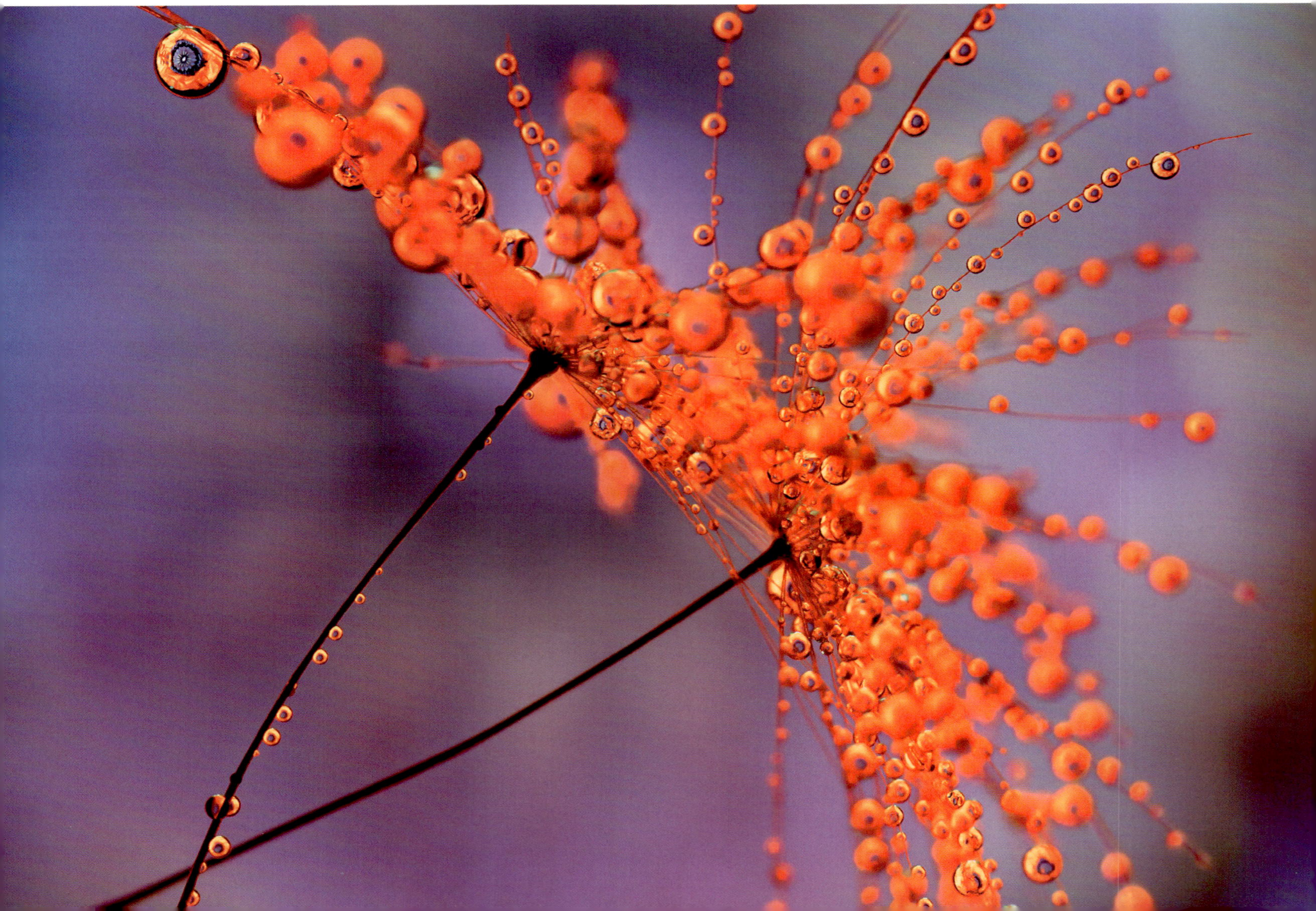

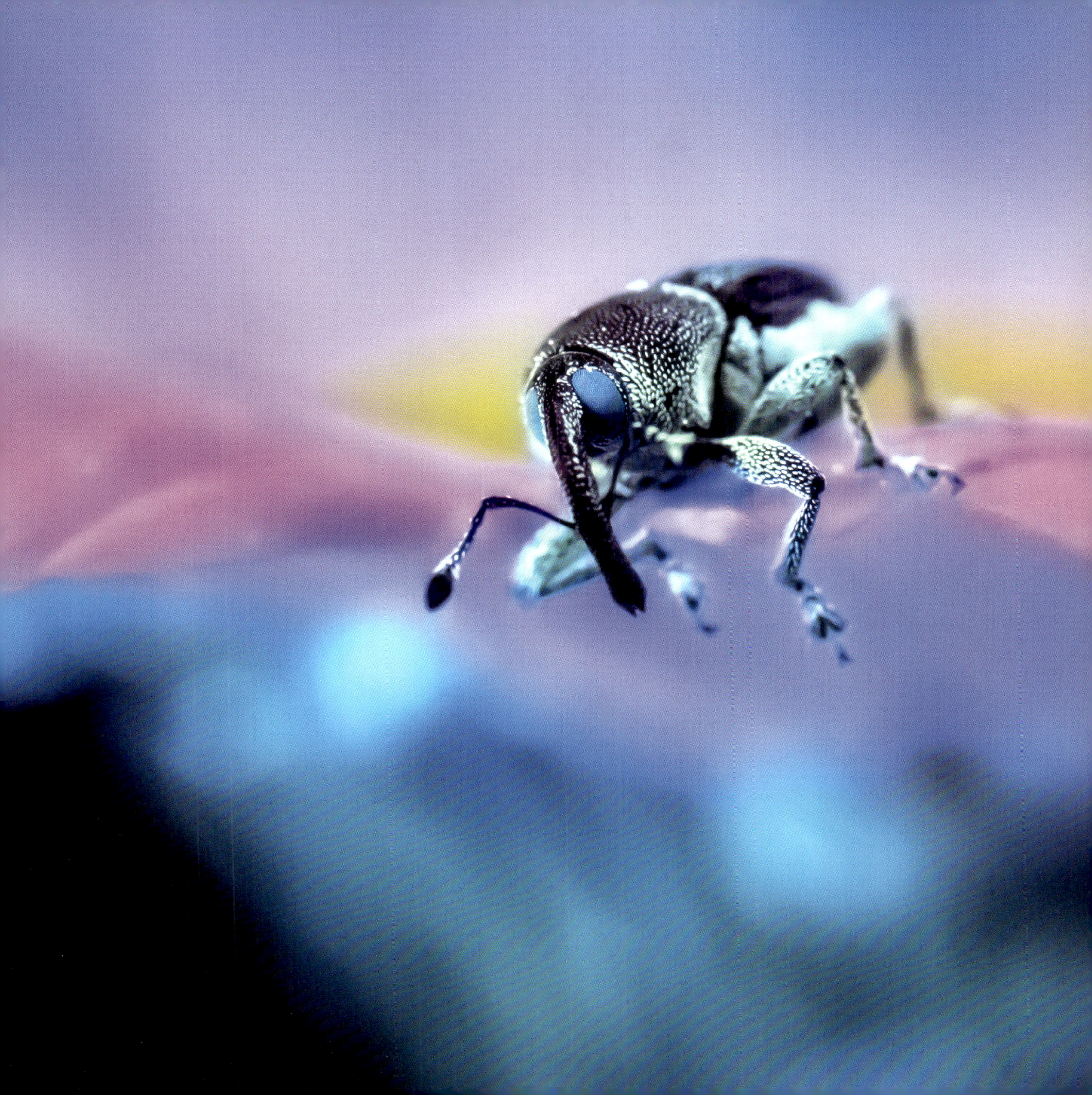

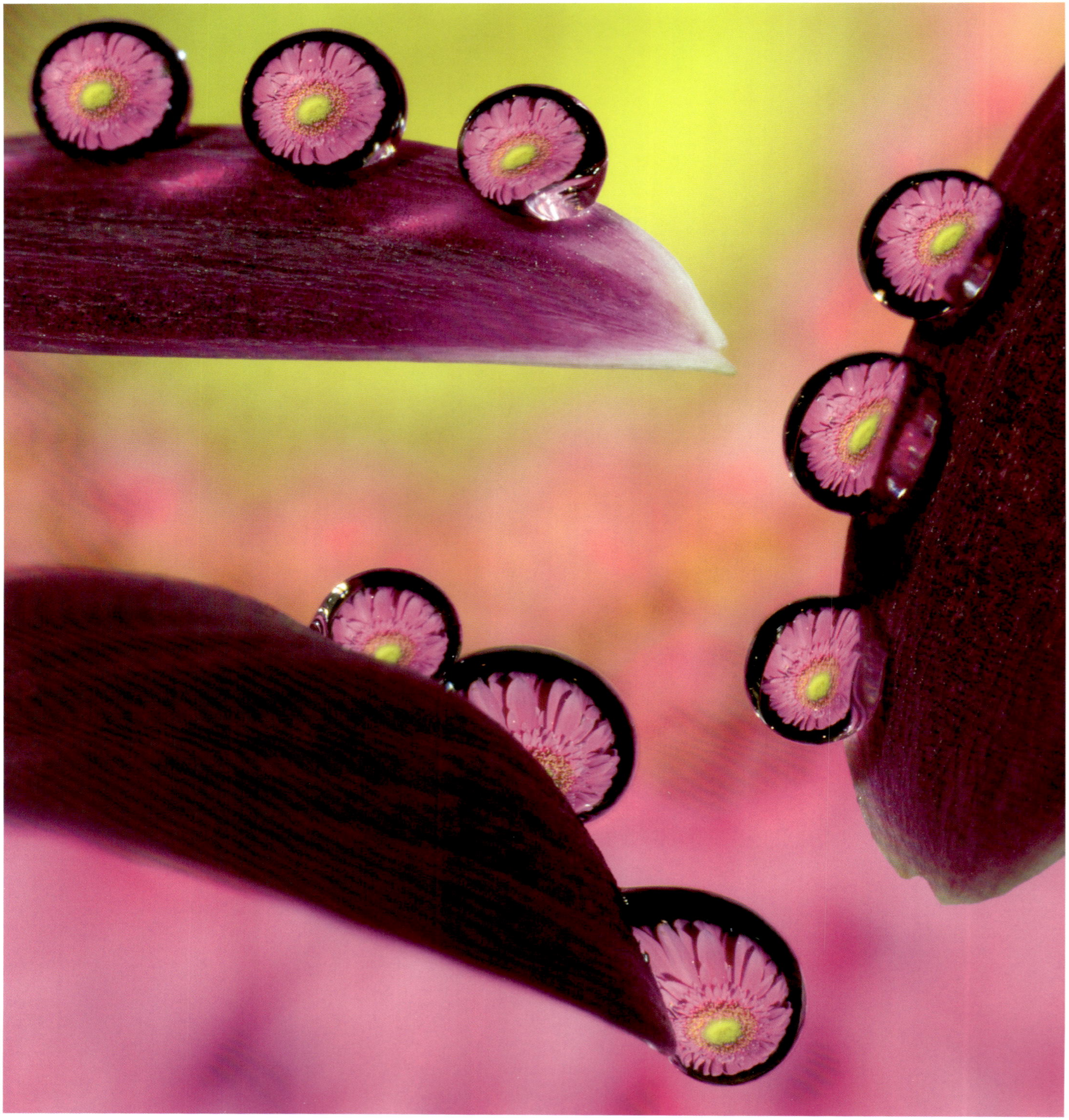

Foreword

by Ted Kinsman
Associate Professor of Photographic Sciences
Rochester Institute of Technology
Rochester, New York

Sir Isaac Newton developed the science of optics and published his work in 1672, some 152 years before the invention of Photography. Newton's famous words "If I have seen further it is by standing on the shoulders of Giants" rings true now more than ever. As photographers we build on the advances of those that come before us. In either technical endeavors or artistic expression, it is important to understand the photographic techniques that have come before us. By understanding these basics, the photographer is able to extend into the unknown or the unexplored. The techniques, ideas, equipment, and artistry presented here all swirl together to make the world of modern photography. In this text, Don Komarechka presents techniques and equipment developed by the giants in the world of photography.

Here Don shines as a brilliant photographer, creating a book that goes far beyond what a cell phone camera can do. Don's passion for macrophotography, built on his strong sense of design, enables him to create some of the most stunning macro images of our modern times. Beyond the beautiful images is rock solid description of how these images were created. This book is a testament to Don's ability to explain relatively complicated photographic techniques in a down-to-earth style.

Preface

As a child, I was always curious. I loved the science experiments my dad would concoct, from a “carbon snake” to a “Jacob’s Ladder” – the high voltage variety. We nearly killed the cat during that last one. This did not translate into a love of theoretical science, barely passing high school physics and failing calculus twice. I loved the practicality of things; seeing things happen by my own efforts was entertainment.

My father was a good man, but one far from perfect. While he had a lifelong love of photography, he also had struggles with depression, alcohol and addiction. When his health was declining towards the end of his life, he handed me an envelope. It contained $1,000, something of a “living will” he said, a last request. He wanted to see me happy – to enjoy whatever it was I wanted. I had no interest in photography, but my father was living three hours away, alone, and I wanted to make him happy.

The next day, I bought a camera.

It was a point of bonding for my father and me; I learned much from him beyond photography, but using photography as a medium. Before long, I was teaching him about the modern digital workflow, what RAW files were and how to get the most out of these “machines”. I still had no grasp of the art of photography; that would come well after my father had passed away.

He taught me curiosity, and he taught me the beginnings of photography. This started me down a path of exploration, continuously asking “what if?” and reveling in my mistakes more than my successes. I became a practical tinkerer in the visual arts, something I would have never imagined possible.

We all come to photography from different points of view, backgrounds and reasons for exploring the art. In general, we might start exploring landscape, portraiture, street photography and more. We take a taste of everything, and see what fits us best. The majority of my professional work has been in the macro photography realm, not because I like small things but because I love exploring the unknown. I enjoy being curious about the world around me, revealing details that previously I could never perceive. It's the same satisfaction I get from infrared photography and astrophotography, but with the infinite possibilities of the universe at our feet.

By whatever means you have arrived here, whatever path has brought you to macro photography as a passion or just a passing interest, you're in good company.

Macro photographers inherently play by a different rulebook. We face challenges that no other genre of photography will face – the lack of depth of field that portrait photographers are so keen on losing. The methods used to achieve focus, techniques for lighting, and general creative control we have over our images diverges from most other areas of photography. Sometimes the work can be purely documentary, showcasing the natural beauty all around us in its unmodified splendour. Sometimes we become artists before ever picking up the camera; we create tiny sculptures and scenes that are then immortalized in an image to share with the world. This book aims to explore it all.

Some areas of exploration you might be familiar with: snowflakes, water droplets, insects. Other areas you may have never thought of experimenting with: stereoscopic 3D, ultraviolet, cross-polarization effects to create crazy colours! I've gone to extremes in some macro niches that I don't think anyone will explore, such as sending 30,000 volts through a flower. Even if you don't care to make your own discoveries in any one area, I hope that the overarching adventure discussed across the entire book will inspire you to think differently.

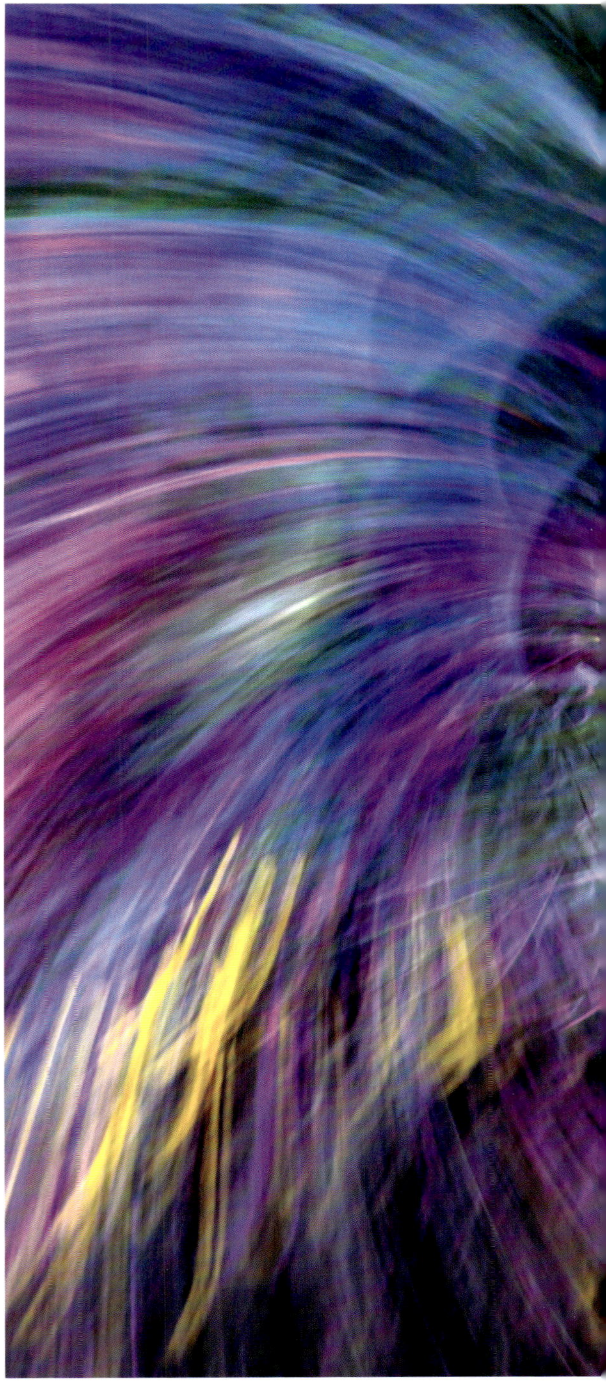

I have written at length about macro photography techniques, often associated with a post on social media, immediately after shooting something I personally considered interesting. Even if the work didn't meet with much fanfare, there was always passion in the curiosity, and this has become a foundational element in my work: sharing every "secret", every ingredient, every technique, equipment, process and the mistakes along the way. For the past 10 years, I've been giving it all away, and now you're reading it in the form of a book – the biggest project of my professional career.

The book was crowdfunded, surpassing 600% of the initial funding goal. A runaway success, in part because of the decade of work serving as a clear indicator of the quality of content it would contain. Thousands of people have put their faith in this project, and I cannot thank you all enough.

From my first snowflake photographed in December 2009 to writing this book a decade later, I feel as if I have only just begun the journey. The camera is not just a tool to capture an image, it is a tool to discover more about the world around us. There have been many times I've spent the day shooting and have not captured anything worth sharing; there have been trips taken for the purpose of photography where the adventures were far more valuable than the images taken. The main goal of my photography, aside from the joys of teaching others, has become satisfying that childhood curiosity. It's amazing how freeing it becomes when you're not chasing an image, but rather exploring an idea.

Sincerely,

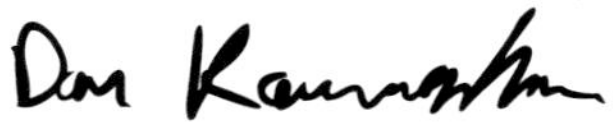

Don Komarechka

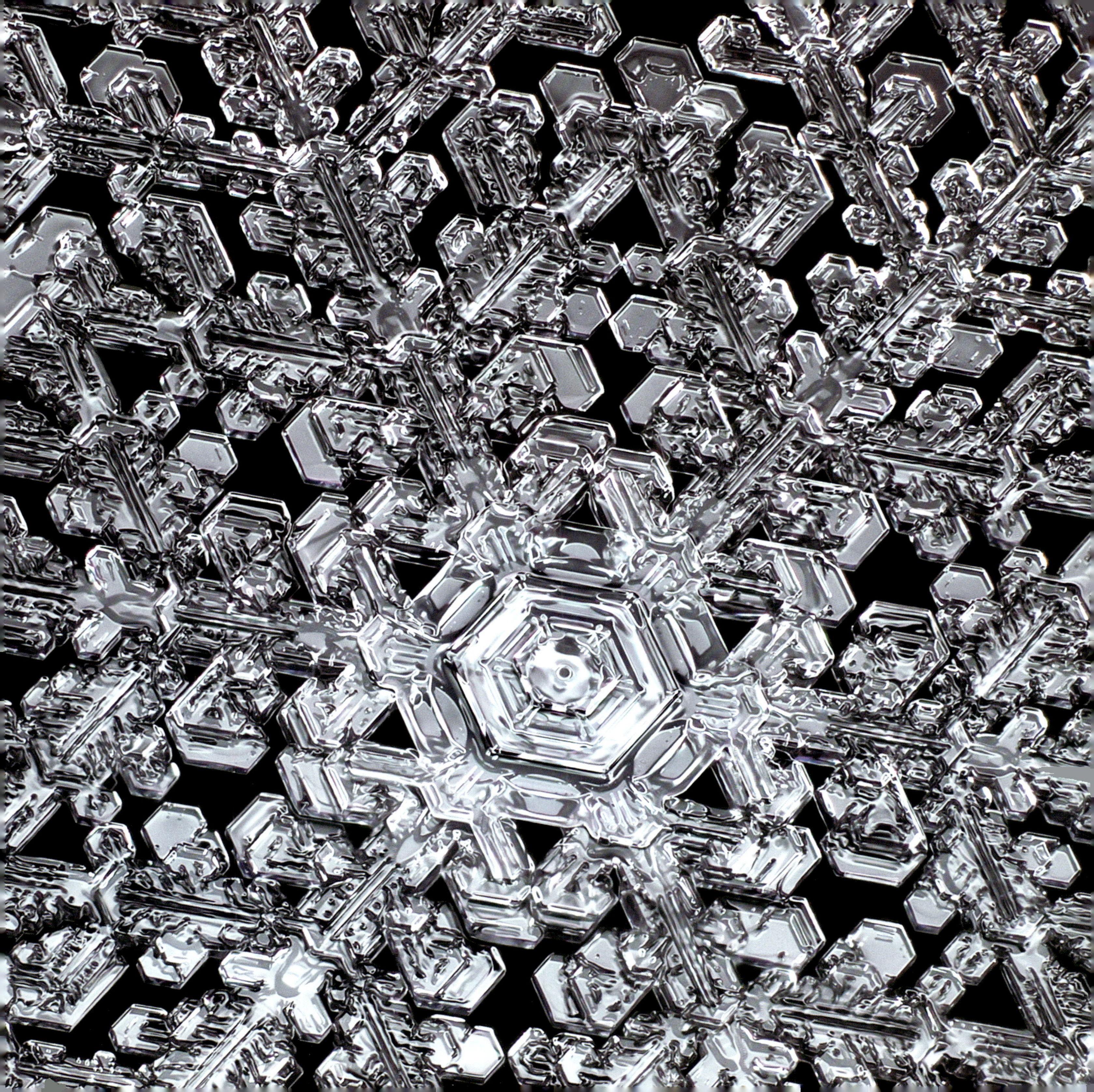

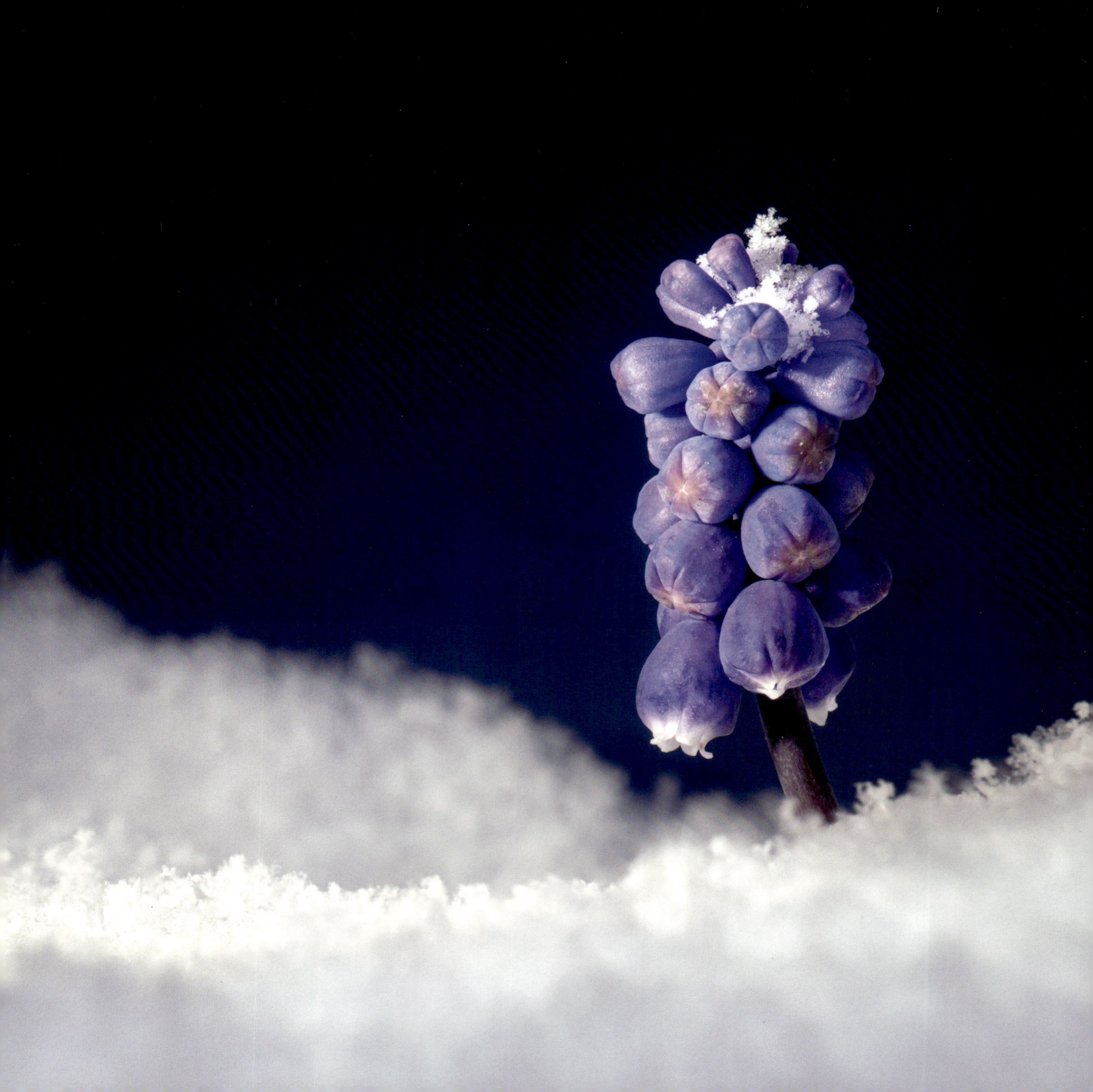

Introduction & Equipment

The term "macro" is a strange one. Macroeconomics, for example, is very large scale: interest rates, national productivity, inflation. "Macrocosm" is a noun that describes the entirety of a complex structure like the universe. One could easily arrive at the conclusion that macro photography involves taking photographs of very large things!

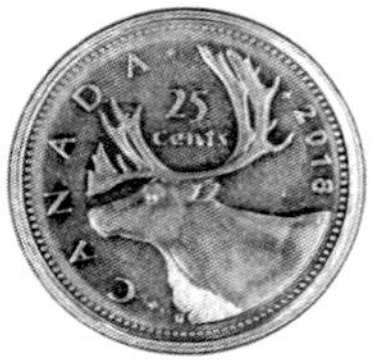

Macro photography, by its original definition, referred to an object being "life size" on the frame or sheet of film. Take the coin on this page, for example. If you were to take an actual quarter and place it over top, it would be a perfect fit. The Canadian 25-cent coin measures precisely 23.88mm in diameter, which would barely fit inside the frame of a full-frame camera with a sensor measuring 36mm by 24mm.

Try it! Set your macro lens to 1:1 magnification, which is often the closest focusing distance of a dedicated macro lens and you'll see the coin just avoid the edges of the frame. It is the same size in reality as it appears on the camera sensor. If you have a smaller sensor, you'll notice that at full 1:1 magnification that you are only able to capture a portion of the coin in your frame. By the same logic, the size of the coin hasn't changed, but the size of the sensor has. It is still appearing as life size, but the smaller sensor has a perceived magnification increase.

This could be imagined another way: what if you took a 35mm film camera and shot the photo, and held the coin up to the developed negative? Perfect fit. Now take a smaller camera like the cute Pentax Auto 110 which shot frames measuring only 13mm x 17mm. Let's pretend that a macro lens was available for this camera, and we shot the same coin. You'd only get a portion of it in the frame, but if you held up the developed negative to the physical coin, all of the features would fit perfectly. It's life sized!

This, however, is a very narrow depiction of macro photography that has been trampled on by photographers and manufacturers alike. For example, have you ever seen a zoom lens with the word "macro" on it? As of this publication, no zoom lens exists that is capable of 1:1 magnification; the term is used as a

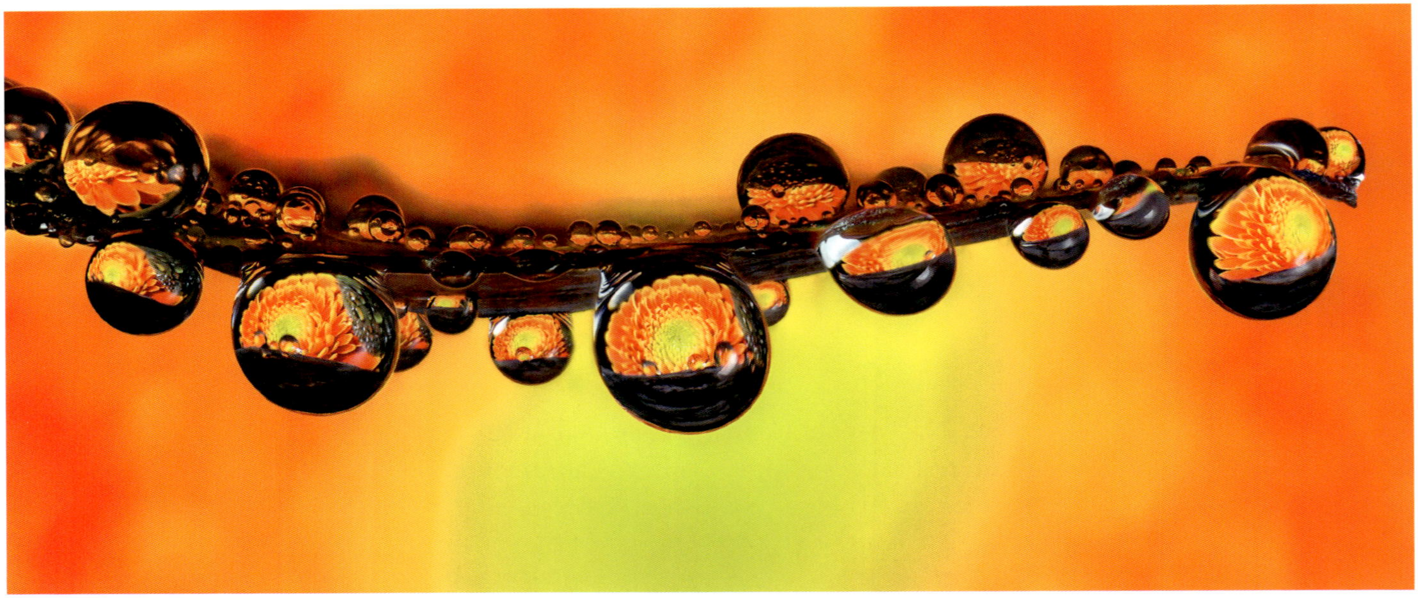

way of indicating that the lens has a closer focusing distance than the average lens in its class. Canon produces one of my favourite lenses, the Canon MP-E 65mm F/2.8 1x-5x Macro Photo. This lens starts at 1:1 and then gets much closer – where the main purpose of the lens is to generally shoot beyond "macro". Nikon calls all of their macro lenses "micro" lenses, which isn't accurate either. What a mess!

Let's define things arbitrarily. Everyone else does anyhow. Macro photography is the capture of something close-up, oftentimes closer than we would see it with our own eyes.

I'll make a subjective proclamation: if your primary subject is eight centimeters (3 3/20") or smaller, you're shooting something small enough to be considered macro photography, regardless of the size of your sensor. Send hatemail to don@komarechka.com.

Now that we've established the general criteria, here comes the fun part: how do we get close? Beyond that, what challenges will we face when we get even closer? This is where things get exciting and problem-solving can offer up some inventive solutions that kick-start the creative process!

Getting Closer

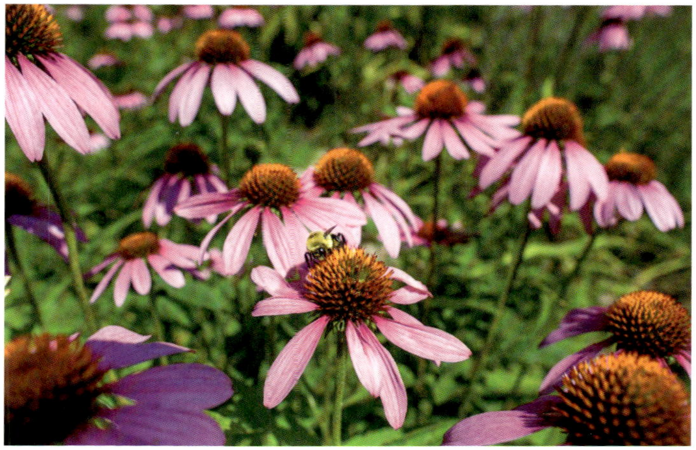

We have an interest in tiny things, but how do we capture them? The first step is to focus our cameras closer – even if you're shooting with a smartphone there are plenty of options! We start this journey looking at ways to augment your existing equipment to enter into the macro realm.

There are three primary ways to use your existing lens: **close-up filters, extension tubes, and bellows.**

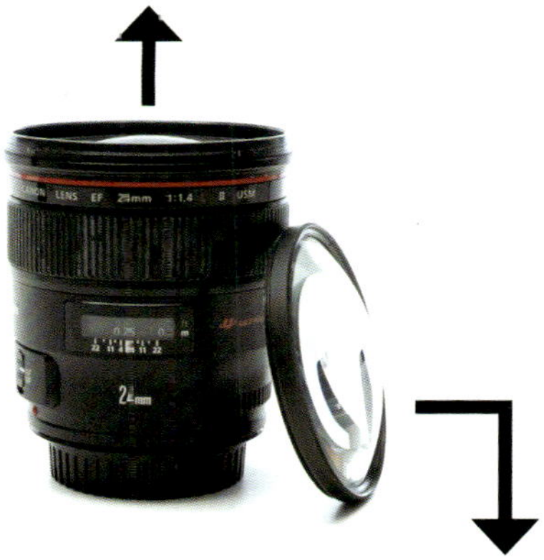

Imagine looking through a magnifying glass: it does what it's supposed to do – magnify things! These are usually simple optics and while the center of the image is sharp, the edges fall off quickly. You can get sets of these simple lenses for your camera for a few dollars on marketplace websites like eBay or Amazon, but be wary of the trade-off: you get what you pay for. You'll be compromising, sometimes to an unacceptable level, to increase your magnification. Some lenses handle these better than others, and based on the price it might be worth the knowledge gained from experimenting.

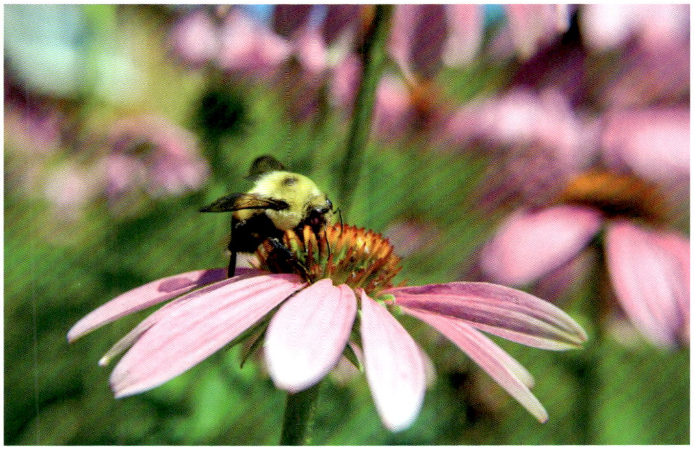

In this example, the Canon EF 24mm F/1.4L II lens – decidedly not a macro lens – is equipped with a +10 diopter close-up filter on the front. The resulting images are straight out of camera, each at the closest focusing distance of the lens. Hey, it works! The corners might be soft, but we often have smooth backgrounds in macro images anyhow, so it might just be the ticket.

There are even better filters with fancy multi-element designs, if this approach seems convenient to you. Raynox has their 150 and 250 filter sets (the magnification effect varies) and Canon has their 500D filter. These cost significantly more, but can offer better optical quality. Even so, whenever you add glass to an existing optical system, you're pushing it beyond its intended design and the quality will suffer. This is also why I dislike UV filters when they aren't needed on your lens.

Even close-up filters or lenses for your smartphone can bring you into the realm of macro photography. Here's an image taken with a "Moment" macro lens attached to an iPhone 11 (*right*). You're not going to get the most impressive results when inspecting all of the tiniest details, but this just illustrates how accessible macro photography is!

Extension tubes and bellows on the other hand, are a way to shift the entire focusing range of a lens closer to the front element. This method has no optics – just a hollow tube between the camera and lens. Because there is nothing "in the way", it's often preferred to close-up filters as the image quality remains incredibly high. Setting the lens to infinity focus might now only result in focusing a foot from the front element, and closer focus settings on the lens will become increasingly more magnified.

Herein lies a problem, and it's the primary frustration for first-time extension tube users: If you add even a small tube to a wide-angle lens, you might shift the focus so far forward that the focus point theoretically ends up somewhere inside the lens, and nothing you do will allow you to find focus. Usually sold in sets of two or three from companies such as Kenko (my recommendation), you can feel confident about putting the whole set on a lens 90mm or longer. For shorter focal lengths, you'll need to set aside some time to tinker and experiment with what works best.

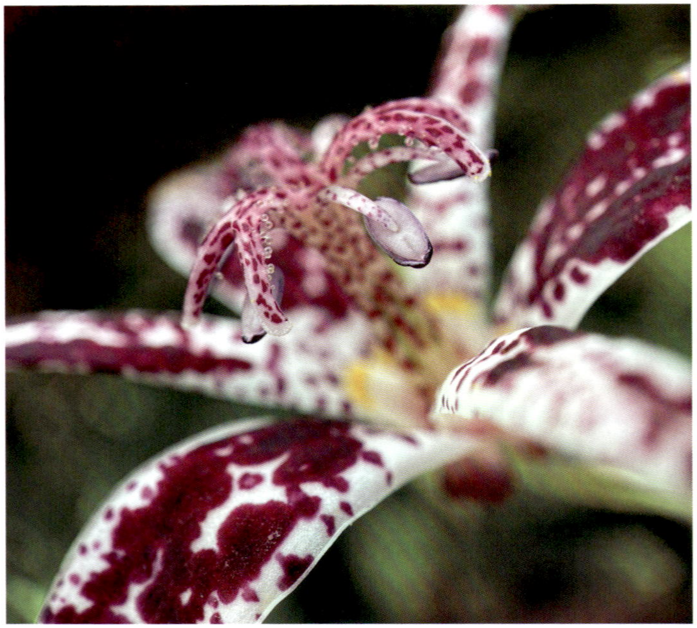

Bellows are effectively a variable length extension tube and have been a part of photography since the early era of film photography. Lenses could only focus by moving the entire lens closer or further away from the camera. Want to shoot a landscape? Condense the bellows all the way. Portrait? Push the lens further away from the film plane until your subject comes into focus. There aren't many manufacturers that make "automatic" bellows that transmit information between the camera and the lens, and I am not aware of any that are truly affordable.

Which option is best? Extension tubes tend to be my personal go-to focus modifier to get closer with any lens. Any lens becomes a macro lens, and a macro lens will push past 1:1 lifesize!

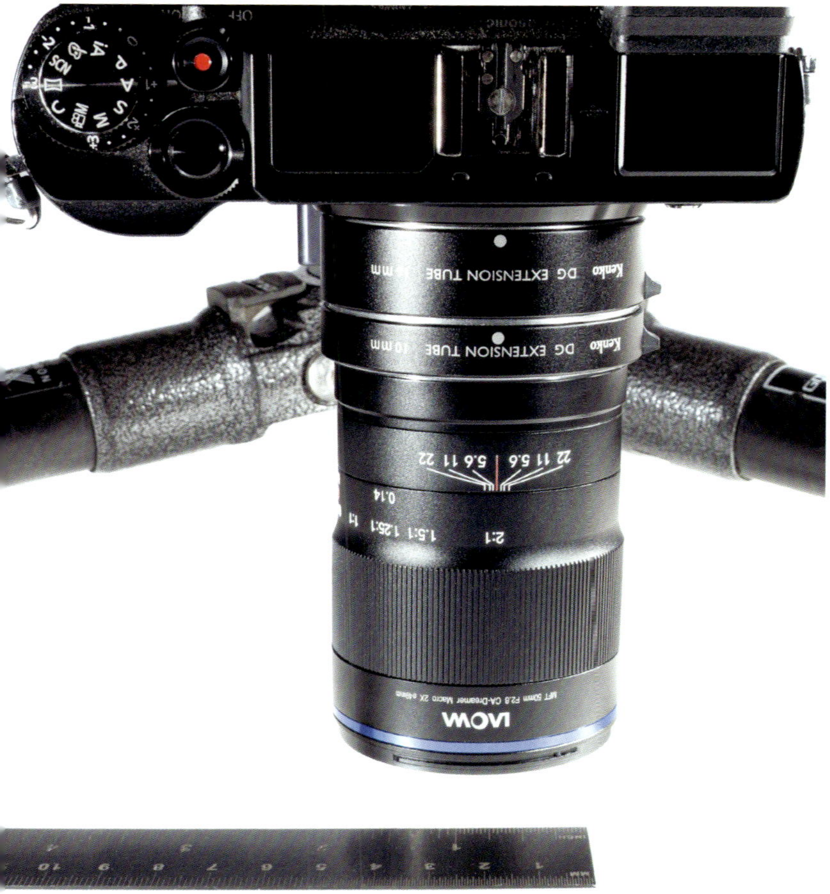

Above: How much magnification does a Micro Four Thirds camera have with a Laowa 50mm F/2.8 2x macro lens plus extension tubes?

Below: The longer lines are millimeters. Roughly 5mm of coverage: 17.3mm / 5mm = 3.46x magnification.

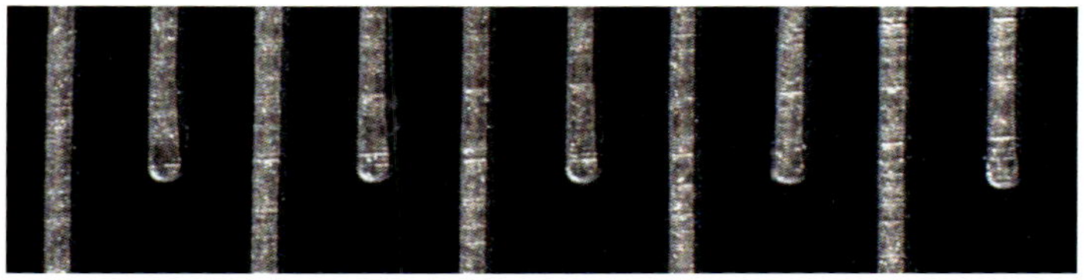

How Much Magnification?

As soon as you start modifying a lens, you'll question exactly how much magnification you're now capable of. What if you add a close-up filter and extension tubes to a macro lens? How big will your subjects be in the frame? Is there an equation to calculate this? There probably is, but it would rely on so many factors, some of them very difficult to identify. The simplest solution is to photograph the millimeter markings on a ruler, and do some very simple math. For ultimate convenience, there's just such a ruler on this page:

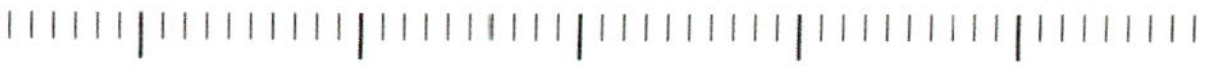

The process here is simple. You just need to know the physical horizontal size of your camera sensor. Here are some standard sizes:

Full Frame: 36mm

Canon APS-C: 22.3mm

Nikon/Sony/Pentax/Fuji APS-C: 23.6

Micro Four Thirds: 17.3mm

Fuji GFX: 44mm

Equation:

$$\frac{\text{physical horizontal size of sensor}}{\text{number of millimeters you see in the image}}$$

If you shoot a full frame camera with a macro lens set to 1:1, you will see 36 millimeters in your resulting image. If you see 22mm after adding a set of extension tubes, then 36mm / 22mm = 1.63. This would be your new magnification factor! How close can you get?

Lenses

This is where things get insightful, opinionated and ultimately subjective. There are so many options for macro lenses on the market, what should you choose? We'll break them down into different categories with sample images to try and establish what best suits your style and subject.

I can't stress this enough: don't get hung up on exact manufacturers and models. This section of the book is not designed as an ultimate review of all available gear, which is constantly changing as new lenses become available and old ones become discontinued. Some are available on multiple camera mounts, others are not. I am not going to decide what your favourite macro lens is for you any more than I can tell you what car to buy. If you already own a macro lens, it's likely a darn good lens!

Vintage

Macro photography does not benefit as much as other photographic genres when it comes to the latest advancements in autofocus and image stabilization. Some lenses from decades past can be just as good as their modern counterparts, and others can offer interesting quirks such as "soap bubble bokeh", where out-of-focus specular highlights can appear circular with the outer edge brighter than their centers. The crowning champion of this effect is often regarded as the Trioplan 100. Why does this lens receive such fanfare?

The Trioplan 100 is a simple "triplet" lens design, originally created by Hugo Meyer in 1916 and based on the Cooke Triplet design, patented in 1893. We're going back a long way. This simple triplet design was used for decades before modern optics began to replace it and offer up a more "accurate" version of reality. It's this uncomplicated basic three-lens design that gives the "Trio"plan its name, and the characteristic bokeh that has a surreal, dreamy feel in the right scenario.

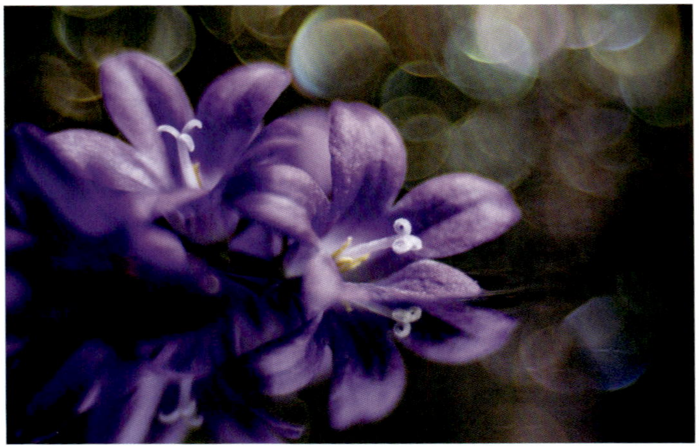

Trioplans are manufactured today by OPC Optics, which owns the Meyer Optik brand, and they come with a high price tag. Remember that these lenses are just simple triplets, and many lesser-known lenses – including projector lenses – can give you the same effect. Other lenses with similar optical behaviour include *Primotar, Primoplan, Diaplan, Domiplan* and others. Search online for "soap bubble bokeh lens" and you'll find the trials and tests of other photographers. Most of these lenses are not natively macro lenses, so grab a set of extension tubes to shift them into this close-up realm.

Other vintage lenses can include the Canon 20mm and 35mm "macrophoto" lenses from 1976, which require a bellows system to mount to your camera and can achieve 10:1 magnification. Olympus has similar

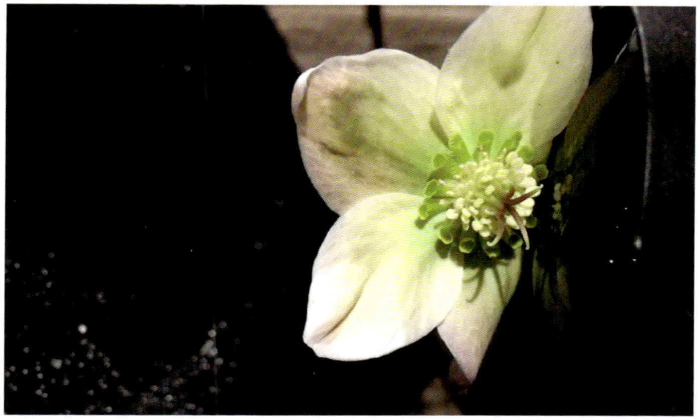

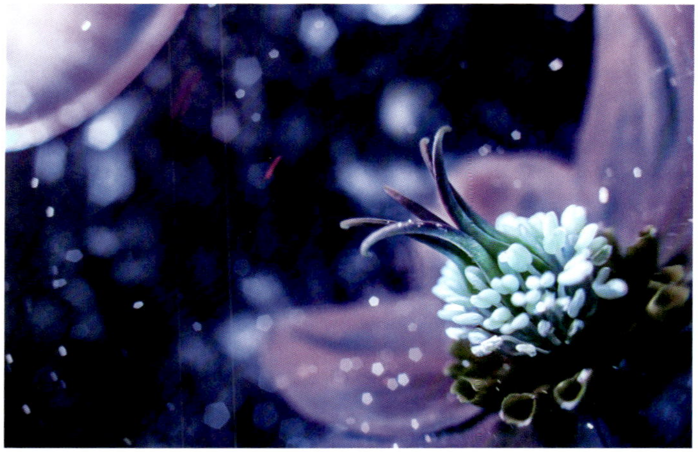

Top: Infinity focus becomes the front element of the lens when you add a 12mm extension tube to the Canon 15mm F/2.8 fisheye lens.

Bottom: The resulting image in ultraviolet fluorescence.

lenses, though for such extreme magnifications you would be better off to use modern microscope objectives at around the same cost. This is covered in a later chapter.

Wide Angle

Macro lenses with shorter focal lengths have not always been common. Venus Optics has produced a 15mm lens as well as their unusual (and partially waterproof) 24mm "probe" lens. These lenses are not for general use, much the same as a fisheye lens would feel out of place in most scenarios. They offer up the ability to shoot an environmental portrait of an insect, or to make a mushroom tower like a tree. I'll be honest – I own both of these lenses and I haven't found a real practical need for them. Your creative ideas may differ! I have, however, experimented by putting my Canon 15mm F/2.8 Fisheye lens on a 12mm extension tube. Infinity focus became the front element of the lens, meaning that I had to "smush" my subject against the front glass to have anything in focus. If you're up for a challenge and enjoy finding a way to use these tools, you'll have far less competition to contend with.

Compact

Macro lenses with an effective focal length of roughly 35-60mm are generally considered "compact", offering up a small size, more intimate focusing distances and are generally more affordable. They don't handle extension tubes exceptionally well, but they can be a useful tool to showcase the separation of subject features rather than compressing details together. Getting closer to your subject will definitely provide an interesting feel, but it's not for all subjects and is not my "go to" category of lenses.

Normal

There is a reason that the majority of macro lenses on the market cover an effective focal length of between 70mm and 120mm. For 1:1 magnification, anything around that 100mm focal length feels about right. This "Goldilocks focal range" features lenses from every single manufacturer, the working distance (distance from your subject) is suitable for studio and field shooting, and they handle extension tubes very well.

There's a lot to like here, but with so many options you will quickly be struck with "analysis paralysis" when diving into the specifications and making comparisons. A few initial considerations: even the best image stabilization system on a macro lens will be far less effective for close-up work, and even the best lenses struggle with nailing autofocus all the time. To that end, I almost always rely on manual focus when shooting my macro imagery and there will be an abundance of discussion on focusing techniques later in the book.

The best value here? I've got to hand it to Tamron with their 90mm F/2.8 lens – without "VC" (vibration control). Yes, there are technically better lenses. However most of the benefits, even from this lens's more expensive sibling, are not realized by the majority of macro photographers. It's a perfect example of a lens that's affordable (USD$450), versatile, and offers up sharp results when stopped down to apertures common for macro work: F/5.6 and smaller.

The truth is, you genuinely cannot buy a bad macro lens in this category, so buy whatever your brand allegiances dictate and your wallet will allow. I shot with the Canon 100mm F/2.8 lens for years and it served me well.

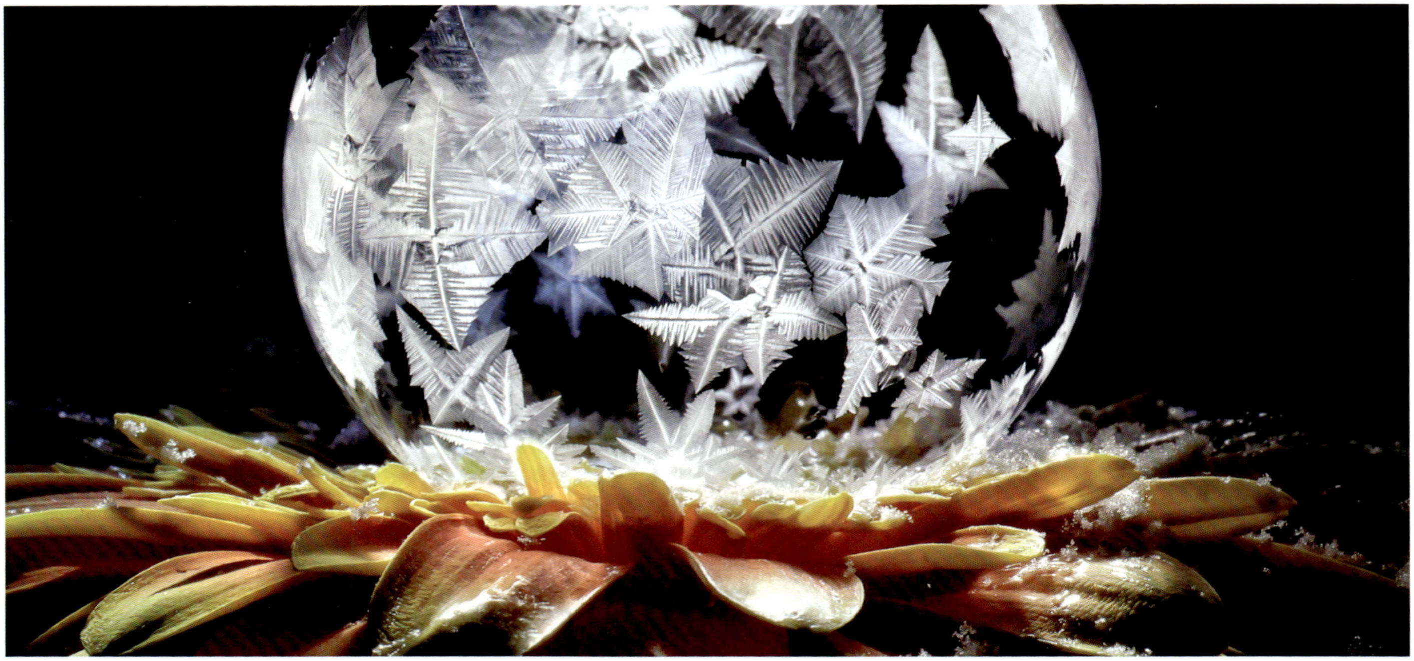

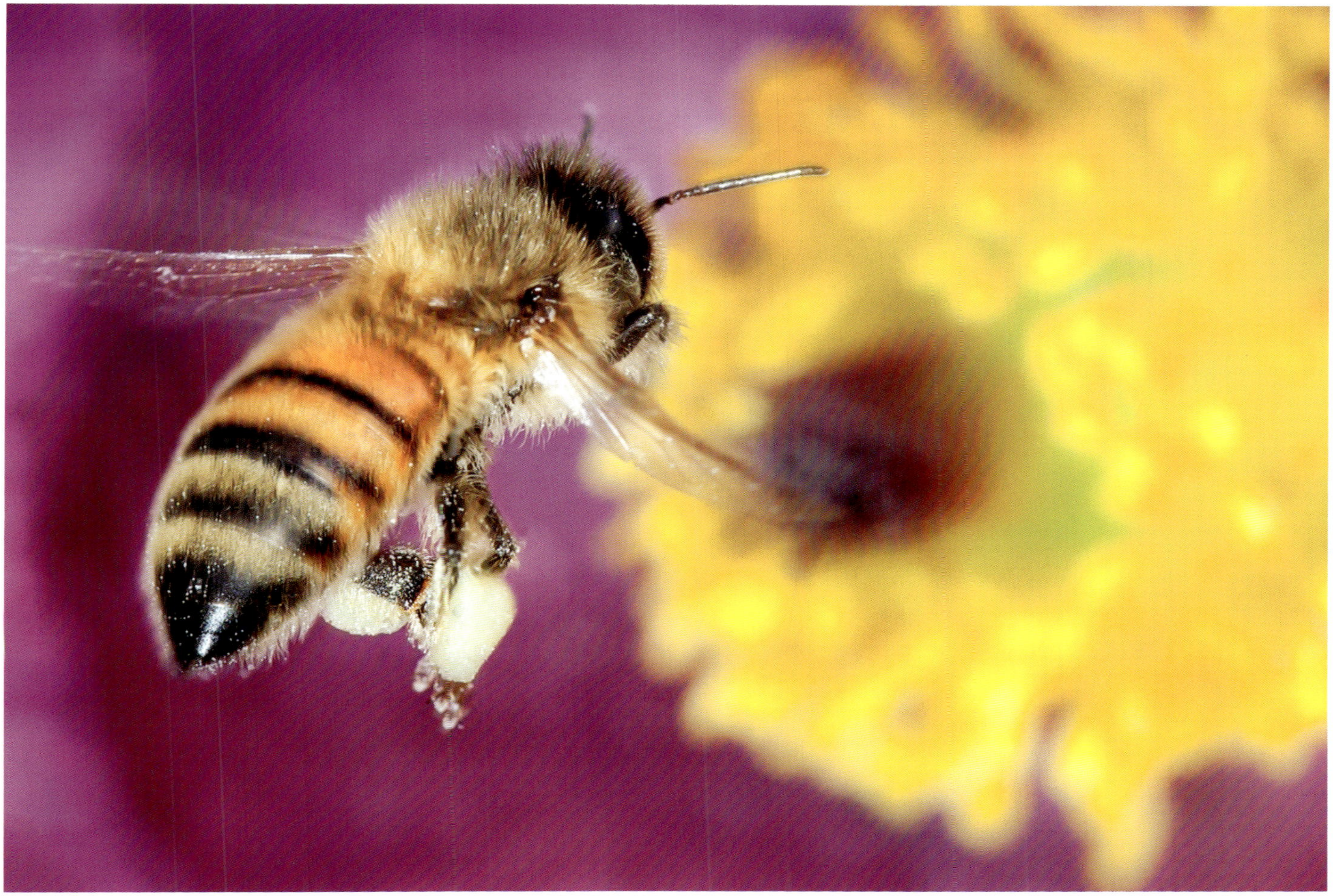

Telephoto

There's something unique about the depth of field and subject compression you get when you enter the realm of 150-200mm macro lenses. The look is always smooth, controllable and easy to work with in the field. Insects are often unaffected by your presence because you are working farther away from them, and it can be easy to place a specific splash of colour right where you want it in the background.

These lenses are slightly cumbersome to work with in the studio, and extension tubes have a less significant impact of magnification than "normal" macro lenses. Those detractions aside, it can be an excellent tool for shooting out of the studio – I've even used the Canon 180mm F/3.5L to photograph bees flying in and out of flowers. My current favourite is from a much lesser-known brand, the Irix 150mm F/2.8 – a manual focus but electronically controlled aperture lens for various mounts and a great price point with exceptional results.

High Magnification

There used to be only one player in this category, the Canon MP-E 65mm F/2.8 1x-5x Macro Photo, originally released way back in 1999 and still a current lens in the Canon lens portfolio in 2020. For nearly two decades, there wasn't any competition and photographers of competing brands were left to find more exotic solutions to break well past the 1:1 magnification barrier. This is my most-used macro lens, though it is also one of the most challenging macro lenses to get familiar with. In fact, a search on eBay for copies of this lens yields numerous used copies that have been used only a handful of times. Many photographers give up on it too quickly.

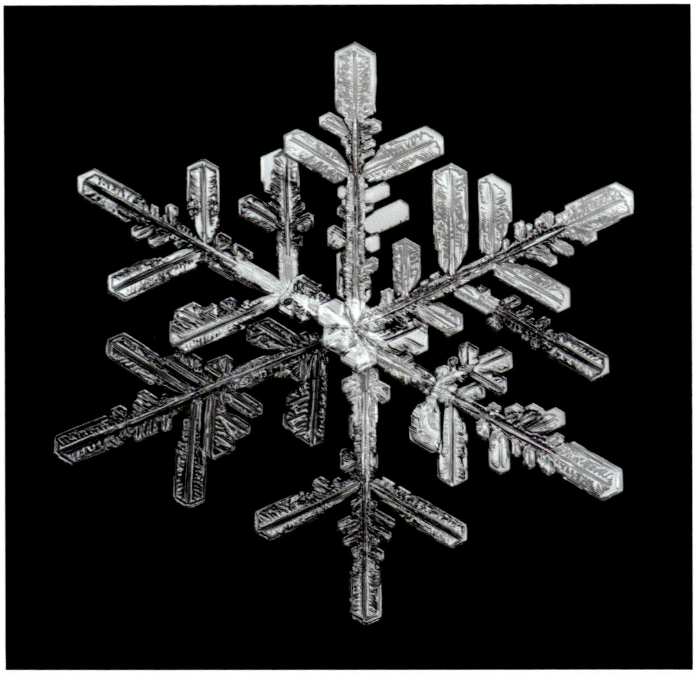

One of the main reasons why? Every lens in this category has no focusing mechanism at all. Not a lack of autofocus, but a lack of manual focus too. To achieve focus, photographers need to move the entire camera forward and backward – or move the subject in the same way. This approach is counterintuitive initially, but you'll come to realize that this is functionally the best way to shoot many macro subjects.

Venus Optics has a number of lenses that break the 1:1 magnification barrier. The Laowa 60mm and 100mm 2x macro lenses are wonderful, as is their Laowa 25mm 2.5x-5x lens. With much jubilation, these lenses are available for a wide variety of camera mounts.

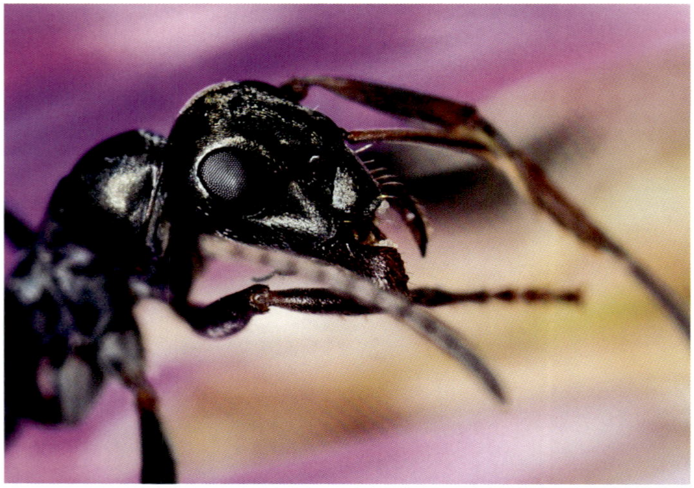

Just prior to publication, Zhong Yi Optics started shipping the Mitakon Creator 85mm F/2.8 1x-5x Super Macro lens, and it's every bit as good as the Canon MP-E 65mm at half the price and available on a variety of lens mounts. Finally, without having to resort to reverse-mounting lenses or microscope objectives, this category has matured. And, there's plenty to explore at the extremes.

Microscope Objectives

Don't tune out just yet! This is far more approachable than you might think from both a cost perspective and ease of use, so long as you understand how things fit together. Microscope objectives are optics designed to peer through a microscope at very high magnifications, but they can be easily adapted to use with any camera.

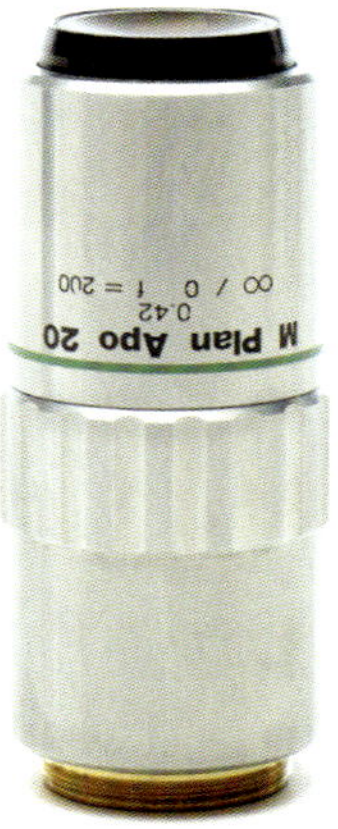

First off, the best series of objectives to use for this is the Mitutoyo Plan APO objectives, available from 1x to 100x. These are infinity corrected objectives (of which there are many less expensive options found on used marketplaces), which is key to equipping them to your camera. An infinity corrected objective means that it can be equipped to a base lens, set to infinity focus, and it will relay the light perfectly through to the camera sensor.

20x objective (above) *attached to a Lumix GX9 to fill the frame with just a few grains of pollen* (below).

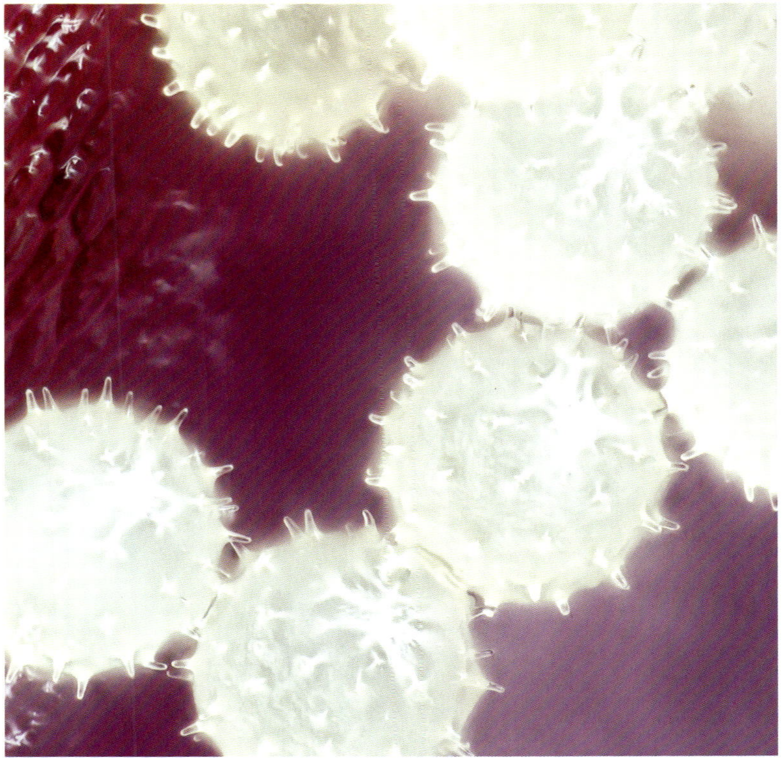

These objectives have a marking of f=200, which denotes that they need a base lens of 200mm, set to infinity. **That's it.** Just get an M26 (the thread on the objective) step-down ring to whatever filter thread is on a lens you already have at 200mm, and you're set. The image in the lower right of the pollen grains from a Rose of Sharon flower was taken with a Canon 100-400mm telephoto zoom lens set to 200mm!

These lenses tend to have the very best resolution possible, at a compromise of depth of field – there is no aperture diaphragm. There are ways around that, but you really want to be secured on a tripod with these lenses, hopefully on a focusing rail with focus stacking in mind… all ideas we will get to shortly! Still, the initial concept is simple, especially if you already have a 200mm lens in your camera bag.

Lighting

My first year with a macro lens was a frustrating, uneventful one. While trying to overcome the challenges of a shallow depth of field by shooting with smaller apertures, I was beaten up by other problems. With so little light entering the lens, I traded shallow depth for blurry images. Not an improvement! It was only when I discovered the value that instantaneous light adds to the equation that I began to truly embrace the wonders of the universe at our feet.

There are a number of ways to proceed here, and the best options, thankfully, are not the most expensive.

Ring flash or twin flash?

There are two dominant varieties of macro flashes: ring flashes which contain two semicircular lights in a ring that is mounted to the front of your lens, and a twin flash that has two independently positional lights at the end of your lens, both of which can be operated off the lens as well.

There is some debate as to the usefulness of ring flashes for some subjects. It's particularly unhelpful when illuminating a subject with a spherical surface, which will generate two semicircular catch lights on a water droplet, the eyes of a spider, the shell of a ladybug, etc. They perform exceptionally for most other subjects, even down to extreme magnifications like snowflakes, where a twin light would be less effective.

I use a ring flash for everything unless it shows some level of incompatibility with the subject, and an off-camera flash with a wireless trigger for other occasions.

Xenon vs. LED

The majority of inexpensive ring flashes use LED lighting, with a few notable exceptions. These LED lights can be used continuously for video work, but for still photography it poses a problem. It all boils down to the duration of the flash.

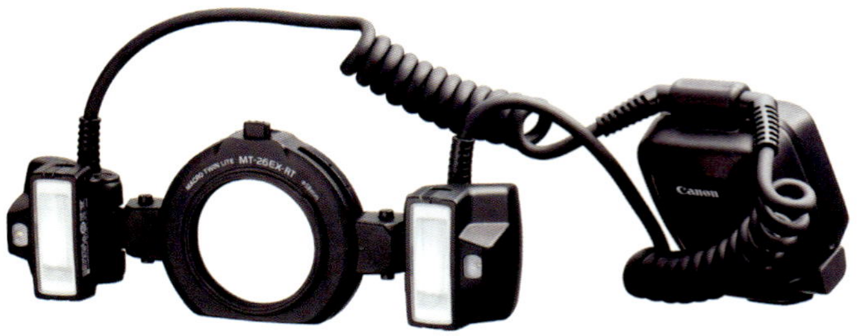

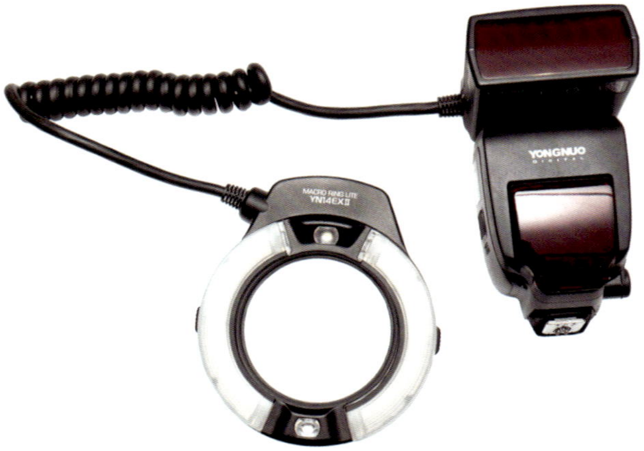

Macro flashes come in two main varieties: twin flashes (above) and ring flashes (right). You'll have success with either system, but my personal preference is a ring design.

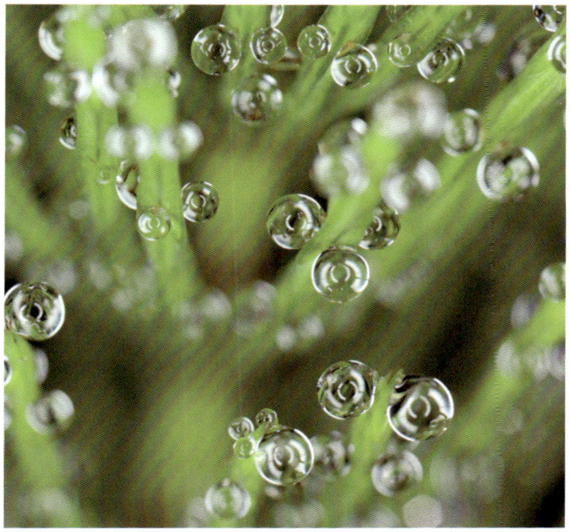

Top: the moment I realized that ring flashes are the worst light source for spherical objects.

Bottom: Using an off-camera flash aimed at the background, distracting catch lights disappear.

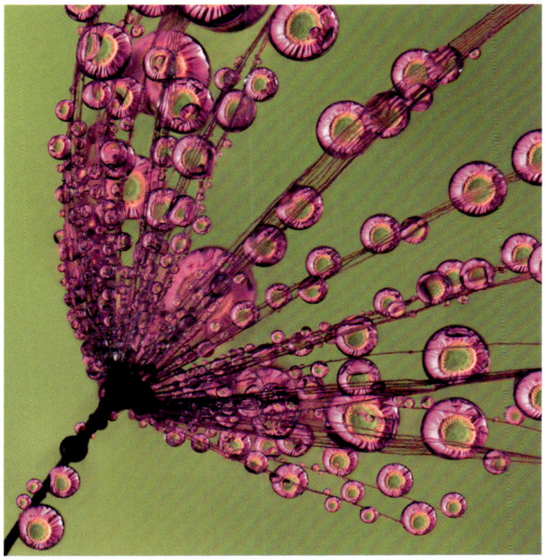

Imagine this: a completely dark room, not a stray photon to be captured. If you set your camera to a 10-minute exposure, you'll get nothing but a black frame. However, if during that exposure you arbitrarily fire your flash, what is the duration of your exposure? 10 minutes, or the duration that the flash was illuminated? If the flash is the dominant light in the image, it's the number we care about. Xenon flash tubes, especially for macro work where they are within inches of the subject, can fire at a speed of 1/20,000 second or faster. LED-based flashes on the other hand? Down to 1/100 second or slower in some cases. This is a huge difference.

You could spend top-dollar on a Canon MR-14EX II ring flash, but the very best option is the Yongnuo YN-14EX II at a fraction of the price. The Chinese manufacturer Yongnuo makes excellent flashes that often imitate those from manufacturers like Canon, and the YN-14EX II is no exception. It also offers magnetically attached colour diffusers and one silly thing that makes a huge difference: they engineered a thermal sensor into it.

That might sound like the smallest thing to opine about, but the Canon MR-14EX II has a thermal limiter to prevent it from overheating – not a bad idea, right? The problem is how they implemented it: with a counter in software. The software in the flash adds up the aggregate amount of light output over a period of time and associates that with temperature… which isn't accurate, especially when I'm shooting outside in -20C / -4F weather and I repeatedly get overheating warnings. These can be reset by simply opening the battery door while the flash is on, waiting a few seconds, and closing it again. Inconvenient, to say the least. On the other hand, the YN-14EX II actually measures the temperature, and never stops working due to false alarms.

While the flash is designed for the Canon E-TTL metering system, I use it reliably on my Lumix cameras with a manual exposure selected. It's by far the best macro lighting tool to overcome initial hurdles and frustrations.

Off-camera Flash

If you already have a speedlight, you can pick up an inexpensive wireless flash trigger. I'm partial to the simplest of designs, full manual control without any bells and whistles. The Vello Freewave LR is one that I use in my studio with great success. I find this preferable to a macro twin light, as the flashes are more powerful and can recycle faster, and the inexpensive Yongnuo YN-560 series of flashes work wonders.

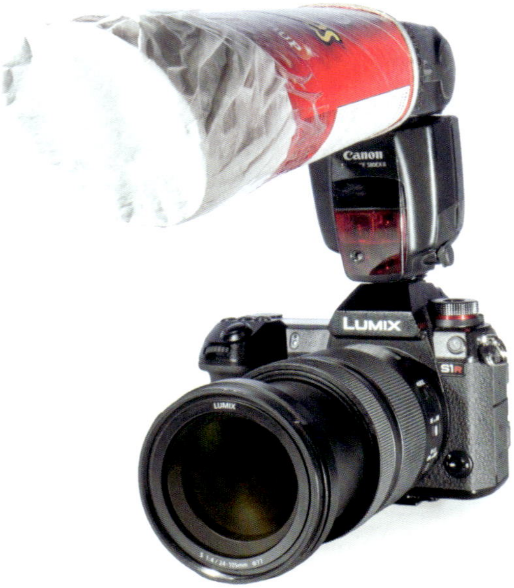

Even just the straight, directional light from this configuration can be a great way to light certain macro scenes. When a ring flash doesn't work or isn't convenient, off-camera flash can be a wonderful tool. It's also something that you can easily tinker with, experimenting to see how modifications to angle, distance and diffusion will affect the look of your image. There's no substitute for practice here. Go ahead and spend an hour experimenting.

What about a Pringles can?

Yes. Involving a Pringles can in photography at all sounds like a ridiculous idea, but read on and decide for yourself. The inside of these tubes are lined with aluminum foil, which works very nicely for bouncing light around. If you cut off the bottom on a 45-degree angle, and cover that opening with a diffuser (wax paper, coffee filter, paper towel taped in place), it can function as a novel light modifier, making it appear like the source of your light isn't coming from the top of your camera but directly above your subject.

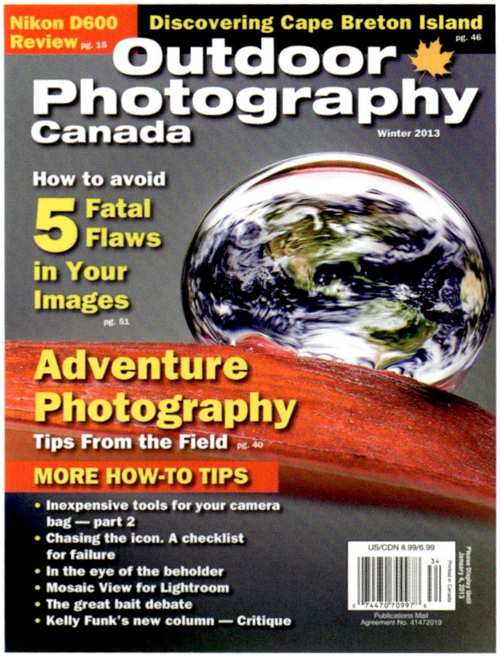

This cover image (above) was shot with a Pringles can as a light modifier.

An image shot with this "tool" was selected as a magazine cover – it's not just a gimmick! Though, I would offer one piece of advice: if you're using it in public, it might be a good idea to cover the outer surface with gaffer's tape, so that people don't question your sanity (as often).

LED Flashlights

In an effort to contradict myself, I also use extremely bright LED flashlights regularly. The high-resolution mode on the Lumix S1R cannot operate with flash, so out of necessity, I have explored these options. It also provides you with a "what you see is what you get" type of light, perfect for stills and video – so long as you're not getting blurry images.

There are a number of good brands out there, but every flashlight I have purchased from Nitecore has been exceptional. Some LED flashlights have a refresh cycle that is imperceptible to our vision but appears as bands of horizontal lines, almost as if you were experiencing a flash sync problem. Lights rated to 1000 lumens or brighter are strongly recommended, with either the SRT7GT or the TM03 CRI – as of publication – being the best all-around options.

The SRT7GT has a very nice analogue brightness control up to 1000 lumens, but also includes dimmer red, green, blue, and ultraviolet LEDs which can be used for light painting or other experimental work. The red light also comes in handy if you're taking a break from macro photography to shoot the night sky, as red flashlights do not harm your adjusted night vision. It might ruin other photographer's images though!

The TM03 CRI is a "tiny monster" flashlight, capable of up to 2800 lumens with a CRI (Colour Rendering Index) that is higher than most flashlights, making it ideal for photographic purposes. It requires a quirky battery that's designed exclusively for this flashlight, but it's the best continuous macro light source I have discovered to date.

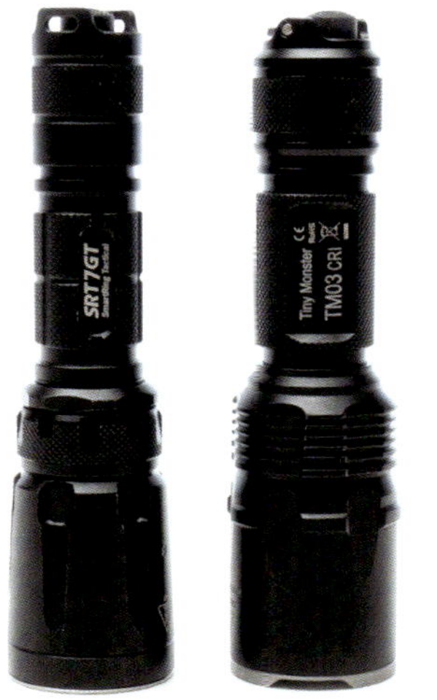

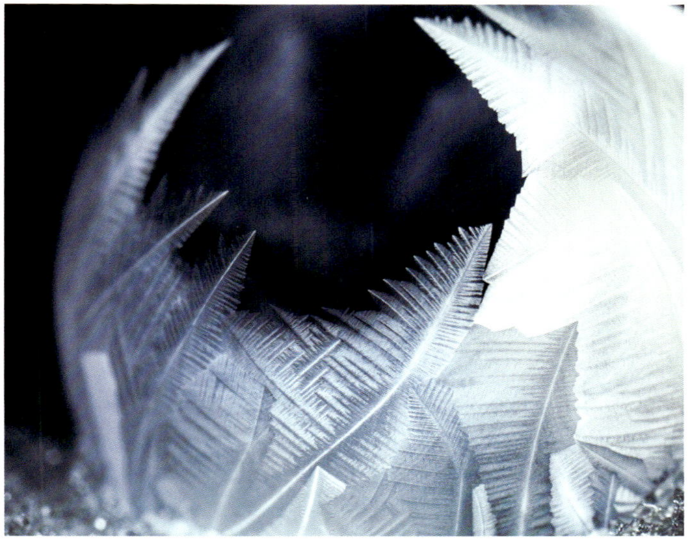

Natural Sunlight

Of course, this is always an option, and it's the light source we're likely to start shooting in! However, bright sunlight can create harsh shadows that make for distracting images. The background is often as bright as the foreground, preventing adequate subject separation. You can modify the sunlight by filtering it through a white umbrella or putting a small disc reflector underneath your subject to improve the results, at which point you're back in the game – controlling the light.

Pay attention to where you position your background as well – subtle shifts can allow you to find a darker or more colour-contrasting background to compliment your subject better. Even in the same lighting conditions, survey the options around you to see how the natural puzzle pieces will fit together better!

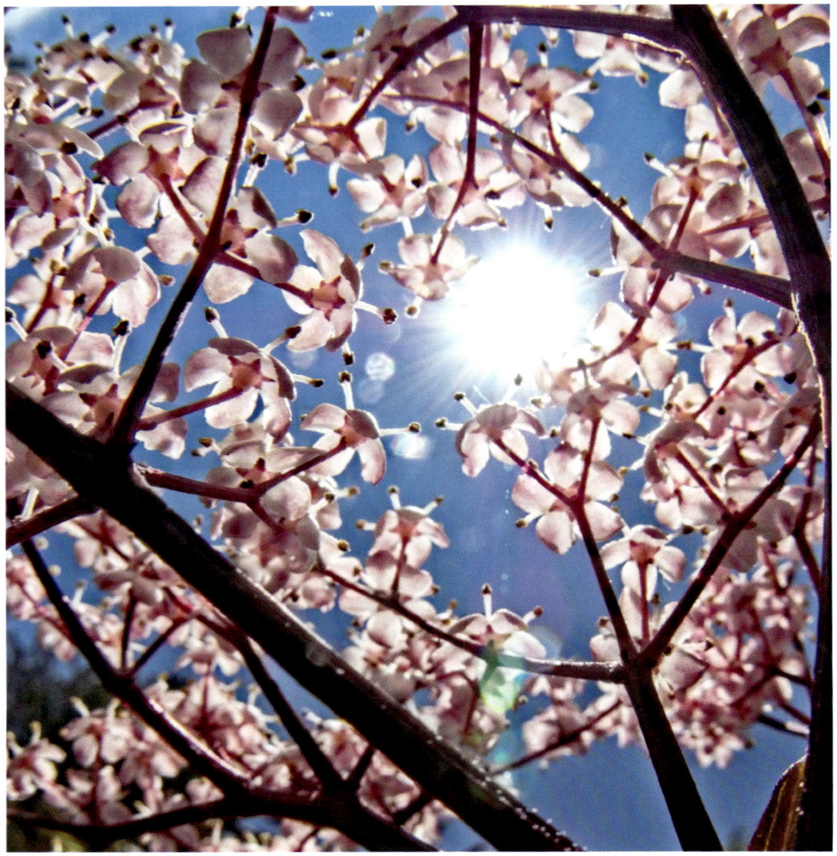

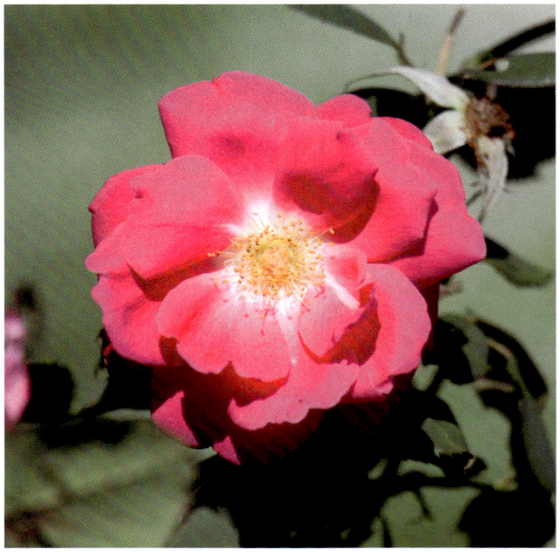

Sometimes the sun is a necessary element in the frame, like these blossoms seemingly reaching towards the light. Backlit subjects can be magical! However, direct, harsh sunlight might not play very well with your subject.

Take the rose on the left. It is the epitome of a terrible flower photograph, with most of the problems originating from how it was illuminated in the bright sun.

Fun fact: The flower was much redder than you see it. Colours can shift in bright lights, especially reds, because the red photosites on the camera sensor are over exposed even though the green and blue photosites are properly exposed.

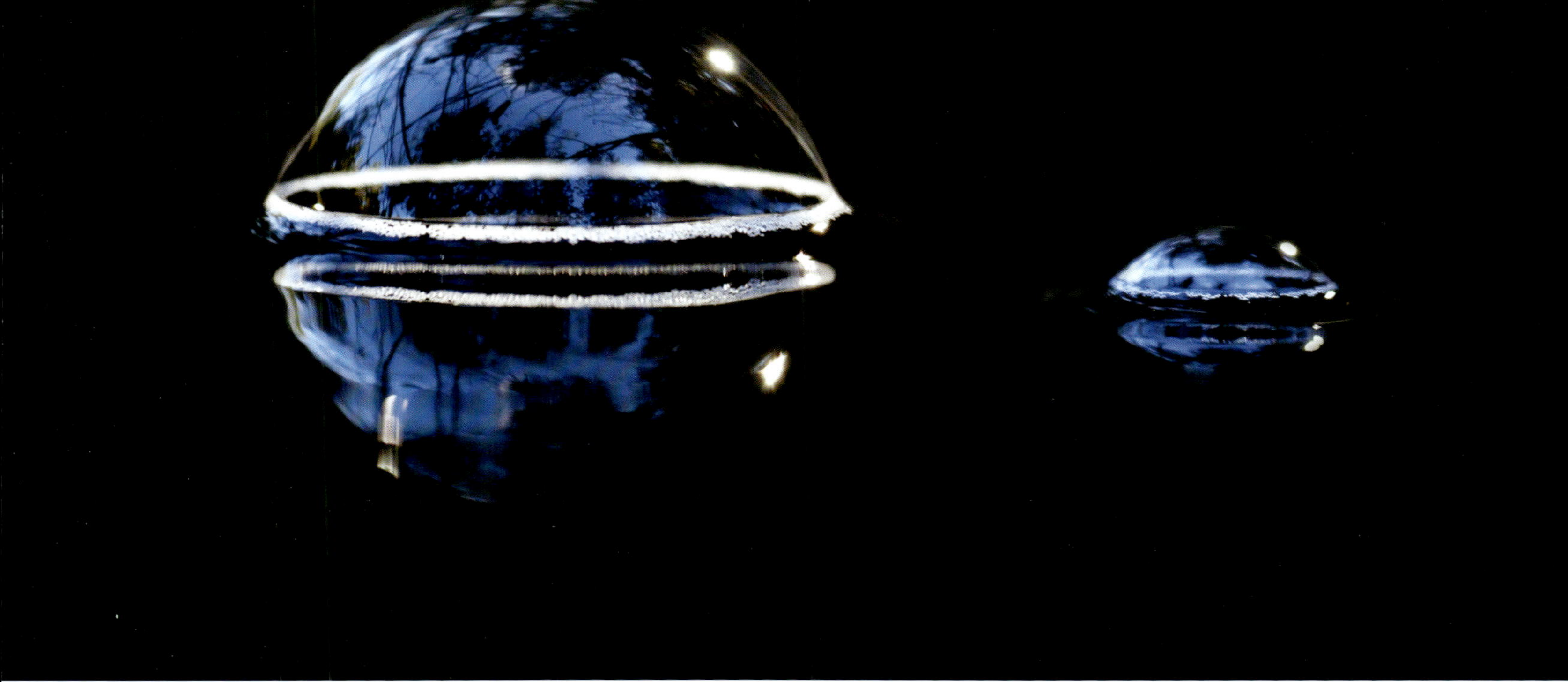

This image, "Young Worlds", illustrates the value of natural light macro photography. It wouldn't be possible without the sun illuminating the blue sky and canopy of trees. It was photographed using the Canon EF 100-400mm f/4.5-5.6L IS USM lens, with extension tubes attached to make its closest focusing distance even closer. Shot at 400mm, it also proves that telephoto lenses can make for interesting macro lenses in the right scenario.

There is no perfect lighting solution. It depends on where you are and what you want to achieve with your image. Understanding the options, as you'll see as they are used throughout this book, will help you evaluate the best lighting option for your ideas.

Exploring all options is the best way to understand when each of them will come in handy – sometimes essential – to the photograph you're trying to create.

The Technical Basics

Photography, in its best form, is a mesh of science and art. You need both. For science, you need to understand the technical elements that affect the image – depth of field, diffraction, exposure, focus, magnification and more. On the artistic side, there are so many considerations from composition, colour, contrast, understanding what "beauty" is perceived as, narratives and storytelling elements and beyond.

The deeper you can weave the mesh of these two elements, science and art, the more magical your images will become.

Some of this can be learned as theory, but it only becomes useful when you begin to experiment and understand what works, but more importantly what doesn't work. You can tinker away on your own with no one judging your experiments – it's all part of the learning process. There are no real failures here so long as you learn from mistakes. With the theory presented here, I heartily suggest you take it to some practical tests and experiments of your own. The more familiar you are with all of these ingredients, the better you will be able to predict how they interact.

Understanding Depth of Field

There are three primary considerations for how much depth of field – the amount of the scene in focus in the resulting photograph. The size of your aperture, the focal length of your lens, and the distance from your subject all have an impact on how much you'll get in focus in a single frame.

There is no "correct" answer for how much depth of field you want. Some images look exquisite with only the tiniest sliver of focus! Others appear too diminished and unable to tell their story without all of the proper visual ingredients depicted. Sometimes the middle ground is the best – giving enough detail while allowing the background to fall off into abstraction. This is an artistic choice that can have a dramatic impact on your work, often revolving around the background detail in the image. I'll repeat this a number of times, especially when we enter into thoughts on composition: the background is one of the most important elements in a macro photograph.

Aperture

This is the most common influencer of depth of field, and it's the reason why lenses with very wide apertures are prized by portrait photographers. The wider your aperture (smaller F-number), the less you'll have in focus. For larger subjects, having a soft background can help simplify an image; for smaller subjects, shooting with wider apertures isn't always ideal. The narrower your aperture, the more you'll have in focus… to a point. Read on how diffraction can interfere with your image quality on the following pages. Having everything in focus isn't always the goal, but this is the most often adjusted setting to control depth. **Remember this**: The smaller the F/#, the less you'll have in focus and the more light you'll let in.

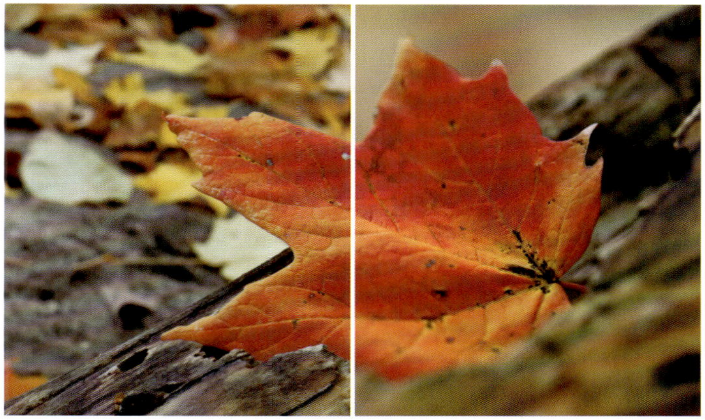

Canon 100mm F/2.8 USM Macro. *Left:* F/32 *Right:* F/2.8
Which one of these is correct? Likely somewhere in between.

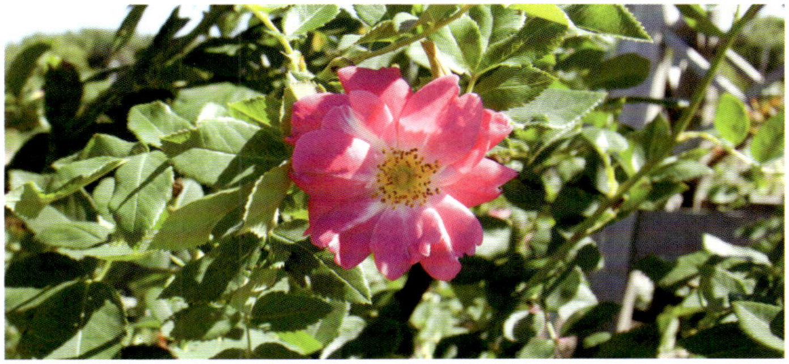

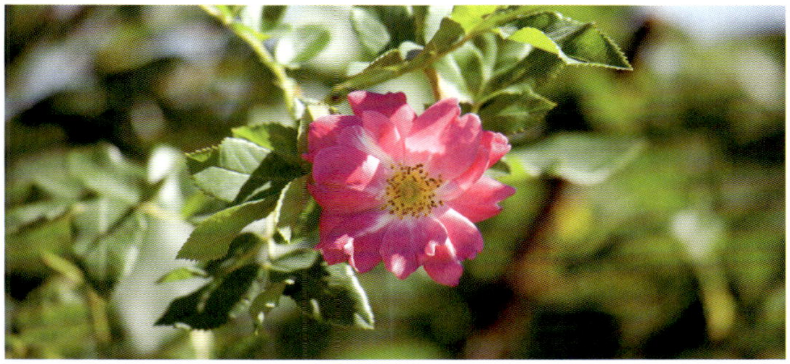

Left: Canon 24-105 F/4L @ F/10, 24mm
Right: Canon 100-400 F/4.5-56L @ F/5.6, 400mm

Focal Length

Longer lenses inherently have less in focus at the same aperture setting than wider-angle lenses. Some macro photographers prefer telephoto macro lenses for precisely this reason, while others are enamoured with greater sharpness across the frame (including the background) and might opt for a wider lens. There is merit to both approaches, but understand that your focal length has a direct impact on the amount of focus in the image. This cannot be overlooked.

Controlling depth of field involves more than one variable at a time. Changing your aperture can soften the background, but adjusting your focal length can simplify the background in other ways. This is partly due to a shallower depth of field, but also because of a narrow field of view behind your subject.

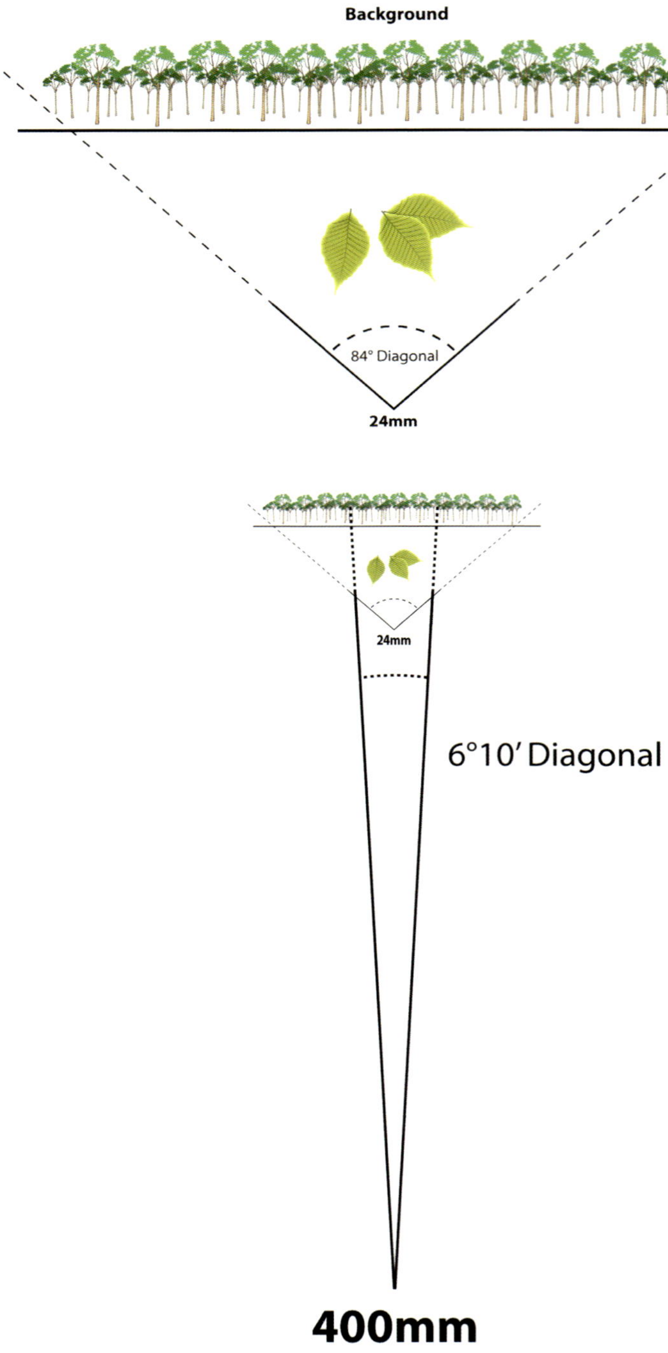

The Forest for the Trees

Maybe not the correct usage of this idiom, but we need to take a look at how focal length and framing have a particularly important impact on our work. Scenario: You're standing in a forest, trying to isolate some leaves against a background of trees. What focal length do you choose? You could get right up in front of the leaves with a wide angle lens, or you could deliberately shoot from much farther away, zooming in with telephoto reach to achieve the same framing. What happens when you try all the possibilities? You'll find out what you like the best.

Controlling focal length, as mentioned on the previous page, also has an impact on the contents of the background, not just how much of it is in focus. Since your field of view will change with your focal length, a telephoto lens can allow for a more precise selection of what is included – and excluded – from the background. You can use this to frame your subject appropriately based on whatever is behind it.

Let's examine what happens as we change our focal length gradually from 24mm to 400mm, with all images taken at the same aperture: F/8.

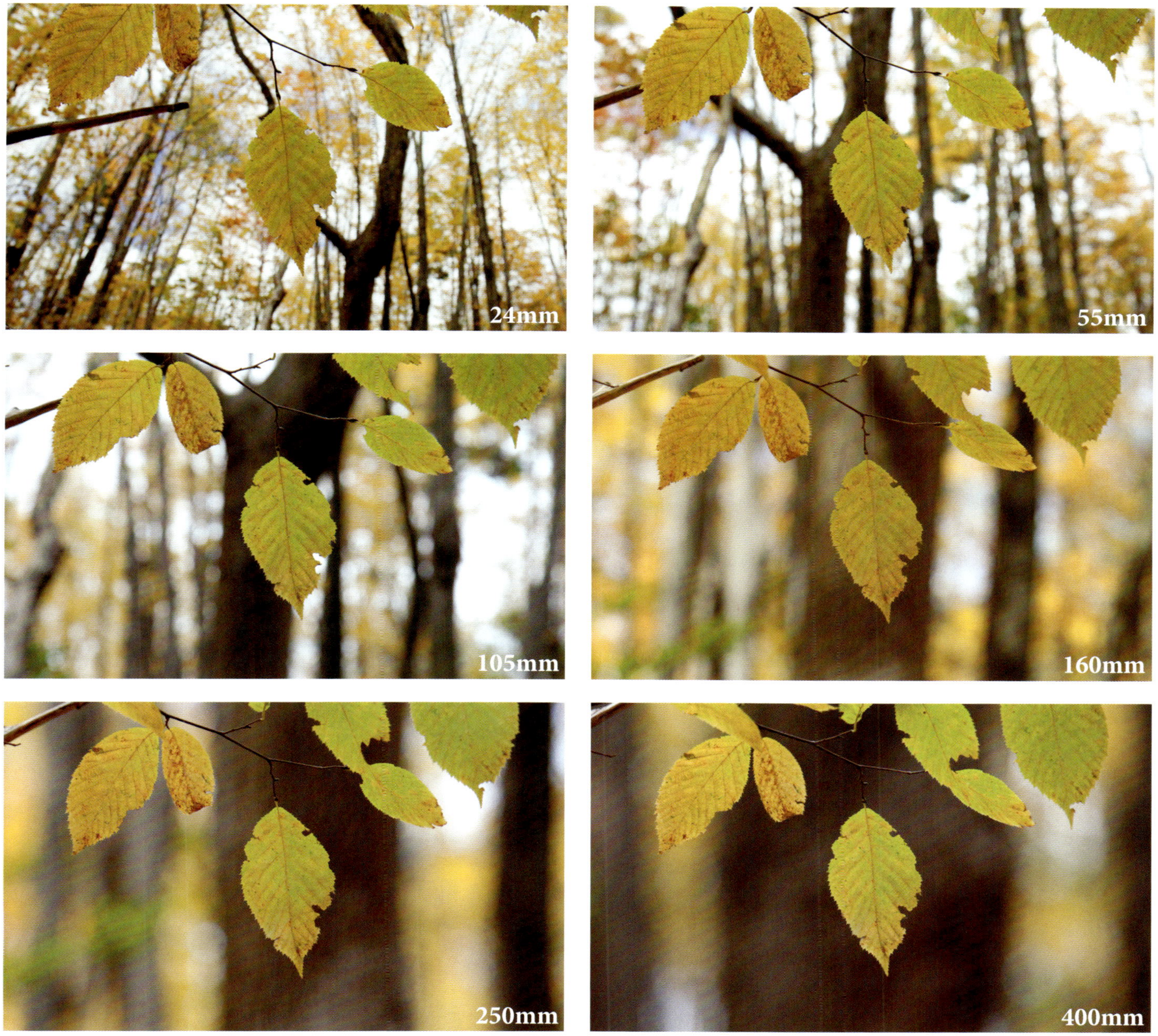

Which one of these is correct? It's all personal preference! My personal favourite is either 160mm or 250mm in this scenario. I rarely choose the extremes, but I know what I enjoy the best because I have experimented beyond that comfort zone. Focal length and distance from your subject, together, can be very powerful tools.

Distance From Your Subject

As a landscape photographer, shooting at F/8 might present you with everything in focus, except for elements that might be in the extreme foreground. F/8 to a macro photographer on the other hand might result in an inch of useable focus – or less. The closer you get to your subject, the shallower your depth of field will become. While it might be your intention to fill the frame with your subject, it can be advantageous to leave a little extra space. Cropping in from modern cameras is a viable technique to increase your depth of field. How many pixels do we really need?

As a part of the creative process, I don't get bogged down with equations to calculate depth of field. This statement might be blasphemous to some! There are some great online calculators to identify exactly how much depth you'll get with a particular aperture, focal length and focusing distance... but does an absolute value matter? Practicality is important here, so the best idea would be to do some homework: get a feel for how these variables impact your images through your own experimentation, and understand what you find the most aesthetically pleasing.

It can be as simple as taking a test shot while out shooting insects, and establishing if you have too little or too much in focus. From there, identify which of these three variables will have the best impact on your photograph. While the technical details are important to understand, the final image shouldn't only be a technical exercise – it should be a work of art.

Still, we find ourselves pushing up against technical limitations when we focus exclusively on the visual component of our images. One such example is not grasping the limitations we face with very small apertures, and it almost derailed my own adventures in macro photography! **It all started with a question:**

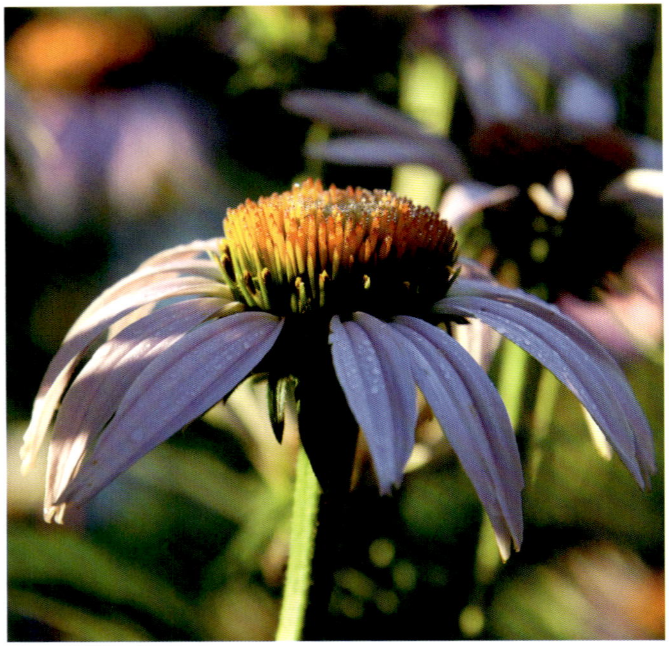

Top: Image photographed at F/8.

Bottom: Image photographed at F/9, same flower but at a closer distance and higher magnification. Note that the depth of field is much shallower.

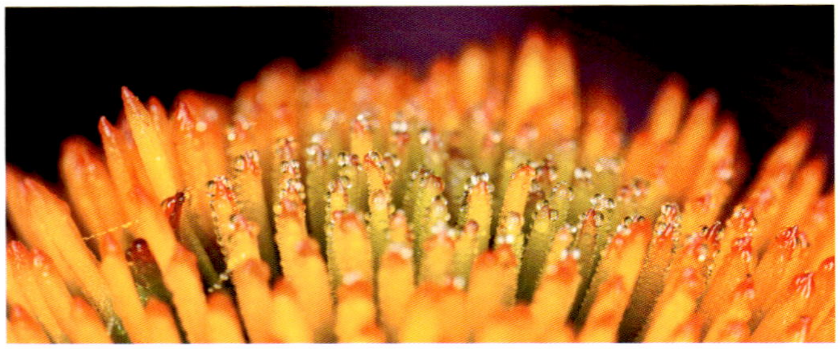

Why Can't I Shoot At F/96?

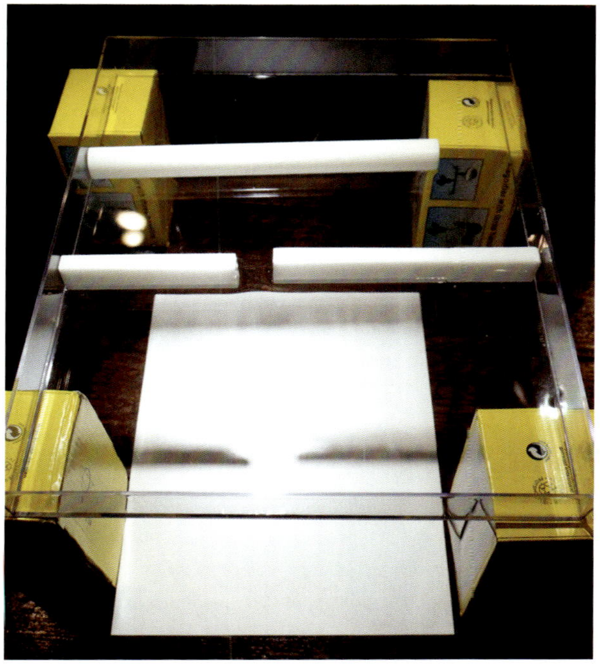

It's a simple question, albeit one I asked as a naive beginner in the world of macro photography. The logic was sound – if my depth of field is too shallow, why not just adjust a variable you can control such as your aperture to fight back? Shooting with an incredibly small aperture would give me some added depth that was taken away by getting closer to my subject, right?

This logic does not account for "diffraction". Diffraction is the process of a wave bending as it passes through an opening. The wider the opening, the less "bendy" the light becomes. The wave at the edges of a large opening will still be bending off course, but the wave passing through the middle will be less affected by diffraction. The smaller your opening, the more the wave will bend off course. I'm using the word "wave" here, not "light", because we can see this explained visually using a ripple table with water – a great way to visualize the wave nature of light.

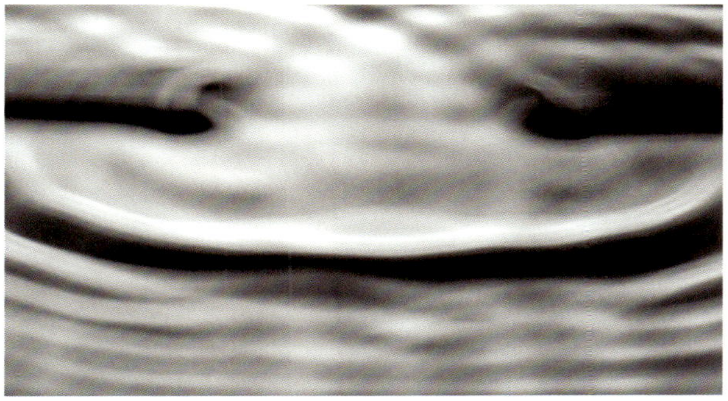

Ripple tanks are a very modest experimental tool; you may have used one in a high school science or physics class. Using a small amount of water with a light shining down through to a piece of paper below, you can get exact visuals of what happens when a wave encounters an obstacle. Consider this opening to be analogous to the aperture in your lens. With that comparison in mind, it's easy to see that the smaller you make your aperture, the further light will bend away from its intended target. This is where the problems start.

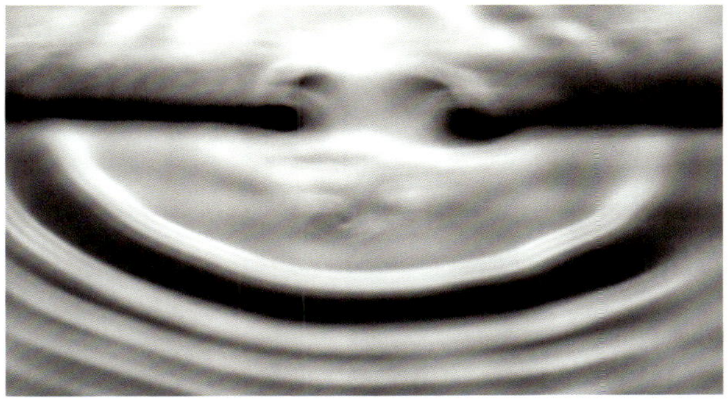

Top: Simple "ripple tank" experimental setup.

Middle: Larger opening (aperture) allows plenty of water (light) pass through unaffected.

Bottom: A smaller opening (aperture) causes more of the wave to bend.

Bring this concept back to photography: The smaller you make your aperture, the more light is going to bend when it passes through this opening and onward to your camera sensor. There is no avoiding this; the physics of light hasn't changed in nearly 14 trillion years and I doubt it will become more cooperative in this scenario. That wonderful "bright idea" of shooting with such small apertures suddenly meets with frustration.

In one of the most extreme examples of this, we see the diffraction pattern created by pointing a blue laser at a pinhole (*right*). The pattern generated through optical interference is called an Airy Disc, though we rarely see it so perfectly presented in our photographs. Imagine that the grid placed over the laser image as dividing lines between photosites on your camera sensor. Light that should only be hitting the central photosite is spilling off to its neighbours. Light that should only be hitting a neighbouring pixel will spill over into the central pixel as well. Effectively, things start to colour outside the lines. Not good!

Can we see this in real-world examples? At the most extreme magnifications I have seen this in some of my snowflake work, shooting at 12:1 magnification and looking incredibly closely at some high-contrast edges, we can see the same patterns emerge. One would think that shooting with your aperture set to F/2.8 would surely avoid such problems, but herein lies a frustration that macro photographers face: **the more magnification you shoot with, the smaller your effective aperture becomes**. *Say what?*

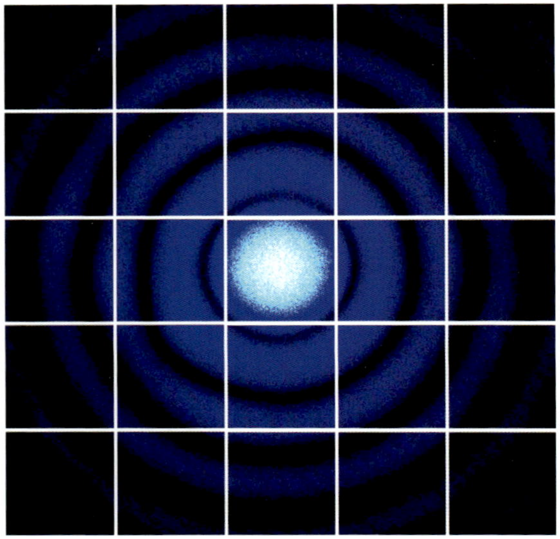

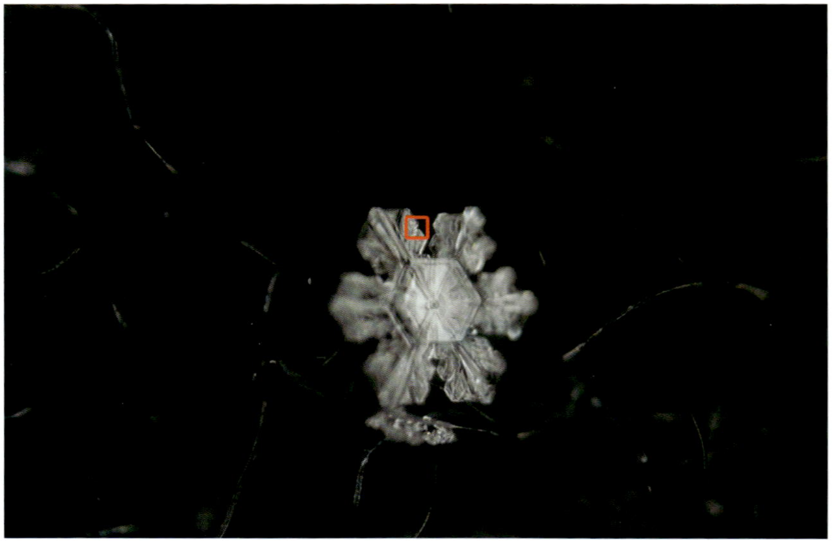

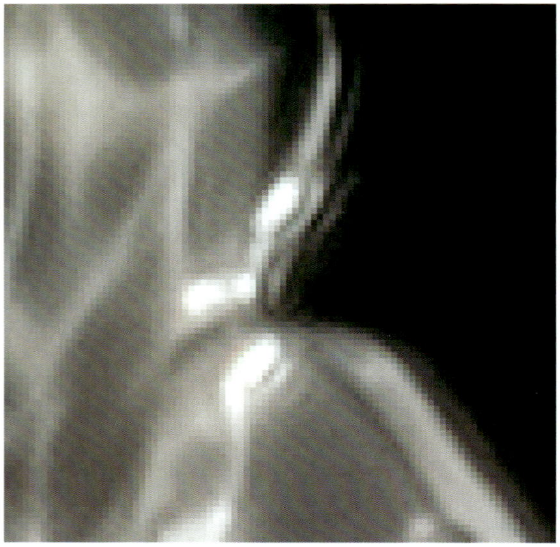

Effective Aperture

The greater the magnification you are shooting with, the more your aperture will deviate from the number you set on the lens or through your camera. This was such a foreign concept to me in the days after I purchased the Canon MP-E 65mm F/2.8 1x-5x macro lens that I thought I had purchased a "bad copy" of the lens – one that shouldn't have passed quality control testing. I was about to learn something.

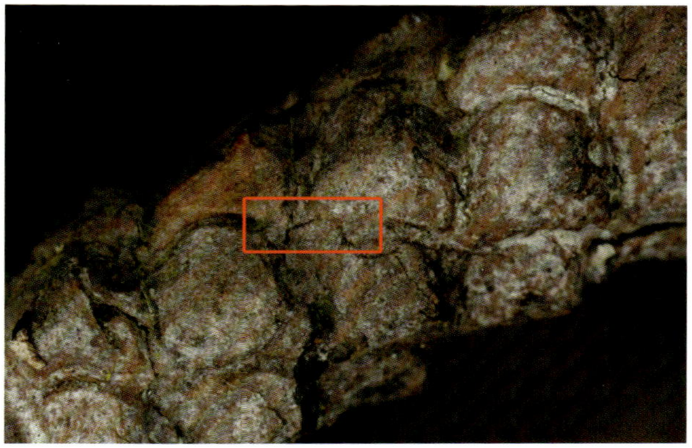

It's a terrible image, even if it was sharp it couldn't be saved! But why was it so much softer than expected?

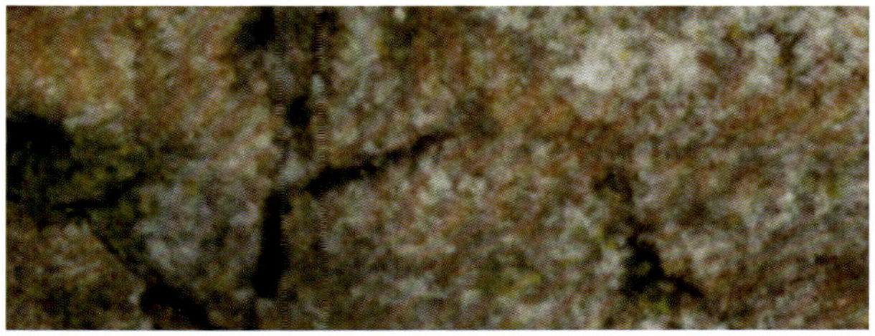

Using standard photography logic, shooting at F/16 shouldn't pose a problem – and when you're testing a lens like this, go to the extremes of 5X! It was November, and a nature walk produced bland subjects – tree bark and lichen mostly, but good enough to keep my enthusiasm up for my new ~~toy~~ tool and partake in a "test drive" of sorts. The results were beyond soft, but in a perplexing way. The image seemed decent in the viewfinder, actually having more detail to my eyes than the final image! Clearly something was wrong, but I was missing important details.

The first detail should have been obvious: when looking through the viewfinder, the aperture blades are wide open. Only when pressing the shutter (or engaging a "depth of field preview" feature) do the aperture blades snap into the selected value. When seeing the image with my own eyes before taking the photo, I was seeing an F/2.8 image, but pressing the shutter resulted in an F/16 image. However, those values aren't what they appear to be – it's all based on magnification.

f-number	1×	2×	3×	4×	5×
2.8	5.6	8.4	11.2	14	16.8
3.2	6.4	9.6	12.8	16	19.2
3.5	7	10.5	14	17.5	21
4	8	12	16	20	24
4.5	9	13.5	18	22.5	27
5	10	15	20	25	30
5.6	11.2	16.8	22.4	28	33.6
6.3	12.6	18.9	25.2	31.5	37.8
7.1	14.2	21.3	28.4	35.5	42.6
8	16	24	32	40	48
9	18	27	36	45	54
10	20	30	40	50	60
11	22	33	44	55	66
13	26	39	52	65	78
14	28	42	56	70	84
16	32	48	64	80	96

Page 8 of the manual for this particular lens (*previous page*) revealed the secrets for me, which I looked through one last time before packing the lens up to return it.

First, we need to realize that the F/stop that is dialed in to our lens is only relevant at infinity focus, and when you focus closer than infinity this number is no longer accurate. Many Nikon cameras will automatically calculate this new effective aperture as you get closer and closer to 1:1 magnification on their camera bodies, if you've ever been curious why F/2.8 becomes something closer to F/5.6 automatically as you get closer to your subject.

The basic rule is that by the time you get to 1:1 macro magnification, you've lost two stops of light. The Canon chart shows this – F/2.8 becomes F/5.6. For every magnification factor you add from here, add an additional stop to your effective aperture. This simple rule works for most lenses to get a ballpark idea of where your aperture is going to be:

Effective Aperture =
Dialed-in Aperture x (1 + Magnification factor)

So, for Infinity focus at F/2.8 you would be F2/8 x (1+0), or… F/2.8! That checks out.

Where this becomes useful is when you are shooting at 1:1 life-size and beyond. F/16 effectively becomes F/32 at 1x magnification, which is where you might begin to see the effects of diffraction in your images. Using extension tubes, close-up filters or a lens natively capable of shooting closer? Watch out, this sneaks up on you quickly!

To be fair, the actual equation is a little more complex. It factors in the entrance and exit pupils of your lens as a "pupil ratio" or "magnification ratio". Do a quick test: with your lens off the camera and both front and rear caps removed, look through it from both sides. Does one opening appear bigger than the other? The actual ratio can be difficult to measure (my own basic tests yielded wildly inaccurate results), and very few manufacturers ever publish these numbers; just taking a look will tell you on what side of the scale you are.

For example, Looking at the front of the Laowa 25mm F/2.8 2.5x-5x macro lens reveals a bigger "pupil" than looking in from the rear of the lens. This means that diffraction might creep in even sooner. In contrast, the wide-angle Laowa 15mm F/4 Macro has a larger pupil seen from the rear, meaning that F/16 might not translate into F/32, but maybe closer to F/25.

Using a bit of algebra we can calculate the pupil ratios used by Canon to make their chart, and they all mostly hover around 1, meaning that the entrance and exit pupils are mostly equal. Telephoto macro lenses will have a much smaller exit pupil and can be prone to the effects of diffraction even earlier than normal-range macro lenses. Manufacturers generally do not share this numerical value with consumers, and it varies based on focal length and focus distance.

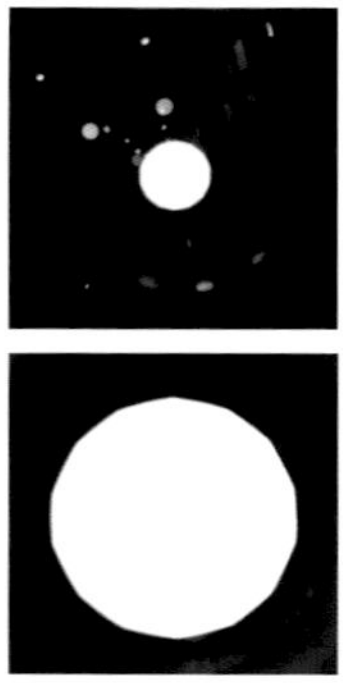

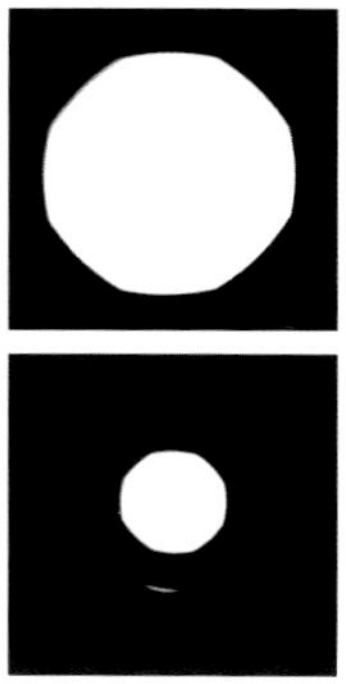

Left:
Pupil of Laowa 15mm F/4 (top entrance, bottom exit)

Right:
Pupil of Laowa 25mm F/2.8 (top entrance, bottom exit)

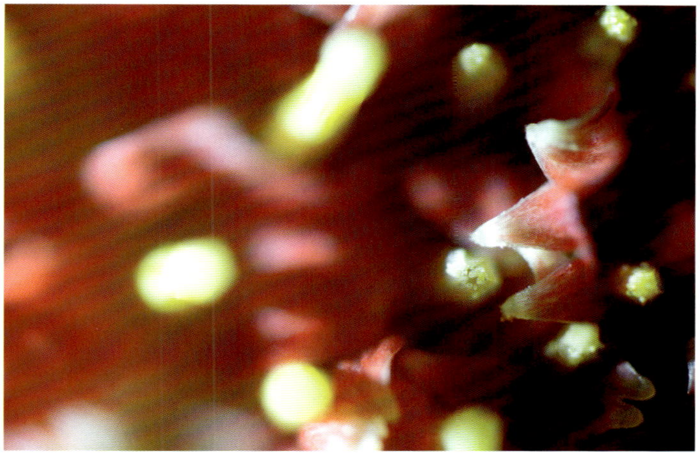

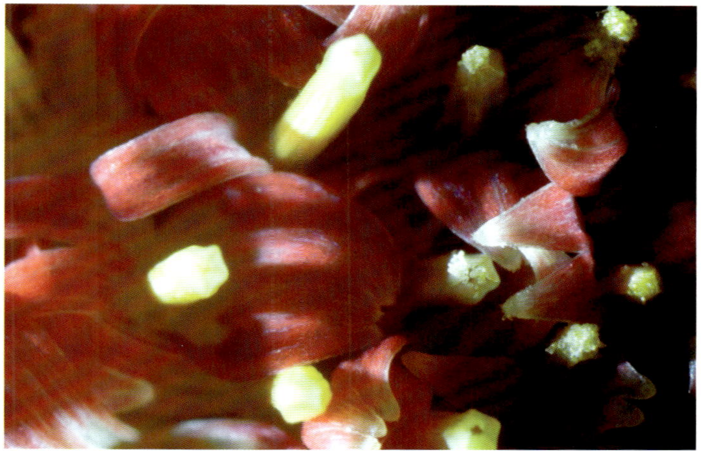

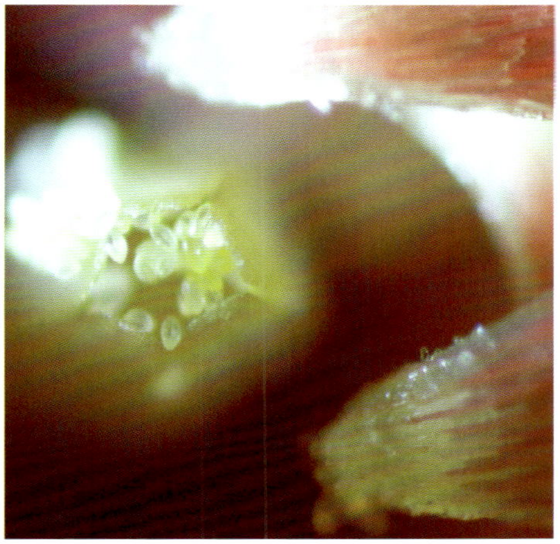

"But what does all this frustrating math mean!?" – I hear your screams. Don't worry. Here's a simple, practical example. Above is the same subject photographed at two different apertures with the Canon MP-E 65mm F/2.8 1x-5x Macro lens. On the left, we have an aperture of F/2.8 (effective aperture of F/16.8). On the right, we have an aperture of F/16 (effective aperture of F/96). Compare the details!

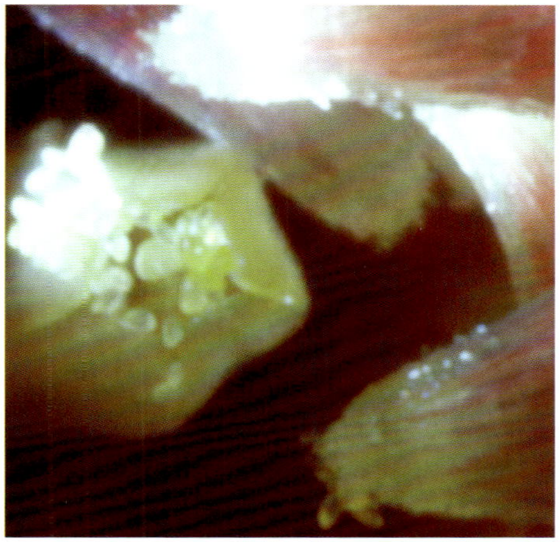

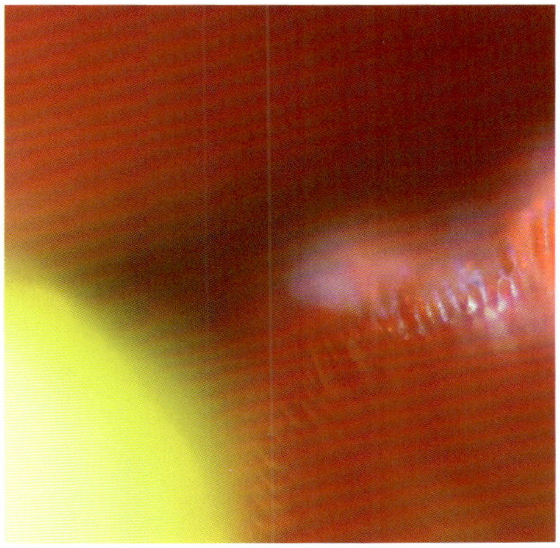

On the left, we have a very shallow depth of field but maintain critical sharpness through a very shallow "slice". On the right, our depth of field is greatly improved… but dive into the details and you'll see that you've just sacrificed every bit of detail in the process. Yikes.

The lesson? The closer you get, the wider you should set your aperture.

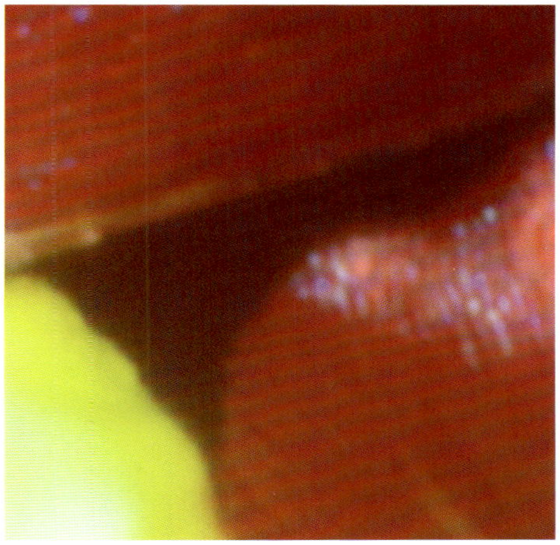

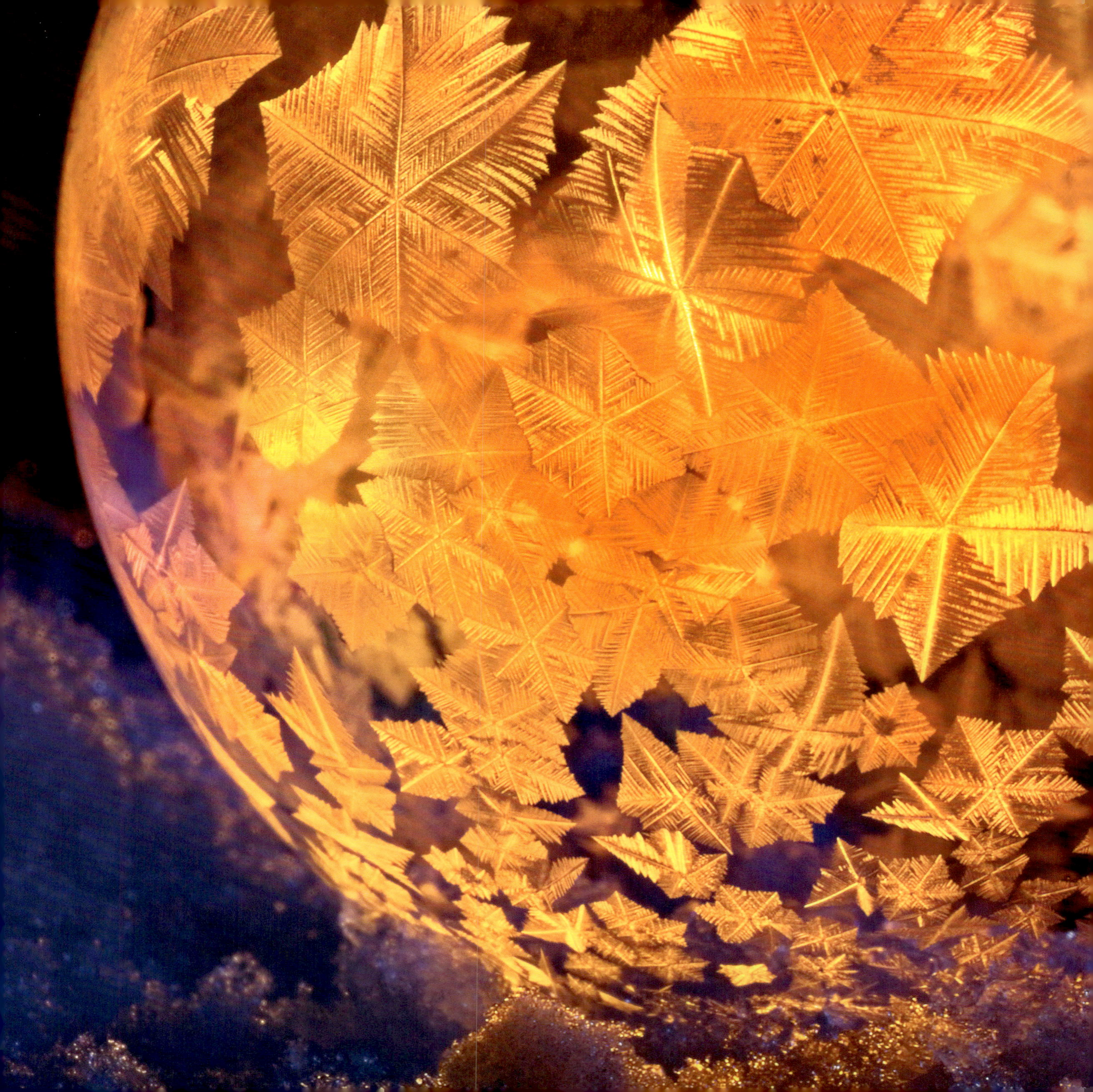

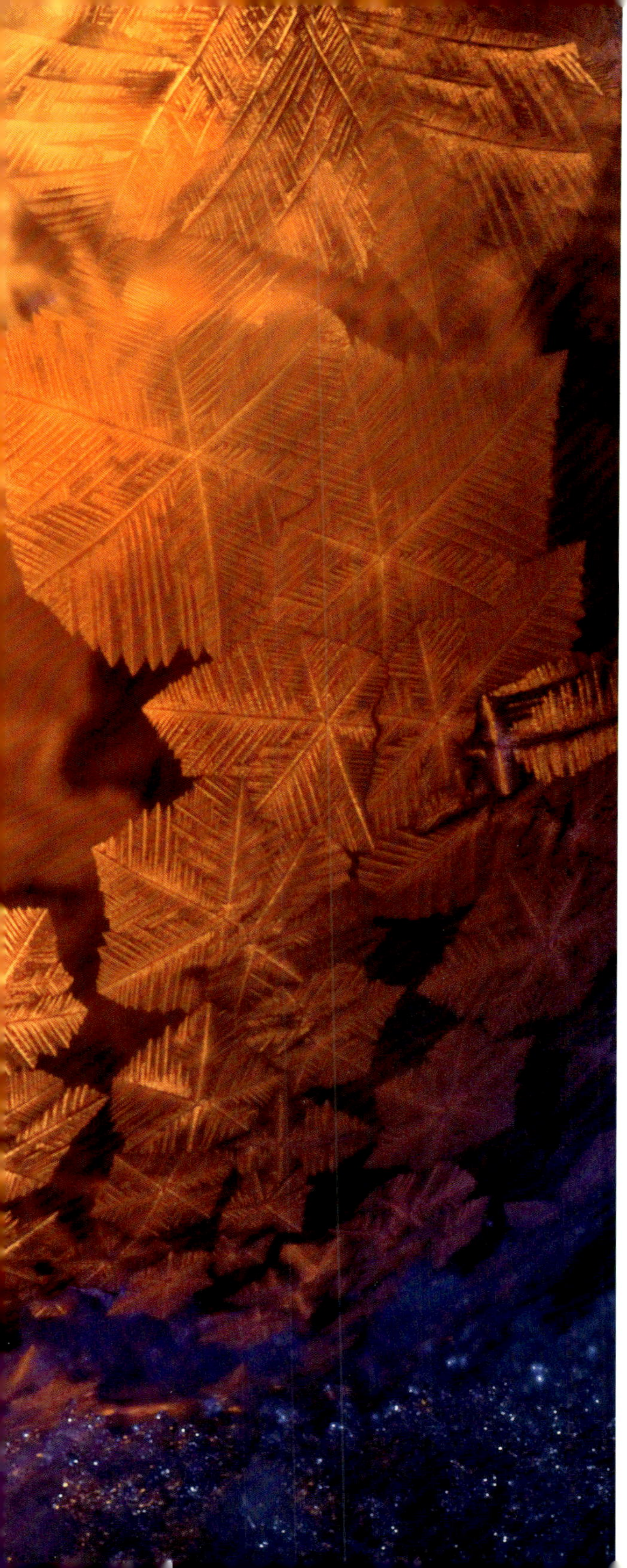

Take a deep breath, you just made it through one of the most technical elements of macro photography – and I intentionally didn't even write the most complex equation for calculating effective apertures. You can get lost in all the minutiae resulting in not being able to see the forest for the trees; finally a correct use for that idiom!

There are a lot of "moving parts" in macro photography. So many variables to consider, and the ways they interact can oppose your intuition. Consider this like solving a puzzle: at first, you have a grand idea to create the image on the box, but the individual puzzle pieces need to be identified and stuck together in a precise way. Once you've mastered the technical activity of putting it all together, you're likely just replicating someone else's work. Only then can you understand the process, and apply it to your own art.

Up to this point in my career, I never had to worry about pupil ratios. It was an important thing to some, but practically it was a puzzle piece that I didn't need to know. Essentially, I just had a basic understanding that the closer I got to a subject, the smaller my effective aperture would get and if my results were softer than I liked, then widen up the aperture. Knowing theory is one thing, but this is a "tools based" approach to creativity, where you gain knowledge and then try to find a place where it is applicable to you. Instead, I genuinely believe in a "goals based" approach, where you encounter a problem and research the solution to the point at which it solves your problem, then move on. Leave stones unturned if you don't need to look under them to find your answer. Revisit technical problems only when they become a barrier for your photographic idea to be the best success it can be, and you'll keep weaving science into art as it's needed.

Lumix GX9, Leica DG Macro-Elmarit 45mm F/2.8,
F/22 ISO 200 1/250
Less than 1:1 magnification, effective aperture closer to F/32.
It's all about finding your balance!

Focus

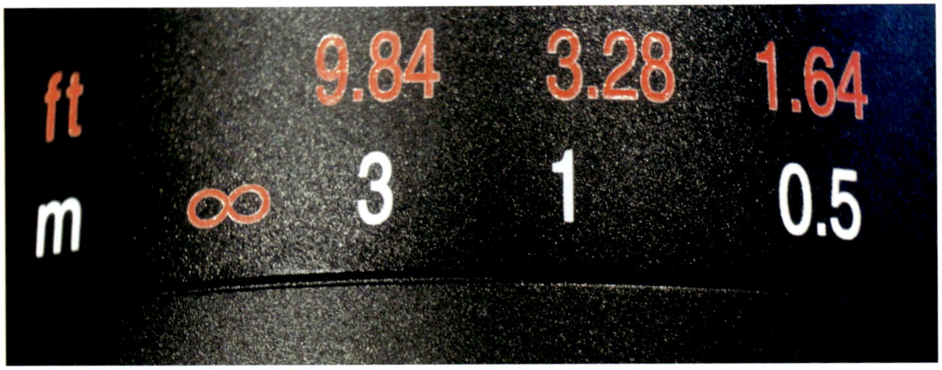

We've established that we need to tolerate - if not embrace - a shallow depth of field. The closer you get to your subject, the shallower your depth will be. How do we ensure that our narrow sliver of focus falls in the right spot?

The latest advancements in autofocus technology are difficult to adapt to macro photography approaching 1:1 magnification and beyond. Take a look at the barrel of your lens and notice the distance markings for focus. The spacing is key – the distance from infinity to 3 meters is smaller than from 3 to 1 meters, which in turn is smaller than the distance needed to turn the lens from 1 meters to 0.5 meters.

What does this mean? The lens has to spin further, moving the lens elements over a greater distance, the closer you get to your subject. It might be fast and accurate to focus on something far away, but the closer you get the slower the focus movement will be, and the more precise it needs to be as well. This sets us up for frustration, because the lightning-fast autofocus we enjoy for sports photography is less effective on a macro scale.

The best technique to consider for macro photography is to physically move the entire camera and lens forward and back. This is even more important when you are at higher magnifications, with most high magnification macro lenses not even having a focusing system at all!

My own initial research had indicated that this was best done on a "focusing rail", a tool that sits on the top of a tripod and lets you methodically adjust the focus to hit precisely the point you required. Immediately I realized the impracticality of this – it might work well for still life subjects in a studio, but what about flowers in the field? Insects? Snowflakes? Freezing soap bubbles? In practice, it's easier than you might first realize to handhold the camera and move in very small increments without the aid of a tripod.

In fact, the vast majority of the images in this book were taken without a tripod or focusing rail at all. They were taken with a simple technique: sway back and forth ever-so-slightly until you find focus where it needs to be.

You'll want to be well anchored while still allowing yourself to move forward and back, and this is achieved with a number of techniques:

Hold the end of the lens, not the base of the lens.
If you place your left hand at the end of the lens where you would typically have the filter threads, this will help prevent the subject from jumping around the frame. Imagine this: the back of the camera is steady but the front of the lens is jittery – but your subject is in front of the lens, not behind the camera. Hold the

end of the lens or the edge of macro flash attached to the end of the lens as often as possible.

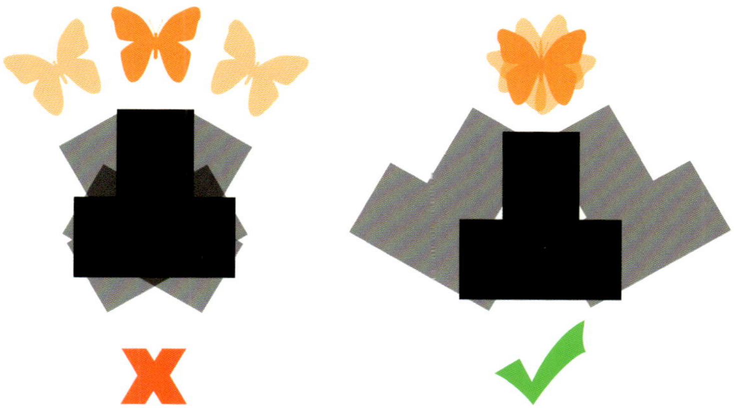

If the camera is shaking / moving at the back, the front of the lens can potentially move so significantly that your subject might be out of the frame! Grab the end of the lens and keep it stable, and you will find that your subject stays in the frame more frequently.

Use your viewfinder.
If your camera has a viewfinder, either electronic or optical, use it. "Smushing" your face against the back of your camera adds an additional point of stability. Using Live View features can be very helpful in scenarios when you're locked down on a tripod, but if the camera is in your hands, the pressure against your face will help steady any tremors you have.

Brace your hands/arms against anything available.
When shooting in studio for water droplet images or any other tabletop macro work, it's easy to rest my wrists on the edge of the table and "slide" the camera forward and back. In the field, a post, a tree, the ground itself can all be helpful. Look for anything around you that you can rest on. Ironically, this is sometimes a tripod that I have set up to hold a flash; the camera isn't on the tripod, but I can rest against it to aid in handholding.

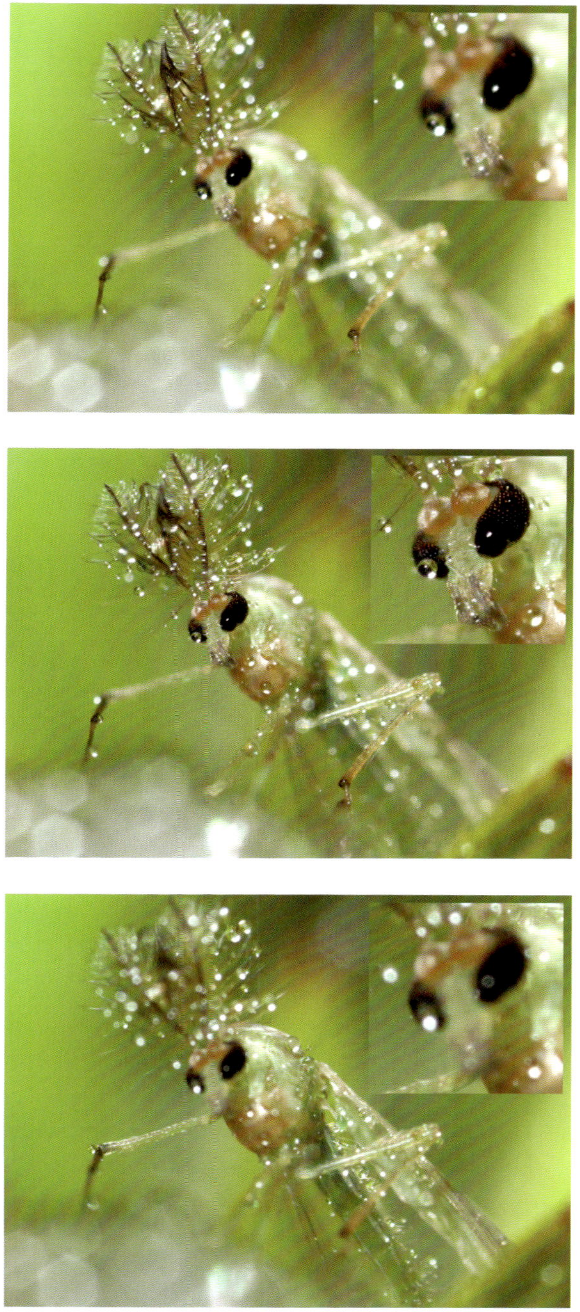

Sway through your expected focus point while shooting continuously to nail focus in at least one frame. Take 20 shots to get the right one!

Press your elbows against your chest.
Don't have anything to brace yourself with? Simply tucking your elbows into your chest will limit the unwanted movement in your arms.

Shoot continuous bursts.
This flies in the face of conventional photographic logic from the film era where every frame cost money. For this technique to work effectively, you need to start taking photographs while introducing a slight movement forward and away from your subject, passing through the point of critical focus that you're hoping for. This means you may need to take 20-30 images to get exactly the shot you need. See the examples (*previous page*) of a small Chironomid using this technique, with critical sharpness and focus falling on the eyes in the middle frame.

What's the advantage?
Why? Why would you go through all of this trouble and chaos, adding unneeded frustration to your life? It's far more freeing in terms of composition and much faster when dealing with transient subjects.

For composition, you now have the ability to move around the subject as the center of rotation rather than wherever the camera is mounted to a tripod. This is not only helpful in orienting the camera to achieve the most beautiful background, but it also allows for quick changes to achieve surface reflection on subjects like snowflakes, or proper alignment of water droplets and backgrounds for refraction photography. As soon as you realize that a tripod is not a requirement for certain subjects, you'll stop getting bogged down with the technical elements and feel much more immersed in the artistic elements of your photographic adventures.

Some subjects are simply uncooperative, whether it's an ant that refuses to sit still or a snowflake that will melt or blow away if you take too much time. Working quickly can make the difference between getting a usable image and getting nothing at all.

This technique of handholding the camera isn't right for all subjects: working in the dark for ultraviolet fluorescence, using a microscope objective, setting the camera to capture a falling water droplet, "high resolution" modes and more. Beyond these scenarios, I highly encourage you to take your camera off the tripod and move it around for focus! It works, the proof is in the images you see in this book.

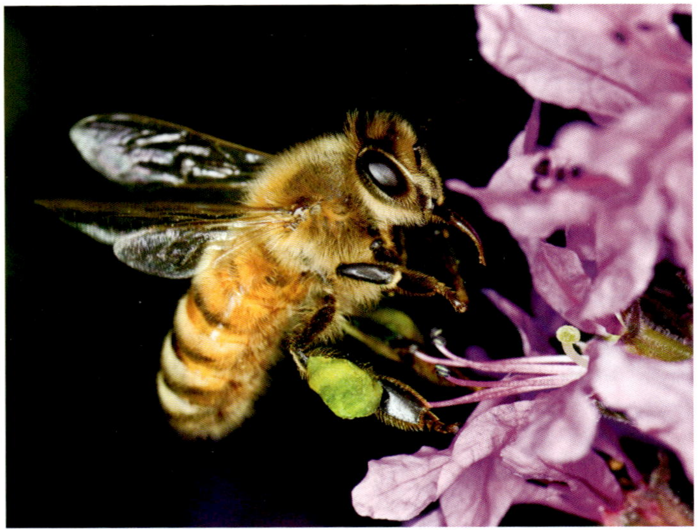

Canon 5D mark II, Canon MP-E 65mm F/2.8 1x-5x Macro, F/11 ISO 400 1/160

Try chasing a bee around on a tripod! Of course you could wait for the bee to fly into a perfectly staged flower, though your opportunities to shoot will be few and far between.

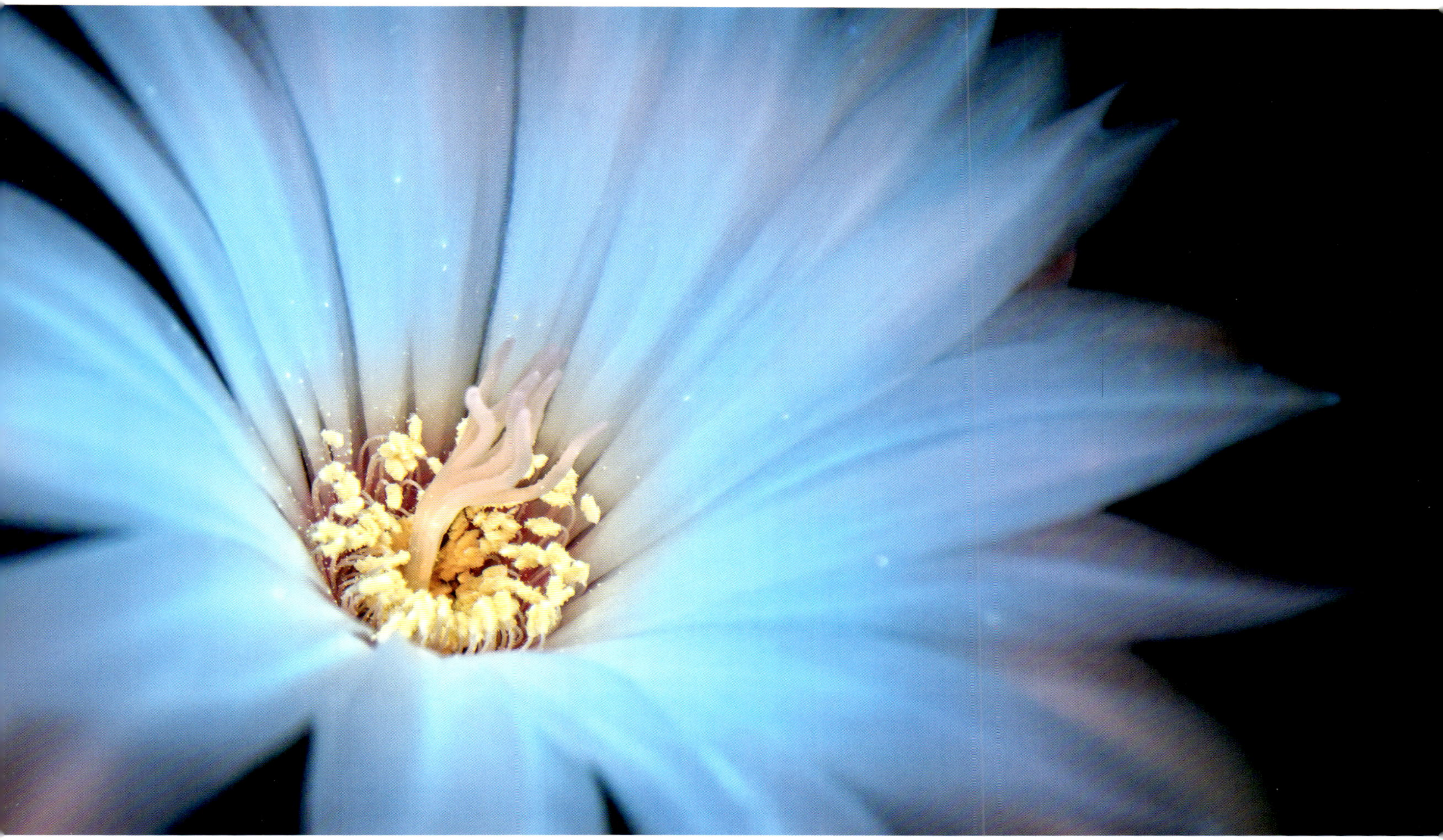

Macro photography is often synonymous with chaotic variables. Small changes in position, focus, or the movement of a subject mean you have to embrace that chaos and work with it, hedging your bets by drastically overshooting. This isn't always the case, and for subjects that are defined, stable and approachable, I give in. Use your tripod.

This succulent bloom (*above*) is photographed in ultraviolet light causing it to fluoresce. The lens used was the Laowa 24mm F/14 Probe Macro lens, with a very small barrel that wouldn't interfere with the petals at a close distance while still giving a wider-angle feel and allowing the petals to "spread out" across the frame. This isn't a lens that is easy to handhold, and the subject was static.

In scenarios where you can get away with being "locked down", do it. Make this the exception if you are able, as shooting with the camera in hand allows for more creative approaches to your subject and a rapid ability to experiment with new angles and ideas. It's fuel for the creative process.

Pushing Focus Farther

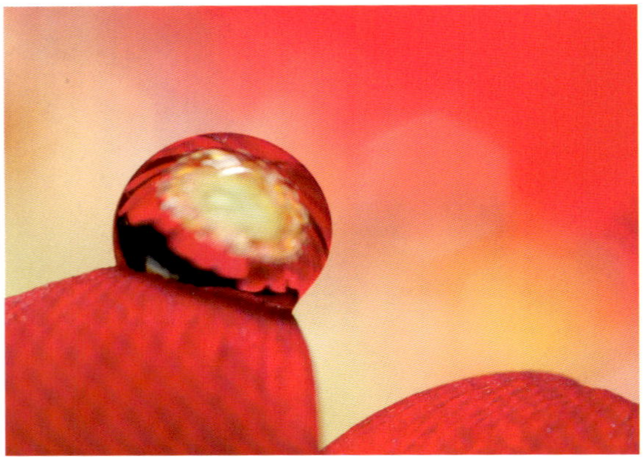

Even if you hit the proverbial nail on the head and get focus exactly where you want it to be in a single image, you'll find yourself craving more focus – more depth. We've discussed how this can be detrimental in a single photograph due to the nasty physics of diffraction, though there are a number of ways around that. The most common approach is a technique called "focus stacking" and the process of editing for stacking is discussed later in this book. We're at the point in the technical journey where we can start thinking about this – we may have just captured the necessary material for this process.

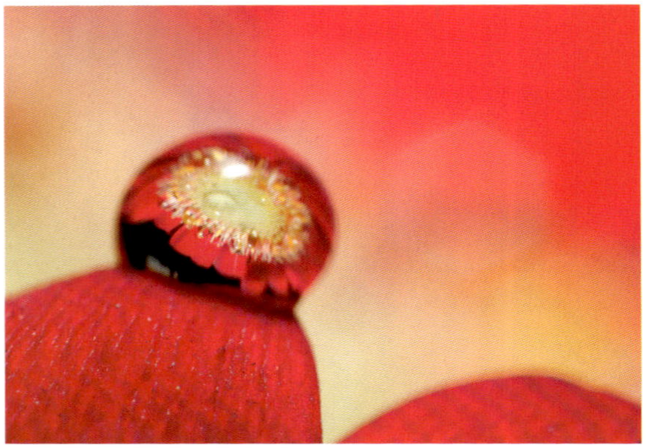

If you're shooting many images in the hopes that one frame gets the best possible focus, you'll also be capturing many adjacent slices of focus. This can prove quite useful – don't immediately discard the images that slightly miss the mark. These images can be combined in software very easily to extend the amount of the image that appears in focus. Even if you only add an extra image, you can improve your focus without compromising on image quality. Adding more images adds to the depth.

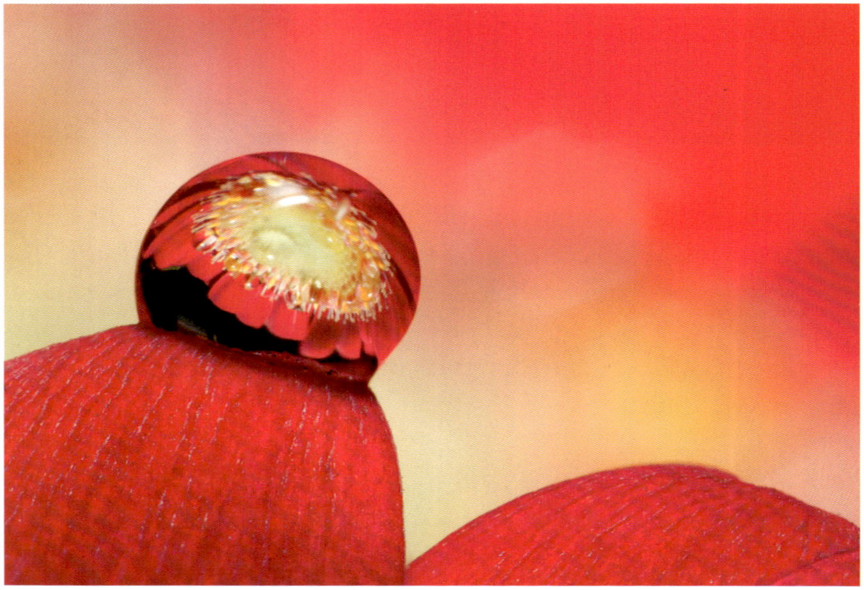

What does this look like? Take a look at these component images (*top right*) of a water droplet refraction photo. In one image, the outer edge of the droplet is crisp and sharp, but the refraction is soft. Next, you have a sharp refraction but you trade that for a blurry edge of the droplet itself. These images and a few additional frames were captured by continuously shooting the subject while very gently moving the camera forward and back. Every shot you take could be the equivalent to a puzzle piece to put together an even better image. Even if you're not concerned about putting together such a puzzle at this stage of your macro photography journey, know that you're gathering the ingredients that can be utilized later.

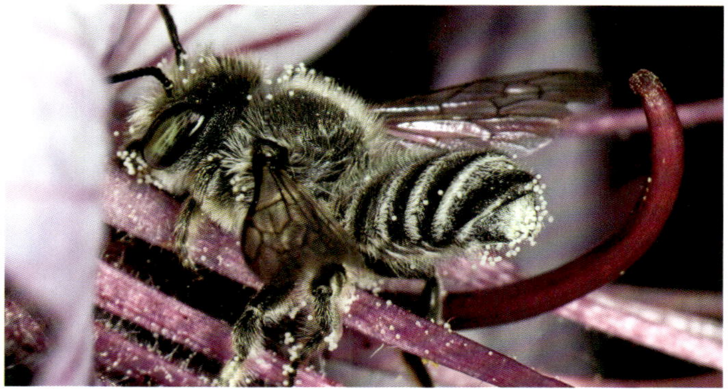

It's also important to remember that the amount of movement here is minimal; the camera has to move the same distance as the thickness of the subject, which could even be less than a centimeter across all needed areas. That distance is slightly more for this thread-waisted wasp (lower right) from the end of its abdomen to the tip of the antennae, but the range of movement for shooting is just from the front to the back of the subject. Notice how the cedar falls out of focus in the background? Even if there was just a bit of extended focus around the eyes, this image would be stronger than just a single frame of detail.

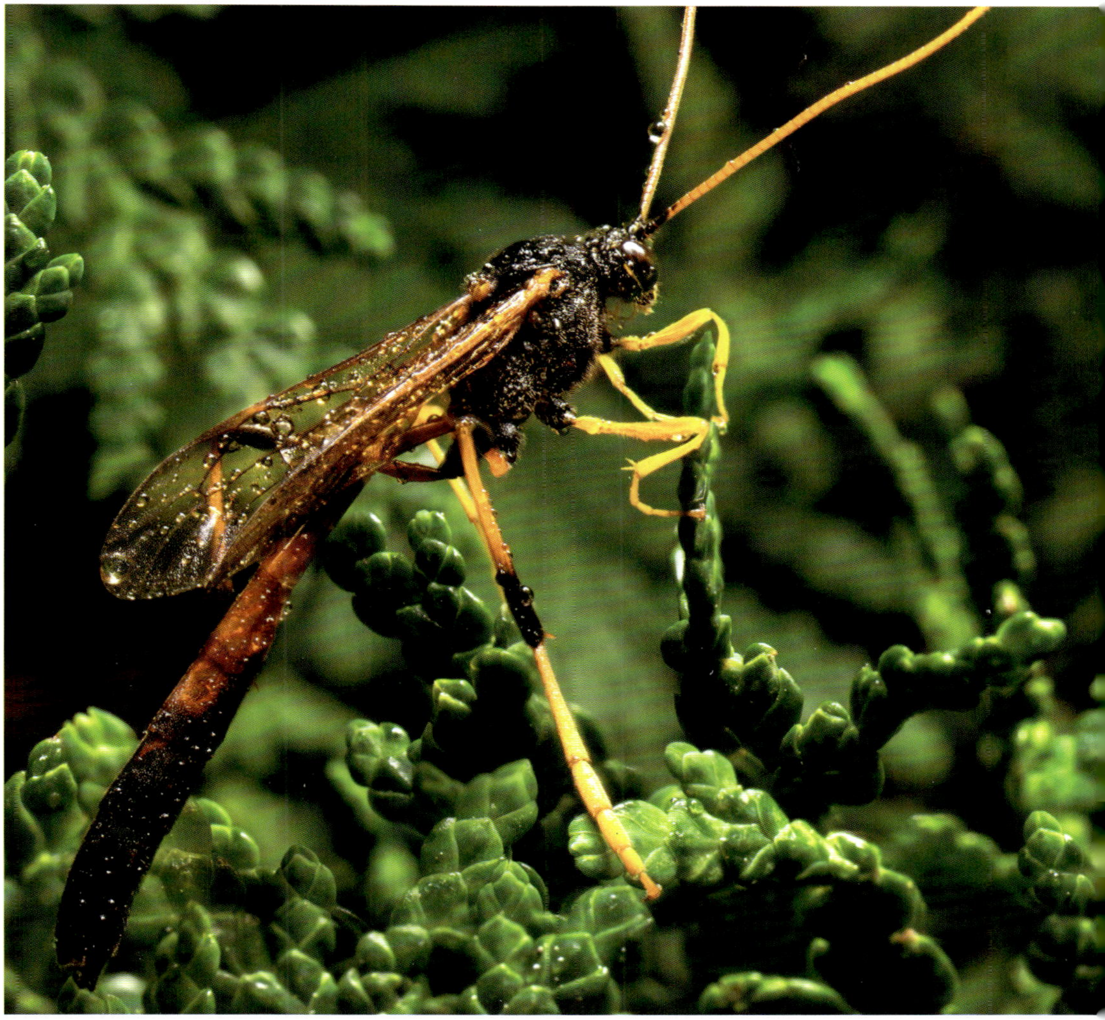

Keep in mind this is not something you always need. The leafcutter bee (top right) is shot as a single frame, with the body mostly in focus and the wing tips becoming blurry. The image survives this very well, keeping focus on the eyes!

Top: Canon 1DX mark II, Canon MP-E 65mm F/2.8 1x-5x Macro F/11 ISO 100 1/25sec
No focus stacking

Bottom: Canon 1DX mark II, Canon MP-E 65mm F/2.8 1x-5x Macro F/11 ISO 100 1/25sec
Focus stacking, 11 frames

Embracing the Chaos

The process of handholding the camera for focus on a snail or a Praying Mantis is entirely different from handholding the camera while trying to capture a bee in flight. The more chaotic the subject the more frustrating it's going to be. Here's a number of common mistakes and how to avoid them.

Problem: Out of Focus
Solution: Practice and shoot more frames.
You'll get a feel for how close you need to be from your subject – a term we call "working distance" – with practice. It will slowly become more intuitive for exactly where you would need to be.

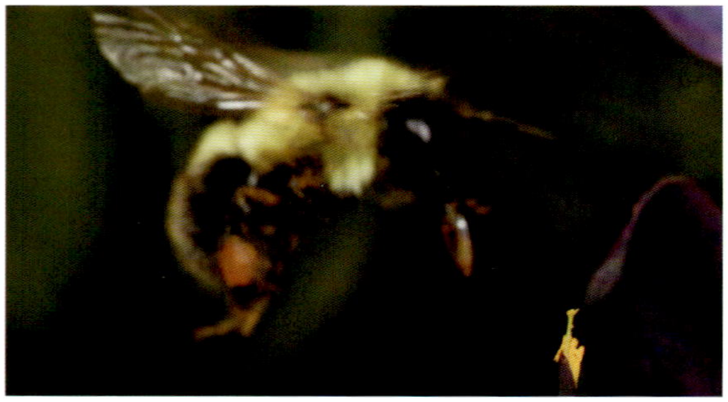

Problem: Out of the Frame
Solution: Practice and shoot more frames.
The more you follow a subject around, the more you'll learn their behaviours. Many bees will only stay in a flower for a certain window of time before flying to the next. Anticipate this and start shooting just before you expect the bee to leap into the air. You'll get a lot of images with no movement in the hopes that you get a dynamic and in-focus image.

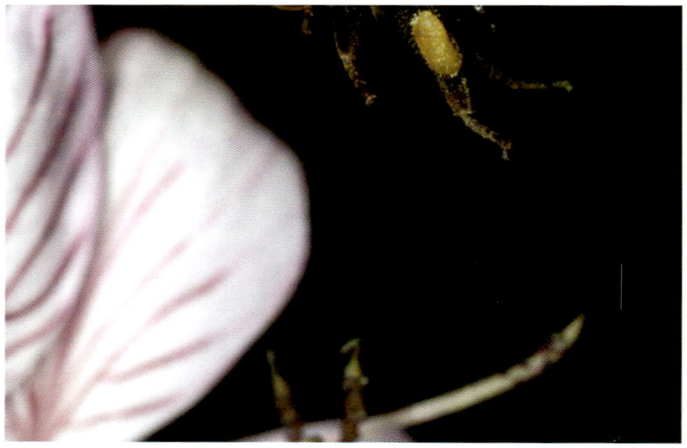

Problem: Motion Blur
Solution: Shoot with macro flash.
Nearly all of my outdoor insect imagery is shot with flash. The ideal tool for my own tastes is a ring flash that is unclipped from the front of the lens and held with my left hand which is also lightly touching the end of the lens. It's all in the wrist!

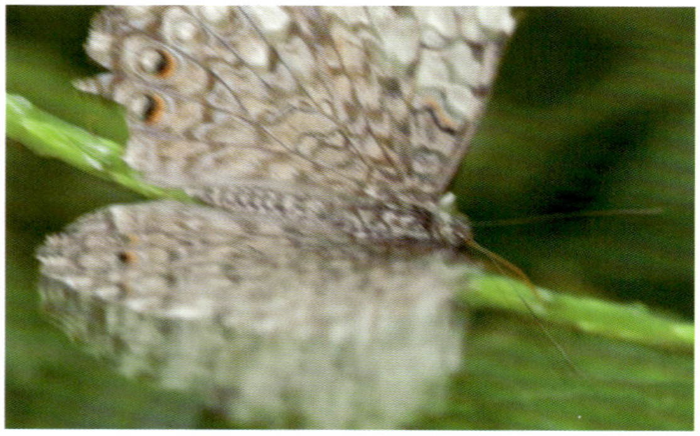

Problem: Dark Frame
Solution: More power!
Most flashes cannot keep up with the rate of continuous bursts from modern cameras; after a few images, you might see intermittent dark frames where the flash simply was not recharged enough to fire. Add an external battery pack such as the Bolt CBP-C1 to add much more power to your flash. It'll keep up.

Problem: No Winners
Solution: Shoot more.
My personal average in chaotic action macro is roughly 100:1. One hundred images to get one I'm generally content with. Sometimes that number is much higher, occasionally spending hours shooting and ending up with nothing useful.

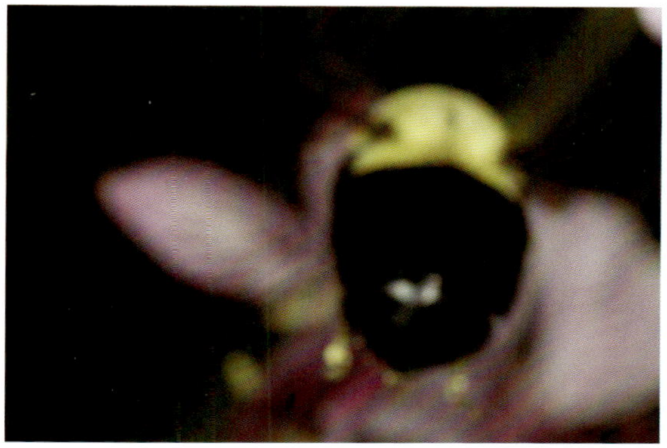

Just seeing the final "good" images from a shoot does not properly illustrate the sheer number of frames required to get there. The best results come to those who shoot more bad images – the harder you work, the luckier you are.

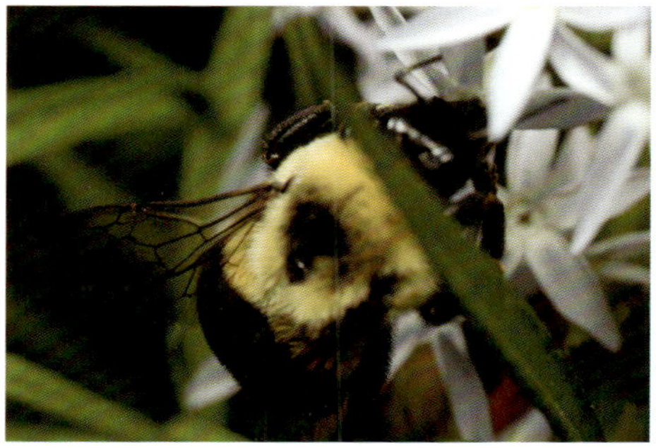

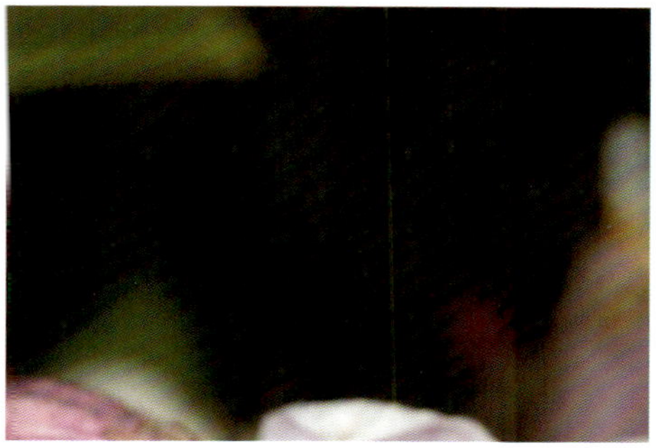

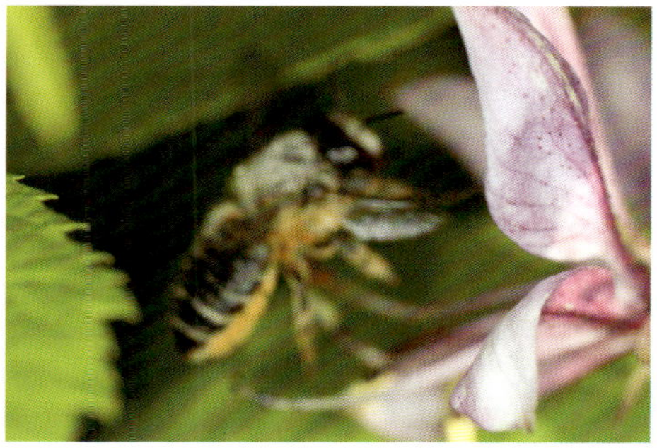

None of these images are even remotely successful, yet they are all stepping stones towards the images that would eventually become portfolio-worthy. Even after mastering specific techniques, the truth is... **you need to embrace the chaos.**

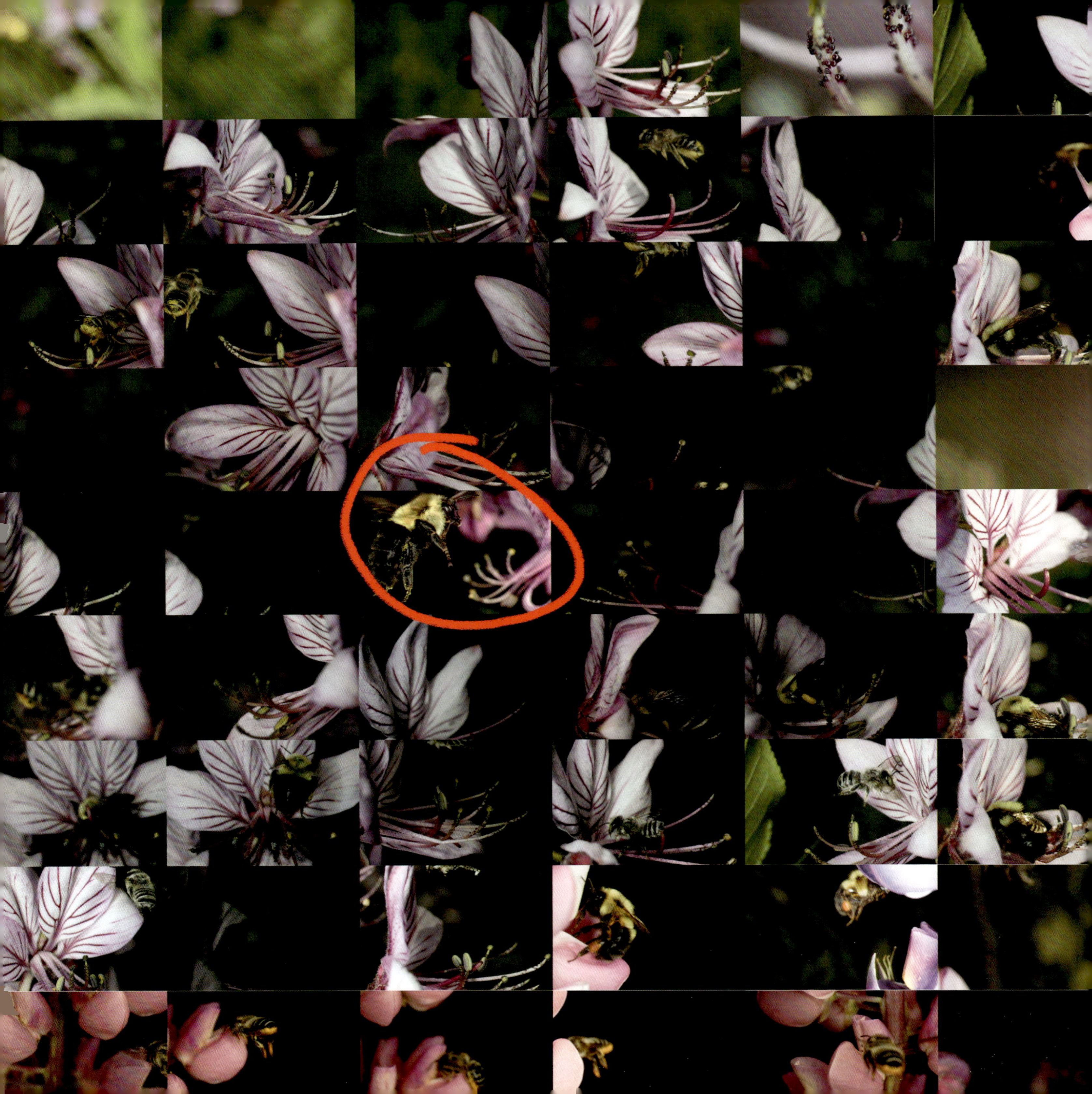

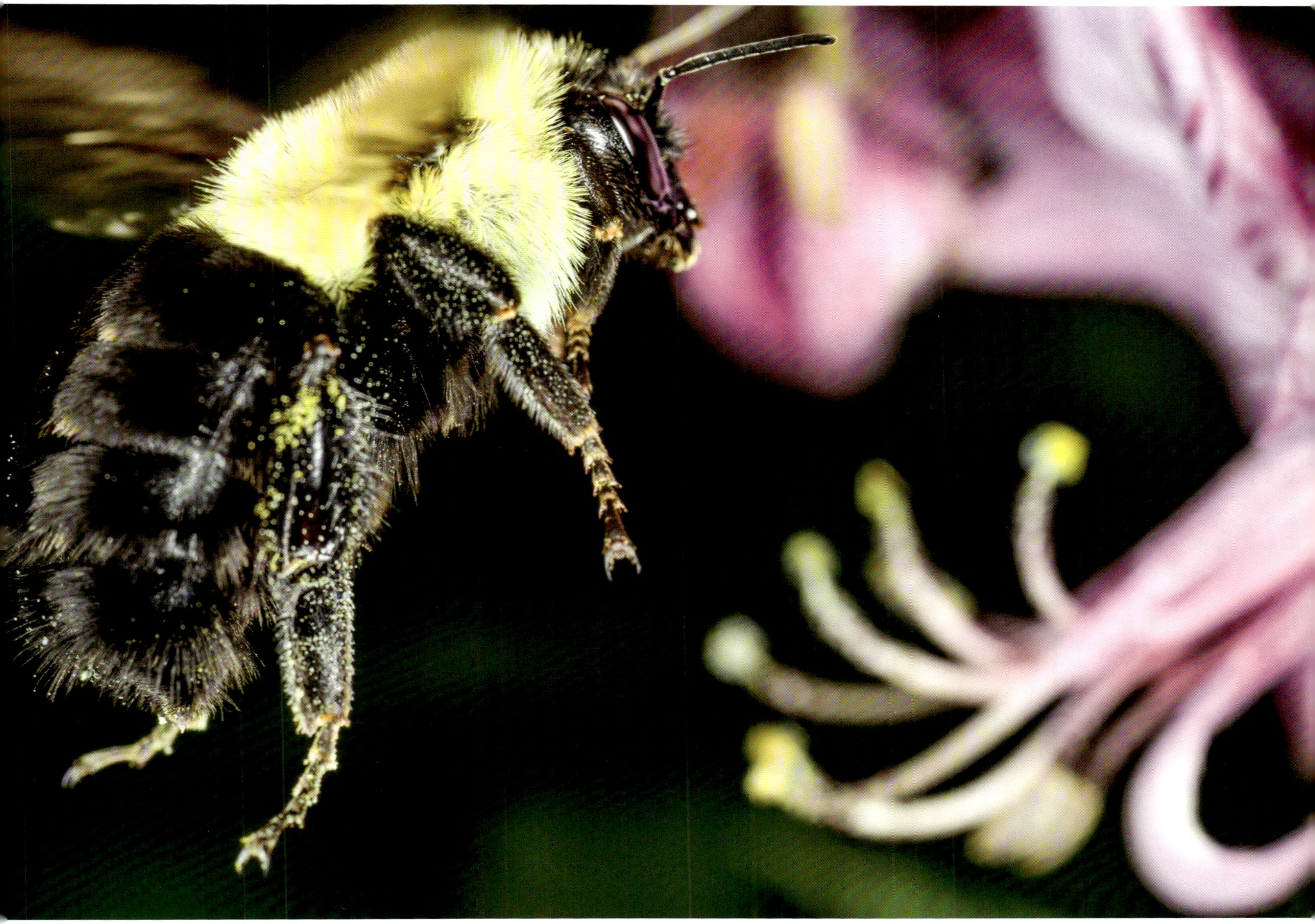

Canon 1DX mark II, Canon MP-E 65mm F/2.8 1x-5x Macro F/13 ISO 160 1/250sec

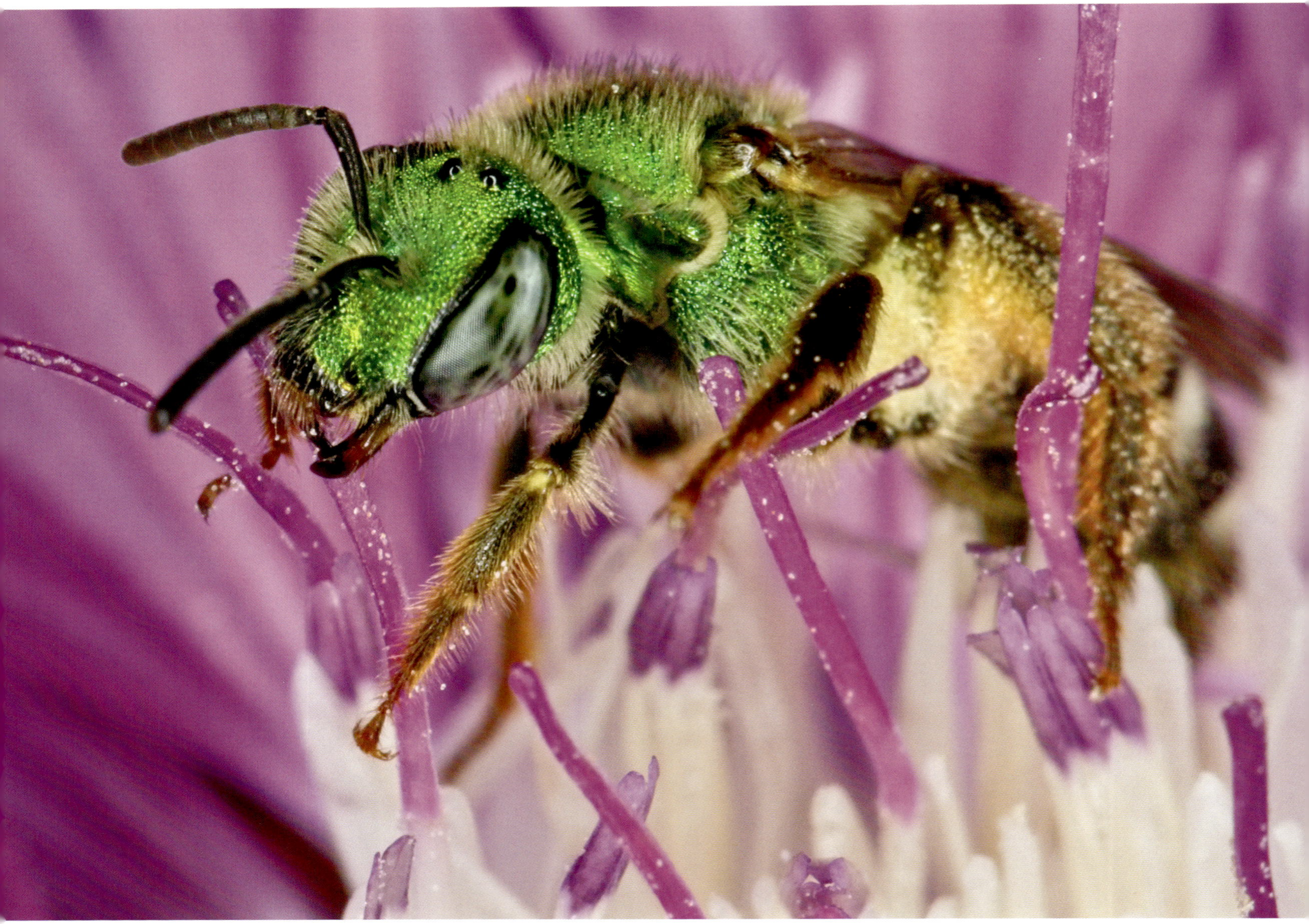

Lumix GX9, Leica DG Macro-Elmarit 45mm F/2.8, F/13 ISO 200 1/160sec

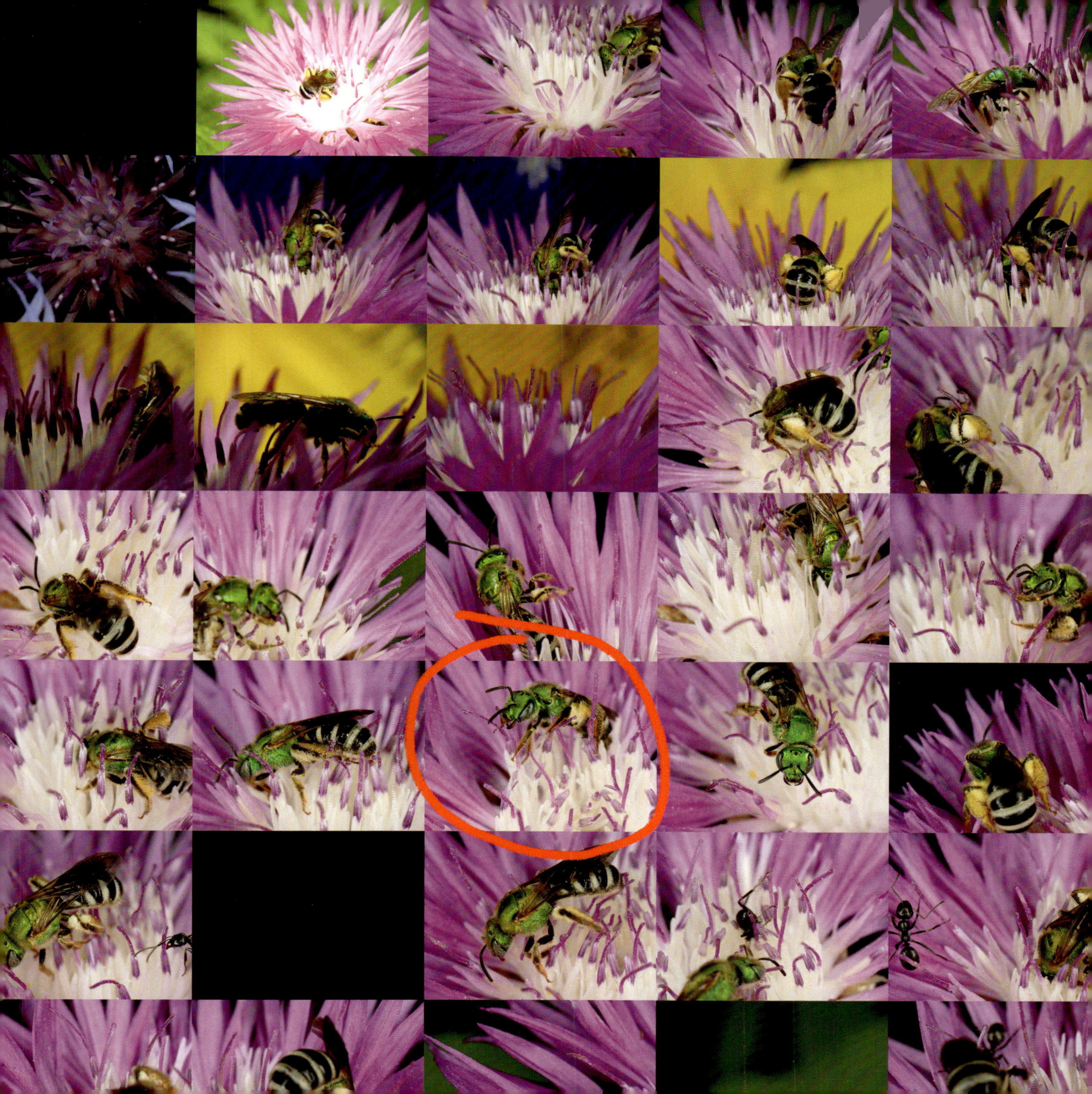

Composition

Macro photographers don't just have a technical rulebook that differs from general photography, we need to explore different paradigms in the realm of composition as well. The fundamental process is the same – we need to create an image that both captivates and engages someone viewing it.

Here are five simple concepts to keep in mind every time you are composing an image. You don't need to hit every point, but the more of them you can manage to check off this list, the more powerful your image will become:

- **Tell a Story**
- **Lines, Shapes and Colours**
- **Simplify**
- **The World is not 5 ½ Feet Tall**
- **Fascination Factor**

Some of my images clearly miss the "story" and are firmly in the documentary category, such as snowflakes. They make up for this with their fascination factor however, still creating a strong image. If we investigate each of these concepts separately we can start to understand what makes them important to the process of composing a macro image.

Tell a Story

Search for narratives within every subject. Many macro subjects can be difficult to anthropomorphize, so this can be a challenging prospect at times. It's easier with insects that are mobile and moving about their day – try and tell their story in a way that we can connect to.

Can a flower on its own tell a story? Sure! Spend some time looking for interesting angles, any potential uniqueness that identifies that flower as dissimilar from the others. What are the surroundings? Interactions with insects and spiders might be part of the narrative. It could simply be that the flower is growing up towards the sun, which was the initial thought I had when I encountered a healthy cluster of Shasta Daisies. These daisies grow much larger and taller than the common wild variety, so it was easier to get the camera at a low angle and shoot up.

You almost never get the perfect image immediately –

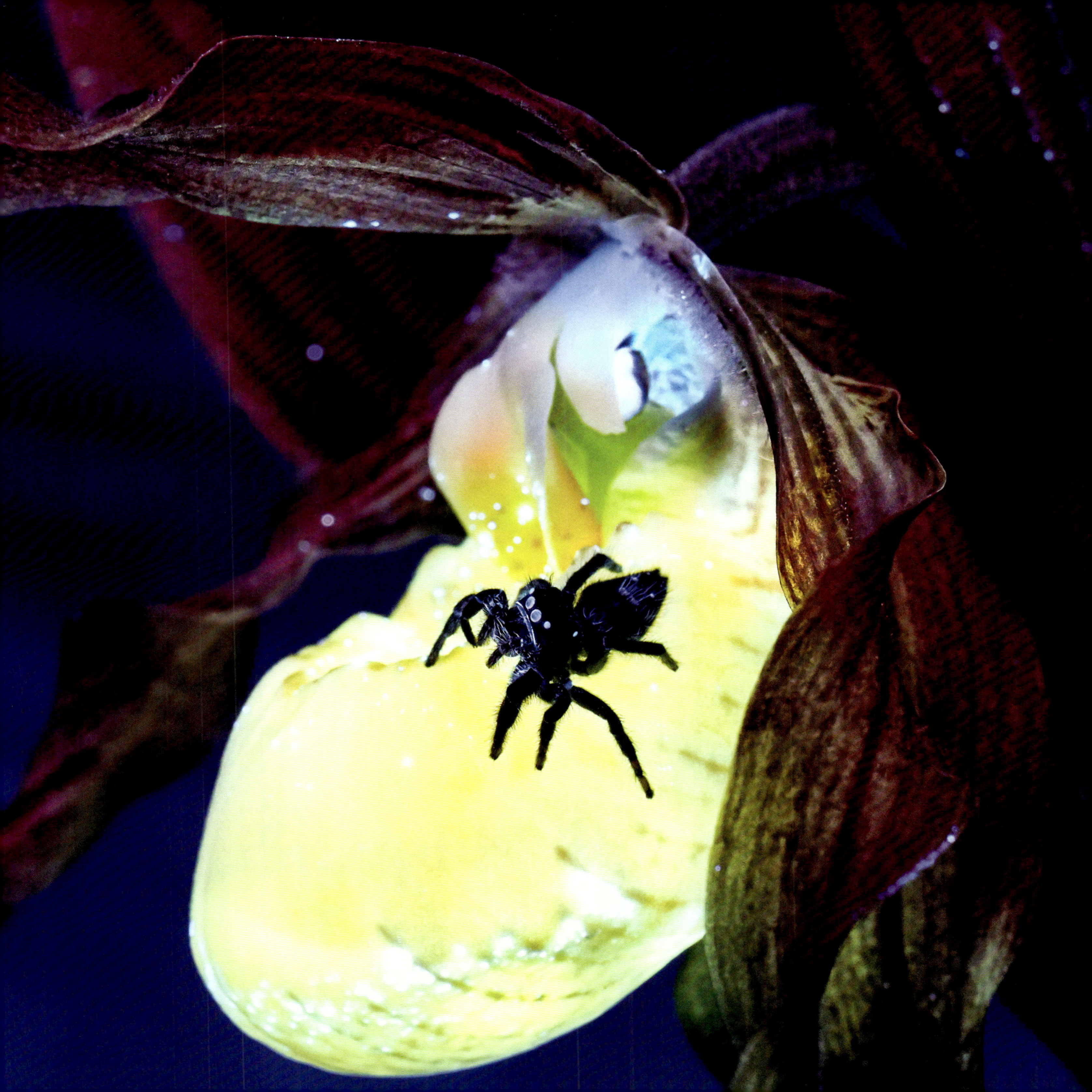

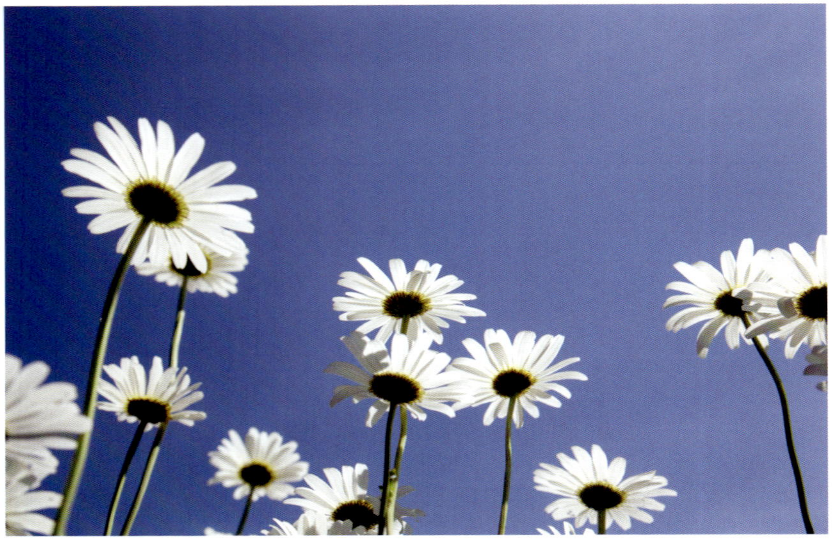

it's an iterative process. I wasn't happy with my first image – it was okay, but far from great. Why? Asking yourself this question is integral to the creative process – every image has something that can be changed if not improved. The answer came to me quickly after studying this image for a few seconds: I have a series of vertical lines within a horizontal frame. Nothing seems to connect. What could I try next?

If the image was to be shot vertically, not only would I have the benefit of the stem lines flowing better with the image, but I'd be able to get the sun in the frame – another strong element to tell the story! I excitedly dug the camera back into the dirt, this time in a vertical orientation. The results were… better? But still not what I was after. Why?

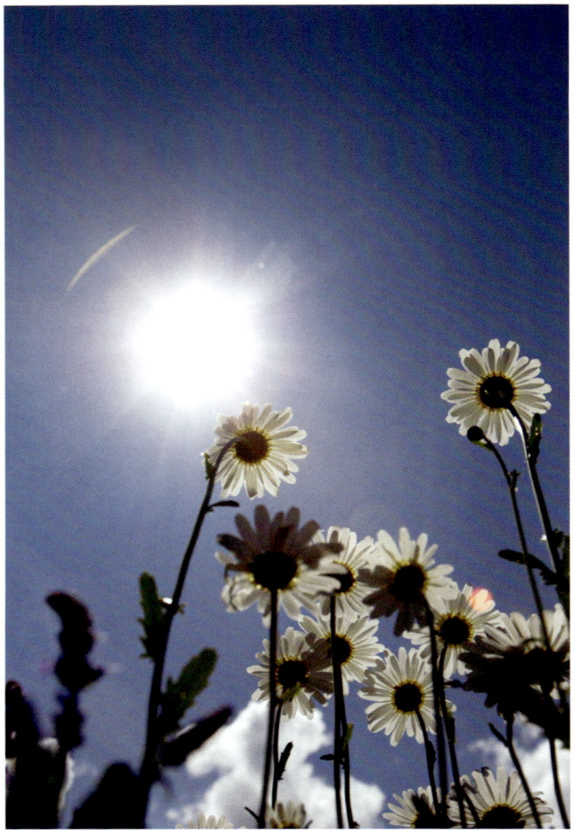

The sun ended up being too bright – taking too much of the attention away from the flowers. There was also clutter in the foreground that needed to be cleaned by moving some flowers out of the way or recomposing the shot from a different angle or with different flowers; the creative process continued.

Faced with the challenge of a slight breeze making the exact flower positions erratic, my goal was to place the sun right behind the flower. With a little luck, one of the frames had a slight beam of light coming through between flower petals.

This iterative process often happens far more than two or three times before I arrive at what I consider a successful image. Many times I am forced back to the proverbial drawing board to contemplate how to approach the concept differently – sometimes leaving an idea for weeks or months before having the breakthrough required to make another attempt. Sometimes that attempt fails, too. I have ideas that I have been sitting on for

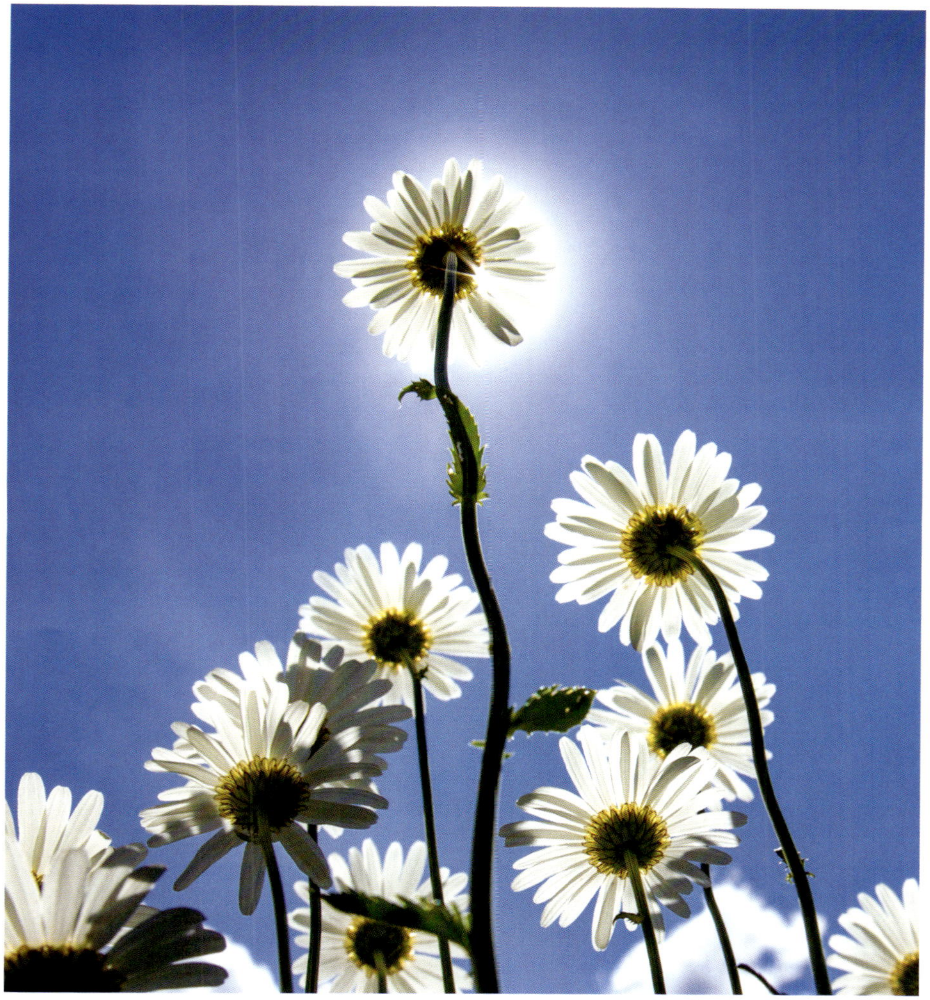

Canon 1DX, Canon 24-105mm F/4L @ 40mm F/13 ISO 200 1/640sec

years because I just can't identify the technical or creative breakthrough required to make them truly shine.

It took me a long time to embrace this creative flow, not really caring about the final image but rather just the next step to getting there. The first step in this process is almost always sparked by a story that I've decided is worth telling.

One afternoon I was exploring the wildflower walking paths near my city's waterfront. Not sure exactly what I was looking for, other than to find some fantastical macro subject fly right up to me and beg to be photographed. Obviously, this didn't happen. Still, I was hunting for a subject that could eventually lead me to a narrative. This is a process that starts well before I take my camera out of the bag. No grandiose chronicle seemed to be taking part in front of me, but then I saw it: tiny red beetles. These Spotted Lady Beetles (*Coleomegilla maculata*) were just in the cut grass off the side of a walking path, with nothing interesting around them. Why were they there? I figured I'd wait around to see if any of them did anything interesting.

Over the course of twenty minutes, I sat cross-legged on the grass of a public space staring at these little insects that anyone from a distance would never have spotted. Most of the time their interactions seemed aimless, but eventually one of the creatures meandered over to a dandelion, and I sprung into action.

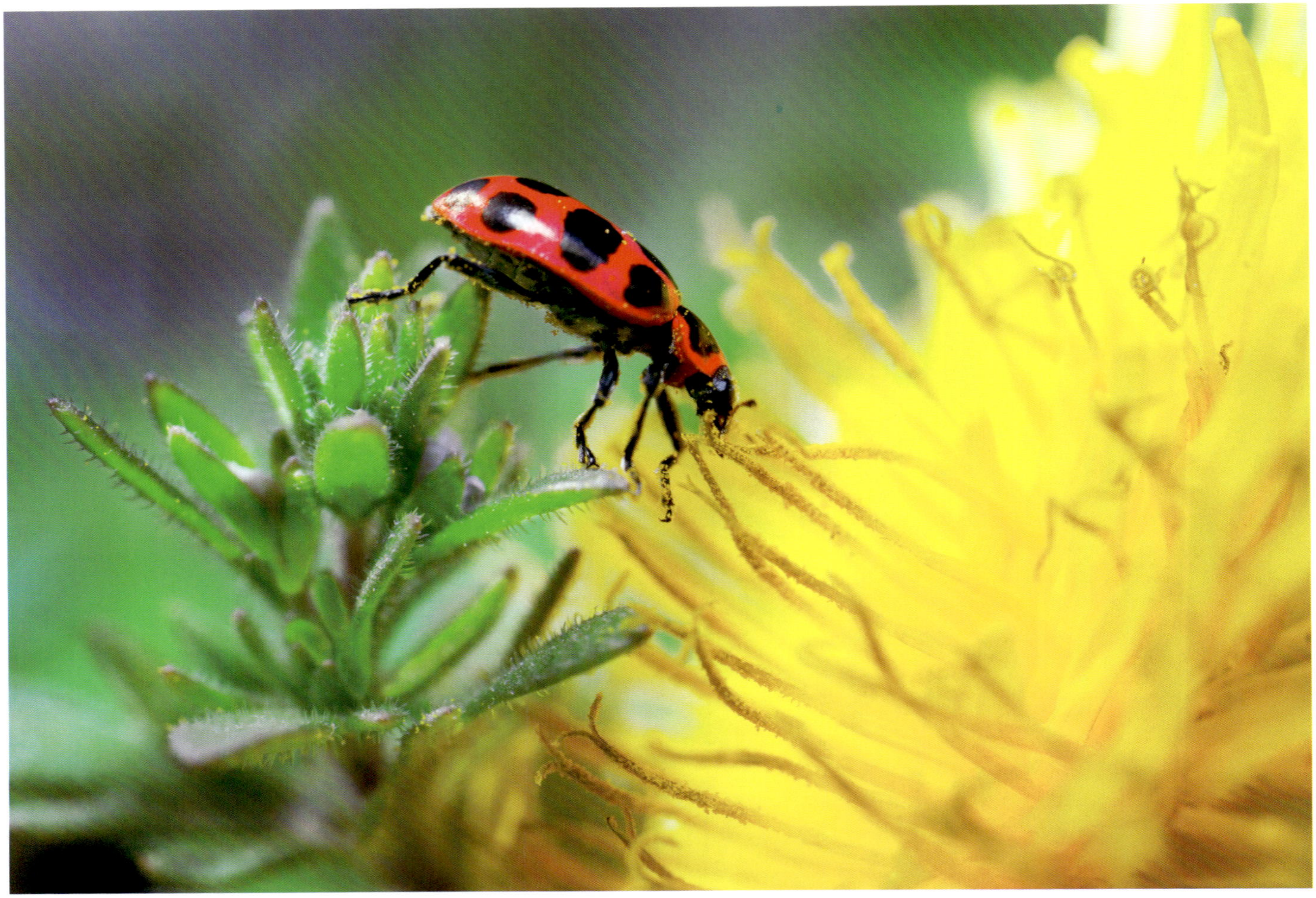

Canon 5D mark II, Canon MP-E 65mm F/2.8 1x-5x Macro, F/7.1 ISO 100 1/200sec

Imagine a photographer wielding a fairly hefty camera lying on his belly snapping off hundreds of frames very enthusiastically. Casual passersby only saw a dandelion as the subject. There is no doubt that my true intentions couldn't have been understood by anyone but myself in that moment – and the moment was captured well. The tiny beetle climbed onto a neighbouring plant to then reach over and down to the pollen; I couldn't have planned it better.

This represents very simple, common ingredients. On their own, there isn't much value. The real value comes with the interaction and how that interaction forms a narrative. The insect becomes more relatable because the camera is shooting right down at their level, not the top-down perspective that we would normally find ourselves observing from. Creating images like this helped me along my own personal journey of discovering the synergistic effect that storytelling has on the components of an image.

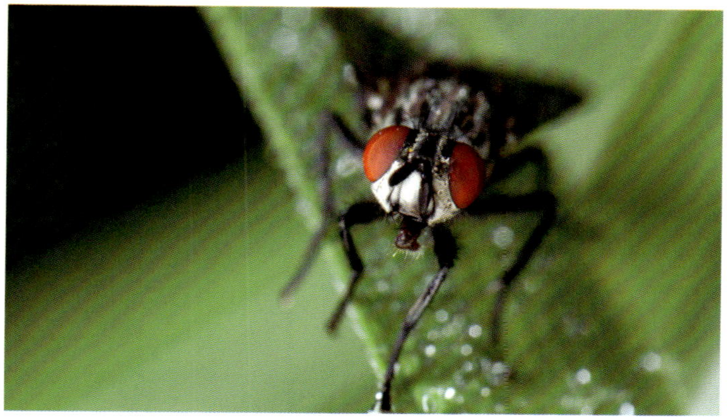

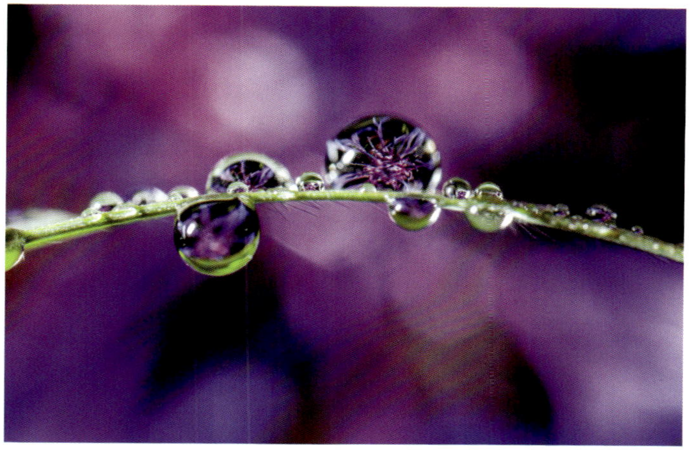

Lines, Shapes and Colours

One compelling element of macro photography that gets overlooked by many is the fact that you often there is no horizon line – or even a definitive sense of gravity. To a landscape photographer that has a horizon line 2 degrees off, the image has a flaw that requires fixing. To a macro photographer, there is a sense of freedom here. We can choose to rotate the frame arbitrarily, sometimes even completely inverting an image and it might not seem broken.

While you can't go to such extremes in every image, there are advantages of exploring a purely horizontal or purely vertical composition. Diagonal lines can be a strong element in a photograph, allowing our eyes to traverse the frame and much more easily connect with our subject. What's to stop you from doing that – even if you make the decision to do so while editing the image? Take the fly image (*left*). This was photographed with the blade of grass in a much more horizontal position, but throwing things off some haphazard angle creates a more dynamic composition. We've all seen flies on walls and ceilings, they don't care which way is up.

Even when dealing with some elements that depict the effect of gravity such as water droplets, you can still get away with significant rotations. On this page is my very first attempt at water droplet refraction photography, using fresh rain drops and a Bachelor Button (*Centaurea cyanus*) flower placed in the background. The blade of grass is nice, but… could you do more with this? What if it was rotated to put the blade of grass on a diagonal, reaching the bottom left and top right edges of the frame? There is a maximum here for how much you can rotate before the droplets will look unnatural, but there is a surprising amount of flexibility.

There are many abstract elements in macro photography that can guide our eyes through a frame. It could be an out of focus background element that offers colour contrast, maybe even as far as intentional camera movement to create blur. Concrete elements can have the same effect, but we must not identify them in concrete terms – rather, always look at their lines and decide how much or how little is needed. This lesson was taught to me by the wonderful Freeman Patterson in his book *Photography and the Art of Seeing*. Originally published decades ago, it's just as relevant today.

There is more to this edit than just a simple rotation. "Focus stacking", explained elsewhere in this book, allows for the depth of field to be increased to bring more of the subject into focus. You don't need everything sharp here, and some droplets on the very left and right are intentionally left out of focus. If the background was sharp, we'd have a muddled mess of an image!

"In nature, light creates the color. In the picture, color creates the light." – *Hans Hofmann, German-American Painter*

That said, the choices that we make both in camera and in post-processing can have a dramatic impact on the final result, without escaping the truth of the image in the process. The droplets in the image below look just as believable as the initial unedited image on the previous page.

Canon 5D mark II
Canon MP-E 65mm F/2.8 1x-5x Macro
F/7.1 ISO 100 1/200sec

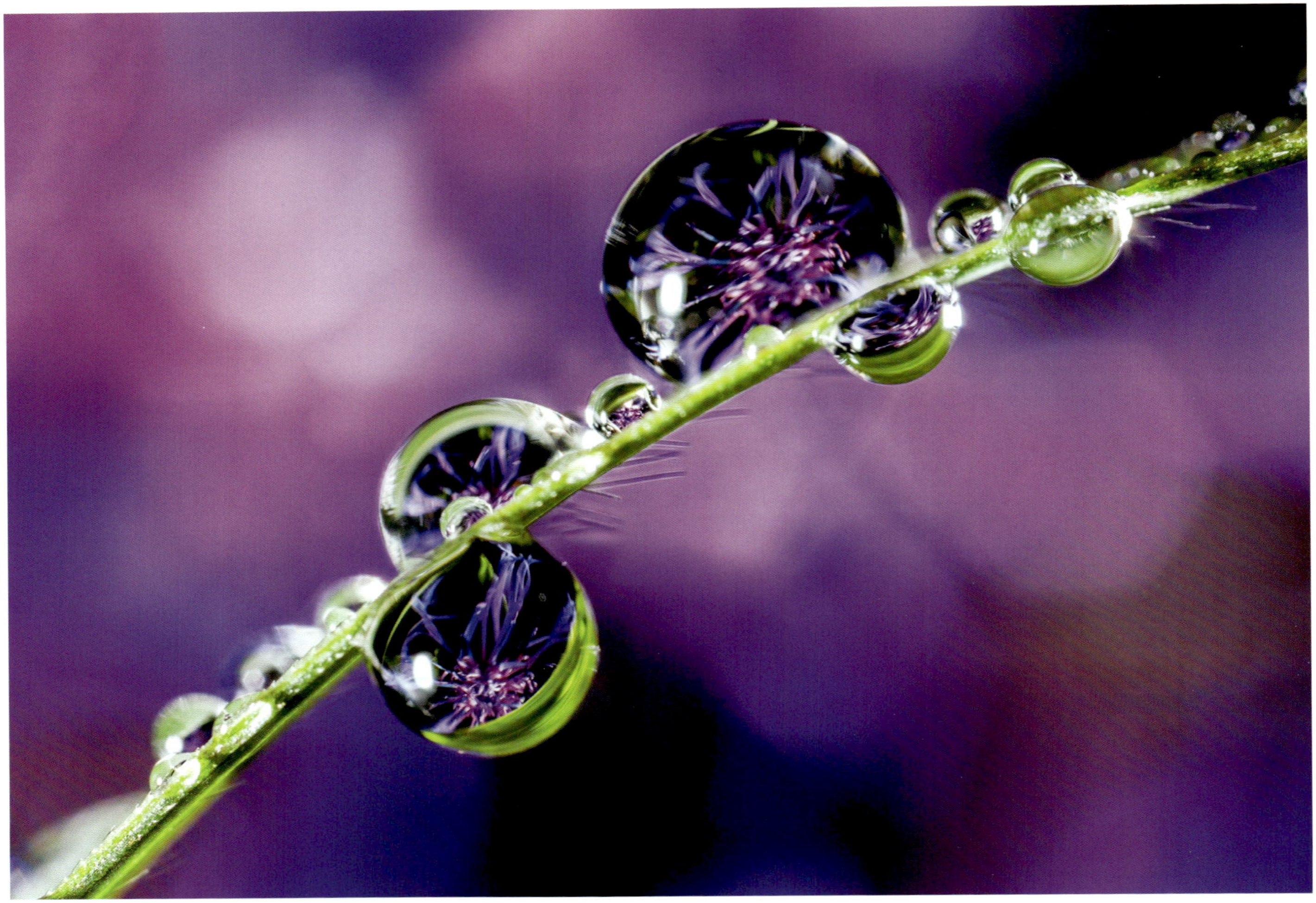

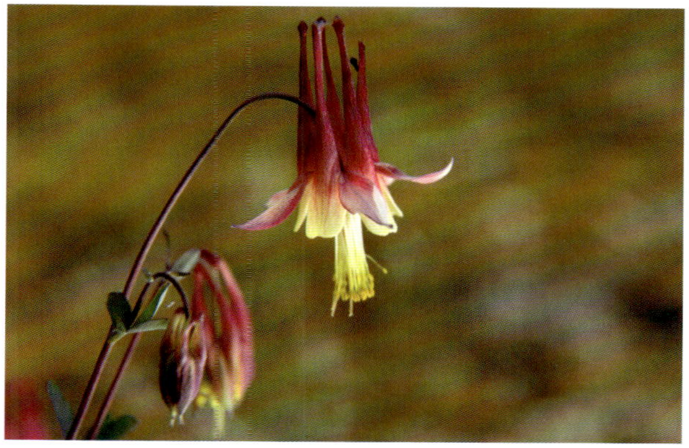

A classic example of in-the-field adjustments pertaining to colour have a lot to do with the background behind your images. This is something of an unsung hero in macro images – the subject defines the image, but the background gives it a stage to perform on. By simply moving the camera to a different position while keeping your subject in the frame, you'll change what is behind the subject. Small changes can have big influences on the image.

This Canadian Columbine flower (*Aquilegia Canadensis*) was blooming in a harsh environment during a drought, with sun-scorched grass surrounding it. This made for a dull grey-brown background that was so similar in brightness and colour to the flower, it became lost in the image. A short distance further away were some evergreen trees, offering up an entirely different background. Darker in colour and much farther away on the Colour Wheel, this was worth exploring.

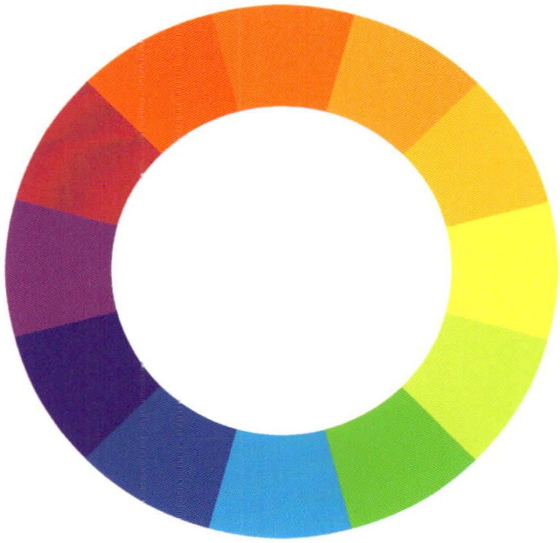

While I don't want to make this a lesson in colour science, I often find that backgrounds that push farther away from the colours in the subject can add contrast and depth to the palette of the image. Keep this in mind and experiment to see what works best with your own sensibilities.

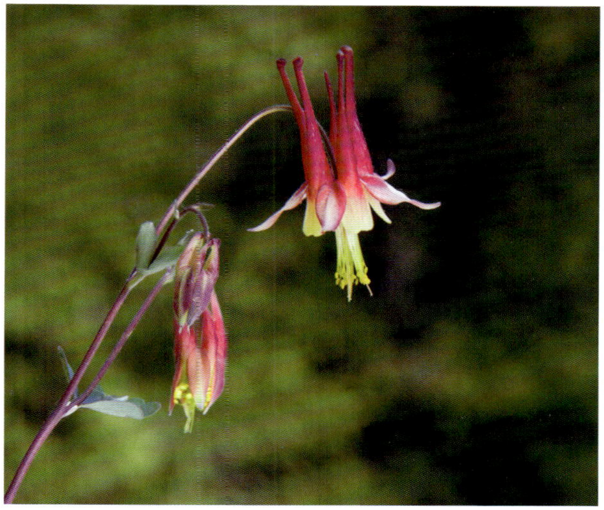

Once you identify your subject and any potential narrative you can discover, the next step would always be searching for the background. Some photographers even carry a series of pre-printed backgrounds around with them for exactly this purpose. This concept of modifying the scene with visual ingredients that are non-native to the scene might cross a line for some people, and I personally prefer to keep things natural… but what if I take disconnected physical ingredients together and create a surreal composition in studio? This is art – define your own methods based on what you'd like the finished image to mean to you.

Canon 1DX, Canon 24-105mm F/4L
F/14 ISO 800 1/125sec

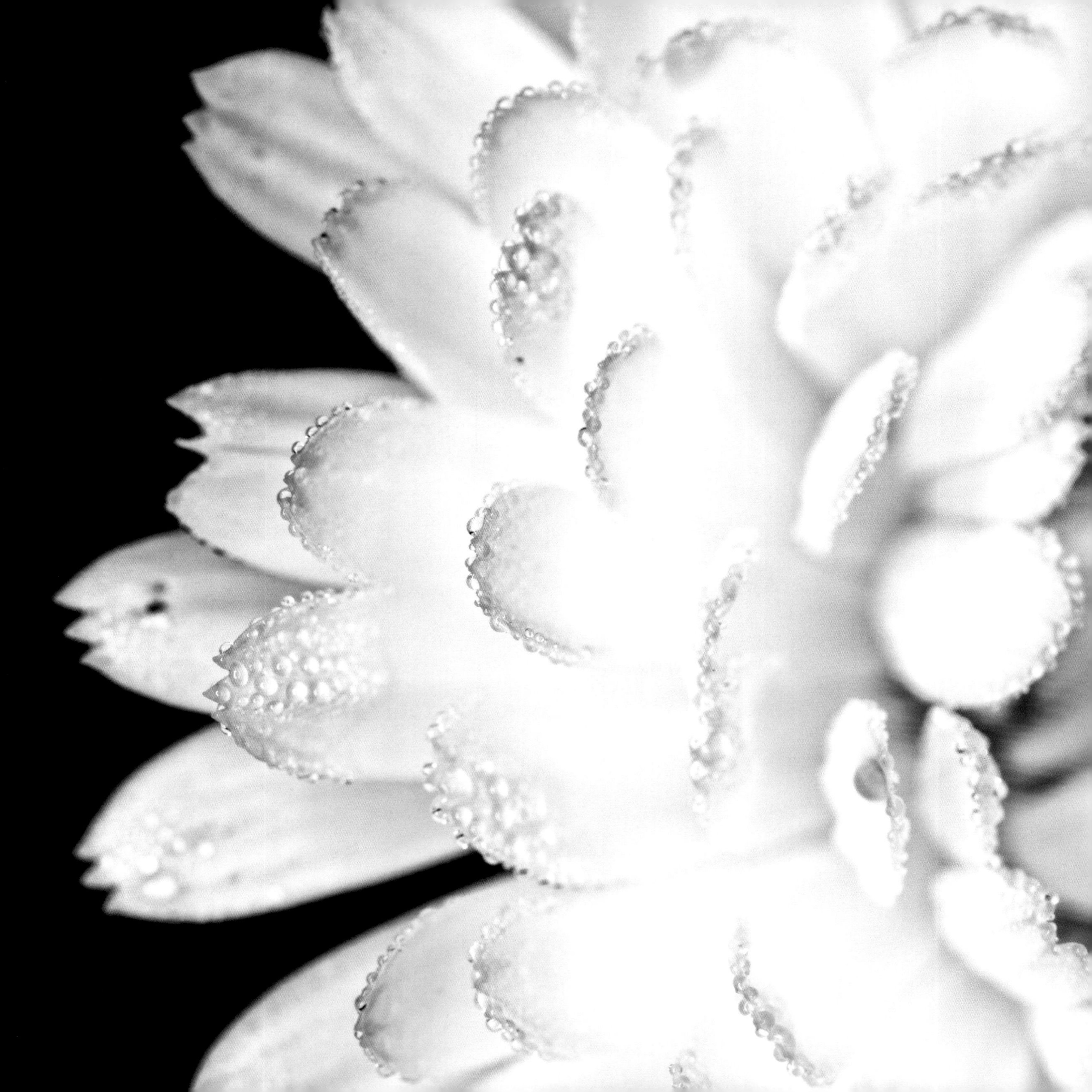

Simplify

Photography is a subtractive art. You have the entire world to choose from, and you need to narrow things down to just the core components that are necessary to make your image successful. Consider this the process that engineers go through when designing something mechanical: make it as simple as possible while still achieving the intended goal. One step too far and you've broken things, but you don't know where that line is until you've crossed it a few times.

Part of the simplification process is making a mental note about what your subject actually is – verbalize it if you have to. For the image on the adjacent page, the subject was not the flower. The subject was the dew drops on the edge of the petals. This distinction is significant as it empowers you as the artist to determine what the subject isn't. How much of the frame that is not directly the subject (or a supporting element) can you remove from the composition?

The entire flower isn't needed. If it was included, the percentage of the image that featured the dew drops would be lower, and the number of drops would make them feel less relevant individually. By only including a portion of the bloom and limiting the aperture to F/9 and not smaller, the inner portion of the petals becomes softer – less in focus. Less relevant to the final image.

Colour is also a consideration when simplifying an image. In this case, the vibrant yellow colour of the petals in reality would have been powerful; colour can easily overpower more subtle elements in an image. It's not all about framing, focus and depth. Sometimes saturation is an element that can be manipulated to build a better image. All of this is about the idea that you need to remove things to ensure that the point of the image is well understood by the viewer without unnecessary distractions.

Simplicity on a macro scale is thankfully an easier thing to accomplish than in other genres such as landscape photography, where it can be easy to "take it all in" and lose track of what exactly the image is supposed to be about. The inherent shallow depth of field and narrower field of view that are hallmarks of the majority of macro lenses will work in your favour. That said, if no effort is placed on thinking subtractively, you will almost always have more within the frame than you intend.

Here's a fun experiment: intentionally take a bad photo of something as uninteresting as you can find. Shouldn't be hard! Then, try to employ some of the concepts that have been discussed so far to improve the image. It's doubtful you'll end up with anything worthy of your portfolio, but the exercise is a valuable one. The easier you can identify problems in a photograph, the easier it is for you to avoid them altogether or identify them immediately after reviewing an image and make adjustments to your composition in the field.

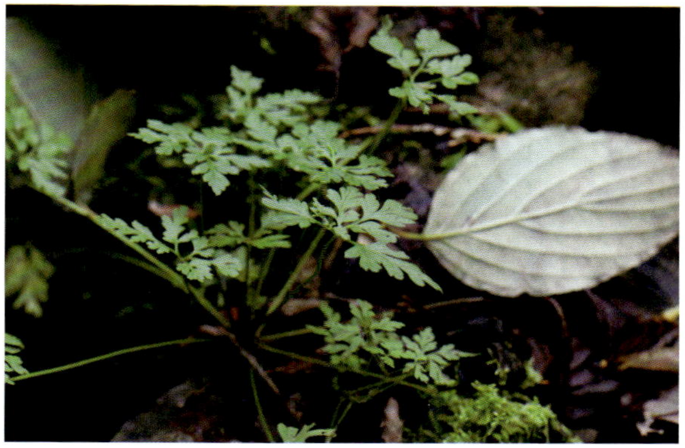

Intentionally the worst photograph in this book.

Some photographs such as the one on the previous page might seem like they are beyond hope. And they are, if your thought process to fix an image comes from cropping or editing after the shutter click. If we start applying these five rules to such a subject, how can we improve it? Obviously there is some confusion about what the subject is, way too much clutter, an uninteresting angle and more. That's okay - look at the image and tear it apart! For every criticism you have, make it a constructive one. How can you put the image back together?

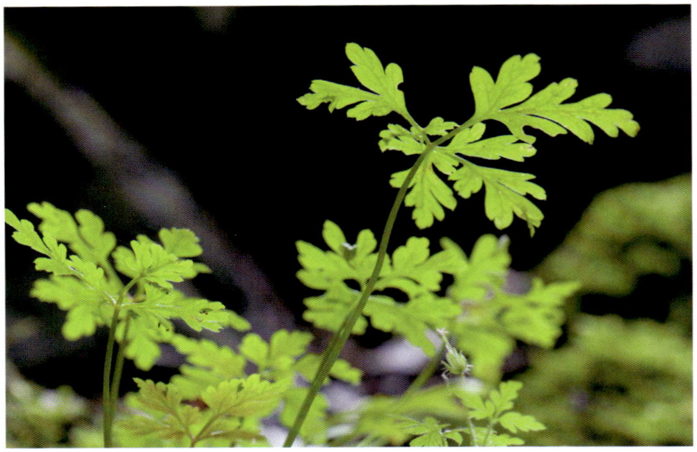

Admittedly, there wasn't much to work with. Sure, the image can be improved, but this is not a photograph that I would share as part of my portfolio. The lesson is worth remembering, however: any image can be improved by keeping this checklist in mind. It's easy to move a garbage image a few notches up, just as it's possible to make a great image into an excellent one.

The World is Not 5 ½ Feet Tall

Viewing the world from our "expected" perspective is boring. It's ordinary! Standing and looking at a beautiful scene from a human angle does very little to tell the story on a macro scale. This same logic is true for children and pet portraits: get down to the level of your subject, and you'll see the world through their eyes. In the macro realm, this can often mean getting right down to ground level.

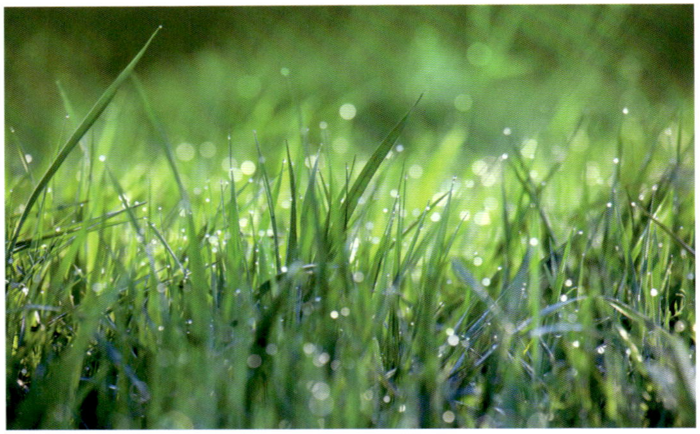

Connecting with your subject is more than just getting it in the frame, in focus and properly exposed. As you can probably tell, most of the items on this list are woven together. Looking back over the past few pages you'll see many images that were intentionally taken at an angle that favours the subject over the comfort of the photographer.

We are exploring the universe at our feet. As such, our viewpoint is inherently not our own. Many of the subjects worthy of placing in front of your lens are completely inconsequential to our daily lives. From an instinctual level, we have no interest in dew drops on blades of grass in the morning or the daily life of an ant. When we use our cameras to make such insignificant subjects much larger, viewable from the standpoint of normal life, they become fascinating.

Remember that we are not just documentarians along this journey through composition. We can capture the world as we see it, changing our technical variables and angles to make it the most pleasing to our eyes, but we also have the ability to become an artist in the process. The daily life of an ant can become much more wondrous with a bowl of water, a passionflower tendril and a flower.

Define your art by your own rules. Checklists such as this along with the "rule of thirds", "golden ratio" and others should not define what you create as a photographer, but rather offer a starting point. Artistic rules are meant to be broken, but they are first meant to be understood.

Sometimes, when all these rules fail you, you might still be giddy with excitement over what you're creating. This is the final pillar to this checklist, and one people often ignore or simply don't properly appreciate.

Lumix S1R, Meyer Optik Trioplan 100mm F/2.8
F/16 ISO 1600 1/125sec

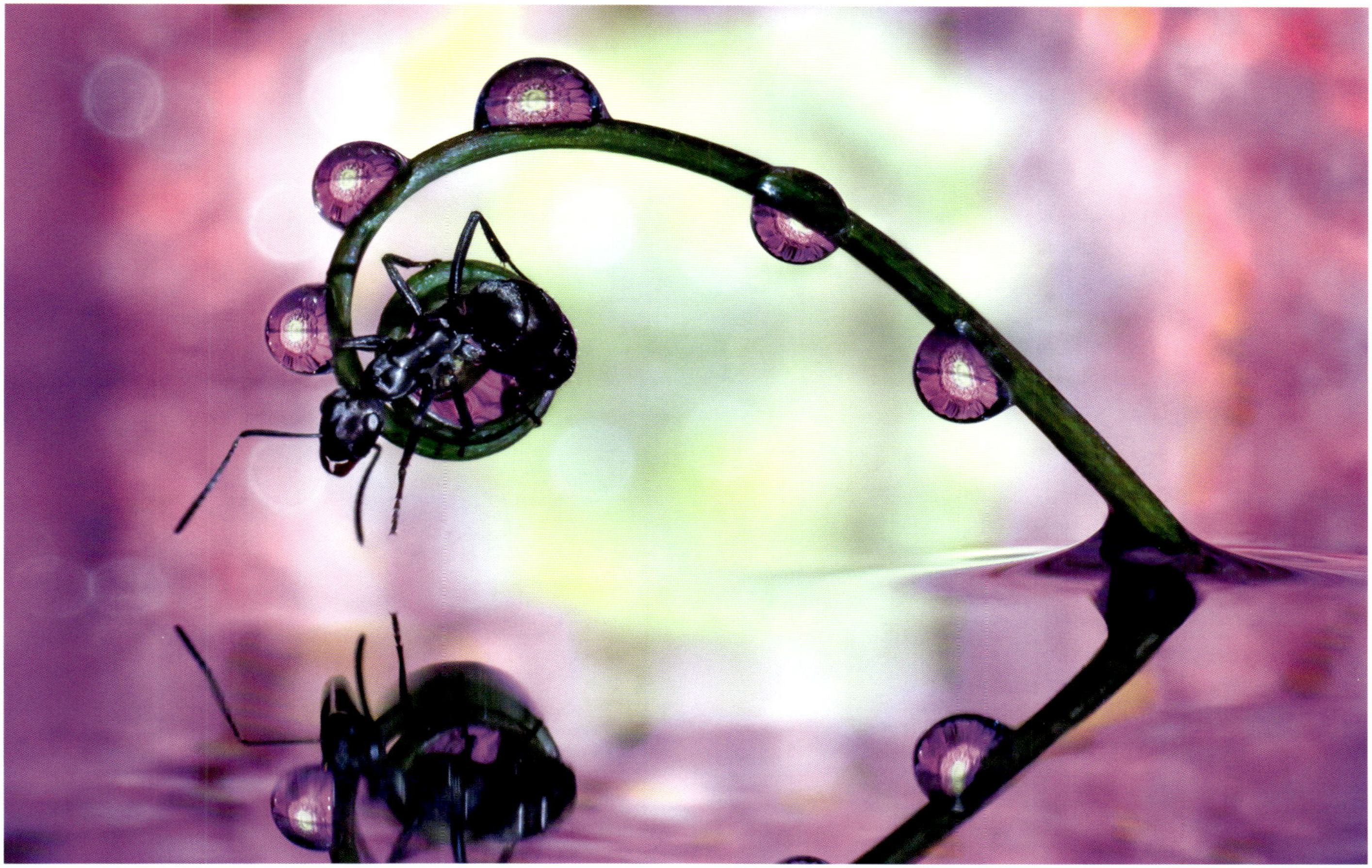

Fascination Factor

Usually associated with the abstract wonders of high-magnification photography, there are many common subjects that often go overlooked that can open your eyes to the curiosities of the natural world. These images may or may not qualify for the rest of the items on our checklist, but that doesn't matter. These are still fun subjects that in their own right have value for simply existing and being discovered by you.

These images often become puzzle pieces. On their own they might not be a useful image, but the knowledge that creating them imparts and the ideas sparked by them will fuel your creative macro adventures. Embrace these. Revel in them. Know that they are part of the creative process that might not end up as a final image, but can lead you there.

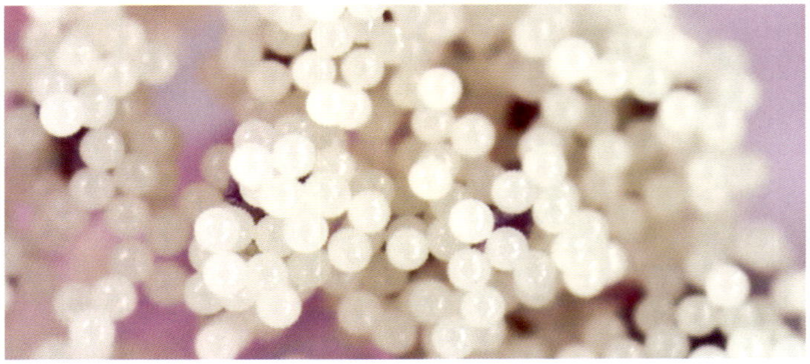

A fun example of this is grains of pollen (*above*). Initial attempts revealed structures that I wouldn't have otherwise predicted – little spikes on their surface, at least in the case of a Rose of Sharon (*Hibiscus syriacus*) flower. The details never end! This sparked something in me – what does the pollen of other flowers look like? The answer is quite varied in size, colour, shape and texture. Individually these images (*adjacent page*) might not have a story to tell, but something appears to connect them all together, even if you as a casual observer have not been told what the subject is.

This can be a fun "what the heck is it?" game. There are so many examples of images that can be hard to identify due to their scale and the lack of any familiar reference in our everyday lives. What does the image (*below*) look like to you?

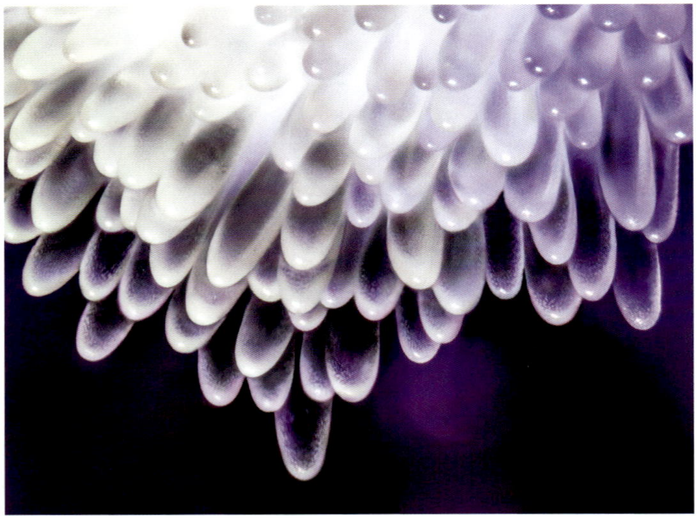

You've seen it a thousand times but never really seen it – the center of the petals of a Pansy. When asked about what these weird structures are, I am often given a response of insect eggs or fish eggs. To this date, no one has successfully guessed what this was from. Albeit a different flower, see below:

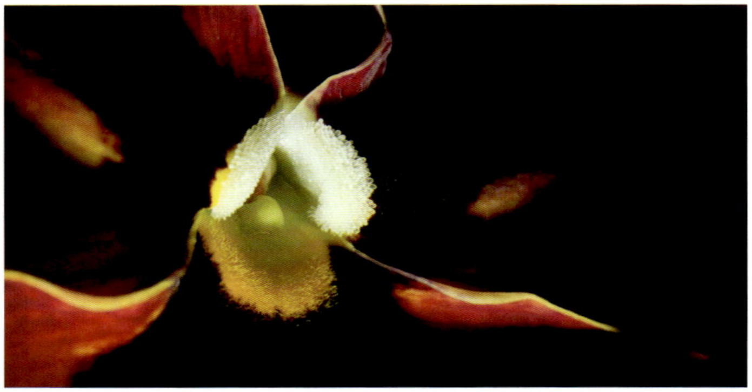

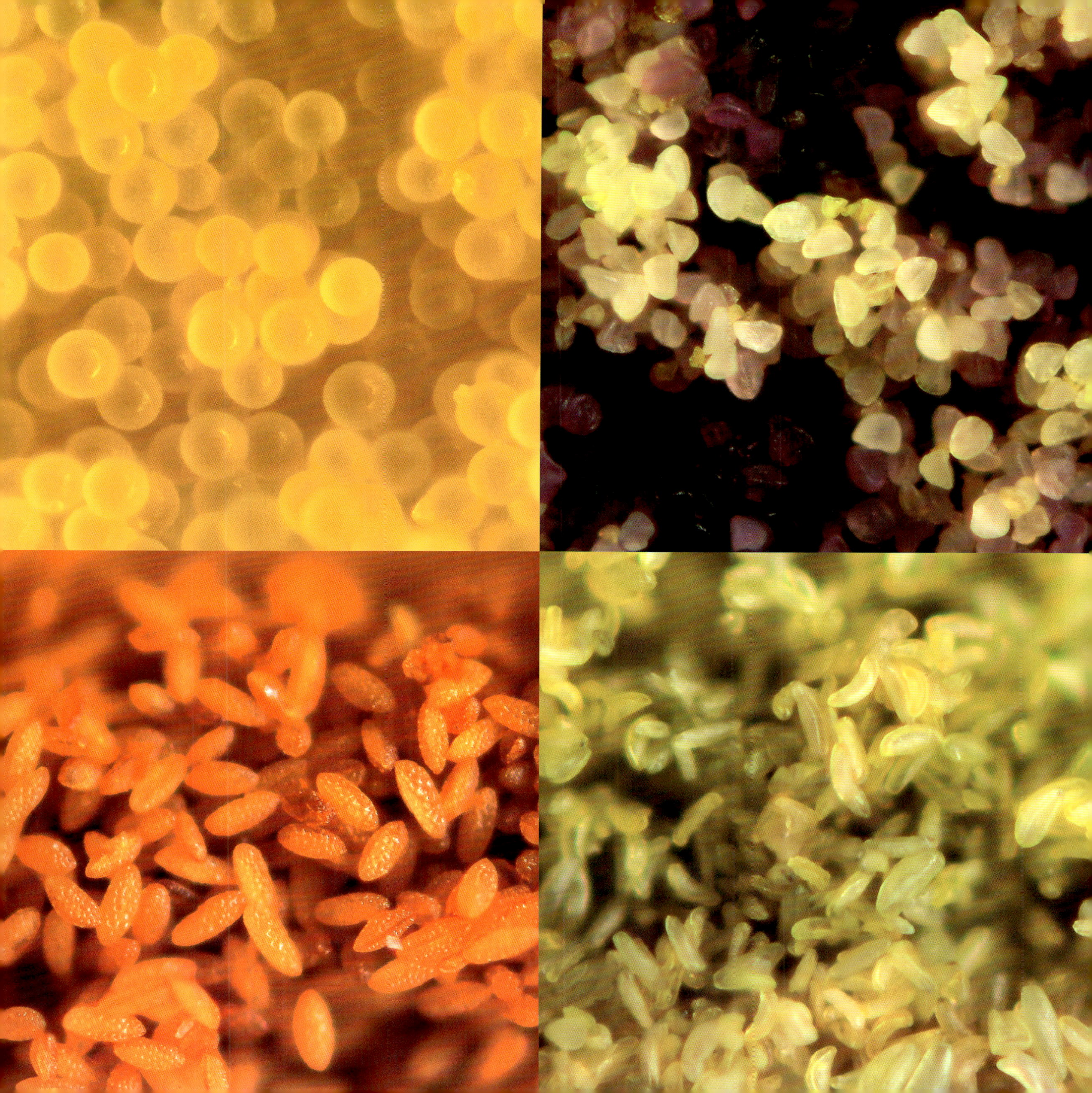

One morning I was walking through a nature preserve, hoping to find some interesting wildflowers. During this walk, I was discovered by a Deer Fly that had every intention of making a meal out of me. With an instinctual reflex response, I slapped my neck when I felt its presence. In my hand, I now had a very cooperative subject; it picked a fight, and I won.

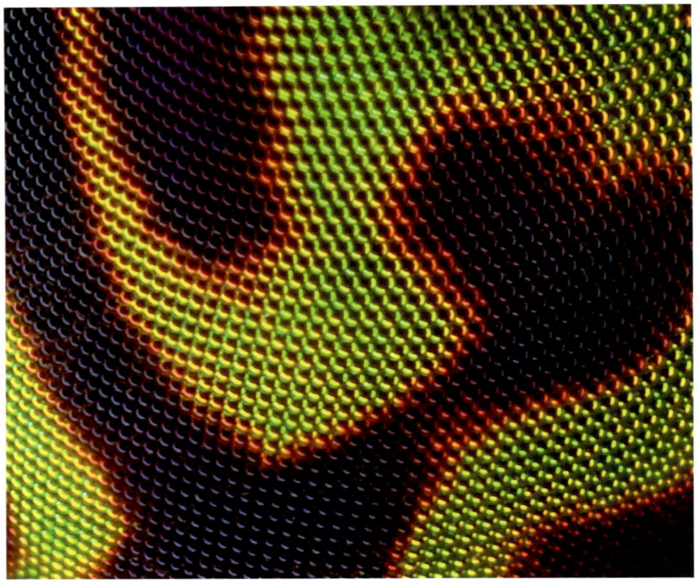

This image (*right*) is the eye of that unfortunate creature. The patterns in the compound eye of Deer Flies and their kin have always appeared enigmatic to me, and I wasn't going to miss this opportunity to capture these optical designs. It was an early attempt at "focus stacking" to get most of the eye in focus, and one of the first images in my portfolio that taught me that the closer you look, the more detail you will find in nature.

Without describing what the subject of the photo is, you might not be able to guess. This is detrimental to any image in terms of its capability to contain a narrative, but that doesn't entirely negate the allure. The "what the heck is it?" game continues!

Often mistaken for ice cubes, the tiniest grains of salt can make for a remarkable subject as well. Just sprinkle some table salt on a black porcelain mug resting on its side, and this is what you'd get. Many minerals on such a small scale will reveal crystal facets and natural geometry that we might mistake for larger subjects. You can even make your own crystals by dissolving salt in water and then letting a small coin-sized puddle of it dry out completely. Will it tell a story? Likely not. It's still worth the experiment.

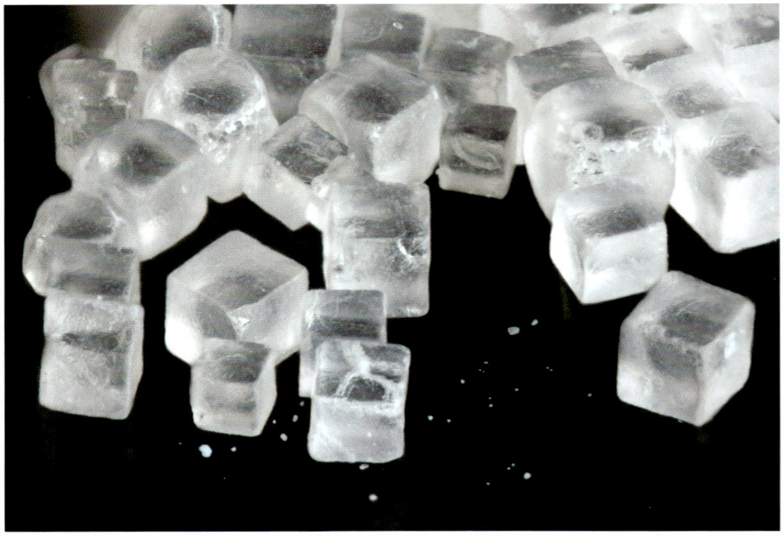

This fascination factor is at the heart of the "what if?" mentality. Essentially, you seek an answer to a question and you don't necessarily care about the result being a successful image, just that you get a result. Celebrate the results as part of the creative journey, even if you keep the results to yourself. I can tinker away in my studio for an entire day gaining nothing but knowledge of what doesn't work to help prepare me for the next attempt.

In the 1910 biography of Thomas Edison titled *Edison: His Life and Inventions*, there is an anecdote from Walter S. Mallory, an associate of Edison. During the time when Edison was researching the possibilities of a nickel-iron battery, Mallory visited Edison.

Excerpt:

> I found him at a bench about three feet wide and twelve to fifteen feet long, on which there were hundreds of little test cells that had been made up by his corps of chemists and experimenters. He was seated at this bench testing, figuring, and planning. I then learned that he had thus made over nine thousand experiments in trying to devise this new type of storage battery, but had not produced a single thing that promised to solve the question. In view of this immense amount of thought and labor, my sympathy got the better of my judgment, and I said: 'Isn't it a shame that with the tremendous amount of work you have done you haven't been able to get any results?' Edison turned on me like a flash, and with a smile replied: 'Results! Why, man, I have gotten a lot of results! I know several thousand things that won't work.'

Thomas Edison often revelled in his mistakes as he knew that eventually it would either lead to a success or a new idea. He was fascinated with process possibly more so than the eventual success.

Sometimes a spark of inquisitiveness comes at unexpected moments. Sitting at my desk about to fill a fountain pen with ink from a bottle, I noticed that a thin layer of film – like a circular bubble – had formed at the top of the bottle. Immediately forgetting what I was doing I raced to grab my camera, as I had noticed the effects of "thin film interference" creating colourful patterns in the ink. The ink was just some ordinary blue colour, but the interference colours were magical.

Is this a successful image? Partially. It's an element in a larger image that I haven't settled on yet. One idea was to hollow out the center of a large flower and place this colour cauldron in the center, but initial attempts

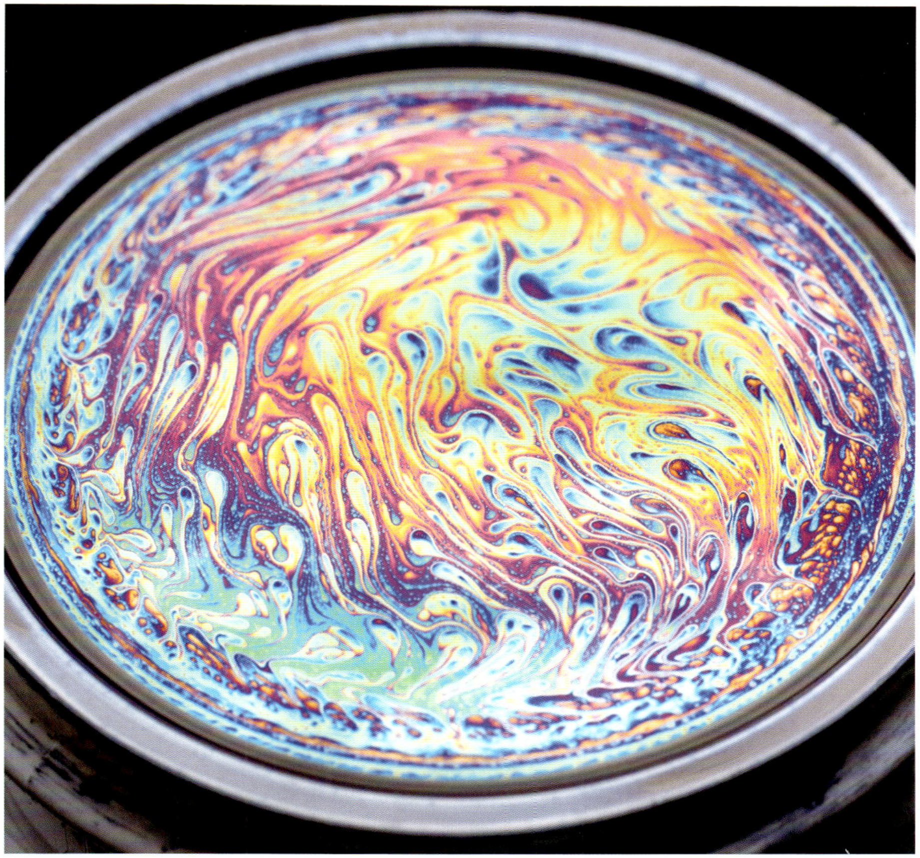

failed when the flowers fell apart. The concept hasn't been revisited, but that bottle of ink sits on my desk just waiting for the discovery of another piece of the puzzle to fit with this concept.

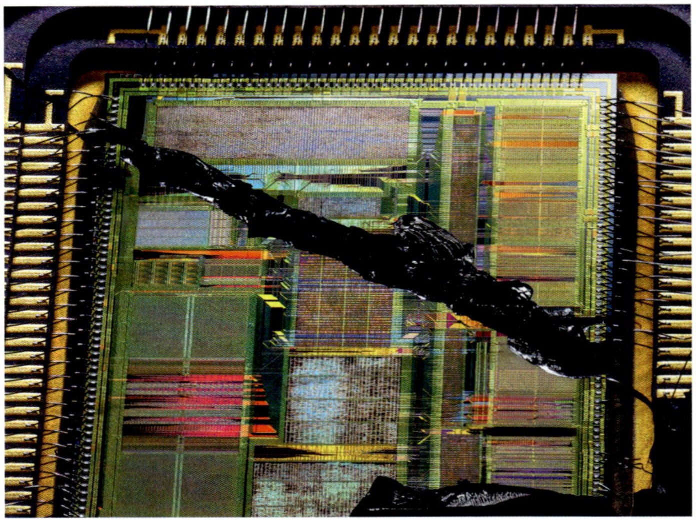

Let your creativity and curiosity combine. What if I try to take apart an old computer processor before I recycle it? Apparently, they're tough nuts to crack open – eventually I succeeded with a hammer, breaking the chip in half while trying to take the top off to see the silicon die of this 486 CPU. Maybe the vast canyon separating the two halves adds a bit of a story, maybe not. I had seen nifty photos of these things before, and now I had my own. Mission accomplished. Might this be a puzzle piece for some future concept? Sure! Why not try and get some very small plants to sprout out through that crack? There are always more ideas to explore and a never-ending supply of curiosities to tinker with. Enjoy the process!

Another "what if?" moment came to me after exploring water droplet refraction photography and ultraviolet fluorescence photography, both concepts that have lengthy chapters of this book dedicated to them. The question was simple: "what if I fill a spray bottle not with water, but with invisible ink that fluoresces blue? What happens if I spray a dandelion seed with it?" Well, you've got your answer (*below*). In hindsight, maybe I shouldn't have sprayed this in my studio where the tables are forever stained with glowing blue splatters like a crime scene.

Some of that splatter ended up on a Gerbera Daisy that was still on the table from a previous experiment. I noticed it sparkling with tiny droplets, and it gained my immediate attention. Adding one larger droplet in the center with a hypodermic needle as a visual anchor, it almost feels like a tiny universe being born within the flower.

This fascination factor can help create a photo that personally inspires you. If you can imagine a way to incorporate other items on the checklist, you'll make magic. At the very least, you should walk away with new ideas. **Always ask "What if?"**

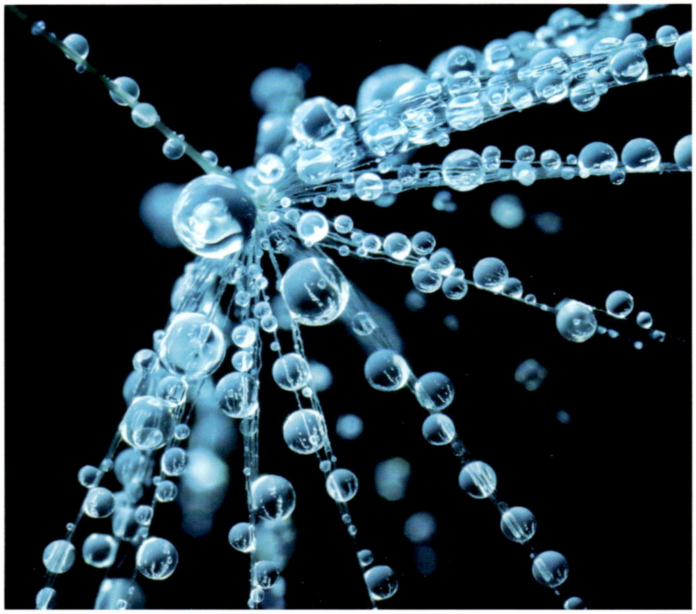

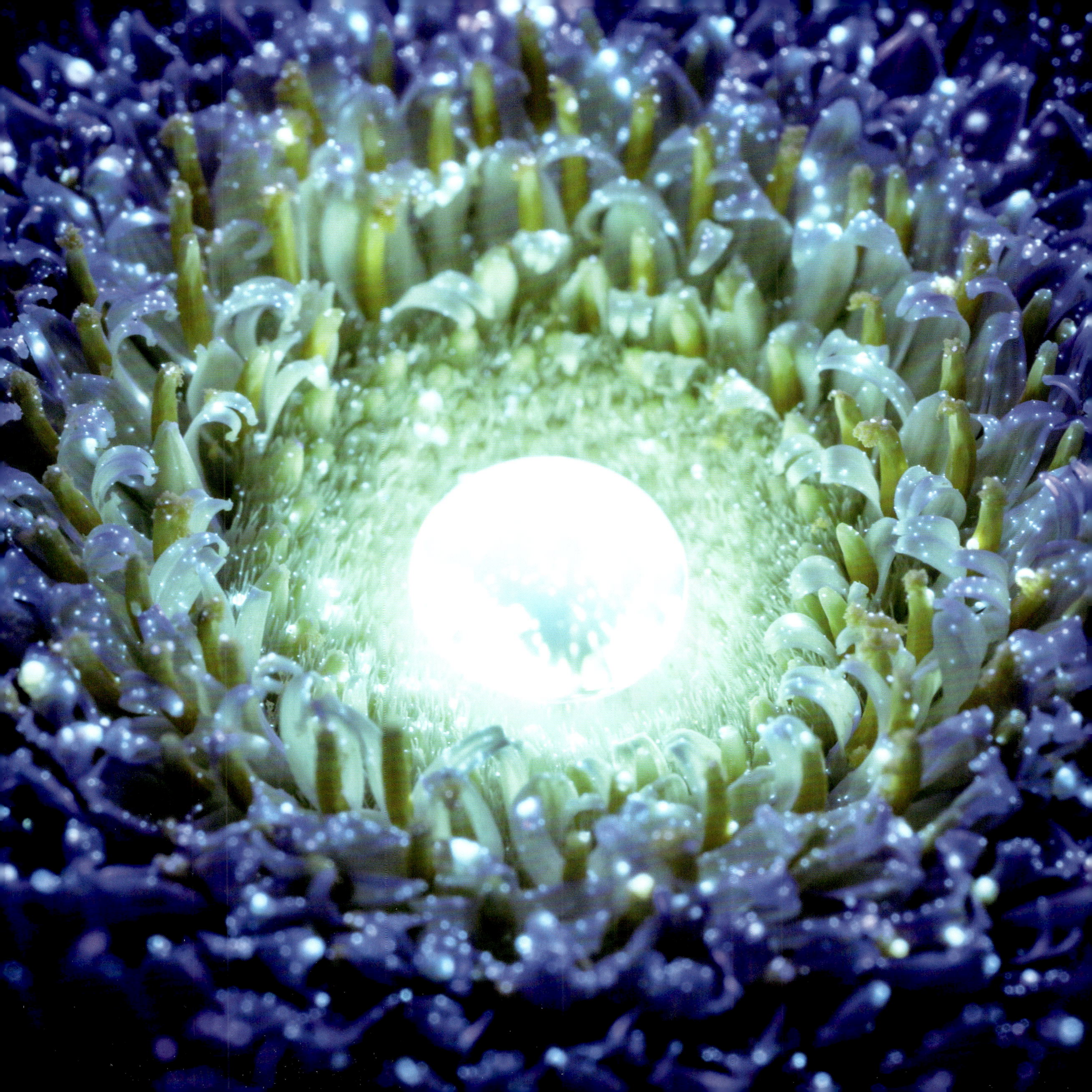

Water Droplet Refraction Photography

You're about to learn a magic trick. At first, this type of photography can feel almost magical – you might have no idea how to accomplish these results and you might think it is beyond your capabilities in terms of equipment and skill. The equipment is simple, and the skills are easily learned. There are a lot of "moving parts", things that need to be in just the right place for these types of images to succeed, but once they are all identified it can be easy to solve problems and get the best results.

This is two art forms at once: droplet sculpting first, photography second. The first set of challenges comes from creating an interesting and compelling subject to which you then apply your photographic skills to document. There are a number of pitfalls that you're almost certain to encounter along the way, so let's start by identifying them and understanding how we can build a better sculpture.

Background Object

Much of the time, I use a flower – most commonly a Gerbera Daisy – as the background that gets refracted inside of the water droplets. These flowers are radially symmetrical and many varieties have a different coloured (or black) center compared to their petals. This offers up a pleasing amount of luminosity or colour contrast between the background and the refractions inside of the droplets. The flowers are also larger, so they can be placed farther away from the droplets and offer up a smoother, softer background.

Distance?

One of the most common questions I am asked about is the placement of the flower in the background and how far to place it from your droplets. This distance can be practically established by a test shot. See the image on the right page? Notice a black border around the flowers in the droplets. Too much black means the flower is too far away; no border, and only seeing the center of the flower and not the petals? Your flower is too close. This level of experimenting will lead to intuition after a few attempts and only minor adjustments are needed to get the right "feel" for the image you're after.

Not All Droplets Are Created Equal

One of the most immediate problems you'll encounter

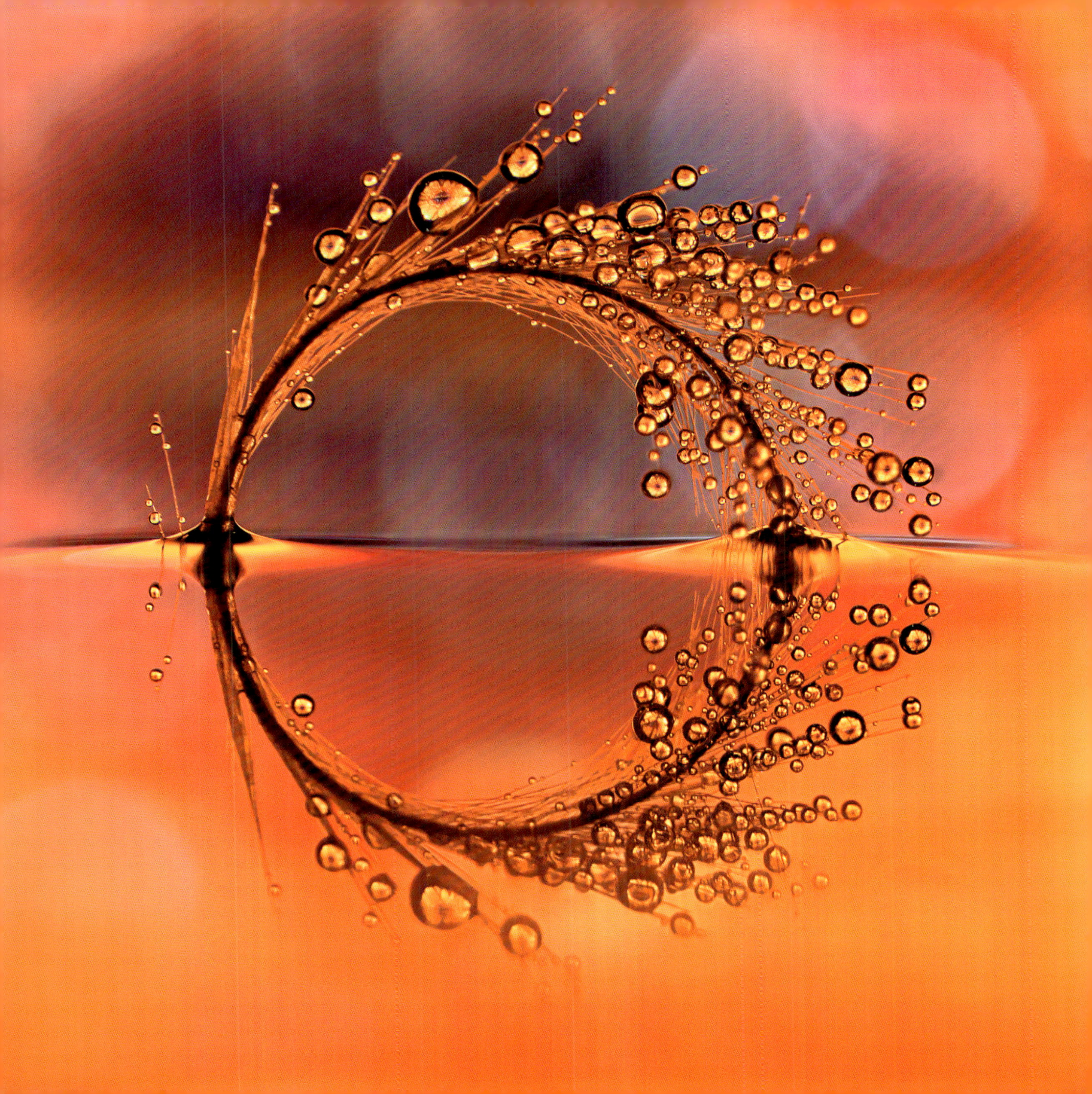

on your first attempt in this genre of photography is that your droplets are not spherical. In order for a droplet to act like an effective lens, it needs to be as spherical as possible. This doesn't always happen, especially when you're using random objects in the hopes of getting this to work. Take for example the large droplet on this flower petal. It's supposed to be a daisy, yet it looks much more like a frying egg. The refraction is distorted because the droplet is flat on the top, though curved on the bottom. This is far from the spherical shape that we're after. If you look closely you might see some of the smaller droplets have a more accurate depiction of the daisy in the background, but the image is ruined by the lack of spheres.

The droplets also need to qualify in another important way: they need to offer a "line of sight" to the background object. If the view through a water droplet is partially obscured, it might only show a portion of the background or none of it at all. In the same image, examine the upper right droplet, partially hanging below the petal but not enough for us to see anything beyond it. Instead, it's functioning like a magnifying lens showcasing the cell structure of the flower. While that's neat in its own right, it's not what we're after.

Our goal then, is to create the most spherical droplets possible that have the clearest view to the background. Thankfully, our choice of materials has a dramatic impact on how easy this is to accomplish.

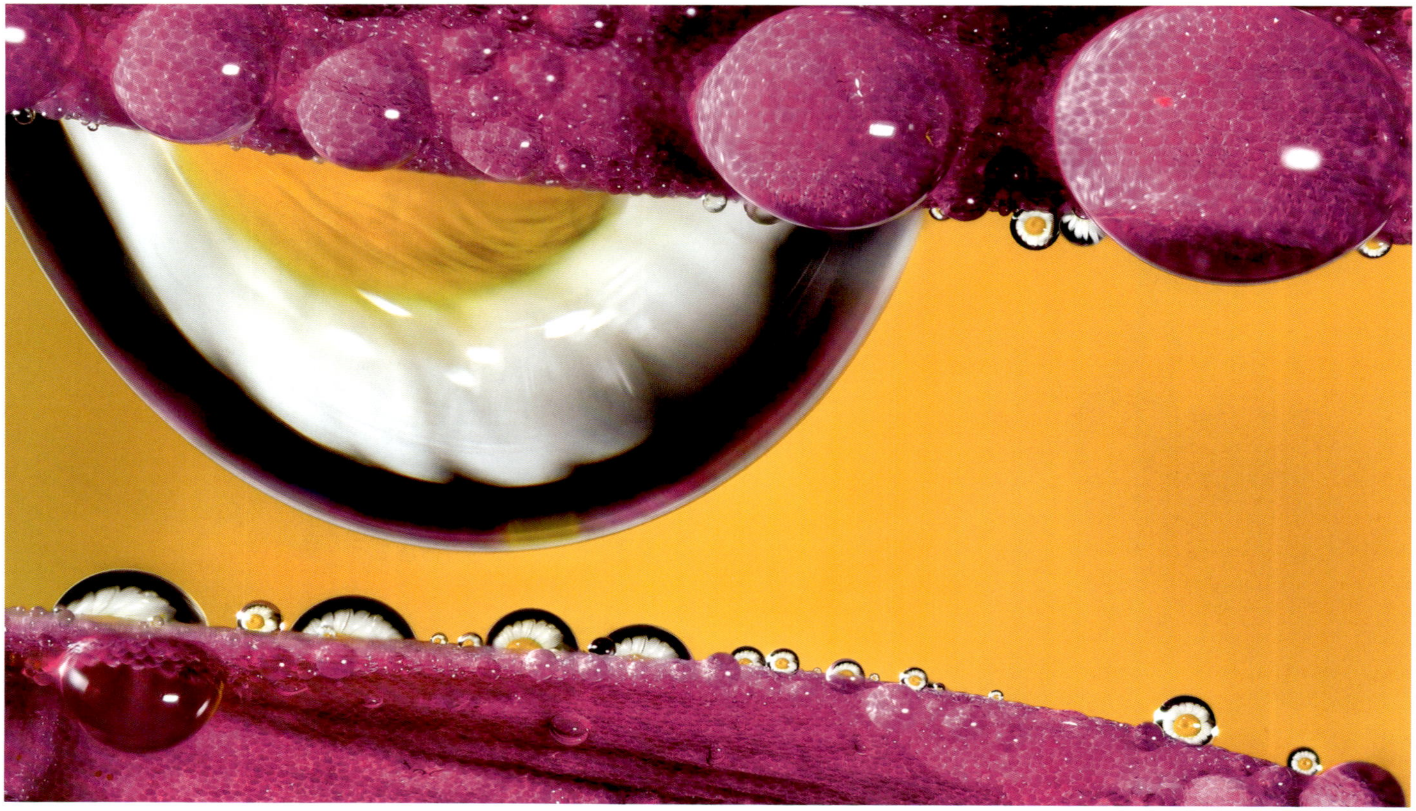

Creating Good Droplets

There has been a lot of trial and error to discover which surfaces will allow the formation of good quality droplets. Initial early successes were found on dandelion seeds and random varieties of grasses, but I sought to compile a rough list of some "go to" objects for myself and others to consider as building blocks for these sculptures.

One such effort involved visiting a local greenhouse, equipped with a spray bottle and a question: do you sell any plants that, when sprayed with a misting bottle, will create spherical droplets? I received a very puzzled look back, and an answer that I'll paraphrase as "maybe, but we don't exactly have a section for that". I then asked if I could use my spray bottle to do my own research on what to purchase, and a firm "No" was received. Further discussions with a manager, which also included showcasing my work in the area of water droplet refractions to date, changed their minds. They insisted on emptying out my spray bottle and filling it with what they knew to be ordinary water, and I have a suspicion someone was instructed to keep an eye on me. The misadventures of a macro photographer seeking the best ingredients!

From this visit as well as plenty of additional first-hand discoveries in the field, I present you with a list of things to start experimenting with:

Wildflower Seeds

Specifically dandelion, Yellow Goat's Beard (also called Salsify), Clematis, Prairie Smoke, and Milkweed… but every wildflower seed that has a "sail" to be caught by the wind and carried off by the wind to propagate will work well. The feathery features of the sail make excellent spherical droplets! If you are going to buy seeds, you'll have to play the long game since no supplier I have found sells them with the sail. This means you'll have to plant them, wait for them to grow and then harvest the seeds yourself – or just hunt for them in nature.

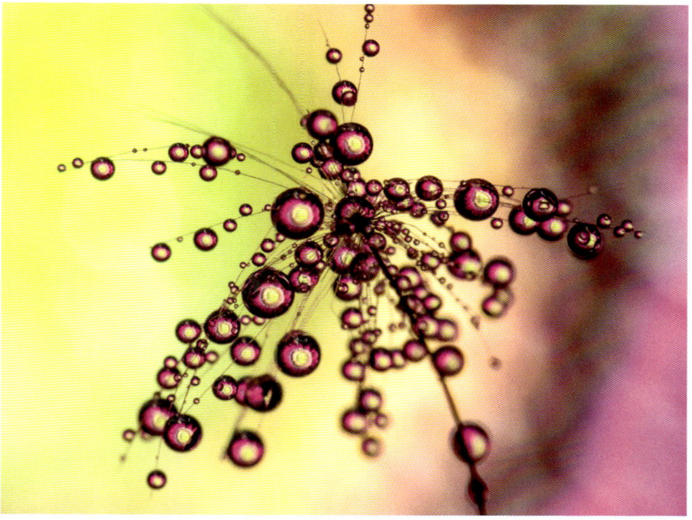

Dandelion seed with Gerbera Daisy in the background. Lumix GX9, Leica 45mm F/2.8 Macro, F/11 ISO 200 1/125sec

Bluegrass

Blue Fescue is an absolute favourite, but any grass that has a powder-like coating on the surface that you can rub off with your fingers will work – it's this powder coating that helps keep droplets spherical.

Eucalyptus

Easy to find any time of the year from craft stores that sell dried flowers, a bunch of eucalyptus will behave much the same way as bluegrasses with a powder coating to give you the best droplets. I find that the youngest tips of the plant yield the greatest results.

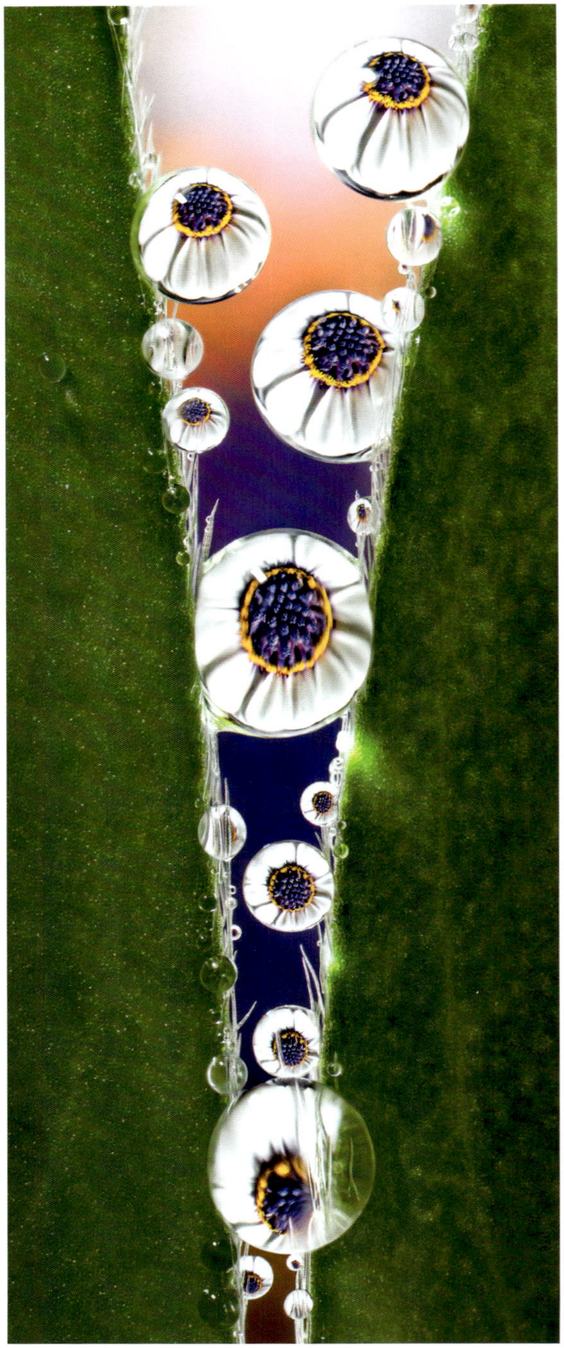

Barberry Leaves

The leaves of the Barberry plant, particularly new growth, can create an array of water droplets on their outer edge. We have some of these shrubs in our yard and when sprayed with the garden hose on "mist" they become a treasure trove of droplets. A small branch can be cut and staged easily.

Lupin Flower

The leaves of the Lupin Flower, which form a beautiful radial pattern, can also be found holding water droplets after a rainfall. The edges of the young leaves have a feathery appearance much like that of wildflower seeds and they behave almost identically when sprayed with water.

Spider Webs

Always a classic, a spider web can hold a heavy amount of water droplets. While this might be controversial advice, you can secure and preserve a spider web for these kinds of sculptures. If you find a large web in the fall, you can collect it by pressing a wooden frame against it. The anchors of the web will re-attach themselves to the fibers of the wood (I've used untreated canvas stretcher bars) and now the web can be brought indoors. The controversy? The spider has to make a new web!

Butterfly Wings

The wings of most butterflies are hydrophobic preventing water from absorbing into the wings and otherwise just sitting on the surface. From a spray bottle this can create an array of spherical droplets, though it can be hard to shoot through them unless they are on the edge of the wing. I have found a number of perished butterflies in nature and have been gifted various sustainably and ethically sourced specimens over the years – though please refrain from capturing butterflies in nature for this.

Left: Leaves of the Lupin flower with African Daisy (*Osteospermum*).
Canon 1DX, Canon MP-E 65mm F/2.8 Macro, F/5 ISO 100 1/250sec

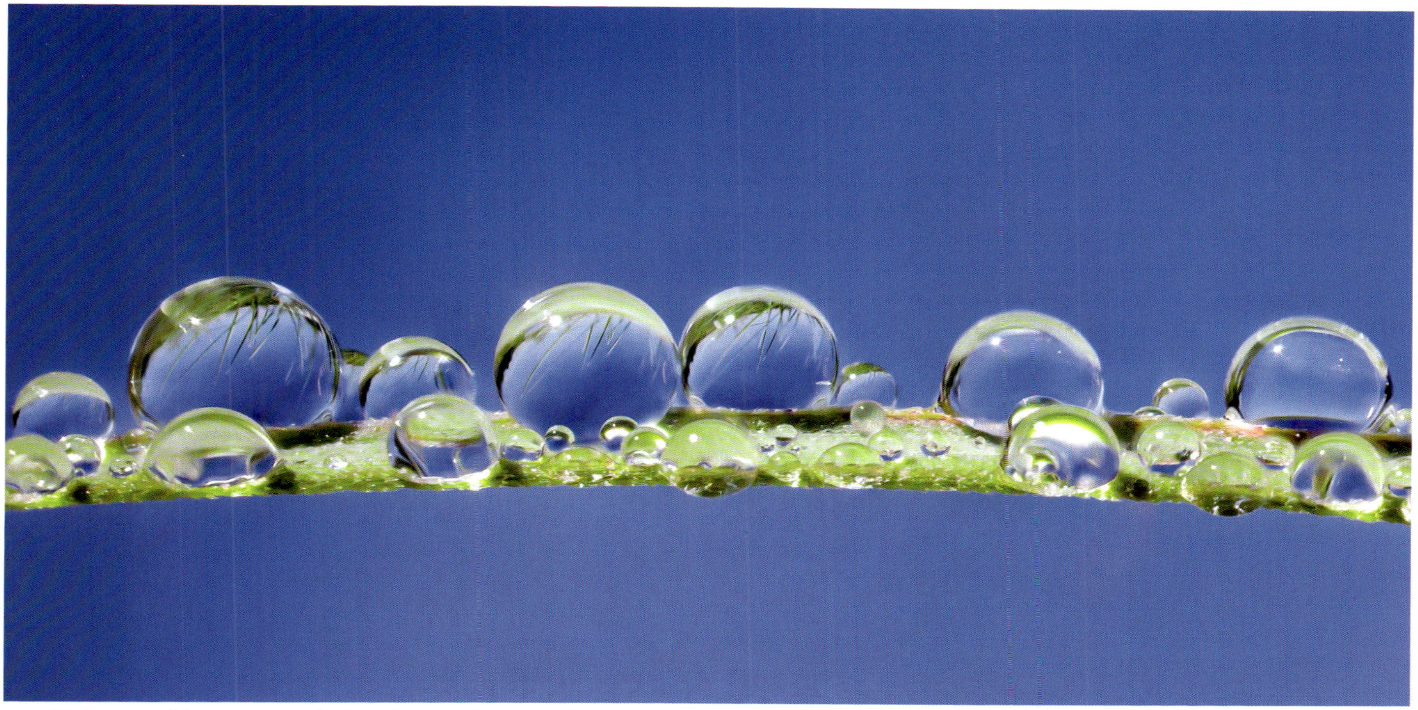

Unknown bluegrass with droplets in the sun. Canon 1DX, Canon MP-E 65mm F/2.8 Macro, F/6.3 ISO 800 1/500sec

Vine Tendrils
Passionflower and Grape vines are some of my favourites, but most fine tendrils will play host to perfect droplets. While they might create droplets from simple mist, they perform best when carefully placing individual droplets with a hypodermic needle. More on this technique on the following page.

Flower Petals
Conveniently, the petals from Gerbera Daisies will allow for spherical water droplets to be placed at their highest point, and stay spherical for at least a few minutes before they begin to flatten. Not all flowers allow for these droplets to be placed easily, as some petals are more hydrophobic than others and cause the droplets to roll off.

Glass
A fun experiment: purchase a bottle of "Rain-X" or some equivalent substance that is designed to make water droplets bead up and roll right off your car's windshield. Rub this into a plate of picture frame glass and spray with water. Keep the glass horizontal and shoot down through it. While the droplets are not spherical, they are round and can function as wonderful lenses.

This list is far from complete – more discoveries are made each year through my own experimentation and undoubtedly you'll encounter your own valuable droplet surfaces when you begin your own tinkering.

To Spray or to Carefully Place?

There are two main strategies for creating the droplets. For subjects like wildflower seeds and bluegrass that are largely hydrophobic, carefully placing a droplet can be a very frustrating process. It's easier to spray these subjects with a misting bottle and hope for a decent array of droplets that you can then modify later if required. Using a spray bottle isn't difficult, but there are two things to remember:

- Do not spray the subject directly, but rather spray above the subject and let the smallest droplets fall down like a fine dew forming slowly. If you aim directly at the subject, you'll waterlog it quickly and larger droplets will easily knock off smaller ones without adding anything.
- You will not spray enough water. Spray more. Even after reading this and following this direction, you did not spray enough water. ***Spray more!***

The spray bottle is just a simple dollar store variety. I have tested some fancy brass spray bottles for greenhouses and they are just as effective, in some ways less effective. Just keep things simple and if it breaks, you'll need to spend another dollar to replace it.

If there is one droplet you'd like to remove, you can take a piece of paper towel spun into a pointed tip and gently poke at the droplet which will be wicked up immediately and is no longer a concern. If you'd like to make a water droplet larger, you can carefully increase the size of it with a hypodermic needle.

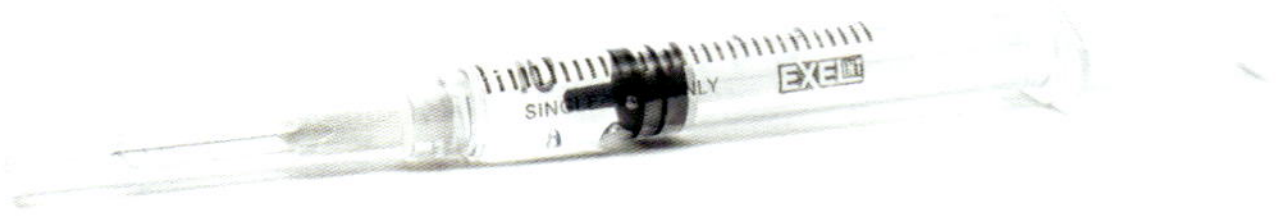

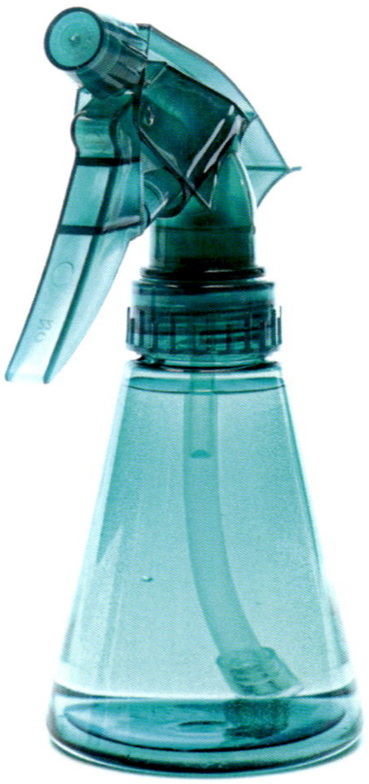

Hypodermic Needle?

You might be surprised to find out how useful a hypodermic needle and a syringe can be to sculpt water droplets. The needle (available with a blunt tip in packs on Amazon and eBay) is hydrophobic – water wants to escape from it more than a plastic pipette or a glass eyedropper, which makes the droplet almost "jump" over to a surface that is a little more water friendly. This can include vine tendrils, flower petals, and sometimes even the very center of a dandelion seed to add one giant droplet to the array of smaller ones.

The smallest gauge of needle is best. Placing water droplets on objects can be a bit frustrating until you get the hang of it – an hour or so of practice goes a long way to supporting your success in this area.

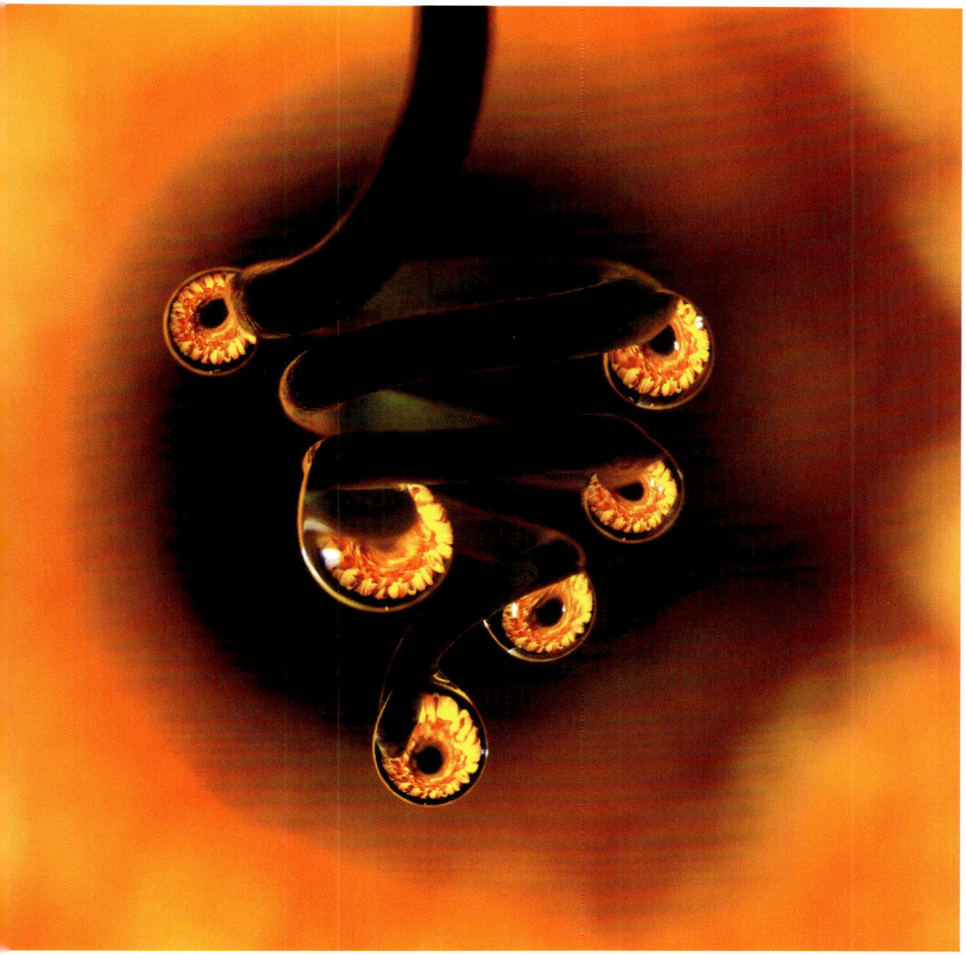

Images on the previous pages in this section were all created using the spray bottle technique. If you decide to try to create droplets in a more controlled manner, you can come up with more "calculated" designs rather than leave the composition up to random luck. Sometimes random luck is better, but the careful placement of droplets can make a difference depending on the subject. Note that one of the droplets, the large one on the left, was uncooperative and would not shift its placement or shape to allow for a symmetrical design compared to the right side. There was nothing I could do to coax it into a different position – sometimes you're just stuck with what you're given.

Could I have gone out to find a different grape vine tendril? Sure! This was the only one after an hour of searching that had such a neat corkscrew character to it, which really helped define the image.

Lumix GX9, Leica 45mm F/2.8 Macro, F/6.3 ISO 200 1/160sec

Note the difference in lighting between the actual photograph (above) and the back of the camera LCD screen (right). The image you're seeing on the back of the camera is without the addition of light to help shape the subject. Additional light will overpower the ambient light hitting the tendril, if aimed at the background. This changes the entire balance of the image. What type of lighting should you use, where should it come from and how should you control it?

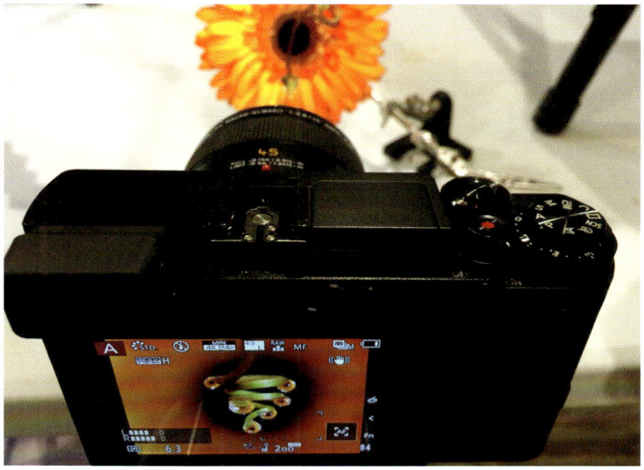

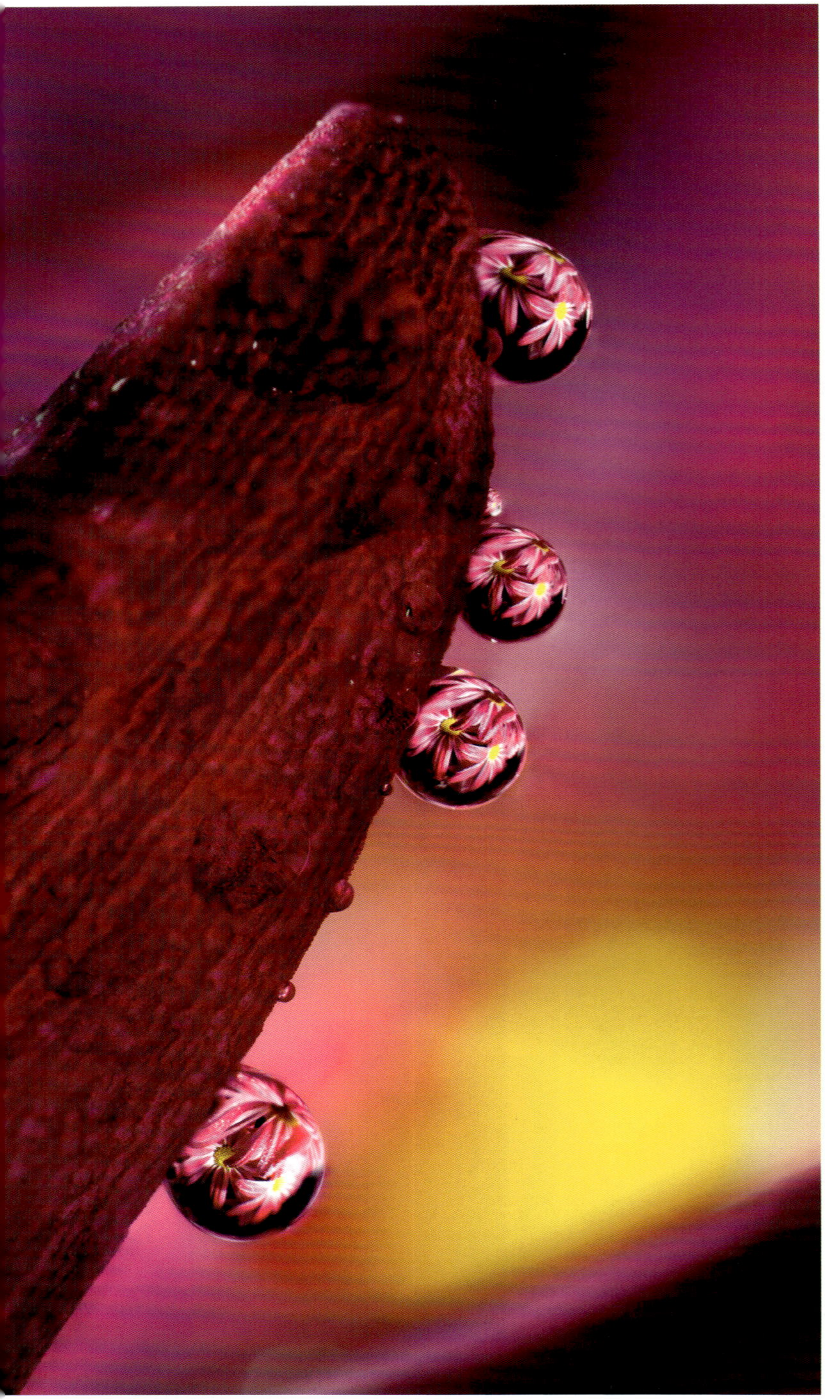

Lighting the Background

Let's start with a simple rule: Put more light on the background than you do on the foreground. In some cases such as wildflower seeds, you might even want the entire foreground in silhouette. The idea here is that we want the water droplets to appear brighter than the surface that they are attached to. Since the droplets themselves are transparent lenses, all of their brightness comes from whatever is in behind them – flowers, thus far in the creative process.

If you keep your light aimed predominantly at the background, your water droplets will have a dramatic impact in contrast to the surface that they are attached to. They'll appear to glow, making them the star of the image. If the light was on the foreground by comparison, the water droplets would be playing second fiddle to their host surface and the fundamental purpose of the image wouldn't be achieved. Yes, there are always exceptions especially when shooting in natural sunlight, but start by following this rule before you decide to break it.

In the image to the left, we see the droplets appearing brighter than the petal they are attached to. You can see a little "kiss" of light on the upper edge of the petal as a small amount of the light from an off-camera flash grazed the petal on its way to the background. This same light also hit the backside of the petal, allowing some light to pass through it and illuminate a portion of the texture of the petal without bringing it to the same brightness as the background. Lighting can be a delicate balance, and even the smallest changes can have huge consequences in the final composition.

Canon 5D Mark II, Canon MP-E 65mm F/2.8 Macro, F/7.1 ISO 200 1/200sec

Lighting Options

If I had been writing this book a year or two ago, you'd have had a firm recommendation that off-camera flash was the undisputed champion to light these scenes. I had used this technique for years to offer the best results without any motion blur, but the technological advancements (read: brightness) in LED flashlights has more than evened things out. You can get pocket-sized flashlights that emit 2800 lumens and beyond with very high quality light. So, what's the real difference?

LED flashlights offer a "what you see is what you get" scenario, where the lighting you see in the viewfinder is exactly what you'll get in your images. Flashes would offer an instantaneous light that could freeze action and remove motion blur, but you wouldn't see a realistic view of the scene while setting up your lighting and subject angles. This made the learning process harder, with a fair amount of head-scratching errors along the way.

While I still recommend the use of flash when you have fast-moving objects in the frame, save yourself some frustration and use continuous LED lighting when things are static. Focus on the artistic elements and don't get hung up on the technical ones.

Glycerine?
If you read tutorials on water droplet refraction photography online, you're likely to encounter many references to the use of glycerine mixed in with water. Glycerine will change the viscosity of the water, which doesn't affect how round a droplet will be but it might help a droplet "stick" better in place instead of rolling off.

I do not use glycerine in any of my images, except for the one on the opposing page. Nearly all the time, glycerine is not necessary and these images are produced with plain old tap water. Glycerine water also tends to dry with a residue that resembles snail slime, which ruins the secondary use for the flowers I purchase for these images. Flowers covered in apparent snail slime do not make an attractive gift for my wife!

Experiment with glycerine if you'd like – it could make some images easier to create but I've learned to live without it.

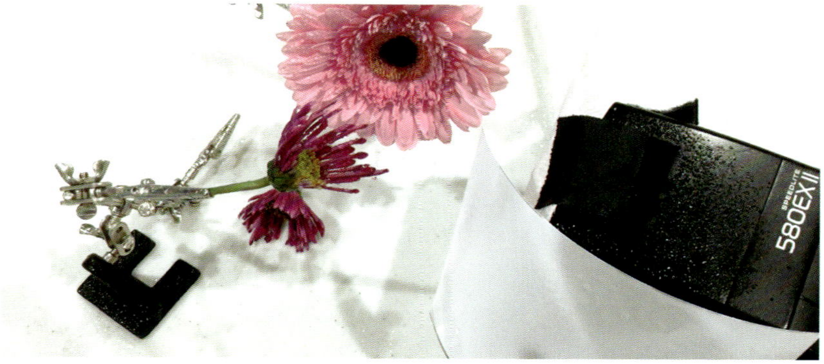

Flash is useful when you know you'll be dealing with motion or otherwise unpredictable subjects. For everything else, use an LED flashlight!

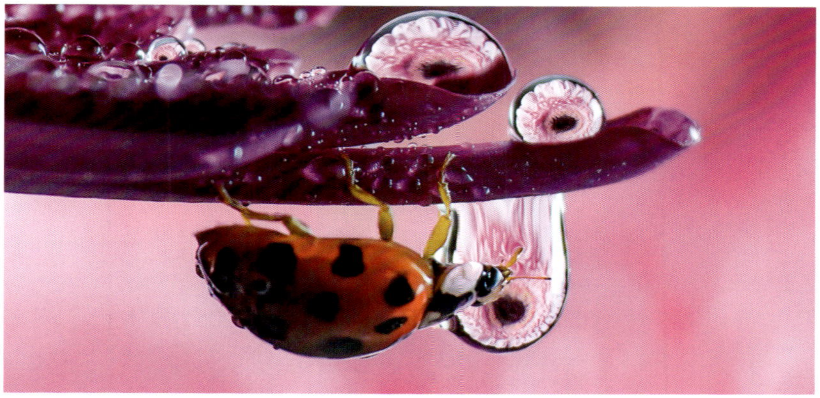

Alignment

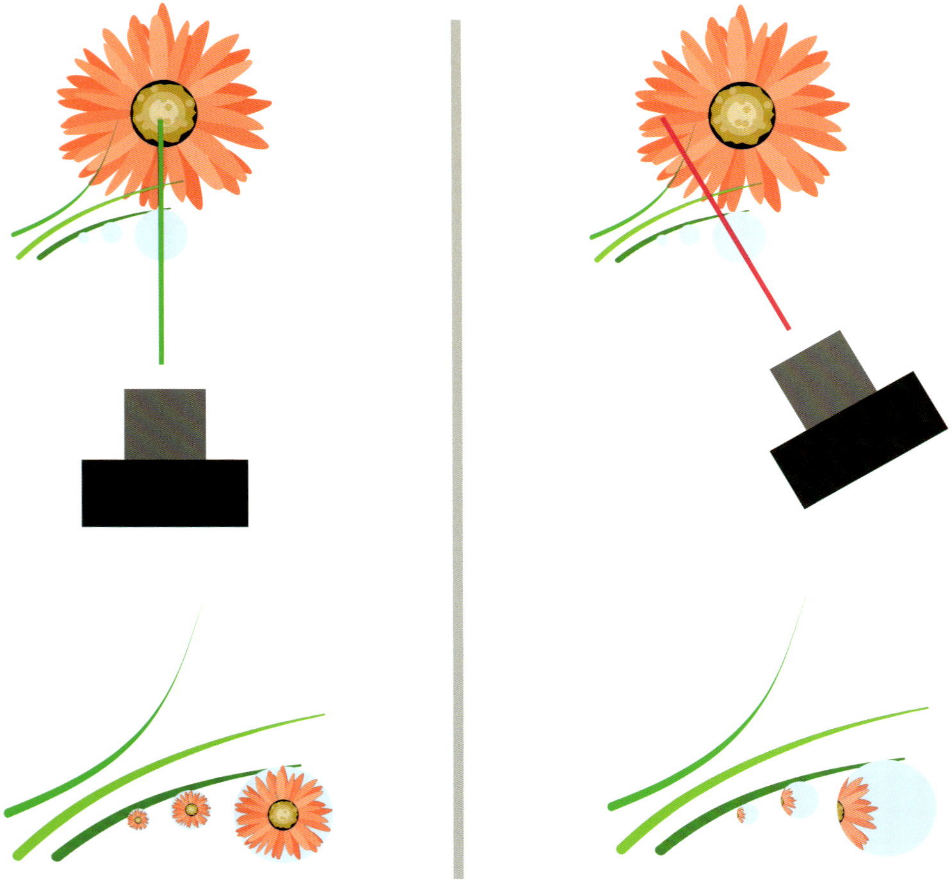

Another "moving part" of water droplet refraction photography is how your various ingredients are aligned. You want the water droplets within the frame, but you need to approach the droplets from the proper angle to keep the flower in the center of the frame, although out of focus. This is easy to see when the flower has a larger darker or different-coloured center which would represent itself as a "blob" in the background. Keep this in the frame, and you'd have a better chance at keeping things in the proper alignment.

This might require you to rotate the camera around with the water droplets being the central pivot point of that rotation. If your camera was on a tripod, the center of rotation would be where the tripod mount is located. It might surprise you to learn that the majority of my water droplet images are shot handheld for this reason. It's far more freeing to be able to move around the scene with your camera in hand using the macro focusing technique of physically moving the entire camera forward and backward, especially when we are trying to maintain high magnification.

If you live and die by your tripod, that's fine. You can reposition your subject in the frame by keeping the camera static and then moving your subject. If you happen to knock off the most impeccable droplet because you didn't want to move your camera, welcome to the club; I've done this many times. Sometimes accidentally setting your camera down on the same table too harshly can make your dangling droplets lose their grip. This is a very transient subject and working quickly will offer the best results.

Equipment for Staging

If you look closely in the behind-the-scenes images in previous pages, you will have noticed a tool holding some of these ingredients together: a "third hand" or "helping hands" tool. These consist of a weighted base and typically two alligator clips on a swivel. Many of them also include a magnifying glass, as the original purpose of these devices is to aid in tying flies for fishing, soldering electronics, fine jewelry work, etc. – we can just remove that portion of the tool and use this nifty tool to help us clamp everything down into place.

A single tool can hold both the flower in the background as well as the foreground subject, but for more flexibility you can use two tools so that they can be positioned independently. At less than $10 per tool, it's one of the least expensive pieces of photographic equipment that I find quintessential to your success here.

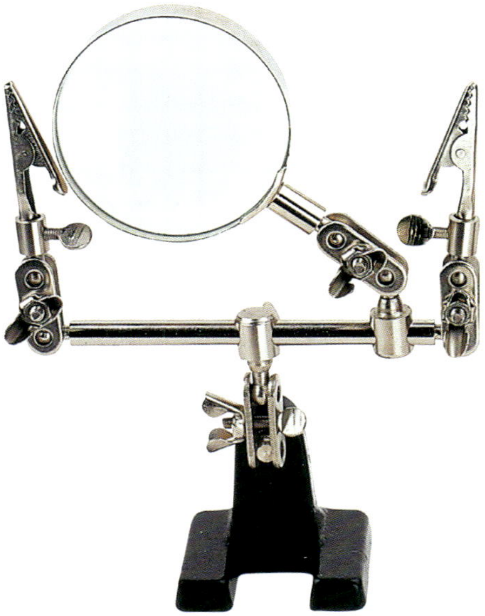

Need something to hold a wildflower seed? A flower stem? Need a flag to block the light from hitting the foreground? Third Hand Tools. Whenever I hold water droplet workshops, these are such an important part of the process that the students get one of these to take home with them. Always have a few of them handy!

Canon 1DX Mark II, Canon 20mm F/3.5 bellows macro lens, F/5 ISO 100 1/250sec.

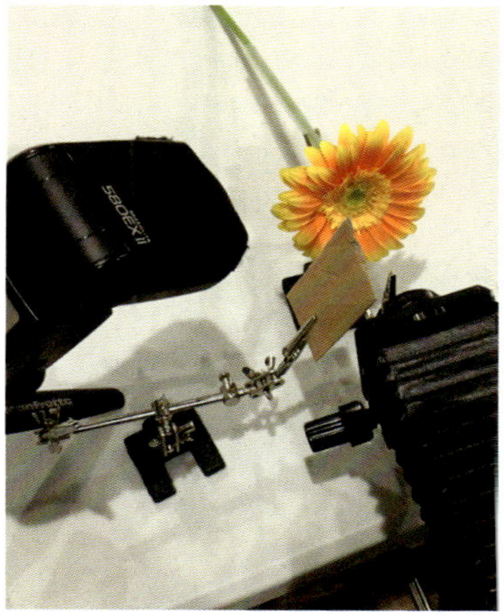

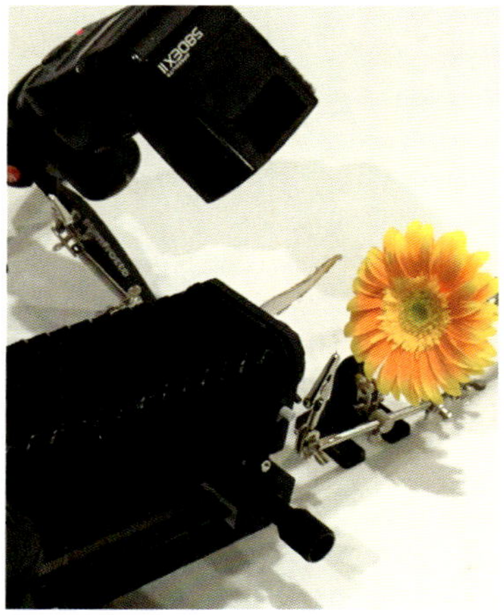

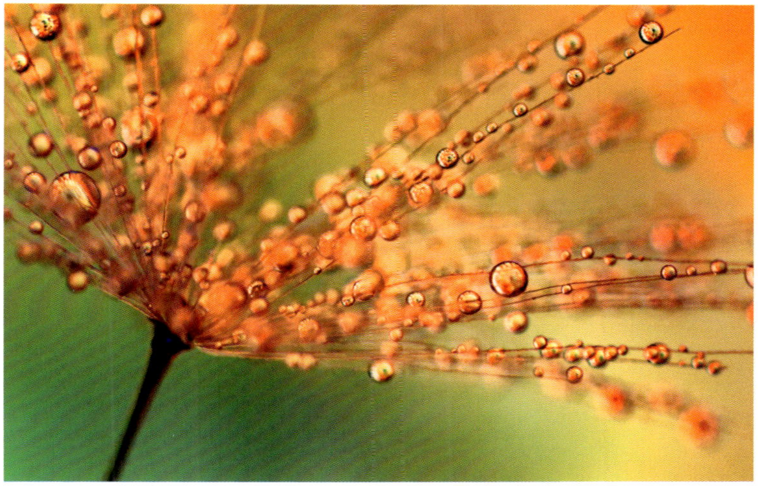

Depth of Field

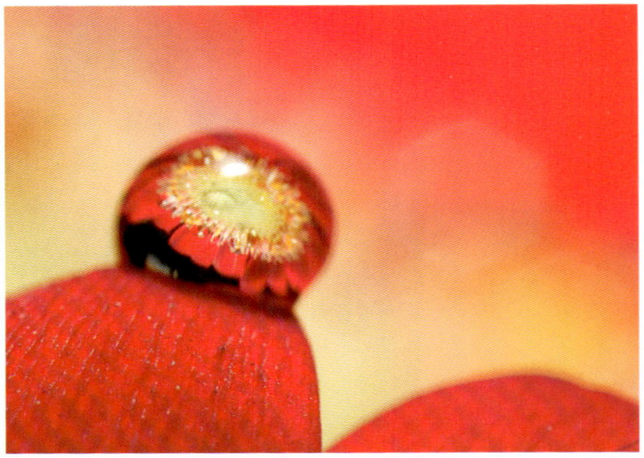

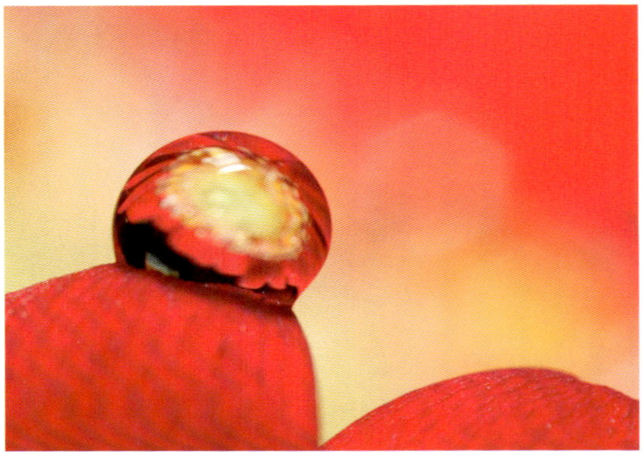

Even F/10 can't get an entire droplet in focus!

Water droplets are tiny. The closer you get, the less you have in focus. It's frequently the case that you can have the refraction in the droplet itself sharp, but the outer edge of the droplet is out of focus. If you were to fill the frame with a dandelion seed you'd have a hard time getting anything sharp! That's not to say that a good image isn't possible, but choosing exactly where your focus falls can have a powerful influence on the entire composition of your image.

Diffraction can play a very negative role in your image quality if you shoot with too small an aperture. Trying to get more foreground in focus can occasionally bring too much of your background into focus. This is especially true if you're using a small flower that needs to be positioned closer to the droplets. You can choose to play with the shallow depth to your advantage, but if you'd like more in focus there are two primary strategies: focus stacking and cropping.

Focus stacking is the traditional method of extending depth in your images. This is discussed elsewhere in this book regarding snowflakes and with a detailed tutorial that also applies here. It's not a magic bullet however, and editing overlapping details can be complex and time consuming. Still, this is the most tried-and-true method of extending your depth.

Like many macro subjects, focus is best achieved by physically moving the camera forward and backward to allow the focal plane to pass through the desired part of the subject. You should be shooting on a continuous burst, collecting dozens of images or more. This approach has two benefits: you can end up with an image with the focus exactly where you want it to be, but you'll also likely have images on either side of that point of focus, which can be combined together to increase your overall depth. Remember that focus stacking doesn't have to make everything sharp (our backgrounds are inherently out of focus with this type of photography), and adding just a little bit of extra depth can solidify your subject.

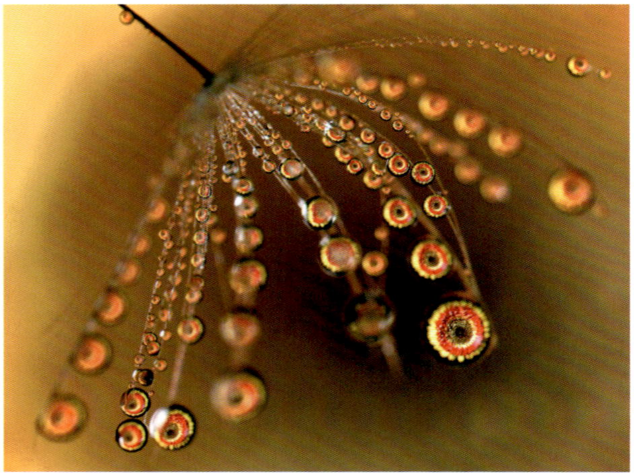

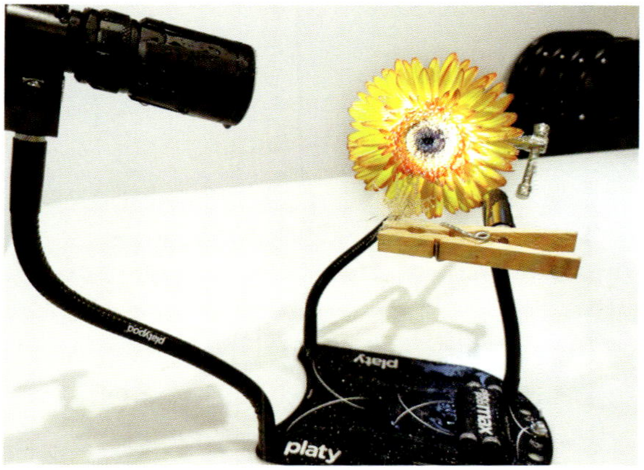

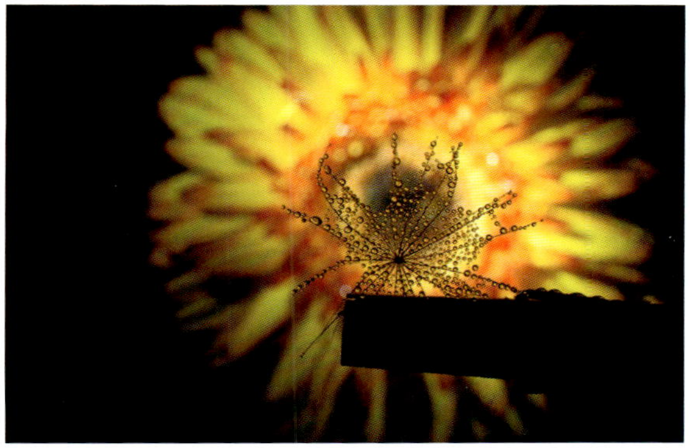

Top: A behind-the-scenes image showing the setup: An LED flashlight, flower, and Yellow Goat's Beard seed all held together with a **Platypod Max** and gooseneck arms, a more robust (and more expensive) solution than the Third Hand tools mentioned on previous pages.

Above: Photograph straight out of camera. Note the intentional lack of magnification.

Right: Cropped version of the image, shot in High Resolution Mode with plenty of detail remaining - no focus stacking required!

Throwing Away Pixels

Especially with modern high-resolution cameras, it might be a better idea do something radical: intentionally throw away pixels! In a move that some may deem offensive, we can increase our depth of field by getting physically farther away from our subject, allowing it to only fill up a smaller portion of the frame. Cropping down to the composition you're after will yield a lower resolution image, but your depth of field can be increased.

High Resolution Mode

The very best use case for this strategy is using the "High Resolution Mode" on your camera, if one exists. This feature on the Lumix S1R takes 8 separate images in quick succession, each one with a slight shift in position of the camera sensor. These are combined together to quadruple the already impressive 47

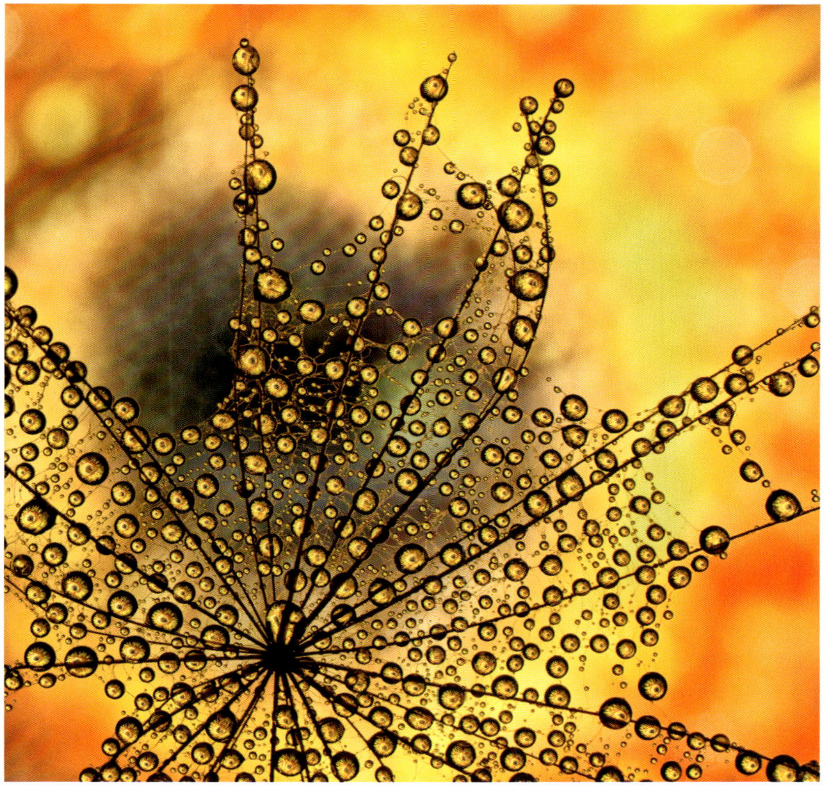

megapixels to an excessive 187 megapixels. I don't need this many pixels – I don't even need 47 megapixels for most of my professional work. This allows me to throw away up to 90% of the image data and still have a very usable photograph with enhanced depth.

This doesn't work in all scenarios. You'll need to have a static subject, a continuous light source, and you must be aware that shooting with apertures even as small as F/16 might allow diffraction to lower the resolving power of your lens. It does, however, allow you to use non-macro lenses as if they were capable of macro magnifications and beyond. Not only does this make macro photography more accessible, it also removes some of the challenges we face with shallow depth.

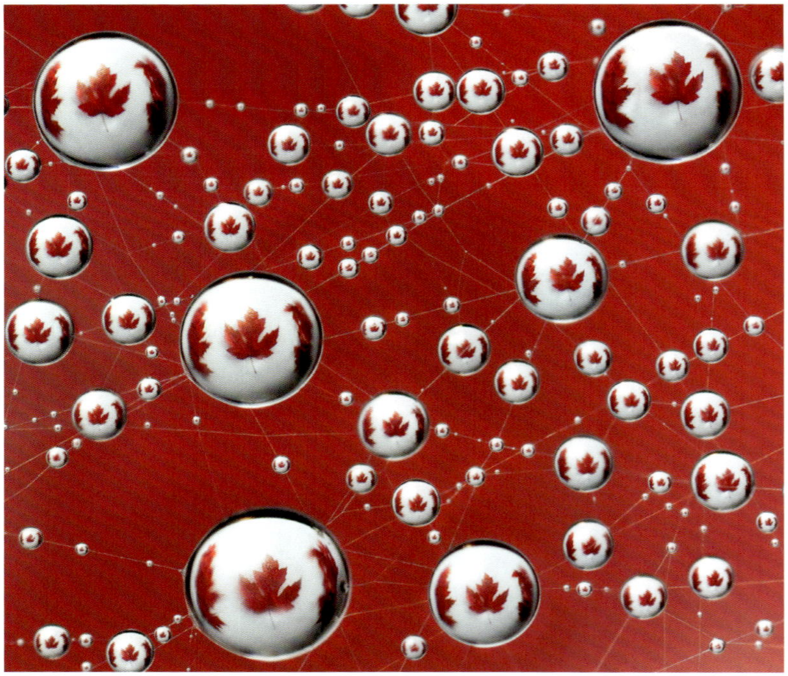

Different Backgrounds

Up until this point, we have been using radially symmetrical flowers in behind the water droplets. This is the classic approach, but you can put anything you'd like in behind the droplets. How about a photograph of fire appearing inside of water? Maybe a single firework becomes a spray of fifty fireworks, one per droplet! Perhaps you have a photo of a butterfly, and you can then place the butterfly on a flower petal, inside the droplet. There are a lot of possibilities to explore – go through your portfolio of images, print one off and give it a go.

I did exactly this with my "Maple Leaf Flag" image, printing a copy roughly 6" long and in a slightly more square crop to fill the droplets better. The result? As a proof of concept it was quite successful!

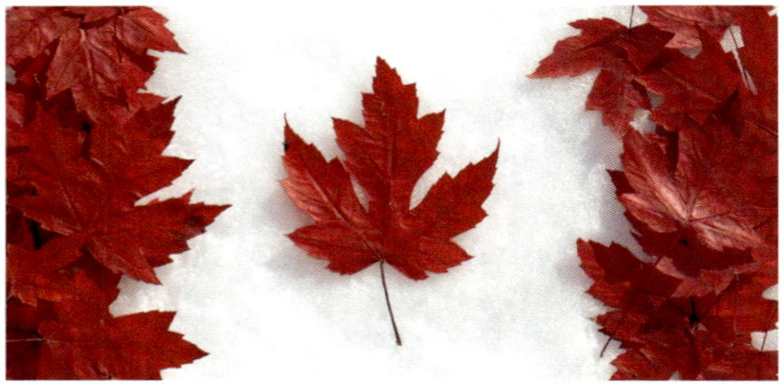

Maple Leaf Flag:
Canon 5D mark II, Canon 24-104mm F/4L F/16 ISO 100 1/125sec

Maple Leaf Flag Refraction:
Canon 5D mark II, Canon MP-E 65mm F/2.8 F/6.3 ISO 100 1/200sec

The Earth in a Droplet

It didn't take long to find a way to use an image beyond a "proof of concept" exploration. Searching through the NASA Visible Earth image archives, I was able to find a map of the earth with realistic cloud cover. Simply printing off a copy of this map and placing it behind a water droplet allowed the entire planet we live on to be encapsulated inside a single solitary drop of water. I doubt I'm the first to attempt something like this, but it became a series of work that I'm eager to revisit at some point.

Download the map for yourself!: visibleearth.nasa.gov/images/57735

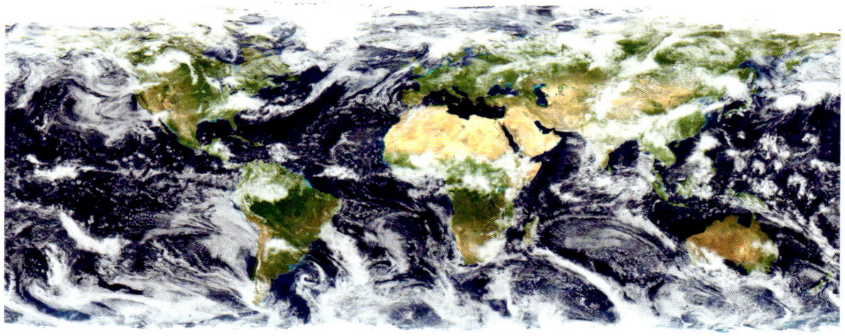

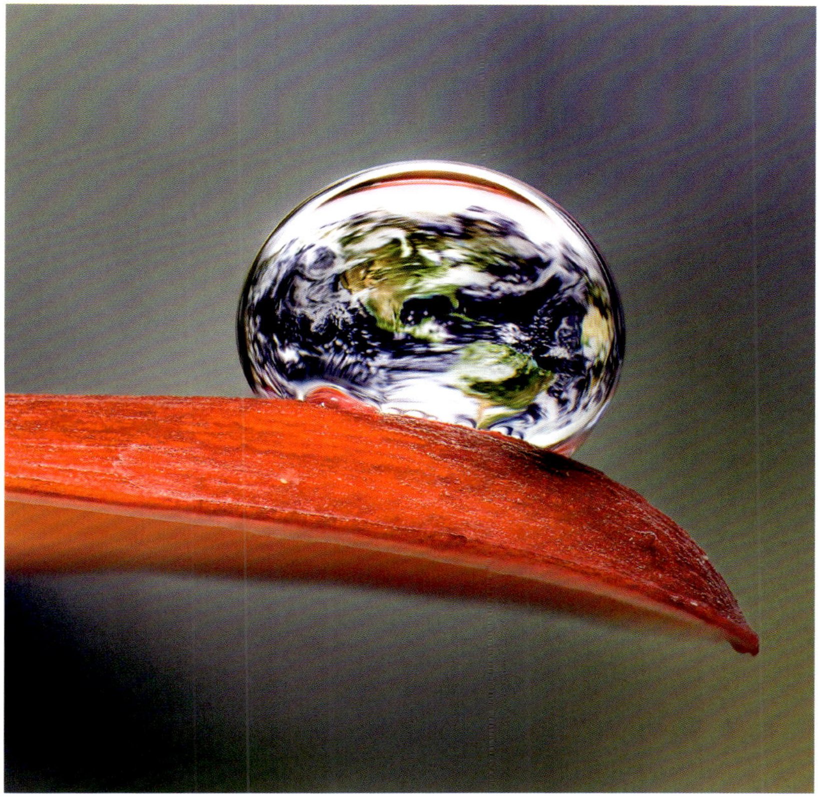

Canon 1DX, Canon MP-E 65mm F/2.8 Macro
F/7.1 ISO 100 1/250sec

Remember – Refractions are flipped! This caught me by surprise, as I never had to deal with flipped images when using symmetrical flowers. My first test photograph of the Fragile Planet image had the Earth upside down in the droplet! It hadn't occurred to me up to this point that the images in the water droplets were always inverted.

The map needed to be placed upside down to pass through the water droplet which would flip it upside right. The image then passes through the camera lens, flipping it upside down again, where software in the camera flips the image back the proper way. You're seeing the image on the page upside right, but in actuality your eyes have flipped it upside down and your brain flips everything back the correct way again. It was in this moment I chuckled to myself and I realized that everyone on the planet is seeing their worlds upside down, but perceiving it properly.

Adding Dimension with Reflection

There are only so many times you can photograph a water droplet refraction image before you have a burning desire to take things a few steps further. How can you keep the subject interesting? I had a creative block here for a while, finally breaking when I decided I would experiment with reflections and refractions in the same image.

This process began with a trip to a thrift store, looking for a large bowl with a flat bottom so that I could accurately place a third hand tool underneath the water, completely submerged. This would allow me to clamp something in the alligator clips to appear as if it was rising out of the water all on its own. If I could come up with an interesting composition, the reflection would be the extra ingredient I was seeking.

The tinkering began. **Hours passed.** If I had known what I was going to create, this process would have been easy. Finally, I arrived at the concept of having a blade of Blue Fescue grass emerging from the water in a shallow arch, and to be covered in droplets. You'll notice the flower in the background – placed with a third hand tool that has a tweezer-like appendage – has no water droplets on it. This was by design; the flower was not in place when the blade of grass was misted, and only put in the proper position once the foreground was "designed".

Remember that alignment is very important. The center of the flower needs to be in the center of the image, albeit out of focus in the background. To achieve this angle, in this instance the flower needed to be halfway submerged under the water's surface. This led to a frustrating "Eureka!" failure moment. Just like Archimedes over two thousand years ago, I had discovered that the water level will rise by the same volume of whatever object is displacing the water.

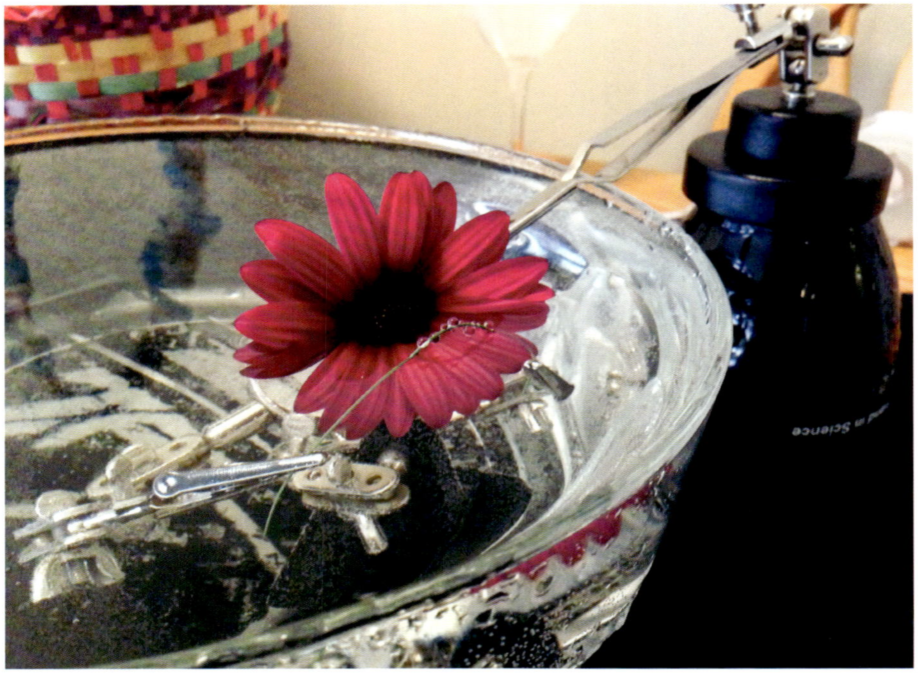

As the flower was submerged, the water level rose and ate all of my droplets that were resting a razor's edge above the surface. Lesson learned, the entire stage was reset with another blade of grass, as good droplets can only be formed on a first attempt. The water level was intentionally lowered, and when everything was placed properly the water was poured back into the bowl to meet the desired level.

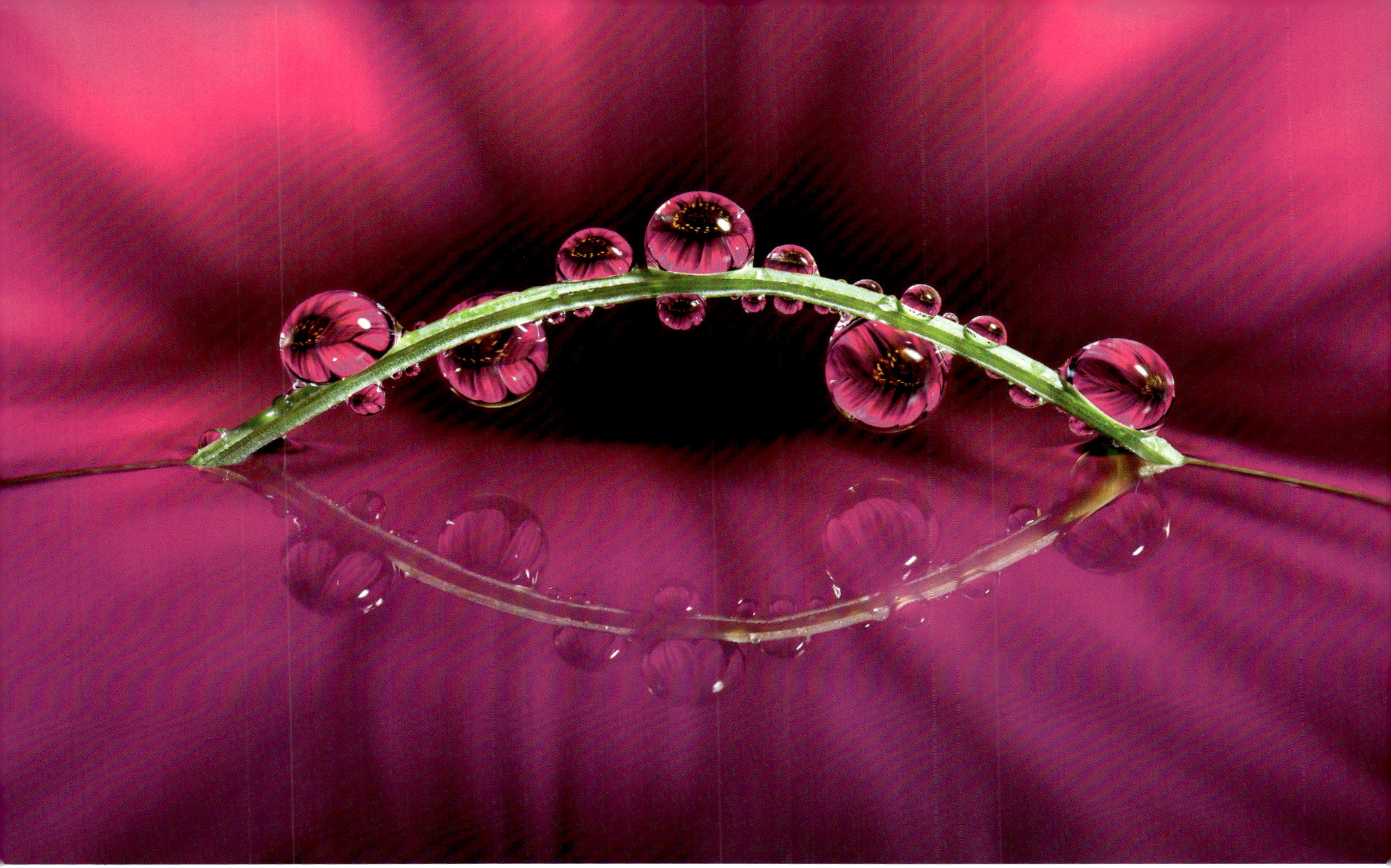

Canon 1DX, Canon MP-E 65mm F/2.8 Macro
F/5 ISO 100 1/250sec

The image is illuminated with an off-camera flash connected by a hotshoe cord, and I had very few flash accessories at the time. For this reason and to experiment with new techniques, the flash was also handheld in addition to the camera. Imagine a police officer pointing both a gun and a flashlight at the same time. The camera (gun) is in my right hand, and my left arm crosses over beneath my right arm, holding the flash(light). It looks tiresome, and if I had only had a light stand and a wireless trigger my task would have been much easier!

Shooting sessions like this often do not result in an image I would publish. They do, however, result in an abundance of knowledge gained and new ideas. Especially from your mistakes there are lessons to be learned. Embrace that idea: revel in your mistakes. Seek them out. You don't grow as a photographer or an artist by getting things right the first time.

Every time I set aside time to play with concepts like this in my studio, I end up with at least five new ideas to explore, and those ideas are more evolved and complete than the concept I started with.

Narratives with Actors

Photographs almost universally have a stronger impact when they can tell a story, and these narratives can be difficult to construct around inanimate objects alone. It's easy to set the stage and the backdrop, but these images can come to life in more potent ways when you have an "actor" in the scene. On such a small scale, we have to enlist the support of equally small characters.

Some such actors are generally cooperative, such as most weevils. This Green Immigrant Leaf Weevil, *Polydrusus formosus*, is an insect easy enough to find in my own backyard to add into the image. They're easy to catch as well, since their defence mechanism when larger creatures approach is to lose their grip on the leaf they were occupying and fall to the ground where they are harder to spot. By placing a small jam/jelly jar underneath the creature, simply give the leaf a tap and they are now under your control.

Let's be clear here: no harm comes to these creatures. They are not frozen or otherwise manipulated. They are generally docile critters that tread slowly and cautiously and that works to our advantage. With ease, they can be coaxed to climb onto a twig and then placed where you'd like them to be. Getting their bearings, I've noticed them stand still for 10-20 seconds before sauntering around. This gives ample time to take any number of photos for focus stacking, so long as you've tested everything beforehand.

Canon 1DX mark II, Canon MP-E 65mm F/2.8 F/11 ISO 250 1/250sec

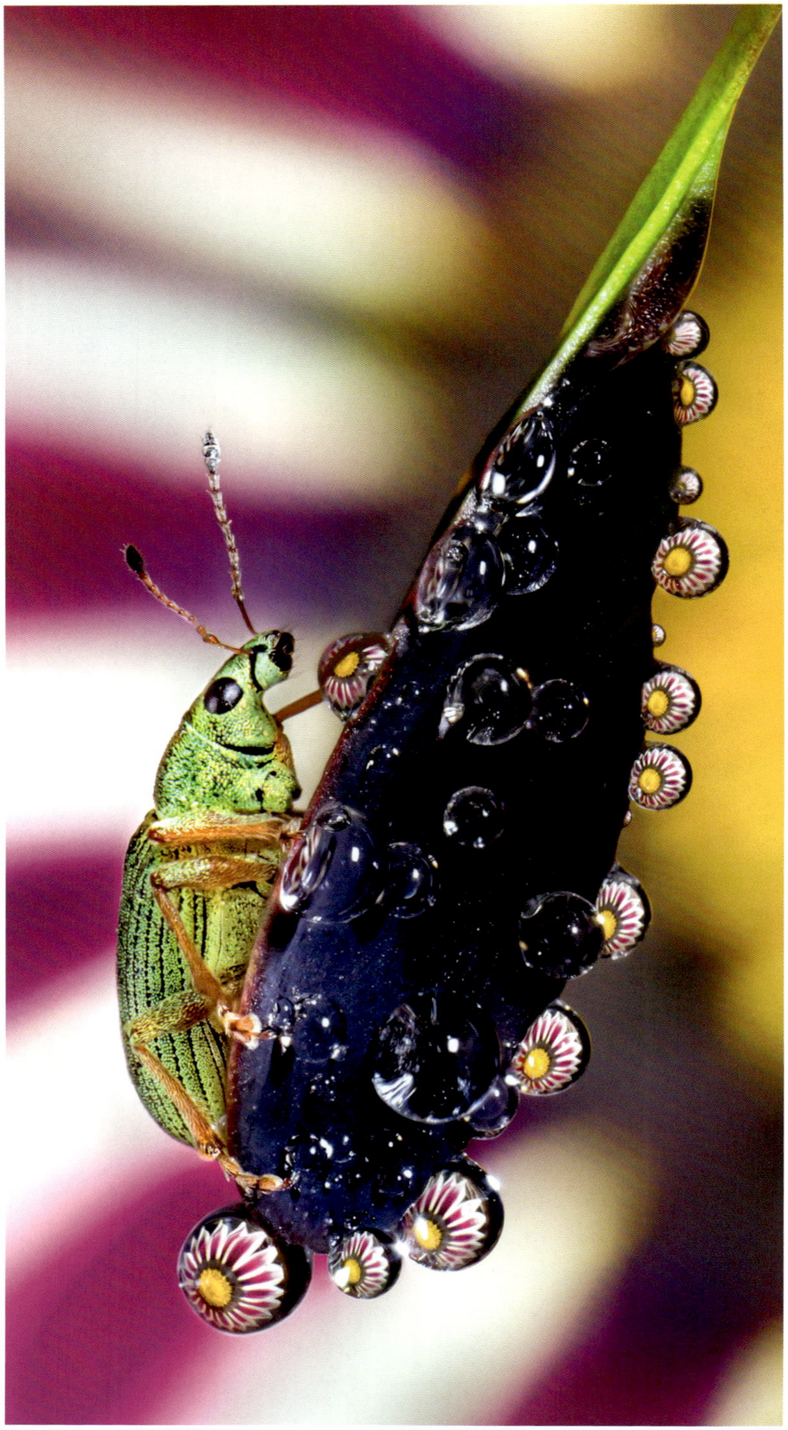

This image is staged with a branch from our Barberry shrubs, with a Gazania flower in the background. It's shot outside, and with an effort to control the lighting a black umbrella is used to darken the area within the frame. I'm also lighting this with two flashes, both off camera: a speedlight and a ring flash. Wait… ring flash? Aren't those incompatible with this subject?

In a manner of speaking, yes. You unquestionably do not want a distracting ring flash reflection on the water droplets. If the ring is positioned such that the droplets are inside the ring or otherwise out of the path of the light, the flash can be used to exclusively light the background flower nice and evenly and without any unpleasant catchlights.

While the flash is locked down and tested beforehand, I can't be certain or confident where the weevil will end up. Will it walk around briefly before stopping? Will it stop at all? The camera is handheld to account for this element of chaos, ensuring that the framing can be adjusted immediately to account for the actions of the actor. Eight images were used in focus stacking, extending the depth to include the entirety of the leaf as well as sharp refracted images inside of each droplet. Manual efforts need to be made to ensure that all of the frames align properly; even though the weevil is relatively static, the antennae will be shifting slightly and create "ghosting" artifacts when combining the images together. This is to be expected when you have a living creature in your frame.

One of the most important considerations here has to do with image angle. Take a close look at the setup shots below. Notice the position of all of the leaves at the end of the branch? None of them match the same angle you see in the final photograph. The actual leaf in question is just intersecting the bottom edge of the ring here, putting it in a much more horizontal orientation. Try this: turn the book 90 degrees counter clockwise and look at the image on the adjacent page. This is the way it was originally photographed, yet it doesn't read nearly as well as the vertical version. The lesson here? These images are not defined by gravity.

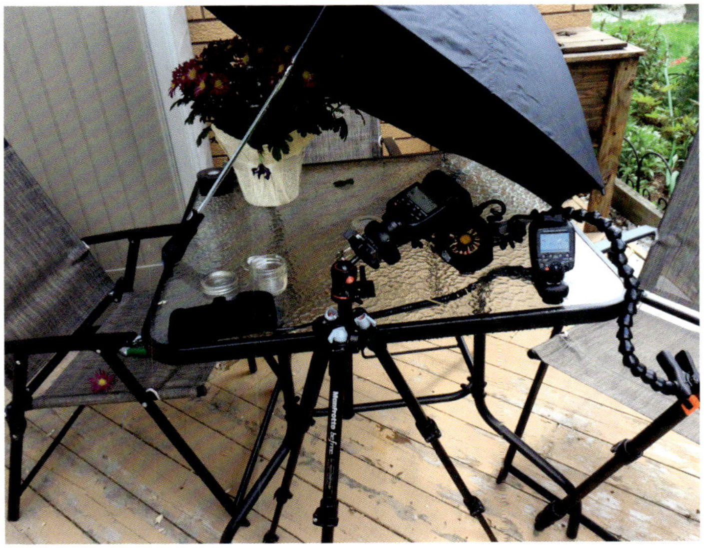

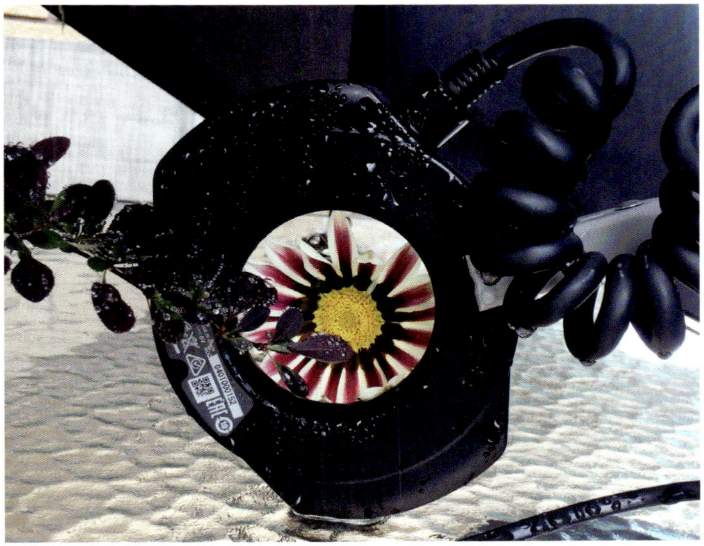

The Evolution of an Idea

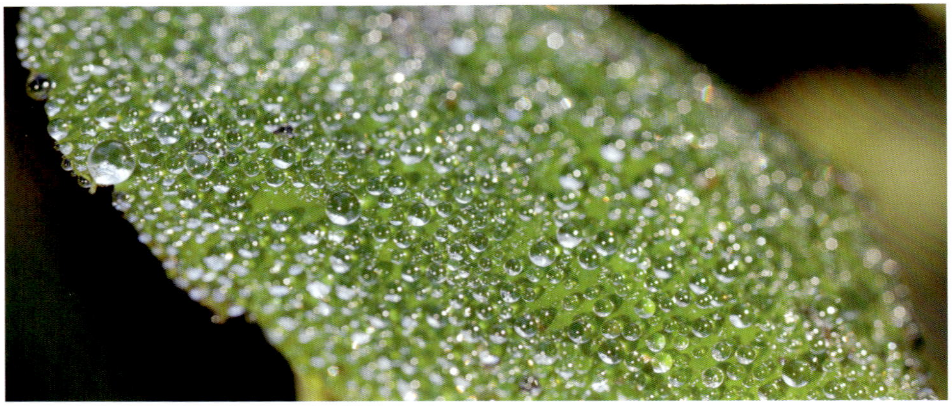

It's been a long journey, originally sparked nine years prior to writing this book when I discovered incredibly spherical droplets at the base of a waterfall. You couldn't do anything with them but document them in their near-infinite numbers, as even adjusting yourself into position would likely send them all flying. Prior to this personal discovery, I had no idea that water could form into such perfect liquid "crystal balls". It would be a year before I began experimenting with my own artistic creations and years before I would be happy with the finished results.

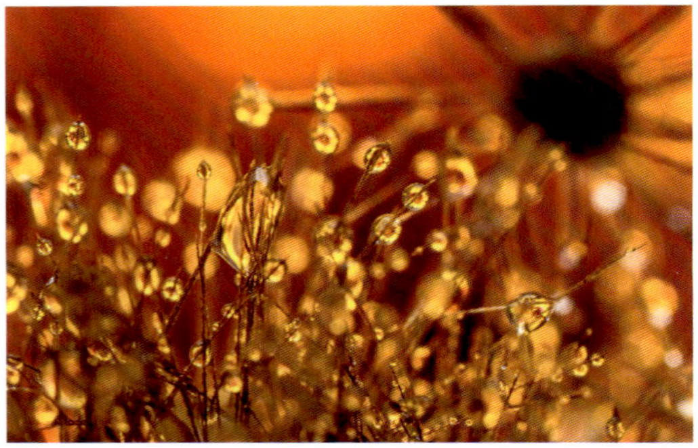

My first attempts were not great. Each time I would experiment, I would recognize ways to improve the results for the next time: more droplets, a different flower, clearer view of the background, on and on my mistakes continued. I don't believe an image is truly a failure if there is something to learn from it, and every hurdle you overcome will likely lead to even bigger challenges.

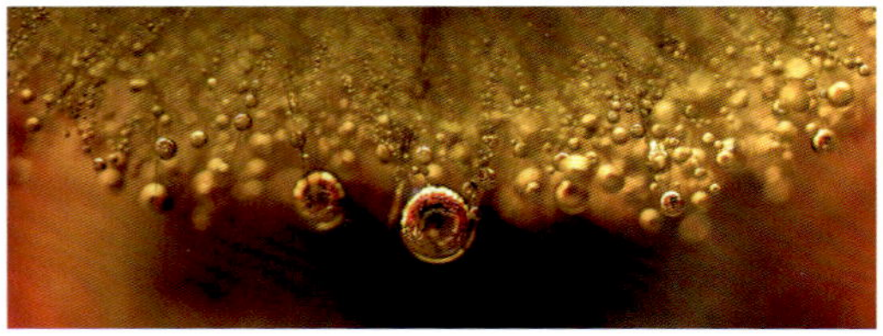

As technical proficiency improved, the focus then shifted towards the art of it all. Water droplet refraction photography requires a beautiful waterborne sculpture to be created by you purely as an artist before the efforts of the photographer come into play. While the photographic skills are indeed an art in their own right, simply wielding a camera will only get you as far as discovering dew drops.

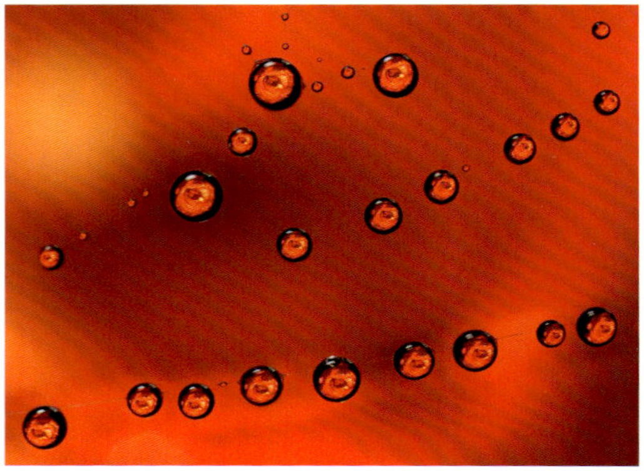

Facing Page: Lumix S1R, Lumix S Pro 24-105mm F/4
F/14 ISO 100 1/80sec
High Resolution Mode + Cropping

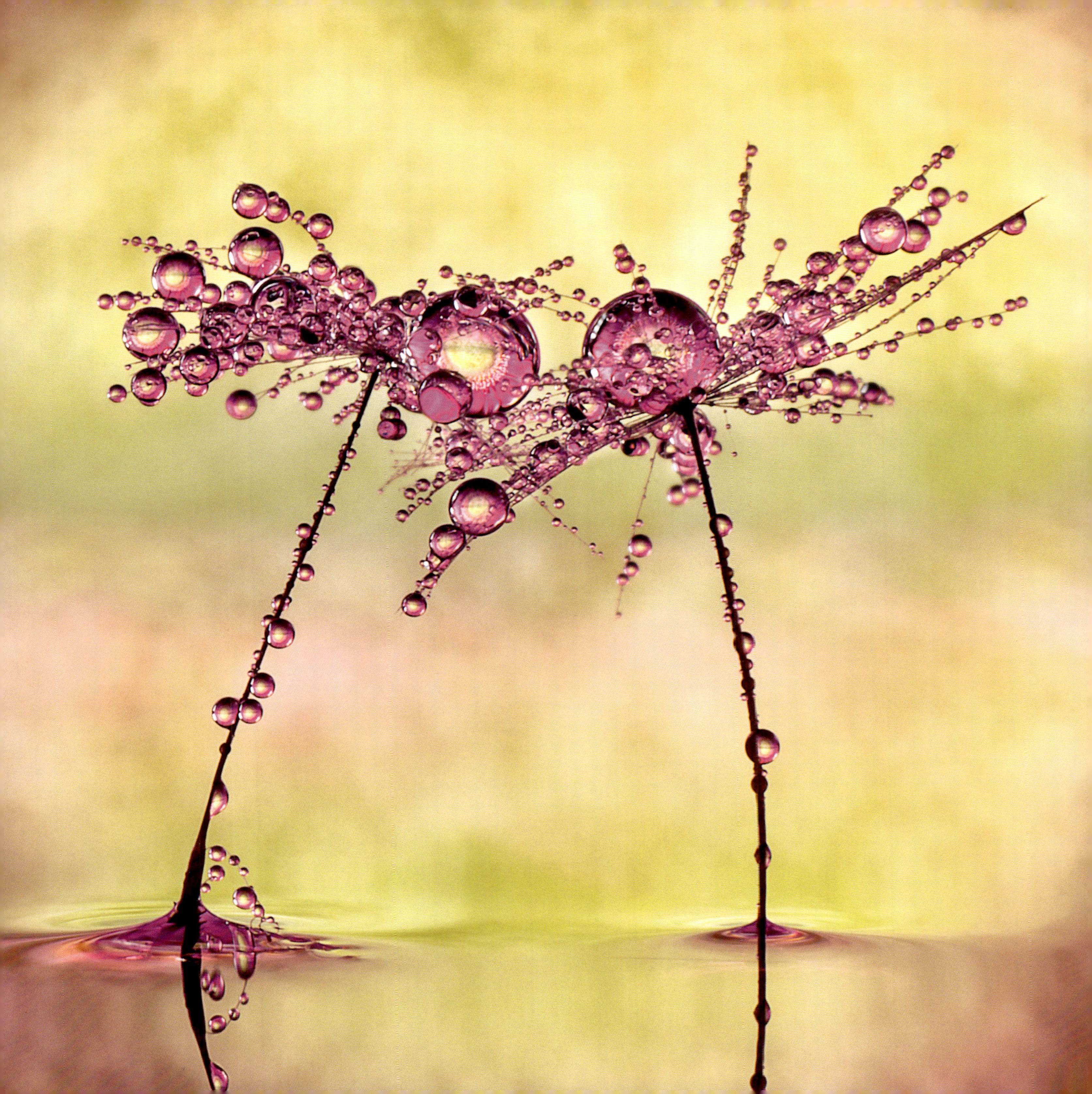

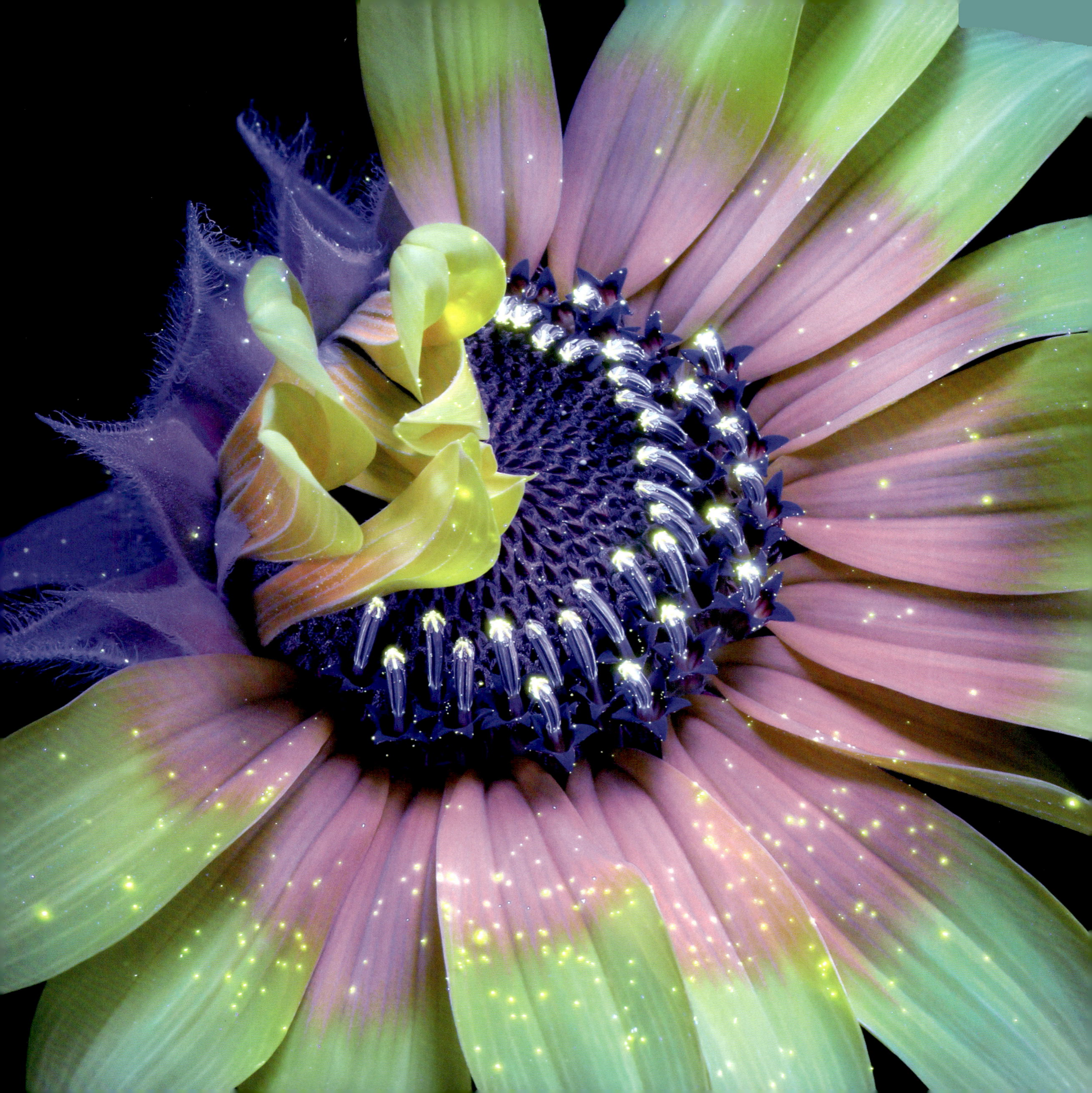

Ultraviolet Macro

The universe at our feet holds many unseen treasures to explore, smaller than we can see with our own eyes. The marvelous discoveries continue when we shift into spectrums of light that are invisible to us – both directly capturing it as well as using it as a tool.

Photography using ultraviolet light is nothing new, but for many years it has resided in the realm of science. Rarely being associated with art, it has been off the radar of many photographers looking to capture the beauty of nature. What was once an obscure niche that required expensive equipment has now become something accessible and captivating for those that choose to experiment in this area. Because ultraviolet photography has not been pursued by many photographers also means that there is an abundance of uncharted territory to discover from an artistic perspective! Where to start?

[1]Linetsky M, Raghavan CT *et al.* "UVA light-excited kynurenines oxidize ascorbate and modify lens proteins through the formation of advanced glycation end products: implications for human lens aging and cataract formation." *Journal of Biological Chemistry*, May 2014. DOI: 10.1074/jbc.M114.554410

Safety First!

This cannot be stressed enough: ultraviolet light can be dangerous; it's why you wear sunscreen when you spend time outdoors. Thankfully the necessary precautions are easy to procure. A pair of UV safety glasses can cost as little as $10, and I recommend you always use them when using ultraviolet light sources. Studies have shown that exposure to UV light can cause cataracts[1], and while the risks here are minimal, why take any risk at all?

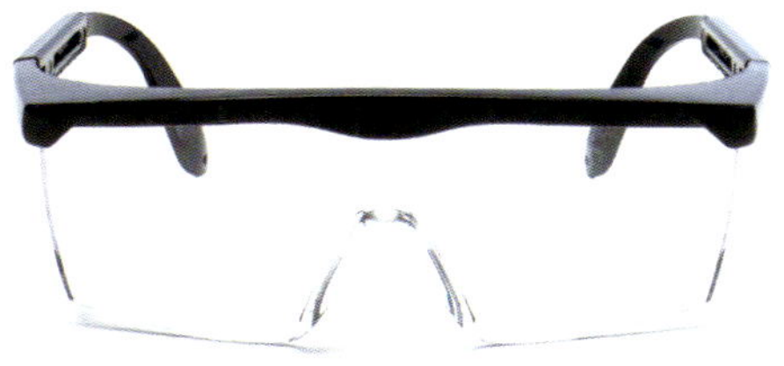

If you already wear glasses to correct your vision, your glasses likely do a decent job at blocking UV light. A simple test would be to put your glasses in front of your ultraviolet light and point the light at a piece of copy paper. If it fluoresces bright blue, UV light is getting through your glasses.

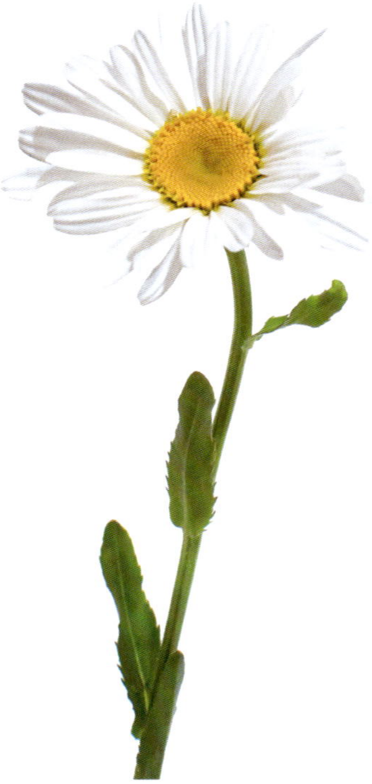

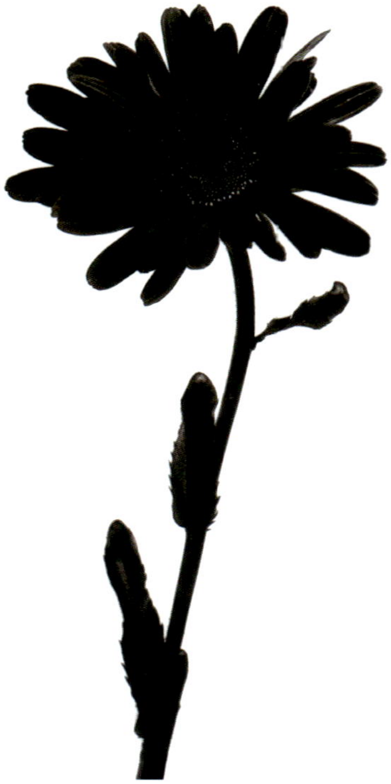

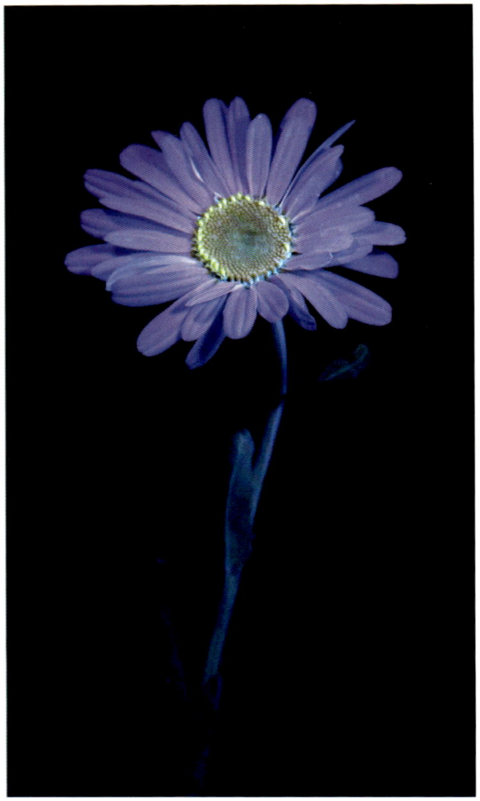

Reflectance vs. Fluorescence

There are two types of UV photography that often get confused. "Reflectance", the direct capture of UV light, requires modified cameras, specialty lenses, expensive filters and ultraviolet lights. "Fluorescence" is what most people will care about: using ultraviolet light to cause a subject to fluoresce into the visible spectrum, and the camera (no modifications or special gear) captures the ordinary visible light that results. This is where the majority of otherworldly images come from.

In the above image, the left flower is captured using plain, ordinary light. The middle image is the result of directly capturing ultraviolet light - many flowers absorb this portion of the spectrum. The right image is often coveted as the most magical, the effect of exposing the flower to ultraviolet light which causes it to fluoresce. This effectively turns the flower into its own light source! Three different ways to look at the same flower, and two of which you've likely never encountered before.

Capture UV Directly – Reflectance

This is more difficult and less rewarding than ultraviolet fluorescence photography. The subjects to explore are more limited and the equipment can be expensive. I'm not selling this well, am I? It's not my favourite. That said, there have been a number of fascinating images created by recording ultraviolet light and it's interactions with the universe at our feet.

What is this good for, anyway? Certain insects can see into the ultraviolet spectrum, and some flowers have co-evolved certain patterns that pollinators can see that are completely invisible to our own eyes. Dandelions are the most common example, with a "bullseye" pattern in the center. The pollen of these flowers absorb UV light while the petals reflect it, transforming the uniform yellow colour we see into something more attractive to bees and other insects seeking out the pollen.

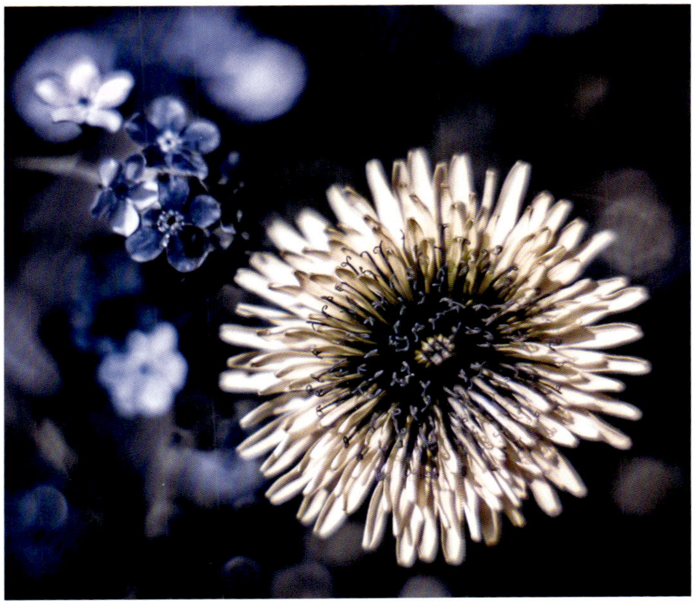

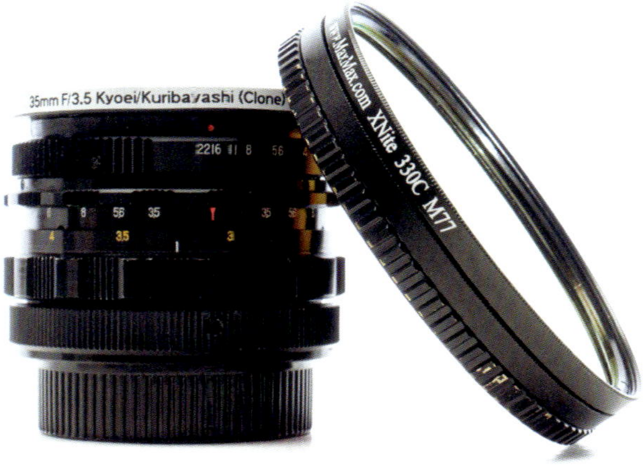

To see these patterns, we need a number of things:

A camera modified for "full spectrum". All camera sensors are inherently sensitive to ultraviolet and infrared light, with filters being placed in front of the sensor to narrow things down to just the spectrum that human vision is capable of (roughly 400nm through 700nm). If you use a professional service to remove these filters such as LifePixel or Kolari Vision, you can capture everything. This produces strange looking images. There's a reason those filters are there in the first place. We can narrow the spectrum with the use of filters to cover just the range we're after.

The best filters for this on the market come as a pair: The XNite 330C and the XNite BP1 sold through maxmax.com. These filters together will remove 100% of the visible spectrum and allow most of the UV spectrum to pass through. More importantly, they prevent infrared light from contaminating the image.

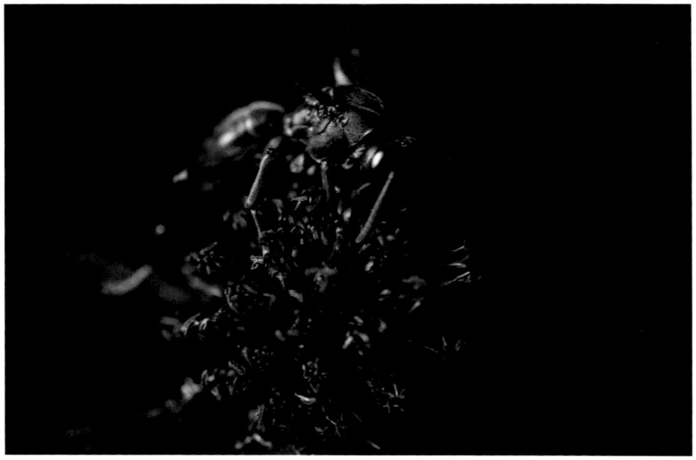

Above: A wasp forages on a flower but we see nothing but specular highlights reflecting back to the camera.

Below: A cluster of crocuses that are normally a saturated violet colour also absorb all UV light! No winners here.

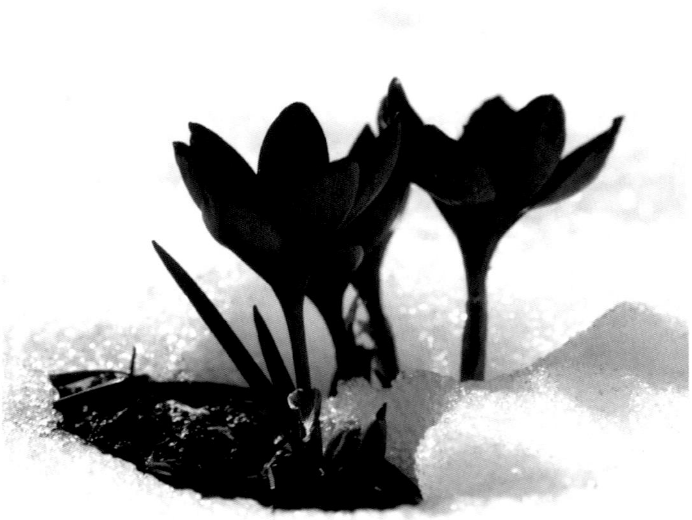

If even 1% of the infrared light from sunlight enters the lens, it can equal roughly 50% of the ultraviolet light – contamination from other spectrums is a real issue and many "UV Black" filters on the market behave this way. These filters can be prohibitively expensive, and the second best option would be the UV bandpass filter from Kolari Vision. Once you pay to have your camera converted, expect to spend at least a few hundred dollars on proper filters.

You're not done yet! You'll need a UV capable lens. Most lenses will block ultraviolet light due to their coatings, the type of glass they are made from and even the glue that sticks certain elements together. The highest transmission UV lenses are made from quartz glass and even in the second-hand market can drain your photography budget by thousands of dollars. Enthusiasts in this area have come with alternatives that transmit high levels of longwave UV light – the kind that can be recorded by modern CMOS sensors. A common inexpensive lens is a Kyoei/Kuribayashi 35mm F/3.5 lens, for which many clones exist that are equally capable for around $100.

Don't forget that you'll need a light source that emits UV light. Natural sunlight can work for this, or you can use some of the options that will be discussed in the ultraviolet fluorescence section where the purity of the light source is of paramount importance. Not so important here, so long as you've got good filters in front of your lens.

And in the end, you're at the mercy of your subject. As you can see to the left, some subjects underperform. It had been a level of frustration coupled with boredom that forced me to put away my ultraviolet reflectance gear for about a year at this point.

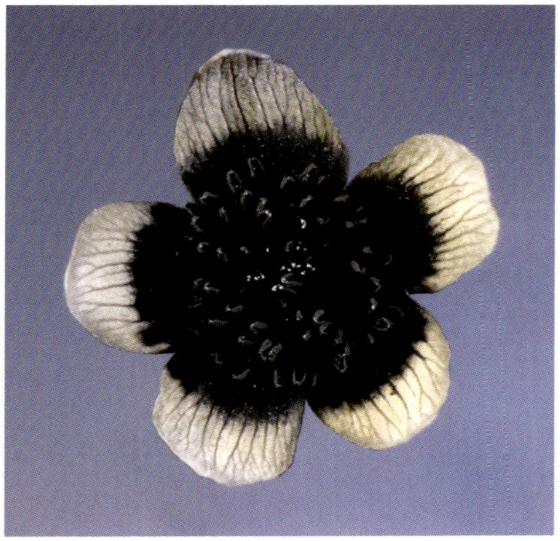

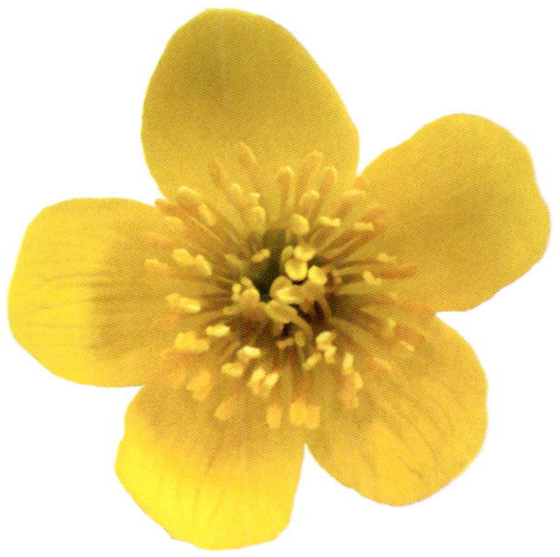

And then, there was a glimmer of hope. Many flowers were in full spring bloom and I took my UV-modified camera out to see if anything would spark interest in this area. Most flowers produced nothing of interest. The Marsh Marigolds in our backyard pond however, produced an exceptional UV pattern.

… but still, it's just a black blob with some dark veins.

I suppose this was more interesting than the plain yellow version, and most definitely better than the infrared version on the right!

This same experiment was conducted with a Snowdrop the next year, one of the earliest blooming flowers. Could there be some hidden pattern to discover? No. In fact, it was even more mundane.

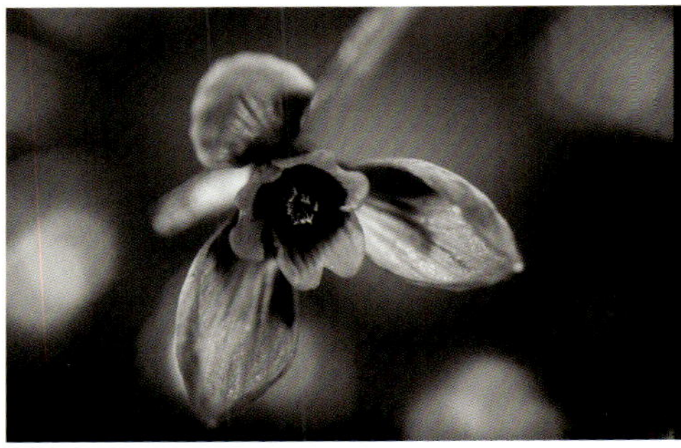

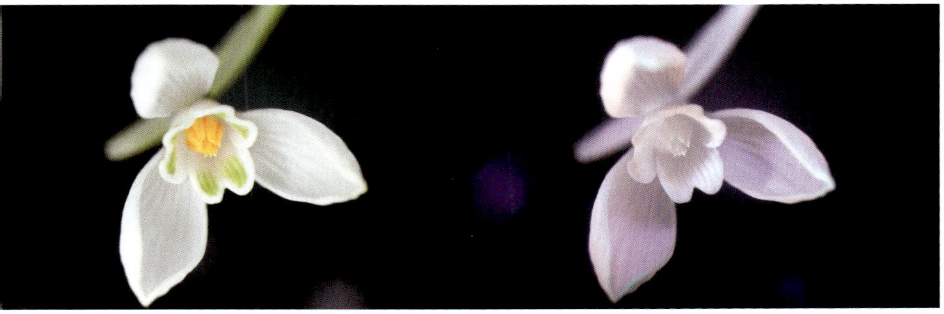

In this moment of disappointment I had a spark of synergy. Images have three colour channels, right? What if I tried to combine my three images, each as a colour channel, into one photograph? The ultraviolet image can take up residence in the blue channel, the visible light image (converted to monochrome of course) can occupy the green channel, and that leaves the infrared for the red channel. Why not give it a shot – at the very least, I'd satisfy my curiosity!

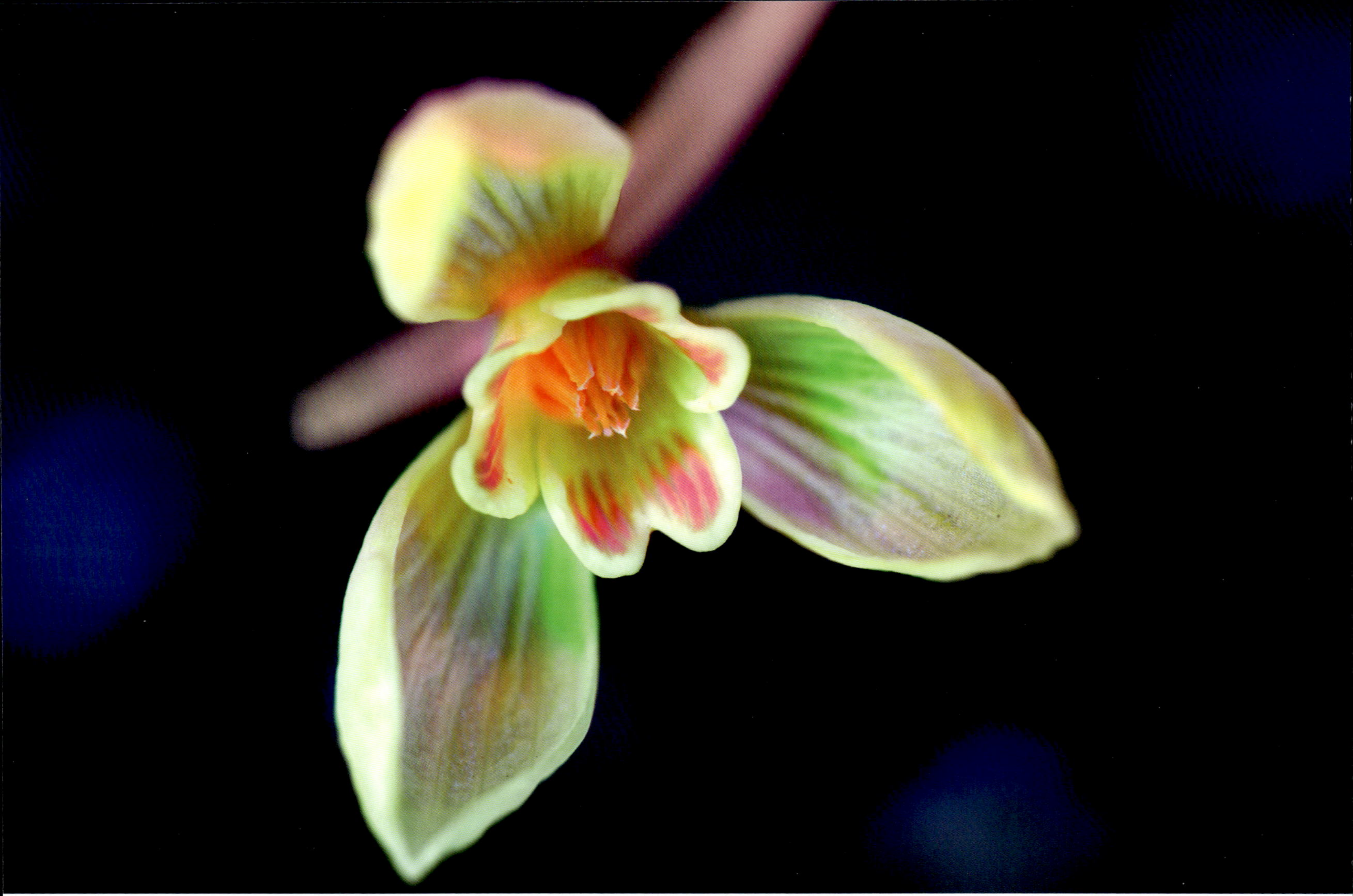

This could have turned out horribly, and yet I'd still be happy. There was some effort involved to line up each channel as different wavelengths of light will focus at different points, and there was some colour corrections required to get here, but I was happy.

Could these be how a bee sees the world? Even our own imagination can only stretch so far – what about compound eyes? Bees have "simple eyes" as well, and might favour certain areas of the spectrum more than others just like human vision has greater visual acuity in the green spectrum. No matter how hard you try it's impossible to truly appreciate the differences in perception, but that shouldn't stop you from trying. Always ask "what if?" and seek out the results, and embrace whatever you get!

There are other ways to embrace the combination of spectrums as well. An early enigma was the patterns found in Forget-Me-Not flowers which gracefully

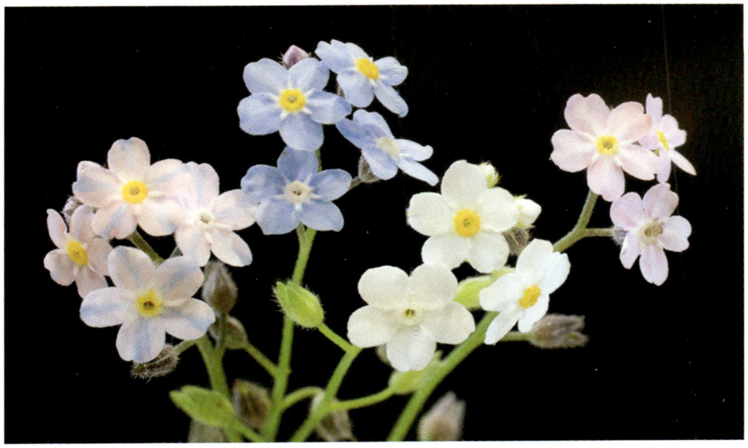

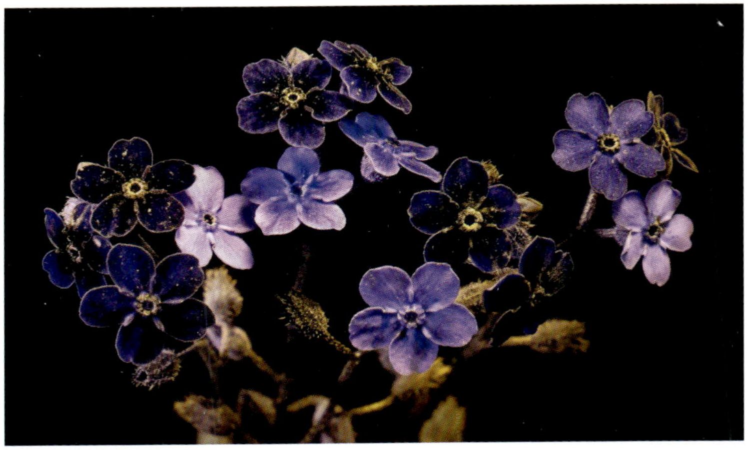

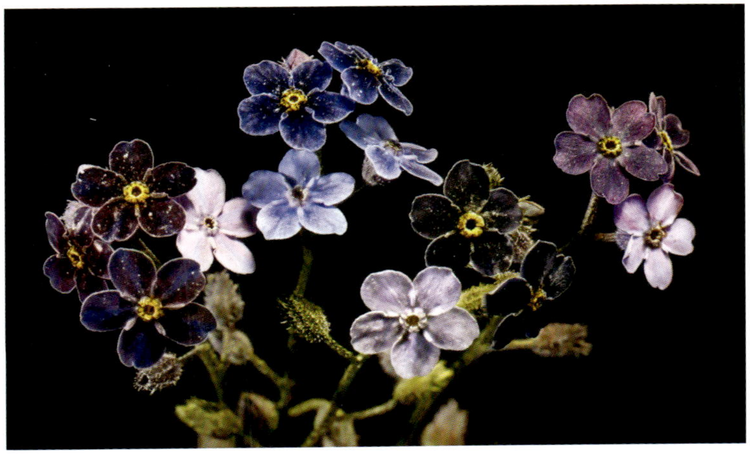

overtake portions of our lawn each spring. Across all of the subtle changes in colours to our own eyes, one thing remains consistent in the ultraviolet spectrum. Some flowers will reflect most of the UV light, while adjacent flowers will absorb the light. This could be attractive to a passing pollinator making it want to come in for a closer look, almost as if sparkling to their senses.

By what mechanism does the flower choose which flowers should be bright and which ones dark? After studying the visible spectrum image (*top*) for some time, a connection was made. Can you spot the connection for yourself? Stop reading now, take a look at the top and middle images and see if you can spot the connection!

It has to do with the centers of the flowers. The yellow-centered flowers all reflect much more UV light than the white-centered flowers. This doesn't explain exactly why, and I don't have the knowledge of an experienced botanist to drill any deeper into it. I can, however, use photographic knowledge to make an interesting image.

The bottom of these three shots is a combination of the top two. The brightness information from the UV image with the colour information from the visible spectrum. This type of experimentation is an attempt at revealing hidden perspectives of the world around us. It's about as interesting as ultraviolet reflectance photography can get. From this point, we venture into the truly magical – and much more accessible – ultraviolet fluorescence photography. Read on!

Lumix GX85 Full Spectrum, Kyoei/Kuribayashi 35mm F/3.5 lens, F/8 ISO 400 1sec

Ultraviolet Fluorescence

This can be "natural" in the sense that the subjects do not have to be modified, though there is no way in the natural world to see this. It requires a pure ultraviolet light source which does not exist in the natural world. It is a glimpse not only into a world that we cannot see with our own eyes, it's a view of the world that no other creature can see.

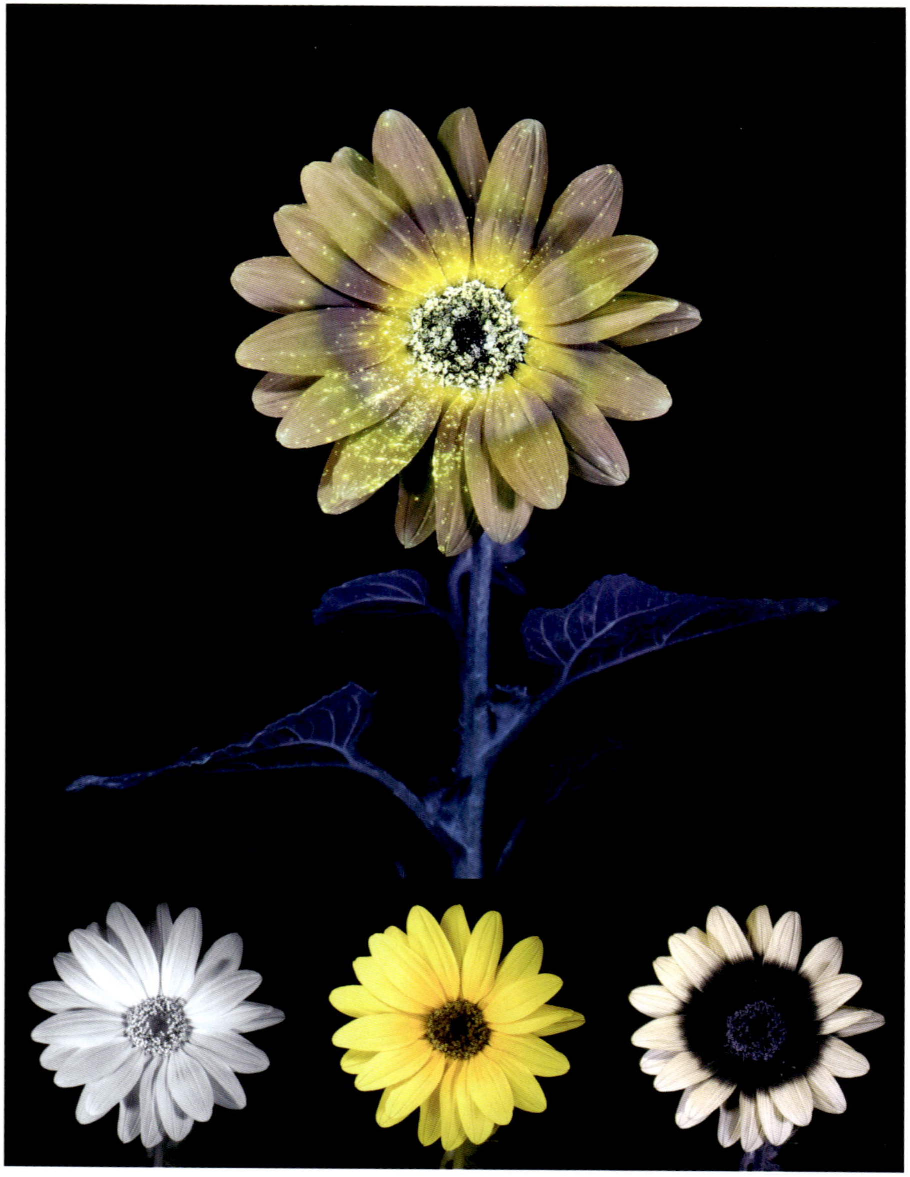

Using a small ornamental sunflower (*right*), we see four different versions. Infrared, visible, and ultraviolet line the bottom from left to right. The black blob pattern seen in ultraviolet reflectance is interesting, but it pales in comparison to the larger image which showcases UV fluorescence of the same flower. The pollen of some flowers will fluoresce under this light and give off light back into the visible spectrum. Everything behaves differently. The flower effectively becomes its own light source, as the visible light is derived from the original ultraviolet light that struck the flower.

What is Fluorescence, Really?

As a brief aside, let's discuss and understand what exactly is happening here. Higher energy light in the ultraviolet spectrum strikes the subject, exciting electrons in atoms in the flower. This extra energy forces the electrons into a higher orbit, but they cannot hold onto this extra energy for very long. It decays back to its pre-existing orbit almost instantaneously (between one billionth and one millionth of a second), in the process releasing the energy it very temporarily stored. We see this energy as visible light and call the phenomenon **fluorescence**.

To be fair, fluorescence can happen at visible wavelengths as well. You can take a specific wavelength of visible light as a source, and using specialized bandpass filters that remove that wavelength from entering your lens you can see how that light fluoresced into longer wavelengths. We're not going down that particular rabbit hole in this book, instead focusing on **UVIVF**: UltraViolet Induced Visible Fluorescence... and maybe taking a step farther into the infrared.

The flowers from an indoor succulent are somewhat uninteresting (*lower left*) compared to the effect we see from ultraviolet fluorescence (*lower right*). The flowers were producing nectar, but with no insects to be attracted to the flowers it simply pooled up in the center of each flower. The nectar also fluoresced, providing faint blue pools of sugary liquid surrounded by stamens which also contained fluorescing pollen.

The effect can be dramatic, but it can also be subtle. In many cases, flowers have no ability to fluoresce and any resulting image is useless. After years of experimenting, this is still something of a crap shoot. Succulents are more likely to fluoresce than the average flower, and many wonderful images have come from flowers in the buttercup family Ranunculaceae. Plants such as tulips offer up no reward, and attempts to

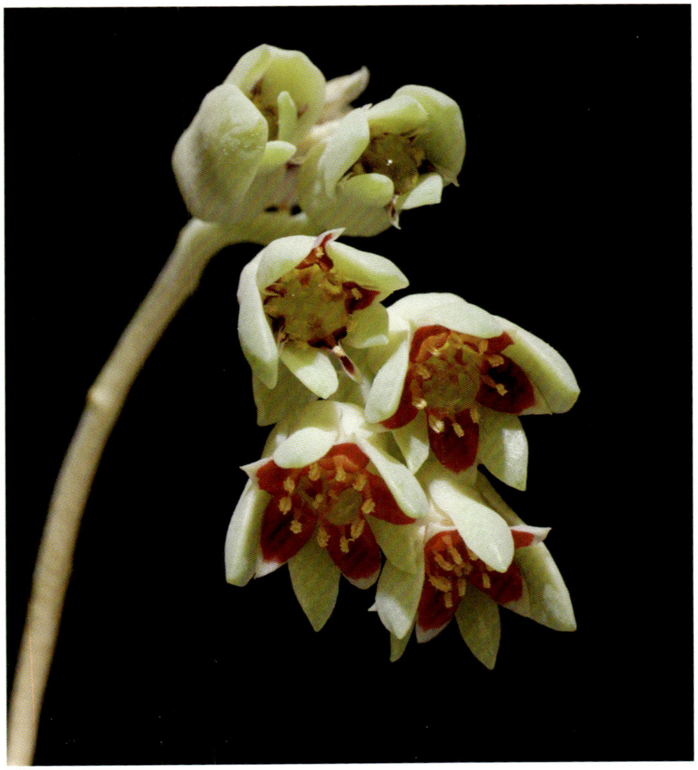

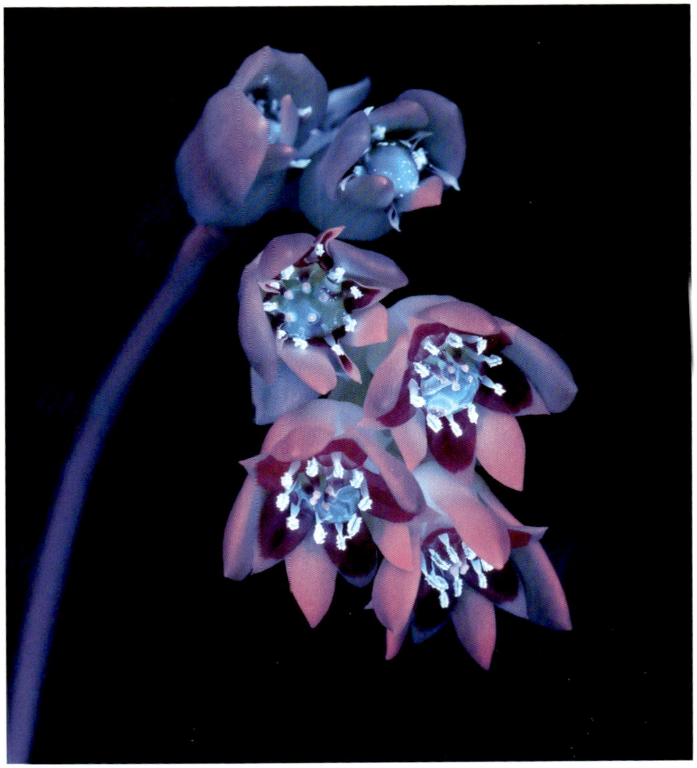

reveal fluorescing magic from Forsythia uncovered the fact that the bark fluoresced more than the flowers. A disappointment, but the process of discovering great candidates for natural fluorescence is an adventure to be embraced. I hunt around in my garden at night with a UV flashlight to identify subjects with the most potential. What happens next?

Once you have a subject you suspect of performing this fluorescence dance well, you'll need to get it into a darkened room – or even shoot outside in situ if it's well past sunset. The key in either case is that you have little to no ambient light when shooting. Any amount of ambient light will contaminate the image, if you're trying to shoot only the fluorescence of the subject as the light source within the frame. You may choose to take a different approach and blend some visible light in based on your own artistic ideas, but at least start in pure darkness. It'll help expose some potential problems with your lights.

One of the biggest challenges here has nothing to do with your camera and nothing to do with your lens. It has everything to do with the "purity" of your light source. If your lights emit any amount of visible light, this will contaminate the scene and you will not end up with a successful image. Some of the worst offenders are UV lights designed to find dog pee on carpets or scorpions in your garage, since these lights will often come at a bargain (<$20) and will also bleed a significant amount of purple and blue light. This makes them largely useless for photographic purposes. The question becomes, what makes the best UV light source? It depends on whether your subject is capable of movement.

There are very few commercially available ultraviolet flashes, and they often cost a considerable amount of

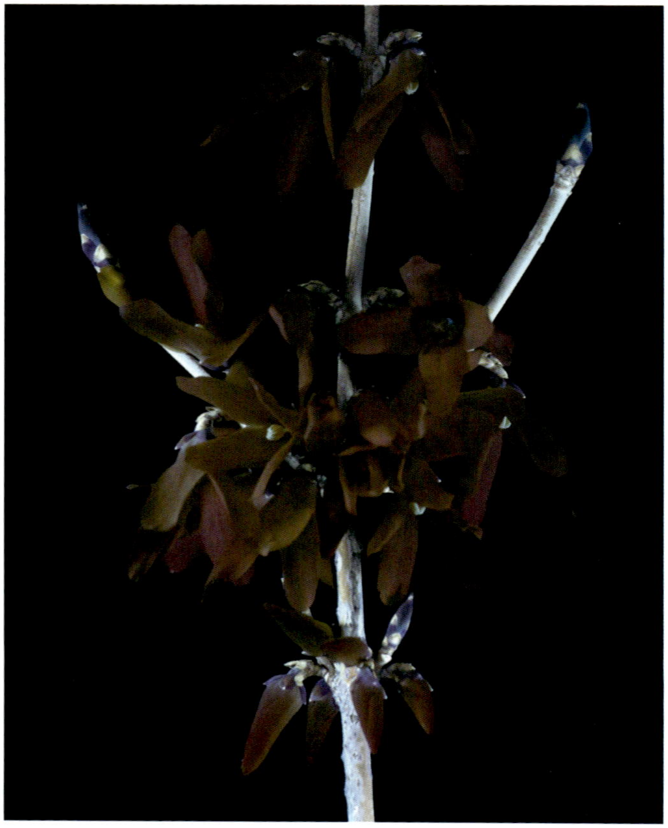

Forsythia (*top*) was a disappointment, as the bark of the shrub fluoresced to a much greater degree than the flowers! I had high hopes for Edelweiss (*below*) as well, but it didn't really impress me. The adventure continues!

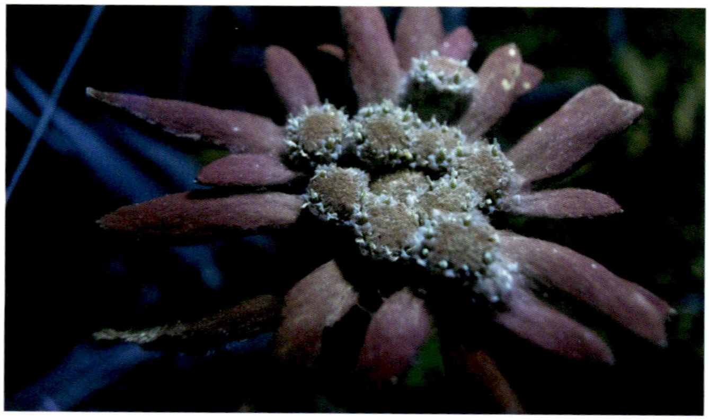

money. You can make your own easily enough, but if you have a static subject you can also use a number of high quality UV LED flashlights.

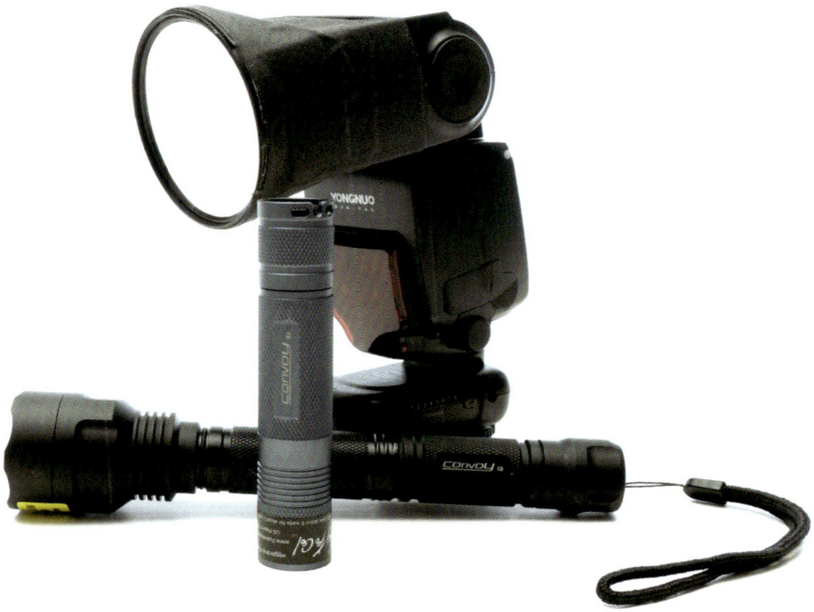

Constructing a UV Flash

Warning: photographic flashes are high-voltage electronics. If you are unsure of how to take the necessary safety precautions, please do not attempt this. All of the flashes that I modify for this purpose are freshly removed from their packaging without ever having been turned on – but even this does not guarantee that the capacitor inside the flash is completely discharged. **Proceed at your own peril!**

Now that I've scared you, the process of converting a regular flash to UV isn't that difficult. I use Yongnuo YN-660 and 685 flashes because they are inexpensive and have a high light output, and the xenon gas used to manufacture traditional camera flashes like this will also emit UV light. This is problematic for standard use, so there are multiple ways that manufacturers prevent UV light from exiting the flash; some manufacturers will use a special glass or coating on the bulb itself, while others rely on the plastic lenses and diffusers in the flash head to block or otherwise absorb the UV light. For these Yongnuo flashes it is the latter, and removing those takes five minutes.

There are two screws on the back of the flash head to remove, and under the rubber circles on the side of the flash head there are some clamps to pry off; the circles come off with a little fiddling, they're just glued in place. The black outer plastic shell comes off in two halves, which allows you to pull out the transparent plastic pieces in front of the flash bulb (they're just resting in place). Put the flash back together the way you took it apart, and now the unit emits all spectra of light.

The next step is to filter it down to just UV, or at least cut out all of the visible light. We don't really care if the flash emits infrared light because our cameras will natively remove that from contaminating our images. There are a number of different filters to do this, some work better than others. None on their own is completely effective, with most bleeding some bit of red or purple light. The best combination I have experimented with involves two harder-to-find filters:

Hoya U-340. These can be found on eBay from a number of third-party vendors. I don't believe that

Hoya actually manufactures these at this point, but anything claiming to be one should be close enough.

MidOpt BP365. These need to be sourced directly from a MidOpt distributor and is the most expensive part of this build. I've purchased filters at a 77mm filter thread size to cover the entire flash head, but smaller filters will work as well – they would just allow for slightly lower light output.

The filters are simply taped on the front of the flash with black gaffer's tape. The order of the filters doesn't matter. You now have an ultraviolet flash at the cost of roughly US$500-600, based on the price and availability of the filters. This is roughly in line with what you would pay for a flagship speedlite from Canon, but allow you to explore an entirely new area of photography.

Using an LED-based Flashlight

Flashes might be useful for photographing the fluorescence of insects or other moving objects where instantaneous light is required, but the majority of images in this area are much more static. Flowers, minerals or other specimens aren't likely to move during an exposure, so we don't need a custom-built flash to explore this. Thankfully, UV flashlights are also MUCH more affordable.

Anything that uses the name "Convoy" is likely to be a good light source, though many of these are manufactured and sold directly from China and the exact components used can vary. Through my experimenting, the **Convoy S2+ and Convoy C8** are both star performers, with a cost in the double digits. Definitely the way you'd want to start with this type of photography.

They do benefit from being filtered just like the flash, but the benefit is very hard to notice in almost all subjects. The amount of visible light bleeding through would only be detected by very dimly fluorescing things. Don't get hung up on this – grab a UV flashlight and start exploring!

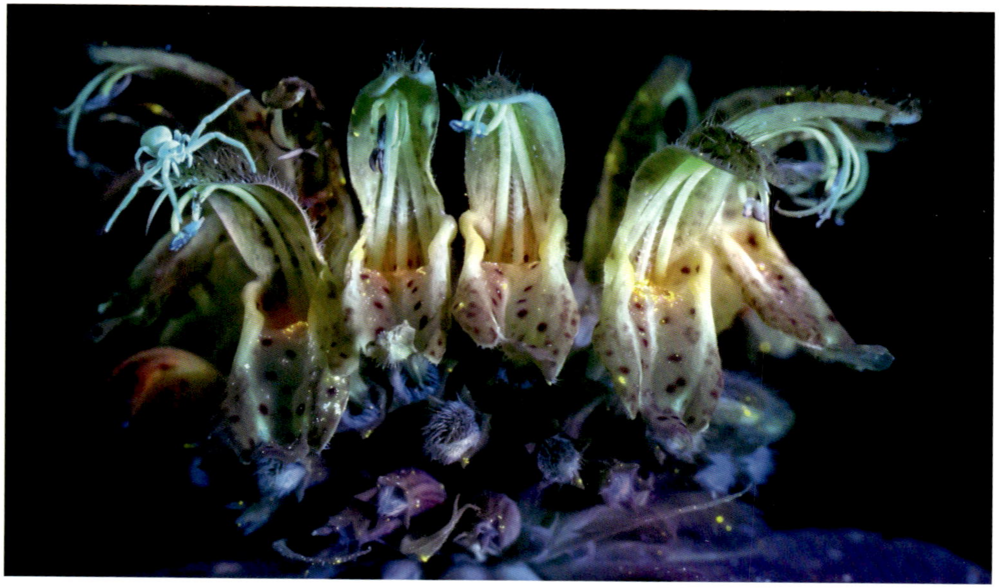

A spider in a Bee Balm flower. Not only does the flower fluoresce with an array of colours, the spider is part of the light show too!

Lumix GH5, Leica DG Macro-Elmarit 45mm F/2.8, F/11 ISO 1600 1sec

Fluorescing Subjects and Equipment Setup

One of the simplest subjects to start your explorations with are flowers. Before discovering the viability of high quality UV flashlights, my initial setups included multiple custom UV flashes – one would suffice, as you could fire it multiple times during a single exposure to get the desired effect. Get technically creative in how you illuminate your subject – know your equipment and what it's capable of. As with almost all areas of macro photography, there is no substitute for your own experimentation.

In the example below, I've cut a stem from our Bleeding Hearts, and positioned flashes (flashlights work too) to cover the subject evenly, but at an incredibly close distance. In this orientation, and at maximum 1/1 flash power, the camera still needed to shoot at ISO 3200 for a proper exposure. Bleeding Hearts don't fluoresce intensely, so a lot of light is needed.

Could you handle this differently? Sure! You could use a single flash and a 30 second exposure, moving it around to different positions and firing it manually during this time, as quickly as it could recycle. You could then shoot at a lower ISO sensitivity and the light might even be a bit smoother – though I like the harder shadows that help define the shapes here. You could do the same type of illumination by moving a flashlight around, effectively applying "light painting" techniques to ultraviolet fluorescence photography.

This reminds me of a quote that resonates with me. These words were said in an era of photography dominated by mathematics and chemistry but it stays relevant when you push the limits of photography by modern means.

Lumix GH5, Leica DG Macro-Elmarit 45mm F/2.8, F/8 ISO 3200 1/200sec

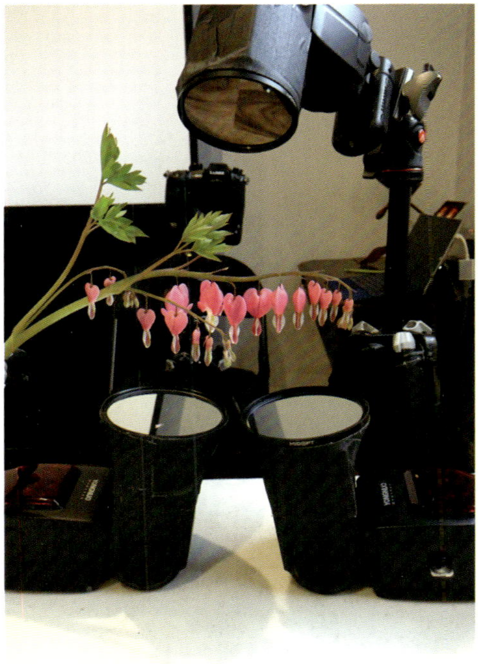

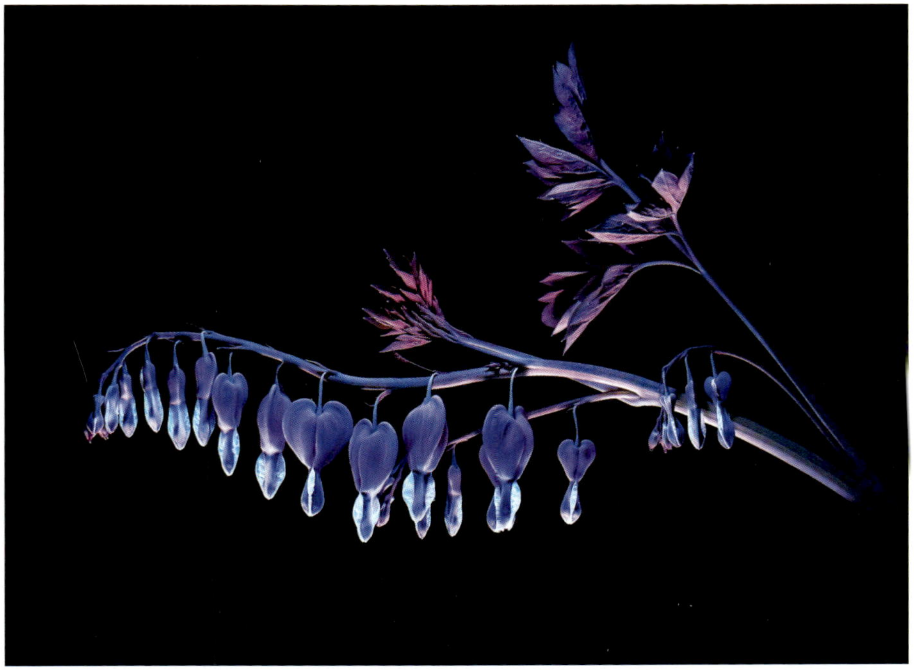

"Light makes photography. Embrace light. Admire it. Love it. But above all, know light. Know it for all you are worth, and you will know the key to photography."
– *George Eastman*

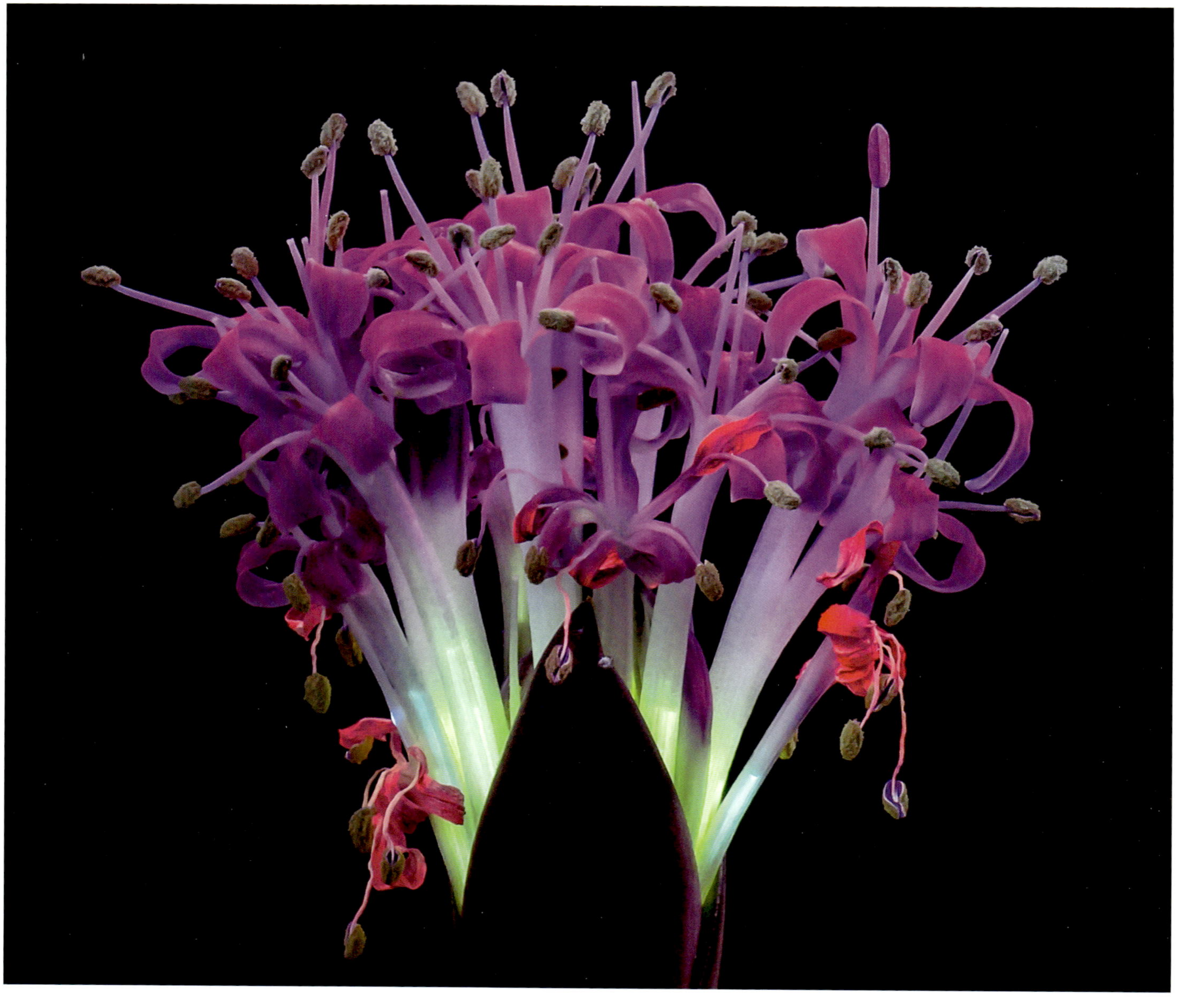

Why were these words powerful to me? Because the more you understand light, the more you can use it creatively in your artistic endeavours. Understanding light is the science-half of photography, and it empowers the creative decision making process.

In search of near-magical subjects to place under my ultraviolet lights, someone suggested I investigate a number of succulents originating from South Africa. A dozen such bulbs were purchased all from different species. Some have yet to flower for a number of years while others bloomed and performed dismally for fluorescence. Some were a huge success, like this *Polyxena maughanii*, seen on the left page as it fluoresces, but it doesn't have nearly the same impact in ordinary light (*right*).

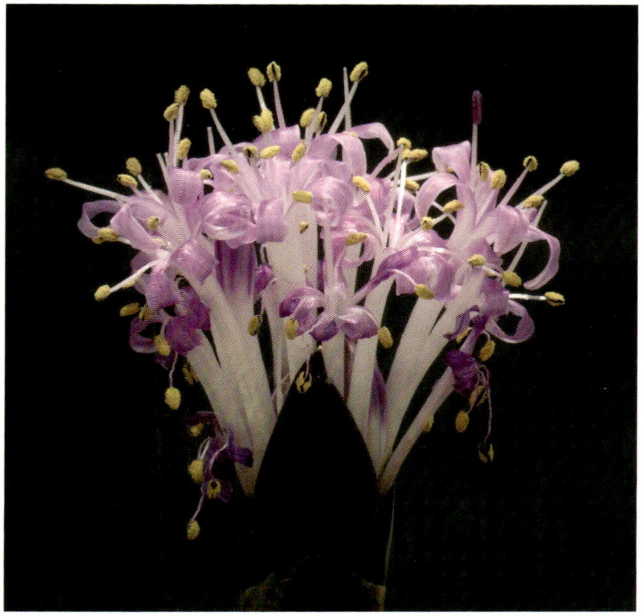

The green throats of the individual flowers were fascinating, and I've seen this with other succulents as well as with irises in a limited fashion. Like a floral aurora of colours, hidden beauty is exposed. This is firmly in the "mad scientist" realm of photography, and there is much more to uncover. Botanic fluorescence across many different species of flowers yields mesmerizing images.

Fluorescing dust specks edited out of the final image:

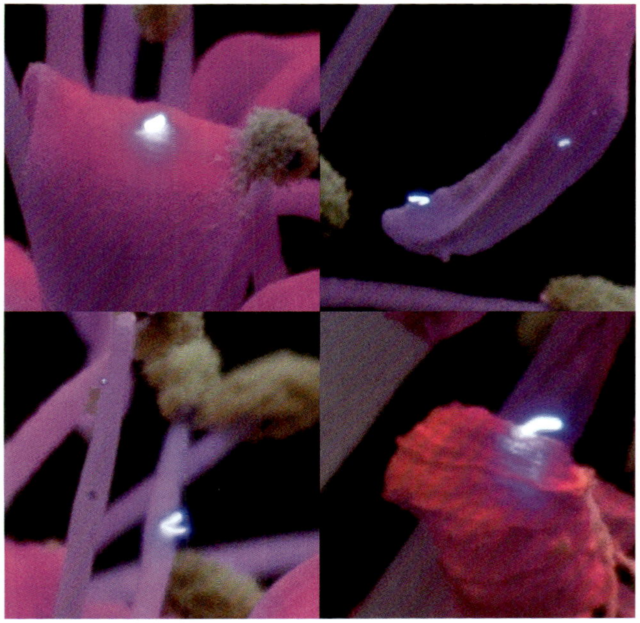

This work is often purely documentary with little done to the subject before photographing and little done in post-production aside from basic enhancements. One consideration for subject preparation, however, is to have a bulb blower handy to remove dust from any flower that may have spent some time inside. Components of household dust will fluoresce intensely, especially fibers from clothing. Ever go bowling under black lights wearing a white shirt? The same effect can be quite distracting for images such as this!

Left: Canon 1DX mark II, Meyer Optik Trioplan 100 F/2.8
F/16 ISO 800 2sec

Exposure and Camera Settings

This technique is unpredictable. We need to take an approach based on a number of factors including how much UV light we have available to us and how long we can afford to make the exposure. The first "test shot" should be to establish how much fluorescence will create a decent exposure, often multiple images are taken to figure out where we need to be. Understanding the exposure triangle is very helpful here for testing.

Initial tests for semi-static subjects usually start with an exposure of a few seconds long using continuous lights but with a very high ISO setting. For the South African succulents on the adjacent page (variations of *Polyxena ensifolia*), the exposure values of ISO 200 and 60 seconds are equal to ISO 6400 and 2 seconds. Rather than twiddling your thumbs in the dark waiting for an exposure to complete with no certainty if you'd be hitting the mark, rebalance the exposure with a higher ISO setting for testing purposes before committing to the final image. Doubling your ISO sensitivity would allow you to cut the exposure duration in half, so we're just taking that a few steps farther to get a feel for what our final exposure should be. I apply the same technique when testing exposures for astrophotography.

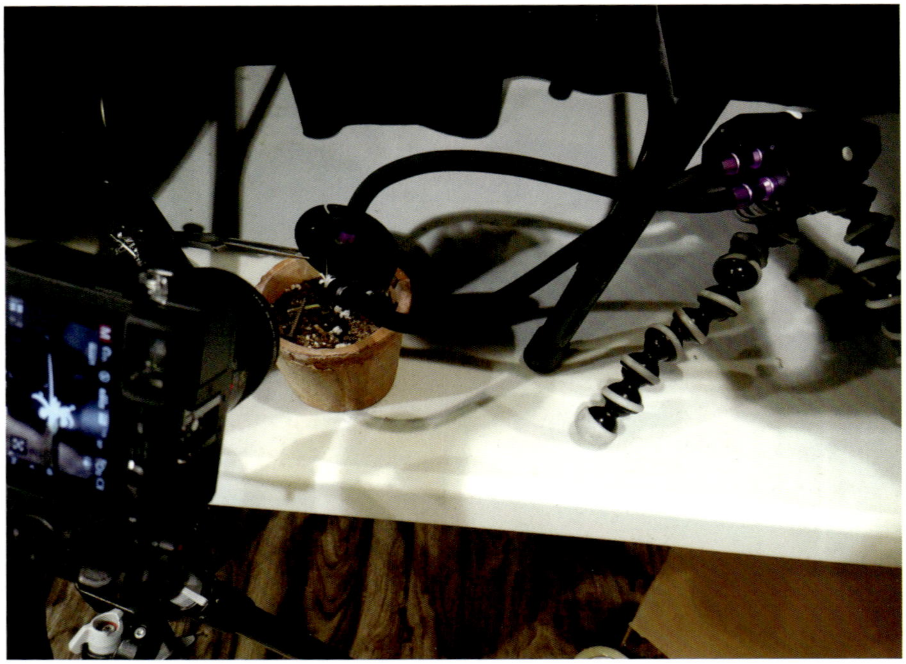

The light source used here is an Adaptalux with two UV lighting arms, very flexible for small subjects but relatively weak output compared to the Convoy UV flashlights, and more expensive. Even though the lights are weaker, in complete darkness the solution can be to simply shoot for a longer duration. These succulent flowers do not move, but some flowers may surprise you. If you pick a Dandelion flower, it begins to fade almost immediately and a 60-second exposure would have motion blur. Some flowers are animated and will "dance" with a slow wiggle, so faster shutter speeds are required. Nigella flowers are a great example of this.

Experiment! Use whatever UV lights you have with high ISO settings and then adjust your exposure variables to provide a higher quality image at the maximum shutter speed your subject will allow. For insects, you'd be hard pressed to use anything but an ultraviolet flash for instantaneous light to freeze any motion. For vibrantly fluorescing mineral samples, you can get away with very low power continuous light, provided that ambient light is at a minimum.

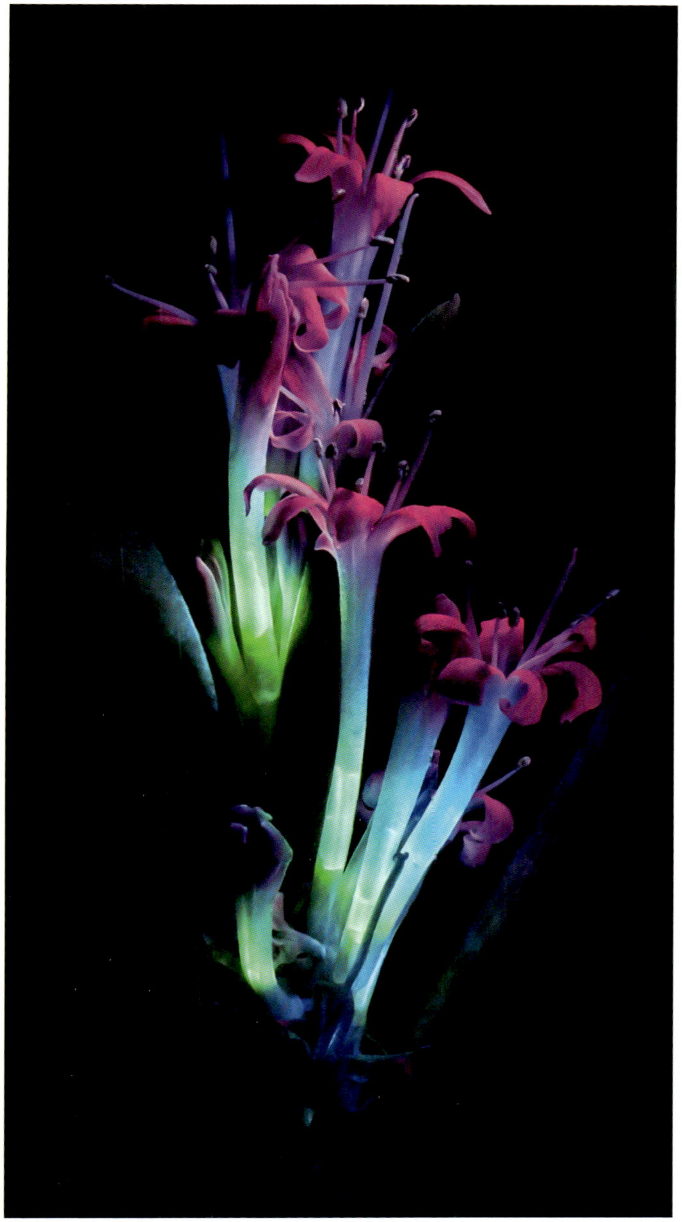

Lumix GX9, Leica DG Macro-Elmarit 45mm F/2.8
F/20 ISO 200 60sec

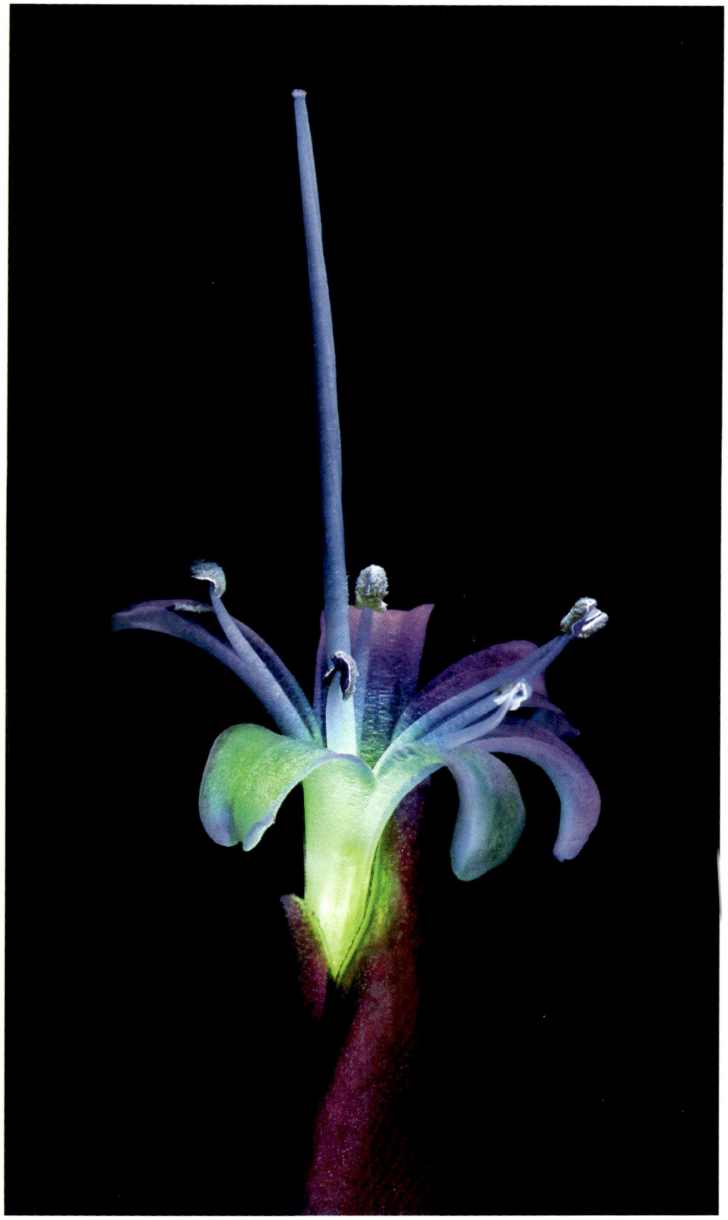

Lumix GX9, Leica DG Macro-Elmarit 45mm F/2.8
F/14 ISO 200 60sec

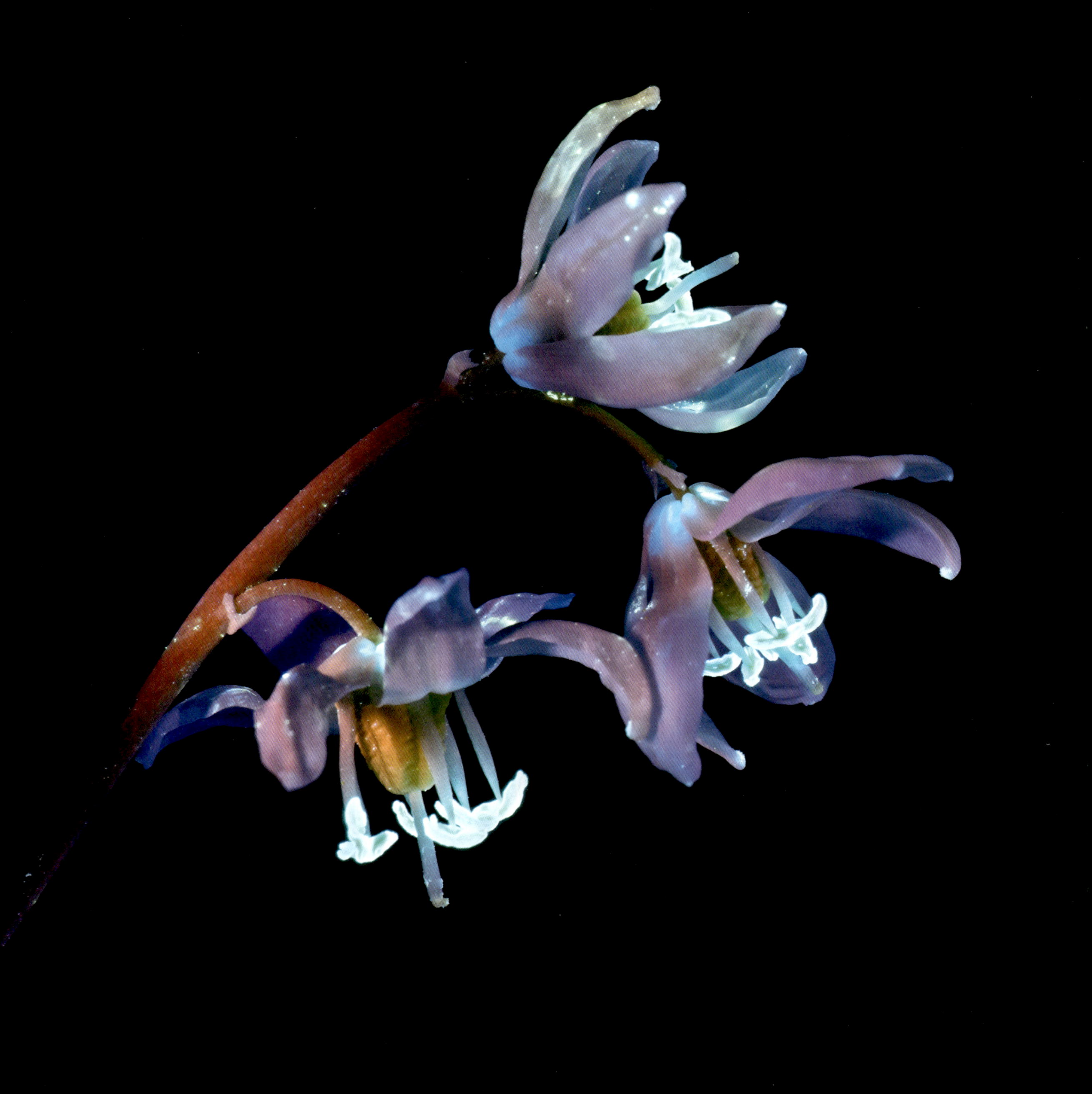

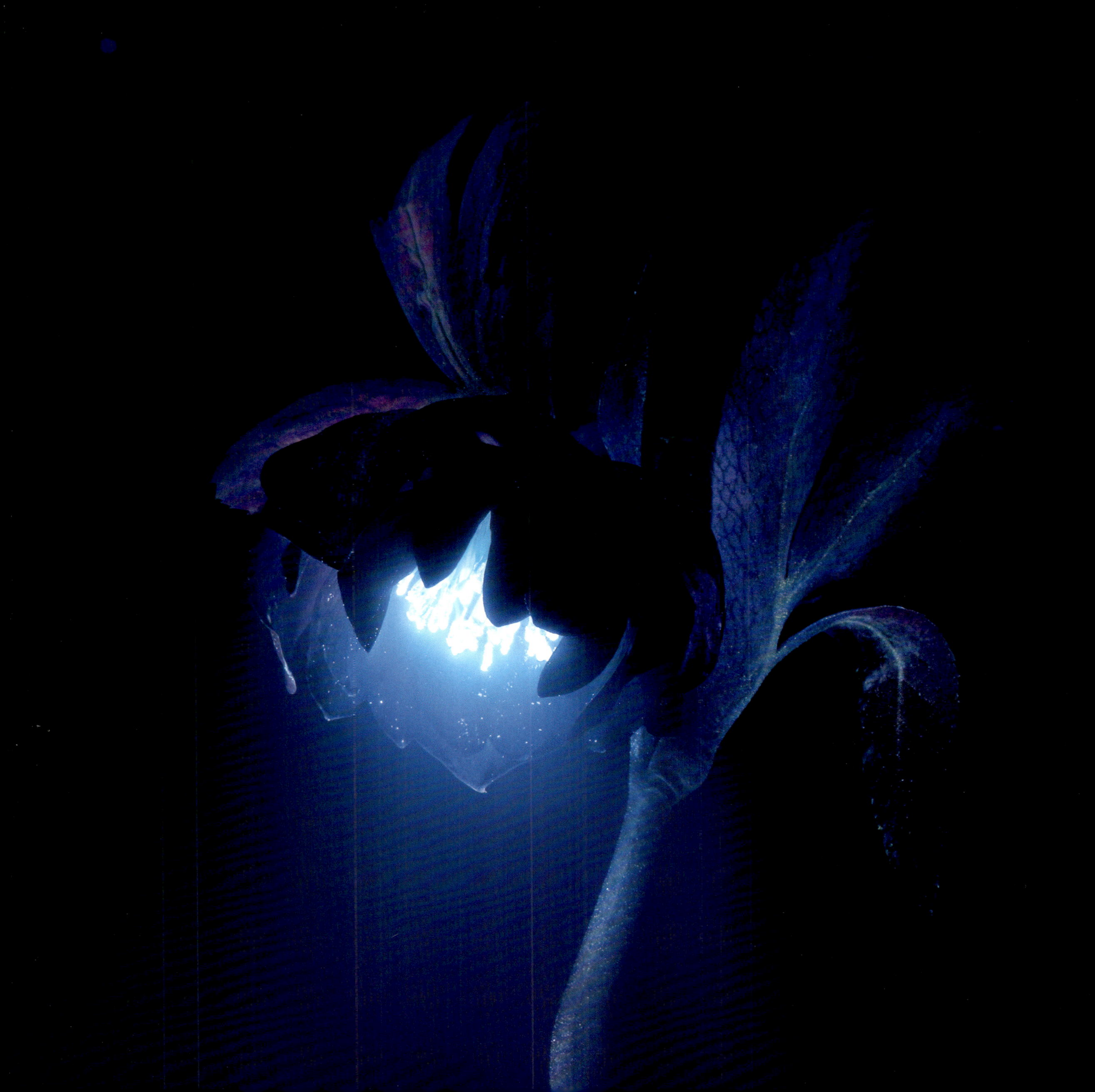

Fluorescent Insects

Scorpions are the first "critters" that most people will think of as being fluorescent. Many people living in scorpion-inhabited regions of the world take care to spot them at night, for safety reasons, with UV flashlights. Certain millipedes can also fluoresce, but these creatures are not common in my area. Cicadas are quite prevalent, however, and can often be found in precarious places. This particular Dog Day Ciacada (*Neotibicen canicularis*) was spotted on my driveway - I almost stepped on her! Thankfully they are docile creatures and can be moved, and it was transported briefly into my studio with a curious thought: **will it glow?**

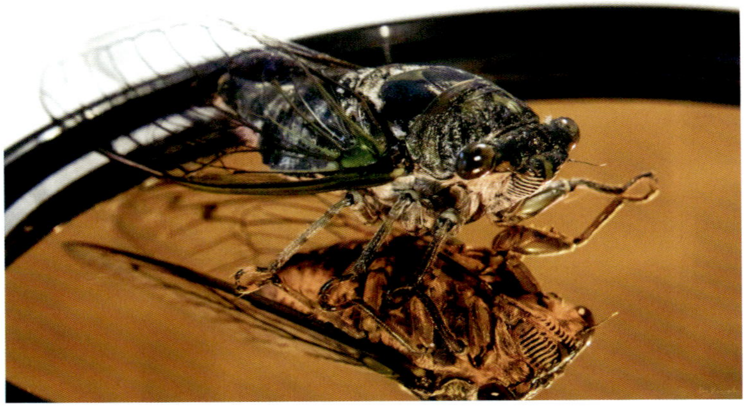

Canon 1DX mark II, EF 24-105mm F/4L @ 105mm F/20 ISO 5000 1/200sec

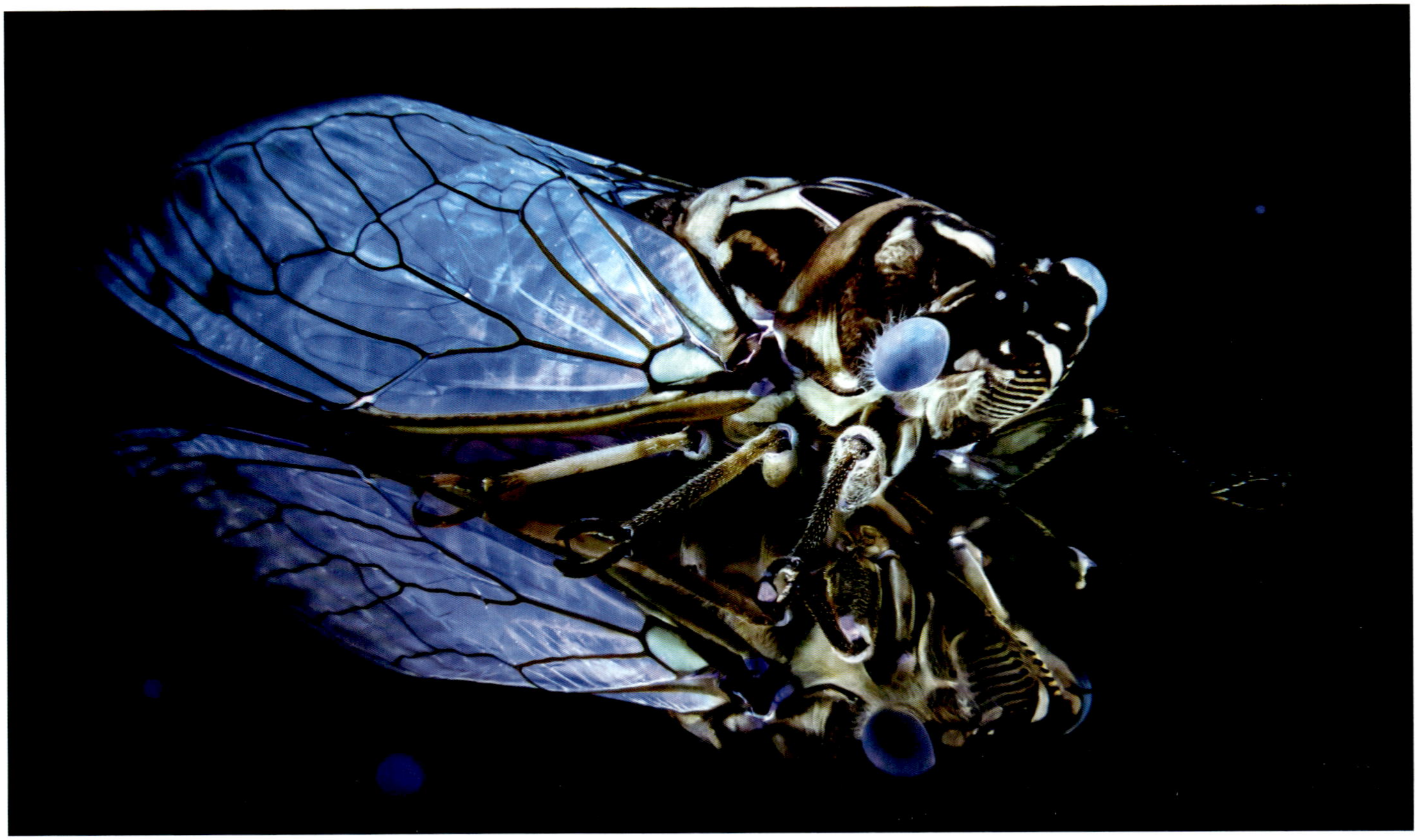

I placed the insect on whatever I had lying around as a mirror – randomly, a 900nm infrared filter that uses optical interference coatings but also can function as a first-surface mirror. Much to my amazement, the normally transparent wings fluoresced with a shade of blue I'd only associate with science fiction. The eyes, normally grey-brown, took on the same colours. I was giddy with excitement!

It's not often that my curiosity is so generously rewarded. The cicada stayed put long enough for me to fire off a number of shots to test the exposure, and beyond to allow for the focus stacking of five frames to extend the focus across the entirety of the creature; notice in the visible-light photograph that the back portion of the wings become soft.

Ultraviolet fluorescence proved itself to be quite supernatural in this instance. It is helpful to remember that ultraviolet photography comes in two flavours: the direct capture of ultraviolet light (UV reflectance) and the capture of visible light that only exists due to excitation from ultraviolet light (UV fluorescence). If we capture the UV light directly from this cicada, the results (*below*) are a grumbly disappointment.

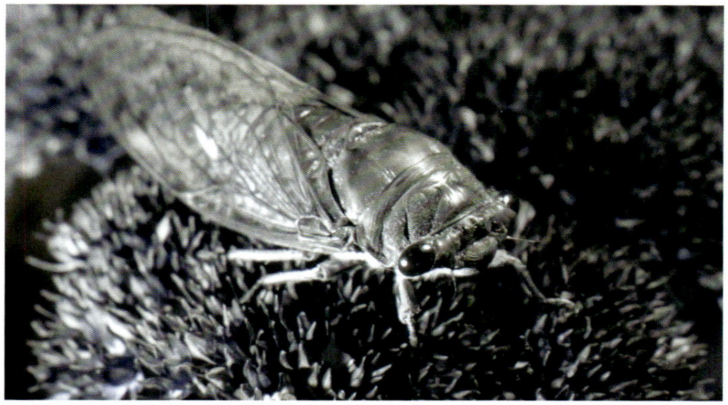

Similarly staged "live actors" in studio include a leaf from our plum tree that was infested with aphids. Luckily a ladybug had discovered this and was feasting, and I had hoped to pluck the leaf and bring it into my darkened studio where the ultraviolet flashes could illuminate the subjects. While not moving quickly, a number of the small aphids were mobile and would have been blurred if I wasn't using flash.

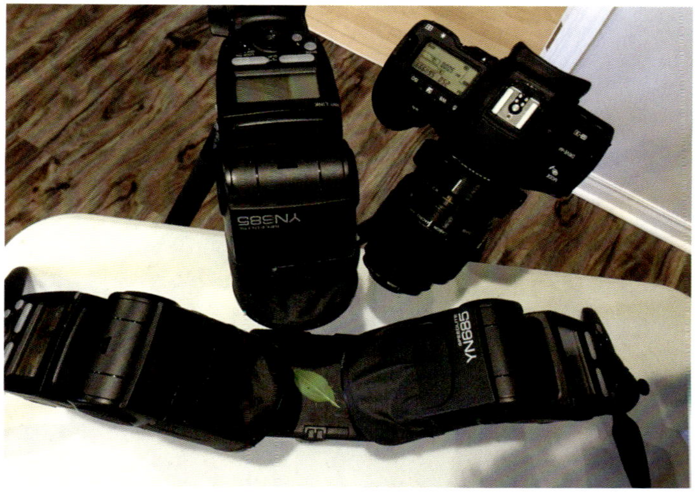

Inverse Square Law

Let's not get muddied up in math here, but the placement of these flashes is important. They are as close to the subject as they can possibly be without being in the photograph. I have even placed lights in such proximity to subjects that they are in the frame but not blocking anything important and can be edited or cropped out. This closeness is based on a rule borrowed from portrait photography: if you double the distance between your subject and the light source, you don't lose 50% of the light, you lose 75%. The light gets reduced not by 1 stop, but by 2 stops.

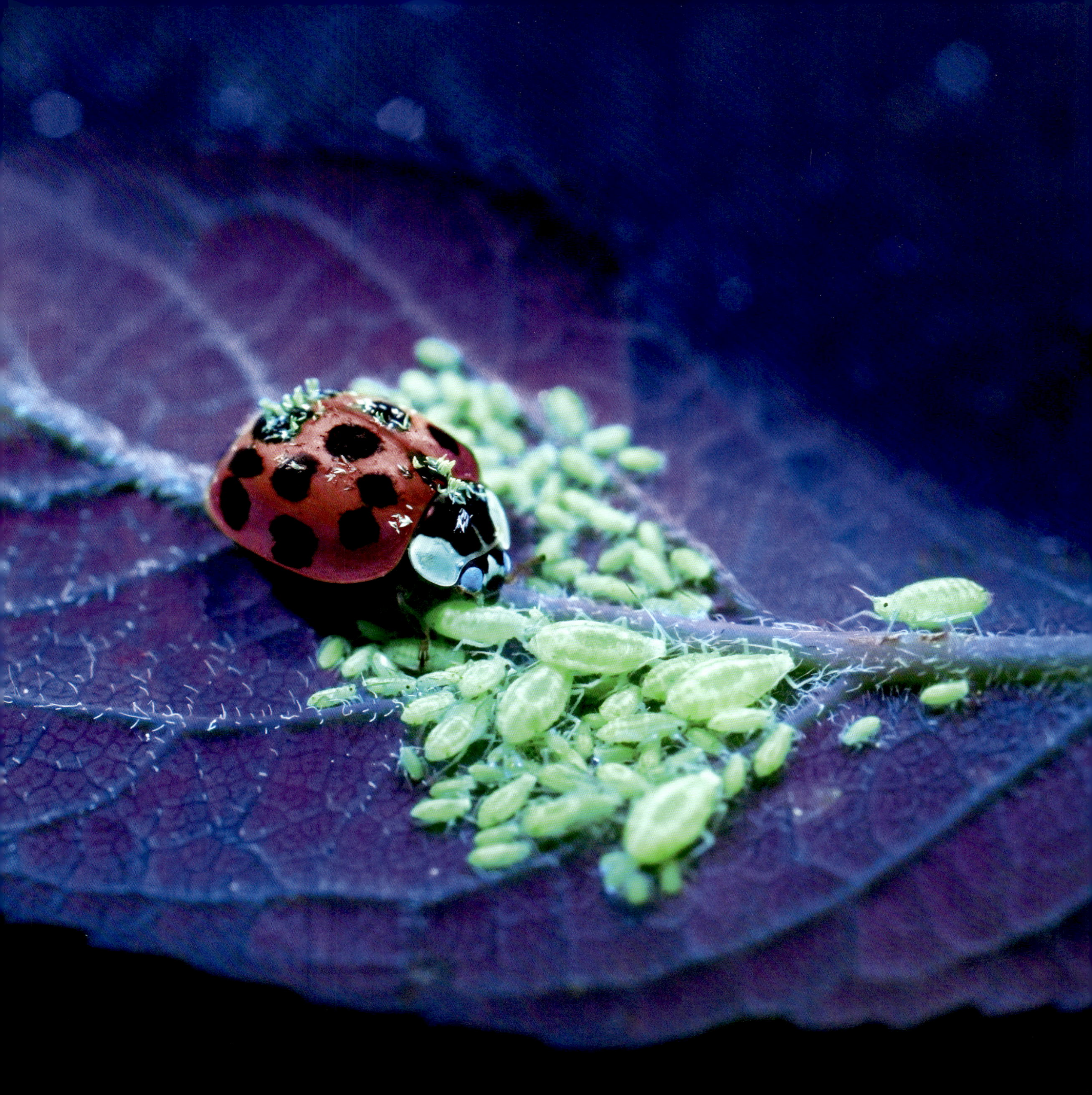

Conversely, if you were to reduce the distance between the light source and the subject by half, you wouldn't just double the amount of light hitting your subject – you'd quadruple it (2 "stops", every stop being a doubling or halving of light). Getting your light source as close as possible while still properly covering your subject can help increase your exposure more than you might expect.

Back to the Bugs

What I hadn't noticed before was the strange growths on the ladybug. This would appear to be a parasitic fungus, *Hesperomyces virescens*, which is commonly found on Harlequin Ladybugs. It doesn't impair the beetle in any way, thankfully.

The same technical process can be repeated with a myriad of subjects, and with an insect component the images take on a stronger narrative. These images are harder to control since the actors in the scene do not take direction very well and it takes a few seconds before the flashes fully recycle from full power bursts. Additional battery packs can be used to shorten the recycle time, but there will still be enough of a delay that continuous shooting is improbable.

What treasures will you find?

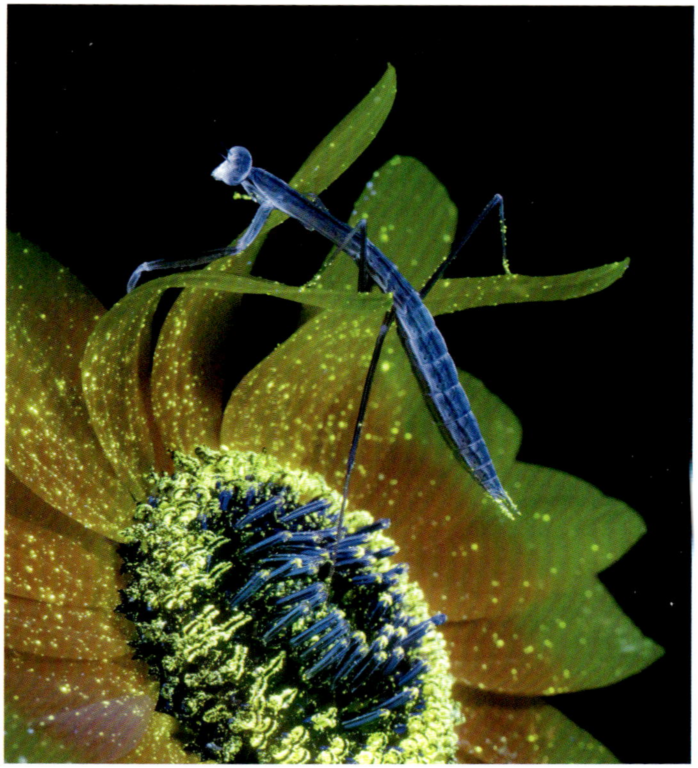

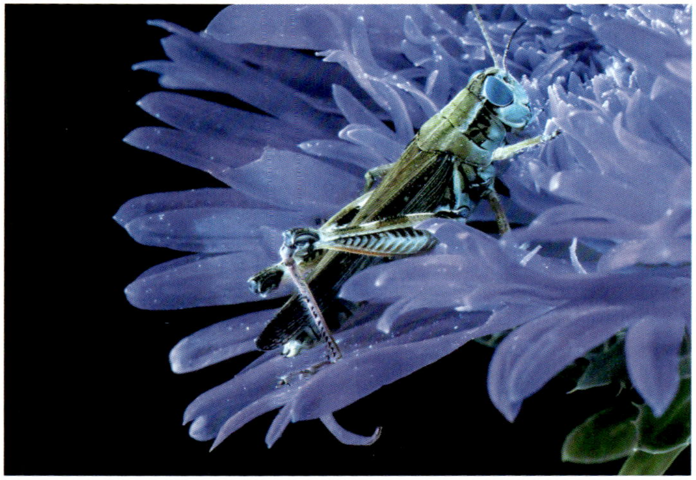

Top and Bottom:
Lumix GX9, Leica DG Macro-Elmarit 45mm F/2.8
F/11 ISO 3200 1/160sec

Left: Canon 1DX mark II, MP-E 65mm F/2.8 1x-5x Macro
F/8 ISO 5000 1/250sec

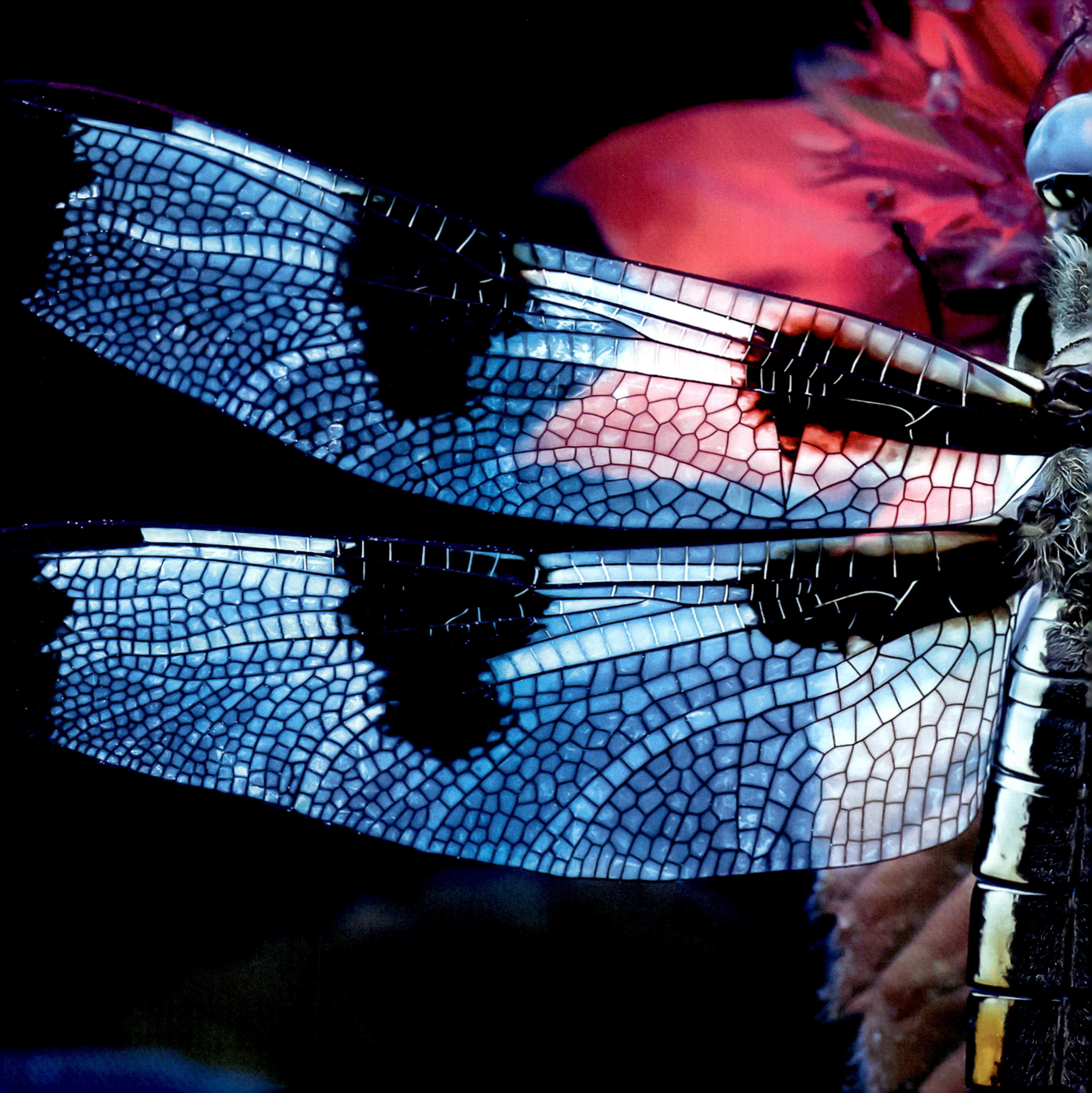

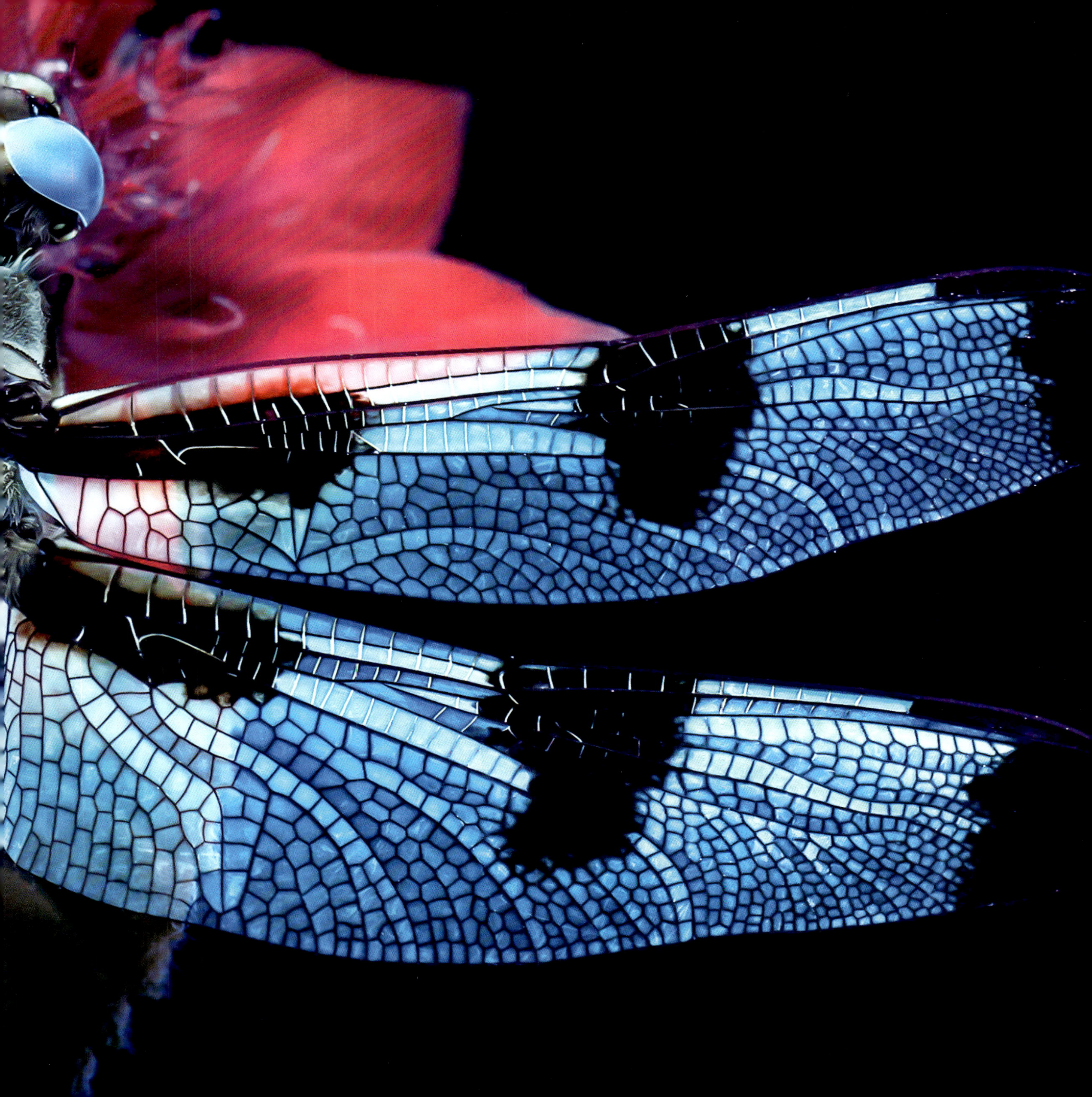

Fluorescent Minerals

Another vastly different kind of treasure comes in the form of minerals that fluoresce vibrantly. While somewhat lacking in the narratives that insects allow for, documenting their natural beauty can be very rewarding as well. Minerals, such as the tiny diamonds seen on these pages (*below left and right*), have impurities that cause them to fluoresce in a variety of different colours. The most common colour of fluorescence from my own research is blue, followed by orange and then other colours vary.

You can compare the gems as seen photographed with visible light (*center right*) and note that a few of them are slightly off-white in colour. Even those that appear clear with a well-defined natural octahedral shape have impurities that cause them to fluoresce – something that might devalue a diamond in the eyes of a jeweler since a pure, flawless diamond will not fluoresce under ultraviolet light.

These gems are absolutely tiny, and also quite affordable. 100 natural rough diamonds of this size can be found for around $20 on eBay, and marketplace websites will also have an assortment of other fluorescing minerals to admire. See the red arrow below? It's pointing to the tiny line-up of diamonds being photographed.

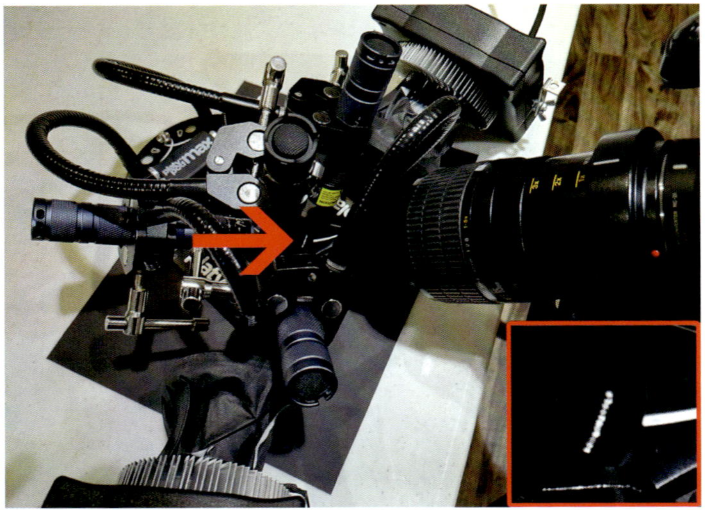

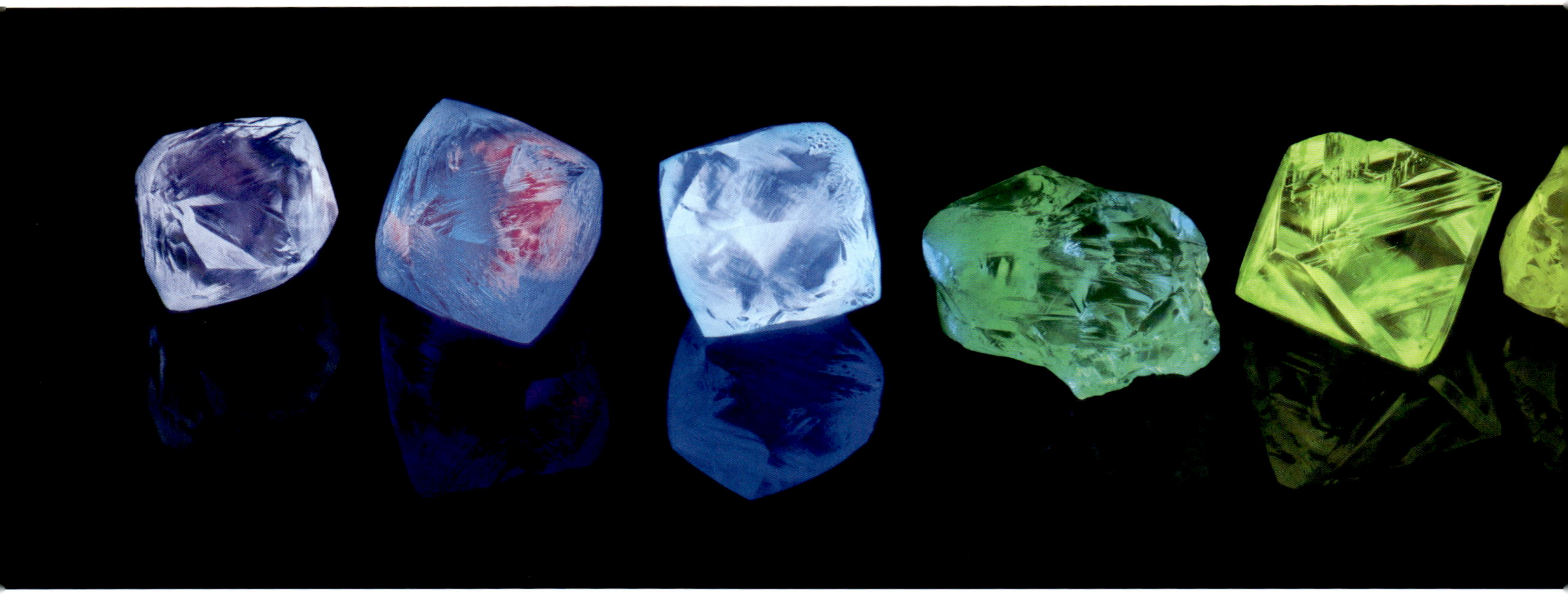

This image was shot on a Lumix S1R in High Resolution Mode, knowing that I would be cropping significantly down on the frame to produce a panoramic style image. This mode is incompatible with UV flash, so an array of UV LED lights were positioned around the gems as close as possible using a Platypod Max, gooseneck arms and crab clamps to keep everything together. Even with excessive cropping down from 187MP, the resulting 60MP image is astoundingly detailed.

I was astounded when I saw an inclusion in the second-to-leftmost diamond that was fluorescing a different colour. Surprises can be found on the smallest scale.

Because of the stable nature and often intense fluorescence effects, mineral samples can easily be explored using continuous ultraviolet lights. In fact, these lights are extremely popular among fluorescing mineral enthusiasts to identify specimens in nature and to show off their collections to fellow aficionados – it's where I first learned about them.

The two larger lights with heatsinks are designed specifically for mineral display cases. These are only adding a small amount of additional light here because of their distance from the subject – remember that Inverse Square Law? I couldn't physically place them

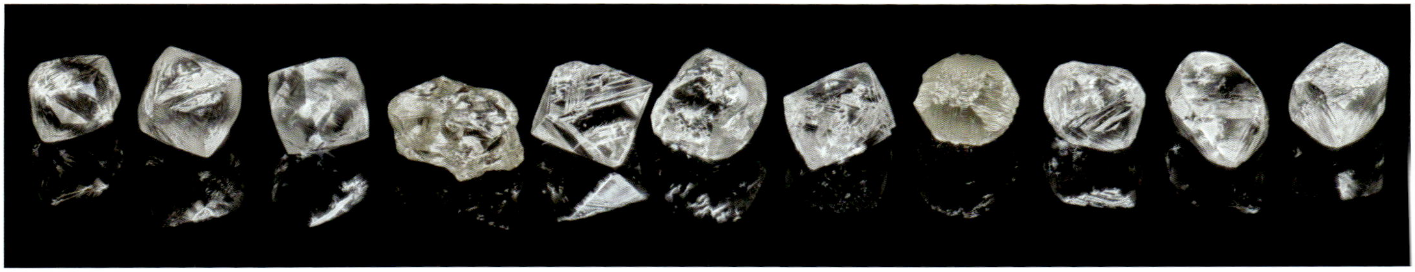

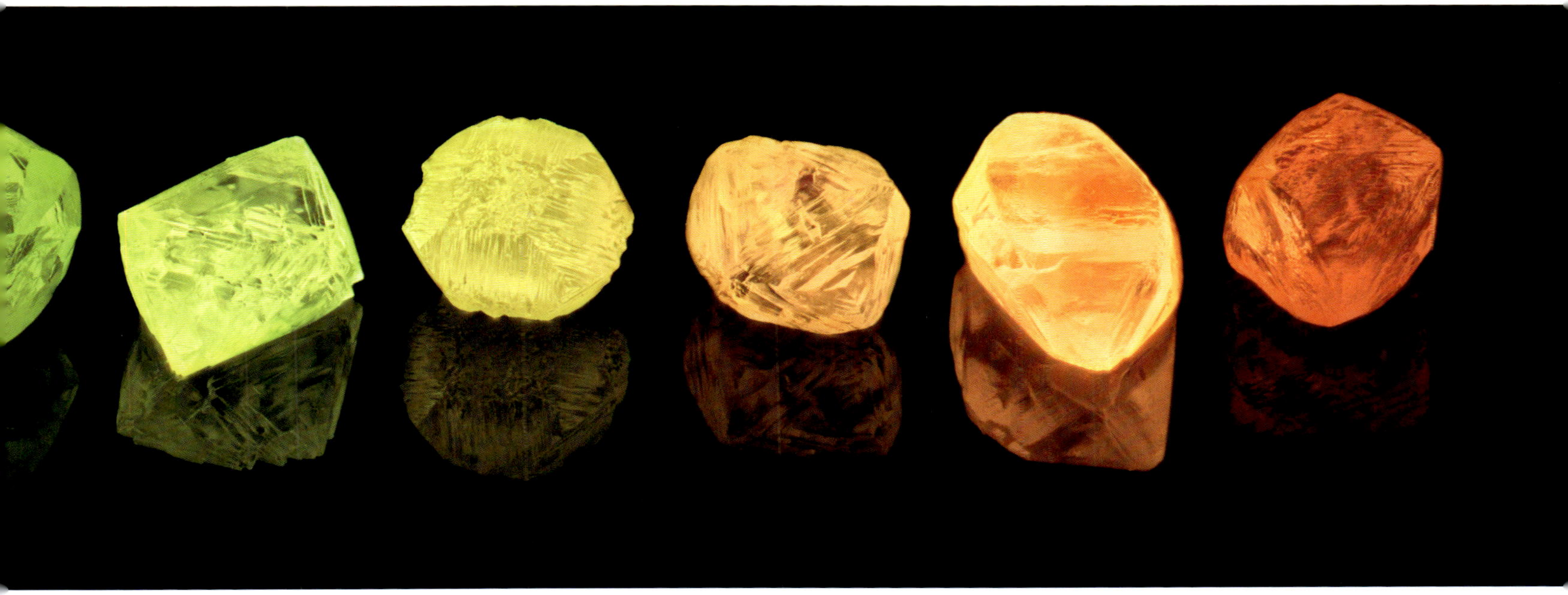

any closer to the diamonds in this scene, and being twice the distance away as the main flashlights they can only contribute one quarter of their output.

Shortwave vs. Longwave

Thus far, all of the UV light sources we have been using are "longwave", meaning that the wavelength of the light is the closest to the visible spectrum as possible without entering into the light we can see with our own vision. This allows for fluorescence in many natural specimens, but some minerals will only showcase their true fluorescent potential with higher-energy, shorter wavelength, ultraviolet light.

Shortwave UV lights are readily available for this purpose, though another warning should be issued: the shorter the wavelength, the higher the energy, and the more damaging the light can be. This is not limited to your eyes, but your skin as well. One of the most effective ways to sterilize a hospital operating room is to bake every surface with intense shortwave ultraviolet light.

Visible Light = 400nm - 700nm

UV-A = Longwave, 315nm - 400nm

UV-B = Midwave, 280nm - 315nm

UV-C = Shortwave, 100nm - 280nm

At this point in my research, I have not discovered any flowers that produce notable amounts of fluorescence from shortwave UV light. Since it would likely do harm to a living insect, they have not been tested either. This puts shortwave UV lights to limited use as photographic tools, but if you can find the right specimen then it might be worth exploring.

My favourite specimen? Ruby that has formed with razor-like crystal "blades" on the opposing page.

Visible Light Illumination:

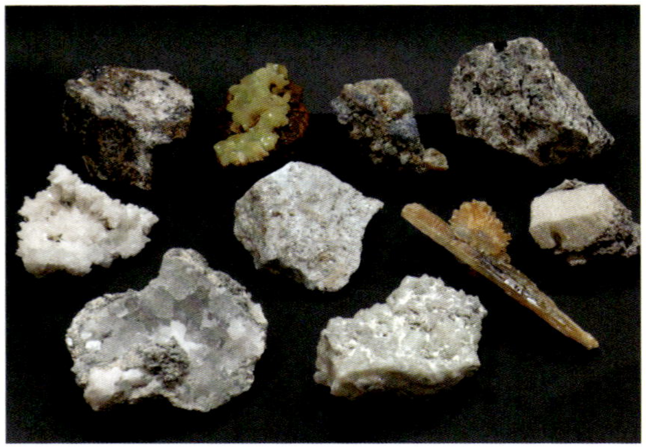

Longwave UV Illumination:

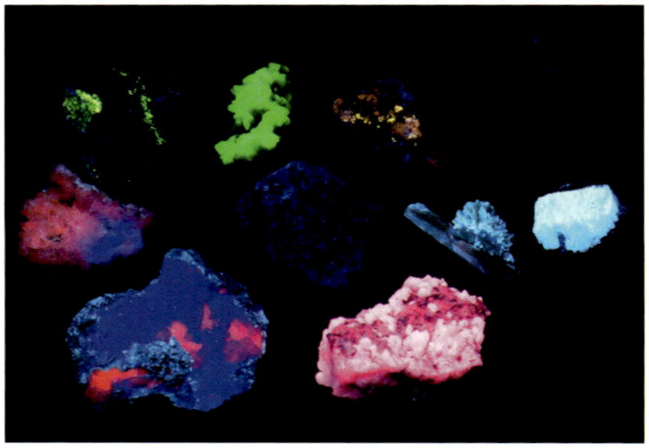

Shortwave UV Illumination:

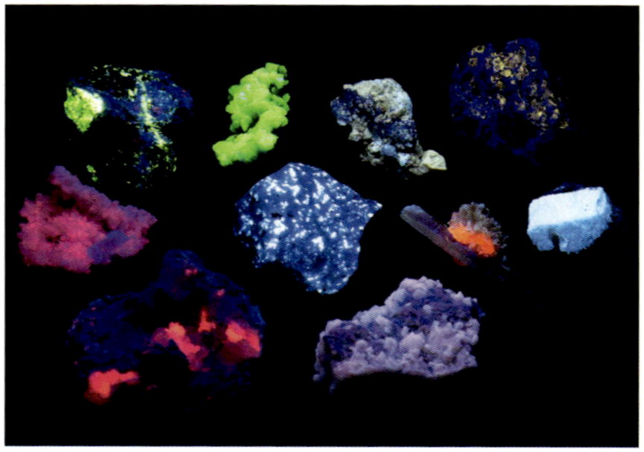

Right: Lumix S1R, Lumix S Pro 24-105mm F/4 @ 105mm F/11 ISO 100 1/2sec

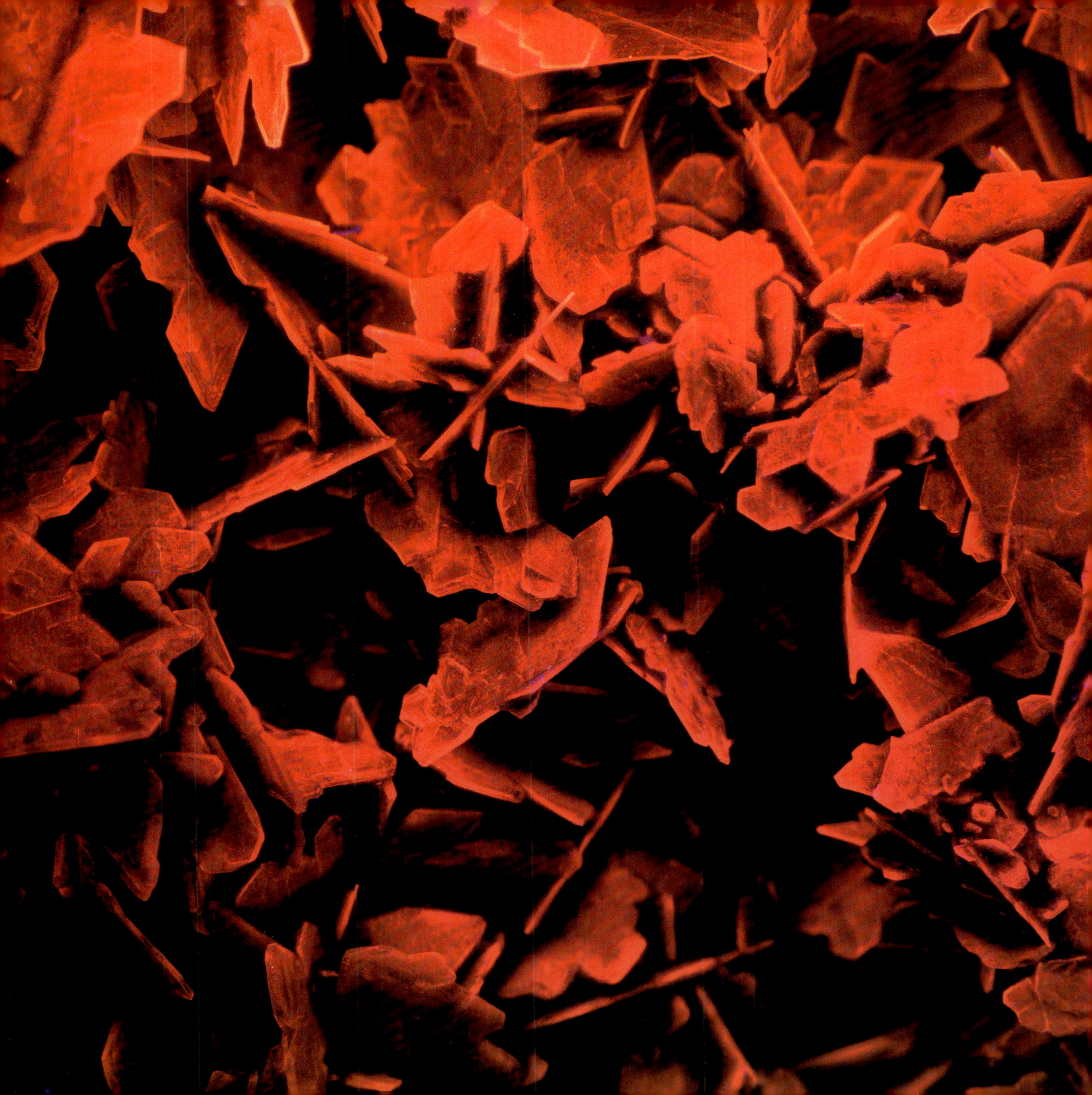

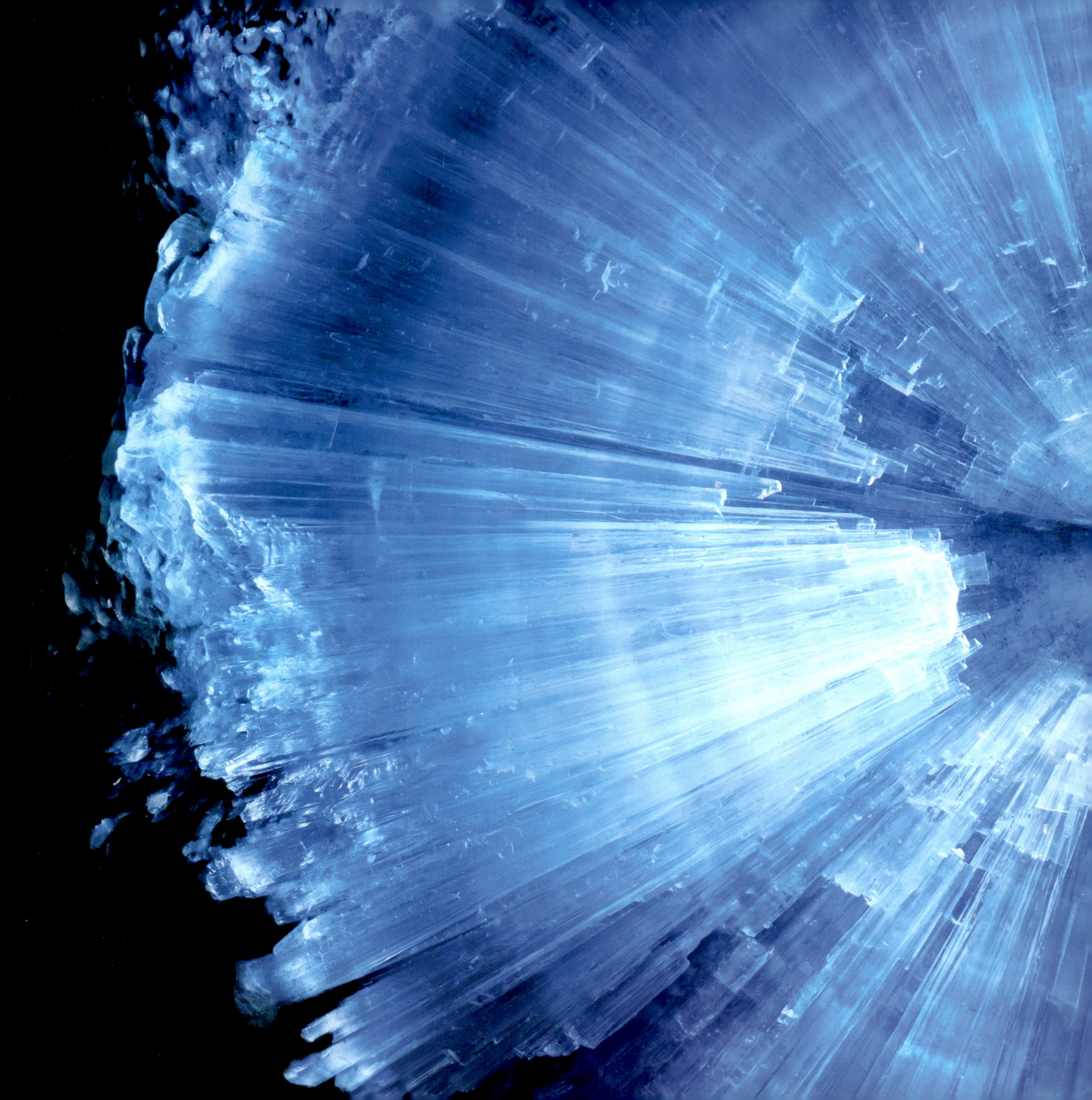

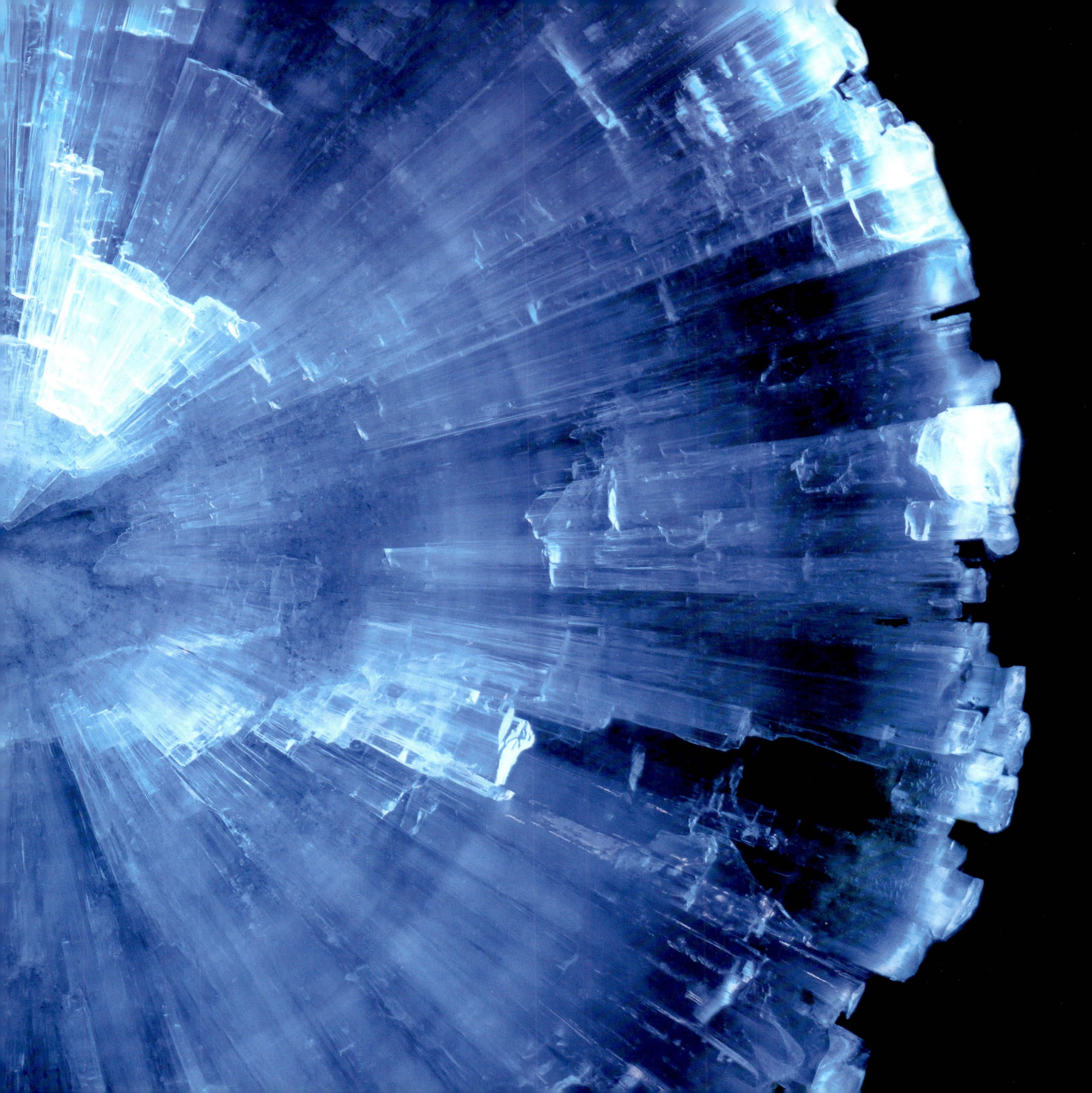

Living on the Rocks

While mineral specimens on their own might not have as much of a story to tell to those that do not study them, they can easily be used as an ingredient in a photograph that also includes elements of organic nature.

Certain fluorescent minerals can be easily found as loose faceted gems. A few star performers from my own experiments are Cerussite and Hackmanite (the latter technically being tenebrescent). Cerussite fluoresces a bright yellow while Hackmanite radiates a significant amount of orange light.

The initial test placed a weevil on the Cerrusite crystals, as if to be navigating around some celestial structures. This was a very simple setup, though difficult to control and frame due to the unpredictable path that the tiny creature would take, wandering around the various crevasses and contours. With depth of field being so shallow and a delay between frames of a few seconds, it was a challenge just to get the subject in focus!

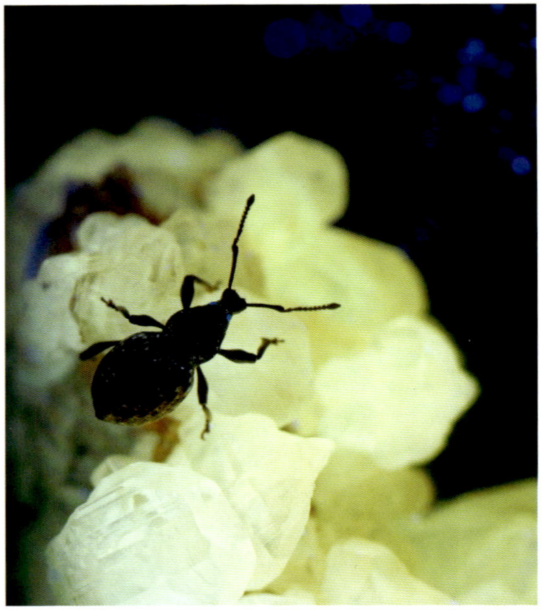

Lumix GX9, Leica DG Macro-Elmarit 45mm F/2.8
F/6.3 ISO 800 1/160sec

The next thought was to wrap a grapevine tendril around the mineral as if it is holding it like a gem, and along comes a bug to investigate the treasure. A neat concept, and with some tiny mineral samples in hand I could find the rest of the ingredients in my backyard. The first attempt used Cerussite and a Shield Bug (also called stink bugs). This worked, but the colour palette wasn't as spread out as I would have liked, feeling more muted than vibrant. Consider this a stepping stone toward the next image, a process that is almost always required to properly explore an idea.

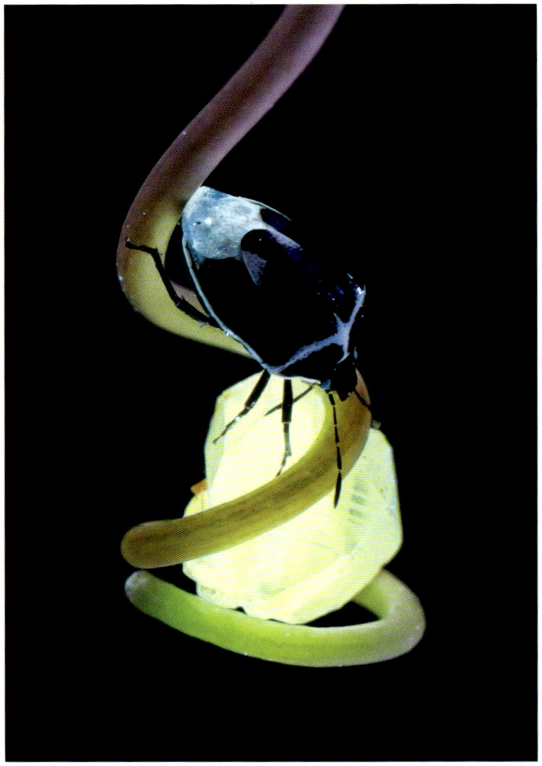

Lumix S1R, Lumix S Pro 24-105mm F/4 @ 105mm
F/11 ISO 500 1/200sec

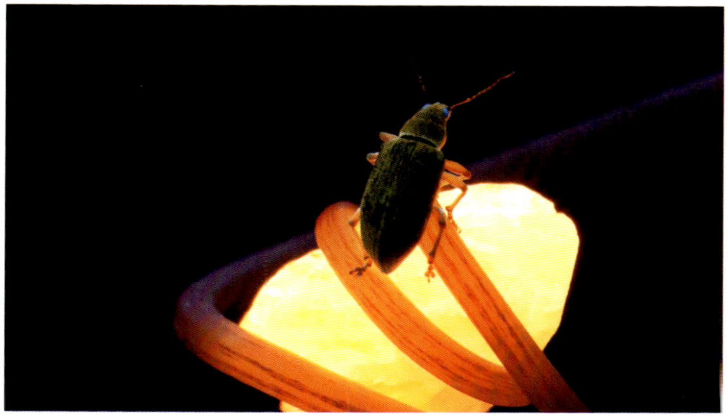

Hackmanite having a more saturated orange colour, and a Green Immigrant Leaf Weevil having a complimentary green shell with fluorescent blue eyes seemed to be the right fit, at least in theory. In practice, it hit the mark! The main actor was still somewhat unpredictable, but there is much less room to move around. In total, roughly a dozen images were made. The first ones featured just the weevil, grapevine and mineral, but then an idea struck me: what if I added some additional atmosphere to the scene? The mineral was clearly glowing, but how could I make that spill off into the air around it to become more noticeable?

The answer: A handheld fog machine called a "*Microfogger*", which uses vaping technology and vegetable glycerine to create "fog" – no inhaling required. Every idea evolves through multiple iterations; some ideas need to be revised, others are promising but can be improved on. This is a constant element in my creative process: **asking "what if?"**

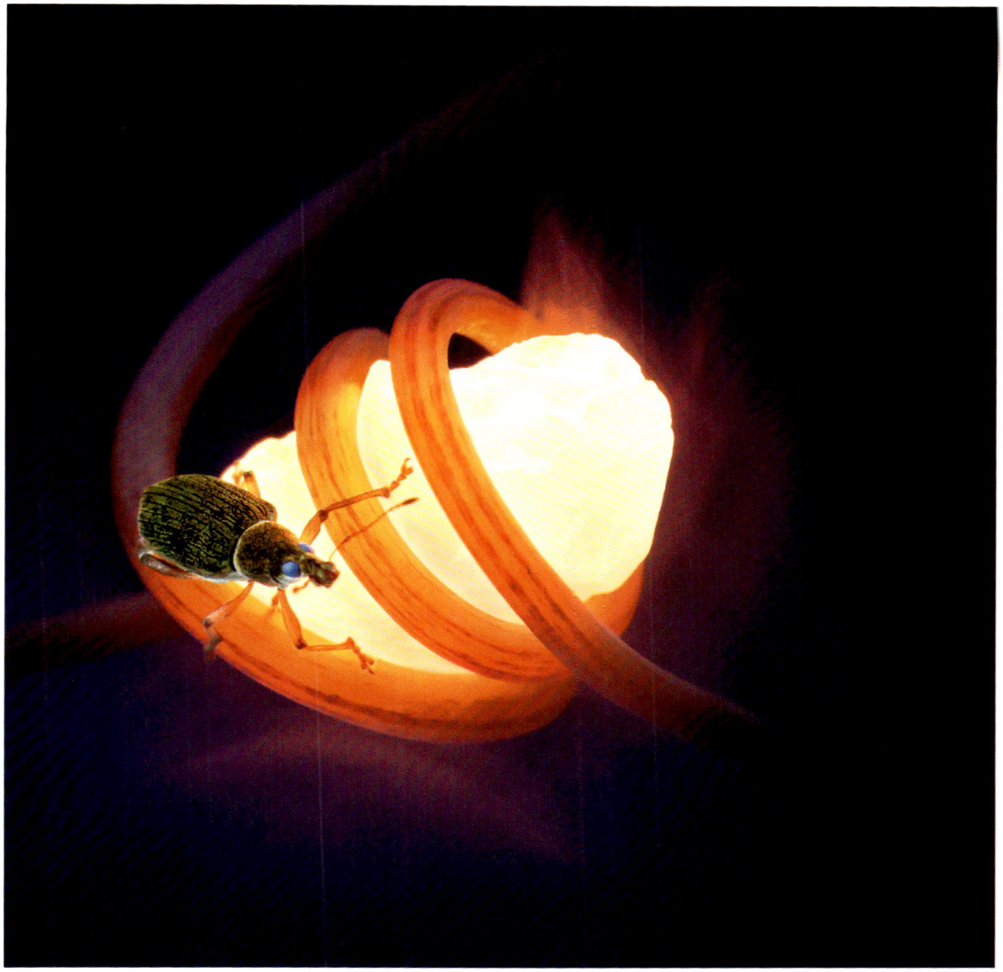

Lumix S1R, Lumix S Pro 24-105mm F/4 @ 105mm F/14 ISO 3200 1/200sec

Ultraviolet Liquid Flow

You've already got the UV lights, so here's another fun experiment to try. This involves a small fish tank (mine is 8" cubed) and fluorescing inks. The fish tank can be purchased from many online sources, just be sure to get a tank made of glass rather than plastic, as plastic tanks tend to fluoresce on their own. The inks are readily available from online sources, often those selling fountain pen inks: two of my favourites being Noodler's Blue Ghost and Noodler's Dragon Catfish Orange… but there are hundreds to choose from.

Due to the different densities of the liquids, we see captivating patterns immerge as you place droplets gently on the surface of the water and watch as they cascade below the surface. This technique is nothing new – it has been used to make photographic art for decades with different ingredients such as coloured milk in water.

The physics here, the *Rayleigh–Taylor instability*, applies equally with both milk and many fluorescing inks. The same physics on a larger scale causes the shapes and structures of mushroom clouds from nuclear bombs and supernovae from exploding stars. Thankfully this experiment is much less destructive.

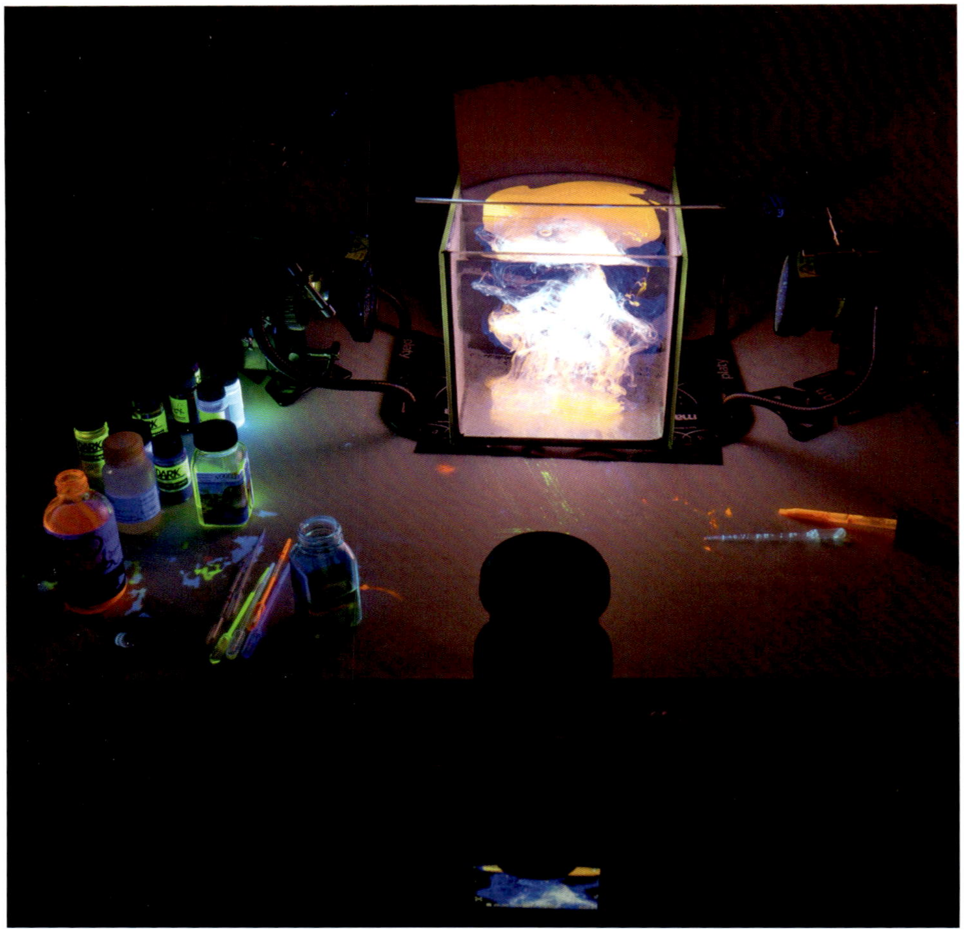

The patterns appear quickly, so it's best to have the camera ready to capture exactly where it's going to appear beforehand. To accomplish this, mount the camera on a tripod and angle it slightly up at the tank so that you have a small portion of the underside of the surface of the water visible. Set the lens to manually focus, and use a focusing aid to determine the exact position you'll be dropping the liquid from. I just used what was at hand, some kebab skewers from my kitchen: one across the top as a drop-line indicator, and one temporarily submerged vertically at the same distance for setting focus.

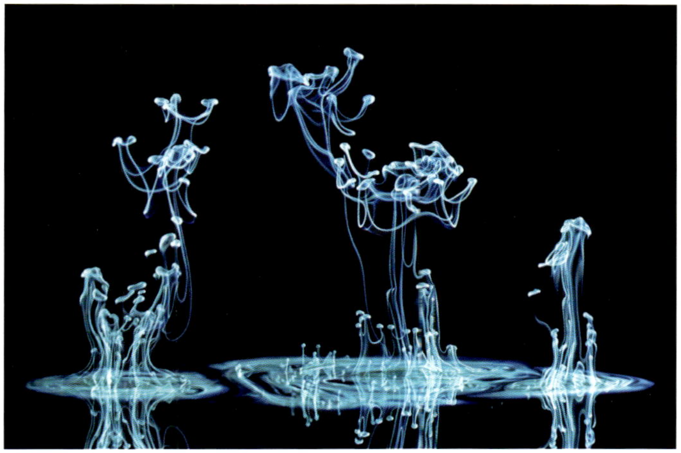

Exposures will be affected by how much UV light you can beam into the tank and the fluorescent capabilities of the liquids you choose. Expect that your first tank of water will be used exclusively to test your exposure, after which you will need to empty and clean the tank to start fresh. For these images, the exposures were typically F/13, ISO 1000 and 1/160sec. If your aperture is too wide, you won't have the depth needed to keep things in focus and if your shutter speed is too slow you'll have motion blur causing details to fade away as well.

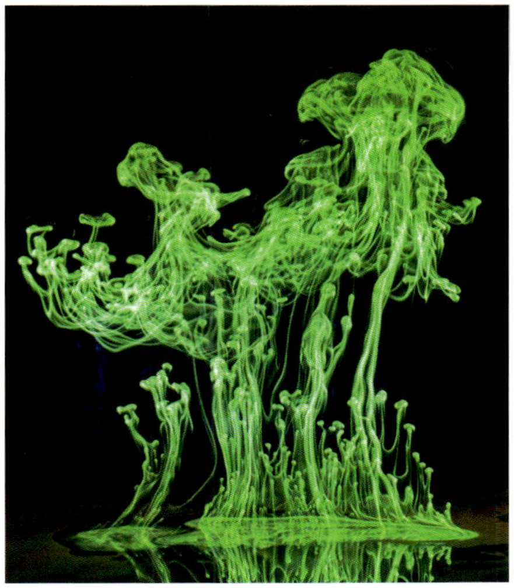

I have found that F/11-F/16 and anywhere close to 1/200sec are ideal, so start there and adjust your ISO sensitivity until your exposure is acceptable. Don't be afraid to punch your ISO level up higher than you would normally as these images survive noise and noise reductions remarkably well. The more UV lights you have, the easier this will be. I have five UV flashlights and two AC-powered lights, but similar results can be easily obtained with just two UV LED flashlights.

Combining multiple inks together can generate remarkable interactions, or the ink from a previous drop might simply pool at the water surface based on how it initially reacts to the impact with water. This is true of Noodler's Dragon Catfish Orange as well as many inks that are alcohol-based and are inherently lighter than water.

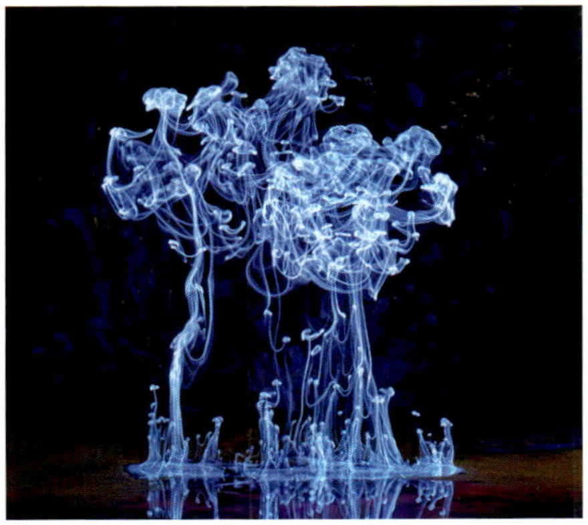

The next step, in post-production, would be to invert the final image so that the liquid appears to be moving upwards into the water. This is done purely based on personal taste, some images might look perfectly acceptable in their original orientation but all of these examples have been inverted. This provides an appearance similar to mushrooms or jellyfish, and the patterns can never be repeated twice.

Be prepared to spend hours experimenting with this. It can be addictive trying to create the perfect patterns and interactions! You're an abstract artist first and a photographer second – even just enjoying the patterns unfold with your own eyes can be very satisfying.

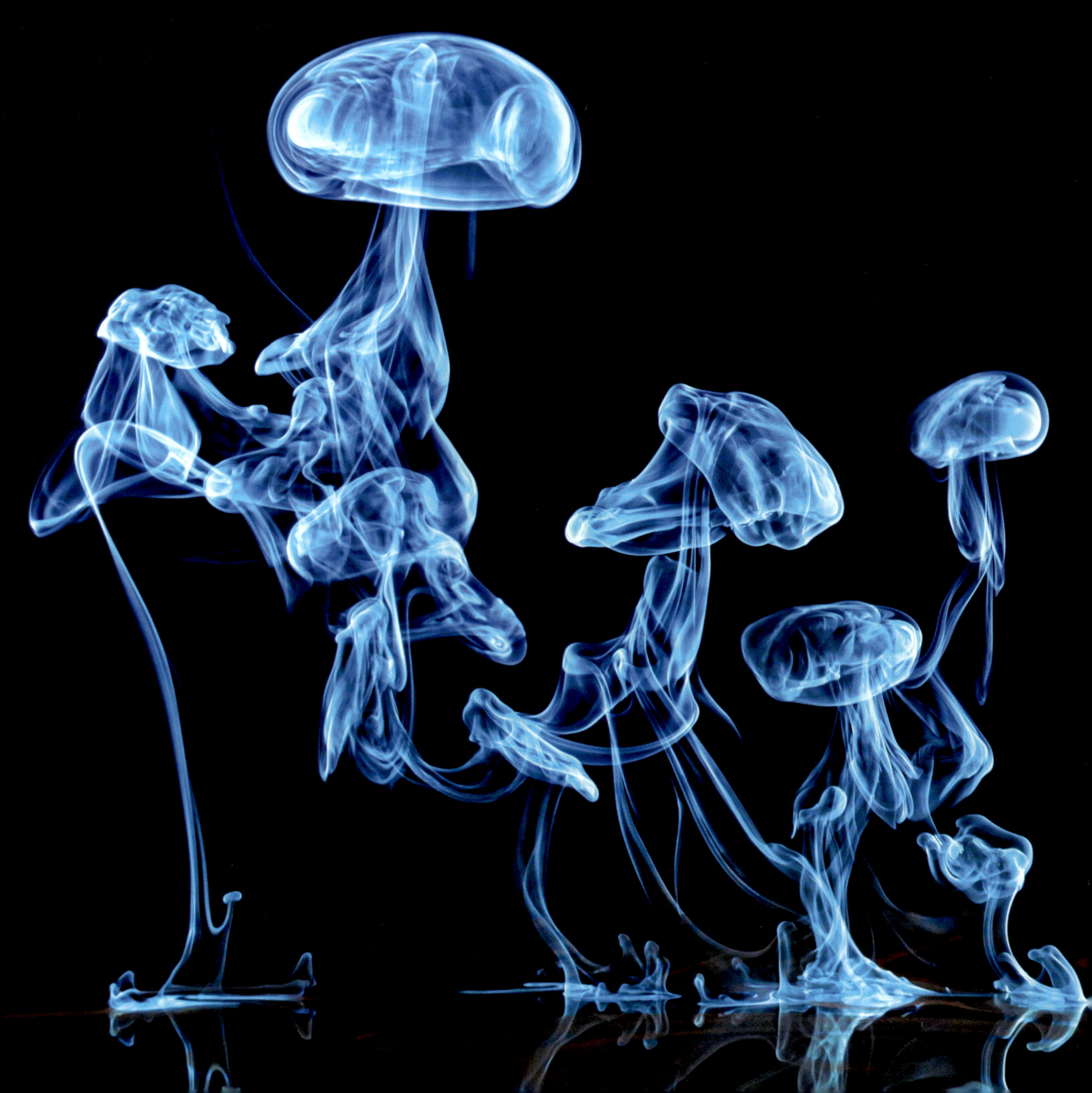

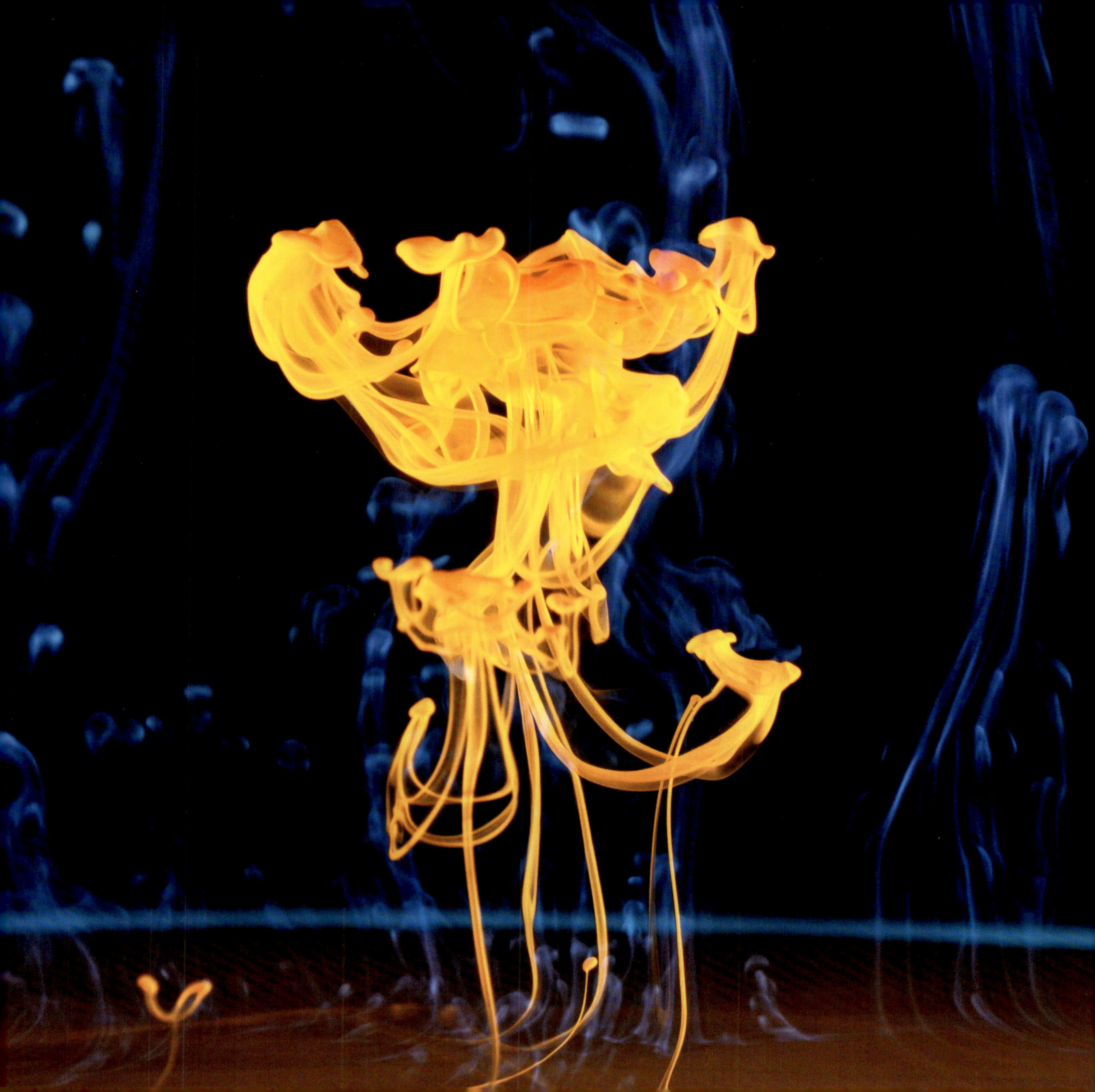

Bokeh

"Bokeh", as defined by Miriam-Webster: the blurred quality or effect seen in the out-of-focus portion of a photograph taken with a narrow depth of field. Its exact definition will vary equally to the multitude of ways you'll hear the word pronounced. In macro photography, we tend to associate bokeh with specific geometric shapes that might be present in the out of focus regions of an image, rather than simply the "smoothness" of these regions.

Not everything falls out of focus equally when it is placed farther away from the focal plane. This statement is an oversimplification to make a point; even though something is out of focus, does not mean it becomes entirely blurry. Bright spots of light can often take on the shape of the aperture of lens you're shooting with, appearing as geometric shapes or circles. This can come in the form of light passing through the leaves of a tree, but the best example of this phenomenon involves "specular highlights".

A catch light in someone's eye is a specular highlight. If you have a direct light source, and it hits a shiny surface, you'll get a very small bright spot of the light reflecting back. I've often admired the sparkling effect of freshly fallen snow on cold winter nights – this is the same effect. When these tiny points of light fall out of focus, they do not simply blur like the rest of the image – this is why artificially blurring a background in Adobe® Photoshop® doesn't look quite as real as if it was naturally out of focus.

In this example (*facing page*), I placed a mineral sample with colourful crystal facets behind a home-grown frost crystal. The mineral, chalcopyrite that has been treated with acid to change its colour from gold to blue, was placed two inches behind the subject. The frost was created overnight by placing an ultrasonic humidifier in an unheated shed on one of the coldest winter days. The effect was impressive – but on their own the crystals were just white on a black background with no real "character".

When I made the decision to shoot with background bokeh in mind, I went to the "holy grail" of bokeh in my lens collection: the Meyer Optik Trioplan 100mm F/2.8 lens. When shooting wide open, this lens offers up a look referred to as "soap bubble bokeh", where

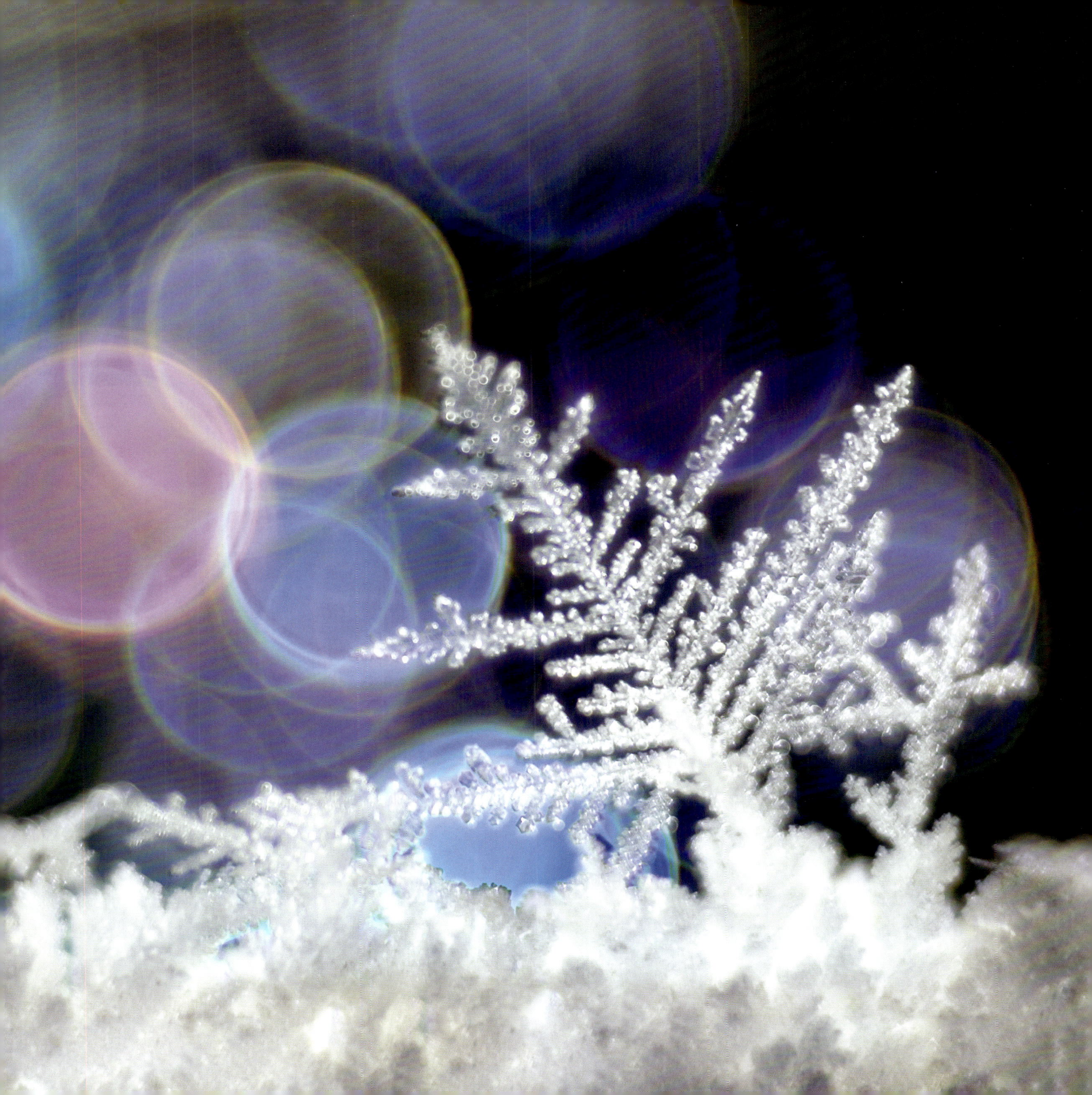

the outer edge of the unfocused specular highlight is brighter than the inner area, making it look like a bubble.

You can do a test with your lens to see what its bokeh characteristics are. The simplest experiments are done using a fiber optic desk lamp. In the dark and close up, photograph the light points with your lens at various apertures, including wide open.

In this example, The Laowa 50mm F/2.8 2x macro lens was used on a Lumix GX9. Wide open, most lenses will exhibit circular bokeh as the aperture blades are not limiting the amount of light entering the lens, and therefore the lens iris is completely circular. When shooting with smaller apertures, you'll notice that the circle takes on a polygonal form based on the number of blades the aperture has. This lens has a seven blade aperture, and thus creates heptagonal bokeh also with seven sides.

The more you stop down the lens, the smaller the bokeh will be. This is partially because the light points are more in focus than at wider apertures, and it will likely have more strongly defined geometric edges.

Try out your lenses! Discover the bokeh quality between macro lenses or the differences with non-macro lenses using close-up filters or extension tubes and traditional

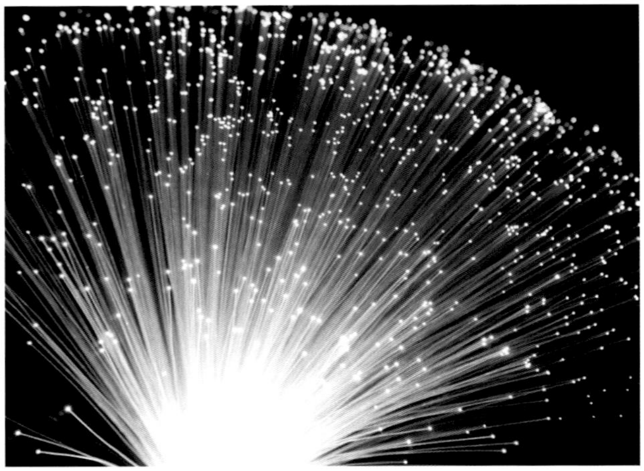

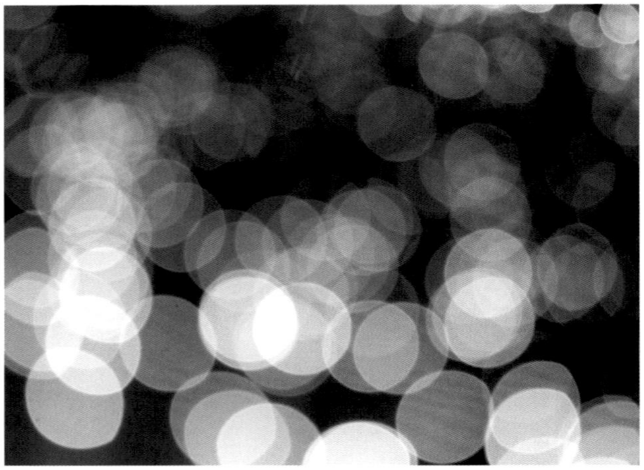

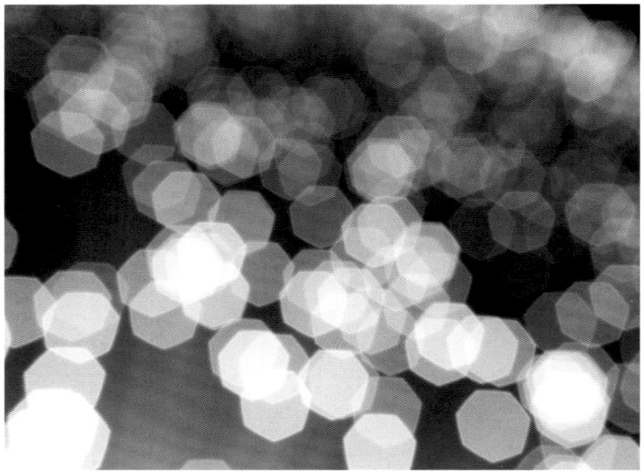

Top: F/6.3 with the lens intentionally focused on the light points from the fiber optic lamp.

Middle: F/2.8 and focused such that the light points turn into large circular shapes.

Bottom: F/6.3, but placed at the same focus point as the middle image to illustrate the 7-sided shapes caused by the aperture in the lens.

macro lenses. Every lens is made differently and will showcase slightly different results. Some lenses will behave beautifully, other will be mundane. You do not need to spend $1000 on a modern Trioplan 100 lens, however. There are plenty of options to consider if you're looking for some magical backgrounds with minimal investment.

The reason the Trioplan 100 creates such beautiful "soap bubble bokeh" has very little to do with the exact lens itself. The lens is a triplet design with three elements to overcome optical aberrations that would otherwise be present in a singlet (one element) or doublet (two element) design. With triplet lenses having been manufactured for over a century, there are plenty to choose from. Some the most readily available and least expensive come in the form of projector lenses. Want to take a gamble? Instead of searching eBay for a "soap bubble bokeh lens", instead look for a "projector triplet" and then figure out a way to mount it to your camera. It may be easier than you think.

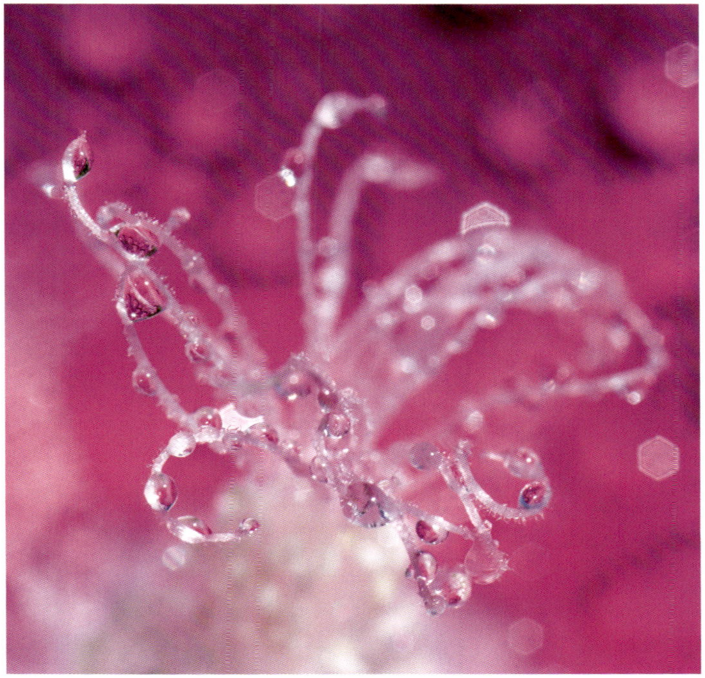

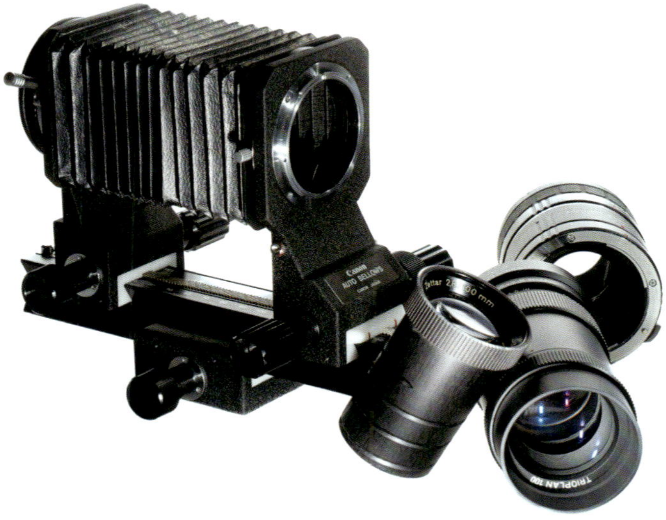

The best solution I have devised comes with the attachment to an old set of bellows. I purchased a set of Canon FD-mount Auto Bellows for under $100 and a triplet projector lens for under $20, plus the adapters to fit this on my Lumix S1R. How does a an old projector lens compare to the Trioplan? Amazingly well.

Top: The Canon MP-E 65mm F/2.8 1x-5x macro lens has a six-bladed aperture. In this image, you get hexagonal bokeh from the catch lights on the out of focus water droplets.

Left: Lens shootout: what performs better, the Meyer Optik Trioplan 100 + extension tubes or an old projector lens?

This first test is a basic example of abstract patterns, but that's why people love these vintage lenses. It's not for the clarity, it's for the quirkiness. What if we take a mineral specimen, this time being a piece of quartz that has been treated with a thin layer of Titanium Oxide? This causes the surface of the quartz to present rainbow colours through thin film interference and can be quite beautiful. Often labelled as "rainbow quartz clusters" by people selling them online, some can offer up vibrant colours of purple and orange.

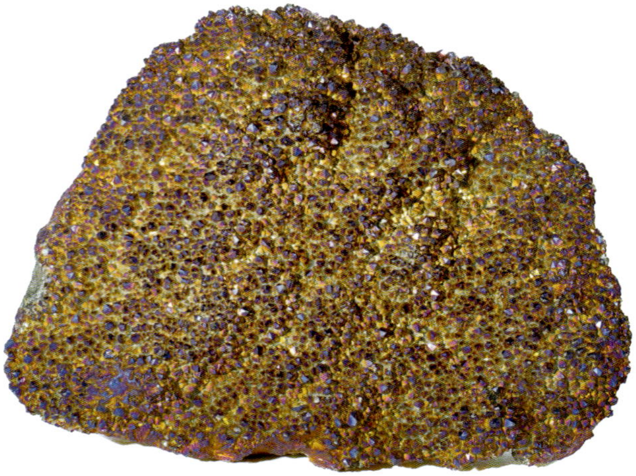

When you shoot these crystals out of focus, the specular highlight reflections from the various crystal facets form into fiery balls of bokeh. The simplistic (and by modern-day standards, flawed) design of triplet lenses when shot wide open result in a similar look. This disappears when you include a smaller aperture, but projector lenses are fixed at their listed aperture with no iris diaphragm to adjust – always wide open. Which image do you like more? Answer that question before you read the next paragraph.

The image on the left was created with the modern Trioplan 100, which costs a significant amount of money. The image on the right was created by sticking an old projector lens in a set of bellows and holding it in place with gaffer's tape. Not an ideal solution, but I personally enjoy the results more. Ironically, there is more chromatic aberration in the outer edge of the bokeh circle in the Trioplan lens than in the projector lens, which appears sharper. Remember, it was only ever designed to function wide open.

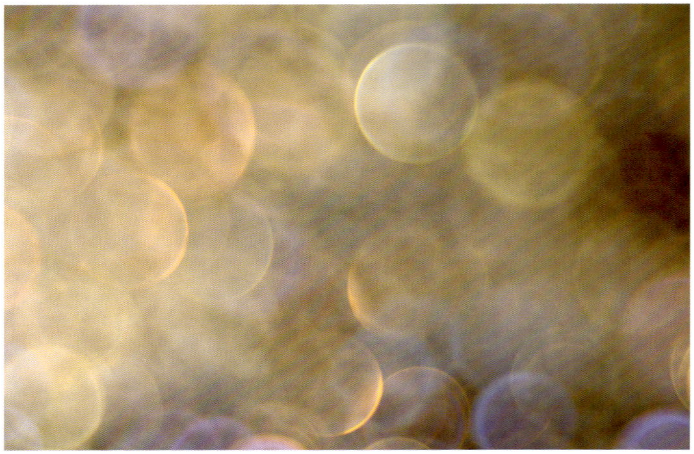

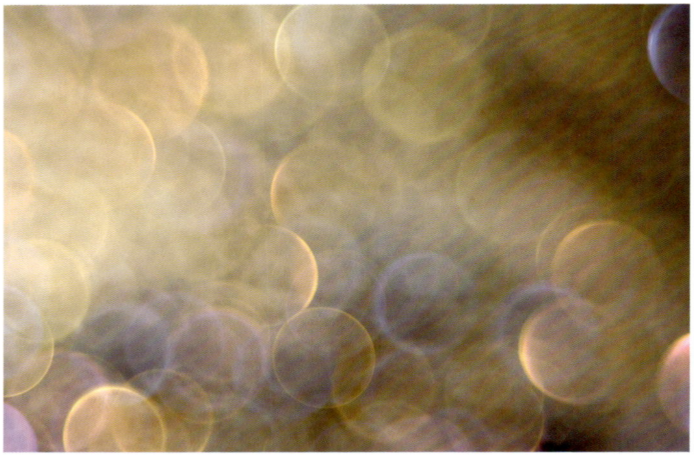

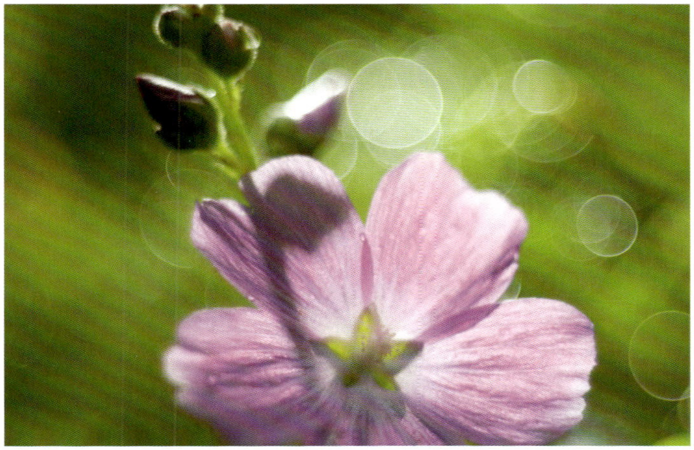

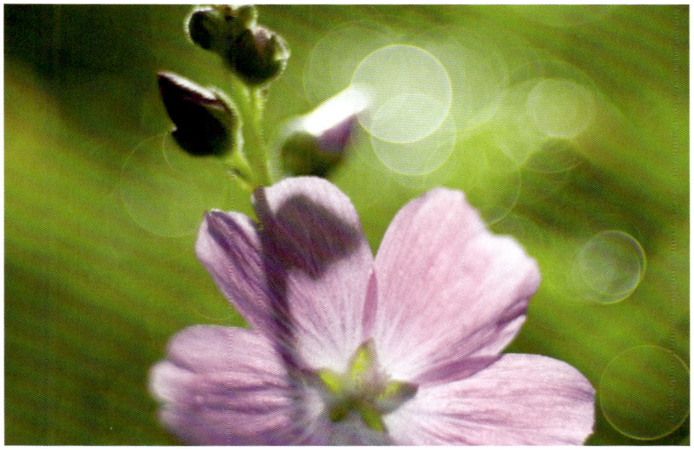

The next test is a quick outdoors example in the garden. I grabbed my hose and set it to the "mist" setting, and then sprayed a patch of grass. The flower was placed with a "third hand tool" behind some droplets that I knew would behave well for the example. Which do you prefer? The image on the left is the old projector lens. The image on the right to compare? The coveted Trioplan 100. These 100mm lenses were designed for different purposes, and both are anachronisms.

Clarity isn't the point of these images. The depth of field will be inherently shallow when shooting wide open, and the optical design is antiquated. What we're seeking is a different way to imagine our reality, to allow the camera to transform our normal perceptions into something fanciful. The bubble effect from the projector lens is sharper and suffers from less chromatic aberrations on the bright edge of the bokeh circles, but maybe that rainbow colour fringe is what you're after? Your choice.

The cost difference is certainly shocking, and I personally enjoy the crispness of the projector lens more. I will make a clear statement here: you do not need a "Zettar" lens. This was a randomly purchased item because it was the least expensive I could find. Any old "triplet", often written in the Cyrillic alphabet as "триплет" as many of these lenses originate in Eastern Europe and Russia, is what you seek.

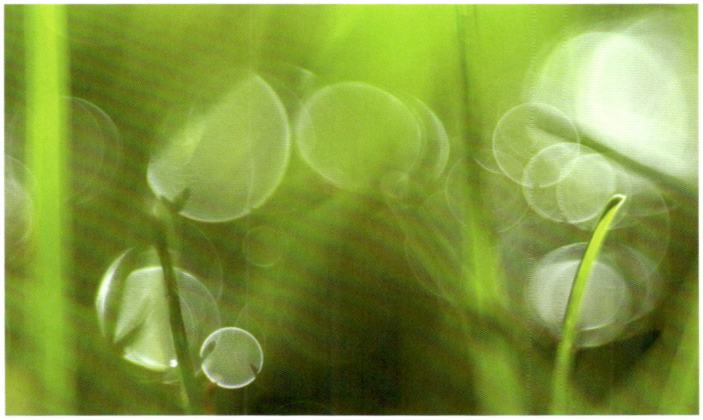

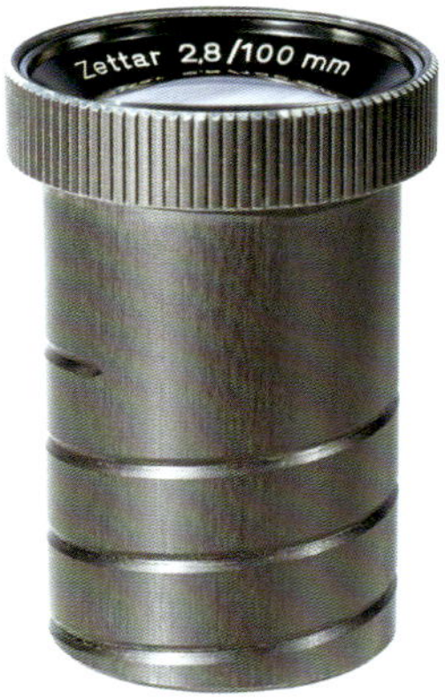

Mucking With Light

We are effectively bending light to our creative whimsy at this point. We've left our own reality behind us, so what does the road ahead look like? Applying the "what if?" mentality to lenses can lead us into some interesting modifications. Many vintage lenses can be modified to produce abstract results, generating painterly, ethereal images to get your creative juices flowing.

MIR-1V / МИР-1В 37mm F/2.8

Originally conceptualized by Mathieu Stern, the front element of this lens can be reversed to create streakingly blurry edges to an image. An easier modification, at least with the copy of the lens that I have, involves simply unscrewing the entire front element group – it's just threaded on. Unscrew, flip over, and shoot. This generates a strange bending circle of light while still maintaining additional clarity. Since these old Soviet-era lenses are inexpensive, it can be enjoyable to just take things apart with wanton disregard to the end result. Is this effect for everything? No. Just like a fisheye lens has a purpose, this particular lens is one I use sparingly.

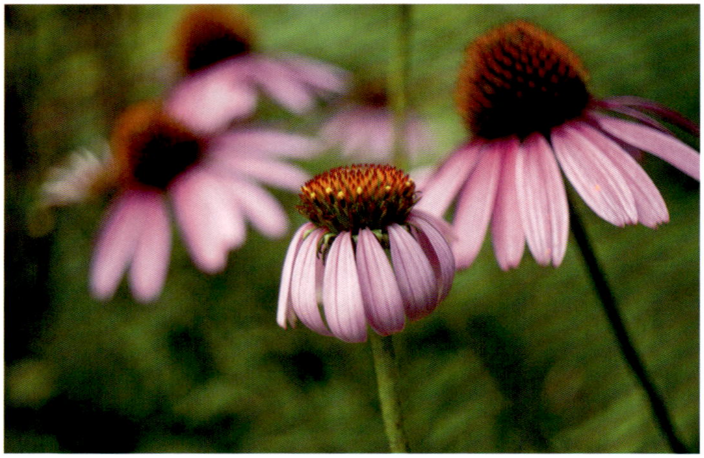

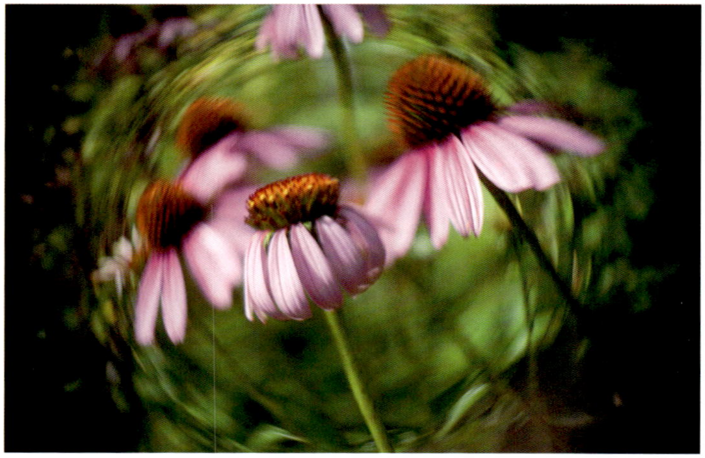

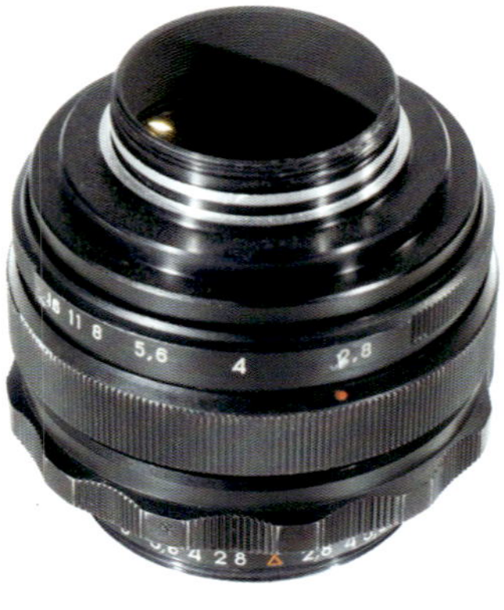

Top: MIR-1V lens with "ordinary" optics.

Middle: Reversed front element group.

Bottom: MIR-1V lens with reversed front section.

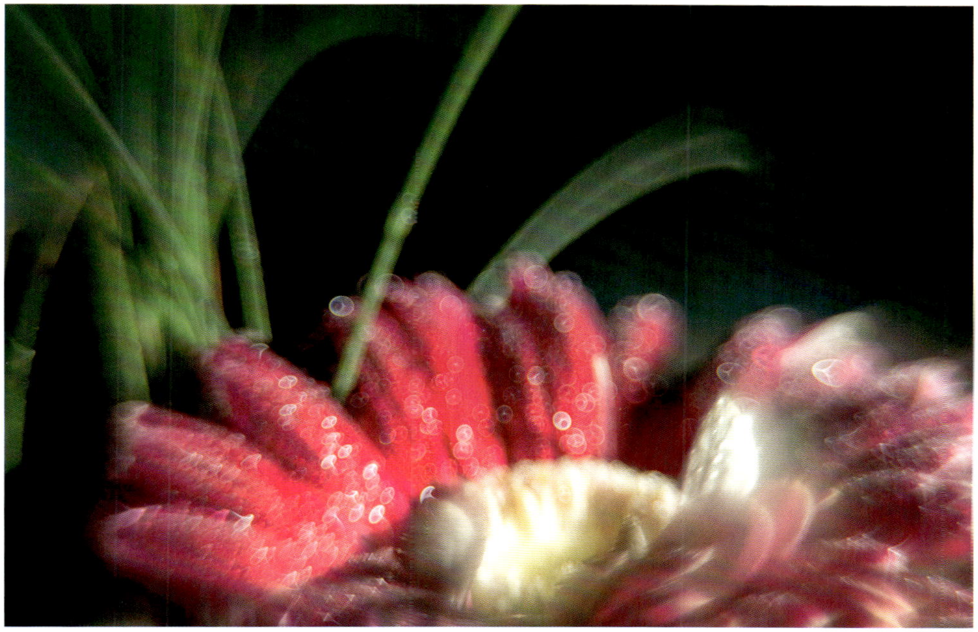

MC Zenitar M2s 50mm F/2

I have Alireza Rostami to thank for this modification, which is more technically challenging. Effectively, we need to flip an internal lens group around – the second last set of optics in four groups. This requires the removal of the rear element, vigorous shaking and banging to knock other internal pieces out, and then reassemble with the inverted optics. The results? "Dreamy" is one way to describe it, like remembering the vagueness of a dream where you can't quite recollect the details.

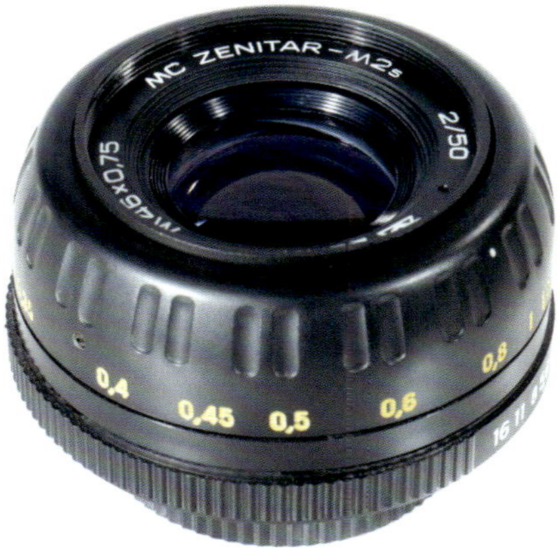

Top: Photograph taken with an inverted lens group on the MC Zenitar M2s 50mm F/2 lens.

Bottom: Modified lens. Because the modification is internal, it doesn't look any different on the outside.

Nothing is sharp. Your subject is oftentimes unrecognizable. Lenses like this allow you to explore abstract creations that take a beautiful background of bokeh and smear it all over the image. Many people who experiment in this area will walk down this path and decide that it isn't their style, since it is quite a distinctive departure in artistic expression. Others will embrace it, and find more ways to explore this "altered light". To that end, entire companies have been founded for the purpose of exploring the artistic eccentricities of bending light.

Lomography and Lensbaby

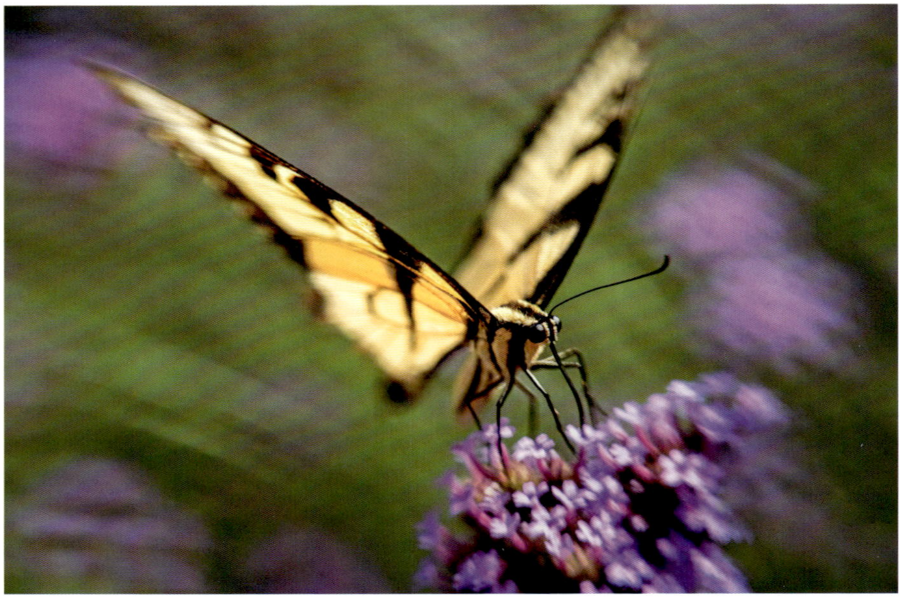

Two companies have taken the lead in producing imperfect lenses for creative effect. Lensbaby evolved as photographer and inventor Craig Strong attached a vacuum cleaner hose to a large format lens as a creative attempt at constructing a tilt-shift style lens with a "sweet spot" of focus. The company has expanded with a huge selection of lenses and accessories designed for you to mess around with light, focus, colour and creativity.

One such lens, the Sol 45, includes "arms" that can be positioned in front of the lens that serve to interfere with light before it enters the lens. This generates the appearance of brush-like strokes in the out of focus details in an image – the bokeh. Whether controlled by careful choice of your subject or by placing things in front of your lens itself, we can be imaginative.

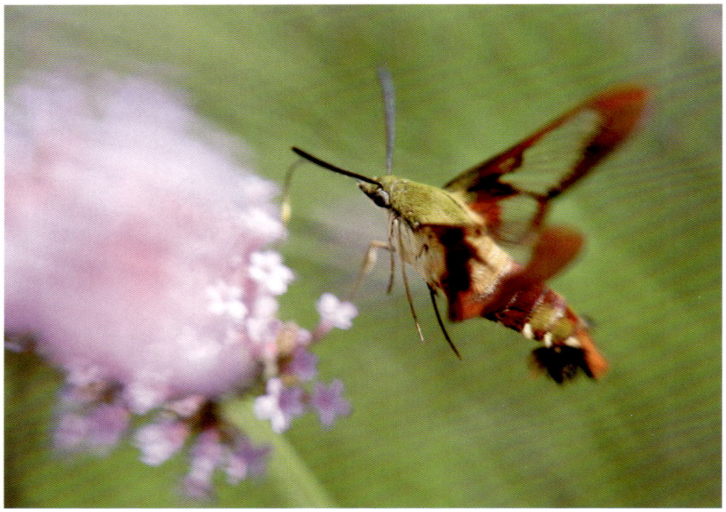

Above: Two images taken with the Lensbaby Sol 45 which imparted a painterly sense of motion to the images.

What if you wanted to soften an image to provide a sense of motion while still maintaining sharp details somewhere? There are many ways to accomplish this; don't let me lead you to believe that this is the only way. It does, however, add a sense of wispiness to images of insects in flight.

Lomography is synonymous with toy cameras, a combined name of "LOMO" and "Photography", the former being a reference to the LOMO LC-A 35mm film camera from Leningrad Optics and Mechanics

Association originally manufactured from 1984 through 1994. It started an entire movement of people enjoying these quirky inexpensive toy cameras alongside Holga cameras manufactured in China. Lomography as a company today continues to sell LOMO cameras and film, but also a series of lenses inspired by vintage optical designs. These lenses would have originally used "Waterhouse diaphragms", which would be drop-in apertures rather than a variable-diameter iris.

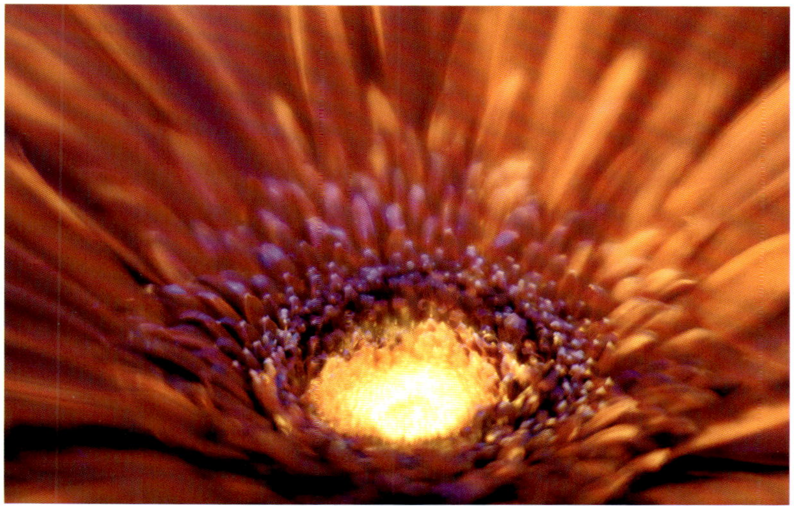

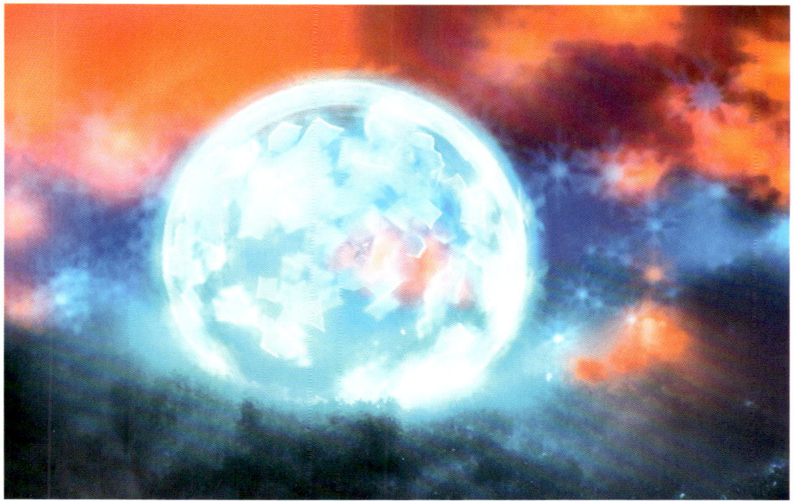

This offers up some experimental concepts that allow you to change the shape of your aperture. We've previously discussed that your bokeh will take on the geometric shape of your aperture, but what if you decide to insert a specially crafted aperture shape? Or maybe one with many smaller holes to intentionally soften the resulting image?

A sieve aperture, also called a diffusion disc, can create soft focus effects. That was used in this image (*top*), depicting a Gerbera Daisy covered in orange highlighter ink and then illuminated with ultraviolet light.

What if your aperture was a recognizable shape, such as a snowflake? In an experiment that I think I went too far with (*bottom*), I ended up with "snowflake bokeh" created by mixing invisible ink and highlighter ink to create an overly magical freezing soap bubble image. Techniques regarding freezing soap bubbles as well as ultraviolet fluorescence are discussed elsewhere in this book. An image like this is a great example of the "creative puzzle piece" approach, wherein the more various techniques you explore, the more ways you'll find to fit them together.

Not all such experiments will be successes. These two images (*above*) were taken with the Lomography

Daguerreotype Achromat 2.9/64 Art Lens, which has only been used for a handful of experiments. Experiments almost always lead to new ideas worth exploring, and more "what if?" moments. Even if something doesn't work out, or you don't feel artistically connected to the results, embrace the process.

This led me to ask a simple question: can I design an aperture that has floating areas of transmission? The answer is yes, and it was a simple contraption to build that was dependent on one key ingredient: inkjet printable overhead projector sheets. Normally transparent, I can choose to print out an aperture of my own design here at my desk. It could be a spiral, a leaf, a heart within a heart within a heart. The more complex you make the aperture, the less you'll see the details, but how many concepts can you think up? The cost of printing out a sheet of experimental apertures would be pennies.

To hold the apertures in place, you can simply tape them to the front your lens – and you can take a simpler approach and just cut a shape out of a piece of construction paper. My invention is a little more advanced but still very inexpensive; It consists of a screw-in aluminum lens cap into which I have cut a hole and framed with some pieces of metal. These metal pieces were originally designed to be hammered onto the corners of books to prevent them from getting damaged. The aperture insert slides right in.

What if I then light my subject with different primary colours from different angles, to double up the strangeness of the bokeh? Can I get some to be red, some to be blue, all of them having a square within a square? Yes. Will it make for a beautiful image? Maybe not. Even still, the sense of adventure I feel when I sit and tinker in my studio is ignited.

Even if the results of an experiment do not impress, you've still gained something in the process. Keep going!

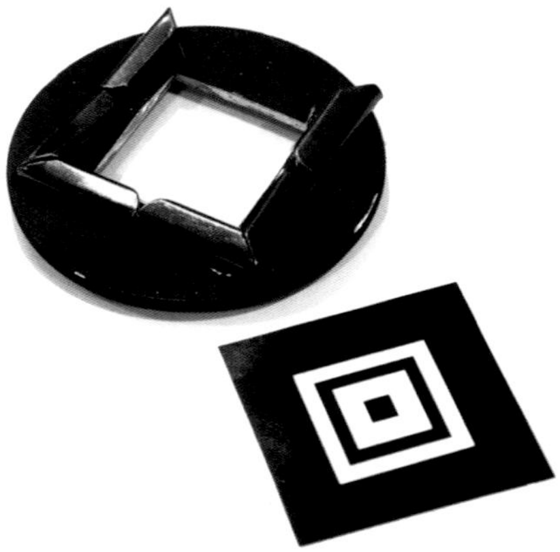

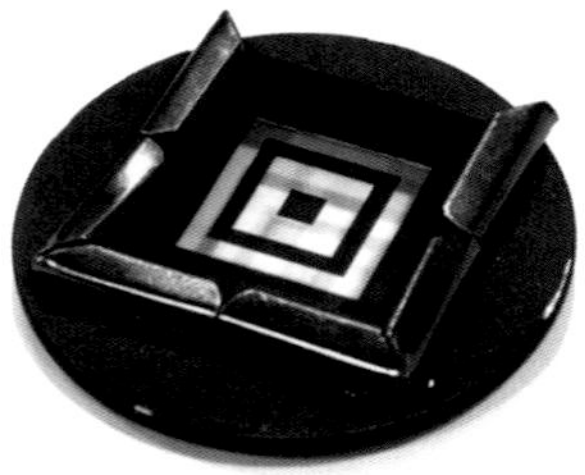

Above: An aperture printed on inkjet-compatible overhead projection material and a home-made holder to fit it on the front of a lens.

Facing page: Image taken with such a contrapion afixed to a Meyer Optik Trioplan 100 F/2.8 lens.

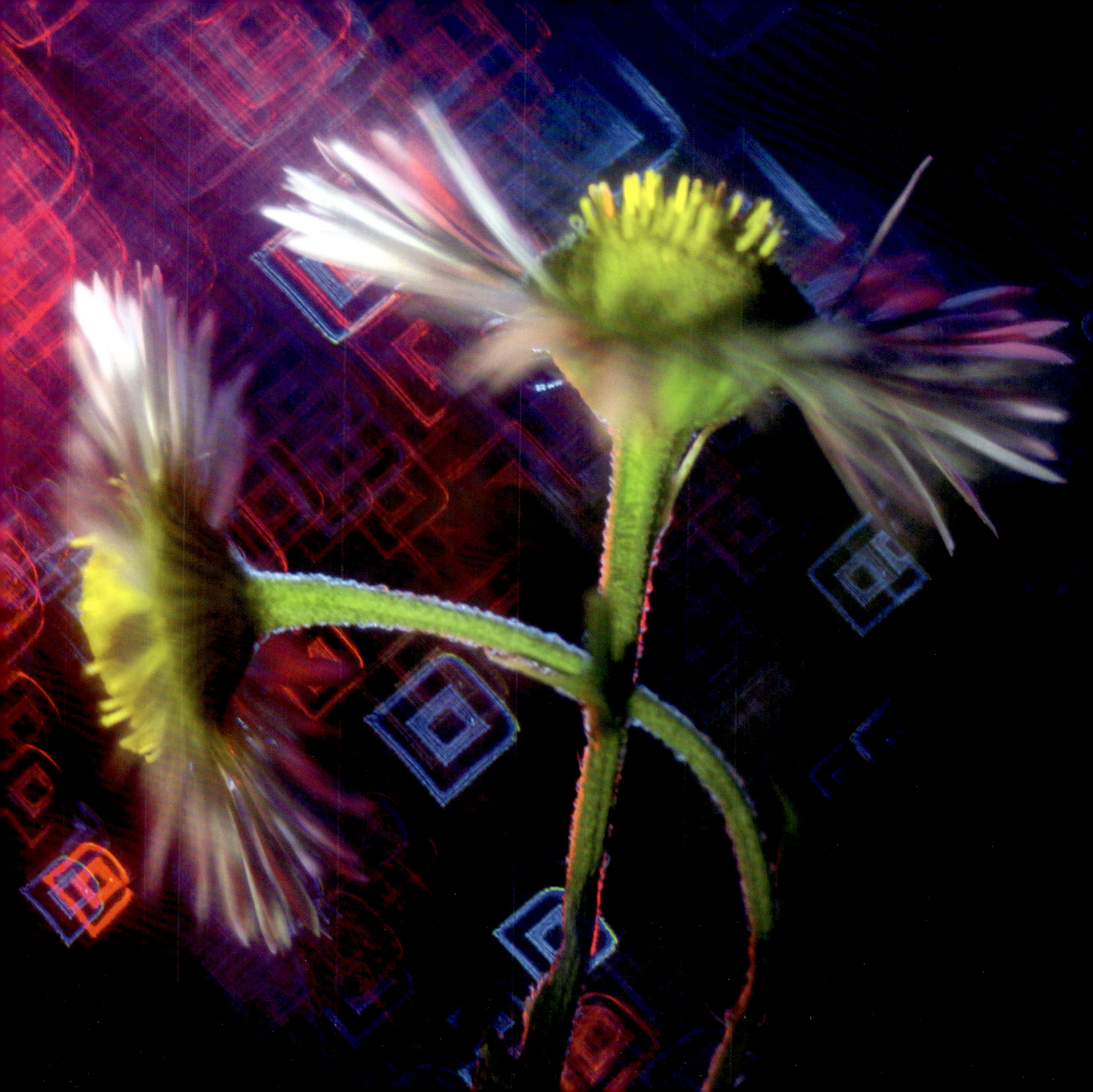

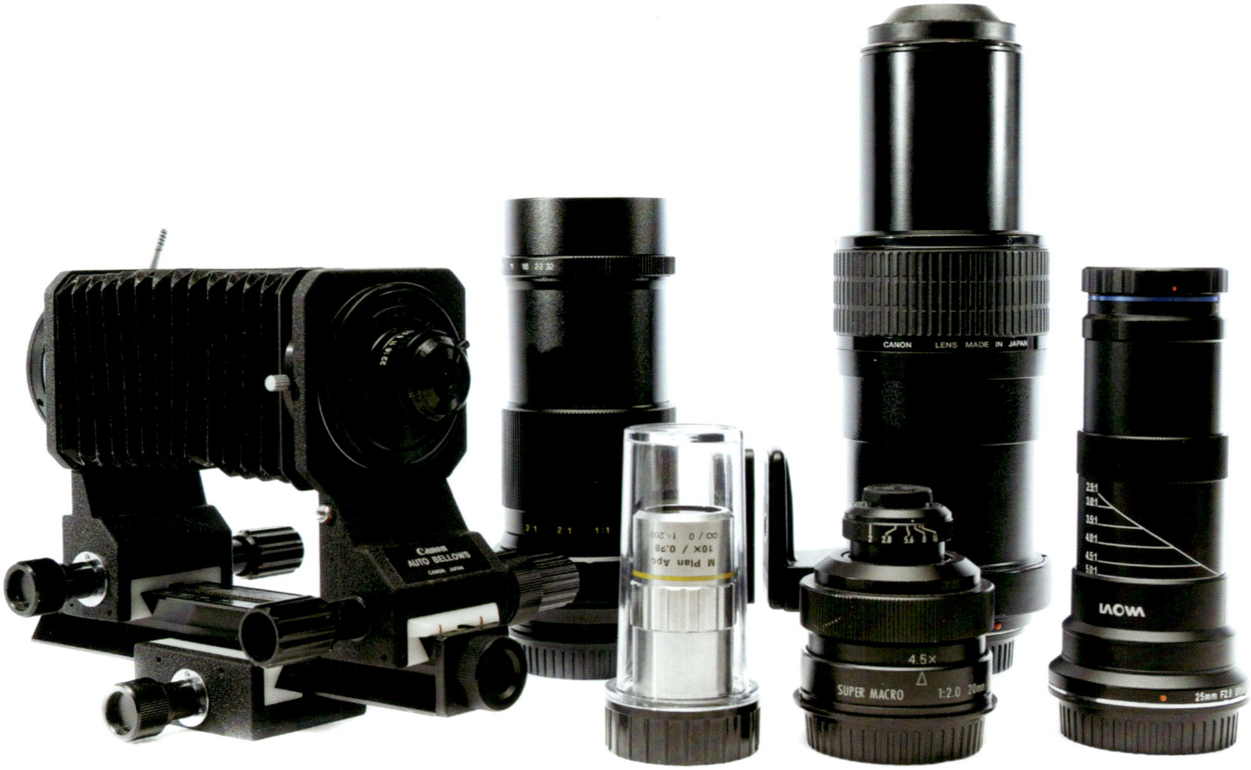

From left to right:
Canon 20mm F/3.5 bellows, Mitakon Creator 85mm F/2.8 1x-5x, Mitutoyo Plan APO 10x, Mitakon Creator 20mm F/2 4x-4.5x (front), Canon MP-E 65mm F/2.8 1x-5x (back), Laowa 25mm F/2.8 2.5x-5x

High-Magnification Macro

Grains of sand. Pollen. The eye of an insect. Snowflakes and frost, of course! There are so many interesting things you could fill the frame with if you just had more magnification – if you could just get closer. Once you feel comfortable enough exploring the 1:1 macro realm, almost everyone looks for ways to get more magnification. Extension tubes and close-up filters might be your first stop on this journey, but it's by no means the end of the line. If you keep going, you'll discover many purpose-built macro lenses that can push to 5:1 magnification and sometimes beyond.

For a long time, there weren't many options for high magnification macro photography without resorting to solutions like lens coupling and lens reversals. The only lens on most photographer's radar was the Canon MP-E 65mm F/2.8 1x-5x Macro. There are other lesser-known options, so let's take a look at how the MP-E 65 compares to more modern and vintage lenses to put to 5:1 magnification and beyond – using a moth wing.

There are six lenses in this test:

- Canon MP-E 65mm F/2.8 1x-5x
- Canon 20mm F/3.5 bellows lens
- Laowa 25mm F/2.8 2.5x-5x
- Mitakon Creator 20mm F/2 4x-4.5x
- Mitakon Creator 85mm F/2.8 1x-5x
- Mitutoyo Plan APO 10x microscope objective

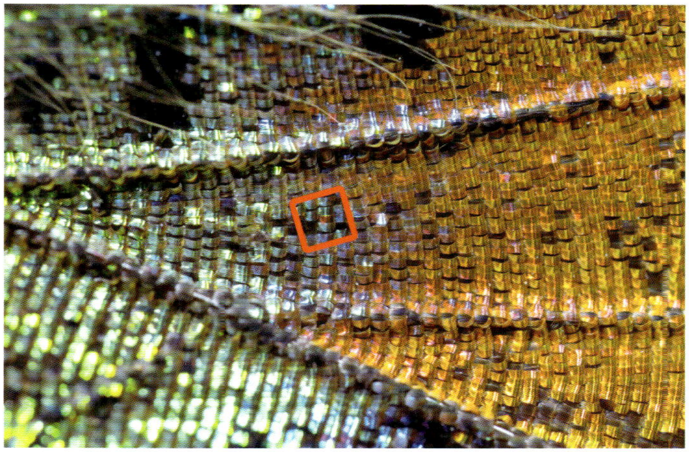

Sample area of study (red square) on a 5:1 magnification image taken with the Canon MP-E 65mm F/2.8 1x-5x lens.

This test involves a portion of the wing from a *Chrysiridia rhipheus*, the Madagascan Sunset Moth. Chosen for this experiment because it has colour scales that transition quickly and vibrantly from one hue to another in a specific area of the wing. The scales also have small lines running down their length, making for a very good test of optical resolution. In order to test resolution, each lens is shot both wide open, and stopped down to F/5.6. All lenses capable of shooting at 5x were set to that, and others were scaled to that size for a more direct comparison. How do these six lenses perform at the limits of macro photography?

Canon MP-E 65mm F/2.8 1x-5x

A workhorse of a lens, one of my favourite macro lenses ever, but a design that has no modern technology – originally debuting in 1999. Still, it's the benchmark in this test. We can see plenty of detail and good colour rendition, and the lines on the scales are clearly visible. While there is some degradation of detail when stopped down slightly, this is due to diffraction. Page 8 of the manual for this lens gives a handy conversion chart from dialed-in aperture to effective aperture, which changes as magnification increases. F/5.6 at 5:1 magnification is actually F/33.6, which would be diffraction limited on the 47MP sensor that these images were taken with. No fault of the lens – we're just bending light too much.

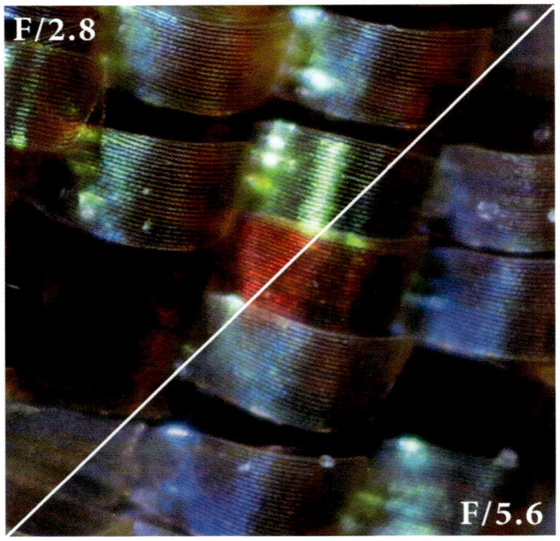

Canon 20mm F/3.5 bellows lens

Originally released alongside a 35mm F/2.8 lens way back in 1976, this lens is capable of 2x-10x magnification on a Canon Auto Bellows. It's a great example of high-magnification technology from over 40 years ago, and can show us how far we've come. Remarkably, the resolving power is quite good. The colours are slightly muted, though to some degree this is due to a change in lighting angle and specular reflection into the lens. This lens requires a bellows to be used properly, so it's a bit big and bulky for every use case. Stopping down brings a loss of details. The hipster vibe is strong with this one.

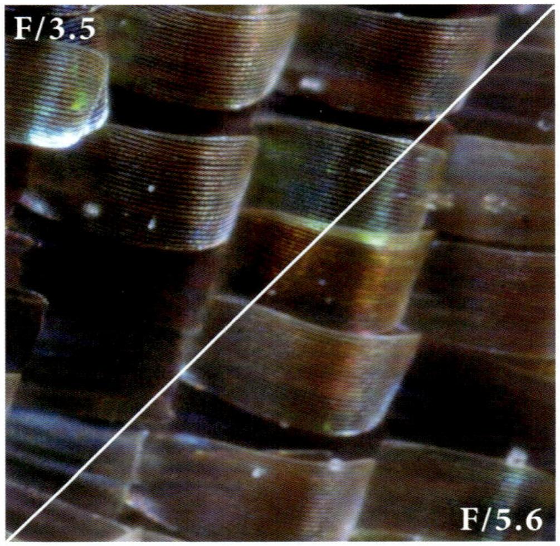

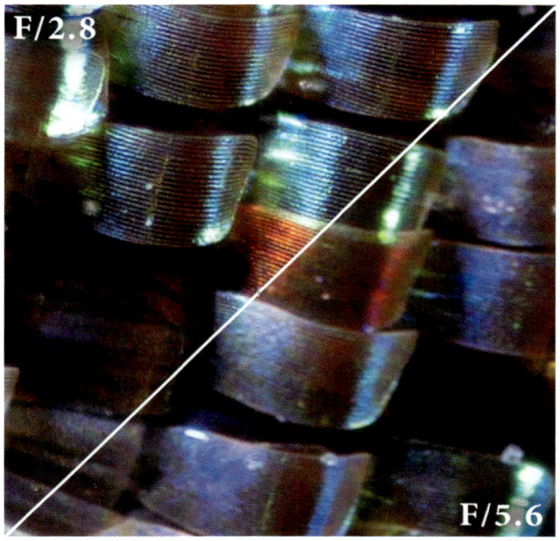

Laowa 25mm F/2.8 2.5x-5x

A newcomer from Venus Optics, the Laowa 25mm macro doesn't have the same level of flexibility in magnification range as the Canon MP-E 65, but it's certainly a contender. Dare I say it's just as sharp? Wide open, anyhow. Detail falls off much more at F/5.6 than the Canon MP-E 65. This lens also does not have a filter thread, a design flaw in my opinion – it makes it difficult to attach a ring flash or macro twin flash to the front.

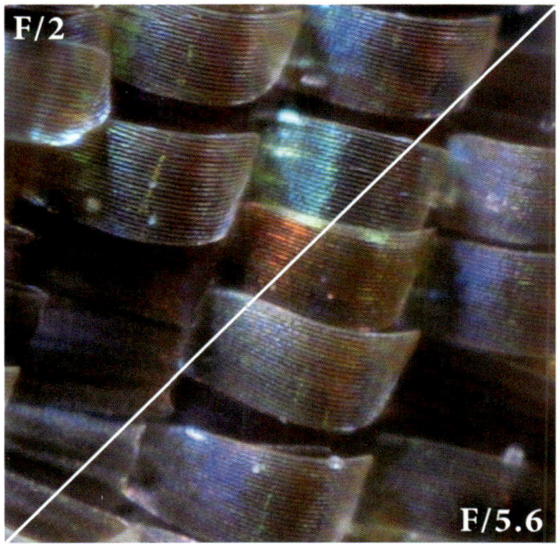

Mitakon Creator 20mm F/2.0 4x-4.5x

The first super macro lens from Zhong Yi Optics, an interesting inexpensive little lens that was confusingly engineered. Why have a barrel adjustment go from 4x to 4.5x? That would be mostly useless to most photographers and greatly increase the engineering cost of the lens. If you're going to over-engineer something… why then put in a THREE-blade aperture? Not sure who out there is clamoring for trigonal bokeh. Optically, it's about on-par to the Canon 20mm from yesteryear, performing better when stopped down. Also no filter thread on this lens, limiting the flexibility.

These tests are done using a Panasonic Lumix S1R full frame 47MP camera body. The pixel pitch on this camera is 4.27μm. Regardless of sensor size, the pixel density is an important consideration for diffraction. If you have a more densely packed sensor, you will notice diffraction muddying your results earlier than F/5.6.

Mitakon Creator 85mm F/2.8 1x-5x

This lens is the whole reason I did this comparison - just announced - and on paper it had the potential to usurp the Canon MP-E 65mm. At half the price! Smaller and lighter! Available in a variety of lens mounts! But there's a catch. The much longer working distance afforded by this lens comes at its own price. When you push the working distance out, you lower your responding power. This might allow you to create photographs that would otherwise be impossible to make, but don't expect details to live up to your expectations on a high resolution sensor. It's a compromise of quality for flexibility.

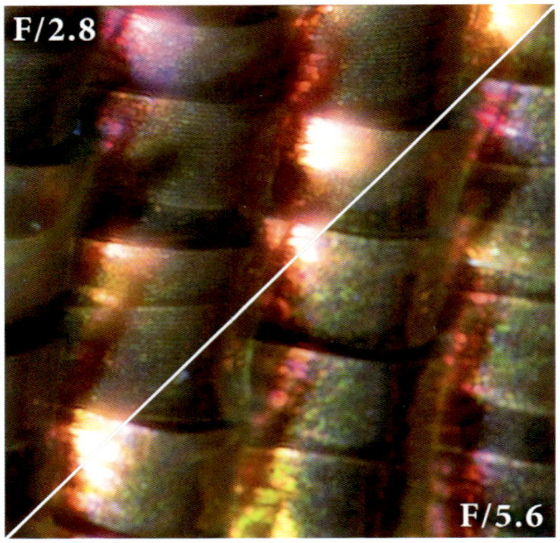

Mitutoyo Plan APO 10x Objective

There are a lot of high-magnification macro photographers that will state that anything beyond 5x should be handled by a microscope objective. I tend to disagree in terms of usability, especially when shooting handheld as these objectives have such a drastically thinner depth of field in comparison, but that's where the increase in resolution comes from. Mitutoyo makes these objectives at 1x, 2x, 5x, 10x, 20x, 50x and 100x, but they aren't often considered when people want a macro lens. Why? Most people don't know how to attach them, but the process is incredibly simple:

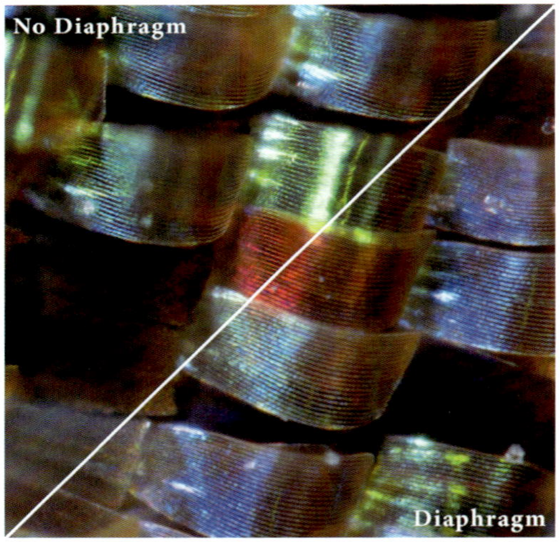

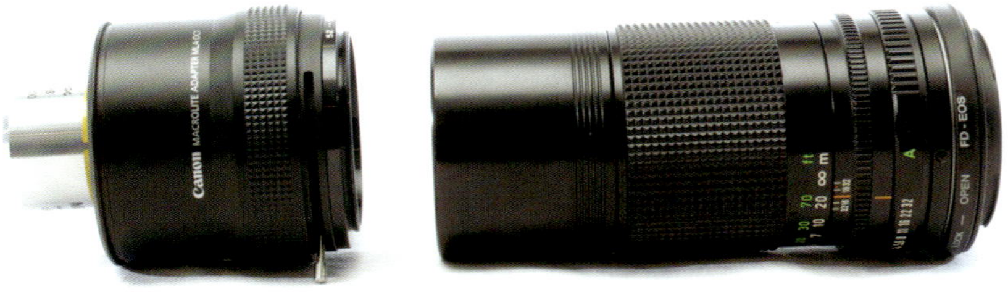

Note: In the image (*left*) you can see a Canon MLA-DC1. This was originally designed for G-series cameras to mount a ring flash to them. It's glued to the step-down ring to allow the mounting of a ring flash around the microscope objective.

First, get a regular lens that covers 200mm. All of these "long working distance" objectives from Mitutoyo state "f=200" on the barrel, but note that this number might be different with other lenses. I didn't have a 200mm lens, so I invested $20 in a Canon FD 200mm F/4 on eBay. You'll just need a step-down ring from whatever your filter thread size is, to M26. **You're done.** Set the 200mm lens to focus on infinity, and you can now shoot with your camera as if it's a microscope. You can even add your own aperture diaphragm between the two lenses to sacrifice optical resolution for a greater depth of field – and you'll want to keep the aperture inside the camera lens always open regardless.

The incredibly thin depth of field here makes it very difficult to handhold the camera. I've photographed snowflakes handheld at 20x and it was one of the most difficult things I've ever had to do with a camera in my hands. Being locked down on a tripod with a focusing rail is the best way to go here. Also – don't buy a new objective. There is plenty of second-hand inventory often close to half of the retail price.

And The Winner Is…

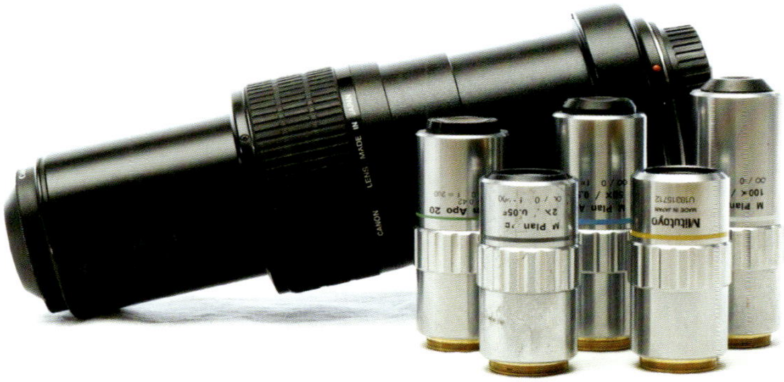

A tie. The Canon MP-E 65mm is still the king of the castle and continuing a 20-year reign, but if you're after the ultimate in resolution and are willing to sacrifice on convenience and flexibility, grab a Mitutoyo microscope objective. The versatility afforded by variable magnification as well as how the lens performs handheld offers enough convenience and ease of use to overcome the additional resolving power of microscope objective for most people. Some of the newer macro lenses from other manufacturers, especially the Laowa 25mm 2.5x-5x are very strong in comparison, but none have yet to take the crown entirely away from Canon.

Yes, yes, this list is not complete. There are many lenses that break the 1:1 barrier now, but this list was looking to the 5:1 range and beyond. Canon, Zeiss and Olympus all had additional bellows lenses, but I figured one would be sufficient for this comparison. Infinity Optical has the TS-160 which can get infinity focus all the way to 16x but it wasn't available and compound microscopes are a headache. Reversal adapters and lens couplers can work too. There is more to this discussion.

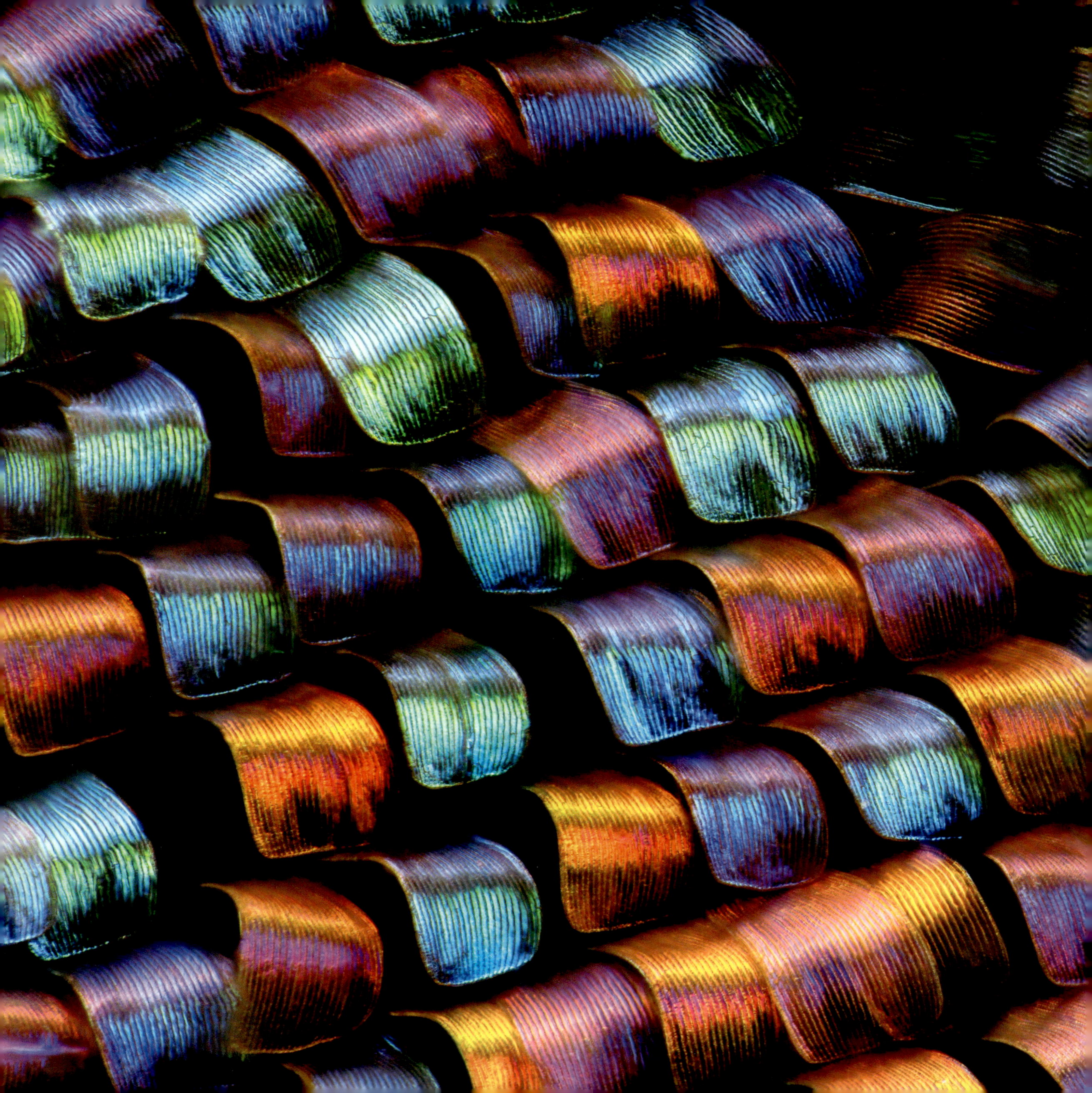

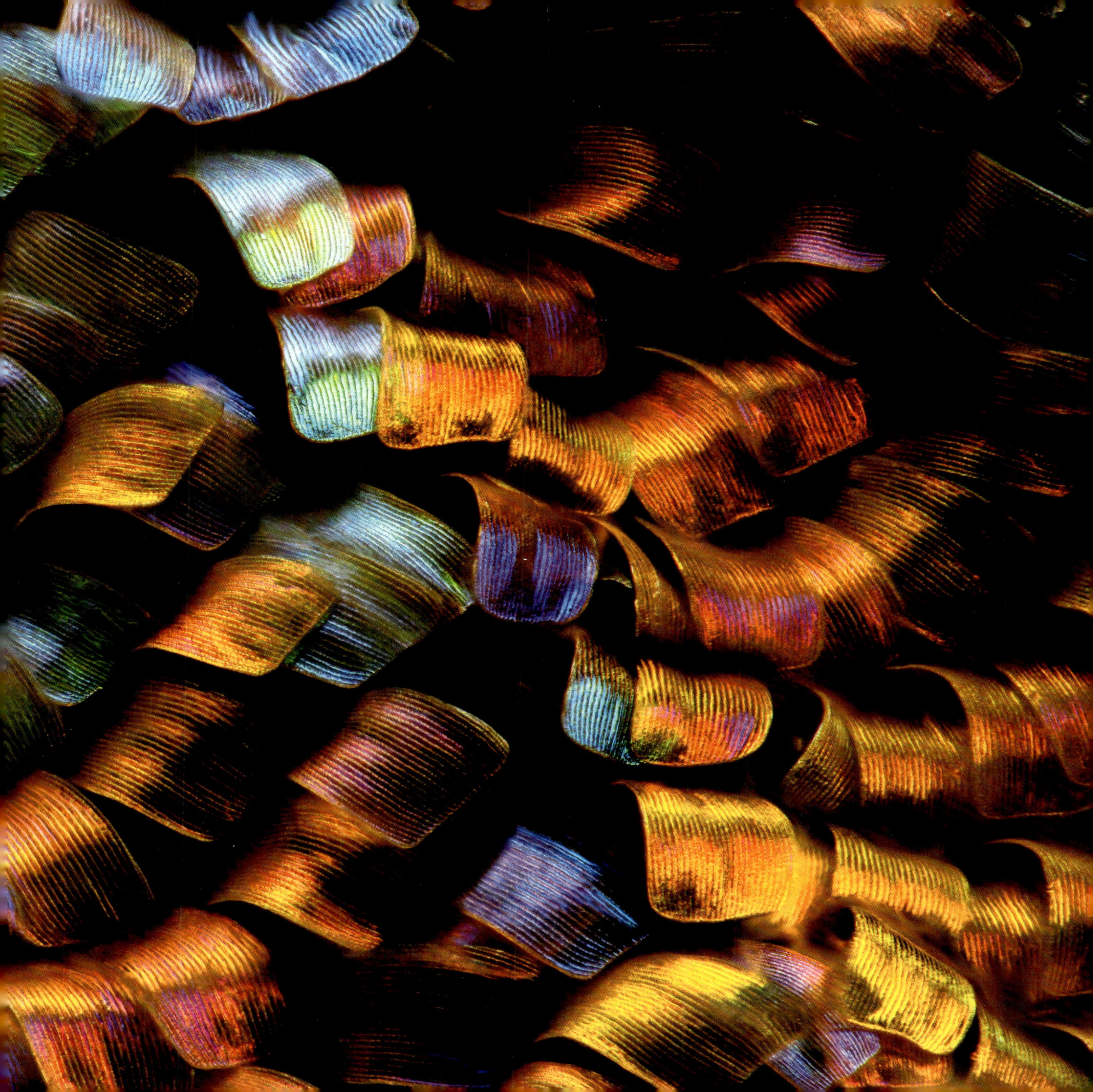

Shooting With Microscope Objectives

This area of macro photography may at first appear mysterious, and it might seem like something you'll pass over in this book. I'm going to write this in bold to grab your attention if you're already thinking that: **DON'T SKIP THIS SECTION**. Read how easy this is, how affordable this is, and what you'll need to consider for shooting and processing techniques.

As stated in the previous pages, you can obtain microscope objectives with as little as 1x magnification – the same as a standard macro lens. These tiny little metallic barrels cannot stand on their own, however – you'll need a little help from a standard camera lens to get things to cooperate.

The Mitutoyo Plan APO series of lenses are widely regarded as the "best", and the used market will present most of them for a few hundred dollars. However, any "infinity corrected" microscope objective will work wonders here, some of which are available with double-digit prices! Do a little bit of digging, and find the right ingredients for you.

Oftentimes your choice of objective is based on what you'd like to photograph. Since adding extension tubes to a regular macro lens might yield close to 2x magnification, most people seriously start considering using these objectives when you deal with smaller subjects, with keen interest starting at 5x and beyond. So, how do you know what you're looking for? Infinity-corrected microscope objectives usually have a number of common markings:

"Plan" refers to how flat the field of the image is. Lesser quality objectives might have the center of the frame focused at a different point than the edges, but Plan objectives keep the focal plane flat across the frame.

F=###, where that number is the focal length of the "tube lens", usually ranging from 160mm to 200mm.

∞ / 0 denotes that the objective is infinity corrected and the "0" refers to the millimeters of thickness of a cover slip used to calculate corrections to the objective. You don't really need to worry about these numbers, other than knowing it's infinity corrected.

0.### is the **Numerical Aperture** of the lens (**NA**). The larger this number, the more resolving power the objective is capable of.

Magnification and Resolving Power

Doubling your magnification doesn't double your detail. There are limits to how much you can actually "resolve", even though your subject is filling the frame to a much greater degree. A perfect example of this is between 20x and 50x with the Mitutoyo objectives. My 20x objective has a numerical aperture of 0.42 and the ability to resolve down to 0.7 microns (micrometer, µm). Compare that to my 50x objective that has an NA of 0.55 and can resolve down to 0.5µm. More than doubling the magnification only results in slightly more detail being resolved. In some cases, objectives with different magnifications will have the same NA and the same resolving power!

I find that 10x and 20x objectives are by far the most useful, and the increase in detail beyond that is rarely worth the extra effort. In fact, every time I try to get something useful out of my 100x objective, I fail.

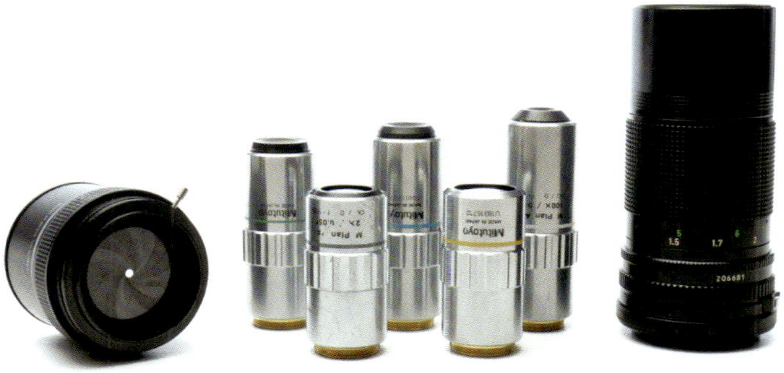

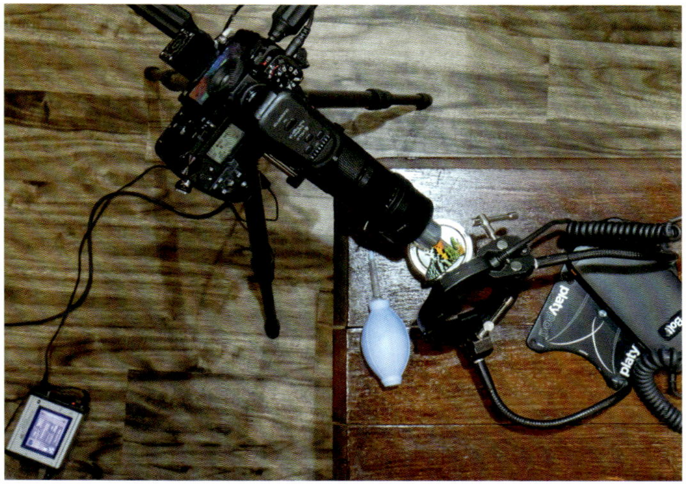

The image on the preceding pages depicts extreme detail in a moth wing. This was shot with a Mitutoyo Plan APO 20x objective (*right*) and the camera setup can be seen in the photograph (*above*). The camera is attached to a Cognisys StackShot automated focusing rail, and lighting is provided by a Yongnuo YN-14EX II ring flash, however it is mounted off camera to achieve a better angle. Ring flashes don't need to be mounted to your lens, in fact, it's completely removed from the camera and wirelessly triggered.

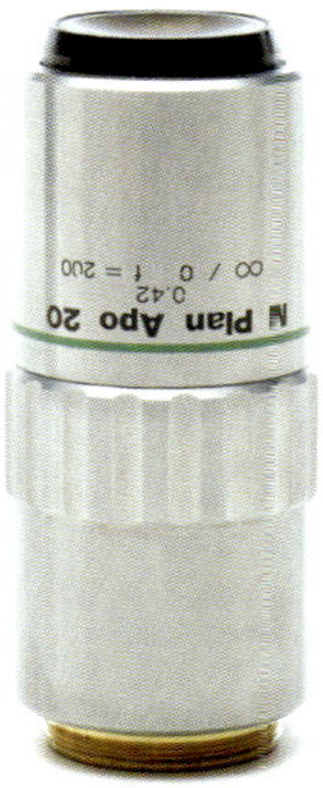

The bulb blower you see is used to clean off the specimen prior to taking the photographs; you'd be surprised how dusty things can get when sitting inside your house, even for a day. The camera took roughly an hour to shoot 991 frames which were later combined together in software to extend the focus.

Focus and Framing

Much like general macro photography, we have challenges related to depth of field. If our depth gets shallower the closer we get to the subject, get ready for some of the shallowest depth of field you can imagine. Hundreds of images might be required to photograph a grain of sand and have it in focus from front to back. This is almost impossible to shoot handheld, though I have applied these techniques to shooting snowflakes with some limited success without a tripod. For nearly all microscope objective work, you'll not only want a tripod but also a focusing rail.

To be precise and to ensure that nothing is missed, an electronically controlled focus rail is ideal, such as the Cognisys StackShot or the Novoflex CASTEL-Micro. This piece of equipment is likely to be even more expensive than the microscope objective you've tracked down, but trust my words: It's incredibly helpful and makes the entire process easier. The StackShot can configure a starting point, and ending point, and the number of frames to shoot.

How many frames should that be? This may surprise some readers, but instead of using depth of field calculators here – where it might be a helpful tool – I just guess. The first few times, I didn't take enough frames and the solution was simple. Examine how much of a gap there was between slices of focus, and adjust the number of frames accordingly. If you overshoot, no harm will come to you – you'll just be wasting memory space and it'll take longer to process the final results.

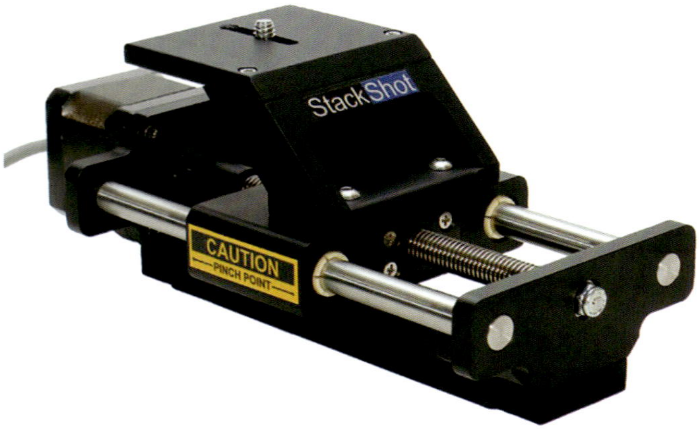

Sometimes just finding the subject in the frame can be the bigger challenge. I will often add a little extra light from an LED flashlight to the subject while trying to find the proper placement in front of the camera. I can find an approximate angle by adjusting the tripod, however all of the fine tuning is done by physically moving the subject forward and back. By shifting the focusing rail to get me closer I can frame and focus very precisely. The smaller the subject, the harder it is to find. **Here's a useful tip:** get a piece of thread and circle it around your subject if it's isolated like a grain of sand. It is very difficult to find your subject without a frame of reference, but if you can find the thread in the frame, you now have a visual reference to where your subject is in relation to it. When you're ready to shoot you can remove it.

Right: A grain of sand that happens to be a faceted garnet from a beach in Oregon - not your average speck of dirt!

Lumix S1R, Mitutoyo 20x objective, 445 separate images stacked.

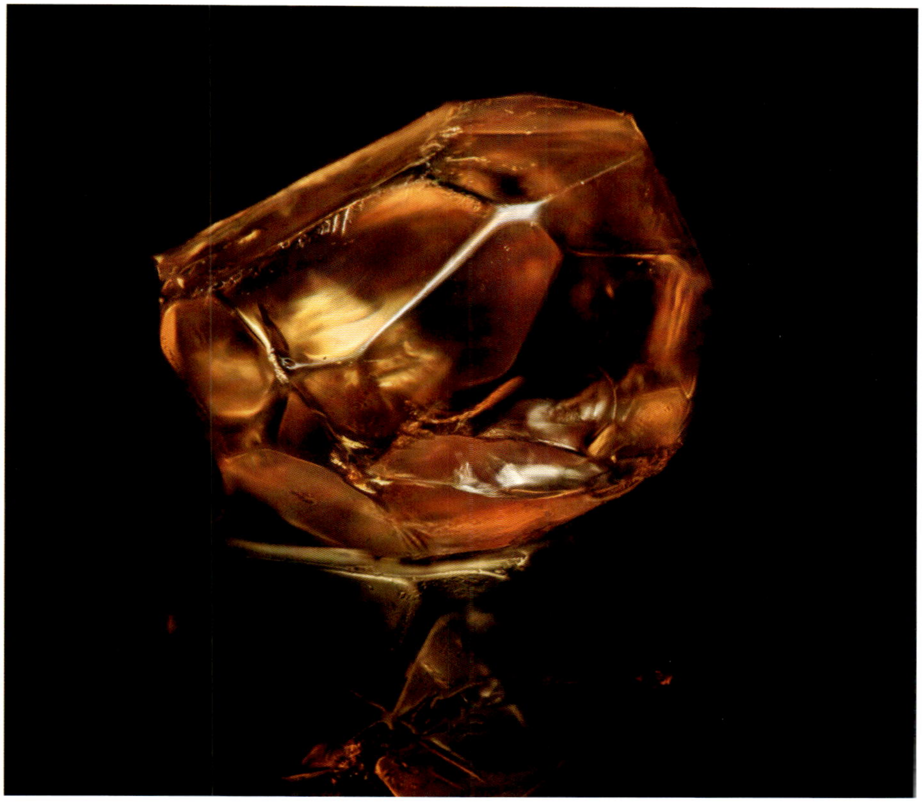

For subjects such as a grain of sand, you have many things to consider. How interesting will it be? This can be a bit of a crap shoot – just like snowflakes, it can be a while before you discover something beautiful. Specific locations might yield better results, though it can be a fun activity in exploring the everyday elements of life around you to see what becomes fascinating under a microscope. Pollen from different flowers all have their own colour, shape, and texture. Seeds from different plants can feel otherworldly, even things you can purchase at the grocery store such as poppy seed.

How you choose to stage and light your subject is also very important. Observe the microscopic garnet on this page (*top right*); It was illuminated on the screen of an old iPhone that was otherwise collecting dust in my office drawer. Many different angles and positions of the ring flash were chosen so as not to have a direct reflection off the gem surface, while still being directional enough to feel as if the light was coming through the mineral itself. Imagine spending hours in your studio, engrossed in the process of properly framing and illuminating a single grain of sand! It was a day well spent, but the process doesn't end with taking the photographs. There is a phenomenal amount of "heavy lifting" still to do, but thankfully your computer will handle the next step – focus stacking.

If you'd like to dive into the numbers and calculate your depth of field based on what microscope objective you're using, here's a primer:
https://www.microscopyu.com/microscopy-basics/depth-of-field-and-depth-of-focus

Focus Stacking at the Extremes

Elsewhere in this book we discuss focus stacking techniques that use Photoshop or ON1 Photo RAW. These tools are exceptional when you have a small number of images, with Photoshop struggling at 100 frames in almost every scenario. Photoshop would outright fail and go cry in a corner if I asked it to focus stack hundreds of images together. Instead, we look towards other tools to handle the focus stacking process for us: Zerene Stacker and Helicon Focus.

Both of these programs are built for the purpose of focus stacking, and they do not load every image into memory simultaneously like Photoshop. They are also pleasantly multithreaded so the work is done quickly. Unfortunately, like Photoshop, the algorithms aren't perfect. This is why each program has multiple ways of interpreting data, it's a good idea to try out the different options on a photograph to see what the best fit is.

Let's use this beautiful moth wing image as an example. This is a single frame from the complete sequence of nearly 1000 images:

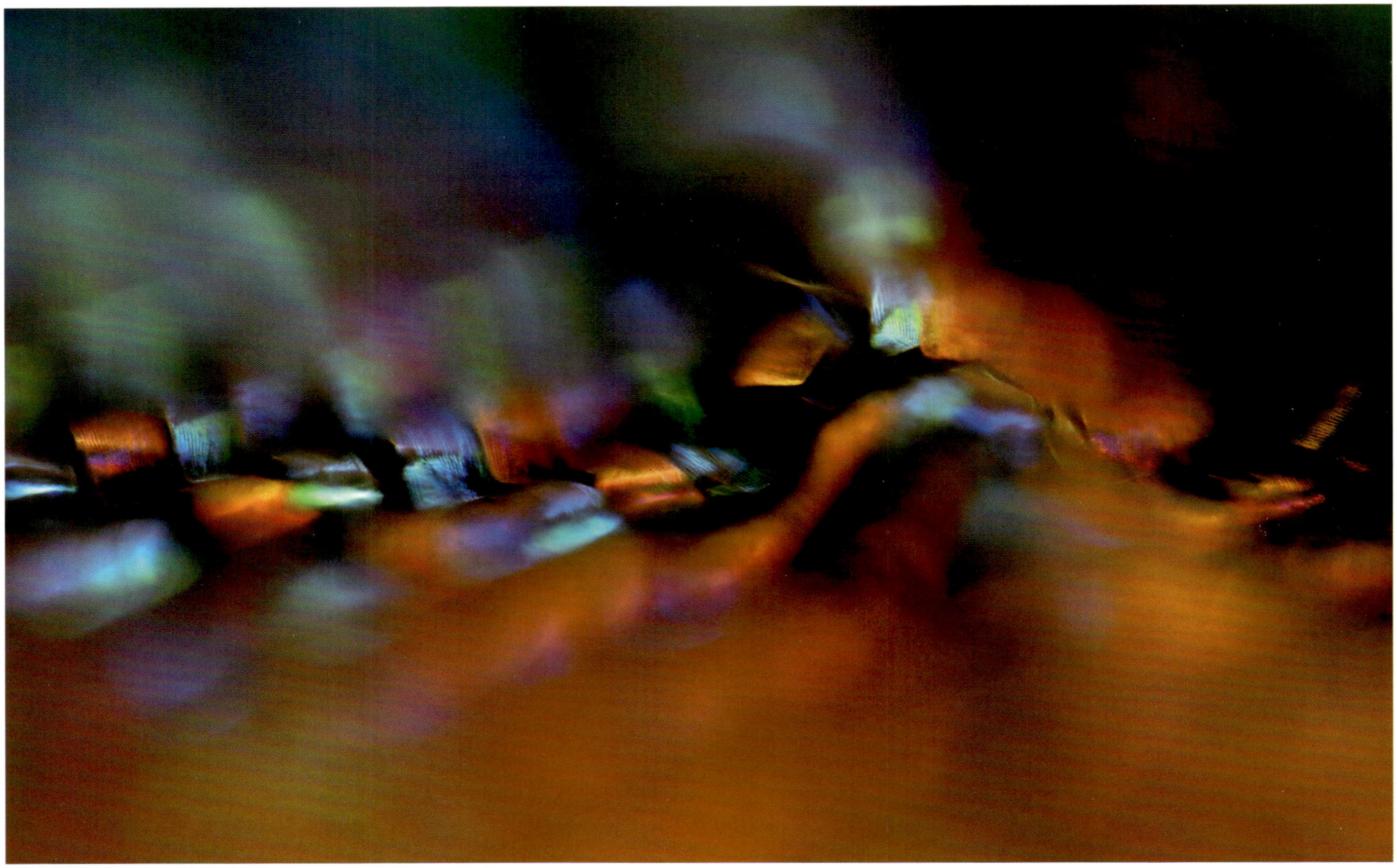

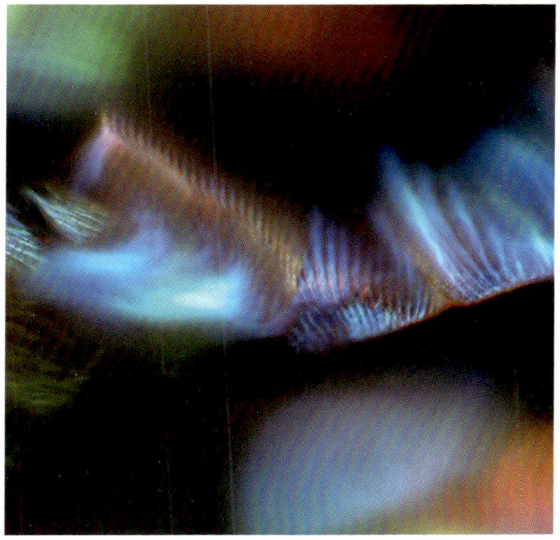

You don't have much to work with! Moreover, the subject inherently has additional challenges. The reflective nature of the scales can cause streaks of colour when they fall out of focus that appear to some algorithms as actual features. The fact that there is a sharp transition in depth at the edge of each scale will also confuse certain stacking technologies. While there may be more difficult subjects to work with, a butterfly or moth wing offers up great examples of how certain methods of focus stacking are simply incompatible with certain subjects. Let's check the results and see which one we would prefer to use!

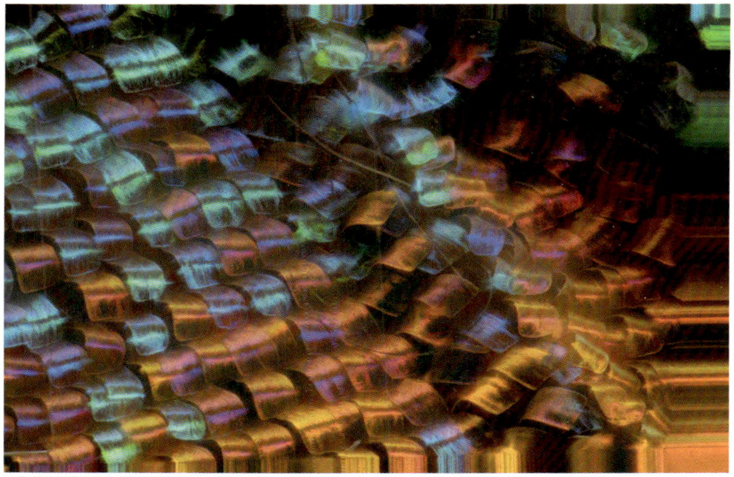

Zerene Stacker PMax
Good results on the edges, except for the coloured flare off the scales which was still included.

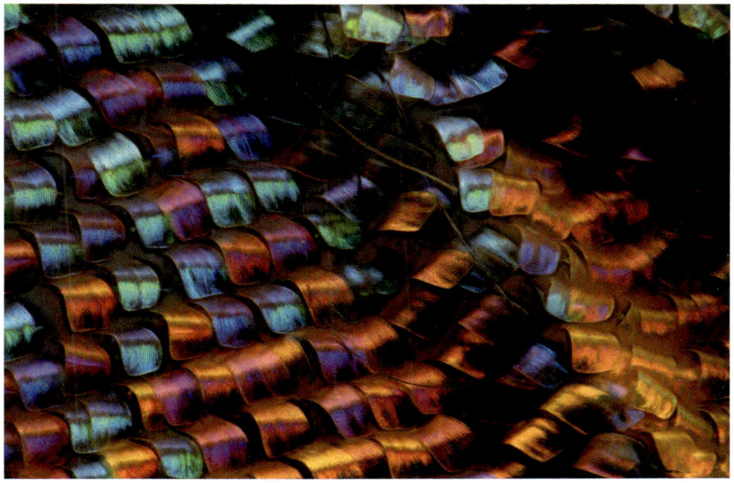

Helicon Focus Method A - Weighted Average
(default settings)
No flare! However, there is a dark halo around all of the scales which would be troublesome to fix.

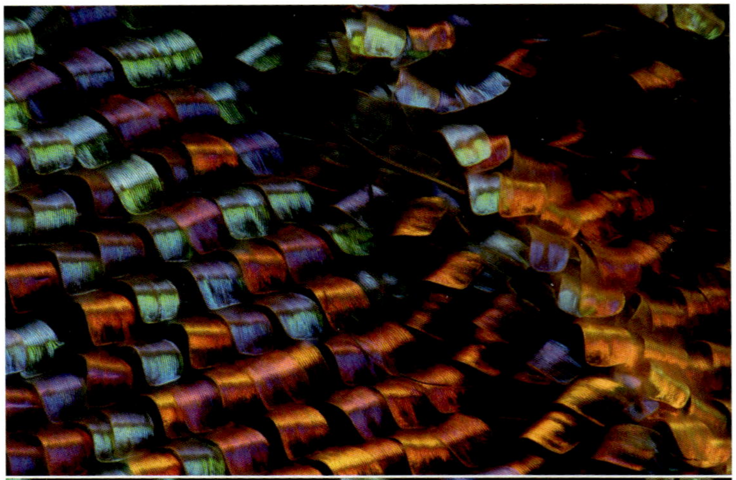

Helicon Focus Method B - Depth Map
(default settings)
Very good! In fact, this one is the best. No flare artifacts and the background / edges are consistent. A great place to start working from.

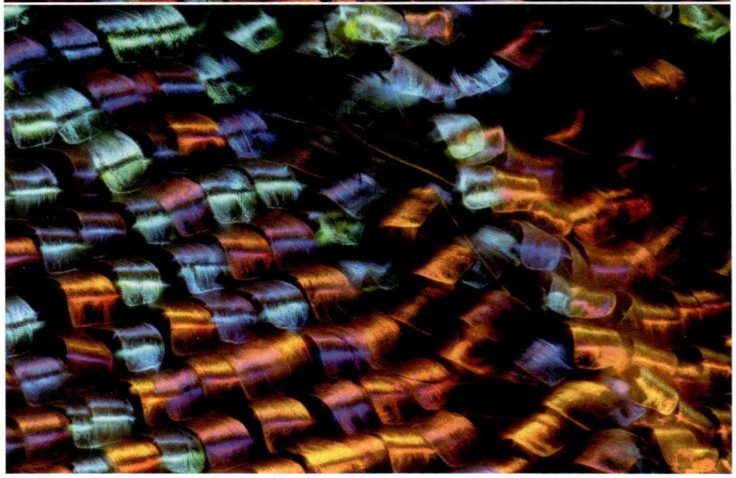

Helicon Focus Method C - Pyramid
(default settings)
Just like Zerene Stacker, this method, which usually works well with large stacks, has offered up coloured flare where there should be none.

These results will not match every subject. I love Zerene Stacker and Method C in Helicon Focus for a lot of work (if I had to pick a favourite, Zerene). But in this case it just didn't give the results that I would like to start editing from. Some of these can take a long time to compute – they were allowed to run overnight and I checked the results in the morning. In the end, Method B from Helicon focus was about as good as it gets right out of the gate. Again, the next time I do a massive focus stack, the right method will likely be something else. There is no perfect way!

While the process starts with the stack, it also needs to be edited, like every image. Cloning out the "hairs" from the moth was tedious and time consuming. Fixing the issues introduced by the stacking process was the same as any other touch-up work I do – removing spots, evening out background tones, just making the whole thing feel seamless. Focus stacking these images can be immediately magical, showing how many tiny slivers of focus build up to a scene that would have been impossible to envision before it all snaps into focus.

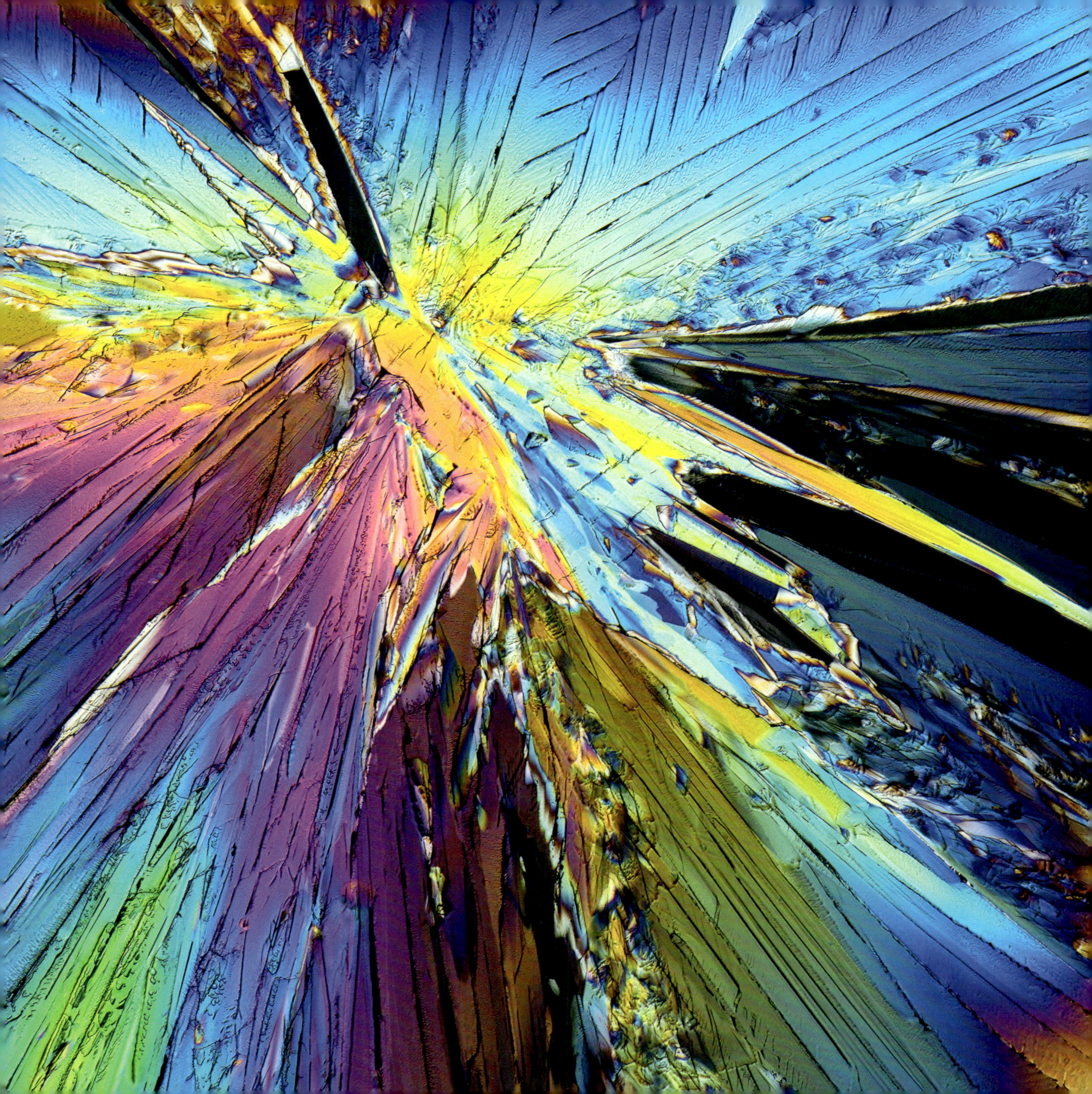

Cross-Polarized Crystals

When I first showed these images to my wife, who is very talented as an abstract oil painter, she was jealous. The patterns and colourful interactions remind me of her work, and here I am with no clue how to hold a paintbrush being able to manufacture similar results in nature. It's easier than you might imagine to create such works of art, but you shouldn't take all the credit: natural physics is the true master of artistry here, we just learn to observe and document it.

The simplest way to get started is to go shopping for a few simple ingredients:

- Distilled Water
- Isopropyl Alcohol
- Microscope Slides
- Pipettes

And the substances to start experimenting with:

- Citric Acid
- Ascorbic Acid (Vitamin C)
- Tartaric Acid
- Methylsulfonylmethane (MSM)

All of these ingredients can be purchased from supplement stores or online in powdered form. **Keep out of reach of children.**

My favourite to start with is citric acid, and the recipe is simple: just add equal parts water and isopropyl alcohol to a small jar, and add citric acid. Keep adding the citric acid until it will no longer dissolve in the solution, which means the water/alcohol mix is holding as much dissolved citric acid as possible.

The exact amount varies based on temperature, so just experiment a little. If you add too much, that's fine; just let the undissolved crystals sink and settle to the bottom. You don't need to make a lot of this mixture, as you'll just need a few milliliters to play with. I always make too much and store it for later uses.

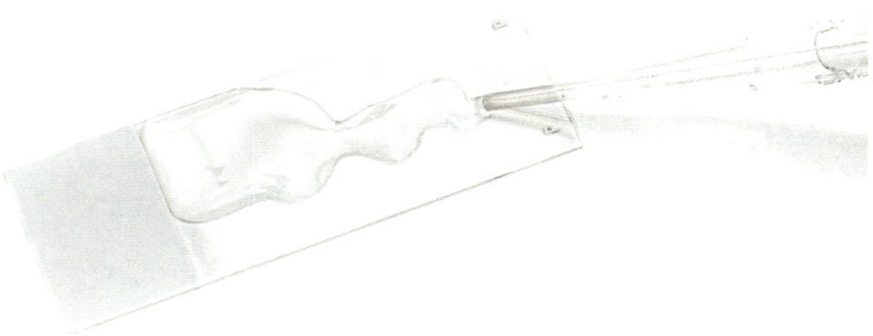

Simply take a pipette, and place the solution on a microscope slide. Then wait. The water and alcohol will evaporate, and when they do the solution will become oversaturated in citric acid, forcing some of the crystals to begin to form. As the solution evaporates, more citric acid will grow into ornate crystals.

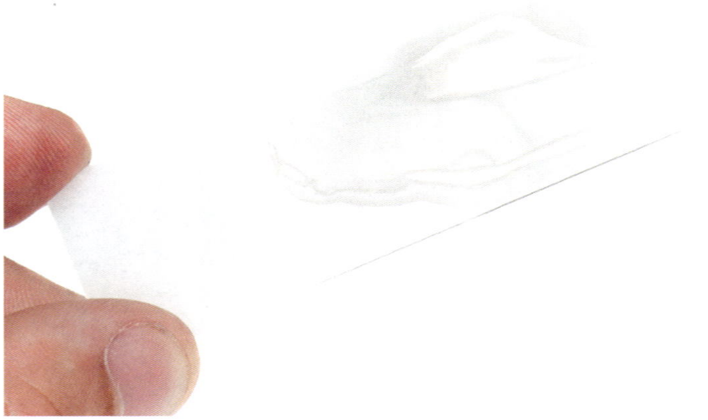

The process can take a few hours. The process can be done with just pure water as well, but the addition of alcohol means it evaporates faster.

Every time you do this, expect different results. If you used tap water, for example, you might see a multitude of nucleation points around the contaminants in the water. This makes the crystal structures harder to see, since there are so many "starting points" and you don't get nice elongated features. Just as every snowflake is different, so too is every microscope slide. Make things easy for yourself; create a dozen at a time before bed and then check them in the morning!

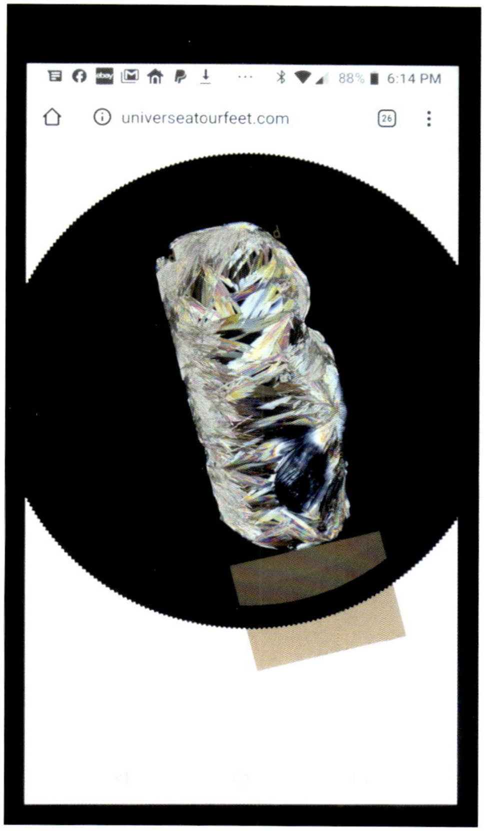

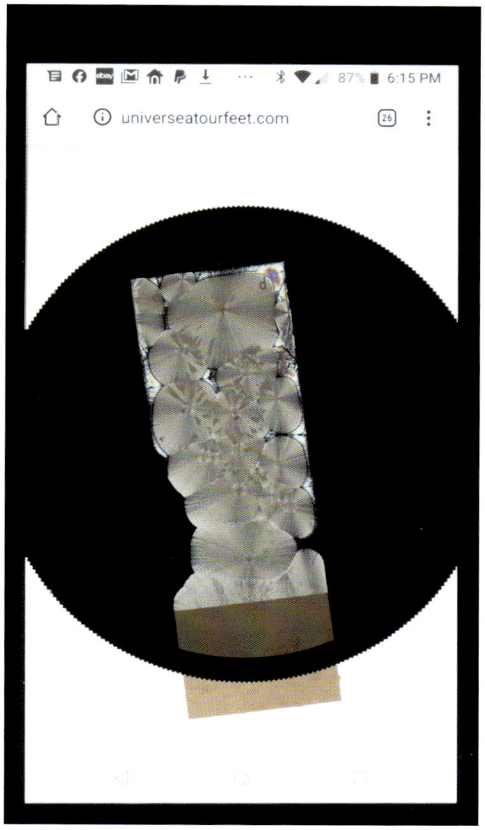

Left: MSM (Methylsulfonylmethane) crystals.
Right: Menthol crystals. These formed too thick to generate interference colours.

We Have Crystals. Now What?

Depending on temperature and humidity levels, it can take between hours and days for your solution to evaporate, providing you with ornate crystal patterns. When dry, take the slide and place it on your phone, displaying white on the screen. Take a polarizing filter and place it on top of the slide. If the phone screen does not turn dark (as seen above), rotate the filter or flip it over. Light will pass through the crystals, hopefully offering you dramatic colours and patterns.

This is a simple experiment in "cross polarization". Your phone screen emits polarized light – every LCD screen does. Imagine a skipping rope, with light going from one handle to the other. It's always heading to the same destination, but the path it takes to get there can be any infinitely variable orientation across 360 degrees. What if light is forced through a tiny slit in only one orientation? It would become "polarized". Bob Mellish did a great job illustrating the concept in this diagram (*right*[1]). If you then put a polarizer in the opposite direction, no light would pass through.

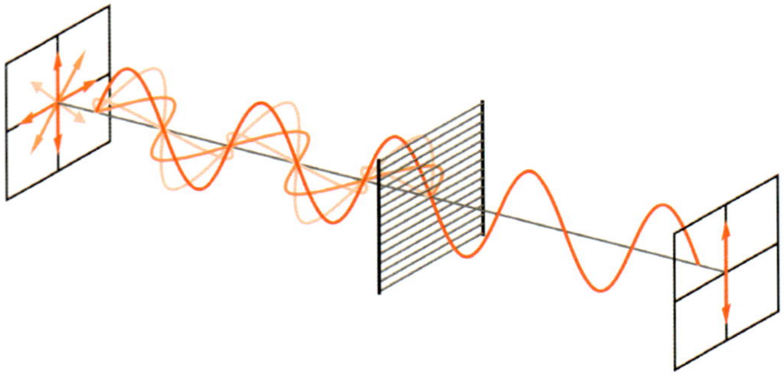

That's what we're seeing with the phone screens with a polarizing filter on top. Without getting into the weeds about the types of polarization, it's important to know that most polarizing filters for cameras are called "circular polarizers" as opposed to "linear polarizers". For this reason, they appear much more effective for this experiment in one direction – hence the possible need to flip the filter over. A quick Internet search can send you down the rabbit hole of polarization techniques and technologies if you're curious to embark on that technical adventure.

So, why does light pass through the crystals? Citric acid creates biaxial anisotropic crystals – those are big words! Fundamentally, when light passes through the crystal, it splits the light into two new (and opposing) polarized orientations that wouldn't match the "blocked" angle by the top filter. This allows some light to sneak through, but there's some fun physics (magic) that happens in the process.

Each pair of polarized light orientations take slightly different paths through the crystal. This means that one will have taken longer than the other to emerge on the other side, pushing them out of sync. When you add in the final polarizing filter, you effectively recombine these separate orientations back into alignment, although out of phase. "Optical interference" then plays its magic trick: some wavelengths of light are amplified, others are diminished through destructive interference. The balance of pure white light is replaced with light favouring certain colours. The colour will change if the crystal has changed thickness or if a neighbouring crystal structure has formed at a different angle. A stained glass effect emerges.

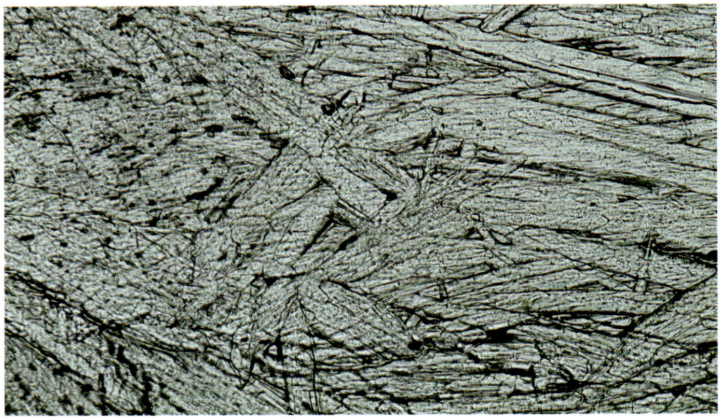

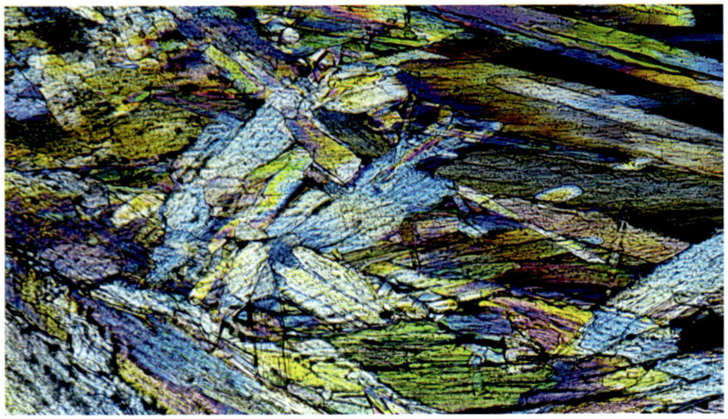

If you spin the polarizing filter, you will change the colours as the ratio of how much light from each of these polarized orientations are allowed to pass through the filter.

Side note: It's this last part, optical interference, that is also responsible for bold colours seen in snowflakes, but through entirely different means.

Photographing Beautiful Physics

These crystals are extremely tiny, so bring your high magnification macro equipment to the table. A Micro Four Thirds camera with a Venus Optics Laowa 25mm F/2.8 2x-5x macro lens would yield the same equivalent magnification of 10x on a full-frame camera. Anywhere from 5x through 20x magnification would be worthwhile to explore this subject. You do not need a dedicated microscope objective and expensive polarizing microscope, you've effectively made one out of your phone.

Tripods are essential to acceptable results at these magnifications, allowing you to focus on finding the best part of the subject by sliding it around in front of the lens. Ideally, a focusing rail will help you achieve focus, since no lenses capable of these magnifications have focusing abilities. Position the tripod such that the camera is pointed directly down at the phone screen and focus with the rail. If the slide isn't completely parallel to the focal plane of the camera, you might need to combine a few frames with focus stacking techniques. Your subject is mostly two dimensional.

Top Right: Tartaric Acid crystals at 50x magnification.

Facing Page: MSM (Methylsulfonylmethane) crystals, as seen without a polarizing filter (*top*) and with one (*bottom*)

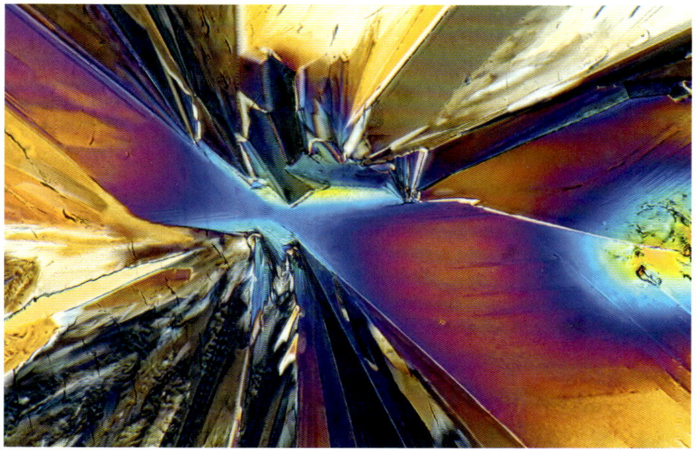

Your shutter speed will vary based on the brightness of the screen and amount of magnification, but to ensure best results, consider the following camera settings:

- Remote shutter release or timer. This prevents any motion blur that would be introduced from pressing the shutter button.
- Electronic shutter. Many cameras have the option to use an electronic or a mechanical shutter. Even on mirrorless cameras, the physical movement of a mechanical shutter can introduce motion blur at very high magnifications.
- Low ISO. With everything locked down, it shouldn't matter how long your exposure is. Go for the highest quality results.

What if you have a second polarizing filter and a flashlight? While not required, what if you have the ability to shoot with microscope objectives? The setup becomes a little more complicated, but it's all the same pieces coming together.

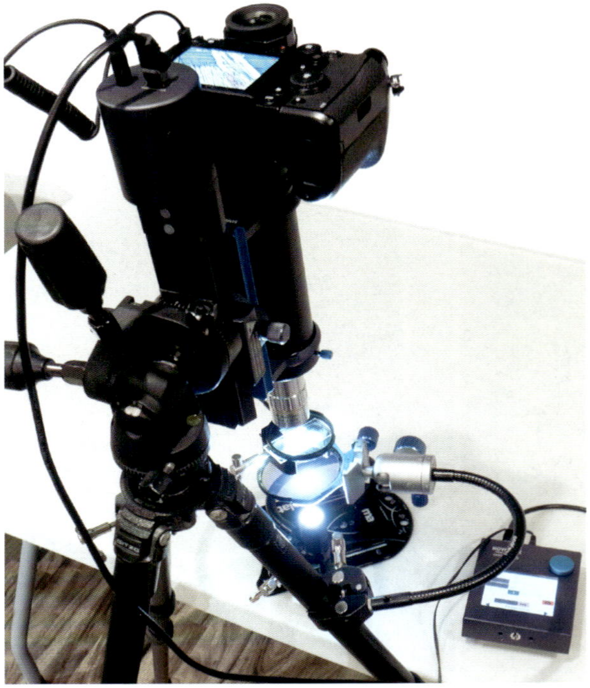

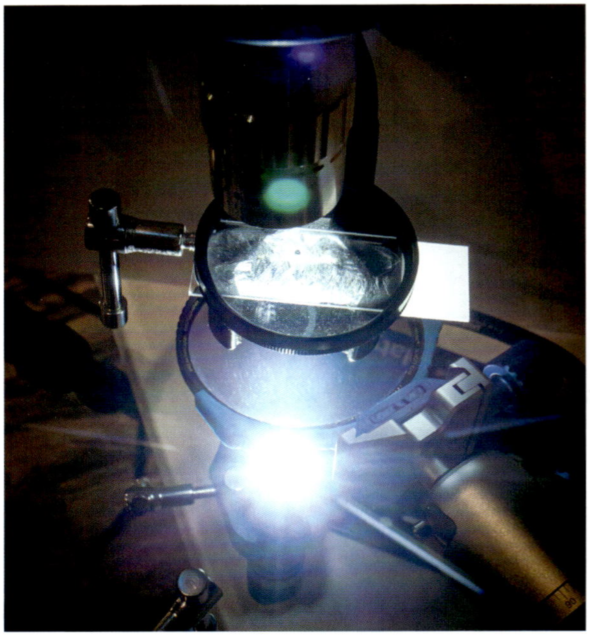

In principle, you are seeing the same setup. We have a light source (LED flashlight) that becomes polarized with a circular polarizing filter. Note that the filter is positioned such that if it were to be on a lens, the lens would be where the flashlight is. Above the light source is a crab clamp that is acting as a platform to hold the microscope slide with another polarizing filter resting on top. Finally, the camera is positioned above, looking down through the light.

Does this all line up perfectly? No. I've always had to focus stack a few frames together. Could I have made this more robust? Absolutely. This is effectively a cobbled together polarizing microscope from stuff I had lying around my studio. And it works! See what you can put together at home.

Important Lesson Learned:
Heat damages polarizing film, including the film used to manufacture polarizing filters. My first setup was simpler, with the filter resting directly on the flashlight. Bad idea. I didn't think this would reach damaging heat levels, but the proof is easy to see in the filter. **Do not place a circular polarizing filter on top of a flashlight for any length of time, or expect this:**

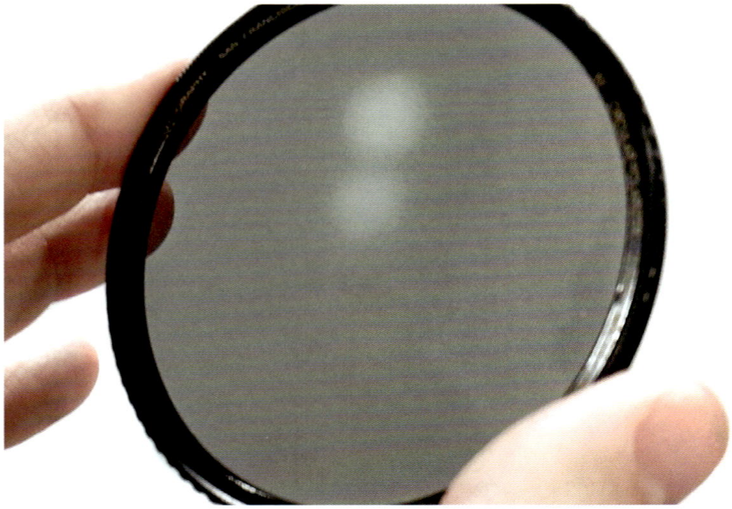

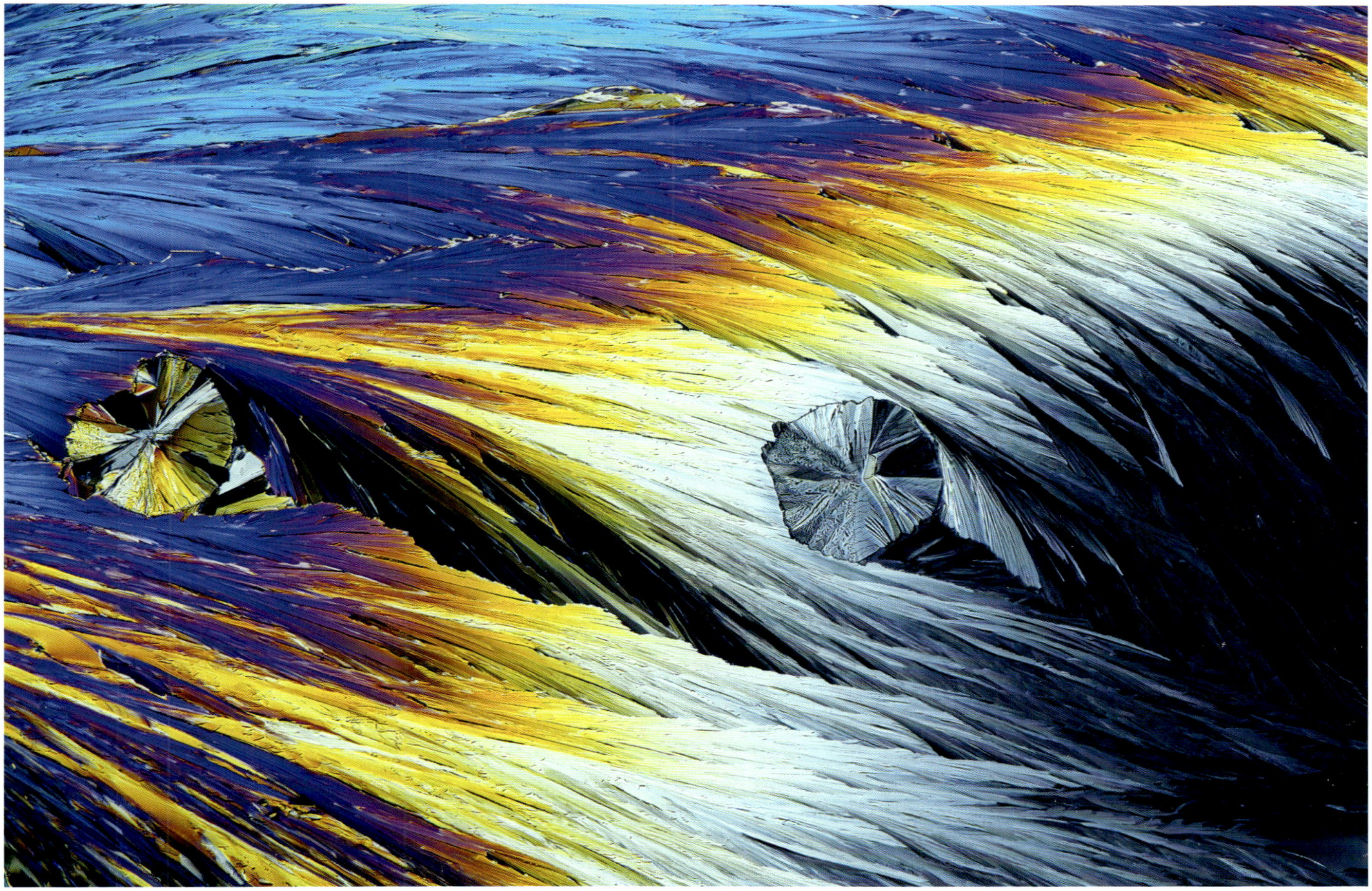

This photo (*above*) was taken with this configuration. These are citric acid crystals, which yield a wonderful variety of colours and sweeping structures. Using a 10x microscope objective to achieve the level of detail, once you have everything set up, the photographic element becomes the easiest part.

Finding something "beautiful" among the complex lines and shapes takes over as a priority when the technical elements become akin to muscle memory. You have an unending array of lines, shapes and colours to choose from. What stays in the frame, what's excluded, and even how the final result is cropped can be time consuming. Hours might disappear as you continue with this exploration for compositions on freshly-crystalized slides. It certainly isn't time wasted, as I find myself constantly enamoured with my discoveries. Even if something isn't worthy of a photograph, dare I say it's entertaining to follow the lines around to see how these puzzle pieces all fit together. Finally settling on a composition, a quick twist of the polarizing filter can change the colours and get exactly what you're after.

Luck is a huge component of this type of photography. Don't expect to do one experiment and be happy with the result. All of the ingredients are inexpensive, so make more attempts at a time and see how they play out. Change the variables among the slides – more or less liquid, maybe allow some to dry faster by placing them in the oven? Use just plain water, or research what liquids a particular substance is soluble in.

The image (*below*) is also citric acid from the same experimental batch as the one on the previous page. How about this one (*facing page*)? Citric Acid. Same batch, different slide. The variations are endless.

What will you discover? Probably significant initial frustrations based on getting good crystals.

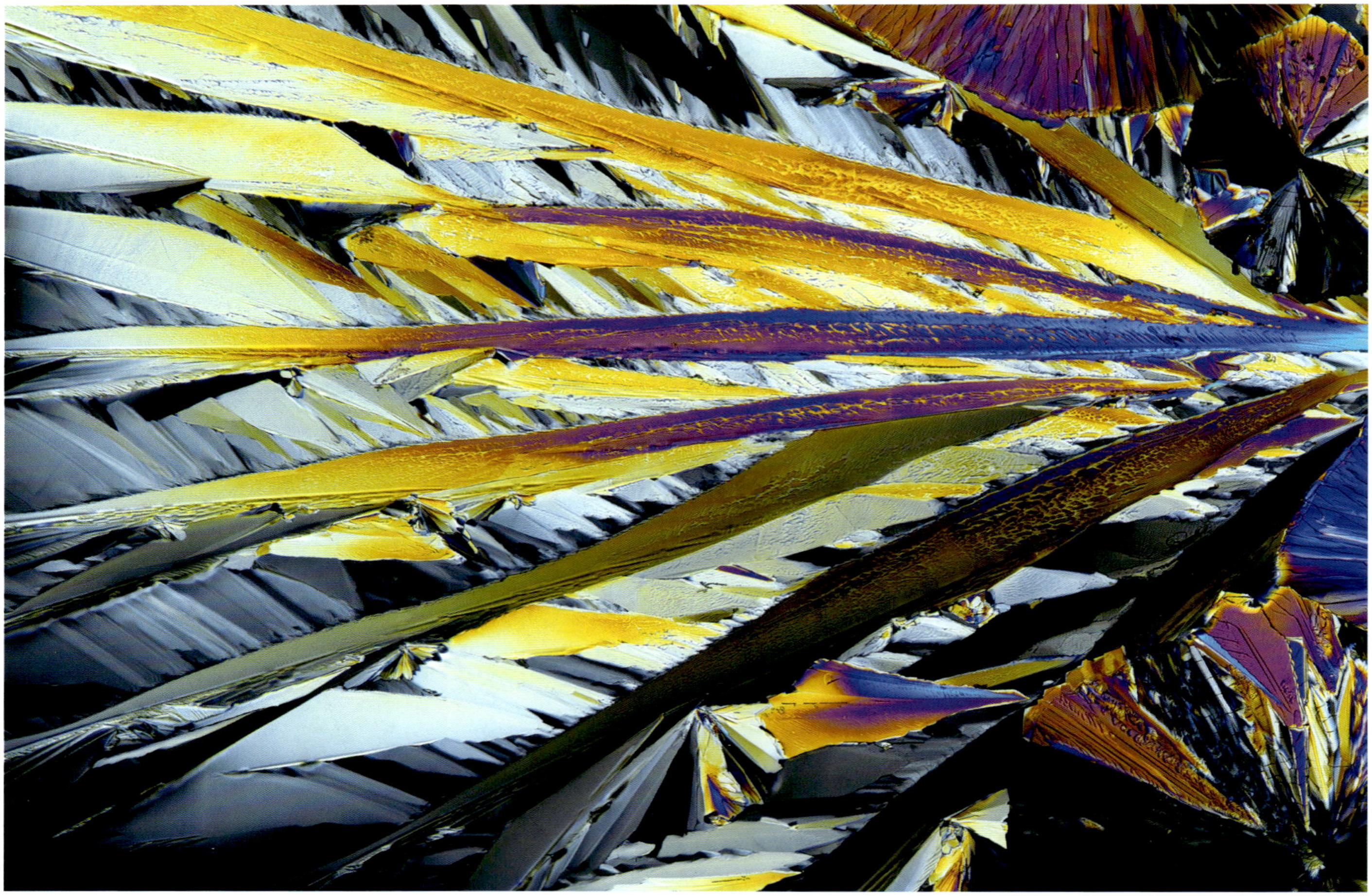

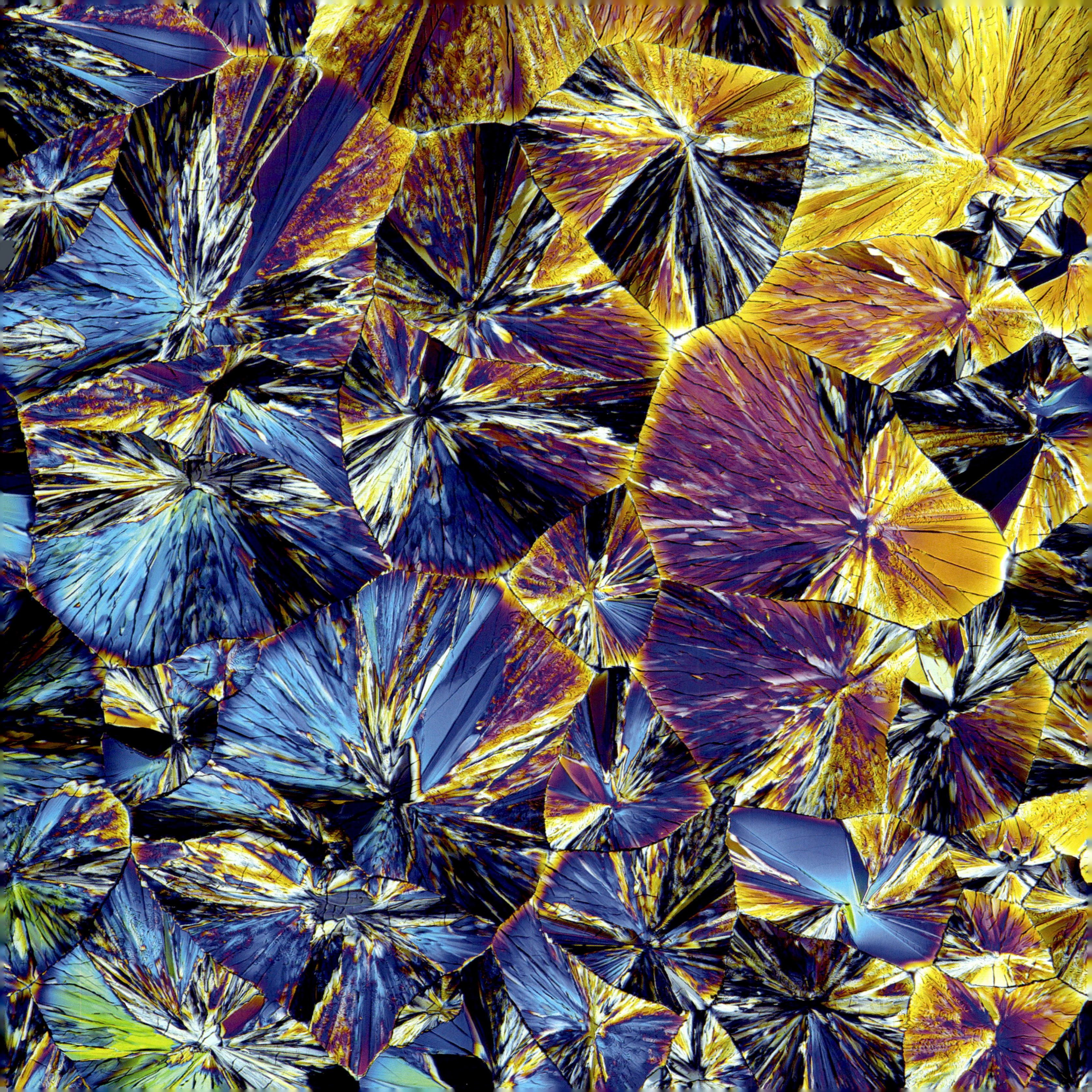

What can go wrong? Plenty! One of the biggest hurdles is getting crystals to form to your liking. If they form too thickly, then you will not see the optical interference "magic trick" that generates the beautiful colours you are seeking. You'll want the crystals to be deposited in a very thin layer, and this can simply take practice.

Top: Menthol crystals growing too thick, too cluttered and no prominent colours.

Bottom: Menthol crystals forming a thin layer.

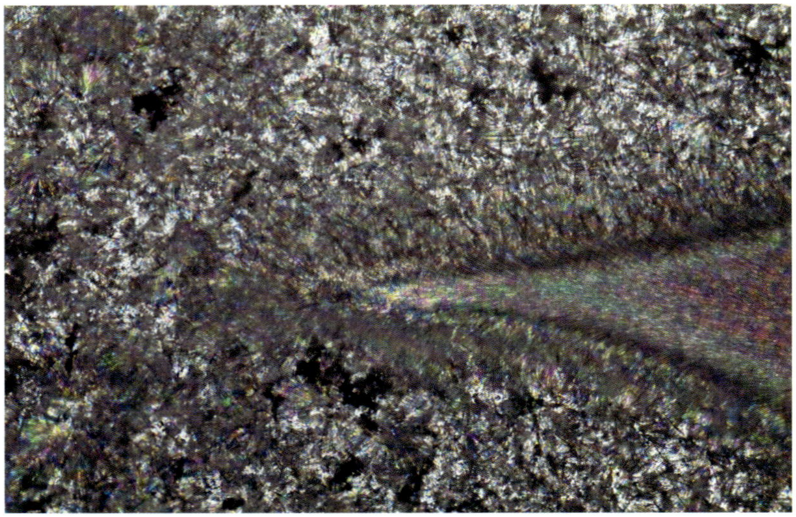

While not the most beautiful resulting crystals, there are few very easy experiments to dial this in with menthol crystals. Menthol has a melting point of around 40C / 104F, and you can directly melt it onto a microscope slide. Do this in a well ventilated area – I have a portable hot plate that I plug in outside. Once it has melted, move it with a pair of pliers away from the heat and onto a cool surface. Crystals will form in ten minutes. You'll easily be able to gauge whether or not you've used too much – you'll see crystals, but no interesting colours.

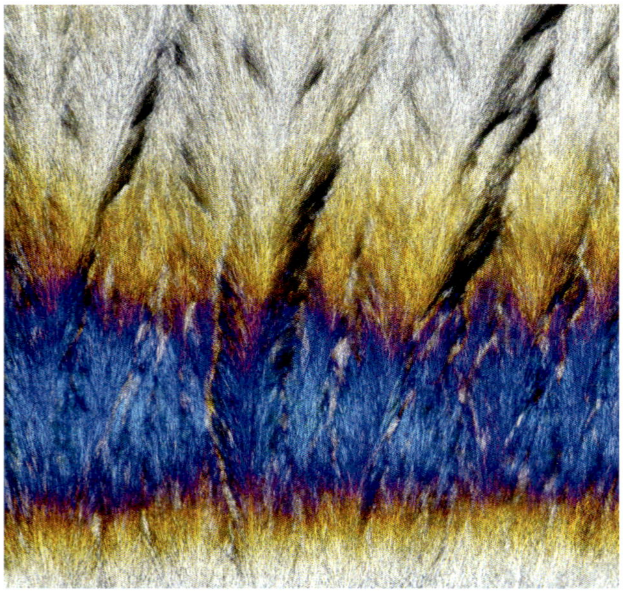

This method should be approached with extreme caution with other materials. Many acids and other compounds will melt, but many have a "decomposition" point at or near their melting point, meaning they break down into other chemicals, some of which could be very harmful. Unless you have a firm understanding of the chemistry you'll be faced with, don't proceed any further down this path.

Some crystals on their own do not yield interesting results, but can be coloured using a "quartz compensator" which generates a rainbow-like band of colours through its own cross-polarization effect that can add colour to your crystals. These devices are not cheap, and I prefer to use the crystal itself as the source of the colours. You can also experiment with a plastic CD case as an alternative colour source without any significant expense. Cheap clear plastics (clear tape also works) offer up a rainbow of colour. Experiment!

There are plenty of ways to take this farther and continue to experiment. Many amino acids and vitamins produce interesting patterns. Sulfamic acid, used to clean grout haze from tiles, produces elongated hexagonal crystals. Simple sugar works as well.

This image (*lower right*) might appear as an oceanic depth map of sorts, but it is crystallized Beta Alanine, an amino acid. The process was the same as the citric acid, but using just water as the liquid for the solution.

This type of photography is not new. Artful scientists have been exploring these beautiful patterns for many decades. Because of the science involved, it might not be on the radar of most macro photographers that discover beauty in nature. The more you know about how this works, the better off you will be to create interesting images using this technique. Much of this knowledge comes from experimenting, and then researching why you didn't get the expected results.

One final tip: If you heat your water, most substances will be dissolve better in it. If you mix your solution to this maximum saturation level at a higher temperature, the crystals will begin to form not only as the liquid evaporates, but also as it cools. This might yield crystals too thick to display colours, or it may allow for some substances to reach a point where interesting crystals can form. **As always, do your research! Be armed with the knowledge of what dangers may be present. Plenty of materials are completely safe to work with, but please ensure you are aware of any potential risks.**

Enjoy the process. Embrace the "what if?" mentality. What if you mix different ingredients together on one slide? What if you use a piece of picture frame glass for a larger surface area to explore? Keep asking questions and stay curious.

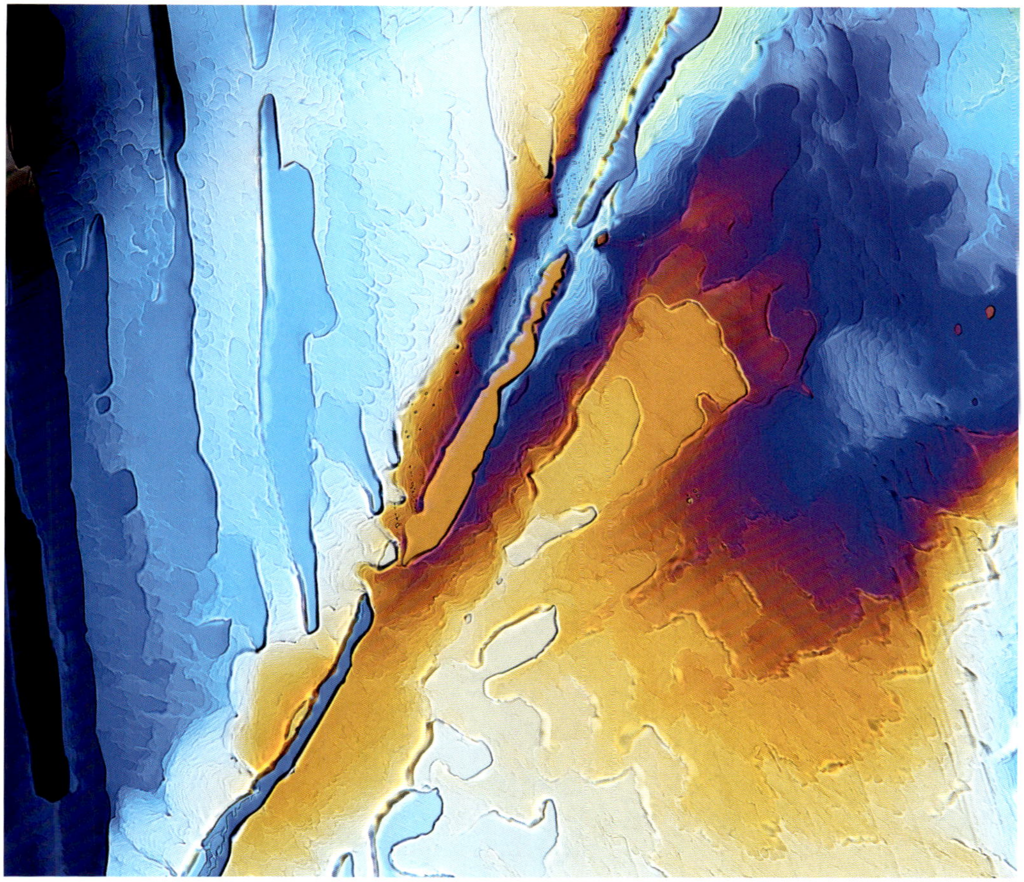

Micrometeorites

Not every grain of sand is the same. Research[1] suggests that between 10,000 and 20,000 tons of micrometeorites fall to Earth each year, though their diminutive size leaves almost no trace of their existence. How do you spot one of these specks of space dust? Just ask Scott Peterson, who graciously loaned me the specimens photographed in this section of the book.

Peterson began his journey of discovery by dragging a magnet through his storm gutters – something anyone with storm gutters can do, and I have no excuse for not attempting this in my own eavestroughs. Many micrometeorites are magnetic, and they can potentially be found with very strong neodymium magnets. You'd be going through significant debris and clutter to find one at home, however. Particles from shingles and decaying leaves will make a mess of your efforts, but it's still possible.

For better results, why not gain access to the flat vinyl roof of a shopping mall? This bit of advice came from fellow micrometeorite hunter Jon Larsen, who has published a number of books on the subject. Find the water drain on the roof and collect some of the sediment from that area, and start searching.

These microscopic "gems" actually originate as tiny (albeit larger than their final form) meteoroids in space, not broken-off pieces of larger rocks that burn up in the atmosphere. Peterson does a great job at describing this: "The size is based on what Mother Nature will allow. If too small then they will burn up, if too "large" they will burn up. So the average size is .2-.4mm. Although there are smaller and larger ones".

This micrometeorite (*below* and *facing page*) is composed of a magnesium-rich variant of olivine, with a much more common name: Peridot. You may be familiar with the green gem as the birthstone for the month of August or just a fancy transparent green cut gemstone. How do you photograph such an exquisitely small crystal ball?

Lighting is a big challenge. Initial attempts (*below*) yielded the crystal structure but failed to showcase the translucency of this specimen. Imagine trying to shape light around a subject that measures only a quarter of a millimeter in diameter. Various techniques were used, but it finally came down to something very simple: the plastic cap from a water bottle.

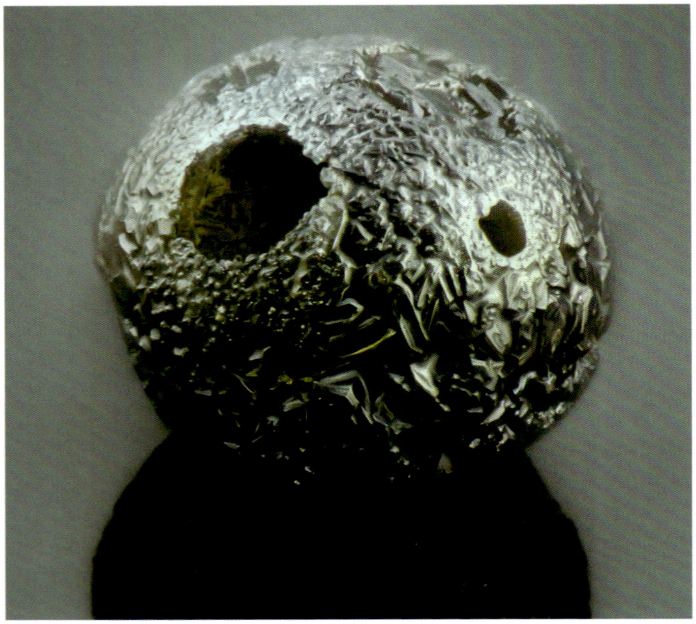

[1]Snelling, A. A., & Rush, D. E. (1993). Moon Dust and the Age of the Solar System. *Creation Ex-Nihilo Technical Journal*, 7(1), 2–42.

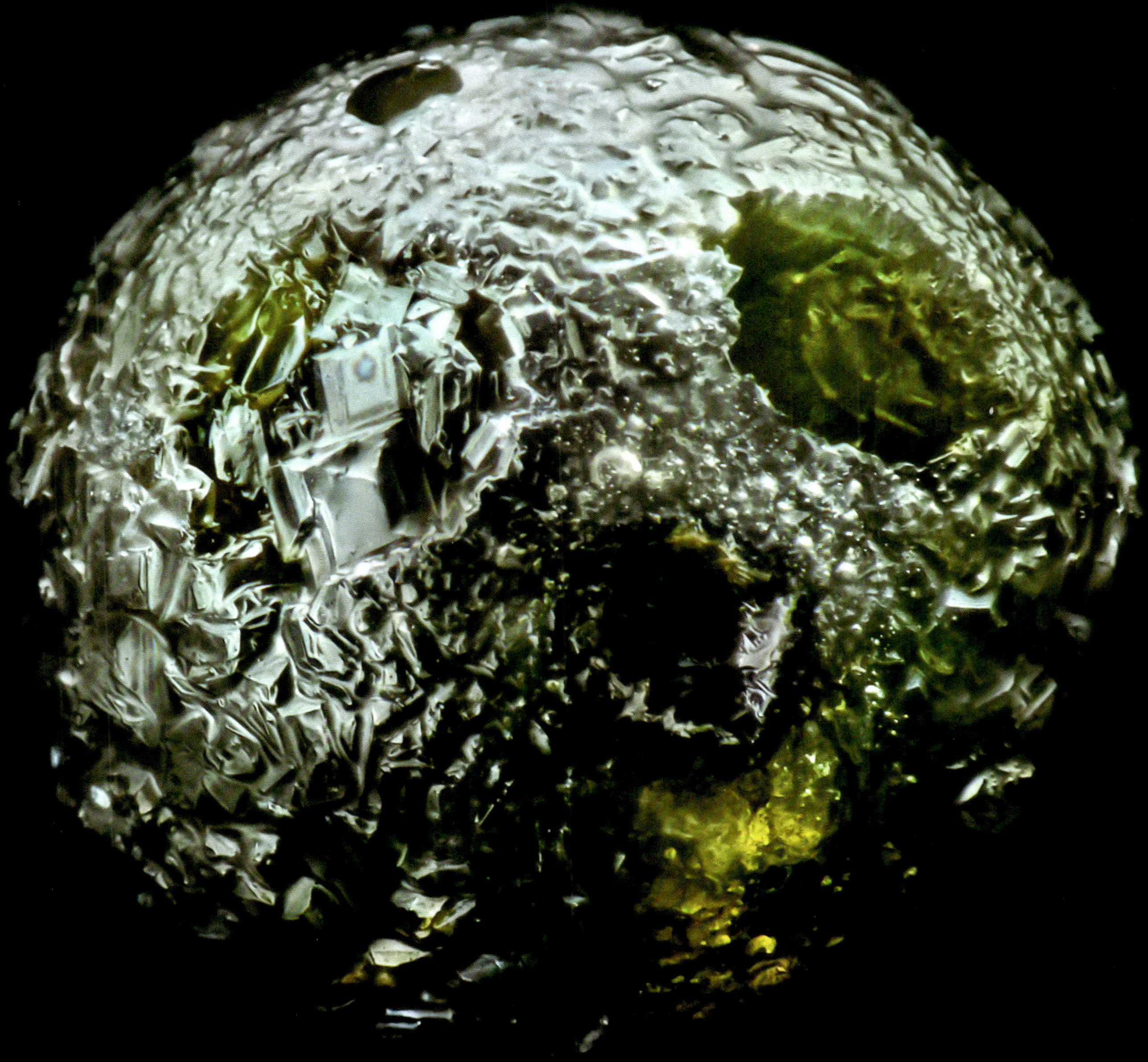

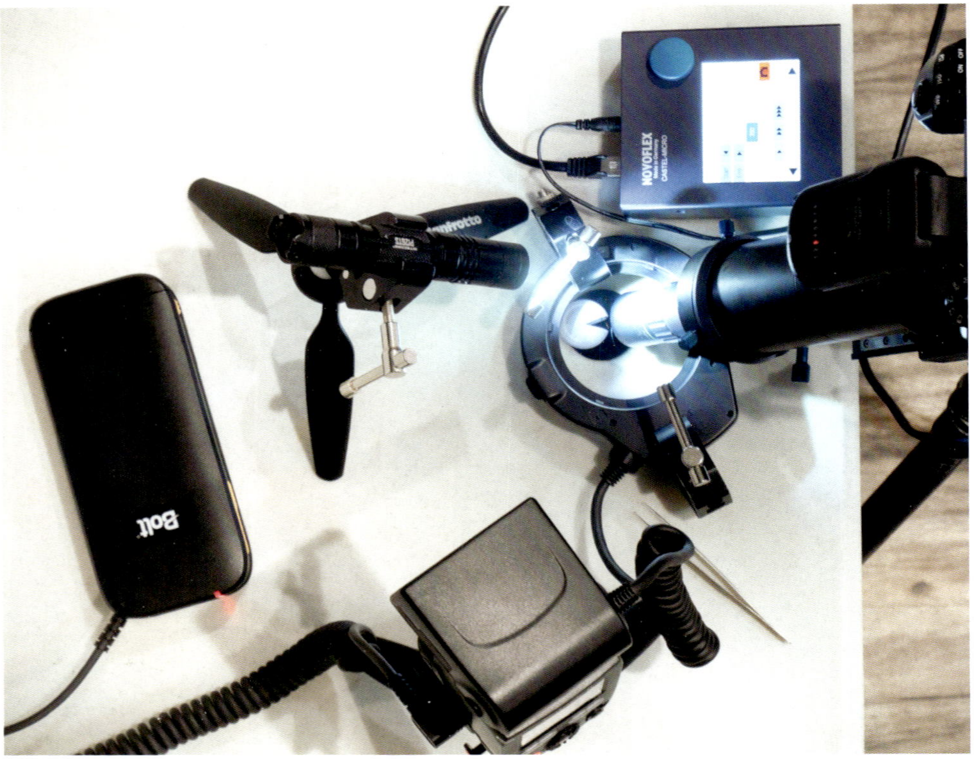

This "behind the scenes" image (*right*) illustrates how everything was assembled for photography. A 50x Mitutoyo Plan APO microscope objective pointed at an invisible speck. That speck is placed on a black glass-like filter and shrouded by the aforementioned plastic bottle cap. There is a wedge shape cut out so that the lens can see the micrometeorite clearly, but the rest of the cap functions as a diffuser for the ring flash surrounding it.

The ring flash, a Yongnuo YN-14EX II, is controlled by a wireless trigger so that there is no tension on the cord leading to the flash ring. Exceptional care is needed to be taken to prevent something from toppling over and sending the micrometeorite flying, never to be seen again. The ring itself is raised above the table by simple means: attaching two crab clamps on opposite ends to function as little "legs" that the flash balances on. It can be rocked forward or back to change the angle of light, and freely rotated around the subject to change all the light angles.

The smallest movements make a big difference. Rotating the ring by a few degrees, tilting it slightly or repositioning it above the subject can all impact how the light hits the subject. The flashlight in this scenario serves no purpose to the final image; it's used as a focusing and framing aid.

These images are also heavily focus stacked. The Peridot meteorite (*previous page*) consists of 428 separate frames. The use of an automated electronic focusing rail is a must for this type of work, and the Novoflex CASTEL-MICRO has been the most accurate system for properly calibrated start and stop points with very minimal frame shifts. Such equipment is not inexpensive – be prepared for an investment.

This is also the perfect subject to help us define the difference between magnification and resolution, as discussed at the beginning of this chapter. The same micrometeorite, although framed at a slightly different angle, has been photographed with both a 20x and a 50x microscope objective (*facing page*). The 20x

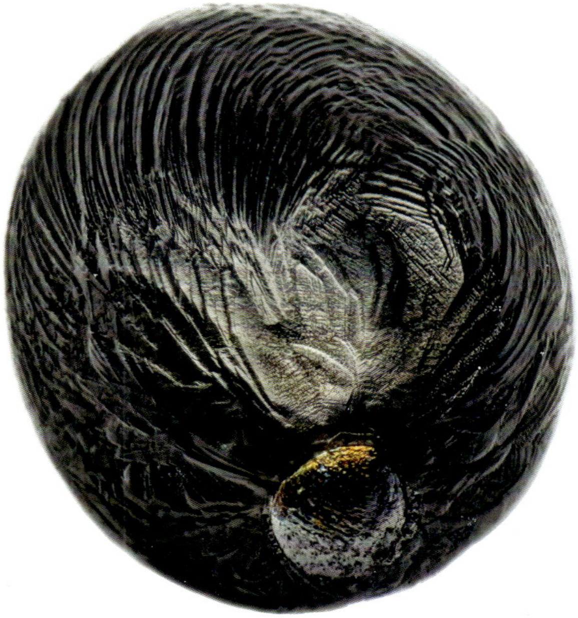

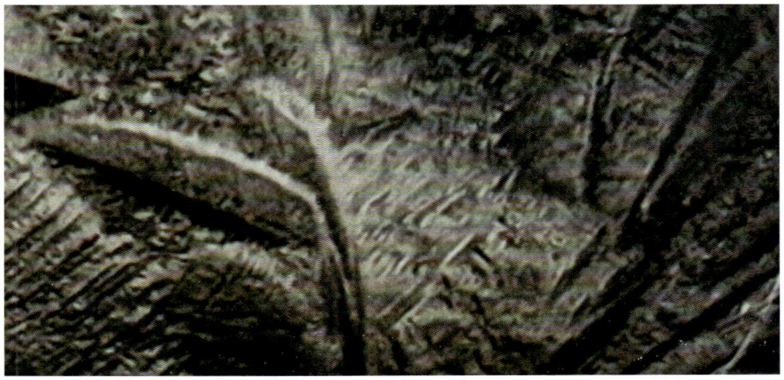

Top: Micrometeorite close details with a 20x objective.

Bottom: The same micrometeorite section with a 50x objective. Slight improvement in resolution on the smallest features.

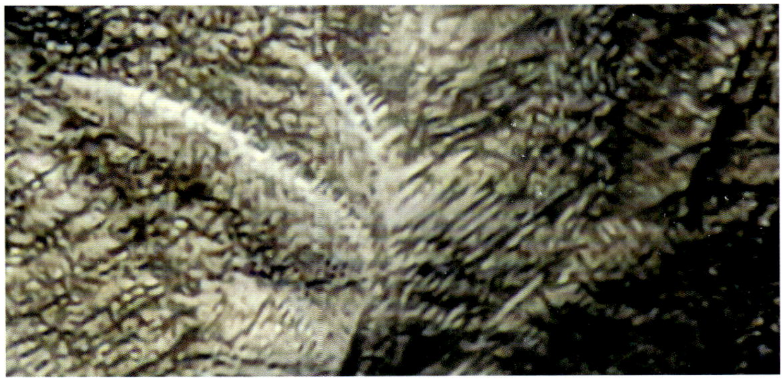

objective has a resolving ability down to 0.7µm (also called micrometers or microns), whereas the 50x objective can resolve down to slightly smaller details of 0.5µm. A significant bump in magnification yields a much less substantial increase in resolution.

To that end, we're reaching the limits of what you can do with optical imaging. A microscope objective with a shorter working distance could increase the resolution, but your options for reflected light photography become more limited the closer you get. We could debate the effectiveness of confocal laser scanning microscopy, but that equipment is simply not suited to this type of work. The 100x microscope objective in the same series of optics has a resolving power that matches the 50x objective: 0.5µm. You would double your magnification but gain no further subject details in the process.

To push beyond these limitations of light, we need to stop using it. If you switch your method of recording an image from "photography" in the strictest sense, we can swap out photos for electrons. Scanning Electron Microscopy (SEM) takes over where conventional imaging reaches fundamental limitations.

I'll be honest: I suspect that almost no one reading this book has access to SEM equipment. Those familiar with the technology will immediately tell me that these images aren't great, as the specimens have not been properly coated for SEM imaging. They were not my specimens, so I took no risks in the preparation of these images. While some might consider the visible charge on the surface of the crystals a defect, I consider it an attractive visual element. The charge is seen as the bright "overexposed" edges.

These images are included to show you how far down the rabbit hole you can go. There is no colour information here, as colour is the result of wavelengths

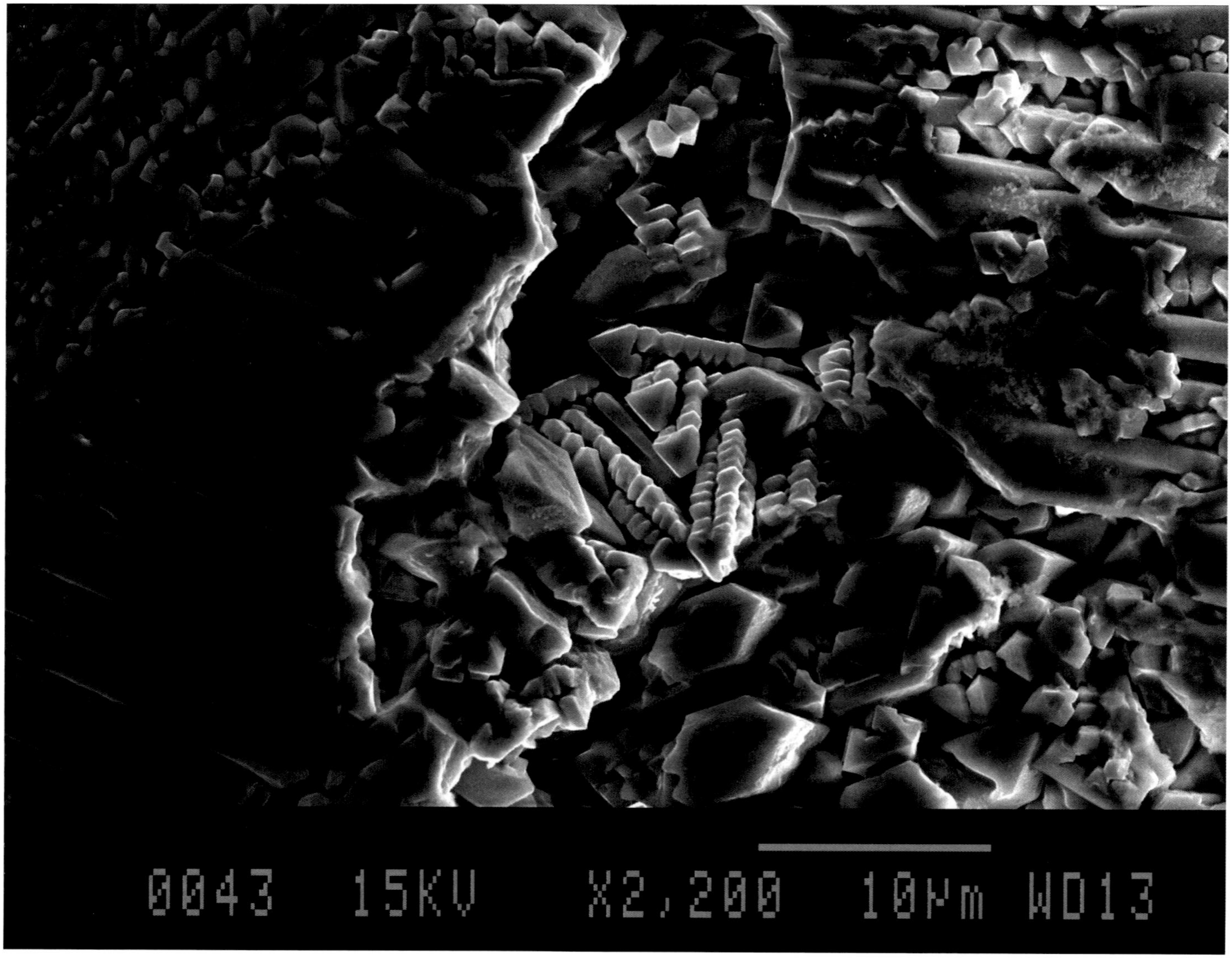

of light. If you've ever seen a colour SEM image, give praise to the person who painstakingly added colour to the image by hand, like colourizing an antique black and white photograph.

Light has limitations – one can only get so close to a subject before the details cannot be resolved any further. High magnification macro photography (microscopy) ends where electron microscopy begins. I once thought myself clever when I realized that I could beat the limits of light with focus stacking, extending my depth of field well beyond what standard optics would allow. When you push even further however, there is no overcoming the inevitable. Diffraction and the wavelength of light itself play a role in this.

0.5μm is the same as 500nm. The wavelengths of visible light run between 400nm and 700nm. Resolving details beyond the wavelength of light itself is possible in some extreme situations, but the closer you get, the more challenging it becomes.

While there is a technical limit on details, that doesn't mean that we have met our creative limits with these subjects. How can we push our creative limits to the extremes? How do we showcase the beauty and the scale of these tiny bits of the cosmos? Read on.

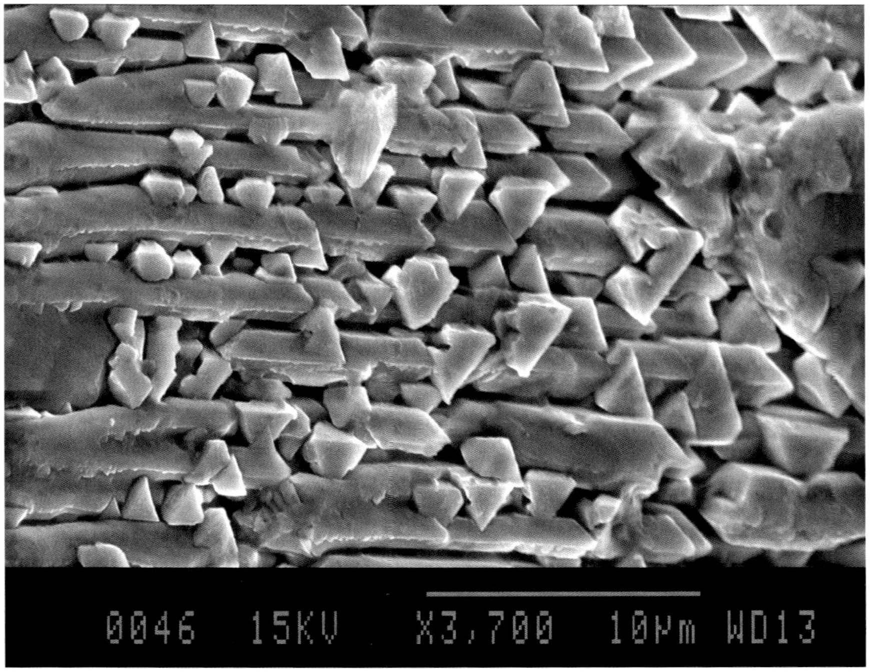

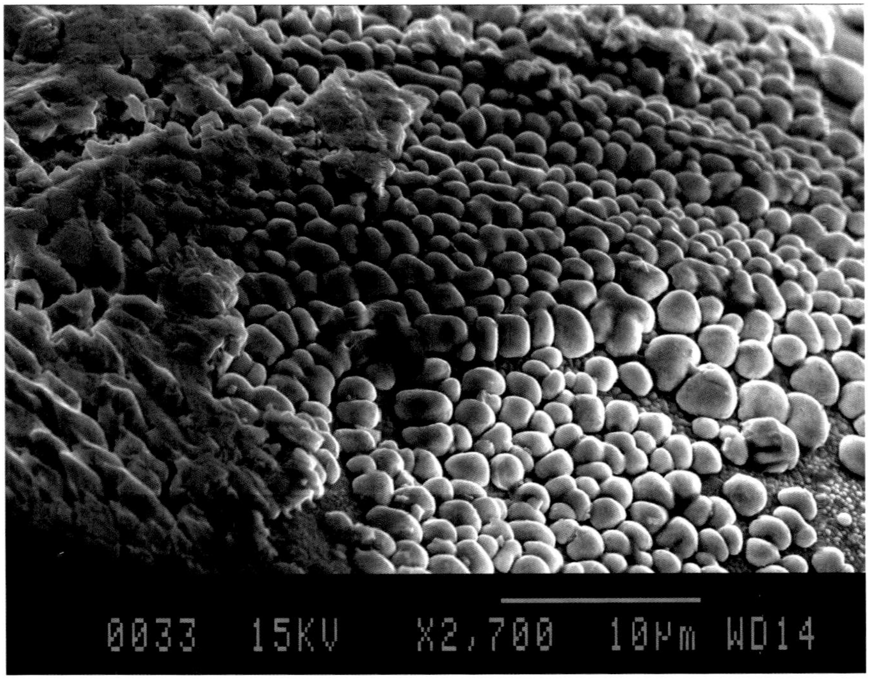

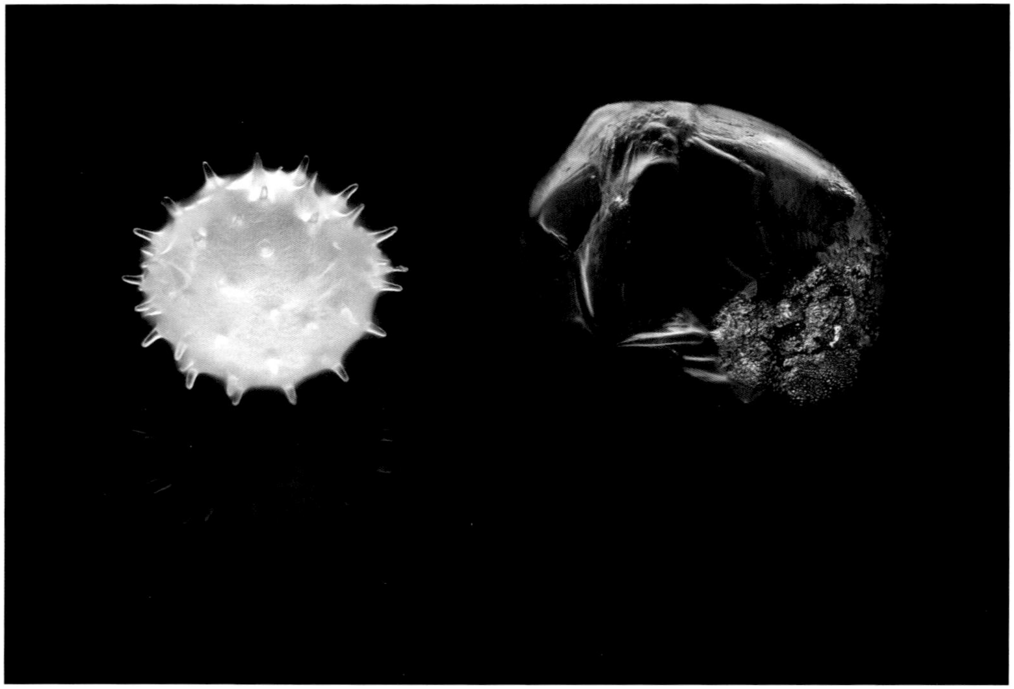

The challenge here is scale. There aren't many interesting compositions to make other than simply documenting the subject. Part of that narrative can be precisely this scale: what can it compare to? The pollen of a Rose of Sharon (*Hibiscus syriacus*) bush makes an appropriate comparison (*right*), as we might have a visualization of how small these tiny bundles of genetic information can be.

Most hibiscus flowers have large, round, spiky pollen that is reminiscent of a much smaller object: a coronavirus. Thankfully they are far less harmful than their viral doppelganger. Placing the two objects on a black glass filter was probably the hardest part here – the pollen wants to stick to things and can be difficult to isolate. Coupled with the fear of accidentally losing the micrometeorite on such a slick surface, the amount of subject manipulation is kept to a minimum.

That said, I have occasionally taken risks. These risks are mitigated by adding additional safety measures, such as placing a piece of white felt underneath the setup. This would hopefully catch any bouncing micrometeorites before they end up on the floor. So far, these extra precautions have not been needed, even when attempting to balance a micrometeorite on top of an equally diminutive faceted garnet crystal (*facing page*). By the end of this endeavour, I was light-headed from holding my breath. Based on my research, this is the first time such a feat has been accomplished, albeit so niche an achievement that I doubt I have much competition in this area.

The further away you get from "ordinary", the more likely you are to discover something new; Macro photography in general allows for far more interpretations of a subject than any landscape photographer would ever encounter. This concept becomes amplified with subjects that require high magnification. The challenges are also amplified, but artful creations can be constructed even at the extremes.

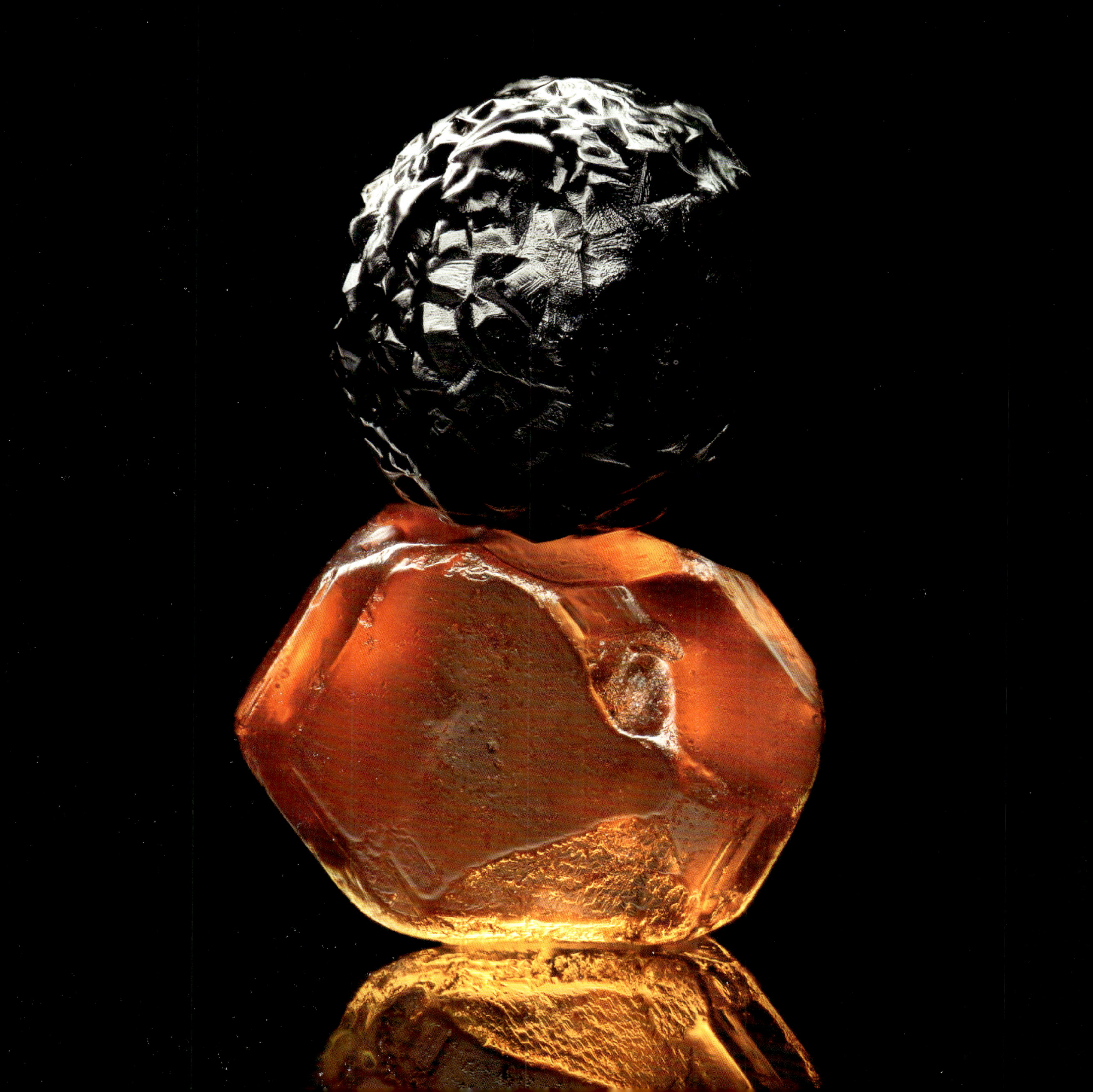

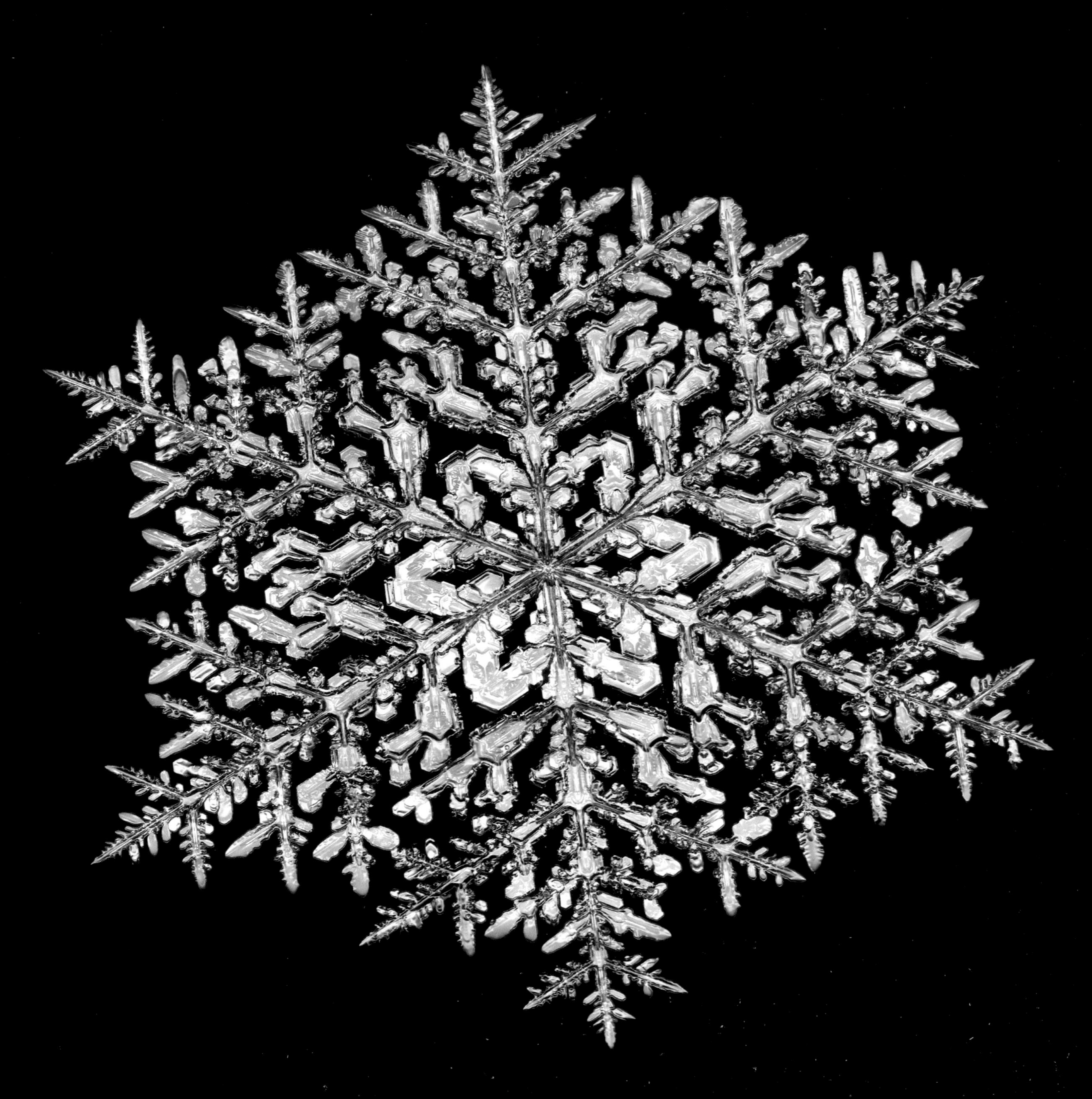

Photographing Snowflakes
and Ice Crystals

The winter months in many parts of the world are typically uninteresting for macro photographers. Flowers, insects, and tiny details in nature all but disappear. Only one faithful subject is left in abundance - the tiny snowflake. Thankfully, "abundance" is an understatement. For nearly half of the year, you'll find countless trillions of them mere feet from the warmth and comfort of home. So, how do you start? How do you capture one of these tiny crystalline subjects and fill the frame behind your lens? The first thing you'll need is an old, black mitten.

Best Shooting Conditions

You'll need more than that, however. The largest snowflakes tend to form under very specific conditions, and searching for these conditions will quickly turn any photographer into an amateur meteorologist. There are a few things to look out for, but there is randomness in the equation that makes most snowstorms slightly unpredictable.

Different conditions produce different types of snowflakes, but you'll have a hard time photographing anything if the wind is too strong. High winds will make it difficult to find and isolate a single snowflake long enough to photograph it. The crystals can quickly blow away, and these conditions often present you with broken snowflakes. The wind will cause snow crystals to collide with one another or shatter on impact with the ground. In comparison, blowing snow consists of the tiniest fragments, as the crystals have been worn down by everything on the ground. Keep an eye out for wind speeds below 10km/h for best results, but don't let high winds stop you if you feel up for the challenge.

Temperature is the next factor to consider. The biggest "stellar dendrite" style of snowflake (*facing page*) is created around -15°C / 5°F, so keep an eye out for similar numbers. The temperature in the clouds where snowflakes will grow is likely different from the ground temperature, throwing a random element into your calculations. Beyond the "peak" temperature, the crystals will begin to grow smaller, but as this book will illustrate, some of the most beautiful snowflakes are also the smallest. If the outside temperature is any warmer than -5°C / 23°F, you'll be faced with quickly-melting crystals - colder is often better.

The combination of temperature and humidity affect the size and shape of snowflakes. A weather system capable of growing large snowflakes would have high levels of supersaturation, so keep an eye on the humidity and not just the temperature.

Clouds passing closer to the ground can also contribute to great snowflake photographs. If the snowflake has less distance to fall, the condition of the snowflake you see will be more pristine. All of these variables come into play in determining the kinds of snowflakes you'll see and photograph. In the end, just follow this advice: **If the weather is cold, calm and snowing, get outside and see for yourself.**

There is a good chance you will rush back inside to grab the camera for a closer look.

Background & Contrast

The background behind most of the snowflake photographs in this book is an old black mitten. This is one of my essential tools for capturing snowflakes. The mitten is usually kept outside, and I place it out on top of any available platform – the side of a barbeque works nicely. The mitten has a few advantages over other possible surfaces, and I've yet to find anything that works better.

The first advantage is contrast. Snowflakes are being lit from above, and so the light source will fall on the snowflake and its background. If the background is too light (such as other snow), the details are lost. A dark background is necessary to make the snowflake "shine". The next advantage is background isolation. Snowflakes will become held in place by a few fibers and will not rest on a flat surface. This means that a large part of the background will be out of focus, and easier to clean up in editing. Trying to remove a solid texture from the background can be a nightmare, but a few stray woollen fibers are easily taken care of.

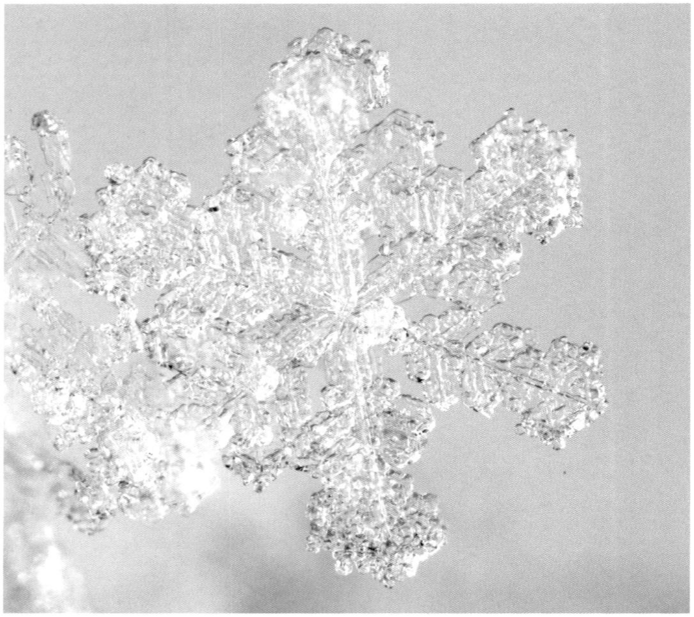

Above: Without a dark background, the details of the crystal are obscured.

Below: The black mitten used as a background for every one of my snowflake photographs , except for the above.

Because the snowflake is caught in fibers, it's often perched on an angle. Most of the images in this book, especially those photographed with a shimmering and bright surface, are intentionally photographed on an angle, and the fibers allow for this very easily. We'll explore that technique shortly.

Finally, the snowflake is only making contact with a few fibers of the mitten. This acts as an insulator from any possible heat. If the delicate crystal had landed on a solid flat surface, there is a strong possibility that it'll begin to melt before you finished photographing it in warmer conditions.

My initial intention for using the black mitten was only for a dark background; it was only after I tried to replace the mitten with something else that I realized the other advantages. Nothing so far (aside from other dark woolen fabrics) have shown a greater advantage, and I have used the same mitten for years – it has become a tradition.

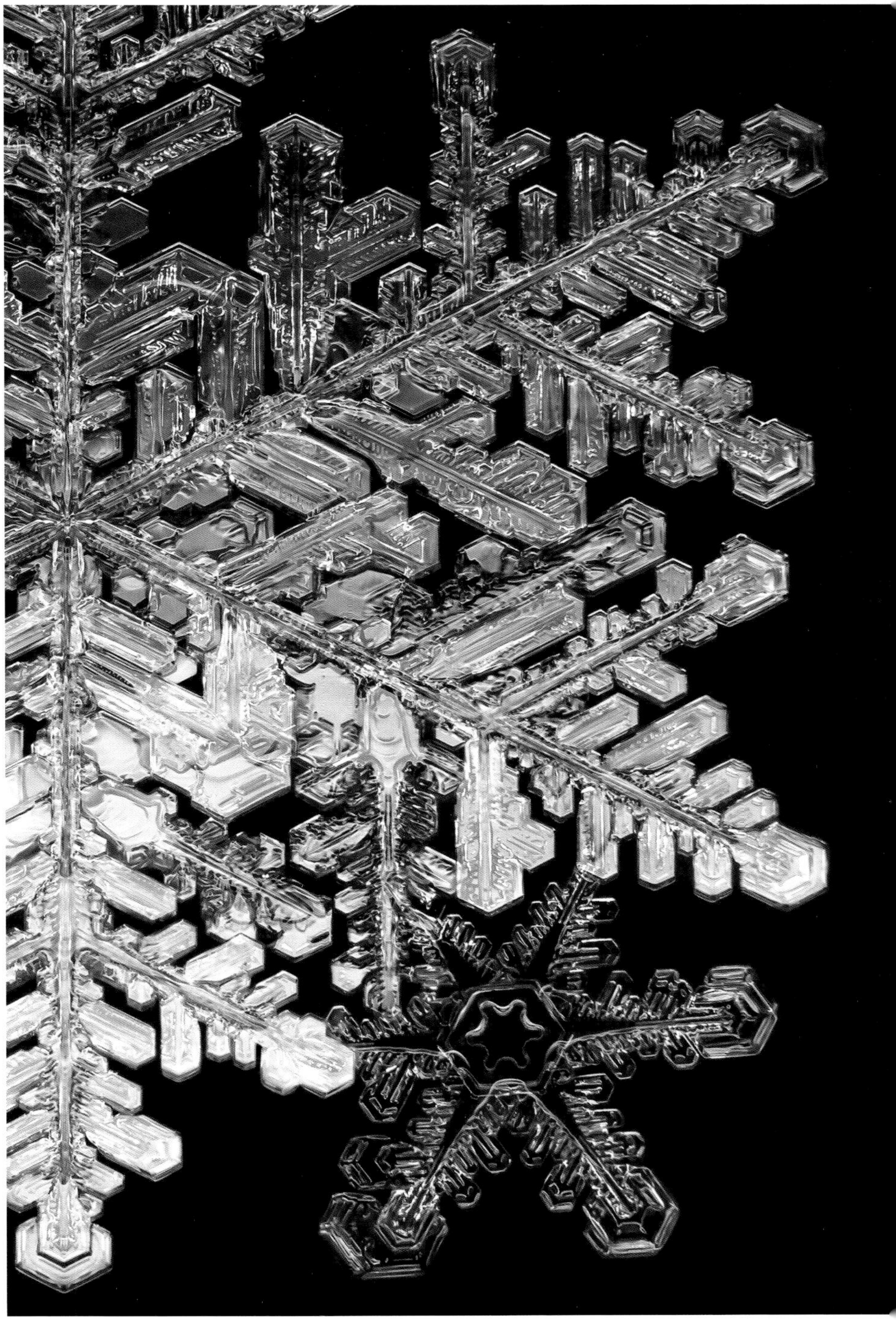

Right: A black background makes the snowflake stand out and shine, if positioned and photographed at the correct angle. Note the smaller crystal at the bottom, which is angled slightly differently, doesn't appear "white".

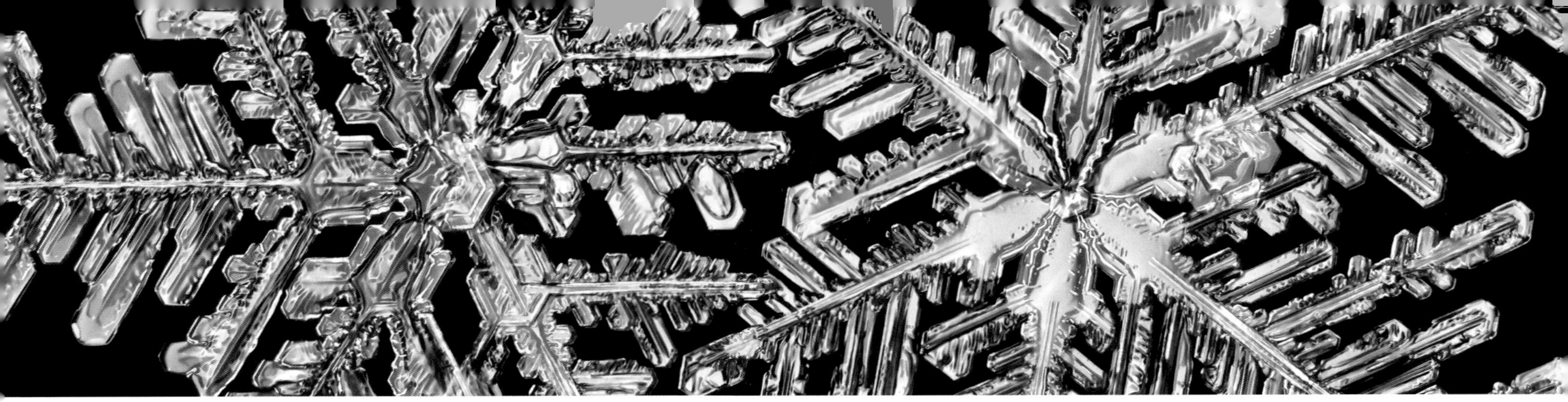

Photographic Equipment

The equipment that I use for photographing snowflakes may appear specialized and somewhat obscure, but the goal is simply to get the highest level of magnification possible. The tiny size of snowflakes puts them just barely viewable in the realm of the 1:1 magnification found in most macro lenses. I have photographed some crystals as small as 250 microns (0.25mm), far too small to be captured using a normal macro lens.

To photograph snowflakes on that scale, I use the Canon MP-E 65mm 1x-5x F/2.8 Macro Photo *(pictured on camera, facing page)*. This lens starts where normal macro lenses stop, though thankfully it's not the only game in town. High magnification macro lenses have no ability to focus (automatically or manual), so I have to move closer or farther away from my subject. This lens starts at 1:1 life-size magnification and continues up to five times that magnification at the extreme.

Other good options for lenses come from Venus Optics: the Laowa 25mm F/2.8 2.5-5x macro lens and the Laowa 50mm F/2.8 2x lens for Micro Four Thirds, providing the equivilent of 4:1 magnification on a full frame camera.

So, you don't have a special high magnification macro lens; what else can you do? There are plenty of ways to get closer to your subject. Close-up filters, extension tubes, and various methods of flipping a lens around backwards can offer a similar experience. I'll describe a few of the most practical methods, but the choices are not limited to what you read here.

Camera Body

The pixel density of your camera sensor can greatly affect the level of magnification you are able to reach. The more pixels packed into the same space, the more detail you can capture. There are limitations to this detail that I mentioned earlier in this book regarding diffraction, a digital SLR with a cropped sensor will have the upper-hand compared to a full-frame camera offering the same resolution. You'll want a camera that is capable of shooting at a high rate of frames per second, as you might end up photographing hundreds of images of the same snowflake.

These camera considerations are all "wants", not "needs". Any digital SLR is capable of photographing snowflakes, and the real challenges come from the lens and lighting. I first started photographing snowflakes on the woefully slow Canon 5D mark II which could shoot at only 3.9 frames per second. I have also successfully shot images using the Lumix GX9 which does not have a lengthy buffer for continuous shooting.

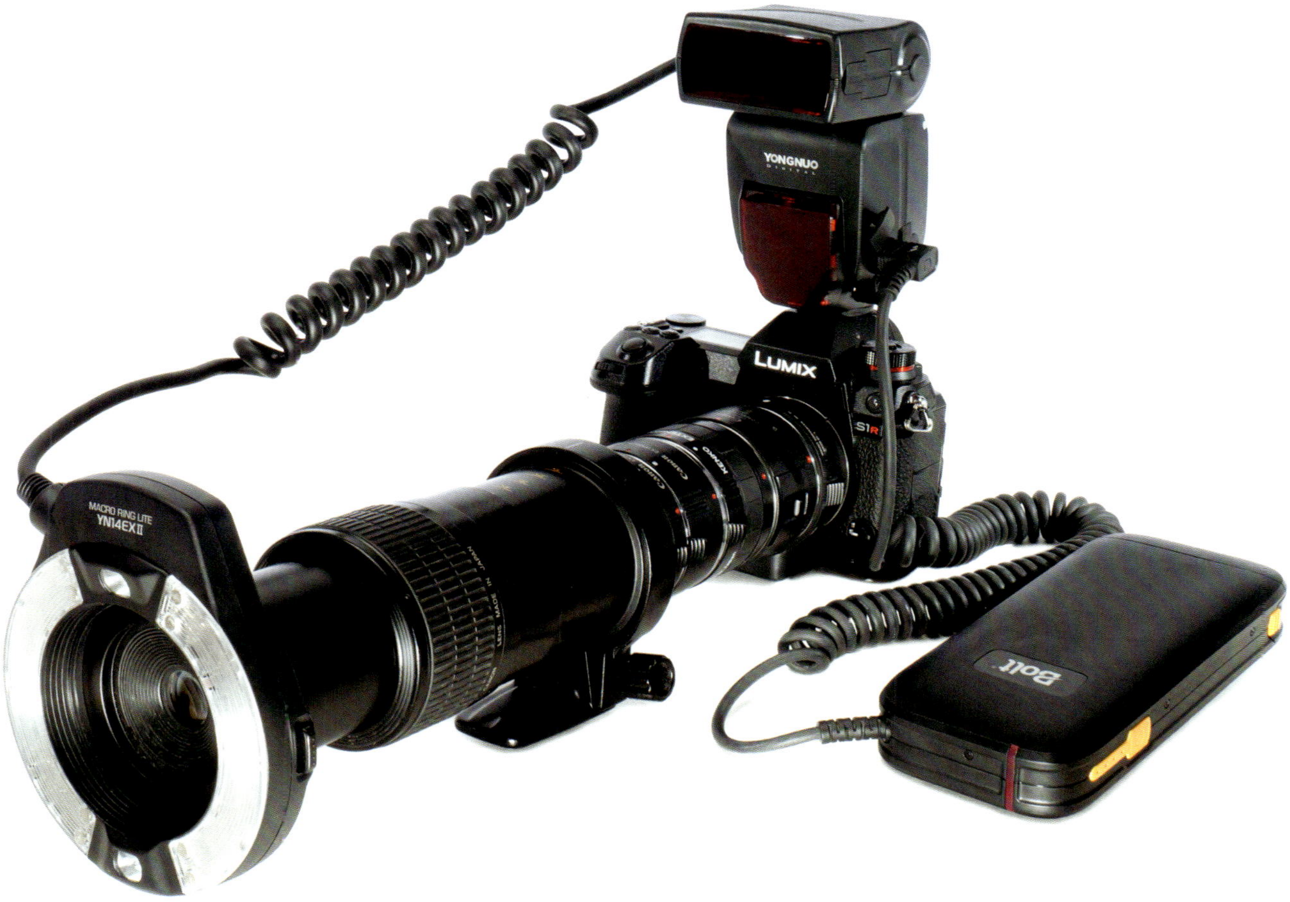

This strange connection of camera equipment (*above*) consists of a Lumix S1R camera body and a Canon MP-E 65mm F/2.8 1x-5x Macro lens, but in between the camera and the lens is a set of extension tubes for further magnification. Also in this set is the now-discontinued Canon Lifesize Converter EF, which functions like a teleconverter for macro lenses.

The combination of equipment is capable of producing magnifications as high as 12:1. If the lens is originally measured at F/2.8 at infinity, it would be two stops lower at 1:1 magnification to F/5.6. For each additional magnification factor, you'd need to subtract one stop of light to arrive at your "effective aperture". In this maximum configuration, that would equate to roughly F/256. Diffraction plays a huge role in limiting the resolution of your images when you push this far.

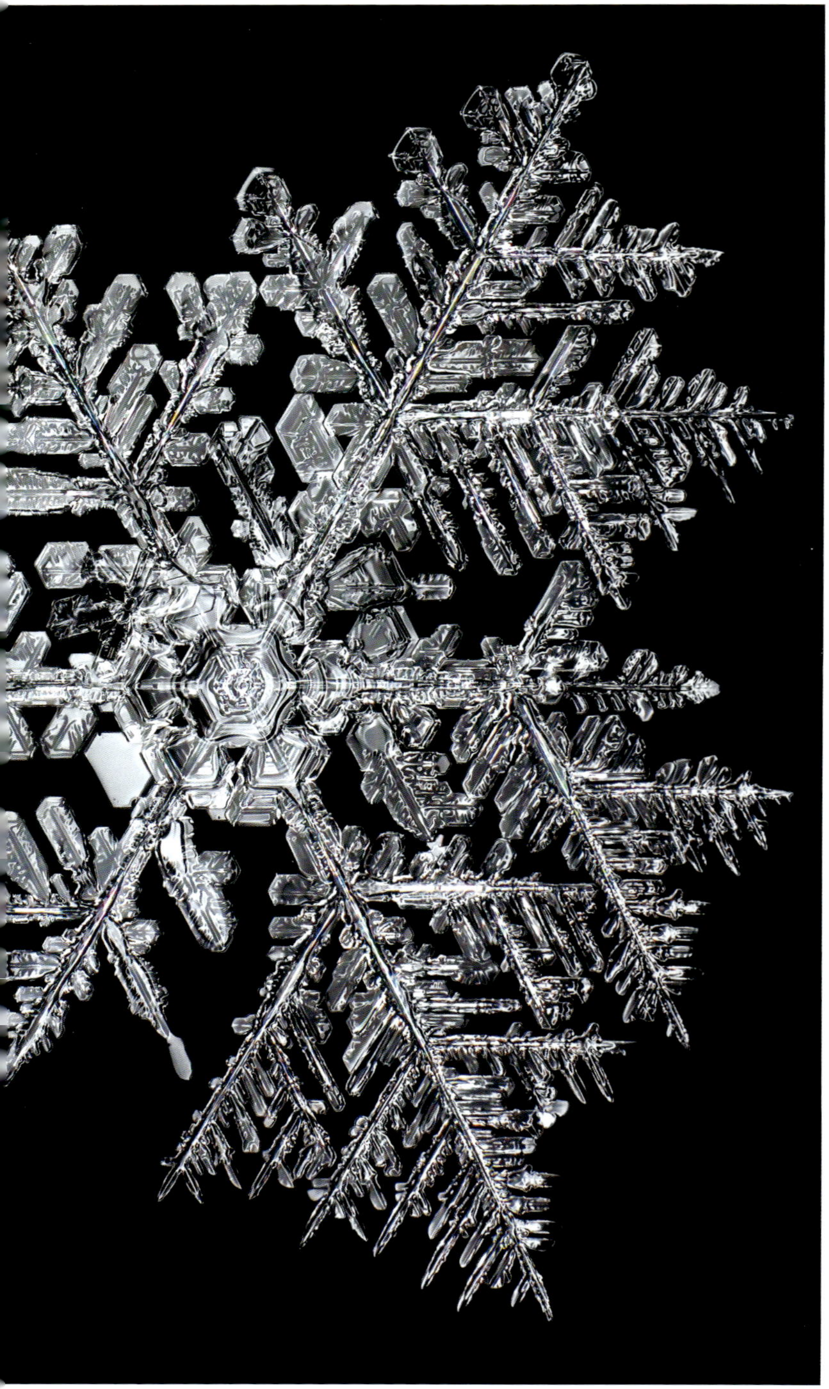

Lighting - Ring Flash
Your next challenge is light. As you've hopefully discovered elsewhere in this book, having a flash handy will save you hours of frustration trying to create a sharp image. With snowflakes, you'll need the light of a thousand suns to illuminate these tiny beauties. Or, a macro flash will also do the trick. The best option is a ring flash, attached to the end of your lens and is designed for subjects that are too close for a normal flash to illuminate. We're working in close quarters with snowflakes and achieving reflected light by other means might not be possible.

Battery Backup
If you tackle the subject of snowflakes like I do, your flash will not be able to keep up on its own. Many ring flashes, including the Yongnuo YN-14EX II and the K&F Concept KF-150 have a port on the side of the flash controller that can accept an additional battery pack. You'll want this to be part of your kit to ensure that you do not end up with "dark frames" where the flash didn't fire.

Tripod or Not?
Macro photography on this scale is not usually done "in the field", but rather in more controlled studio conditions. With a controlled environment and a non-volatile subject, a tripod equipped with a focusing rail can offer a huge advantage when seeking perfect focus at every point needed for focus stacking.

Snowflakes are very dynamic subjects, and because of their nature, a tripod is one piece of equipment you can leave inside. A number of problems arise when attempting to use a tripod to keep things stable:

- Timing is everything, and setting up a tripod in the perfect position takes more time than you typically have. By the time you get the tripod in position, the snowflake may have melted, sublimated (evaporated from a solid state directly to gas), changed position because of the wind or maybe blown away completely. The tiny crystal could also have been covered by more falling snow. From the time you see a snowflake to the time you are photographing it, you will likely have less than a minute for ideal results.

- Choosing the angle of light is very important, and this often means pivoting the camera with the end of the lens anchored in place. This is problematic when using a tripod where the camera is anchored at the base of the body, not the end of the lens.

- The many fine-tuned adjustments required to get the tripod in the exact position might be possible without gloves at room temperature, but step outside into the freezing cold and tripod adjustments become an exercise in frustration.

While my methods of photographing snowflakes do not require a tripod, other techniques can place the camera in a fixed position. These techniques are discussed briefly at the end of this chapter relating to transmitted light, rather than a reflected light approach.

Facing page: A ring flash will provide the light. Depending on it's angle of incidence, the light can either pass through and reflect off the edges, or reflect off the surface of the crystal to create different effects.

Below: Because the surface of snowflakes are not significantly curved no ring-shaped reflections can be seen bouncing back.

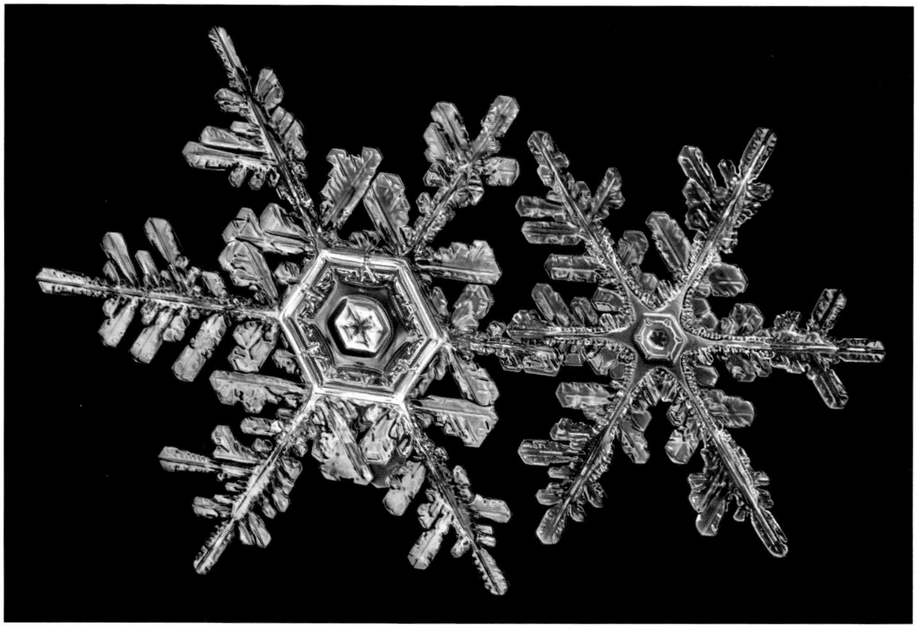

Shooting Techniques

Place the mitten outside during a snowfall and wait a few moments for snowflakes to land (tip: you shouldn't be wearing the mitten). It may take 10 minutes for the mitten to acclimate to the outside temperatures, during which time any viable snowflakes are likely to melt on contact. Following that time, examine the menagerie to see if any of the snowflakes fall into the "beautiful" category. It is common to see balls of ice or crystals covered in frozen water droplets. It may take a few snowfalls before you see crystals worth photographing: big, clean snowflakes with lots of branches.

It is very important to photograph the snowflakes as quickly as possible after they land. In as little as one hour afterwards, the crystals melt or sublimate and the sharp crystal edges begin to degrade. This process starts as soon as the snowflake leaves the high-humidity environment that it formed in. If you've just missed the snowfall by a few minutes (or still shooting after the snowfall has stopped), try to place the mitten gentlly on freshly fallen snow and pick it up again. The fibers will catch fallen snowflakes like Velcro and you'll have a chance at photographing a few more before they deteriorate too far.

Isolating a Single Snowflake

A snowfall will give you plenty of possible subjects, but the problem quickly becomes isolating a single snowflake from the never-ending addition of new crystals. Millions of snowflakes could be falling all around you, and how do you separate just one from the crowd? I love simple solutions.

A small, fine paintbrush. Any art store will have an ample selection, the one I use has a flat row of bristles that are firm but gentle. The gentle nature of the brush should let you clear away unwanted crystals and nudge the desired crystal into the best position for shooting. The paintbrush should be kept outside with the mitten before the snow begins to fall so that they do not transfer any heat to the crystal.

Snowflakes are incredibly fragile, and repositioning or moving them can easily result in shattering or damaging the branches. With practice, you'll soon be able to begin manipulating the snowscape on the mitten without destroying too many specimens. Your efforts might still be rewarded with a perfect snowflake broken or blown away from time to time, but there's always more snow falling.

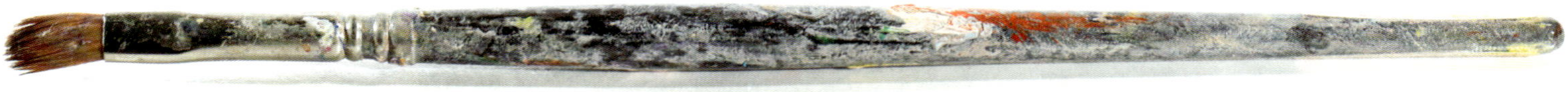

Above: A paintbrush I've used to push around and manipulate snowflakes. As you might be able to see, it's also been used in a more traditional role. Actual size.

Ambient Light and seeing through the viewfinder

As the magnification of any lens increases, the amount of light returning through the viewfinder gets diminished. Additionally, many great snowfalls happen in the middle of the night. You may find yourself in the dark, struggling to see anything through the viewfinder.

Most macro flashes will have something called a "modeling light" that consists of small continuous lights to help illuminate your subject. Knowing where this feature is on your flash, if available, is important. Most modeling lights will turn off after 30 seconds, as well as immediately after you've taken a photograph – this is inconvenient behaviour, but memorizing the location of the modeling light button will come naturally after a few sessions in the twilight snow.

Another good option for photographers is a small LED flashlight. This can be mounted anywhere beside the shooting area with a tabletop tripod to give extra ambient light to the subject and help you hunt for the perfect snowflake. LED-based lights are preferred as they produce far less heat.

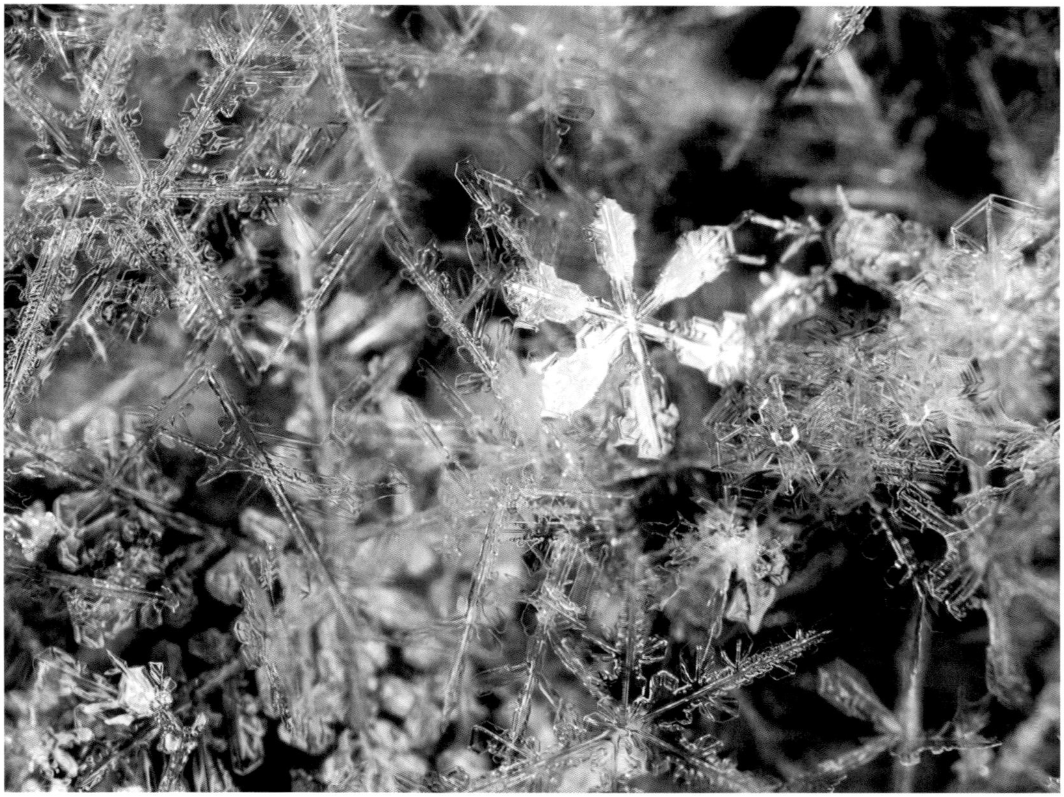

Right: Getting one snowflake on its own can be a challenge - best attempted with a small paintbrush.

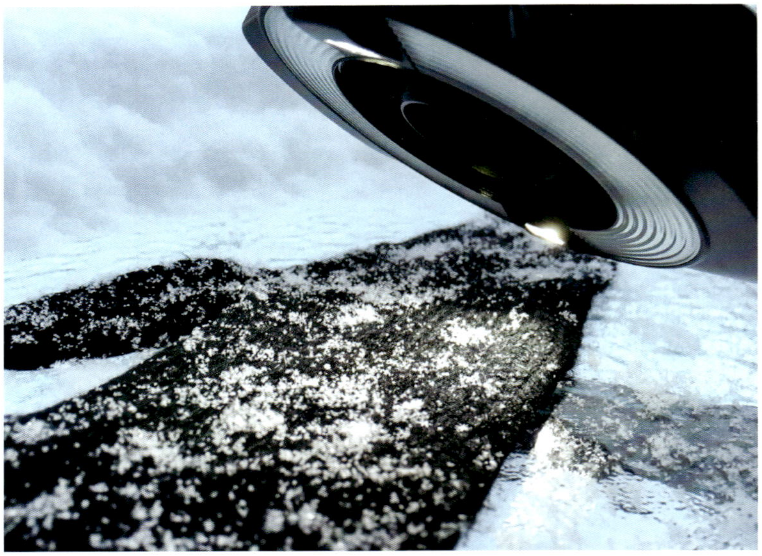

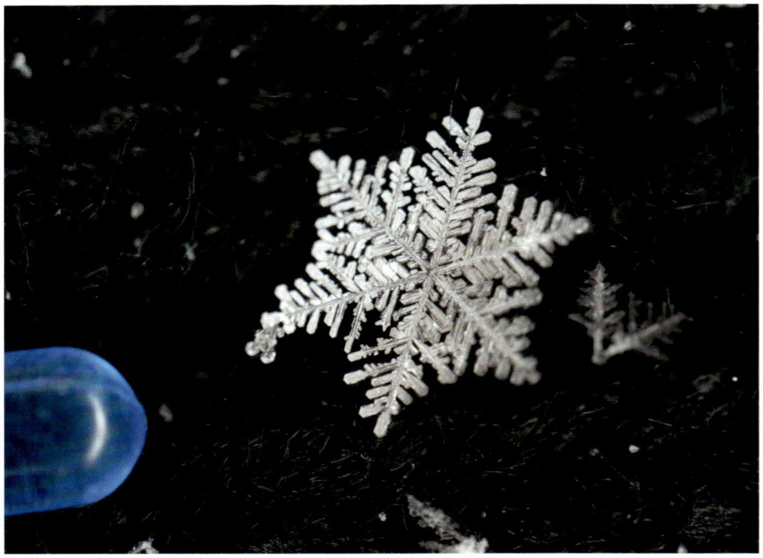

Top: Using a light source to illuminate your collected snowflakes is ideal. This helps you see directly reflected light off the top of the snowflake (basal facet).

Bottom: Use a paintbrush to help you find your snowflake.

Finding the Diamond in the Rough

Using the focus lamps on a ring flash or a separate LED flashlight, you can illuminate the collection of snowflakes you'll be choosing from. I tend to shift my head slightly left and right which will change the "sparkle" on the snow, hoping that my eyes will find the proper angle to make a beautiful snowflake get noticed.

Sometimes these gems are so small, however, that locating them with your eyes is only the beginning of the struggle. Getting them within the frame of your photograph can be even more challenging. Imagine trying to find a small bird on a cloudless blue sky with a super telephoto lens. With no frame of reference, you'll be hunting aimlessly. The same is true with snowflakes, but there's an easy solution: that same paintbrush.

If you place the brush on the mitten with the back end of it right next to the crystal of interest, you can then focus your efforts on finding the brush handle. This is much easier to locate with your eye against the viewfinder, and once it's found you simply follow it to just beyond tip – and your snowflake will be waiting for you there (*left*).

It's perfectly fine if a portion of the brush handle ends up in the frame. So long as it's not overlapping the snowflake, it can be cropped or otherwise edited out afterwards. Once the snowflake is in the frame, we're ready to shoot. How you hold the camera and the lens will have a dramatic impact on your success, and there's a few straightforward but strategic tips to keep in mind.

It's All in the Wrist – How to Hold the Camera

"Working Distance" is a term usually associated with higher magnification optics, referring to the distance between the front lens element and the subject. Most lenses at high magnification will have a reduced working distance, with the Canon MP-E 65mm F/2.8 1x-5x macro lens offering up a distance of only 4.1cm / 1.6", so you'll be right on top of your subject. This has its advantages.

Normally, it's intuitive to place your left hand near the base of the lens. At high magnifications when hand-holding the camera, the best place for you to grasp the camera is at the end of the lens, or on an attached ring flash. Because you are likely to be physically close to your subject, part of your hand can rest on the surface where the snowflake is positioned. This maneuver is pivotal – pun intended.

With your left hand anchoring the end of the lens in place, it becomes much easier to rotate the camera around the snowflake, such that the snowflake is the center of this rotation. It'll stay in the frame as you move the camera body slightly, trying to find the best angle to shoot.

Our goal will be to choose an appropriate angle of light so that it bounces off the surface of the snowflake and directly into the camera lens. Normally this would be called "glare" and you would try to avoid it, but it's the secret to making a snowflake shimmer.

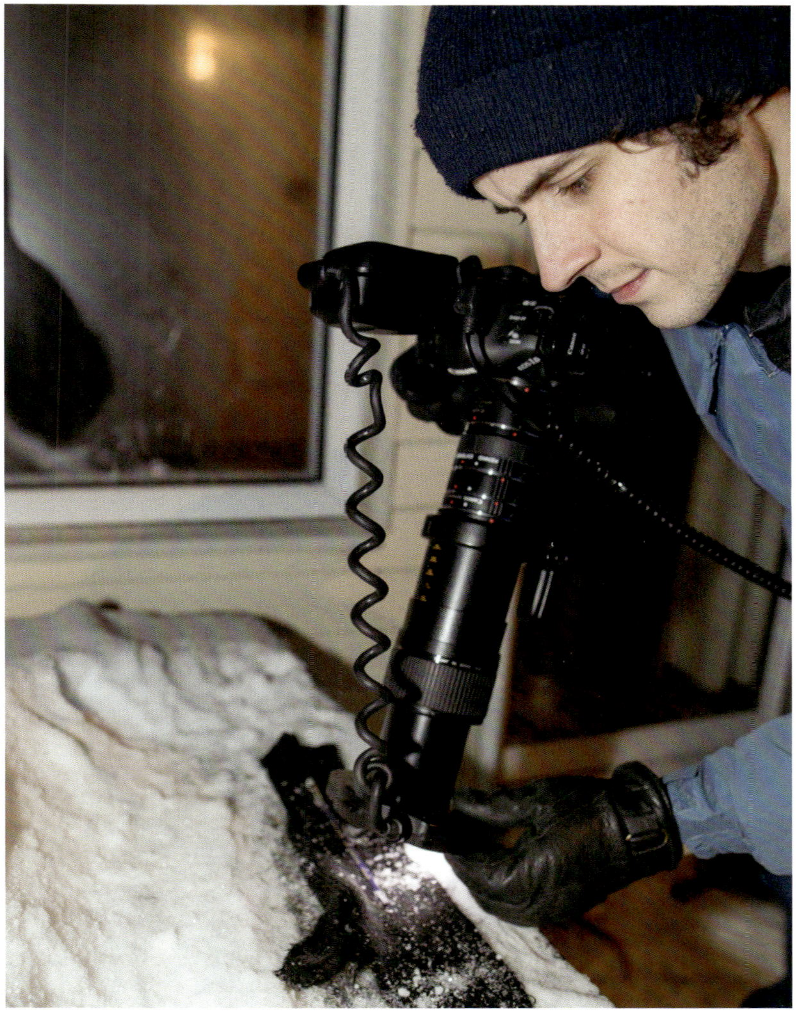

Above: With your right hand on the camera as normal, place your left hand at the end of the ring flash, gripping it with your thumb and index finger, while your pinky and ring fingers rest on the surface from which you are shooting. You are now an anchor.

Camera and Flash Settings

Exposure settings here are fairly standard, and won't deviate much if you follow the same shooting strategy as I do. Keep in mind that diffraction will play a role at higher magnifications, which gets factored into our decision on what aperture to use.

ISO 200. Normally I would shoot at the "base ISO" - the lowest ISO setting available. This allows for the highest quality, and that can be anywhere between ISO 64 and ISO 200 for the majority of cameras. Why shoot at ISO 200 when my camera is capable of slightly higher quality at ISO 100? The quality difference in negligible, but it requires twice the output from the flash. If the flash is overburdened, even with an external battery pack it may not fire for every frame. ISO 200 is the compromise that allows for longer flash bursts and longer battery life.

Flash Sync Speed. Check your camera manual to see what your flash sync speed is – usually somewhere between 1/160sec and 1/300sec. This is the fastest that your camera can operate the shutter with a flash. Choosing this setting would allow for a minimum of ambient light to enter the image, which would likely result in motion blur. Remember that the duration of a flash is much faster than the flash sync speed, sometimes as fast as 1/20,000sec where no motion blur would be possible.

Wide Aperture. Remember that F/2.8 becomes F/5.6 when you reach 1:1 magnification, an effective reduction of two stops. If you add one stop for every additional magnification factor, you can predict a point where diffraction starts to reduce the level of detail you're able to capture. If I was photographing a snowflake at 5:1 (5x) magnification with an aperture set to F/8 as an example, the resulting "effective aperture" would be F/48 when shot with the Canon MP-E 65mm F/2.8 1x-5x lens. Diffraction would be problematic, reducing the resolving power of your lens considerably.

To that end, keep a simple rule in mind: the more magnification you have, the wider you should make your aperture. My standard practice is to loosen up the aperture by one stop for every magnification factor added. F/11 at 1:1 magnification shouldn't cause you any issues, but consider the following – especially if you have a high-resolution camera body:

- 2x: F/8
- 3x: F/5.6
- 4x: F/4
- 5x: F/2.8

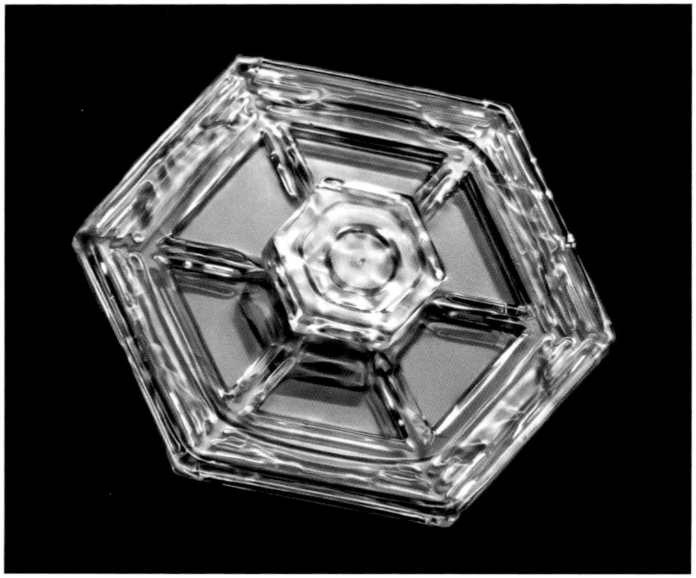

Flash Control Options

How you operate your flash is directly related to what kind of camera you have: a traditional flapping mirror design, or a newer mirrorless camera.

Traditional DSLR: TTL Metering is required for best results. This is due to the nature of how a flash functions: sending out a small amount of light first to measure how much light will be needed, and then sending out the required amount of light for the calculated exposure. It's the TTL pre-flash that helps you here immensely, because it is seen through the viewfinder when you take the photograph.

Without the TTL pre-flash, you wouldn't see anything in the viewfinder except for ambient light, making it impossible to know if you've found the proper angle for good surface reflection. The TTL pre-flash is viewable through the viewfinder while the mirror is still down, which allows you to get an accurate assumption of how the actual flash will affect the subject.

From this point, you'll "focus by strobe". Moving the camera closer and farther away from the subject while continuously shooting, where every shot provides you with a glimpse of how far the focus has shifted. The TTL pre-flash becomes a visual aid, not just a tool for the camera to calculate a proper exposure.

Because the subject is quite bright at the proper angle, and the background is likely to be dark, the calculations that the camera computes might result in an exposure that is too bright or too dark. Take a test shot and review the results, and adjust the Flash Exposure Compensation if necessary.

Facing page: Snowflake photographed at 6:1 magnification, F/2.8, 1/250sec and ISO 400. The ISO was raised slightly as the batteries in the flash were nearly empty.

Mirrorless Camera: Manual flash power is the best option. The advantage of having an electronic viewfinder is enormous; Because you do not have to take your eye away from the viewfinder, you can assess the exposure immediately and the image appears with the proper lighting. No pre-flash required to visualize things properly!

The caveat here is that you will need to manually adjust the flash power to achieve a proper exposure. The required flash power will change as you adjust your magnification, as your effective aperture will be a variable in the exposure triangle. The higher your magnification, the more flash power will be required. After a few shooting sessions you'll get a feeling for where things should be and it'll be easier to predict what the final exposure will be.

In TTL metering, the camera might adjust the flash exposure slightly between shots, creating some variance in exposure. This is usually slight, and is corrected in the focus stacking process. Manual flash power has little to no deviation in exposure, providing more consistent results. Ring flashes from any manufacturer can be used on any camera brand in manual mode, allowing for more flexibility in equipment choice for those shooting with mirrorless bodies.

Advantage for Under-Exposure

There are a few reasons why you might want to keep the exposure a little on the darker side. This may seem counter-intuitive, especially when most images captured by DSLR cameras contain more information in the lighter areas of the image.

The average flash unit will not be able to keep up with the fast rate of fire that modern DSLRs offer. With the average camera able to reach 10 frames per second or faster, you will likely begin to see "dark frames" appear on your camera. Because the flash cannot recycle fast enough to illuminate every image, some exposures are simply skipped.

Snowflakes also have bright areas that can be easily over-exposed. These elements of the crystal can be beautiful, with rainbow colours present as light bends through the prism-like structures. Once these details are blown out, they are impossible to recover. The dynamic range of modern cameras continues to improve, but it's a safe bet to under-expose your image by a small amount to ensure that you'll retain as much highlight detail in the finished image as possible. If you're concerned about noise as a result of brightening things in post-production, these images survive noise reduction algorithms very well.

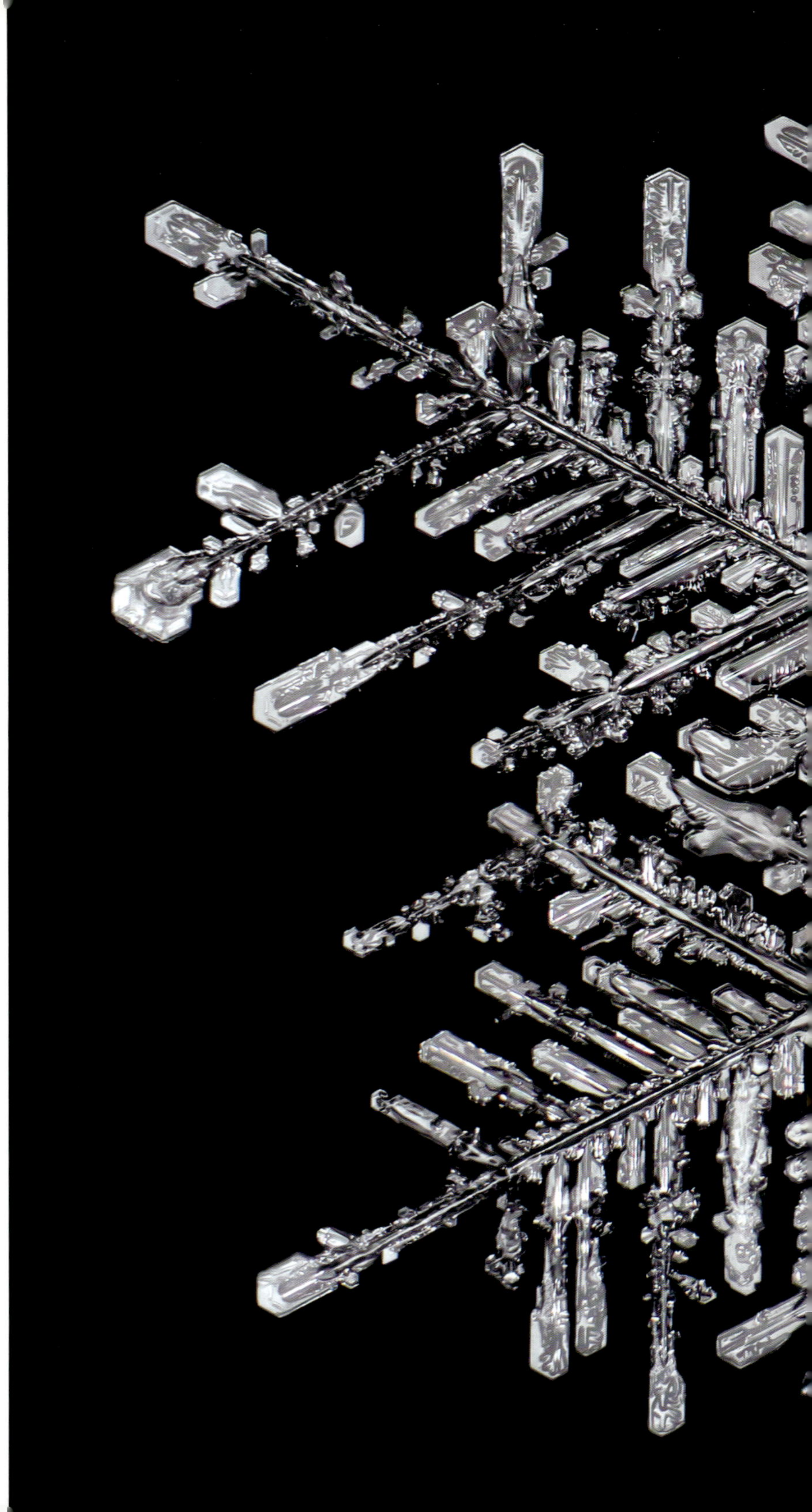

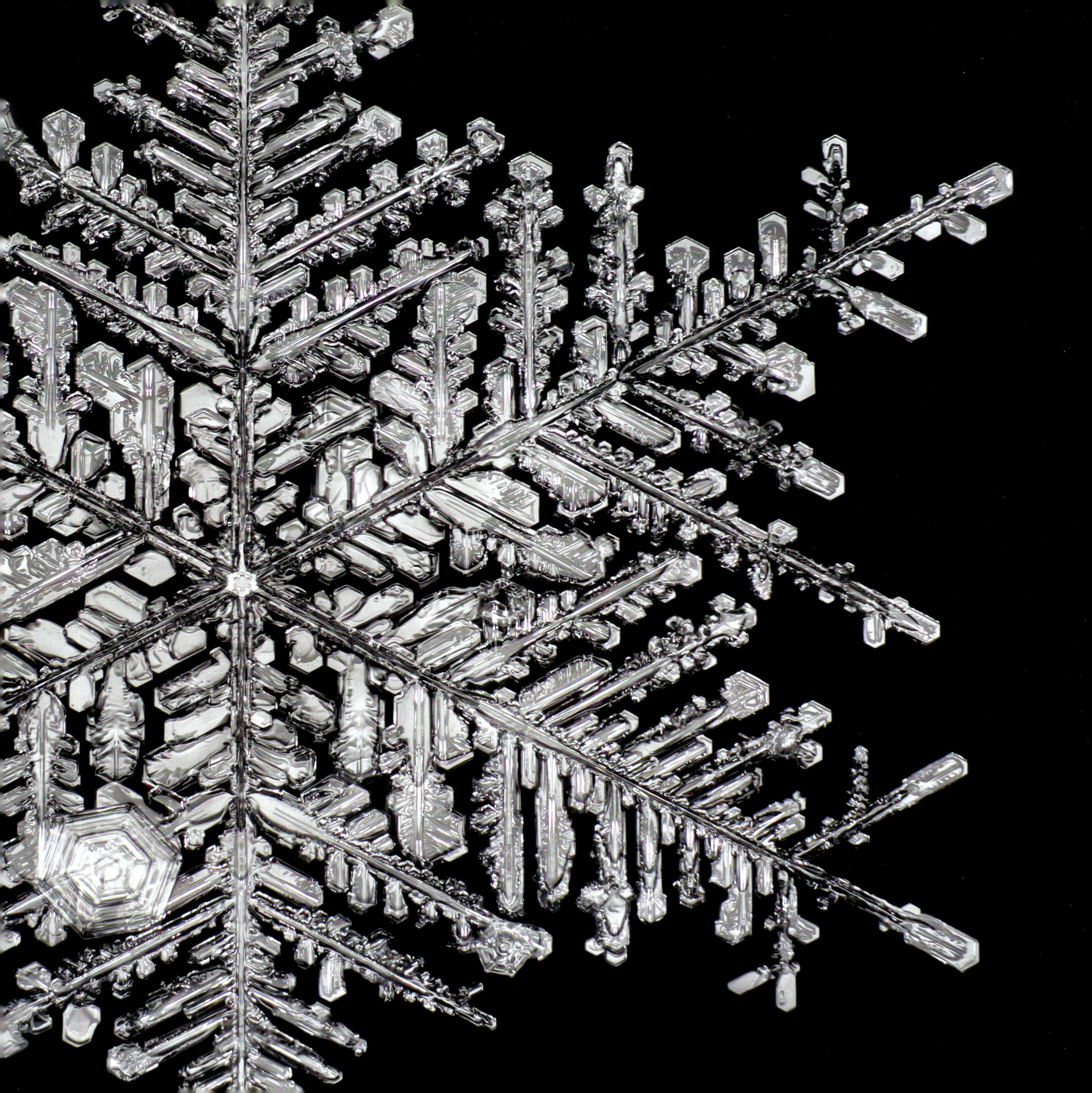

Finding Focus

Getting the snowflake in focus is an additional challenge. Knowing that the camera will need to be shifted in a linear fashion through the snowflake, the best way to accomplish this is by adding some tension. If you pull back slightly with your right hand while pushing forward slightly with your left hand, you can adjust the force slightly on one hand or the other to make the camera move gently and slowly towards or away from the subject.

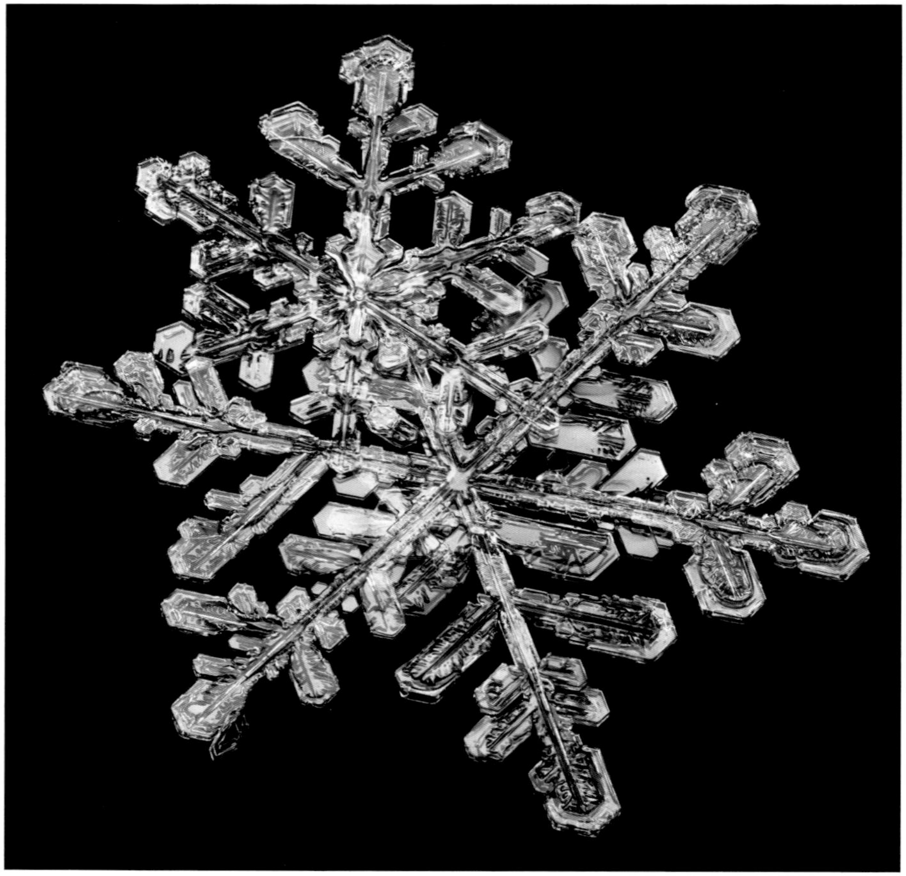

Above: It can be difficult to know with absolute certainty that you've photographed every slice of focus in a snowflake, especially when you discover multiple crystals are "glued" together and have greater depth.

All the Puzzle Pieces

When shooting, I typically start with the entire snowflake out of focus on one end, continuously shooting until the subject is out of focus on the other side. With practice, you might get 80% of the necessary "slices" of focus on a single pass. Do the same thing in reverse, possibly waiting a moment for your camera's buffer to write all of the data from the first pass to the memory card. Pull back through the focus and shoot the same number of frames.

Then repeat once more forward, and backward. I usually make four passes over the snowflake to ensure that I haven't missed any part of the snowflake. This eats up a lot of memory space, and you won't use the majority of the images – you're just making sure that you've got all the pieces you need.

This technique of drastically overshooting for stacking purposes applies to all macro subjects that I photograph handheld, with the

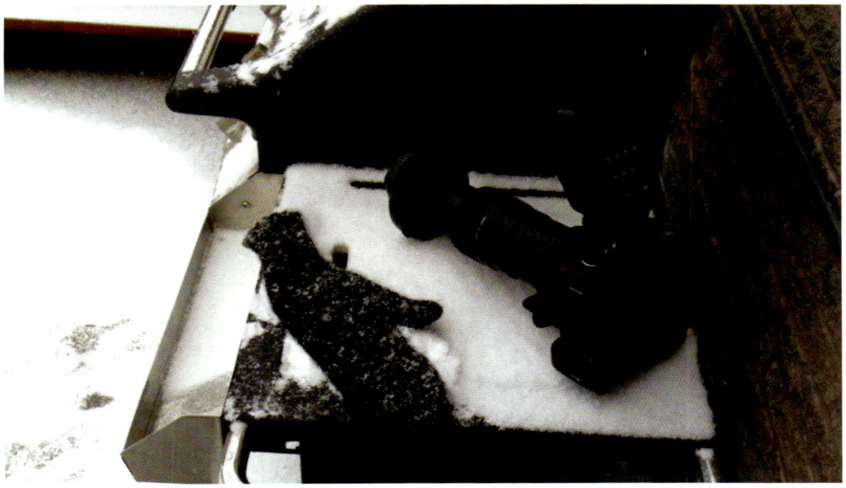

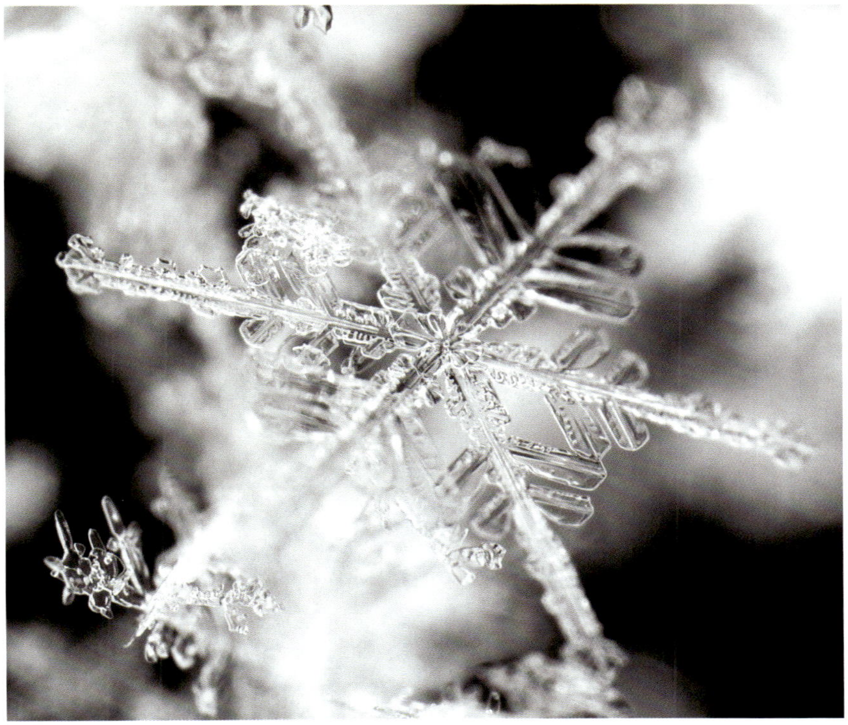

end goal being to combine images together for greater depth of field. It's a lesson that you'll likely need to learn the hard way. Your first attempt, you'll feel confident that you got everything you need, only to discover missing pieces later. Your second attempt will be an improvement, but it would be expected that you are still missing something. After I did this a few times, I learned to overshoot excessively and throw away what I didn't need after the fact.

Your First Snowflake

Seeing your first snowflake image on the back of your camera is an exciting moment. Be sure to look closely at the crystal with your own eyes and compare it to the image you've just taken. The level of detail a camera can capture is far beyond your own vision, and offers a unique and fantastic look into the world around us.

This sense of wonder is what keeps me motivated after spending hours in the freezing cold, with warmth and comfort only a few feet away.

Top Left: The setup used on my first day of photographing snowflakes.

Bottom Left: The image of the first intact snowflake I was able to create in 2009.

Flash Angle

Getting the right amount of light hitting the crystal is important, but we need to be concerned with the direction of light, not simply the quantity. The light should hit the snowflake at the perfect angle for the image we're trying to create. Different angles will produce drastically different results, and the final "look" is entirely in the hands of the photographer.

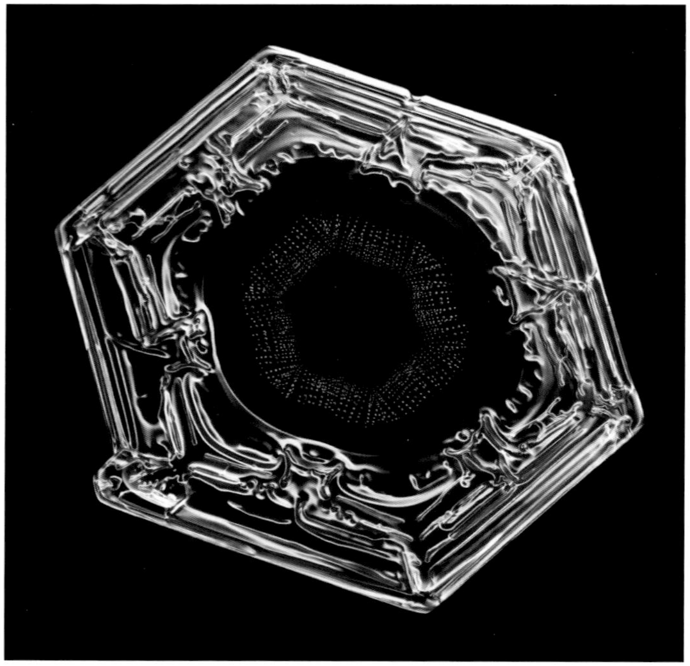

Above: This snowflake is riding the angle between light and dark. If the center of the crystal was reflecting light back to the camera, the subtle colour in the internal bubbles would not be noticeable. The direction of light is key.

Directional Light

Macro flashes and ring flashes are often configured to operate two "banks" of light, and you can control the power ratio so that half of the flash is brighter than the other half. This can help reduce the flash output on the half of the flash that will be at the incorrect angle, which wouldn't serve any useful purpose. By turning the left half of a ring flash completely off, light will only be emitted from the right side.

Holding the end of the lens and/or flash with your left hand, your grip might obscure some of the flash on that side. Remember: "grip left, flash right". The left side of the ring flash can be completely turned off and you'll still get the results you're seeking.

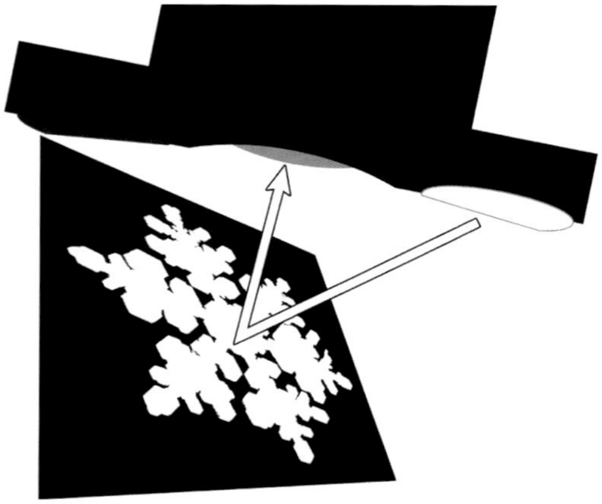

Simple physics, but we need to choose the proper angle for our camera and flash combination to generate reflection (glare) off the structures on the surface of the snowflake. Glare would be something you normally avoid off a window, but we're seeking exactly that in this scenario.

The diagram (*right*) illustrates the snowflake and flash at the proper angle, making this happen. Remember that the angle of incidence equals the angle of

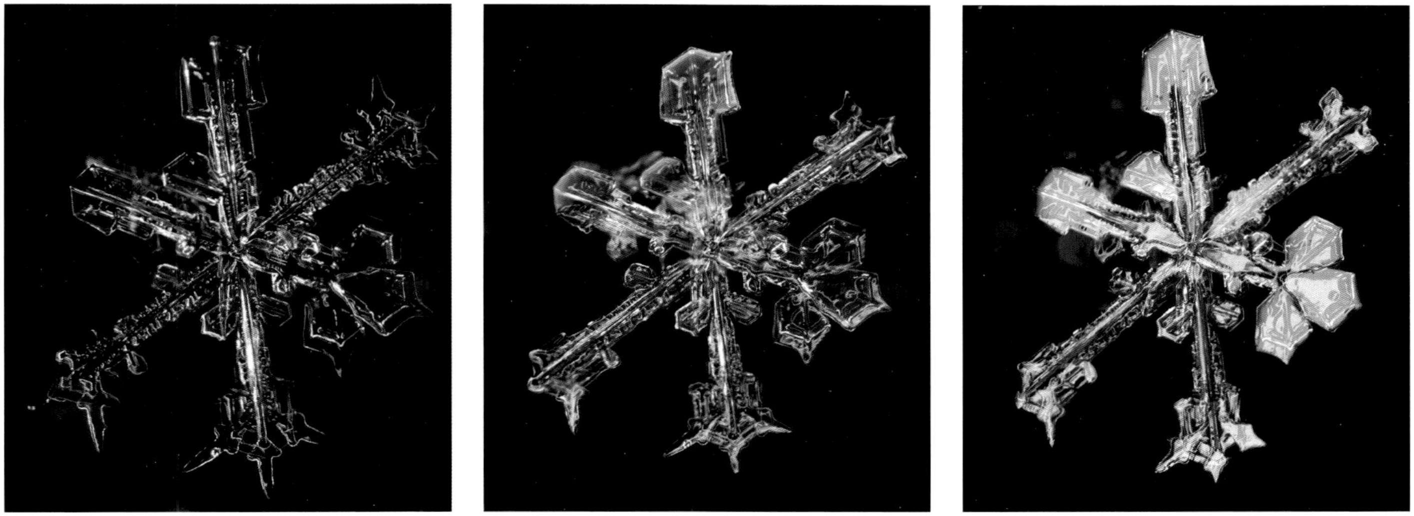

Above: The same snowflake photographed at three unique angles. Each angle offers a different level of reflectiveness to the crystal's surface, revealing different features. The photographer's creative vision should define the final image.

reflection. This means that we need to be "bouncing" light at a slight angle so that the originating point (ring flash) reaches the proper destination (front element of the lens). This exact angle will vary with your working distance, so there no exact angle I can tell you that works best.

Proper angle to the snowflake

Having the left side of the snowflake higher than the right side is the best-case scenario for producing reflection when the light originates from the right side. Most snowflakes will not be in the optimal position by chance, thus requiring a little manipulation.

Gentle adjustments with a small paintbrush will allow you to shift the angle of the snowflake as it sits on the mitten (or other woolen surface). A 20-30° angle seems to be ideal with my equipment, but the snowflake angle depends on the angle of light.

Practice and Adjustment

Take a number of test shots, each time adjusting the angle of the camera slightly. Trial and error is likely required, but you should be able to see how the light is reflecting off the surface of the crystal through the viewfinder. Allow your left hand to anchor the camera in place while you pivot the camera very slightly and take more test images. With a bit of practice, you'll find the best angle at which to shoot.

Every crystal behaves differently. It's worth exploring different angles with each snowflake, as new features will often reveal themselves. Colour contained within the branches is more likely to appear when the surface of the snowflake is transparent, but colour caused by optical interference usually appears when light is reflecting off the surface. You may even be able to find a "sweet spot" in between (*facing page*).

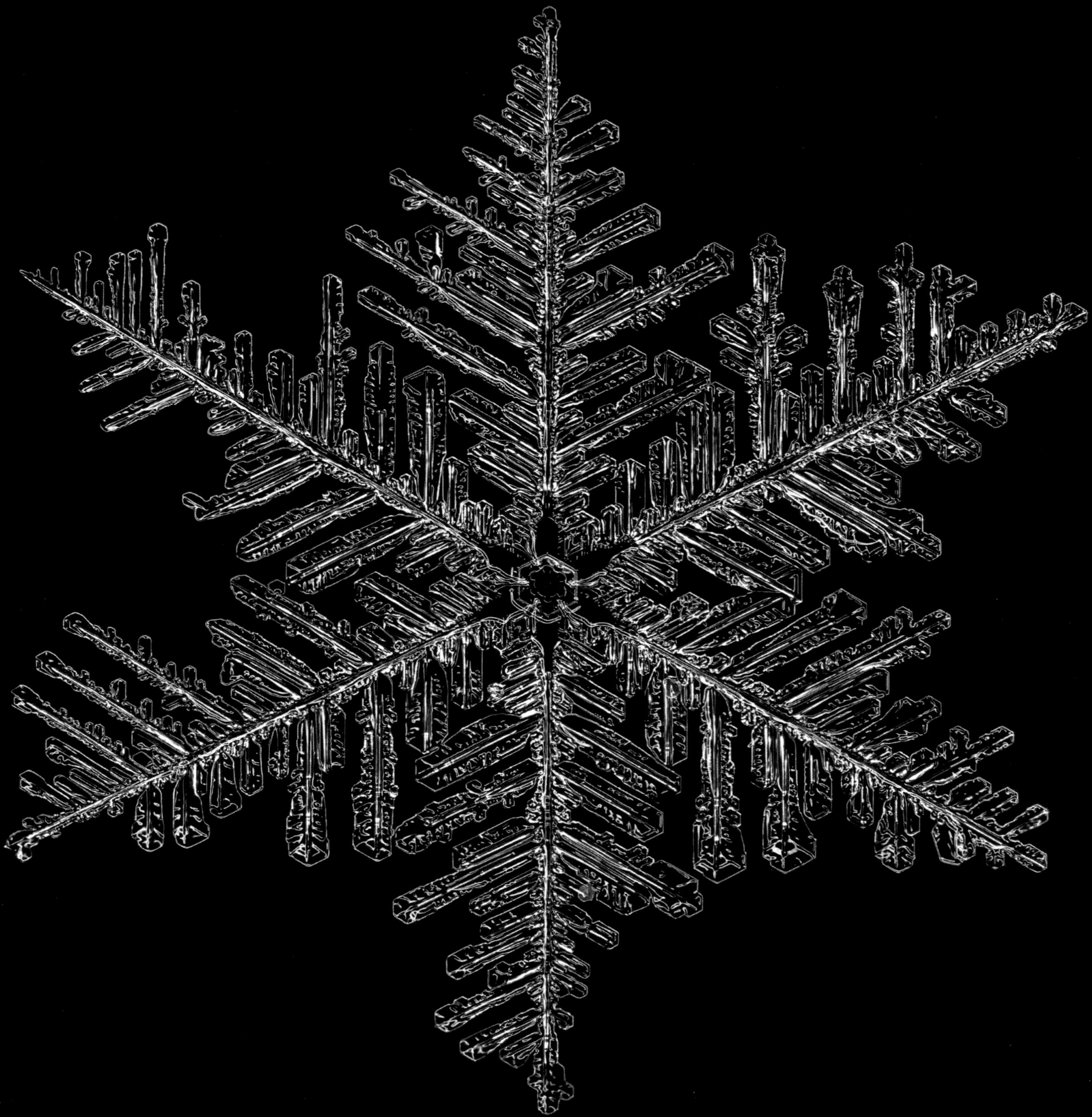

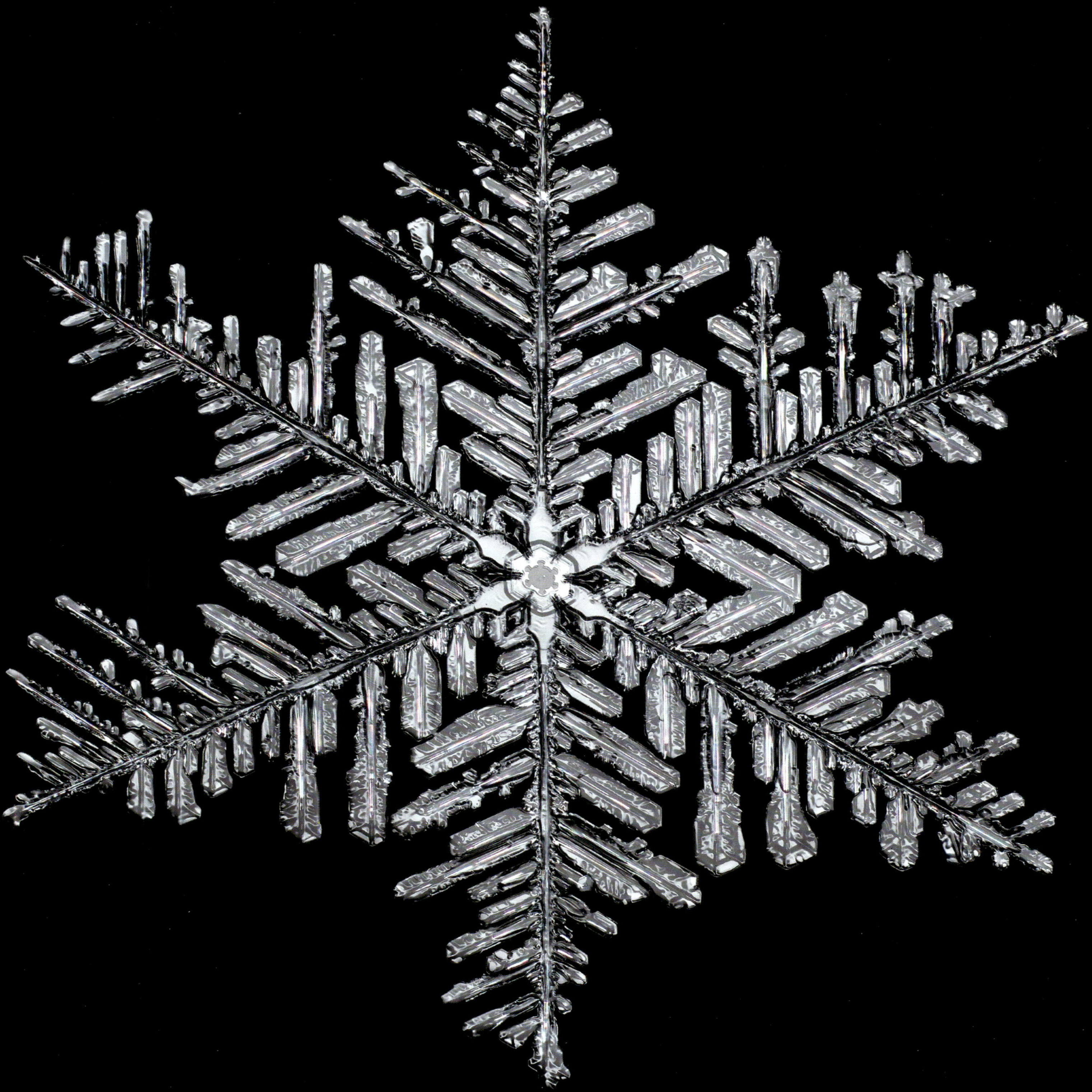

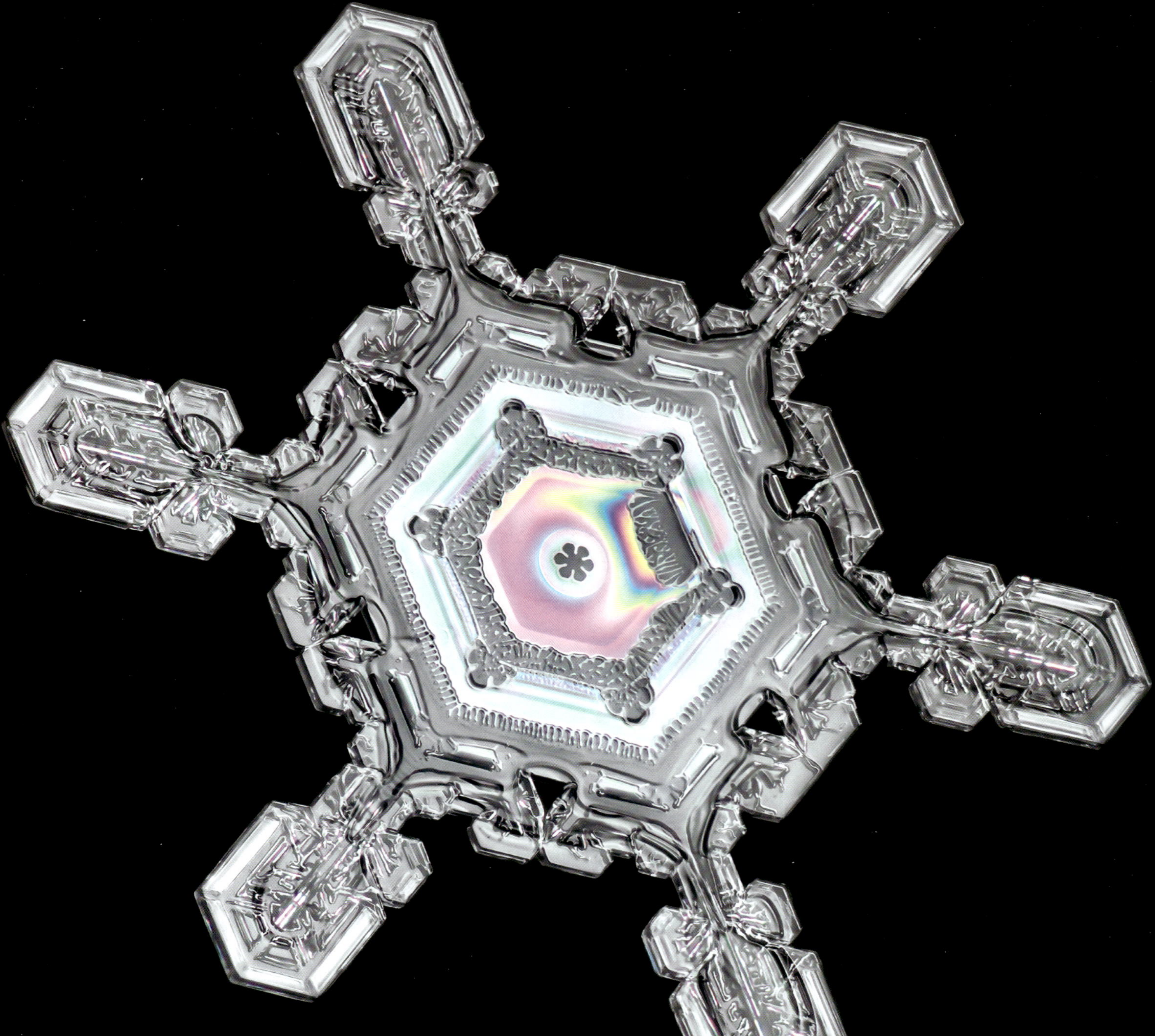

Revealing Hidden Features

The angle chosen can reveal some very interesting structures within a snowflake. The casual observer may see a flat, two-dimensional object. At times, that's true – but photographing a snowflake at the appropriate angle will reveal inner depth and multiple layers. Every snowflake has more detail than we could hope to see without a camera.

Snowflakes often grow on different "planes"; this structure is called a split crystal. A three dimensional design also allows for shadows to be cast and increases the perceived depth if the lighting comes from the proper angle. Surface details also change, showing differences in growth patterns revealed by reflected light.

Colour is affected by the angle of light as well. Some snowflakes do not grow in a manner that is conducive to create vibrant colours, but if the conditions are right and the angle is perfect, rainbows can appear within the crystalline structure.

With enough practice and a bit of luck, you may even find yourself photographing the same snowflake at different angles to show everything the crystal has to offer (*previous pages*).

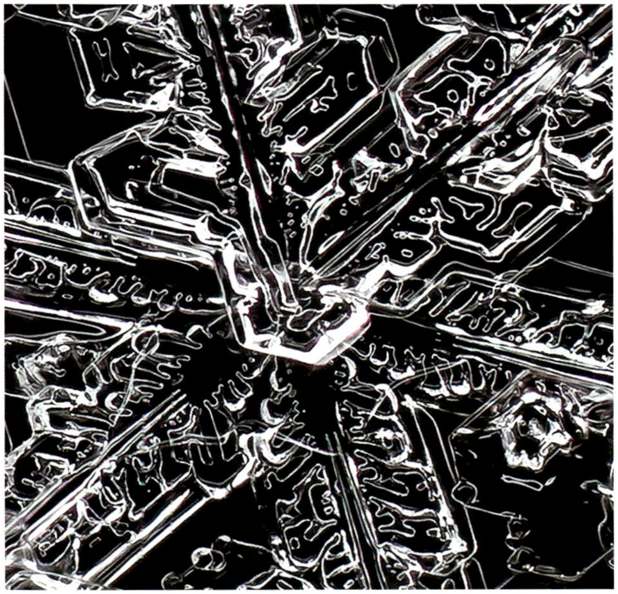

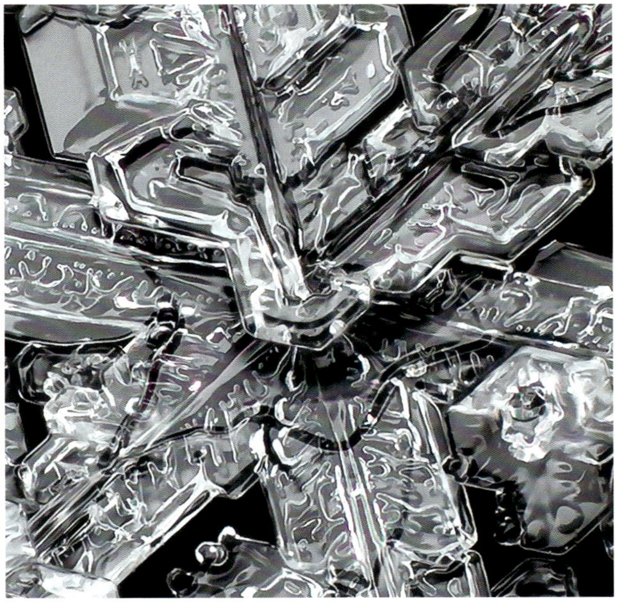

Right: Center close-up. The same snowflake photographed at different angles reveals new features in each image.

Facing page: With the help of a peculiar snowflake, optical interference can generate a spectacular show of colour within the various surface details of the crystal.

Breaking Snowflakes

Snowflakes are incredibly fragile crystals, and moving a snowflake is likely to break it in some way. This doesn't mean a broken snowflake is a worthless subject, however. You can creatively recombine the pieces resulting in a beautiful image with extra depth.

Below is the image of a snowflake straight out of camera *(bottom left)*. This image was a test shot to gauge exposure and the angle of light. I liked the effect, but when I went to find the snowflake again the wind had blown it to a new position. In my attempt to nudge it back to the previous angle, the crystal snapped in two along its center. Carefully moving each crystal piece allowed me to create the illusion of a complete snowflake, but with an important difference: each half was on a different angle. The final image *(bottom right)* was created from the broken pieces.

The angle shifted enough between the two halves allowing the surface reflection to only affect one piece. The final image has a unique appeal that could have only been possible because of my meddling.

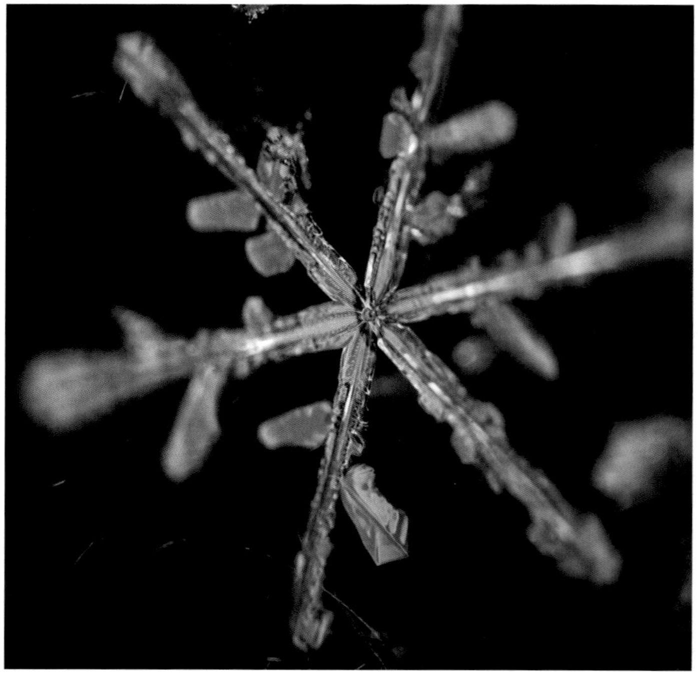

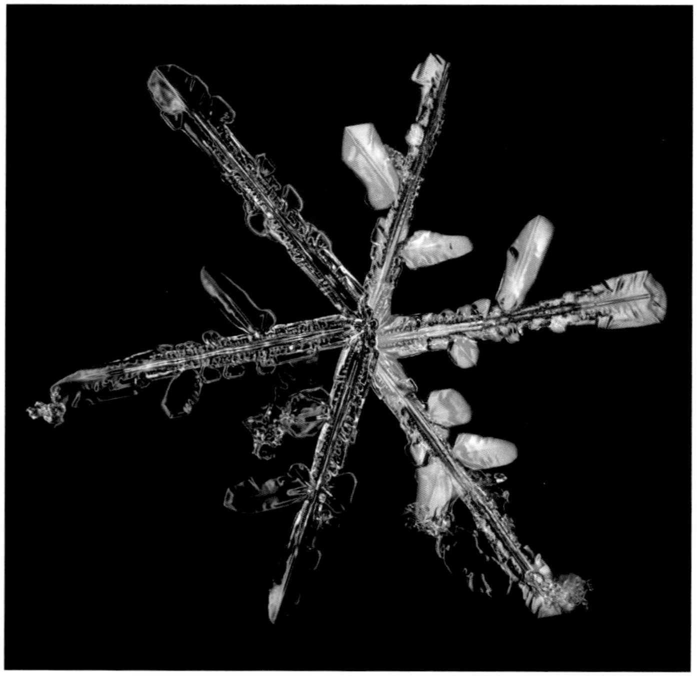

Above: You'll notice that the two images are not in the same orientation. It appears that the image on the right is rotated roughly 180° compared to the original position. This can be done intentionally in post processing to find the best balance within the frame, other times it's due to the repositioning of the crystal. The latter is true here.

Facing page: A broken snowflake isn't a total loss if you can keep the pieces together.

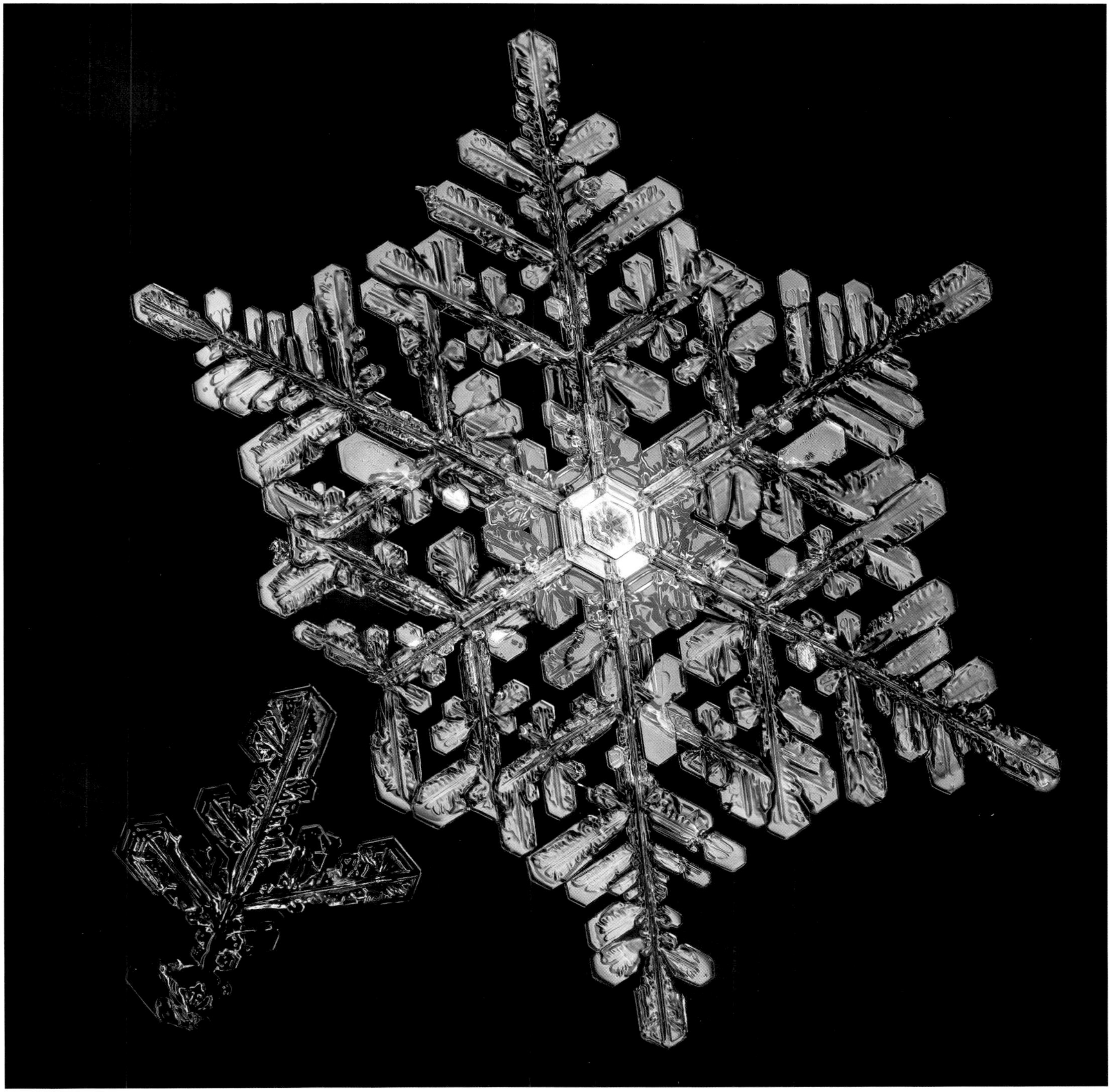

Alternate Method for Shifting Focus
Another technique involves resting the ring flash on the mitten itself, which is possible at the higher levels of magnification. You can then pivot the camera through the focus points needed, which gives an extra level of stability. The results can be a bit unexpected, however. The image (*facing page*) was created using this technique, and it creates a unique effect:

Because the camera and flash are pivoting around the snowflake, the surface of the snowflake gradually changes from reflective to transparent. Every frame would record the snowflake with a slightly different amount of light reflecting back off the surface. These combined together create a smooth gradient.

Overshooting
As previously mentioned, there is no absolute method to determine if you've photographed every necessary slice of focus on a snowflake. There is nothing more frustrating than going through the editing process only to find out that you're missing large chunks of focus. The solution is to overshoot by a large margin.

I may shoot 100-300 images of the same snowflake, even though I might use only 30-50 of them. The extra images give me a safety net to hunt for any missing areas of focus, and this tactic has saved many snowflakes from the digital trashcan. Move through the focus of the snowflake back and forth as many times as you feel are needed, then once more. You'll thank me later.

Extra Batteries, Fast Memory
After shooting for a few seconds, you may notice your camera begin to struggle keeping pace. Fast memory cards should be kept in ample supply, with a full day of shooting generating thousands of images. The fastest memory you can afford will help not only in the field, but also to quickly offload the images. Two cards are recommended if you want to keep shooting while one downloads to your computer.

Imagine those thousands of images, each one requiring a flash exposure. I have multiple sets of rechargeable flash batteries constantly being switched from camera to charger when they begin to show signs of running low (more frequent occurrences of black frames).

Further Stability and Controlled Breathing
You might still find your camera wandering or shaking slightly as you attempt to get the necessary images. In sub-zero temperatures, you will likely begin shivering at some point too. Are there any techniques to keep things even more stable?

I find that controlling my breathing can help significantly. Taking a deep breath and slowly exhaling for the few seconds it takes to pass through the all of the focus points makes the process more accurate. Also, pressing your face more firmly against the camera will help absorb some of the shake introduced by your hands and arms.

Facing page: This snowflake was photographed by pivoting the camera on the edge of the ring flash. A magnification of 3:1 or more with the Canon MP-E 65mm lens makes this focus method very successful, and can create unique lighting effects.

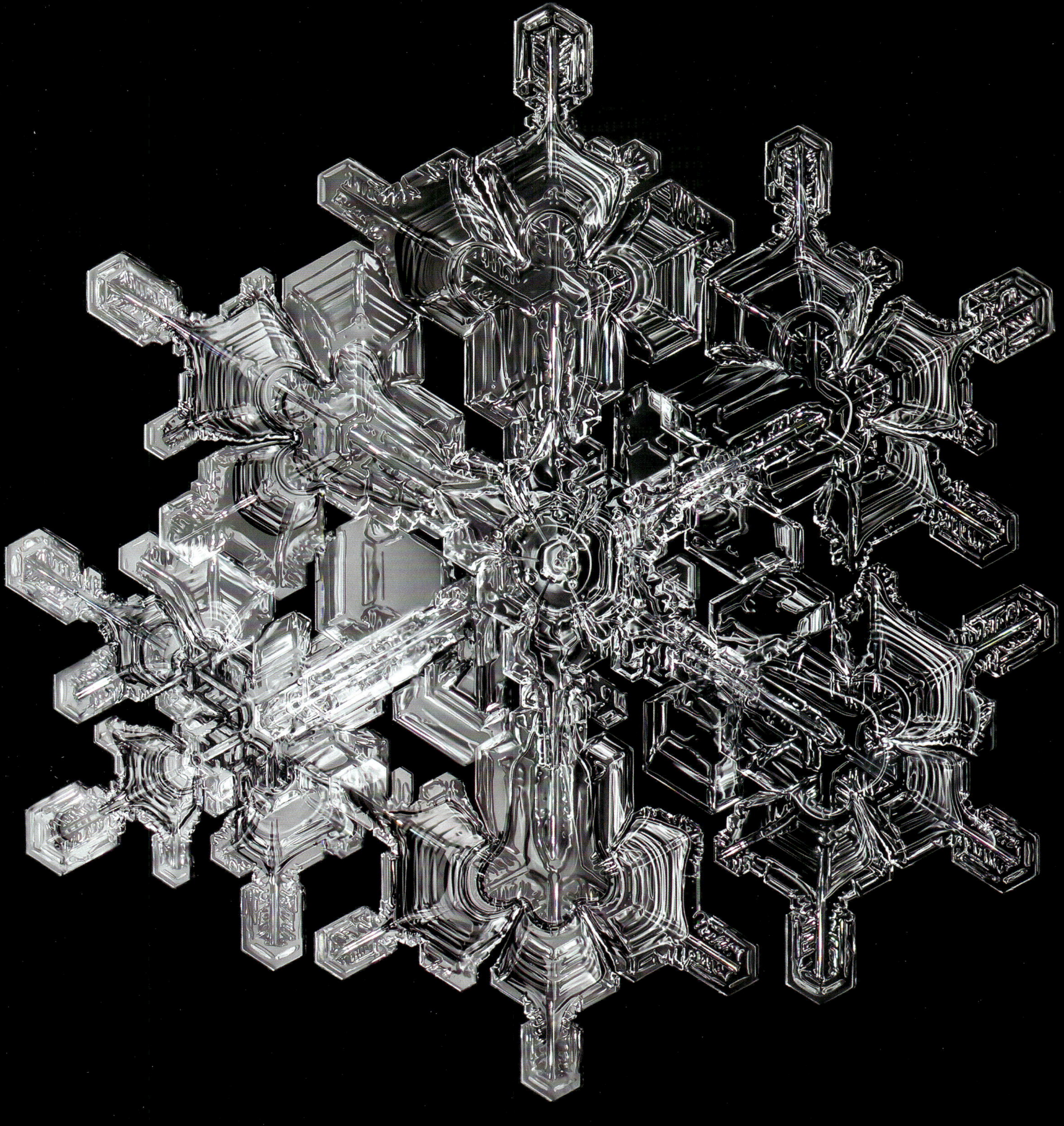

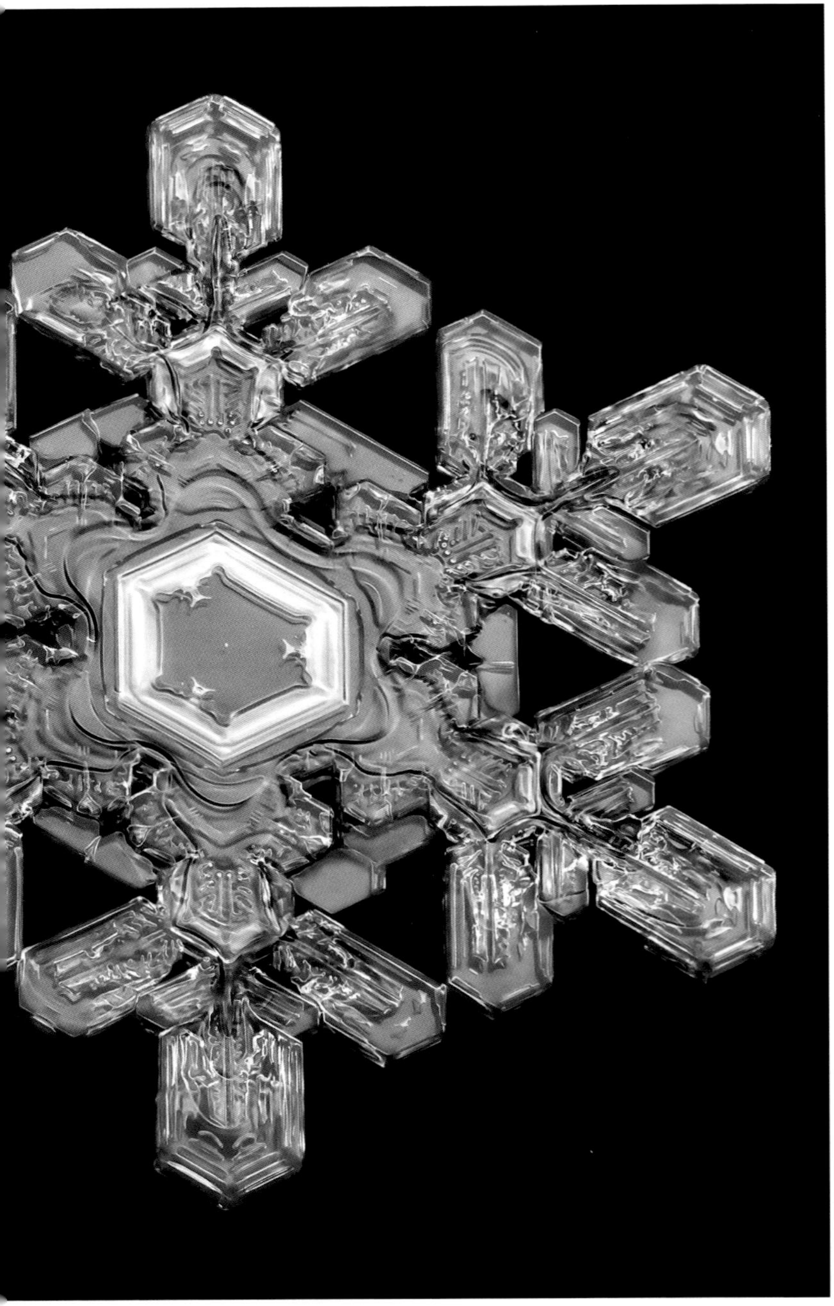

Protecting Your Camera

There are a few things to consider when using your DSLR to photograph snowflakes. Even the flagship cameras from large manufacturers (such as the Canon 1D series) are only rated to work in temperatures as cold as 0°C / 32°F. Any colder and you're on your own, but in practice temperatures warmer than -20°C / -4°F shouldn't give you any trouble for a short time[1]. That said, there are no guarantees!

As the camera becomes colder, the batteries in both the flash and camera body will begin to lose efficiency and perform poorly compared to warmer temperatures. It is always advisable to keep extra batteries either inside your jacket or anywhere else nearby that's warm. I photograph snowflakes in my backyard, so the fresh batteries are kept inside the house.

This brings up another important point – take extra precaution when returning your camera back to room temperature. A rapid temperature change can cause water to condense on the outside of the camera, and potentially inside the camera as well. This is likely the reason why even the most expensive DSLRs are not rated for freezing temperatures. There are a few ways to keep your camera safe from this condensation.

Much like bringing home a fish from the pet store, if you put a camera in a sealed plastic bag before bringing it in, it will add a pocket of cool air that will slowly increase its temperature with the camera. It will also act as a barrier, preventing the camera from collecting additional condensation from the humid inside air.

[1]Michael Zhang (2012). Frozen Camera: What a DSLR Looks Like When Shooting in a -25°C Environment. *Petapixel.* Retrieved from http://petapixel.com/2012/12/20/frozen-camera-what-a-dslr-looks-like-when-shooting-in-a-25c-environment/

My personal solution is to place the camera in an air-tight hardshell case. I bring this case outside with me, and use it as a buffer just like the previously-mentioned plastic bag.

Melting Snow and Weather Sealing

Shooting while the snow is still falling will introduce another problem – water. Some snowflakes will melt on contact with your camera, others may melt with a breath of air. In any case, you may have to deal with a situation where water could potentially get inside your camera.

I recommend shooting with a camera that offers internal weather sealing if possible, otherwise you run the risk of damaging your equipment. That said, the lens and the flash unit I use for this subject are not available with weather sealing; I have had no problems with a bit of care and attention. Keep a dry lens cloth with you and frequently wipe up any excess moisture on any non-weather sealed components, including the pop-up flash cavity if your camera has one.

I have not encountered damage from water, humidity or temperature in over a decade of photographing snowflakes. The risk of such damage is always present, so take as many measures as possible to limit the risk. Be careful out there!

Facing page: Cold temperatures can create certain risks, but the rewards keep me outside for every snowfall, regardless of temperature.

Right: Shooting at temperatures just above the freezing point can have some reward. Exotic types of snowflakes such as columns, scrolls, arrowheads and bullets can be discovered... but you'll have to shoot quickly before they melt!

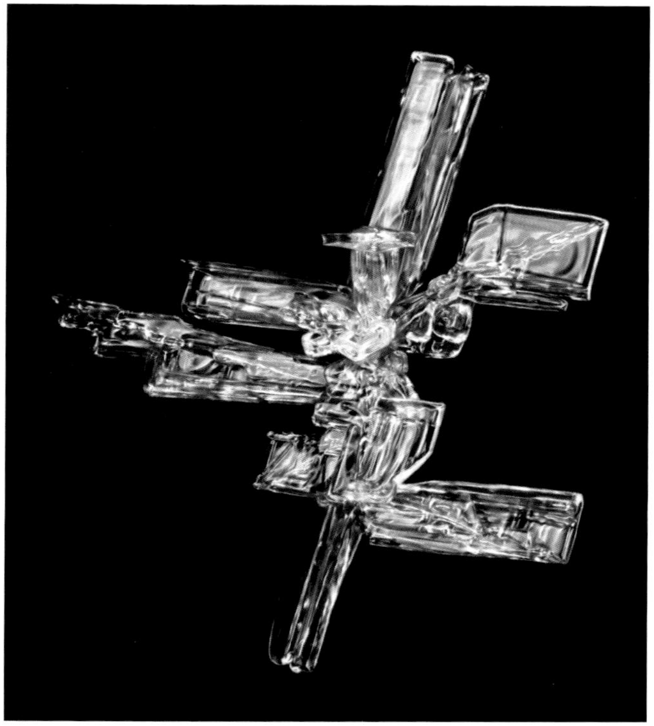

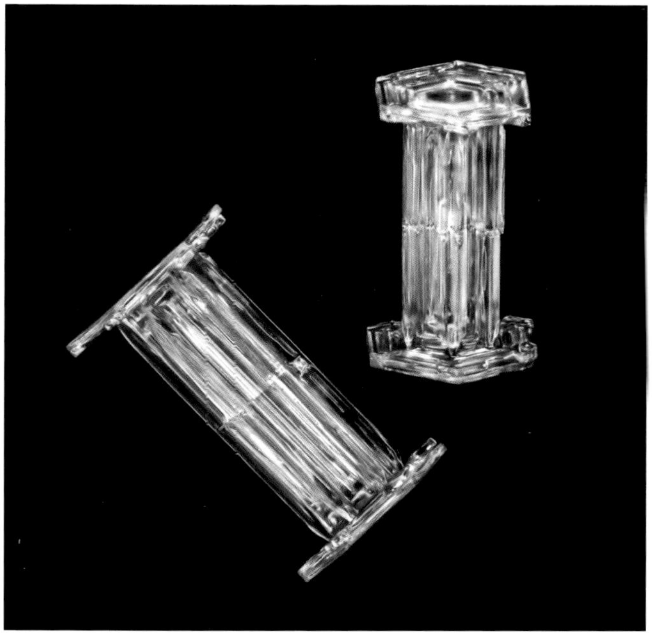

Focus Stacking Not Required

Most of my snowflake photographs are created with the intent to "focus stack", a process where multiple images at different focus points are combined together. This process is time consuming and difficult, and might not be for everyone.

One small slice of focus can reveal enough detail to make a beautiful image. While the entire snowflake in focus has its charm, the small details can be emphasized when the rest of the image out of focus. This technique can be used in a number of ways:

Flat Details: If you choose to shoot the snowflake as flat as possible, more of the crystal will be parallel to the focus plane and appear sharp. You will lose some depth by doing this, but you'll gain more sharpness overall without combining multiple images.

Angle Details: You'll have less in focus, but the details can still be impressive *(below)*. Choosing the proper focus point can be difficult, but not impossible. The shooting techniques used for focus stacking can still be useful, allowing you to cover everything and then simply choose your favourite slice.

Partial Focus Stacking: The idea of focus stacking can be applied only to a small section of a snowflake, usually around the center. This allows for the focus to fade while still retaining many beautiful details.

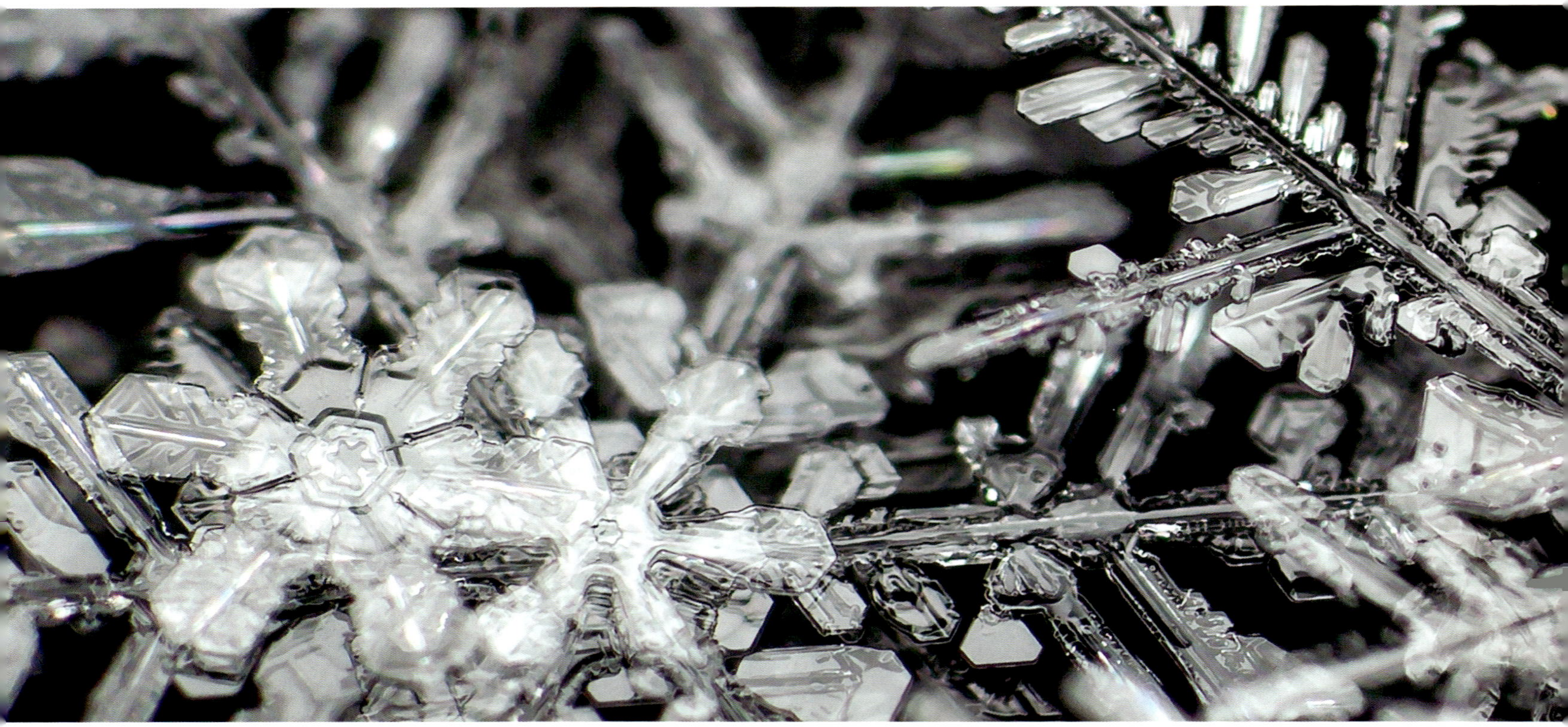

Regardless of the intent, you'll find that your snowflake images can easily stand on their own. As you'll see in the "editing workflow" section of this book, focus stacking can be an involved and frustrating process. I encourage you to give it a try, but rest assured that even a single image can contain its own wonders.

Below: A single frame can contain incredible details. Cropped to show just the in-focus areas, it is a perfect example illustrating that focus stacking is not required for beautiful snowflake images.

Right: Photographing a snowflake as flat as possible will result in much of the crystal being in focus, but some depth is lost by this technique.

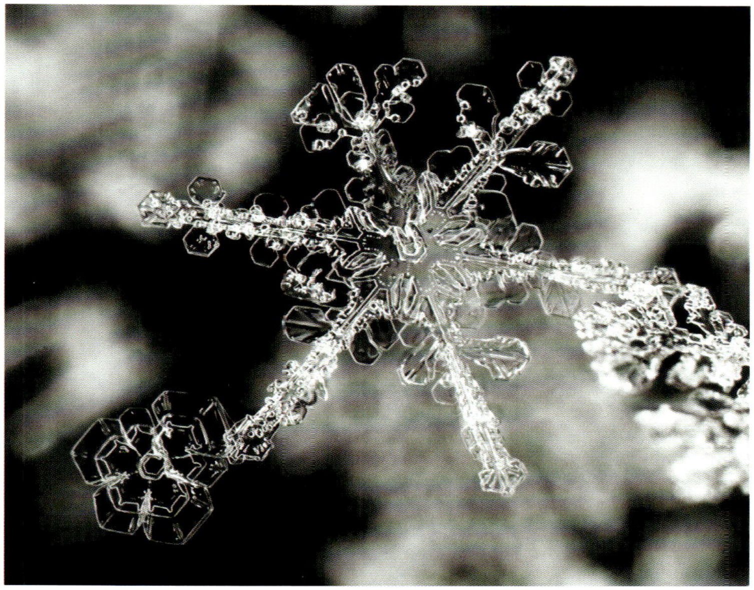

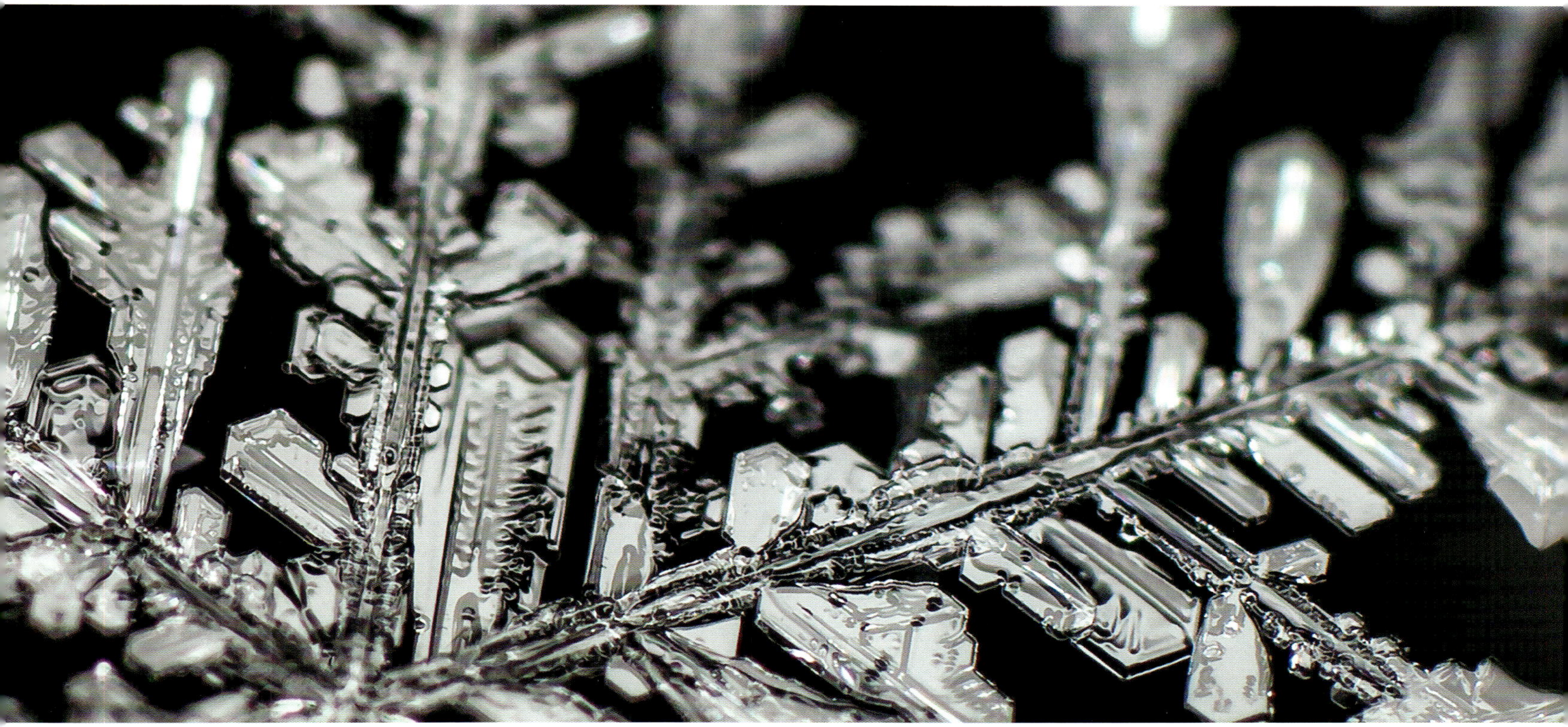

Other Lens Options

While I've talked confidently about the prowess of the Canon MP-E 65mm F/2.8 1x-5x Macro lens, it is not the only lens capable of photographing snowflakes. There are plenty of options available, from inexpensive modern lenses to vintage niche lenses, and the number of high-magnification options available is growing faster now than at any other point in history. Let's take a look at a few options and discuss benefits and drawbacks for each.

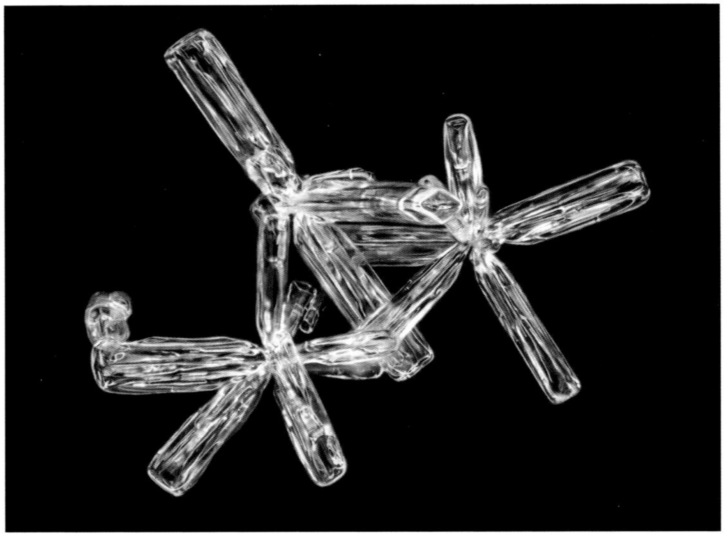

Above: Canon 20mm F/3.5 *Below:* Mitakon 20mm F/2

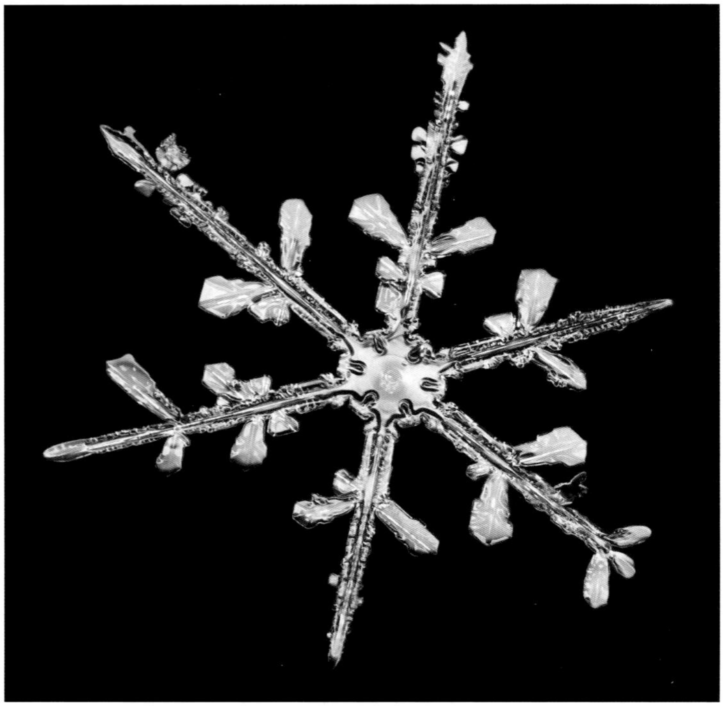

Canon 20mm F/3.5 Macrophoto Bellows Lens
(circa 1976)
Bellows lenses have always fascinated me. Intended to work with the Canon Auto Bellows for the FD-mount cameras built prior to the EOS system and EF lens mount, they can easily be adapted to modern cameras. You can even put this lens on a modern mirrorless system – macro lenses generally hold up well over time.

Capable of reaching 10x magnifications, one of the limiting factors here is that the lens will suffer from diffraction – just like any other lens at such extreme enlargements. The lens (or bellows) also does not have a filter thread, which would be required to attach a ring flash properly to the front of this contraption. Still, an easy solution is gaffer's tape which I utilized in my test. The result?

Decent image quality, not quite on par with the best modern solutions but still quite capable. The bottom rail of the bellows system can be rotated sideways and can function as a handle for easy positioning. Still, I would worry about repeatedly using bellows in the damp environment of falling snow.

Mitakon 20mm F/2 4.5x-5x Super Macro Lens

This lens held a lot of promise, but ultimately disappointed. The three-bladed aperture isn't a huge deal, but it also lacks a filter thread requiring the use of tape to hold things together. Decades after the release of the Canon bellows lens, it doesn't offer up any significant benefits. With a working distance of only 2cm / 0.8", it can also be tricky to find the proper angle to get reflective details without the ring flash running out of room – there's a table in the way.

Mitakon 85mm F/2.8 1x-5x Macro Lens

Opposite of the 20mm lens from Mitakon, their 85mm offering has the longest working distance of any 5x macro lens I have seen: 10cm / 3.93". This has a distinct advantage for snowflake photography, as the angle of incidence can be much shallower, allowing the snowflake to be closer to parallel along the focal plane while still being able to achieve surface reflection.

This is a big deal. It means that fewer images are required for focus stacking purposes, cutting the number of needed frames by at least half. Fewer shots required and a faster post-processing workflow. Seems like a dream snowflake lens, but there are some important technical and procedural drawbacks.

The further away you push the working distance, the lower your resolving power will be at 5x and beyond. This is also why microscope objectives with the highest resolving power also have the shortest working distance. This lens has a hard time keeping up with other lenses in the "detail" category, but what if it allows you to create an image that you otherwise wouldn't have been able to create?

By chance, I happened to be testing this lens with snowflakes when I encountered the perfect specimen of one of the rarest varieties of snowflakes: a double-terminated arrowhead crystal. Arrowhead crystals themselves are exotic and uncommon, but I believe this is the first one discovered to cleanly finish in a point on either side. It's also the only crystal of this type I had any luck getting surface reflections from, which I can attribute to the longer working distance.

I believe this image, the way you see it (*below*), was only possible with the Mitakon 85mm F/2.8 1x-5x Macro lens. One final point of difficulty to consider: the longer working distance makes it difficult to hold the end of the lens while simultaneously resting your hand on a table - unless you have incredibly big hands.

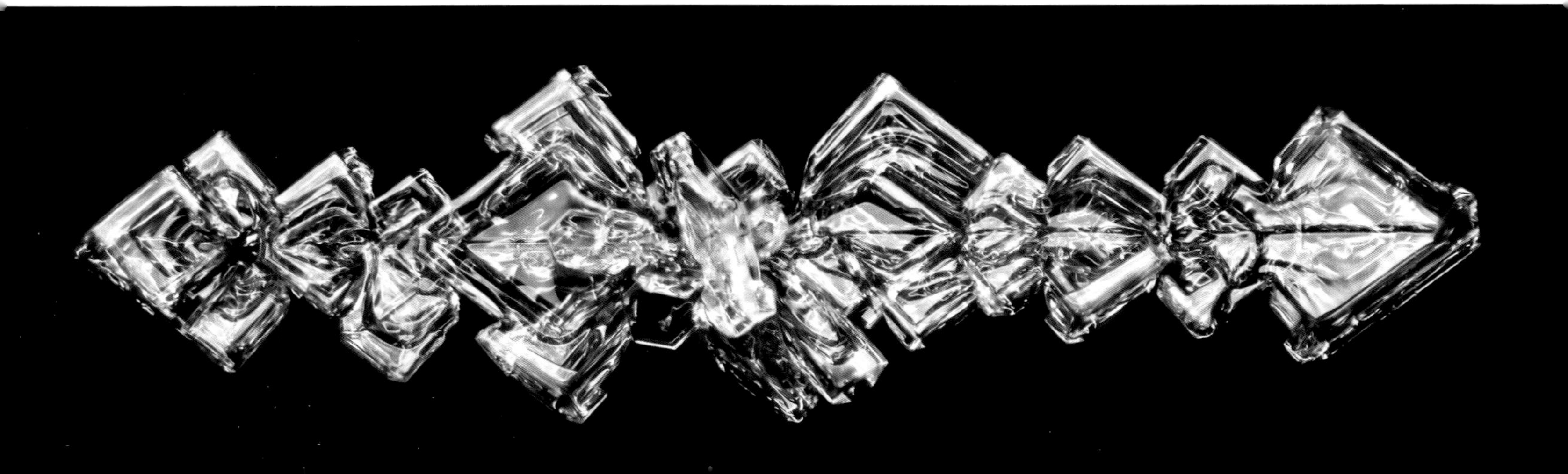

Laowa 25mm F/2.8 2.5x-5x Macro Lens

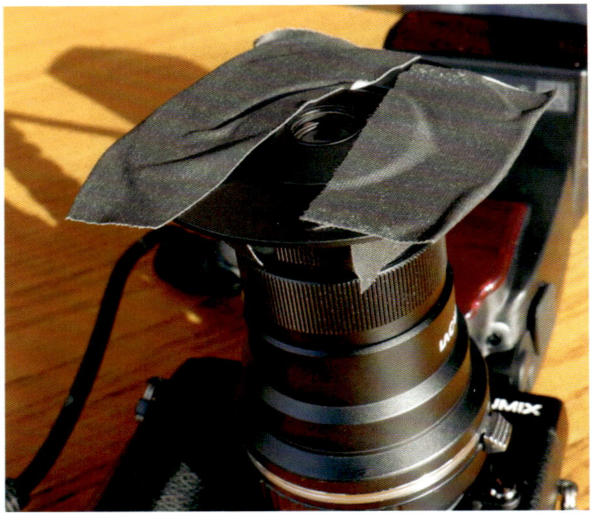

The closest rival to the Canon MP-E 65mm F/2.8 1x-5x Macro lens comes from Venus Optics, the manufacturers of the Laowa series of lenses. It covers the magnification range of the average snowflakes you're likely to find interesting and resolves extremely well. My tests place it slightly less than Canon's offering, but others have said it exceeds this benchmark.

Optically it's great, but there is one frustrating design choice: like others, this lens does not offer a filter thread. Also requiring tape to fix the flash to the front of the lens (*right*), any wiggle of the flash orientation during shooting can change the critical angle of light and might change the look of the snowflake as you try to shoot images for a focus stacked result.

Laowa 50mm F/2.8 2x Macro Lens for Micro Four Thirds

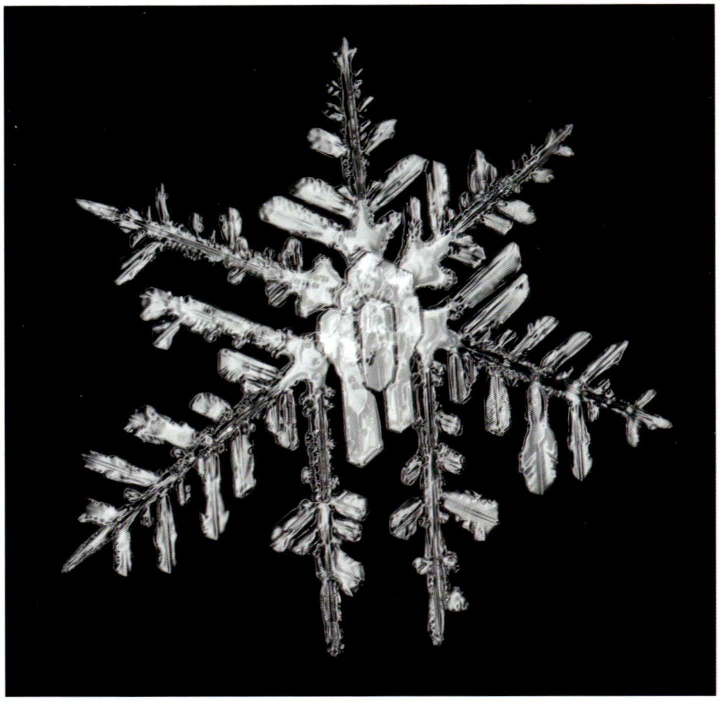

So new to the market that I haven't been able to test it with snowflakes yet, but with other subjects this is a very promising option. A 2x magnification on a smaller sensor with a 2x crop factor results in a comparable magnification of 4x against a full-frame camera. We're in snowflake territory there, and we've got filter threads!

If you shoot with smaller camera bodies and want a lens designed for them, this is shaping up to be a great option. Currently, the cameras that can utilize this lens are limited to around 20MP at the time this book is published. That will change in time, but remember that diffraction is the deciding factor in overall resolving power.

Top Right: It can be a point of frustration to tape the attachment ring to the front of the lens. It works, but it's not pretty. Photo by Jordan Drake.

Bottom Right: The results, however, can be impressive!

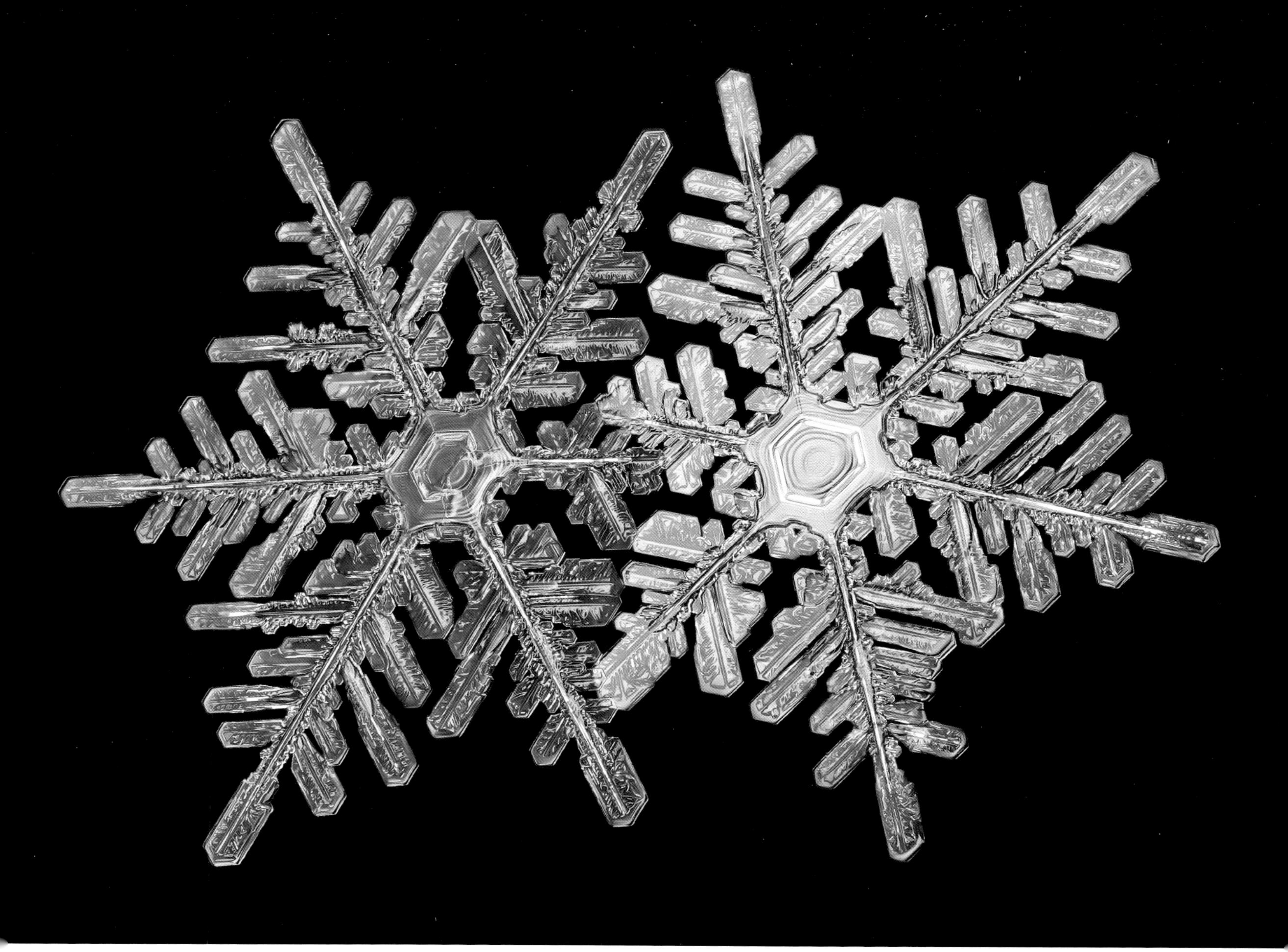

Panasonic Leica DG Macro-Elmarit 45mm f/2.8
My favourite macro lens for the Micro Four Thirds system is this one. Optically phenomenal, although it only gets to a 1:1 magnification. This still mimics what you would see at a 2:1 magnification on a full-frame sensor, and some snowflakes can be quite large. When you get two giant gems "holding hands" and becoming a larger snowflake as a result, you can fill the frame with frozen wonder (*above*).

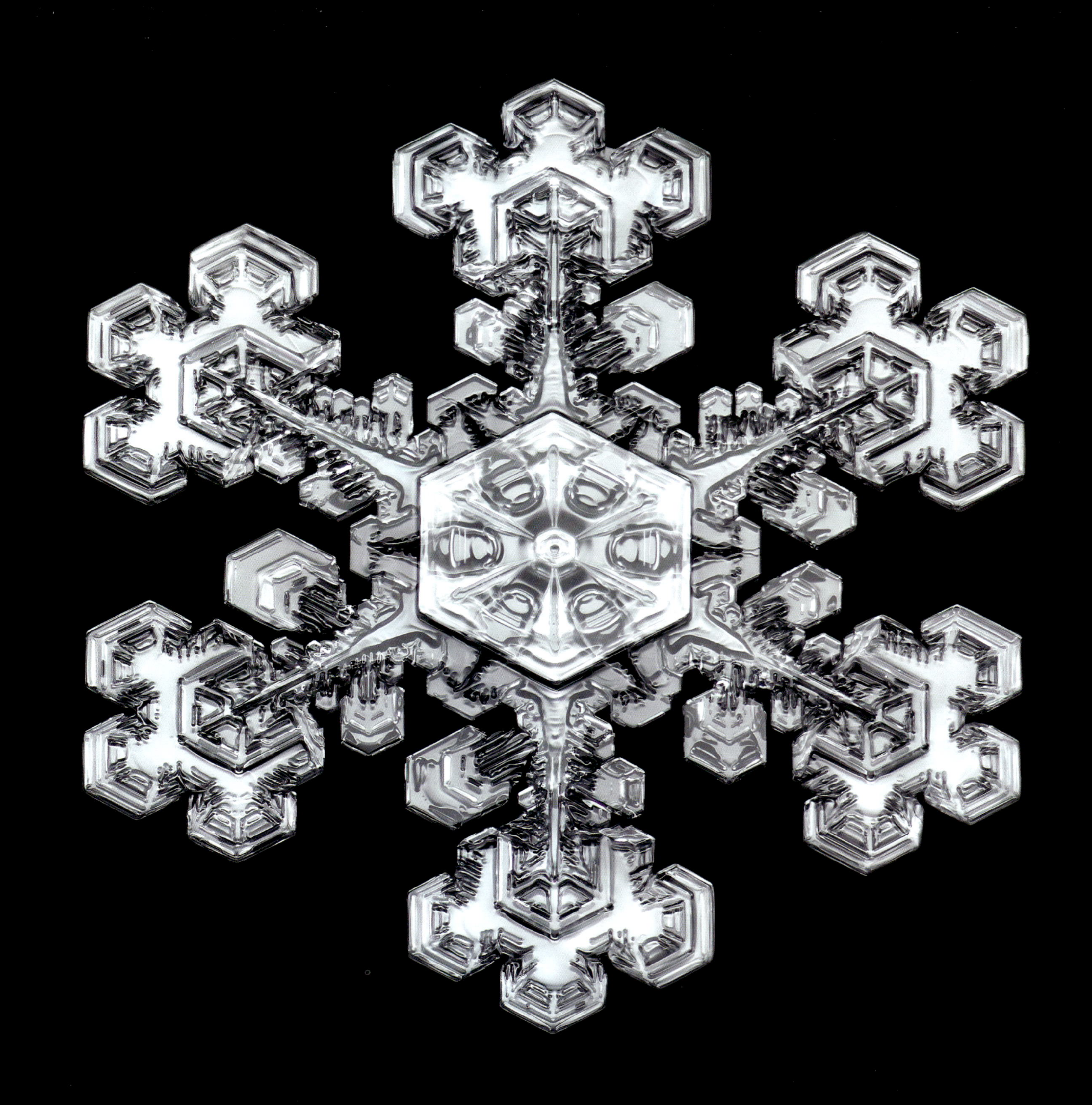

Illusion of Symmetry, Bias on Beauty

Symmetry is beautiful. As such, it's often the case that the most symmetrical snowflakes are seen as the most beautiful. The closer you look, the more deviations from perfect symmetry you're likely to find, but the snowflake still feels cohesively balanced. At least, that's what I want you to believe.

Truthfully, not all snowflakes are symmetrical. Most naturally formed snowflakes are so far from symmetrical that I simply pass them over unless there is some other quirky redeeming quality – volumetric design or vibrant colours. This applies to every other snowflake photographer I have encountered as well: we showcase the crystals that we find the most appealing. This introduces a heavy bias towards your own initial impressions of what you're likely to find when you go snowflake hunting.

Many snowfalls produce ugly snowflakes. I might look over a thousand snowflakes before one catches my attention enough to pull up the camera. You can observe them so quickly and recognize patterns of interest with a bit of training: large centers, hexagons that never grew branches, and symmetrical designs.

Side Note: After a day of "snowflake watching" you'll get what I first experienced as a child - the **Tetris Effect**. Named after the videogame Tetris, which I was somewhat addicted to in my youth. I would often close my eyes and see falling blocks (Tetriminos) and my mind would continue to solve puzzles after I stopped playing. The only other time I have experienced something similar in my life is after a day of photographing snowflakes. They get in your head, and your brain continues the pattern matching process long after you've come inside.

It took me a decade of documenting snowflakes to discover this castle of ice (*facing page*). Be prepared to practice on less-than-spectacular gems, and polish your skills for that unexpected moment when the most beautiful snowflake you've ever seen falls from the sky.

Right: These snowflakes encountered super-cooled water droplets while they were forming, which freeze on impact like little icy warts. The pristine crystalline structure underneath is completely obscured and the symmetry is erased in the process.

This is called "rime" and is a common occurrence. On many occasions I have encountered rime-covered crystals before and after "clean" snowflakes during the same snowfall.

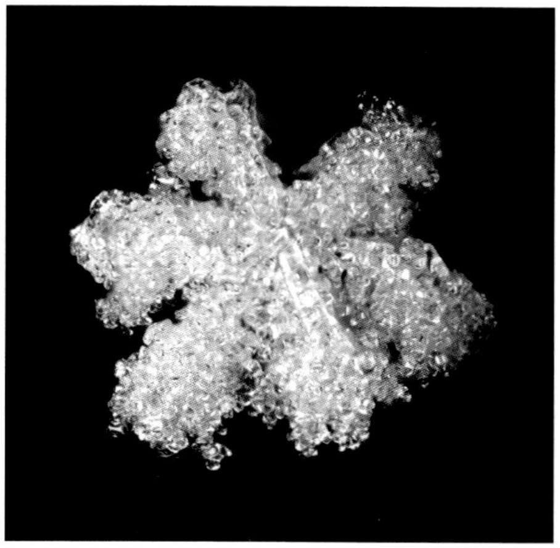

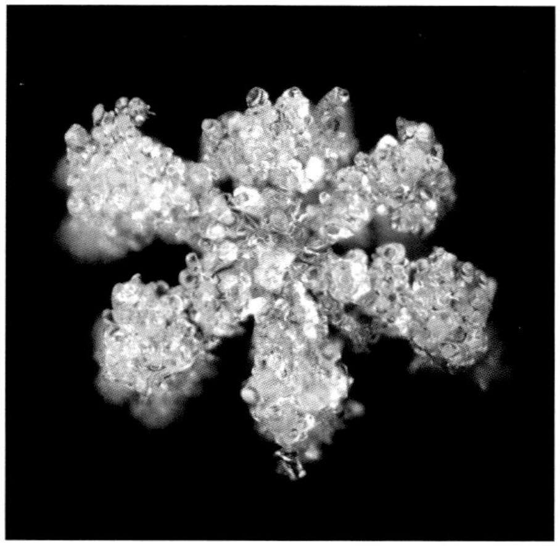

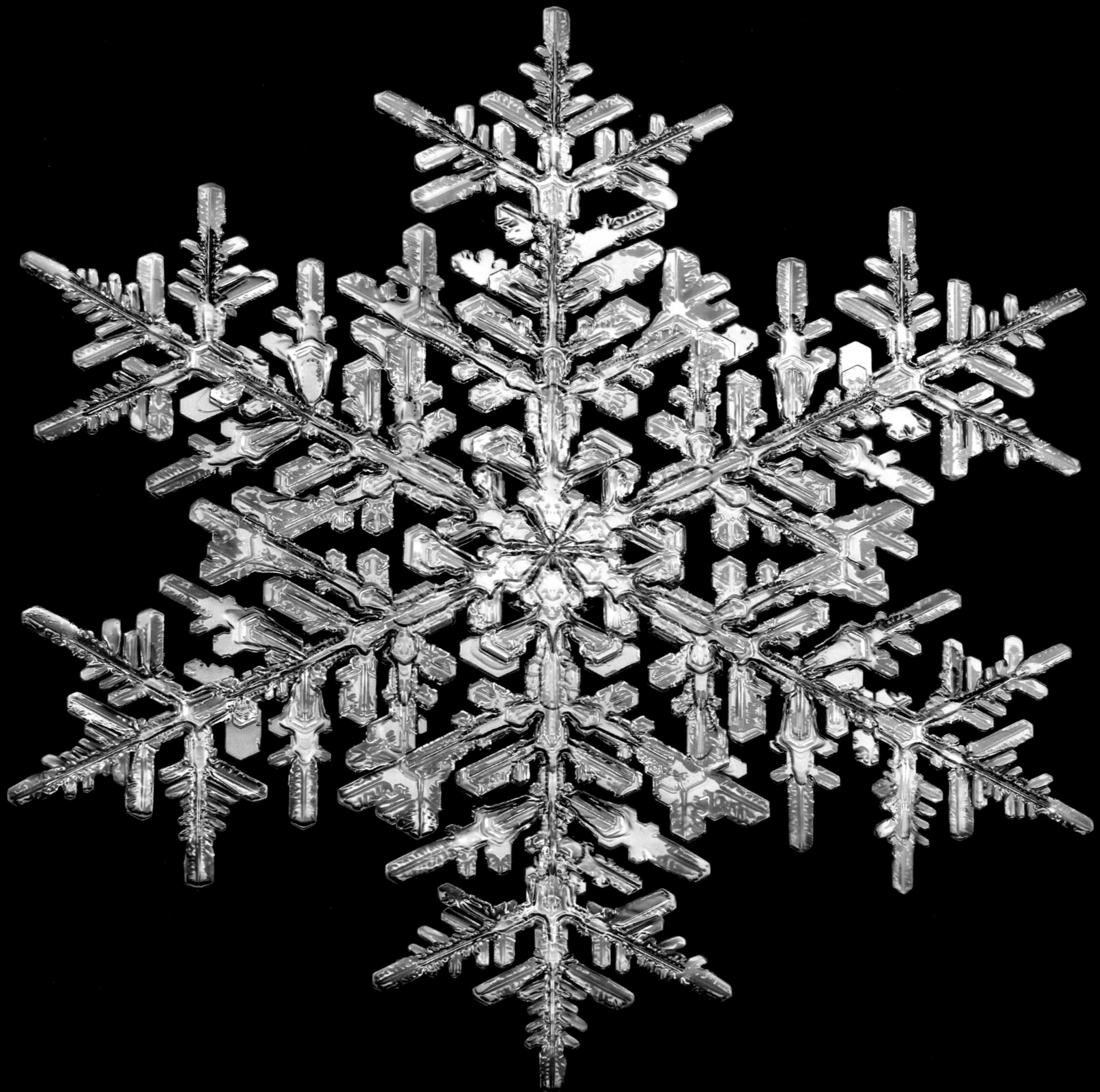

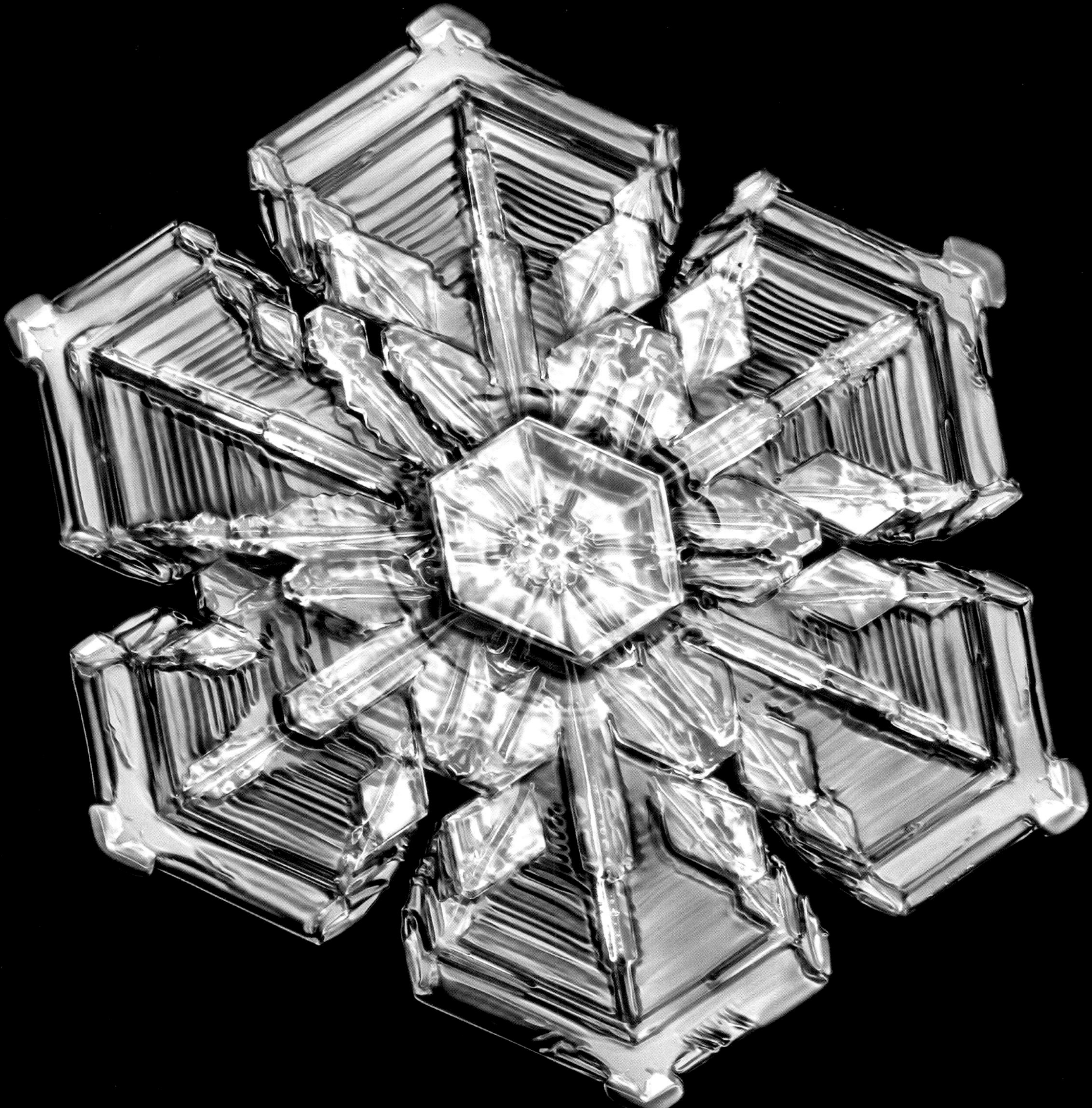

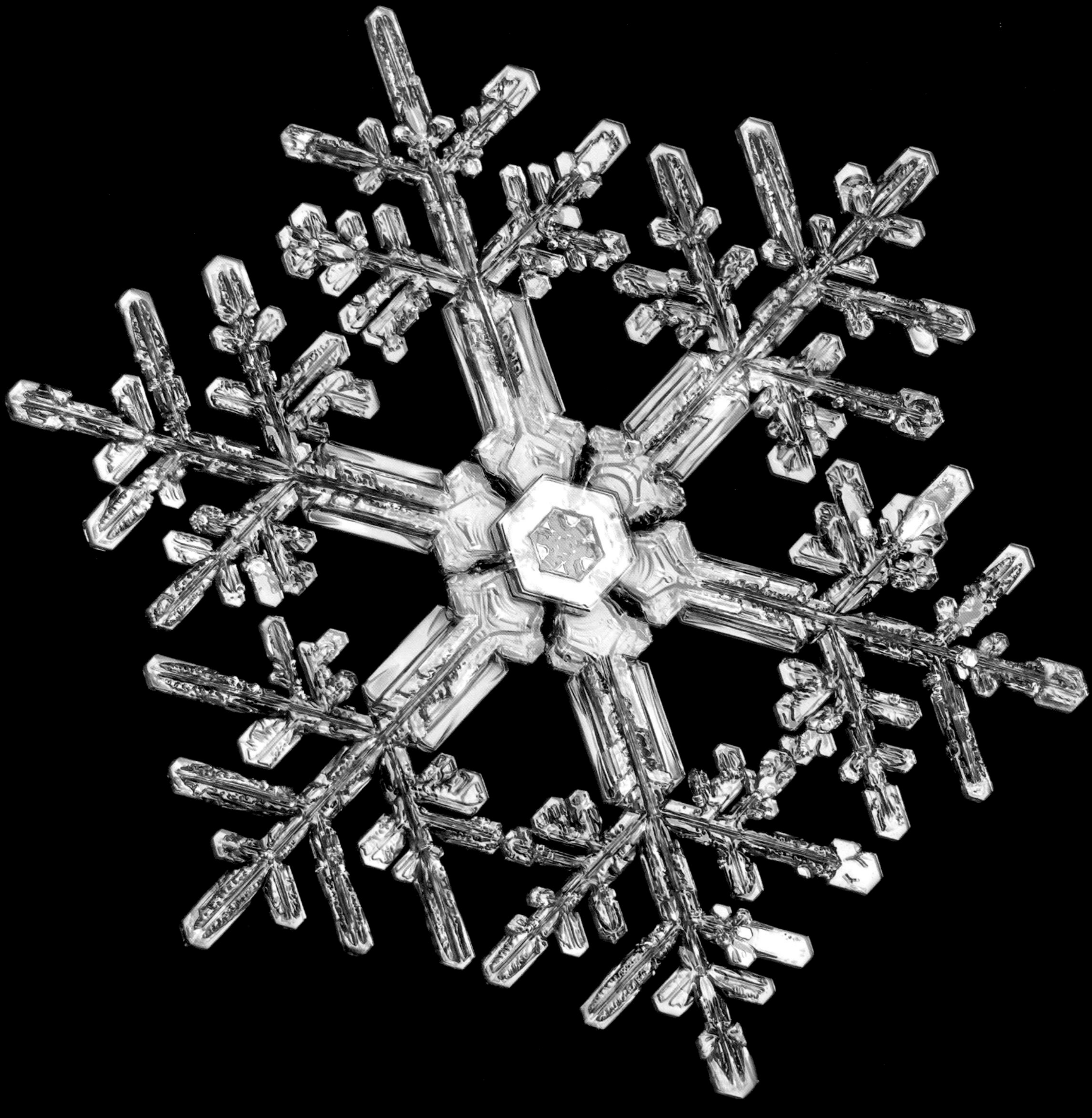

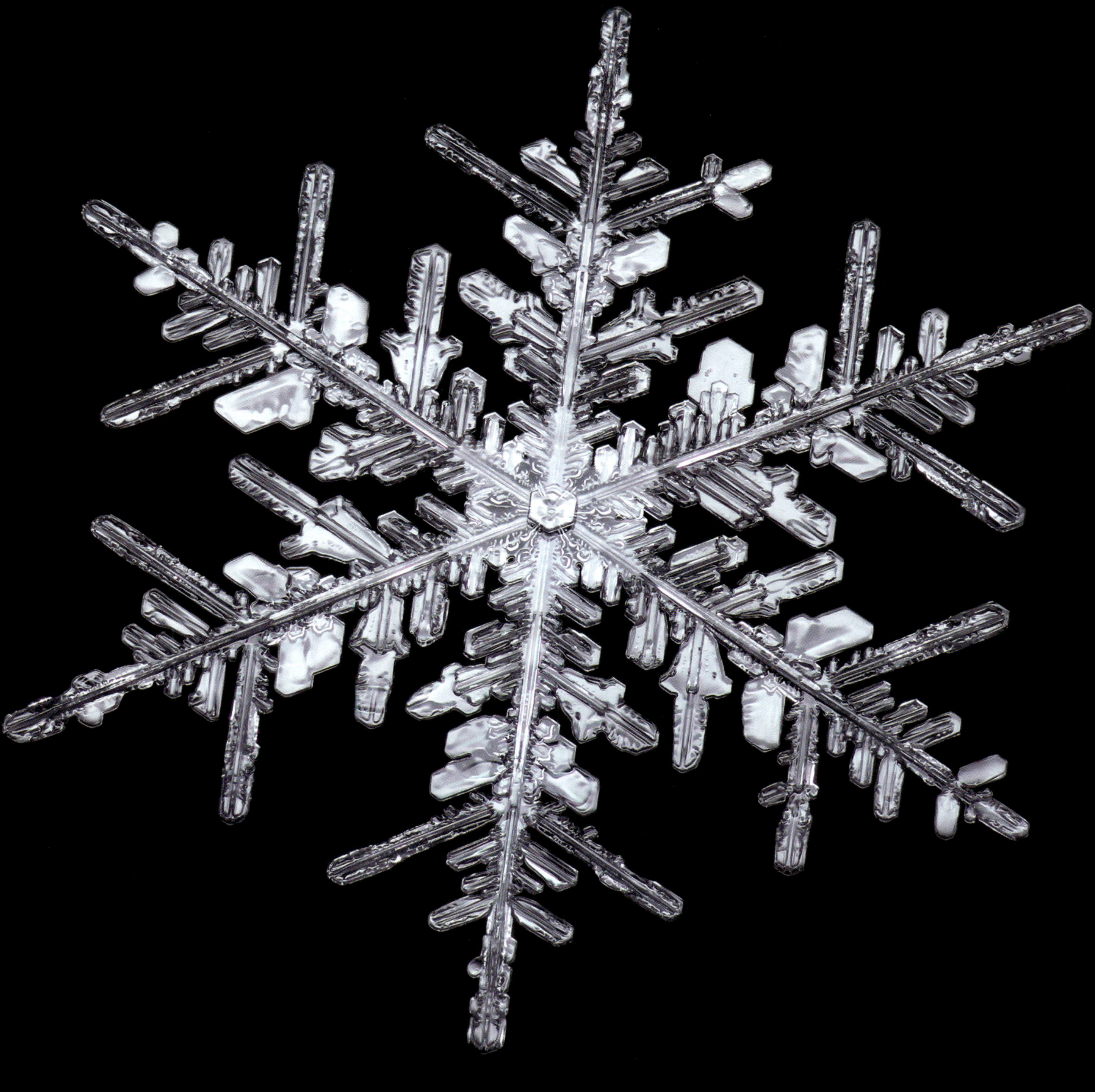

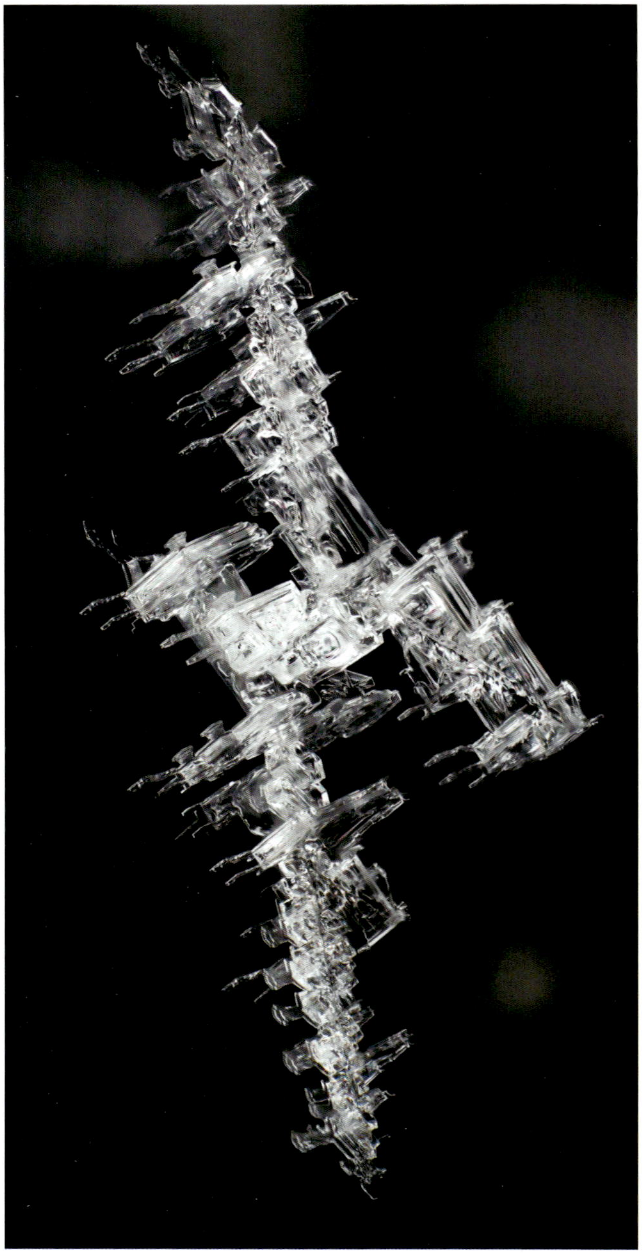

Exotic Snowflakes

Beyond the bias of symmetry, you can discover some truly enigmatic snowflakes falling from the sky. How about this one (*left*)? Does anyone else see it as two Praying Mantids hugging each other? Maybe snowflakes could become the new Rorschach (inkblot) test. This is an example of a number of strange happenings, including arrowhead crystal formations where a molecular misalignment happens at the very beginning of crystal formation and that echoes through the entire crystal structure.

Crystal twinning makes wild designs, and how about column-type snowflakes growing plates on the ends and then back to columns? These bizarre formations are the main reason I continue to photograph snowflakes – it's fun to unravel the mysteries. I might be losing my mind in the process; do you see curling stones in this image (*below*)?

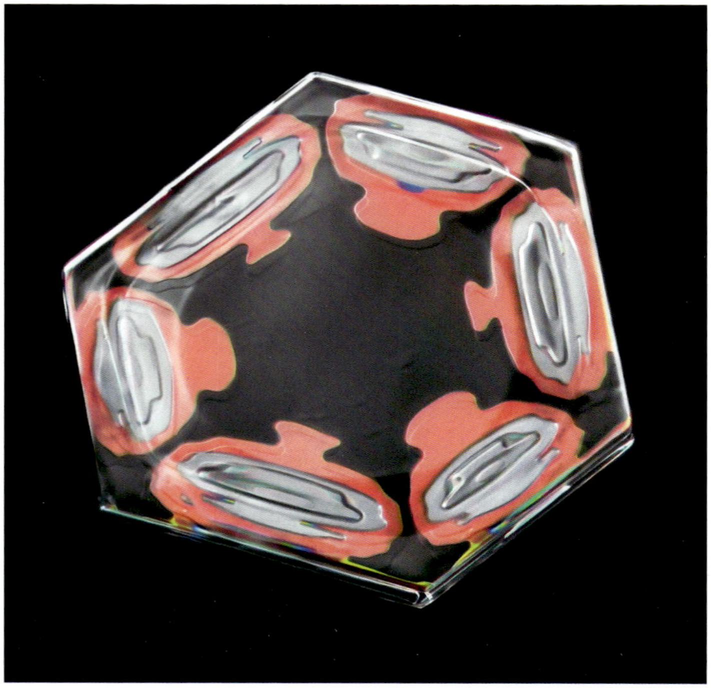

Facing page: How strange can snowflakes get? This is just a small sampling of the oddities that fall from the sky.

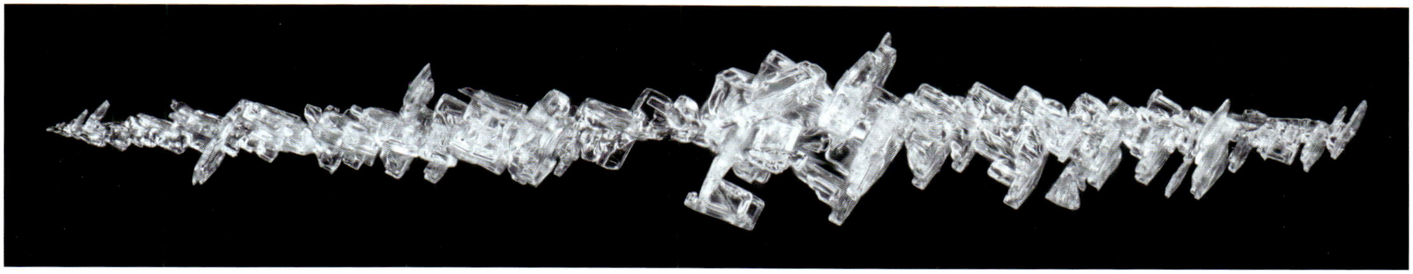

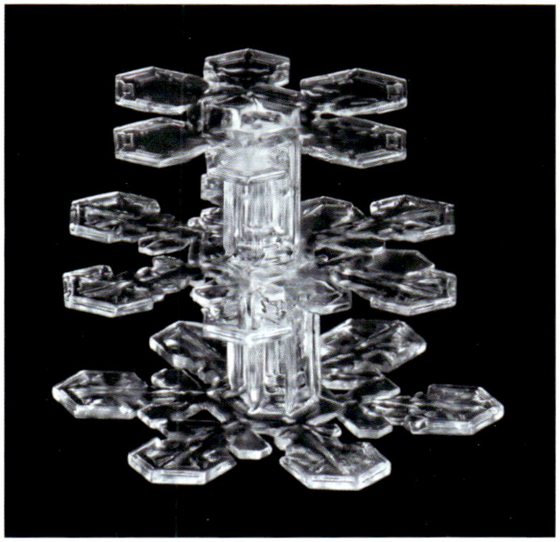

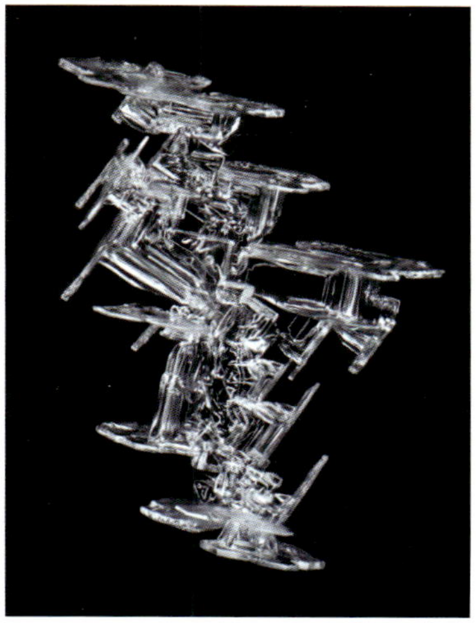

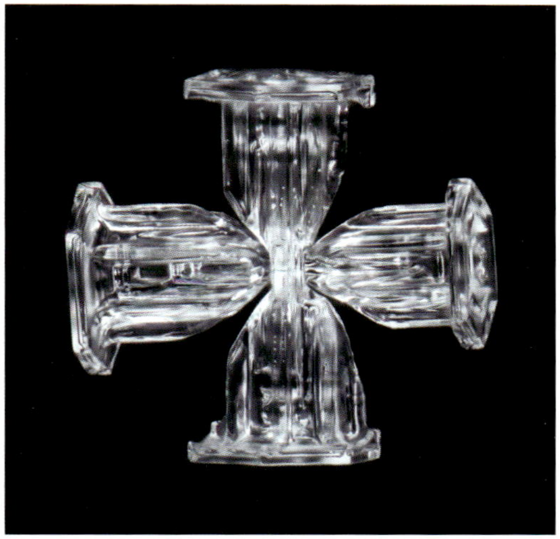

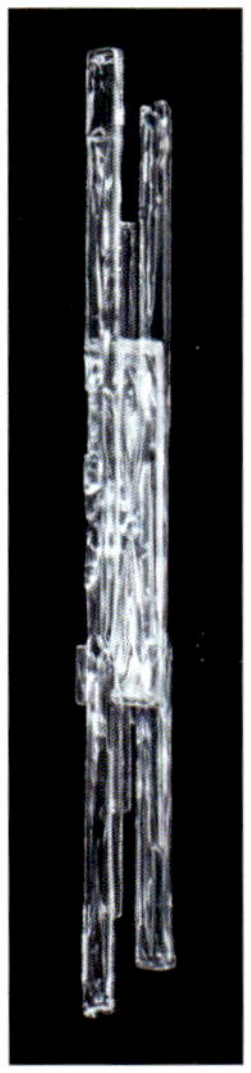

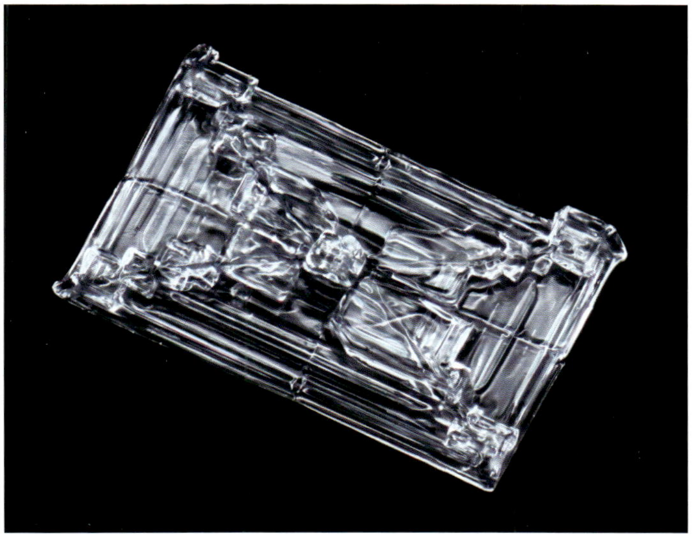

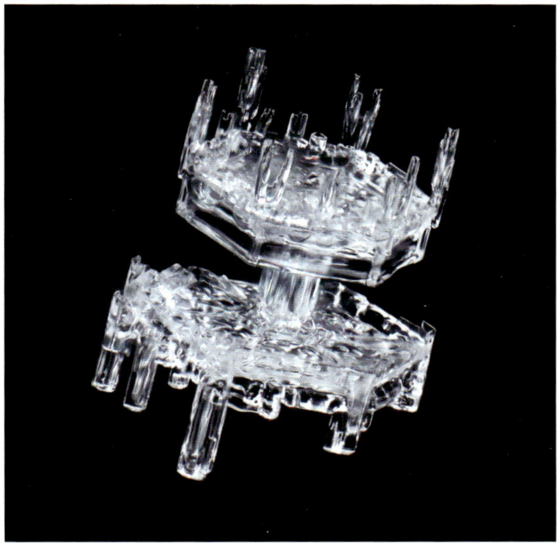

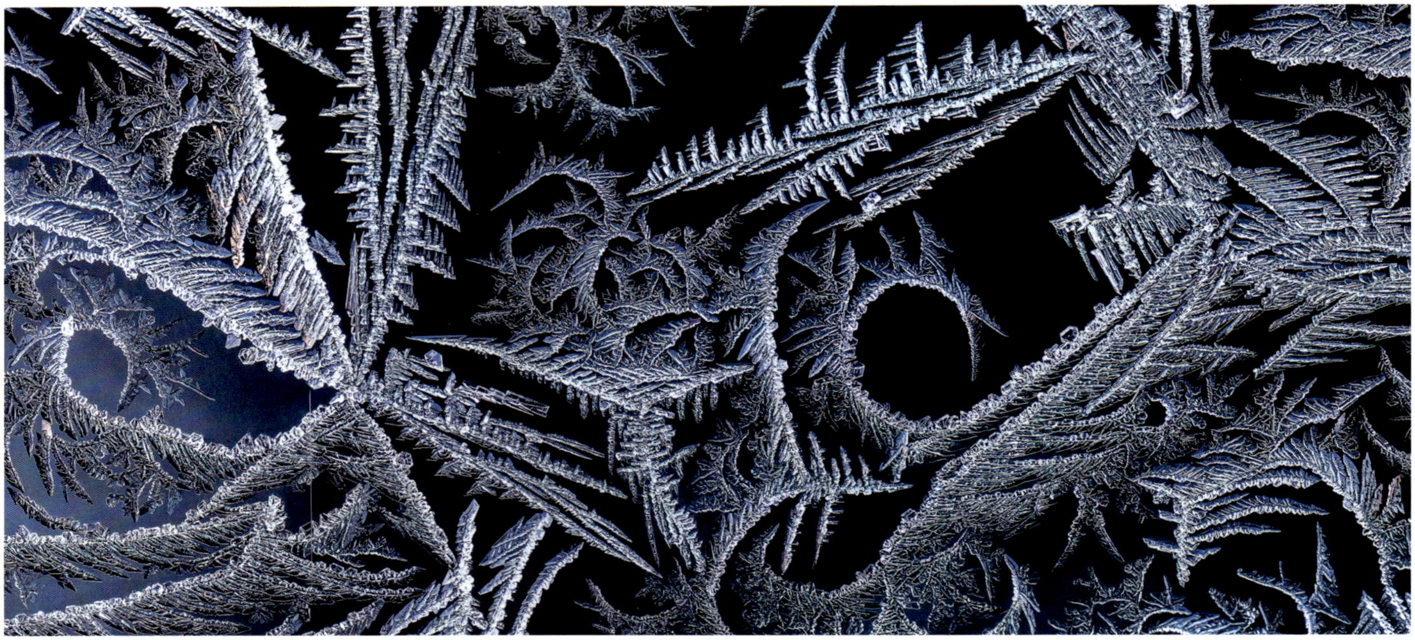

Photographing Frost

My friends and neighbours probably think I'm crazy – and it's easy to come to that conclusion when you watch me photographing frost. While tagging along with a hunting expedition in the Yukon wilderness, I had noticed frost forming on the windows of the vehicles. The patterns were enchanting. It was difficult to find a final composition that worked, as if I was searching for a collection of pseudo-random lines and shapes that all connect together in some meaningful way. It's abstract artwork. Firing off hundreds of frames at a vehicle window will make people raise their eyebrows at you, however; Embrace the awkwardness!

Photographing frost requires a very similar set of skills to photographing snowflakes. The same equipment, the same camera settings, and plenty of patience required for focus stacking. Frost can often be more sprawling or three dimensional than snowflakes, so stacking multiple frames is highly recommended.

Where should you look for frost? As I mentioned, no further than your driveway should give you plenty of options, as frost commonly grows on vehicles during the night in early / late winter. Frost can also be found growing near any source of moisture. This can include caves, air vents, or landscapes frequently affected by fog. Avoid areas near open water or thin ice – there are safer places to find frost on a winter morning.

Different locations can create drastically different structures, and it can be fun to experiment with the possibilities. Frost growing on my car often forms into a Champagne glass shape, where frost growing on a cave wall may take on the appearance of feathers or shells. Even stranger frost could be growing on a spider web, appearing as jagged gemstones strung together. Just as snowflakes come in many shapes and forms, so too does frost; bound by the same laws of physics, it's easy to see similar structures and shapes in each subject.

As with snowflakes, timing is important when photographing frost. As soon as the frost is exposed to sunlight it will begin to melt, quickly destroying its most delicate features. I usually find that the best time to photograph frost is in the morning "blue hour", the hour just before sunrise. You'll have enough light to see your subject, but no risk of it disappearing on you.

Frost is also nearly impossible to manipulate. Because it is usually anchored to a surface at many different points, it can't be moved without being destroyed. Notwithstanding a small twig or leaf that you can relocate, you often have to twist yourself into interesting positions to get the desired angle. By the same virtue, it likely won't blow away on you – but it's a challenge on the same level as snowflake photography.

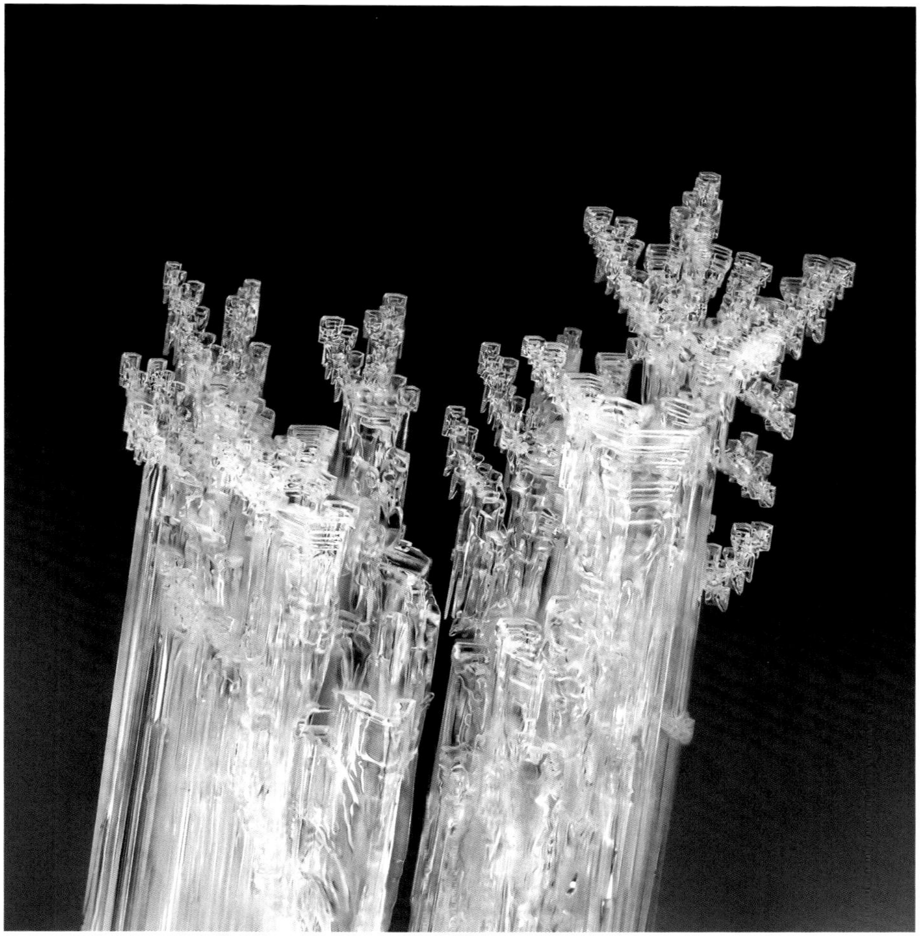

Facing page: Frost growing on the window of a pickup truck in the Yukon wilderness. I may have been ridiculed for the excessive number of images being taken.

Right: Near the entrance to a small cave, castles of frost can be seen growing where the moist warm air inside meets the freezing temperatures outside.

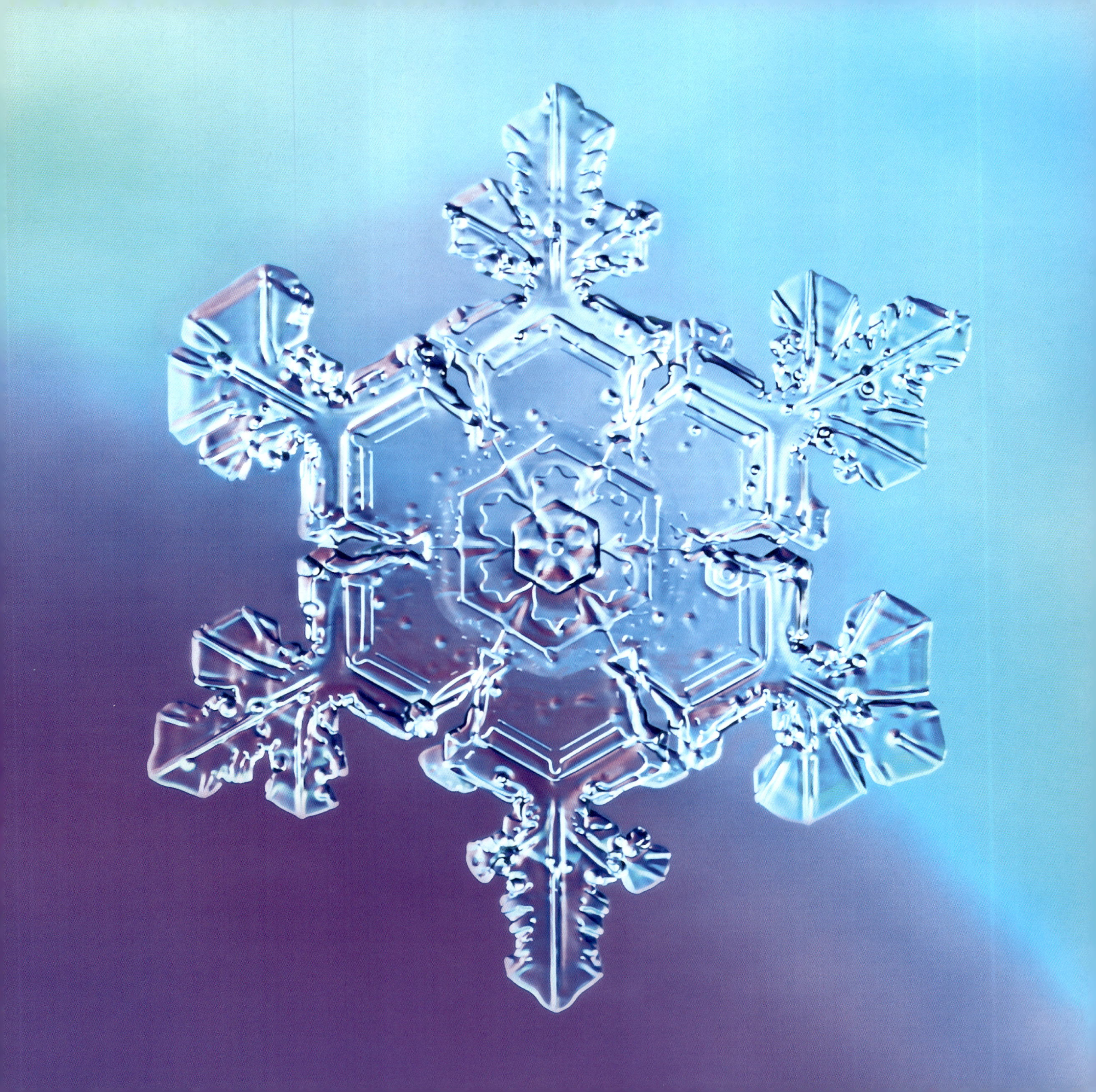

Photographic Techniques of Other Snowflake Photographers

Snowflakes have been photographed for well over a century. One of the most famous pioneers in this genre was Wilson Bentley, a farmer in Jericho, Vermont. Bentley became fascinated with the details of the crystals, and his images are still widely published today. His technique, however, varies greatly from my own.

Bentley would use a large format camera and extended bellows to bring the snowflake into focus. The snowflake was positioned on a plate of glass, and the image was also recorded on a glass plate negative. Light would pass through the snowflake and enter the camera, which is referred to as "transmitted light", coming from behind and through the subject rather than reflecting off the surface. This would have originally resulted in a white snowflake on a white background. Interesting, but unsuitable for showcasing the crystal. I discovered much the same problem, which is why a black mitten is the background to most of my images. In Bentley's case, he had to be a "snowflake surgeon".

Working with duplicates, Bentley would use a razor blade to carefully cut the snowflake away from the background, thus allowing the background to become black (*right*). His more science-oriented contemporaries frowned on this concept as it meant that there could be some decisions made to remove unsightly elements and ruin the scientific accuracy of the images. The general public, on the other hand, fell in love with the series.

Using transmitted light can still be a viable technique today. Using coloured lights, you can see how the snowflake structure bends light and colours become intertwined (*facing page*). This is one of the only snowflake images I have captured using the transmitted light technique. It's a personal choice – I find it far more interesting to see the natural prismatic colours appear in the crystals, as well as the vibrant array of possibilities due to optical interference. That's not to mention the surface details that bring them to life!

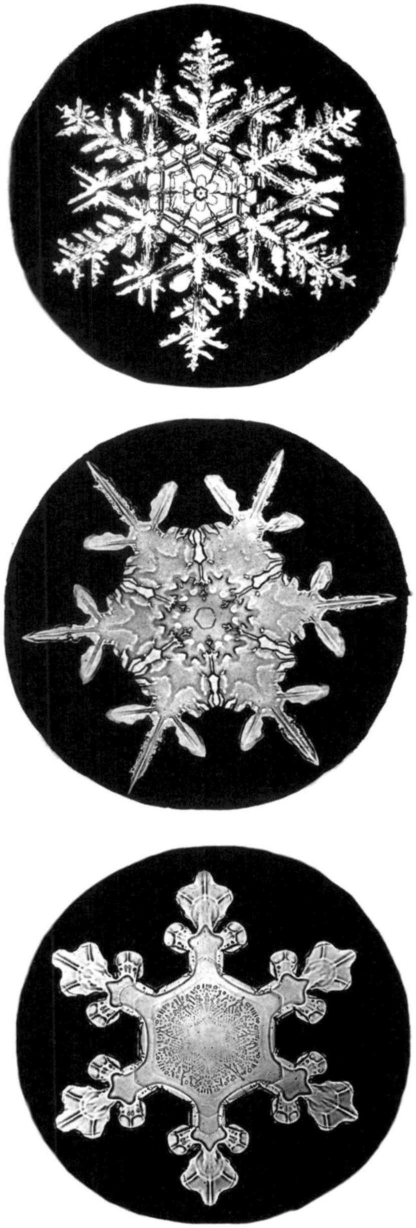

Photo Credit: The Wilson Bentley Digital Archives / snowflakebentley.com

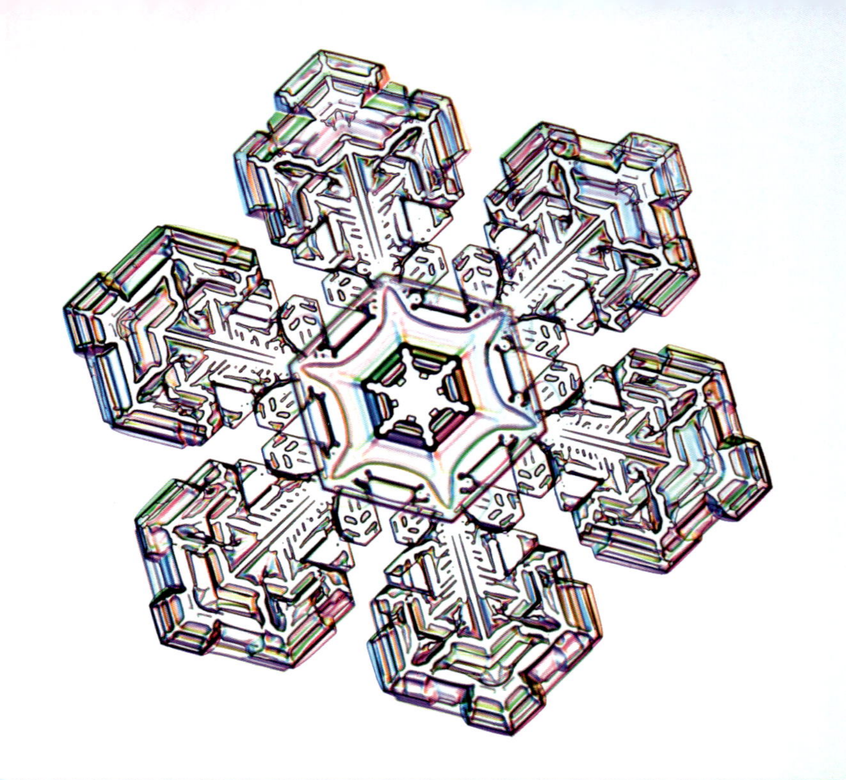
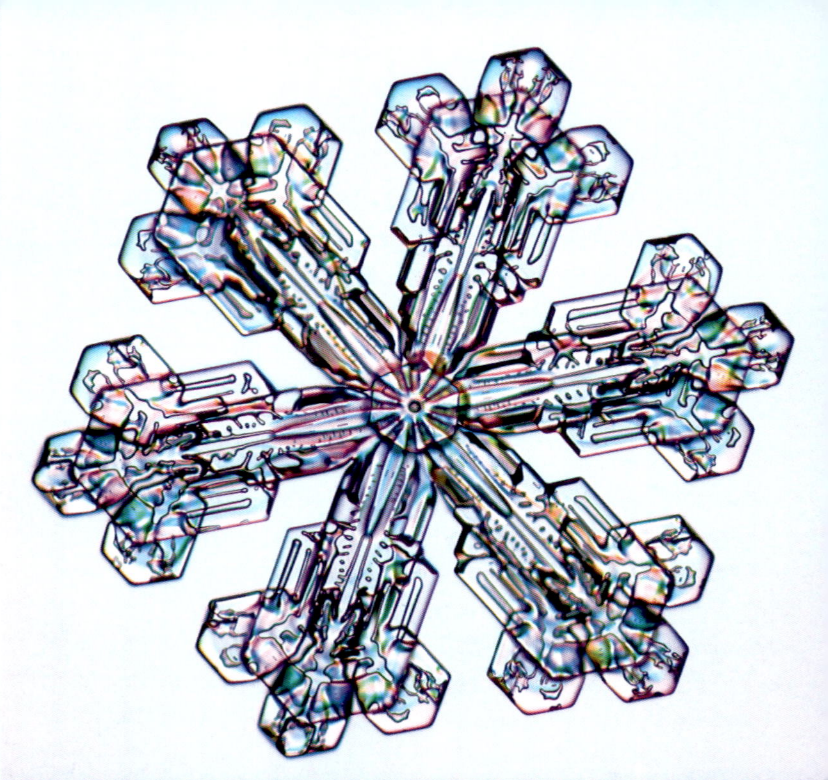
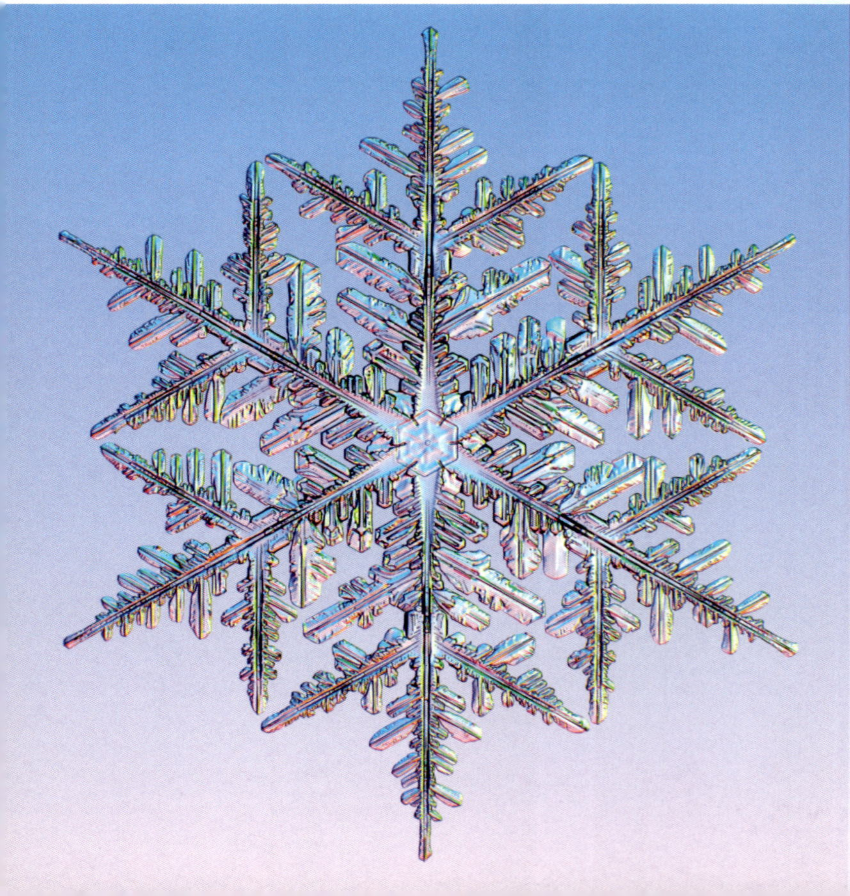
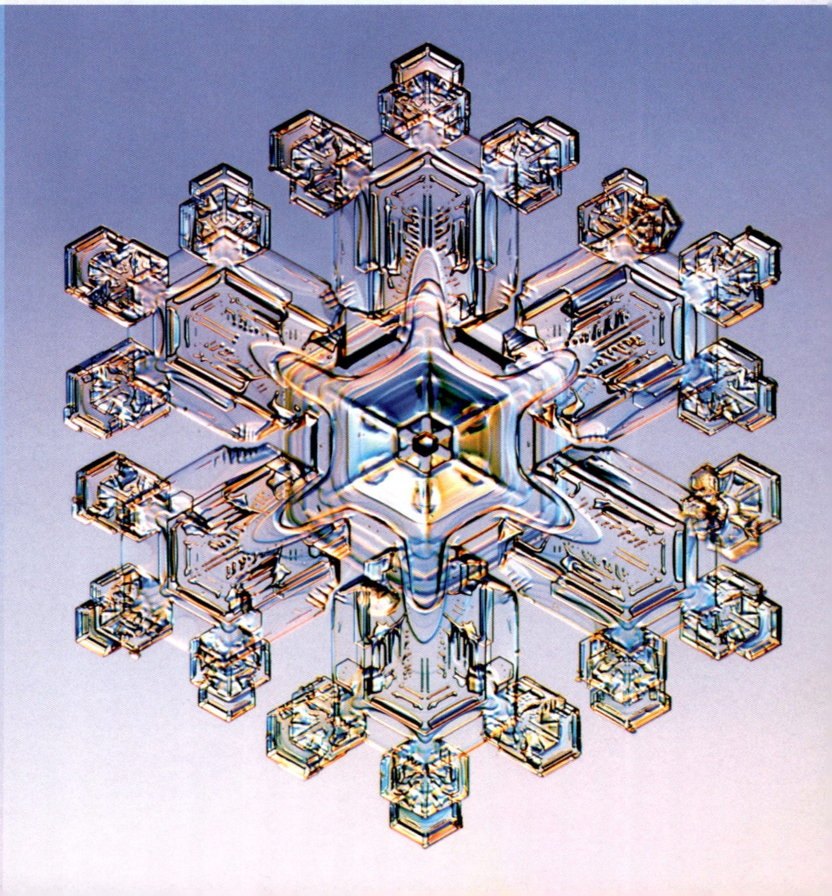

Ken Libbrecht

Ken knows snowflakes. With over a decade of published work in both casual and peer-reviewed science, Ken has seen and photographed more snowflakes than anyone else alive today. When it comes to photographic equipment, he's no slouch.

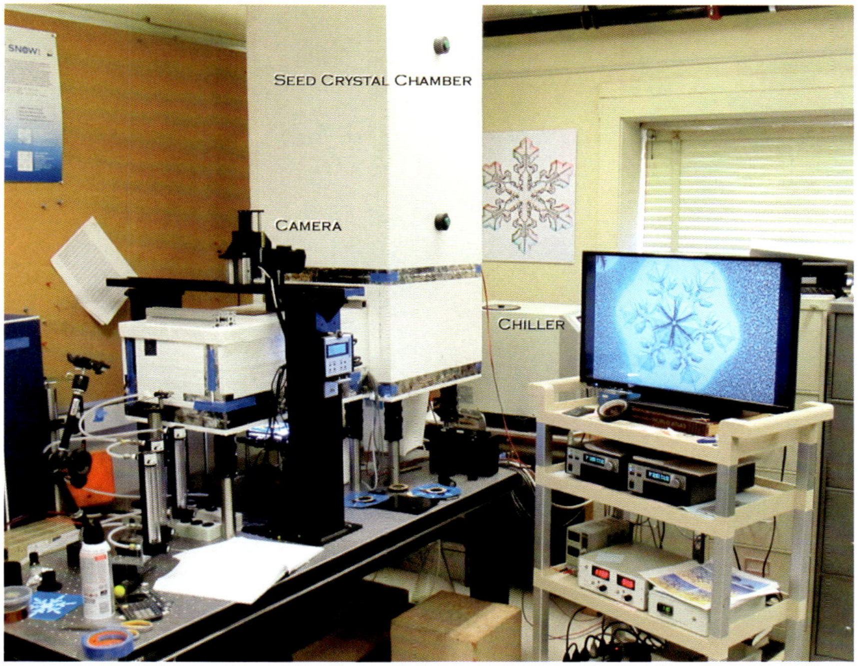

Photographs of Ken's equipment *(right)* can be intimidating. This image contains so many wires and contraptions that may appear mysterious to the average photographer. Gear photographs like this prevented me from heading in the same direction, and instead I focused my efforts on a black mitten.

Ken and I have had many discussions about the physics of snowflakes. He is a wealth of knowledge, and now spends much of his snowflake hunting in his laboratory at Caltech in Pasadena California. He has even taken to growing "designer snowflakes" with carefully controlled adjustments to temperature and humidity. I prefer his natural findings (*facing page*) to enjoy the beauty of nature.

Ken has predominantly used transmitted light to reveal the magic in his snowflakes. This can be done in a number of ways, but always lit from below with the snowflake perfectly parallel to the focal plane of the camera. Only crystals with multiple layers or heavy volume require focus stacking. I envy the simplicity in post-processing as well as the creative control of coloured lights with this approach while still preferring my own approach.

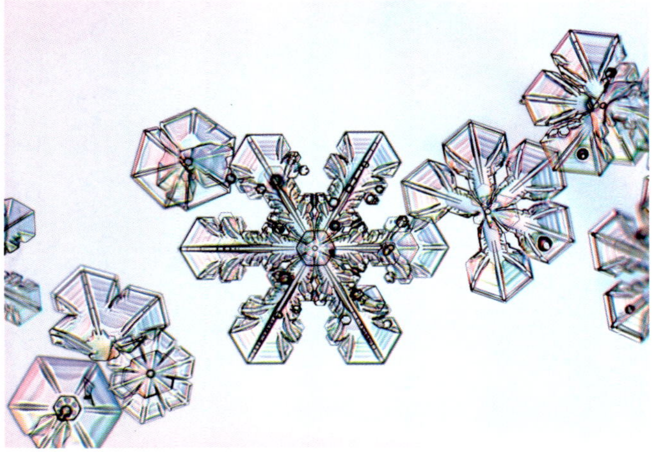

Ken maintains one of the best snowflake-related resources on the internet, www.snowcrystals.com

Freezing Soap Bubbles

Nature's Crystal Ball

Snowflakes offer up infinite variations, but at best all we can do is document them. Freezing bubbles on the other hand can be transformed readily into works of art with equal contributions from the photographer and from nature.

Technically, this subject is far less challenging than snowflakes. We need the proper conditions and the right ingredients, but once we have the formulaic components out of the way we can become artists. These bubbles are much larger than snowflakes, a few inches in diameter, so you don't even need a proper macro lens in some cases. We need to start with the necessities of creating the subject – the recipe for the bubbles.

I cannot take credit for this recipe, and have not been able to source the original creator since it has been so widely shared online for years. There are three basic components:

- **6 parts Water**
- **2 parts Dish Soap**
- **1 part White Corn Syrup**

"White Corn Syrup"? This ingredient, for which glycerine can be substituted, is part of the secret for getting bubbles to survive impact with the snow (or any other object). The syrup will pool at the bottom of the bubble and act like a cushion of sorts, enhancing the survivability of the bubble. Without this ingredient, it's like winning the lottery to get an intact bubble. With this additive, it's more likely a 50/50 success rate.

If you had 100ml per "part", you'd end up with nearly a liter of bubble fluid – probably more than most people would need through the entirety of the winter, so adjust your measurements based on how much you'd like to experiment. Practically, making the fluid in excess volume has a side benefit – the volume of fluid keeps it from freezing quickly outside. Hard to blow a bubble if the liquid has already turned to ice!

This next tip took me two years to figure out: don't use a bubble wand, use a **drinking straw**. If you attempt to blow a bubble through a traditional bubble wand, you'll be setting yourself up for frustration. This method doesn't allow you to choose the size or placement of your bubble, and thereby adds far more chaos for you to deal with. Using a simple drinking straw, you can control the rough size of the bubble and with a flick of

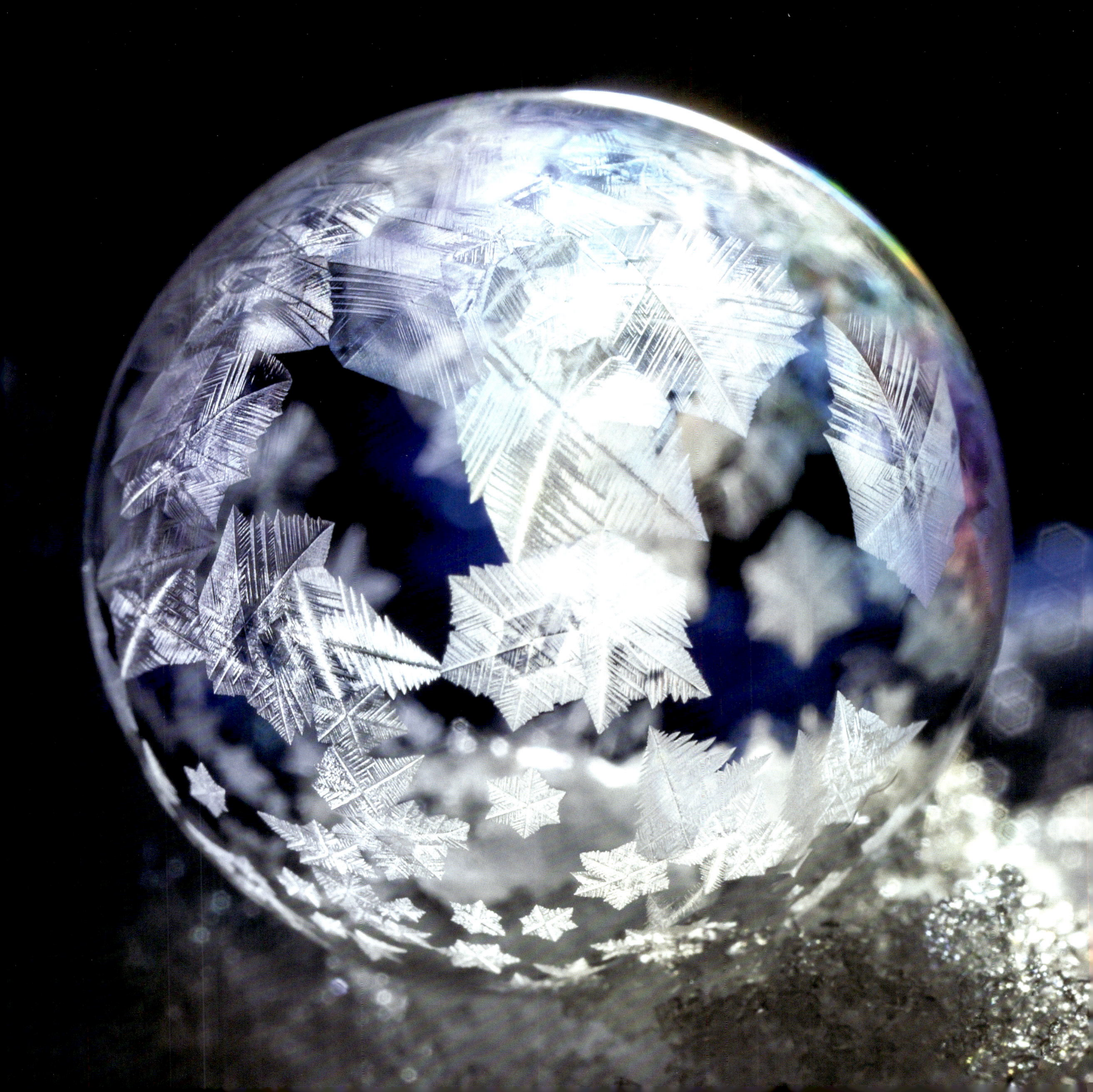

your wrist, have it stuck to the end of the straw where you can carefully place the bubble exactly where you intend for it to be.

You can't head out on any winter day and create these bubbles, however. We need the proper conditions outside:

- **Temperature below -8C / 18F**
- **Absolutely no wind**
- **Usually from dusk to pre-dawn**

If the temperatures are not cold enough, the bubble won't freeze fast enough before collapsing. If there is even the tiniest whisper of wind, the bubble will likely shatter before it becomes solid. This wind can come from ground-level thermals generated by the sun, so it's best to avoid shooting during the day time – it's also much harder to control your lighting.

Picture the perfect weather. You've got your bubble fluid ready and waiting. What next? Lighting. Some people are lucky enough to have a direct view of a sunset for backlighting their freezing crystal balls to dramatic effect, but the same magic can be easily obtained with an LED flashlight.

My typical LED flashlight configuration has a narrow beam at a distance, refocused through a Fresnel lens, also called a "sheet magnifier". This is generally cheap molded plastic and can be found online or in hardware stores for under $10, and will refocus the beam from the flashlight down into a more intense "spotlight".
Any sufficiently bright LED flashlight will do, 1000 lumens or brighter is ideal. In the setup image (*facing page*), you'll see a rather large flashlight – the NiteCore Tiny Monster TM38. This is overkill, and quite expensive, but there is one trait you'll want your flashlight to have: a single diode producing the light. Many flashlights offer clusters of lights to increase their brightness, but when you refocus the beam with a Fresnel lens, you end up with many distinctly separate beams, one for each of the diodes in the light source.

My favourite go-to flashlight for this is the NiteCore TM03 CRI which works well for many other subjects. With a simple "crab clamp" – available online for a few dollars – you can add tripod screws to the flashlight to mount it easily on a tripod as a makeshift light stand.

Notice how intensely bright the spot on the right side of the patio table where the freezing bubble is? This is what we're after. The intent is to backlight the crystal; have the light in its surrounding area become darker. It's advised to place a "test bubble" with no intention of photographing it, but to allow it to freeze solid and adjust the lighting angles so that you can get the brightest "glow" effect while also having the light source outside of the visible image. These angles can be persnickety, and they change slightly from bubble to bubble. For this reason, you may have already guessed it: I prefer to shoot these images handheld.

Part of this reasoning is time. The average bubble will freeze solid in around 10-20 seconds, and the aesthetics of a bubble almost frozen with puzzle-pieces about to connect is greatly preferred to one that has finished the freezing process. You need to work quickly, and be nimble with the angle you shoot from to maximize the "sparkle" of the forming crystals.

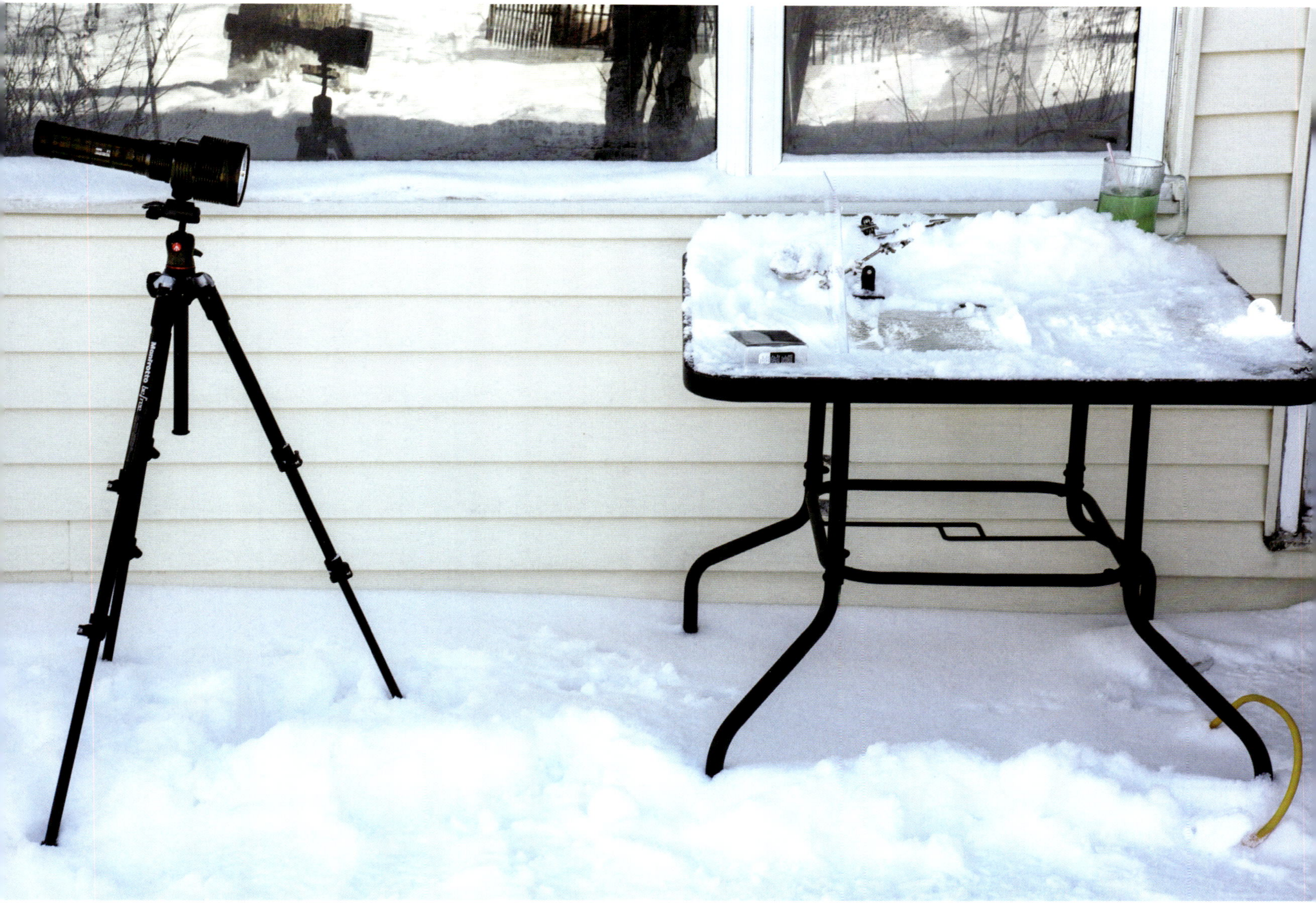

An 1800 lumen flashlight passing through a Fresnel lens on the table (held up by a "third hand tool") to condense the light directly through a freezing bubble that measures a few inches in diameter. Any regular macro lens can accomplish this.

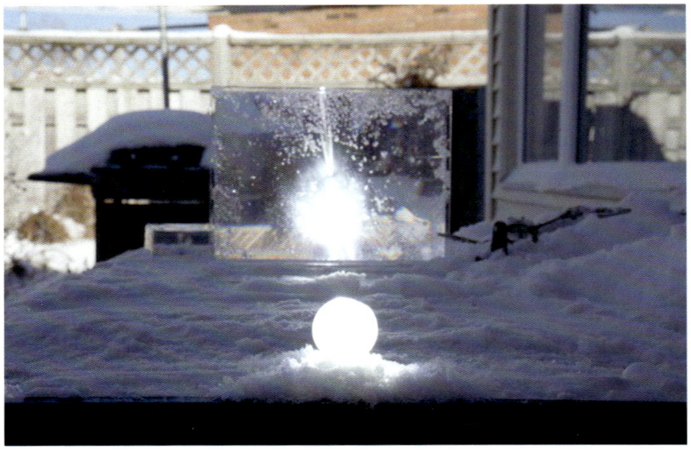

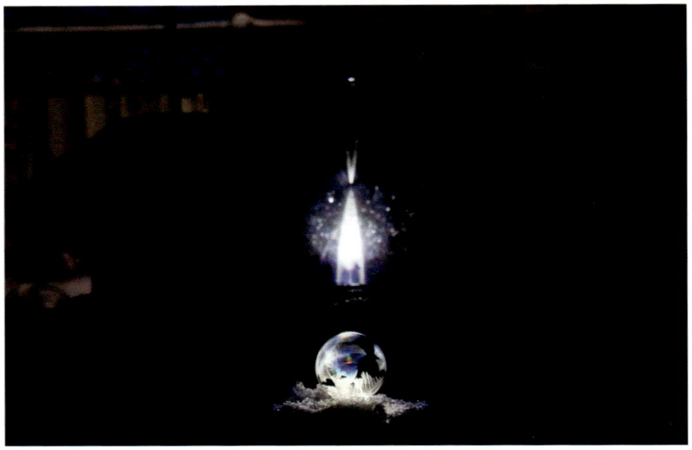

Manual Exposure, Manual Focus

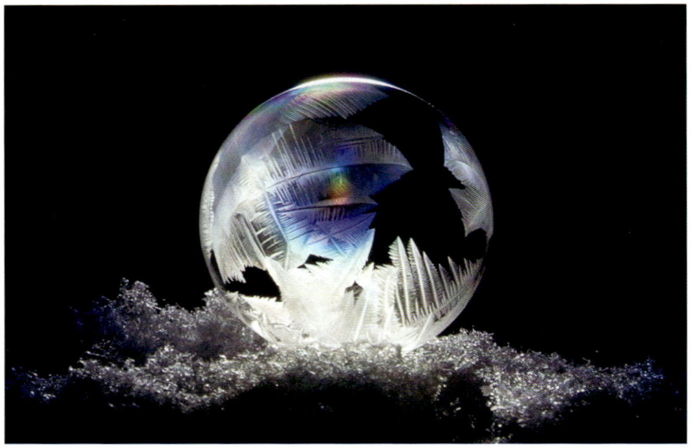

That shouldn't sound scary. I typically shoot freezing bubbles between F/11 and F/22, F/16 being my own personal "sweet spot". These bubbles freeze quickly so a slow shutter speed will not be helpful here. Rarely would I set the camera to a shutter speed slower than 1/160sec, though you want to try and maintain the best image quality and lowest ISO sensitivity. The higher your ISO is set, the lower your dynamic range – and you'll need all the dynamic range you can get.

A good way to establish a baseline exposure would be to start off in Aperture Priority mode and, using a test bubble, figure out what ISO provides an acceptably fast shutter speed. The brighter your flashlight the better off you'll be. Once you capture an image with settings that give you what you're after, dial those values into a manual exposure. This is the same technique I would use when shooting birds with a telephoto lens, especially as they fly in front of backgrounds of varying brightness.

Once the exposure looks good, you're ready for your first trial run. Attempt to place a bubble of the same size in the same place, and shoot in a continuous burst. To achieve focus, use the same technique discussed for handholding, by physically moving the camera forward and back. Autofocus varies in effectiveness from camera to camera, but I've always found it more likely to focus on the back of the bubble than the front – it's much more effective the other way around. Sway slightly as you shoot to offer up some slight variances in your focus position.

For a single bubble, I might create 20-30 separate images as it freezes, often preferring an image near the end of the sequence with the crystals in the farther foreground in focus but without sacrificing too much of the "crispness" of the outer edge of the bubble. With such a dynamic subject, focus stacking is impossible. You need to nail it in one shot!

Lumix GX9, Leica DG Macro-Elmarit 45mm F/2.8, F/13 ISO 400 1/160sec

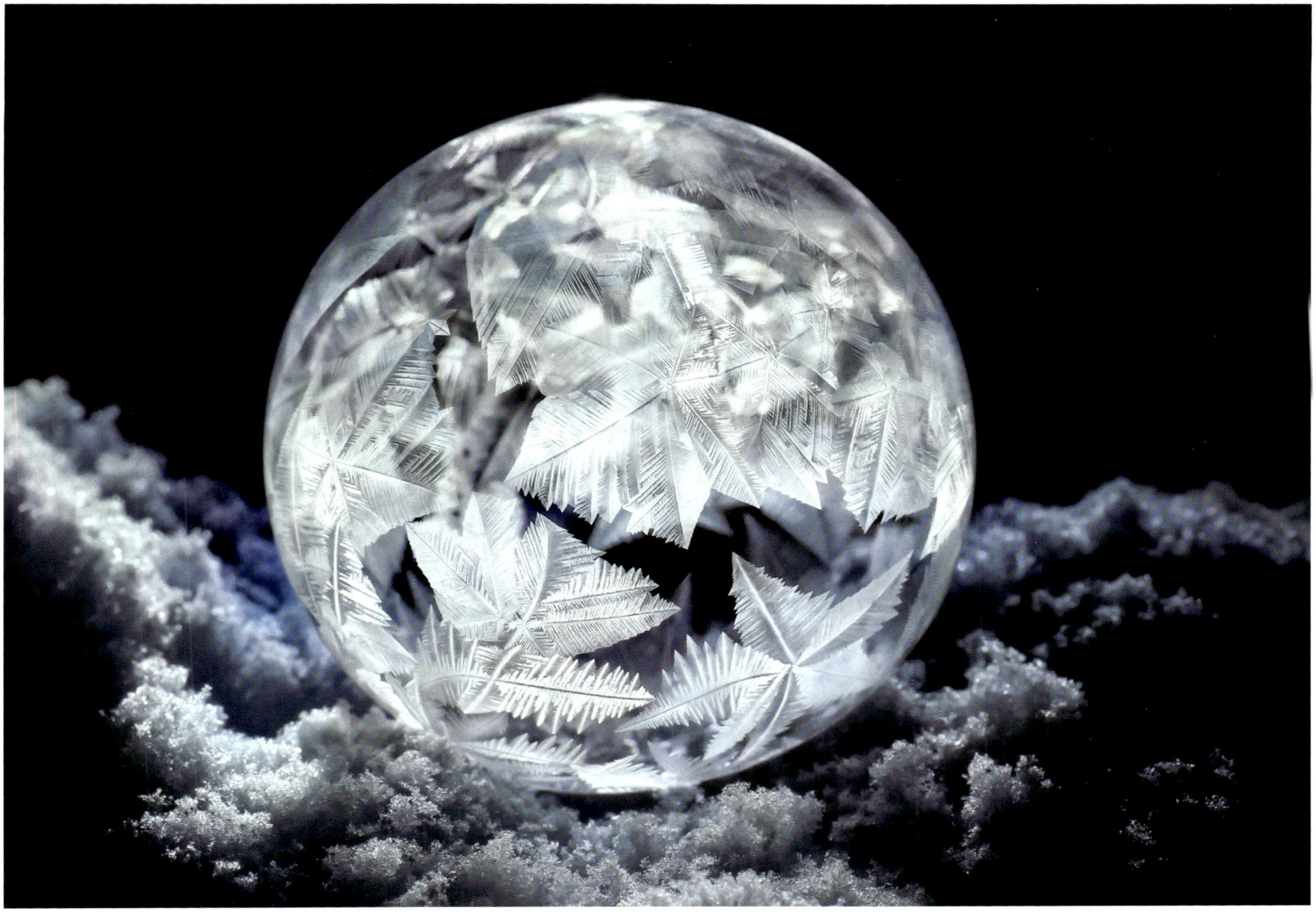

Composition and Creativity

Once you've photographed a freezing soap bubble, you should feel accomplished. There are a lot of moving parts, just like most areas of macro photography, and getting everything to work together can be technically challenging. After that, it's like riding a bike. A bit of practice and it becomes akin to muscle memory and you can rinse and repeat the same process to your heart's content. But...

Right:
Canon 1DX mark II, Meyer Optik Trioplan 100 F/2.8, F/16 ISO 200 1/200sec

Below:
Canon 1DX mark II, Meyer Optik Trioplan 100 F/2.8, F/16 ISO 125 1/640sec

Your heart might not be in it for long. Doing the same thing over and over again – a freezing bubble on snow – can becoming tiresome. Why not switch things up a little? Why not experiment with different surfaces for the bubbles to freeze on? Push beyond my initial experiment with just a bed of snow to, perhaps, a Quartz crystal? The concept of having a crystal ball being seeded by much more solid crystals below it was intriguing, though this setup required a second light to illuminate the dense crystal cluster underneath. It's always helpful to have a few extra pieces of equipment handy when needed! Inexpensive Nitecore P12 flashlights do the trick.

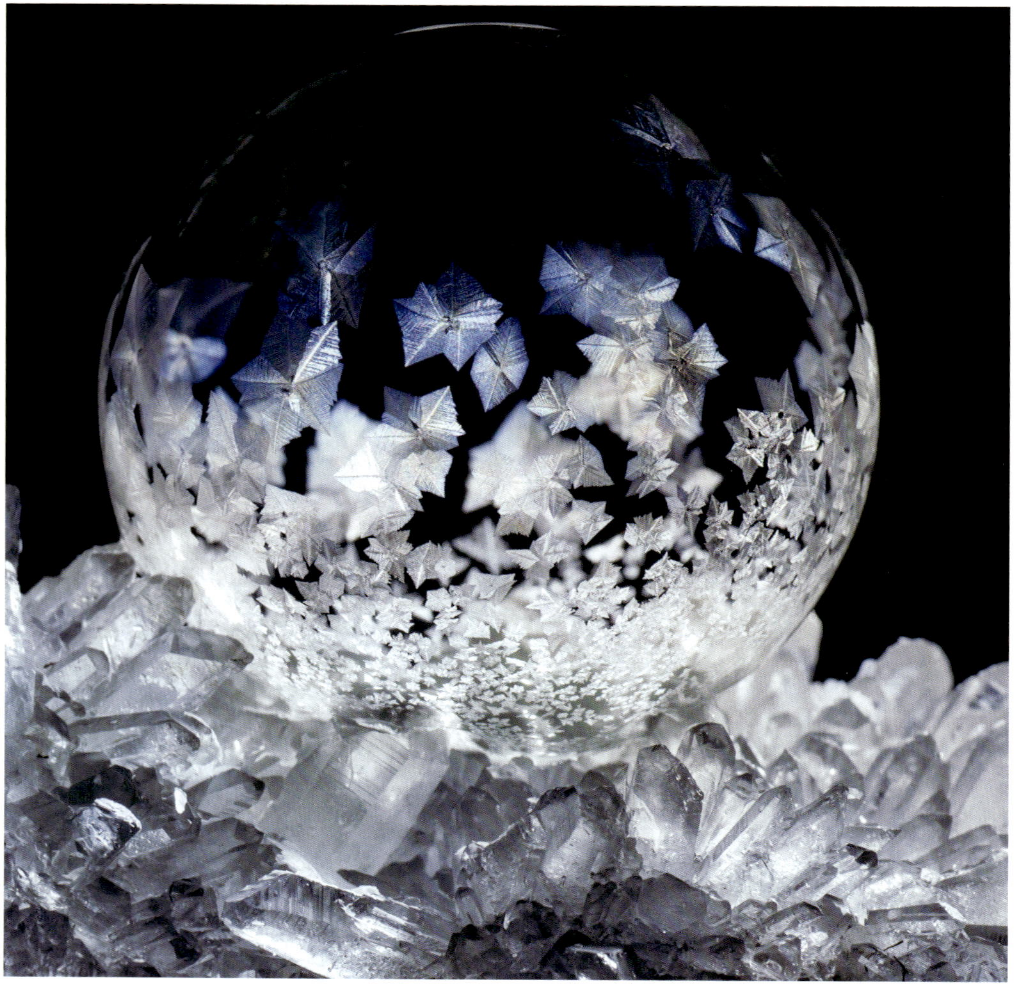

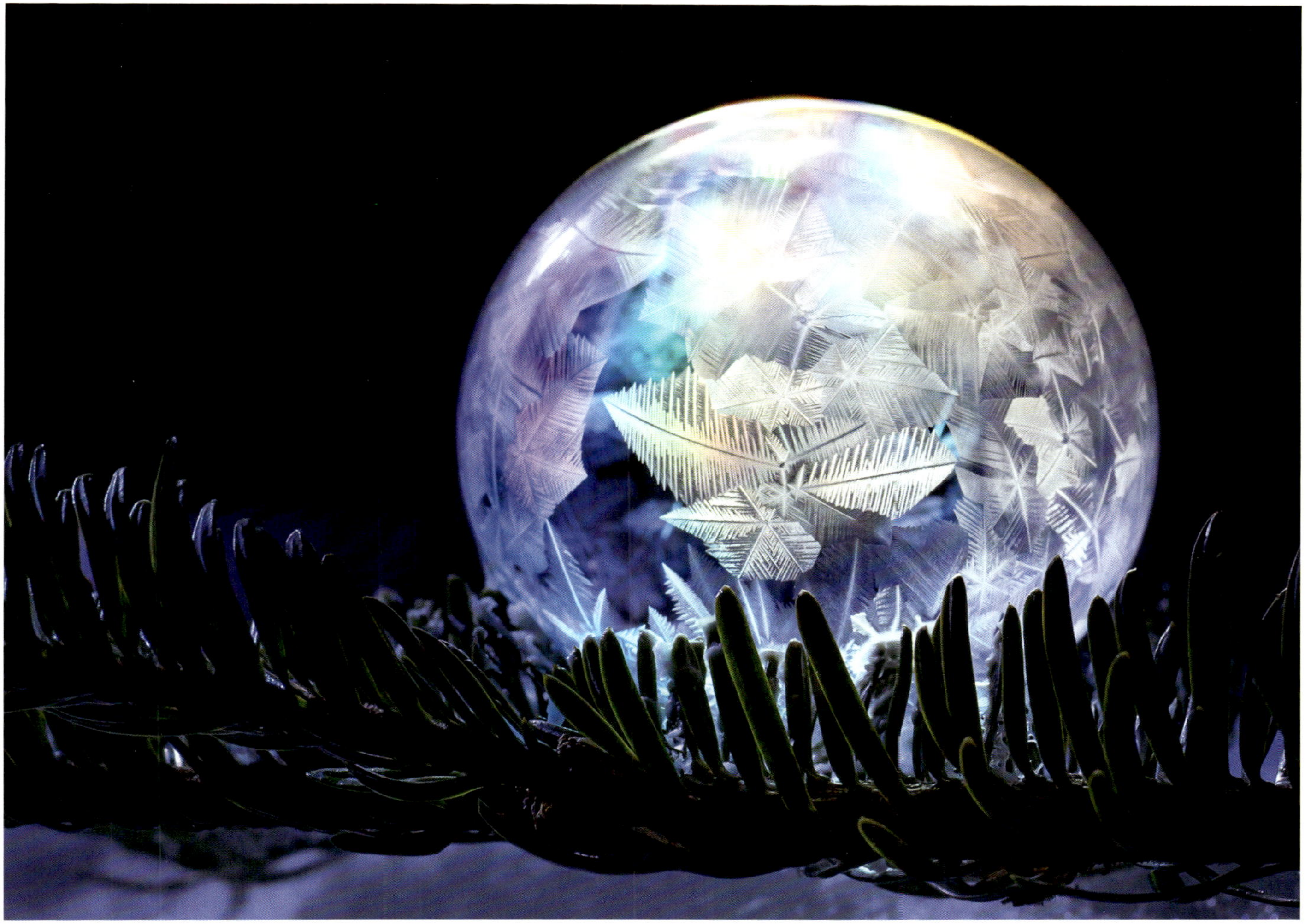

Call me lazy, but one year we missed the pick-up window for our Christmas tree after the holidays, so a displaced evergreen was taking up residence in our garage until the spring yard waste collection. Searching for a subject for another image, the idea struck me to make a freezing bubble appear as an ornamental bauble on the branch of the tree. The first few bubbles popped, leaving a bit of a residue in their wake. This in turn made the surface of the needles more comfortable for the bubbles that would come later, allowing them to survive the contact and freeze beautifully.

The colour in this image is caused by manipulating the angle of the light and the Fresnel focusing lens only – no other tricks required. We can be a little more deliberate with such colour, but these subtle transitions were exactly what the image needed to come to life.

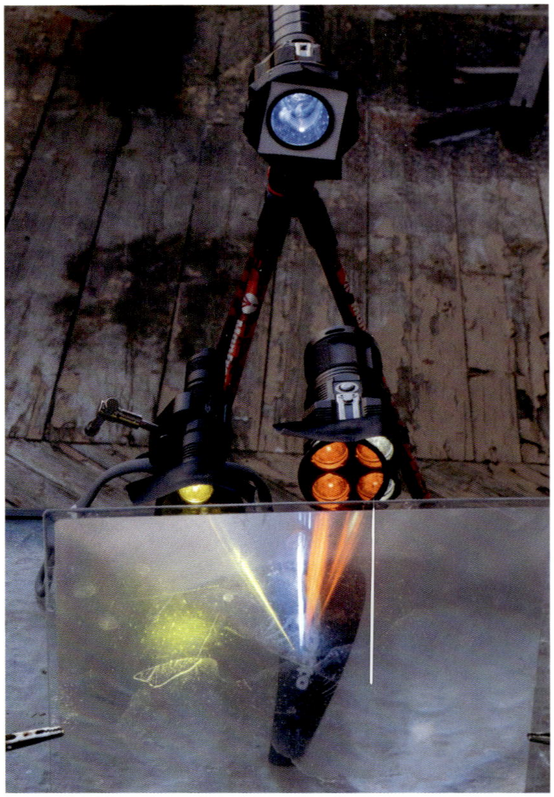

Oops! The bubble popped before I could take the behind-the-scenes image:

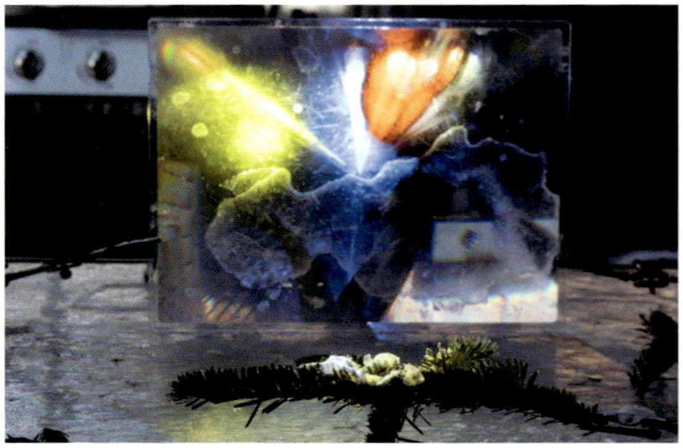

Lumix G9, Leica DG Macro-Elmarit 45mm F/2.8, F/13 ISO 320 1/800sec

Adding Colour

We can influence the colours in these images substantially as part of the creative process. The solution to this is quite simple – buy some coloured lens filters and use Gaffer's tape to attach them to the front of your flashlights. You can even get multiple colours to interact together to form delicate interactions as the crystals themselves interact at varying angles. Simply searching for "color filter set" on Amazon yields plenty of results around the $30 price point. Note that the heat from your LED lights may warp the plastic that these cheap filters are made out of, but they'll still colour your flashlight just fine.

Again, the process can be initiated with a test bubble, where you play around with the angle and intensity of the lights until you get a mix you're happy with. In this case, I was after a predominantly blue image with hints of yellow and orange. It's impossible to predict exactly how the bubble will catch the colours and your results will vary slightly with every attempt as different crystal facets form. Try to plan things out, but embrace the chaos!

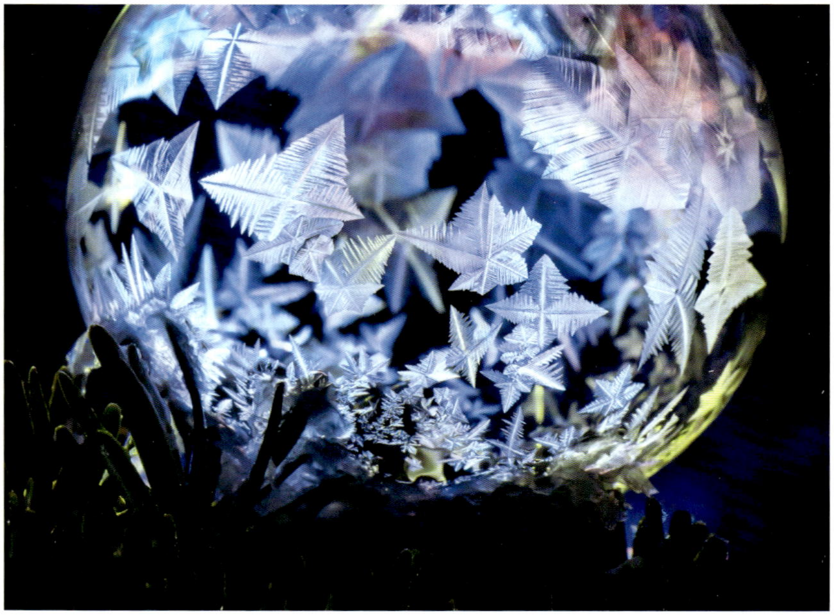

The colours you choose can have dramatic impact. While this image (below) appears to be lit with just an orange filter, there are three lights at work. The primary light is indeed orange, but there is a secondary red light being picked up in some of the upper areas to help the bubble appear more fire-like. To balance things out with a neutral colour to make the intensely saturated warmth feel more believable, a white light hits part of the foreground. This extra light was a necessity, otherwise the image would feel like a white balance mistake.

This particular freezing bubble is resting on some tall grass that had gone to seed in autumn but was still blowing in the wind during the heart of winter.

Lumix S1, Meyer Optik Trioplan 100 F/2.8, F/16 ISO 200 1/320sec

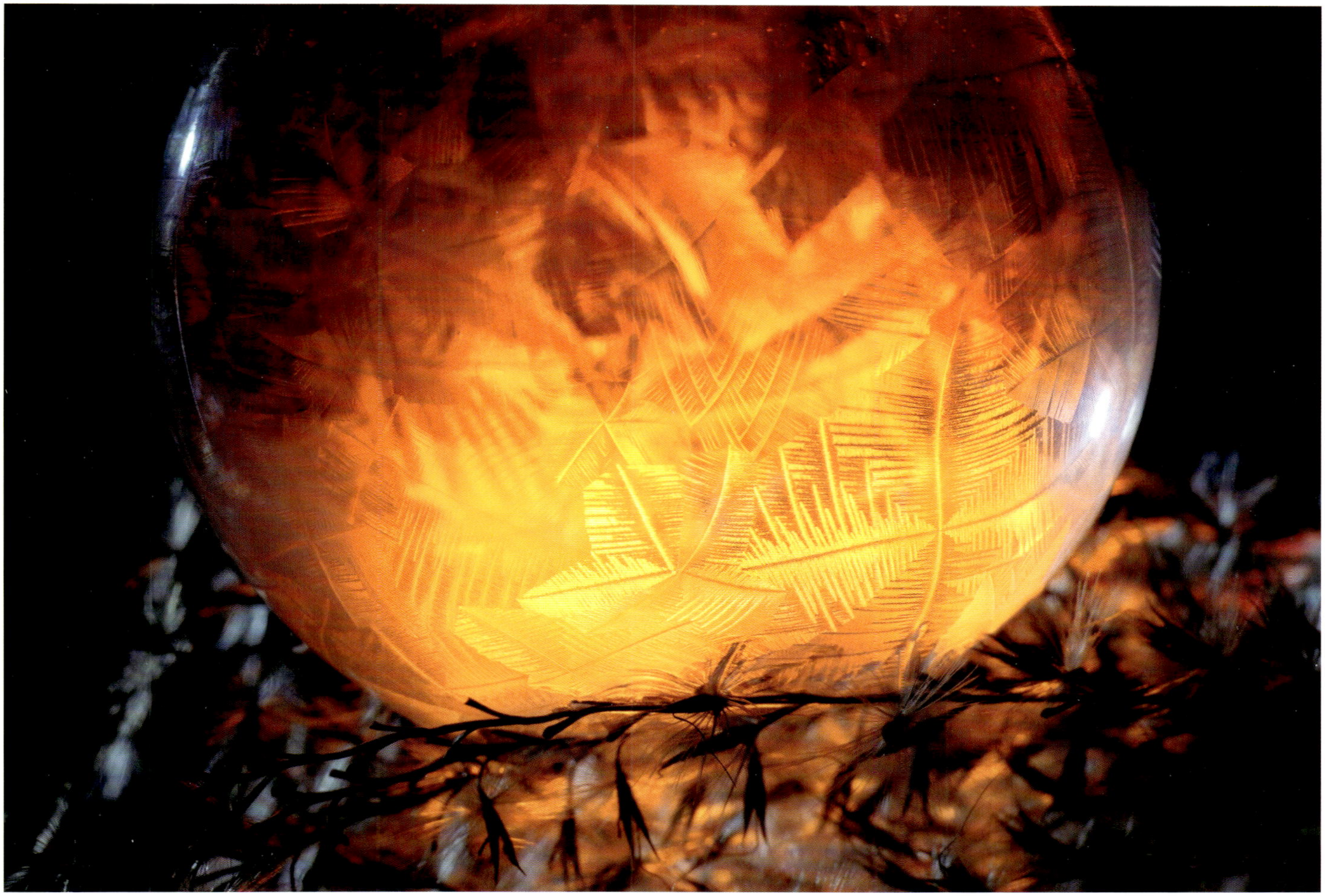

"Mad Scientist" Colour

Want to get intensely colourful? This solution involves getting the cover of an old CD jewel case and some polarizing film. Polarizing film can be purchased in sheets on eBay as replacements for damaged LCD televisions and portable devices. Just search on eBay for "polarizing film" and snap up something inexpensive. If you place the two sheets in opposition to one another, you'll see very little light come through the film. If you then place the CD case in between the filters, you'll get a light show. The effect is called birefringence, but the science lesson for this is elsewhere in the book under (shooting with microscope objectives).

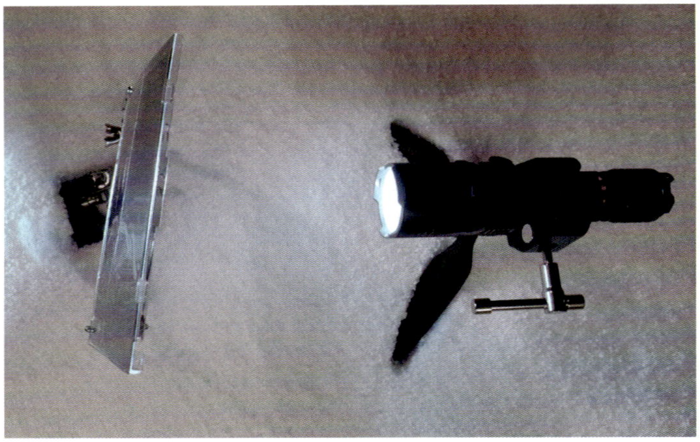

For now, let's just use our new tool: A filter of cascading saturated colours! Place the filter in front of your light source by whatever means necessary – tape, elastics, or maybe just have an assistant to hold it and move it around until the colours connect well through the freezing bubble. Because you are filtering white light down to specific colours, the amount of illumination provided with the filter in place will be less than a bare flashlight, and the total exposure can be less predictable as the filter is moved. So long as you can handle the frigid temperatures, keep tinkering and see what you can come up with!

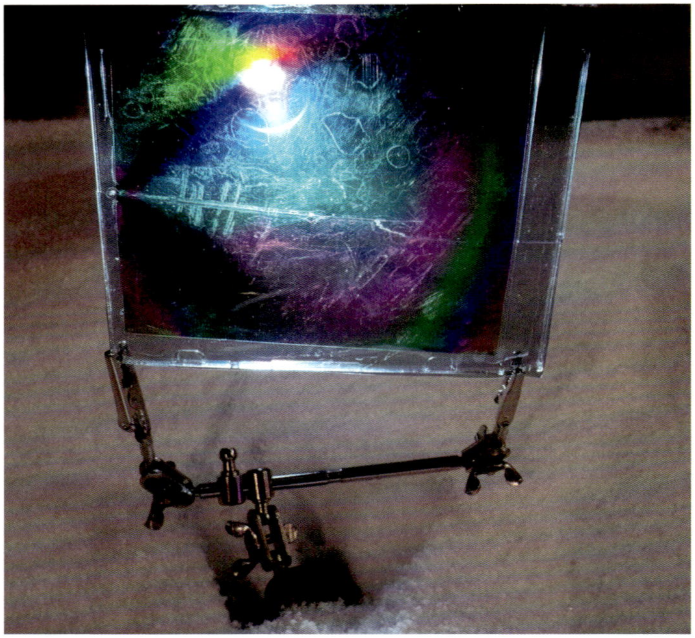

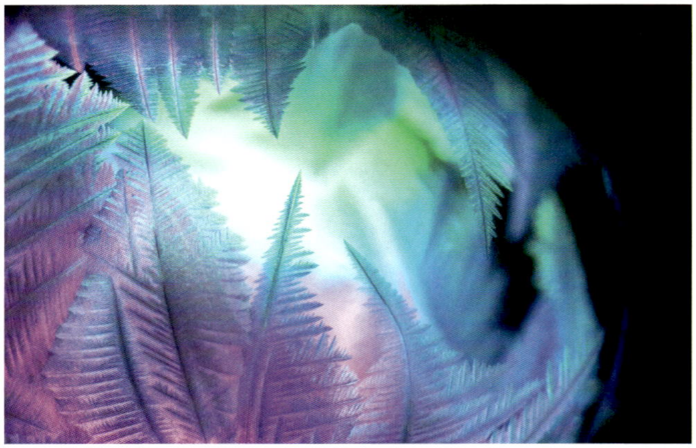

Left: Canon 1DX, Canon MP-E 65mm F/2.8 1x-5x Macro, F/14 ISO 3200 1/1250sec

Right: Canon 1DX, Canon MP-E 65mm F/2.8 1x-5x Macro, F/16 ISO 800 1/160sec

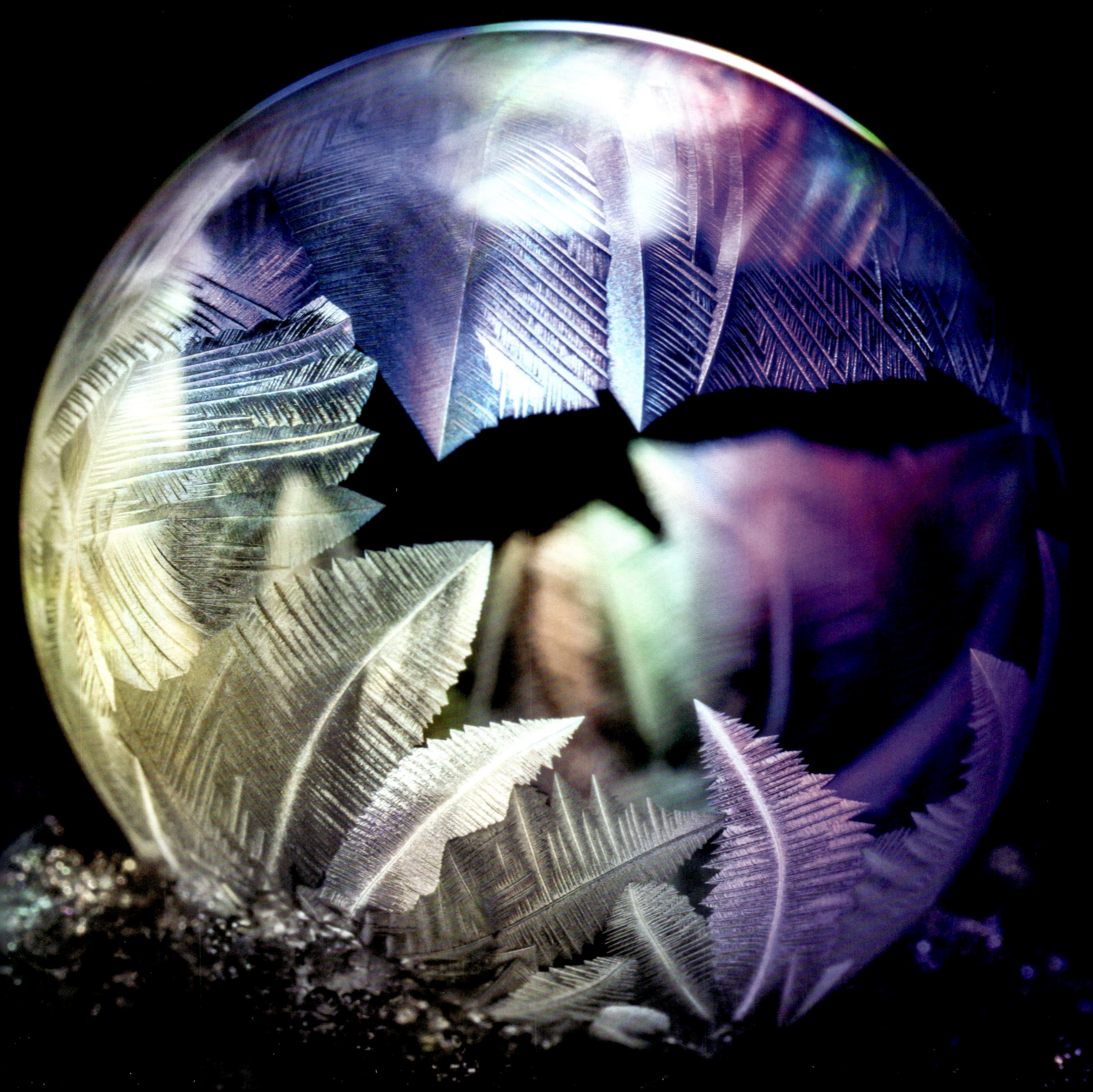

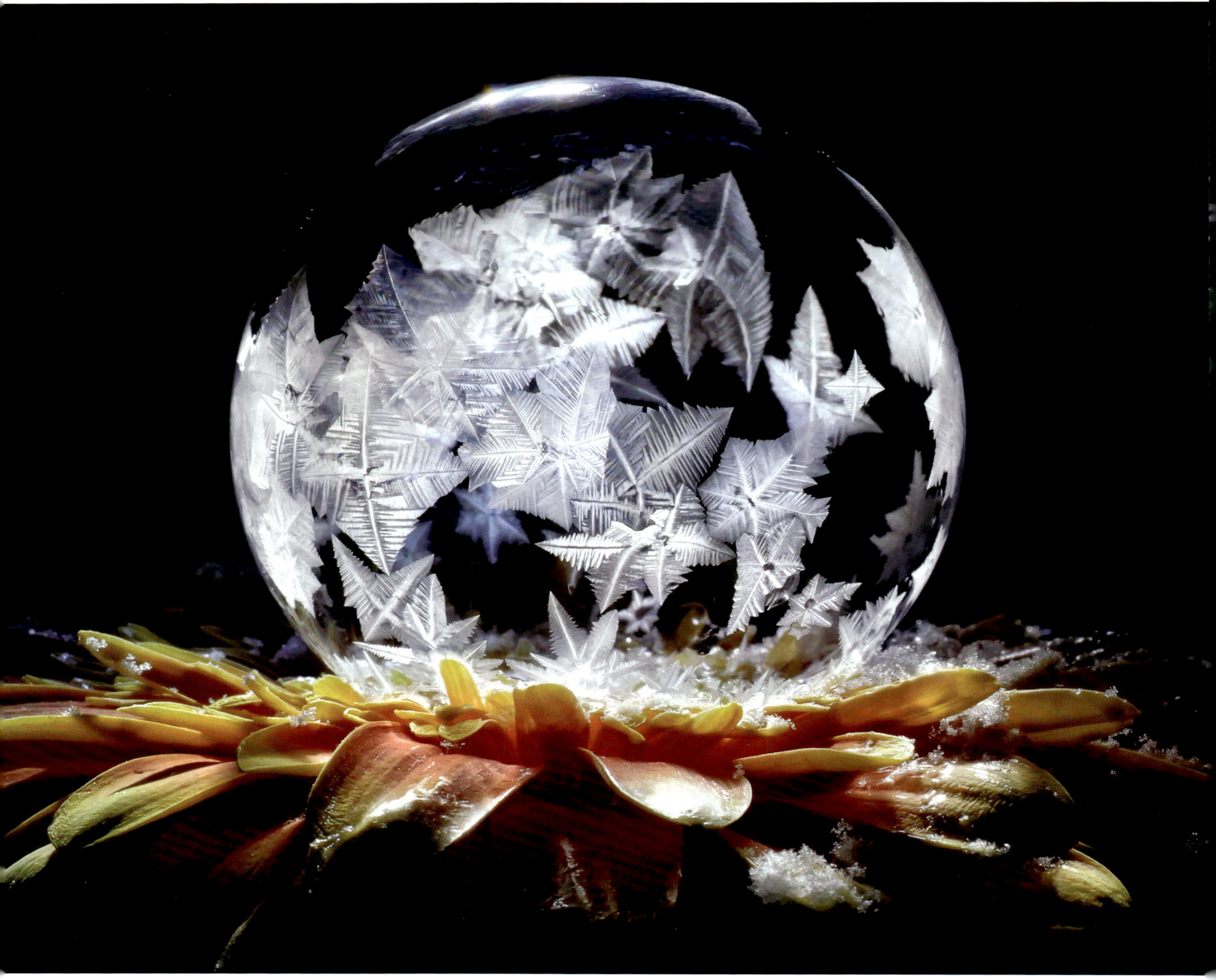

Flowering Frost

The colour in our images doesn't just have to come from filtered light; what if we had a vibrant platform for our freezing bubbles to be presented on? What if we dare to grow such spherical frost on a flower? It's actually easier to do than you might first realize.

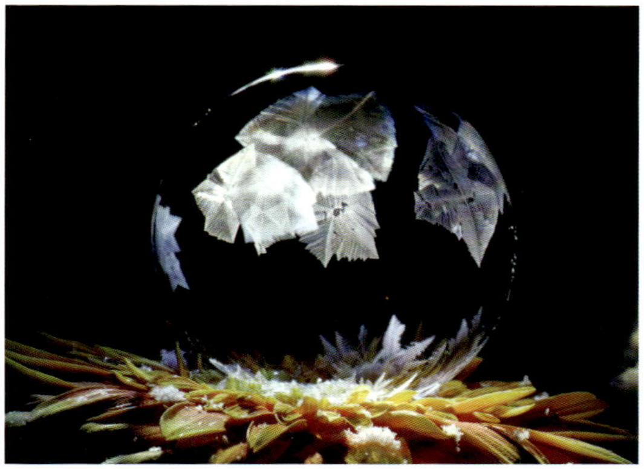

The biggest challenge? Sacrificing a flower for the image. You'll need to leave a flower outside in the frozen temperatures for roughly 30 minutes to ensure that it is completely acclimated to the outside temperature. It will still look lively, but it's now completely frozen and very brittle, and will turn into a blob of mush if you were to bring it inside. Trust me, they cannot be saved once you decide to do this.

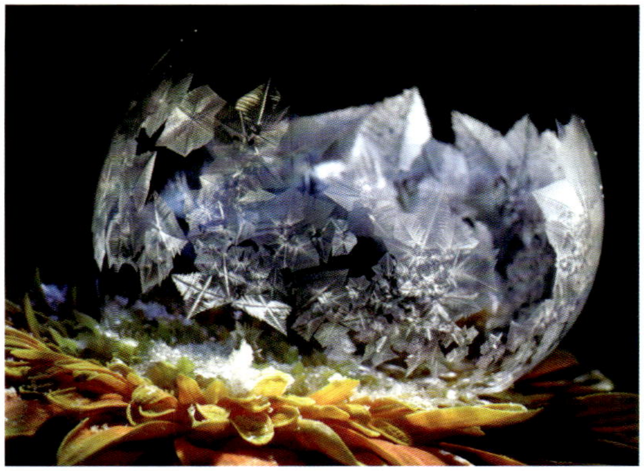

The organic surfaces of the flower, chilly as they may be, still function as a better insulator than the bubble resting on snow. A helpful step to get the bubble to start nucleation of crystals is to sprinkle a small amount of snow onto the surface of the flower, in this example (*left*) an orange Gerbera Daisy. This will help kick-start the process and give more dynamic results. You likely won't get your first bubble to survive, so beware that bits and pieces of the previous bubbles might end up in your next image. This is mostly unavoidable, unless you want to sacrifice an entire bouquet of flowers in the process. This was all multiple attempts with the same flower. Thankfully only four tries were needed.

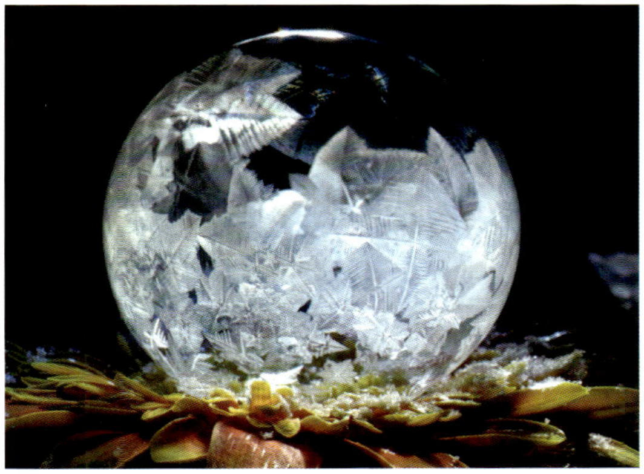

The first attempt (*top right*) was… blah. Not enough nucleation points and slow growth from the bottom. The second attempt (*middle right*) the light wasn't hitting the front crystals right, and it just felt lopsided. The third attempt (*bottom right*) was getting closer – but too blocked up at the bottom with too much space at the top. The fourth attempt (*left*) struck an acceptable balance.

Left: Lumix GX9, Leica DG Macro-Elmarit 45mm F/2.8, F/18 ISO 400 1/160sec

Crossing the Streams

While not quite the same as the *Ghost Busters* reference, what if you were to cross different streams of ideas into a single concept? I've always called this the "puzzle piece" approach to building an image. You might develop some disconnected ideas independently and initially consider that they would never cross paths, but remember the best question to always keep in the back of your mind: **what if?**

What if I could make a freezing soap bubble that glowed from within, as if it was its own light source? They're all glowing, sure, but it's clear to any keen observer that the light is passing through the bubble to make the magic happen. What if its surroundings were clearly being illuminated from the bubble itself and no external light source? This would be possible if the bubble was fluorescent, and hit with ultraviolet light that would create visible light from the subject itself. Magic would ensue, at least in theory.

This became my first successful experiment with UV fluorescence, even though the idea had been in my mind for roughly a year prior with other subjects. Initial attempts however, were merely stepping stones towards an eventual triumph.

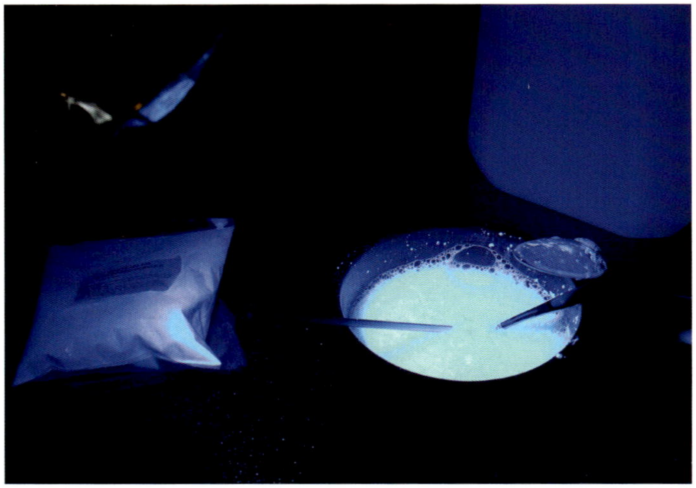

The first steps? Buy commercially available fluorescing bubble solution. I suppose this is intended for the Night Club scene, but the fluorescence was considerably dimmer than I would have hoped. This followed with the purchase of UV fluorescing pigment that matched the fluorescing blue colour generated by the bubble solution, and the experiments began! Mixing up a batch of this curious concoction and setting it outside to see what could be made from it… yielded significant knowledge, but sadly no useful image. Back to the drawing board.

"The cure for boredom is curiosity. There is no cure for curiosity" - *Ellen Parr*

This quote is fitting, though it is commonly attributed to Dorothy Parker (1893 - 1967), an American poet. However, sleuthing done by Garson O'Toole for the book *Hemingway Didn't Say That* reveals that the first use of this quote came in a *Reader's Digest* column in December 1980 attributed to Ellen Parr. According to O'Toole's research, the woman named Ellen Parr could not be tracked down. Indeed, curiosity knows no boundaries and we shouldn't take things at face value without asking questions. Even the facts as presented by others may be inaccurate or incomplete. Explore for yourself and find your own answers!

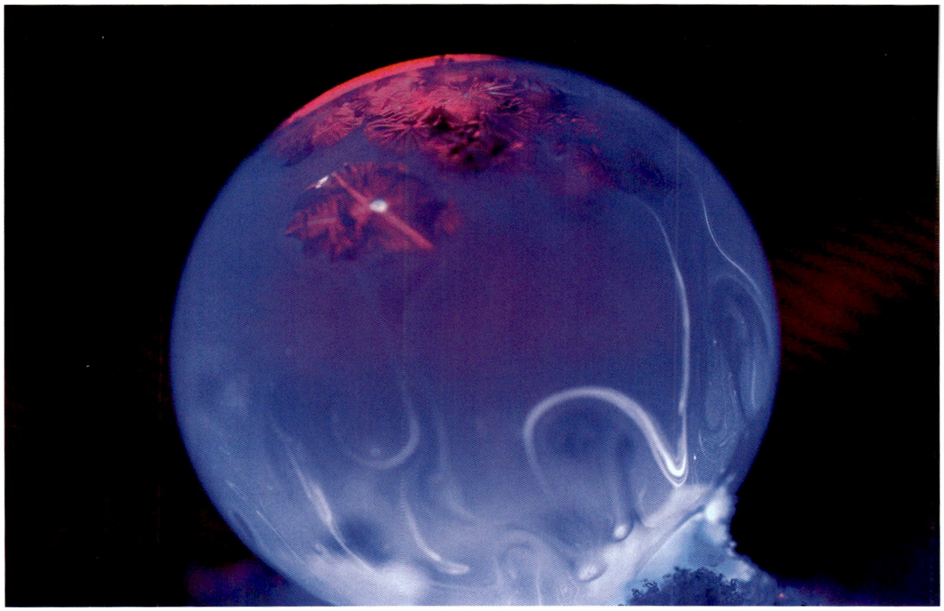

What was learned? Plenty. I could immediately see a spill of red light from the UV flash that I created with recommendations found on the Internet. The process involved removing the plastic lenses / filters from an old flash and putting a "UV Black" filter in front, and that worked! But still some light leaked through. An additional filter was added to allow maximum UV transmission while eliminating the bleed of red light.

Moreover, the bubble solution was not much of a solution. The pigment was not soluble in whatever the bubble fluid was made from (presumably water-based), so the pigment did not behave as expected, swirling on its own and not crystallizing. I noticed that the ice crystals at the top of the freezing bubble had no pigment in them at all, so this clearly wasn't going to work. In searching for a different way to approach the problem, there was a novel answer.

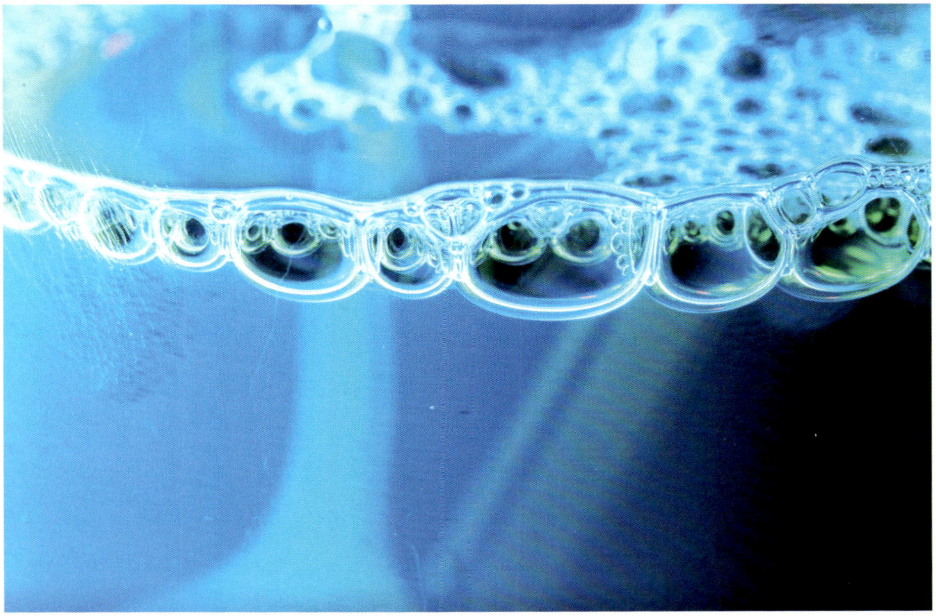

Invisible Ink. Specifically, *Noodler's Blue Ghost* which is available in small bottles and designed to write invisibly with refillable pens but would fluoresce bright blue. When mixed into the bubble formula in place of water, the ink, soap and white corn syrup all blended together homogeneously. It was a transparent but glowing liquid and I was ready for the next attempt.

And the first bubble blown was...

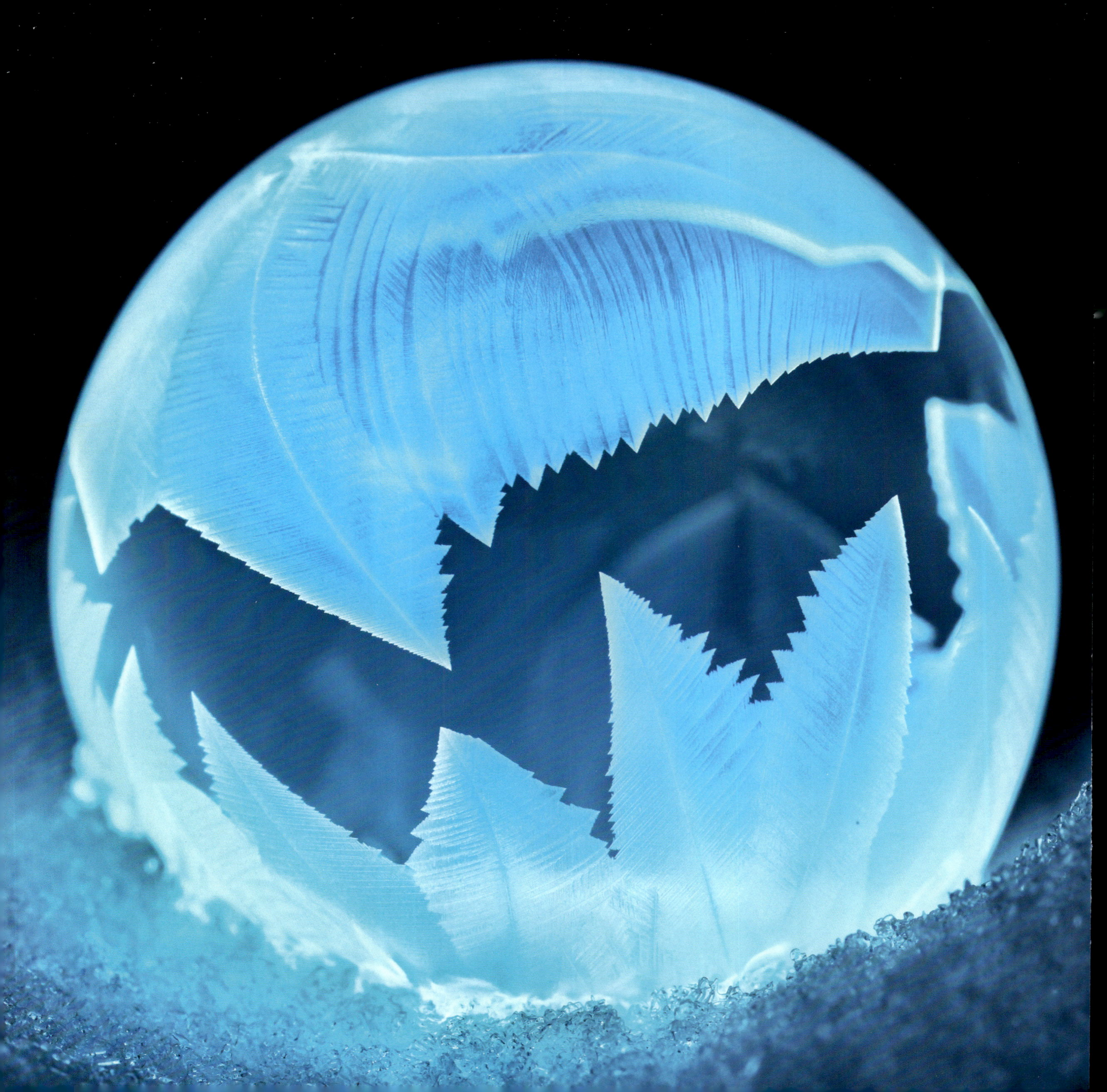

Better than I could have hoped for (*left*). It was exactly as I had pre-visualized and the snow surrounding it had a glow that could not be achieved any other way. The bubble itself felt more solid and there was a clear separation from front to back as my light was aimed at the foreground, not the background for these experiments. Like some alien egg hatching or whatever otherworldly comparison you can make, it hit the mark! I was giddy with excitement.

The spark of curiosity is not that easily sated, however. The same company that creates the invisible ink also makes a wide range of inks, many of them that fluoresce! What would other colours look like? What if colours were combined? The orange highlighter ink I selected failed to freeze into anything useful, and while the green highlighter ink was marginally successful, the resulting image was not. It was overloaded with colour to the point of distraction, not really carrying the same meaning.

I wouldn't call the results (*below*) a complete failure. The image has merit, but part of that value is understanding when you've taken a concept a step too far, or at least a step in the wrong direction. You won't know this until you get there, and you might just discover new concepts in the process.

This doesn't exclusively apply to freezing soap bubbles nor macro photography in general. This is a creative principle that should be embraced even outside of the photographic space. Stay curious and always experiment, even if those experiments meet with initial frustrations. If you keep walking down that path and occasionally head back to the drawing board for new puzzle pieces, you'll eventually arrive at an image that no one before you has created.

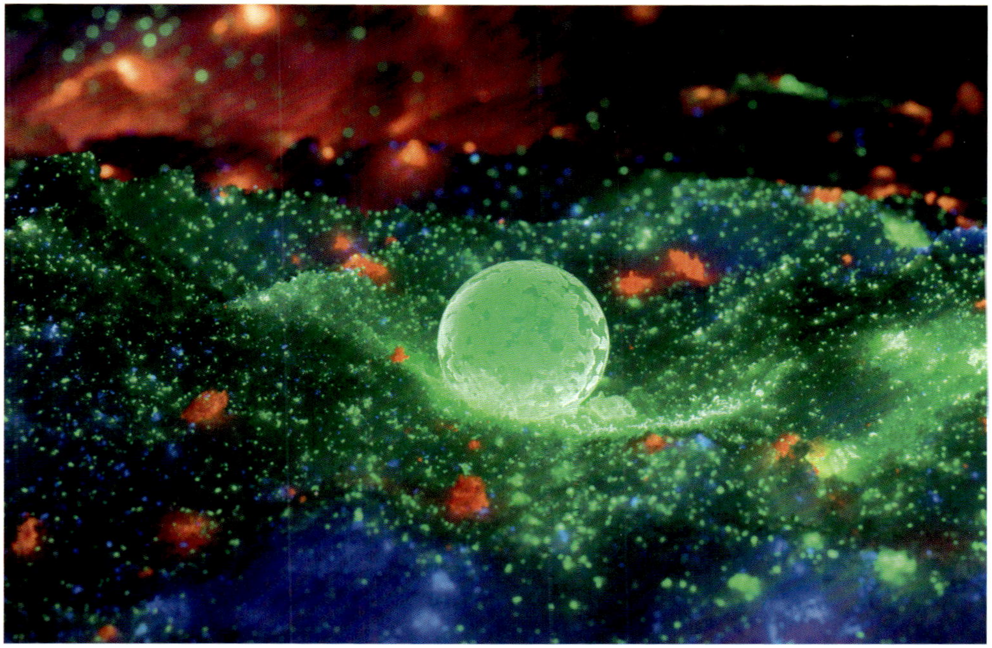

Left: Canon 1DX, Canon MP-E 65mm F/2.8 1x-5x Macro, F/16 ISO 250 1/250sec

Right: Canon 1DX mark II, Meyer Optik Trioplan 100 F/2.8, F/16 ISO 800 1/200sec

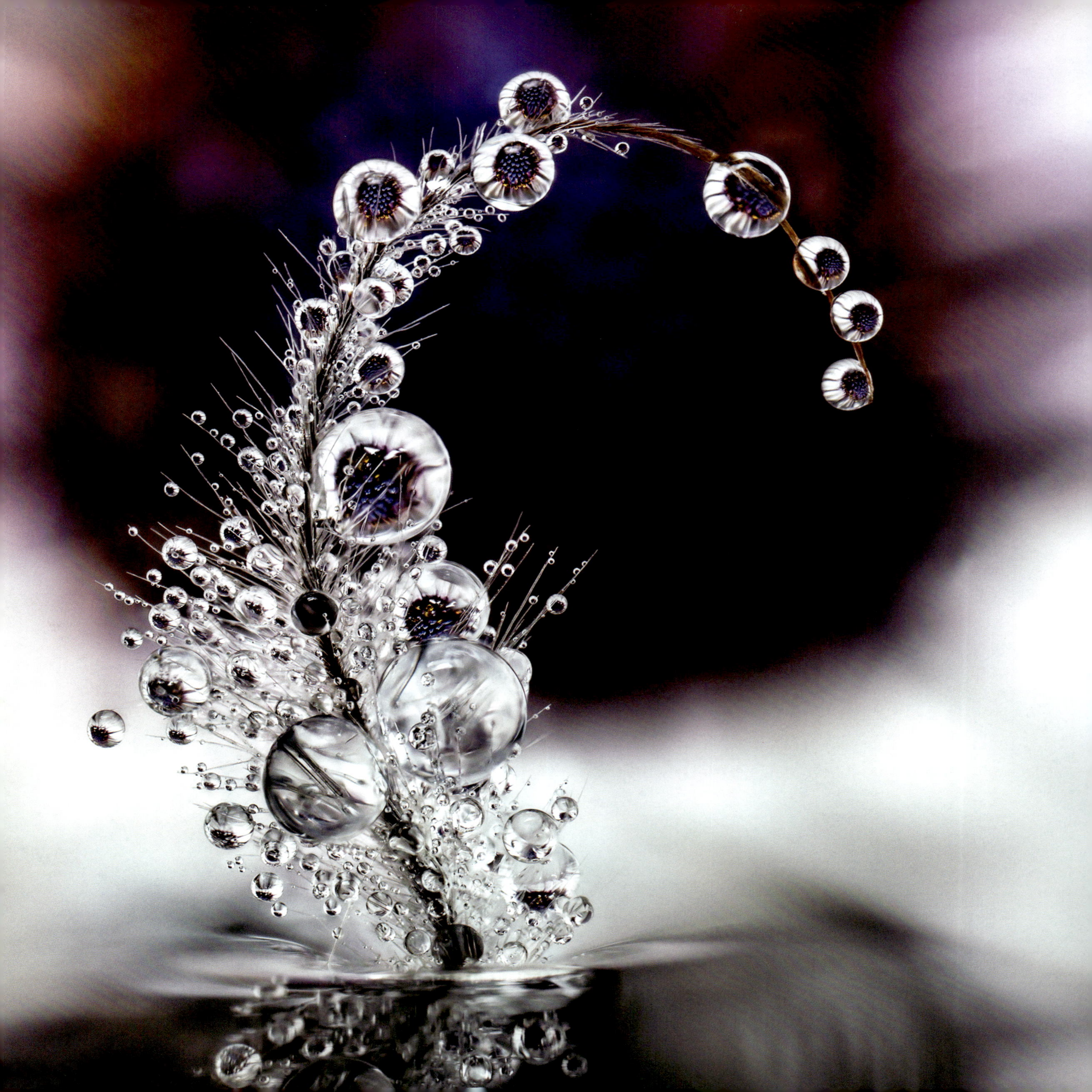

Masterclass

Some images require a unique approach, or they utilize an assortment of skills that would be difficult to place together from individual bits of knowledge. Welcome to the "Masterclass" for a select number of images to dissect exactly what went into their creation. With a foundation of knowledge for the discrete techniques covered in this book, we can put multiple concepts together for further creativity.

Some images will have taken a day to produce. This time does not include the gathering of all previous knowledge with the subject and concept that may have led to mistakes, from which solutions were discovered. Occasionally the photos in this section will offer a number of quick and simple "ah ha!" moments, other times you'll join me down the rabbit hole of curiosities, multiple attempts and arriving at a finished image.

The process for creating an image is not universal. You cannot walk exactly in my footsteps and create the same results. The goal here is to allow you to see every step of my own creative problem-solving process to inspire you, and to adapt it to your own ideas. What better place to start than with the image featured on the cover of this book?

Essence of Reverie

The creation of this image started as the evolution of a concept previously executed successfully, with a blade of blue fescue emerging from the surface of water. This image is featured in the Water Droplet Refraction section of this book. What if, instead of a blade of grass, we used a wildflower seed? The tiny "hairs" on such seeds produce very spherical water droplets.

"Prairie Smoke" is a wildflower that produces seeds with a long "spine" from which many tiny hairs emerge, as a full seed head they look like wispy smoke. Not unlike the seeds of a clematis but more elongated, it was easy to draw a parallel to the previous grass experiment. The comparison was so strong that it led to the initial idea for the image before it evolved: what if the seed was positioned in such a way that it was creating an inverted arch, where the middle was nearly touching the water and bringing the reflection closer at this point? This would connect the compositional elements in the center rather than on the sides.

In theory this would be beautiful, in practice it just didn't have the impact I was hoping for. Further experimentation with this exact concept might have yielded better results, but when I don't feel completely inspired by an idea, I change my approach and see if something else has more of a spark of inspiration.

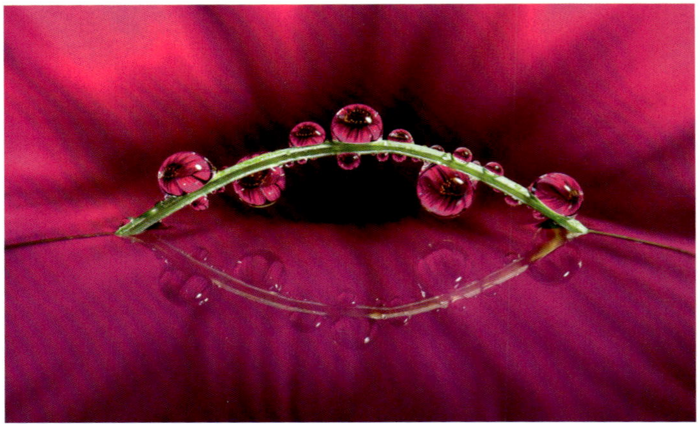

Top: "Hidden World", the original inspiration for "Essence of Reverie" depicting a blade of grass emerging from water with it's reflection underneath.

Bottom: A rather inspired attempt at inverting this concept with a Prairie Smoke wildflower seed.

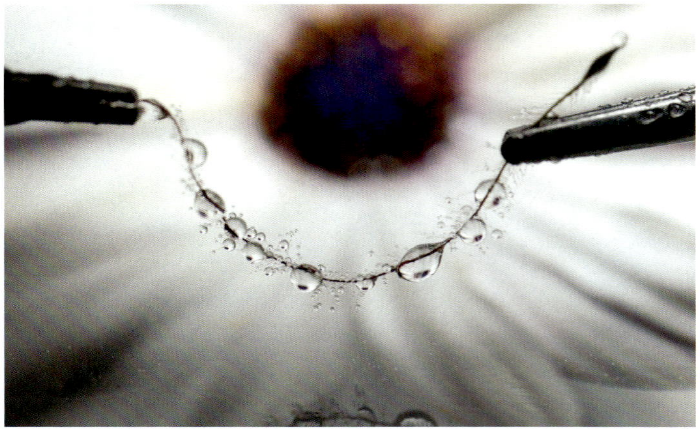

I knew I had the right ingredients here – just looking at the close-up of the seeds themselves revealed very beautiful refractions of a blue-eyed African Daisy (*Osteospermum*) which was selected from the garden store specifically for the blue center. Whenever you are constructing a water droplet refraction image, the colour of your flower is a critical design choice. It defines the colour palette for your image, and flowers with a different coloured center than their petals usually perform best.

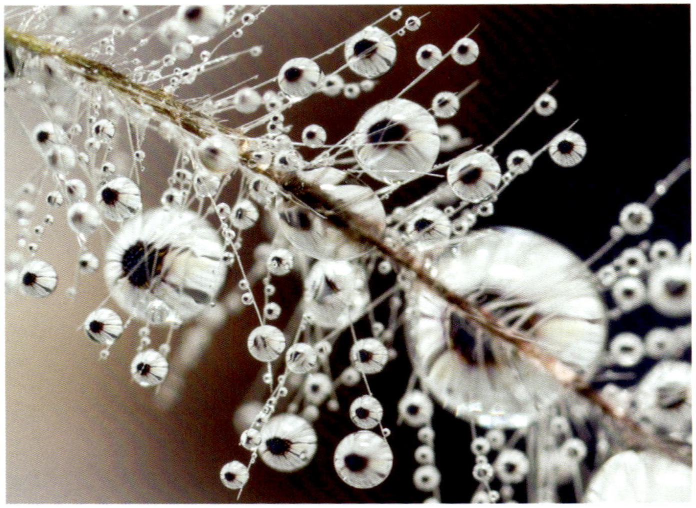

These seeds are behaving well, the background will have the needed splash of colour, but how can it all be arranged so that we make magic? A few hours go by, experimenting with different ways to position the seed above the water. Many of these seeds, when sprayed, would "animate"; the spine of the seed would curl, changing its orientation to the camera and the flower and would drastically change the composition. After a variety of arrangements with one seed, multiple seeds and different flowers, the final image began to solidify: I didn't need the entirety of the seed, they get too long and unpredictable. What if just half of the spine was used, with a curl already established?

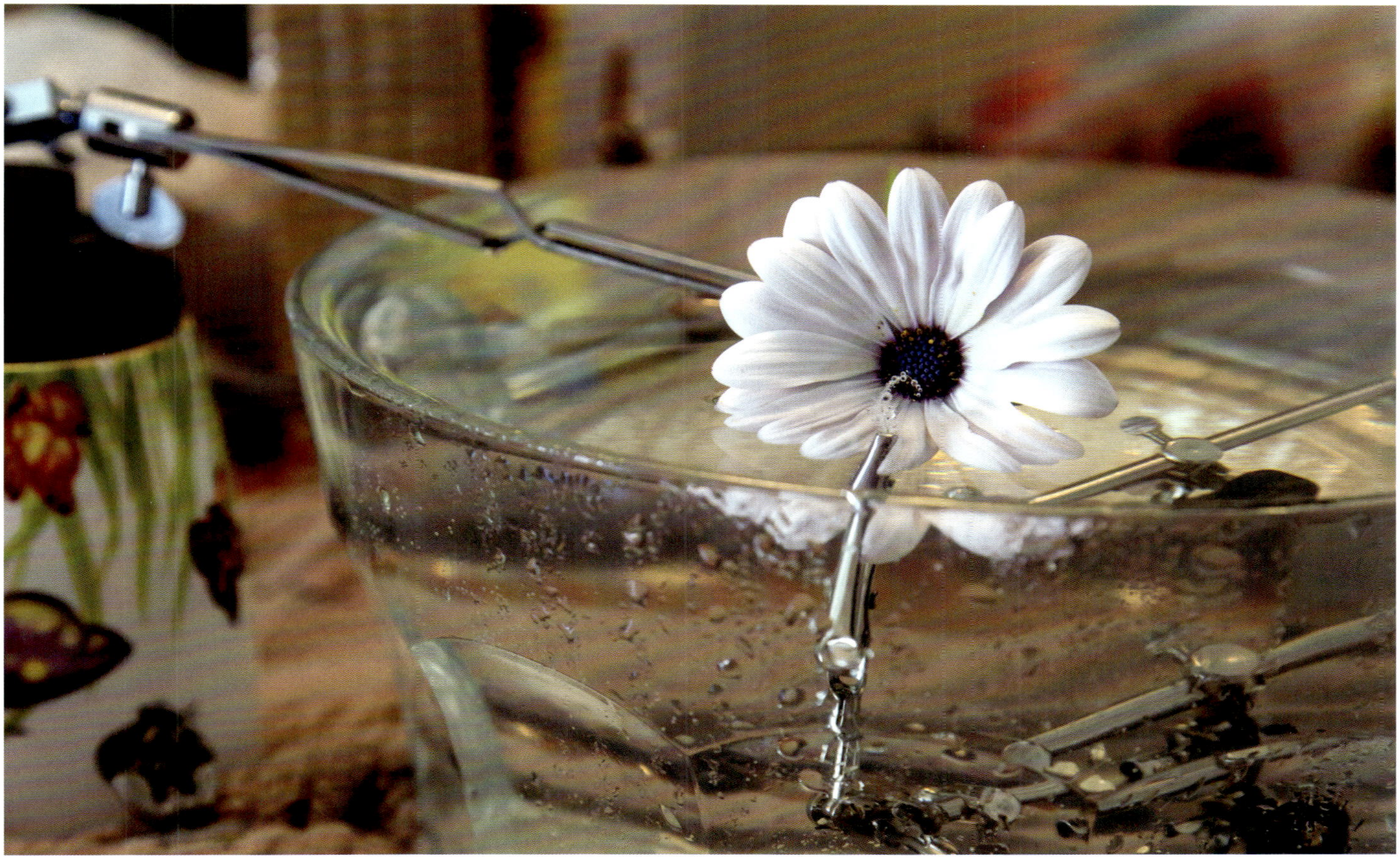

This image was created on my kitchen table with the most basic equipment to construct the final image. A glass bowl purchased from a thrift store, selected because it had a wide, flat base that would be conducive to placing a "third hand tool" into the bowl, fully submerged but stable. Another third hand tool, also referred to as "helping hand tools" with a tweezer-like appendage, was used to position one flower, partially submerged and centered, behind the seed. This second tool wasn't at the right height, so an overturned coffee mug was just the ticket to raise it to the proper level. Use the tools you have at your disposal. I often use whatever is within reach.

Once the visual elements were in order, a spray bottle on a fine mist setting was used to inundate the seed with tiny water droplets, many of which would stick on contact and stay spherical. A simple spray bottle from a Dollar Store is all that's needed here; It's all I've ever used when misting seeds and other surfaces to create water droplets, with the exception of my garden hose when I'm outdoors.

At last, I have a subject worth picking up my camera to photograph! Having shot a few practice images along the way, I had a sense for what settings my camera should be configured to.

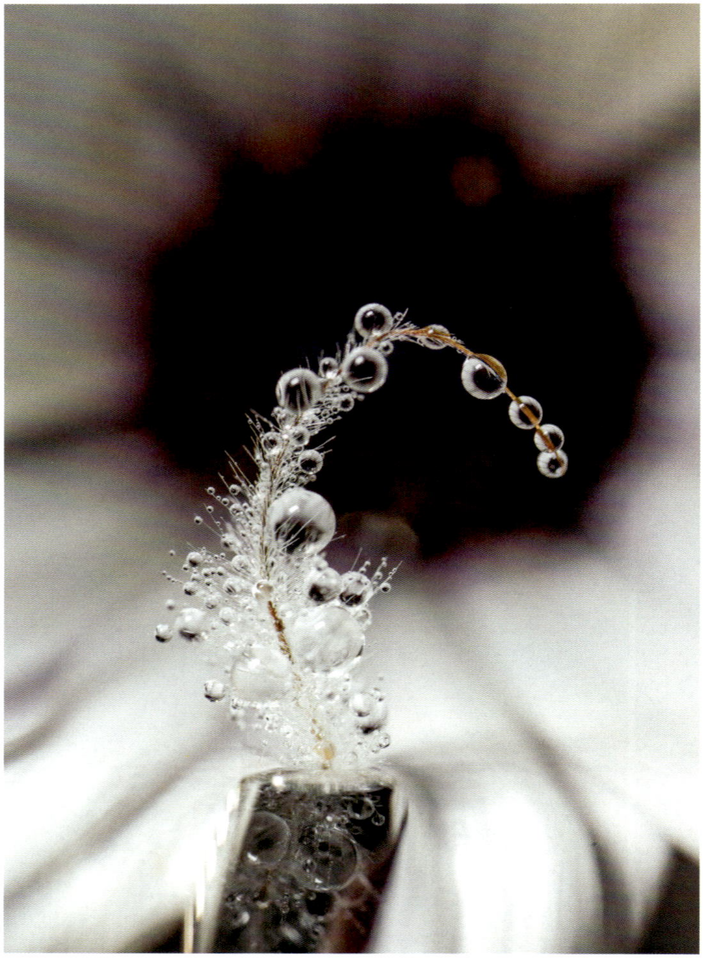

Because African Daisies are much smaller than their Gerbera Daisy counterparts that I usually use, the flower needed to be placed closer to the seed to fill the droplet refractions properly. This in turn would make the flower in the background more in focus than desired if I was shooting at F/8 or F/11. Part of the beauty of these images requires that the background remain soft, but the foreground reveals the flower inside the droplets. While a smaller aperture would be preferred for greater depth of field in the foreground, the compromise needed to be made at **F/5.6** to allow for the background to remain soft. Focus-stacking techniques would then permit greater foreground focus across multiple frames.

Knowing that I would be shooting with off-camera flash, a lower ISO setting is preferred. **ISO 200** was chosen for great image quality, while also allowing the flash to fire repeatedly without draining too quickly at a high frame rate. This was before I discovered the practical use for an external battery pack, but it wasn't a significant compromise from shooting at ISO 100.

With a shutter speed set to the flash sync speed of **1/200sec** and the flash operating in E-TTL mode for a proper exposure, the first image was taken and inspected. Problems. Problems to be solved quickly.

Both primary problems involve the surface of the water. First, that clamp! It needs to be hidden beneath the water, completely invisible. In order to facilitate that, the reflection on the surface of the water needs to be stronger. With a subject actively evaporating, this image was shot handheld – no tripod – in order to make changes as nimbly and swiftly as possible.

The flash was aimed more towards the background and less on the foreground, which eliminated the light hitting the clamp, especially on the left edge where specular highlights would still be visible through any surface reflection. The flash was also handheld in the

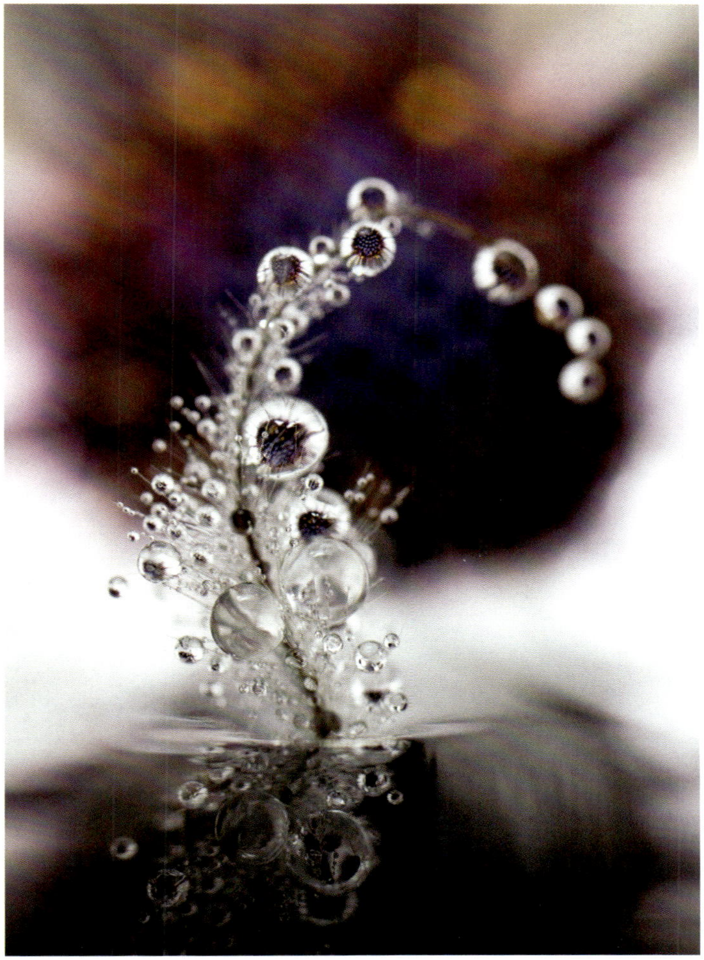

same fashion that a police officer might hold both a gun and a flashlight, my left arm is wrapped in front of my right arm, resting the end of the camera lens on my arm and using my wrist to adjust the flash angle.

The camera was positioned lower, so that the surface of the water was closer to perpendicular to the focal plane. This allows for stronger reflections off the surface of the water, a tip that can translate into waterfront landscape photography as well. While doing so allowed for the reflections to supersede the clamp in the composition, the shift in angle also meant that the entirety of the curve of the seed could no longer be seen within a single frame.

It could also have been due to the seed moving slightly – like all of the other seeds had done – between the initial test image and the start of the proper shooting sequence for focus stacking. A single frame (left) won't cut it – multiple images need to be combined together to get focus across the entire width of the seed. Slightly swaying forward and back as I shoot continuously, I aim to shoot past the seed in either direction, just slightly, to be sure that I gather all of the necessary focus slices.

Because this process is done handheld, I have no certainty of how many images are needed or if I have collected all of the needed focus slices to complete the final image. To this end, I drastically overshoot. For the final shooting sequence, over 180 frames were shot but only 20 were used. Could you imagine if I had missed a necessary slice of focus in this image because I didn't shoot far more images than I needed? I can always throw away frames I don't need after the fact.

Experiment and tinker extensively to create the best subject worthy of your photographic efforts, and then work as quickly as possible to document your creation in the best possible way with all of your skills as a photographer. Two art forms co-existing with synergy allows for images such as this to be made.

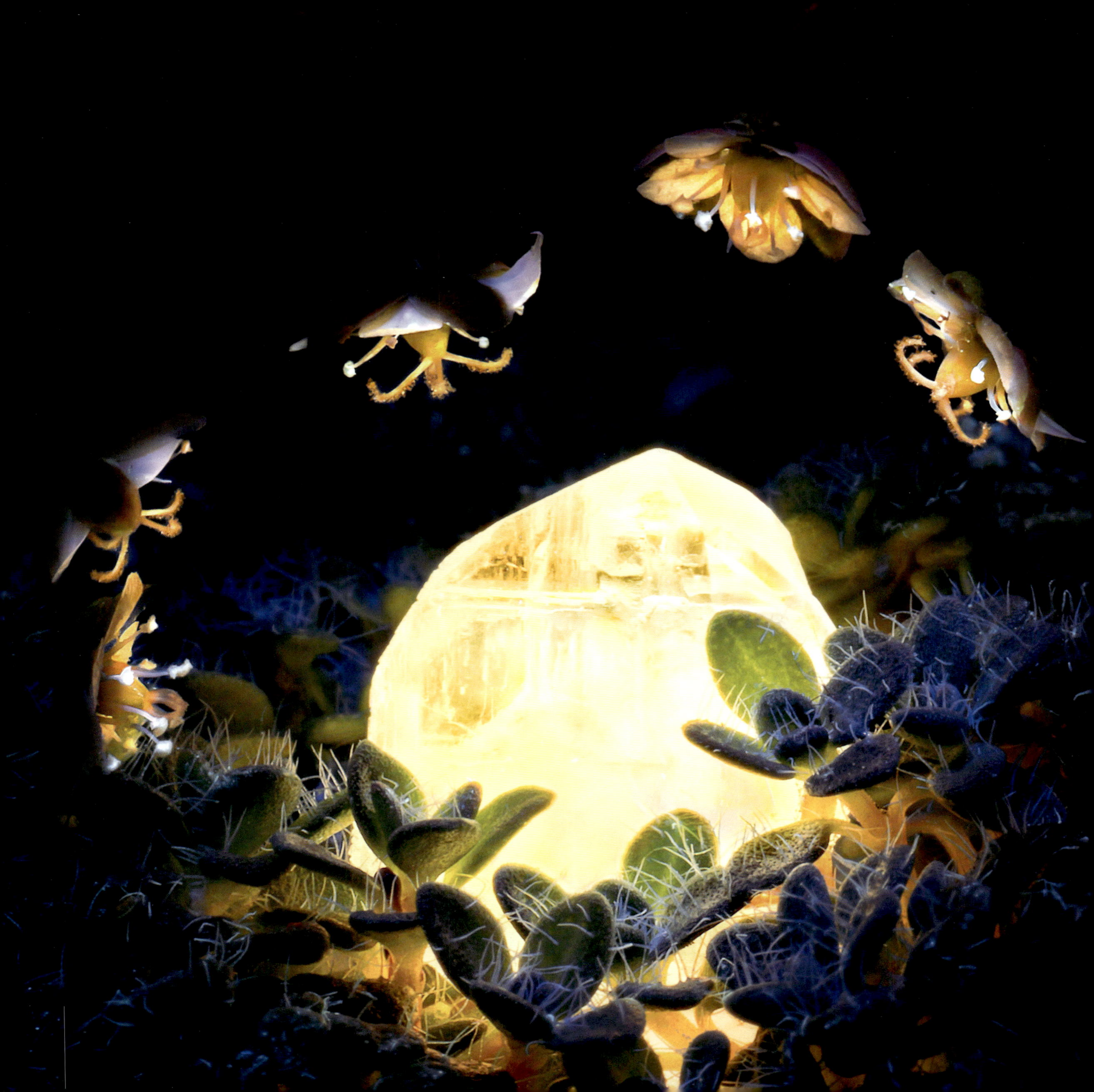

Midnight Sun

I had this story in my mind for over a year before finally experimenting with it: a glowing rock appearing as a source of light for the surrounding plants; a surrogate for the sun. Flowers bend over to reach towards this precious stone rather than the sun itself.

Let's start by listing the ingredients here:

Cerussite: a lead ore that fluoresces a sun-like shade of yellow. This was an eBay purchase for around $20 for a cluster of these tiny crystals, many of which could easily be removed without damaging them. One particularly bright terminated crystal stood out for me, and I placed it into this scene.

Creeping Thyme: The crystal is nestled into this wonderful groundcover – $5 at my local garden store. I figured it would have enough depth, and the tiny little hairs would catch some of the fluoresced light off the crystal.

Irish Moss Flowers: The same garden store, also for $5, had a few Irish Moss plants for sale; One of them had begun to flower. I knew I needed flowers roughly this size based on the crystal size, and their long stems (relative to the size of the flower) would make them easy to position using Third Hand Tools. Delightfully, their pollen also glowed faintly white!

The process began with a simple arrangement: put multiple ultraviolet flashes as close to the subject as possible, just outside the frame. In a room with near-zero ambient light, the fluorescence should produce enough illumination for the final composition.

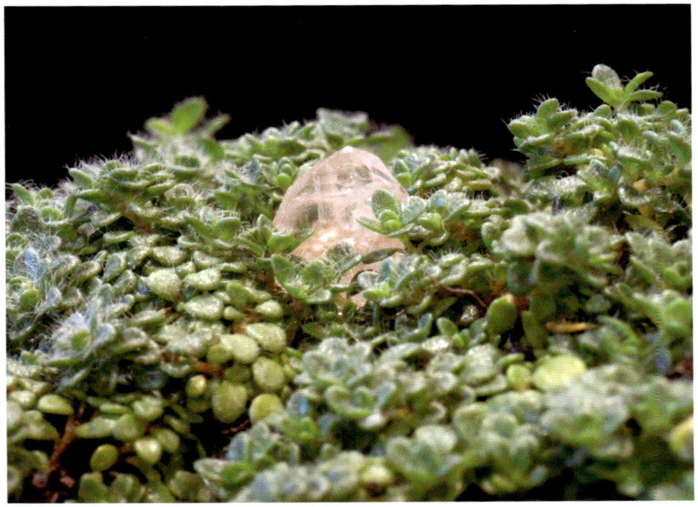

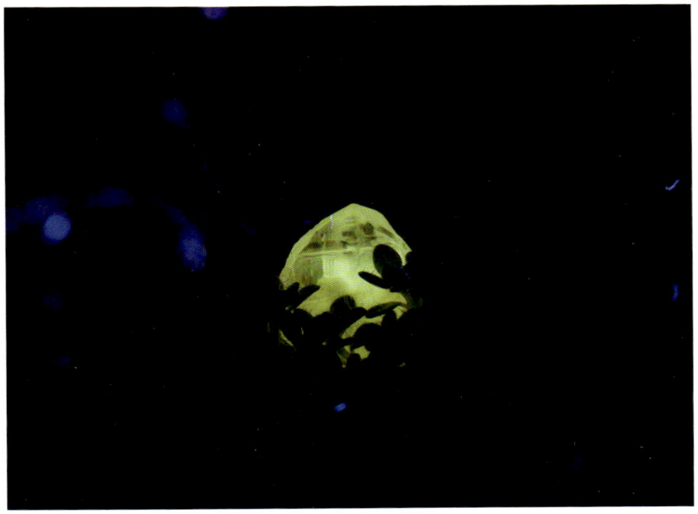

Top: Visible Light image of placement of Cerrusite in the Creeping Thyme.

Bottom: Illuminated with UV flash, the first test is promising, but nowhere near the desired brightness at ISO 400 with UV flashes firing.

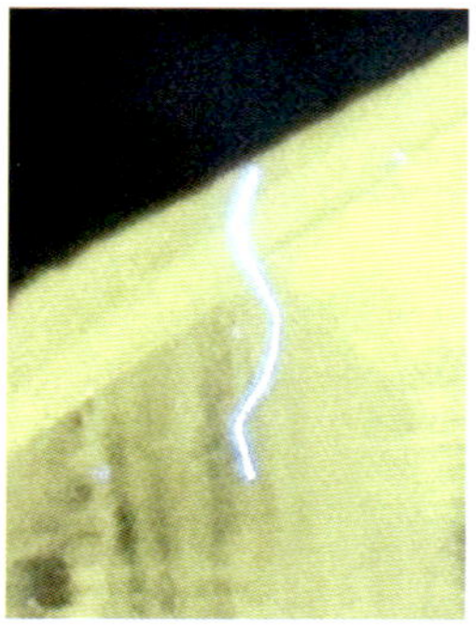

Unfortunately, these flashes at point-blank range at full power still resulted in a dimly-lit image. To add insult to injury, specks of dust and synthetic fibers on the subject constantly remind me how fluorescent they are (*left*) and need to be removed with a bulb blower or a toothpick. This can be tedious, but it's always best to fix this before you shoot.

Knowing that my subject would remain static, a novel idea came to mind. What if I were to set the camera to expose the scene for **30 seconds**, all the while I manually fire my flashes by pressing the "TEST" button on my wireless flash receivers immediately after they completely recharge? With the wireless receiver off the camera and in my hand, it wasn't difficult to continually blast the subject with UV light. Such intense illumination allowed me to shoot the image with the base **ISO** of **200** on the Lumix GX9, while also achieving maximum depth of field at **F/18**.

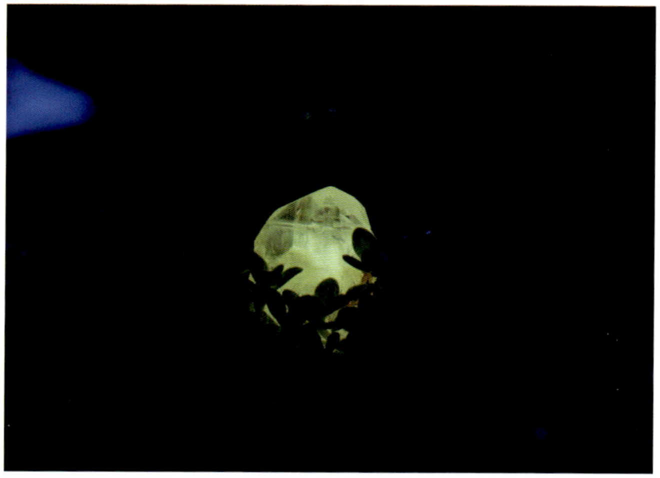

An image like this takes a day to create, from sourcing the components, experimenting with composition, and finally overcoming technical challenges. The flowers, for example, were carefully picked and placed with clamps that would not be visible within the frame. This allowed for the precise positioning of each flower, which were required to fall through a very narrow plane of focus surrounding the fluorescing mineral. If a flower was out

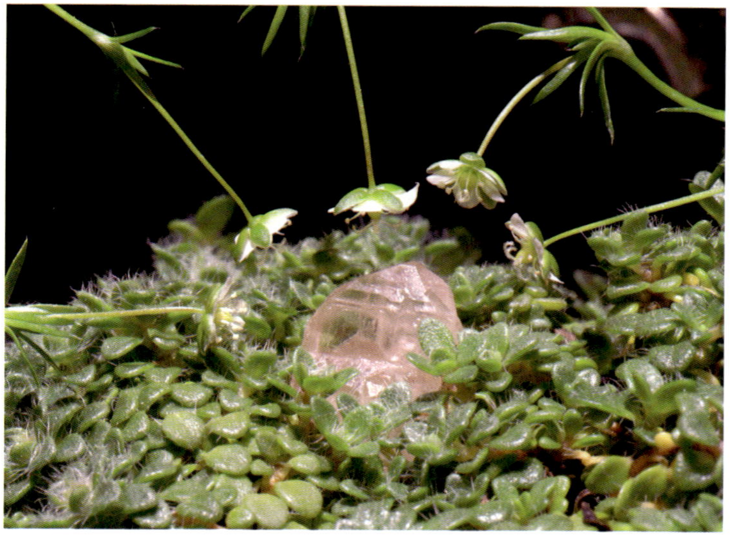

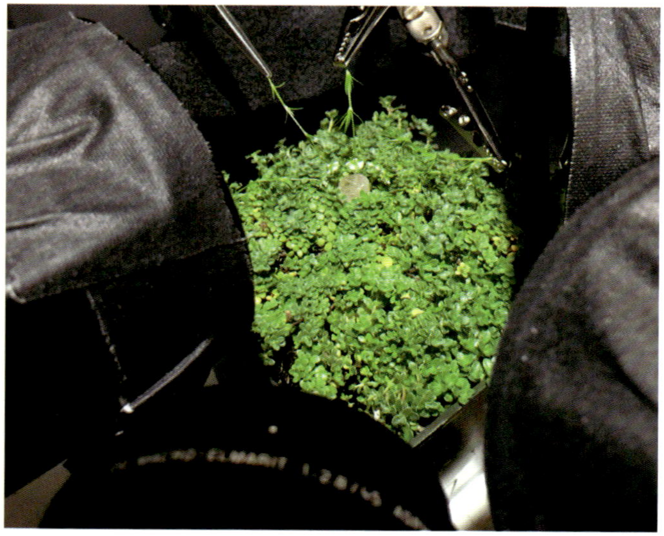

of alignment, it would be noticeably out of focus. While focus stacking is always an option to overcome this, it's always good practice to get the best possible results in-camera.

Some important enhancements were done in editing. The stems of each flower were straight, but the narrative needed curved stems to make it feel like these flowers were reaching in. Quick work with the Liquify tool in Photoshop handled that nicely. To enhance the concept of this mineral providing light for the plants, the sides of the Irish Moss flowers facing away from the crystal were darkened, as were the lower corners of the frame. Editing was done in Photoshop and partly in ON1 Photo RAW.

Sometimes you just need to finesse an image with classic tools like dodging and burning to get the proper feel. Other times you need to use modern structural enhancing algorithms to enhance specific textures. Every part of an image like this requires local attention to bring out the best elements. Don't be afraid to take an hour or two to apply the finishing polish on an image worthy of your attention!

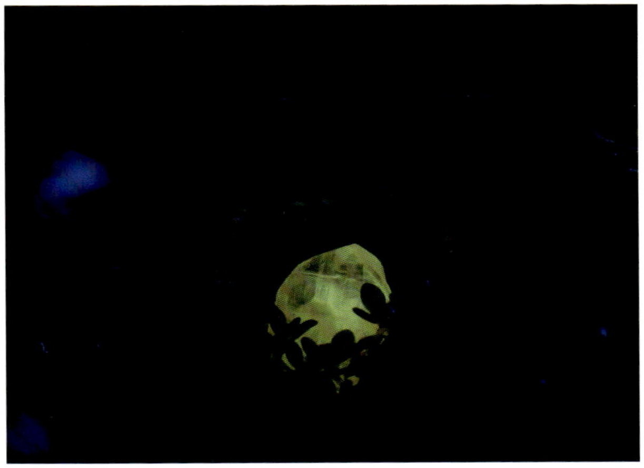

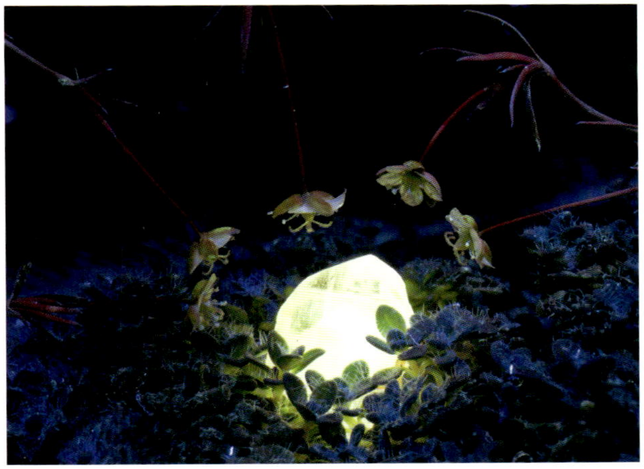

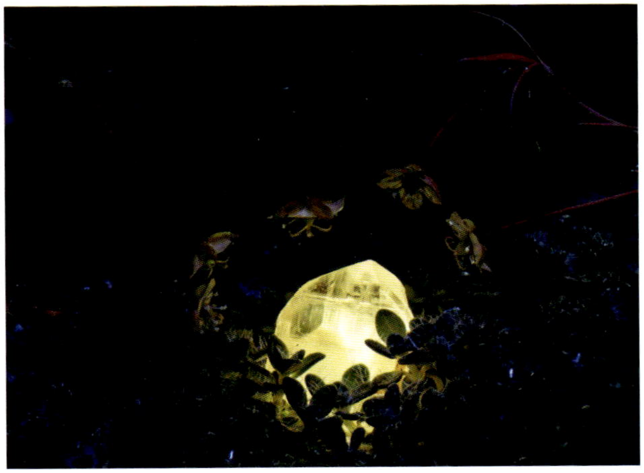

Top: The flowers are aligned and the frame is set, but the exposure is much too dark.

Middle: A 30 second exposure with repeatedly firing flashes provides enough light to illuminate the frame with the mineral fluorescing among the plants.

Bottom: Basic adjustments in Adobe Camera RAW allow for the recovery of detail in the mineral and white balance correction. From here, more extensive edits take place to bring about the proper balance of light and contrast.

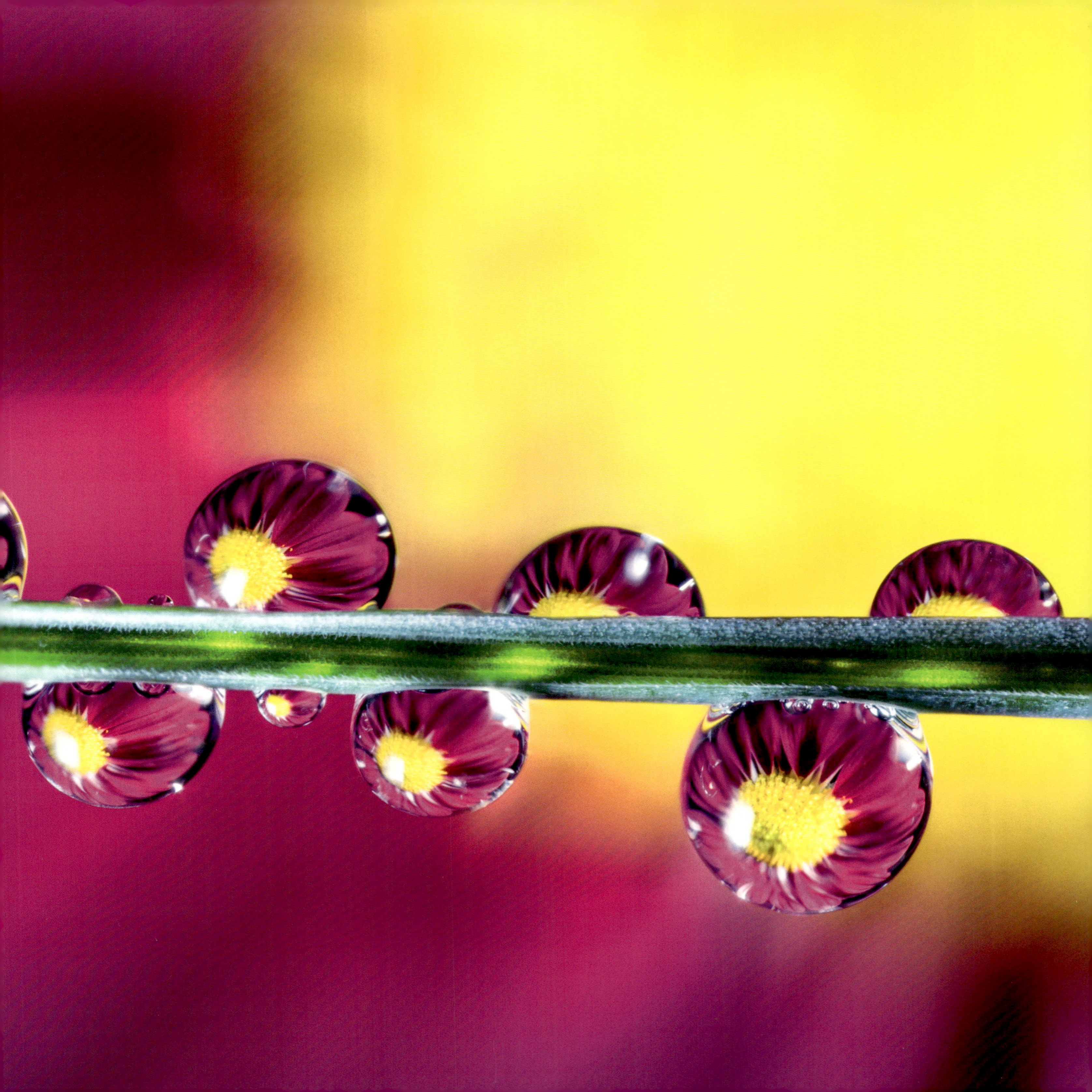

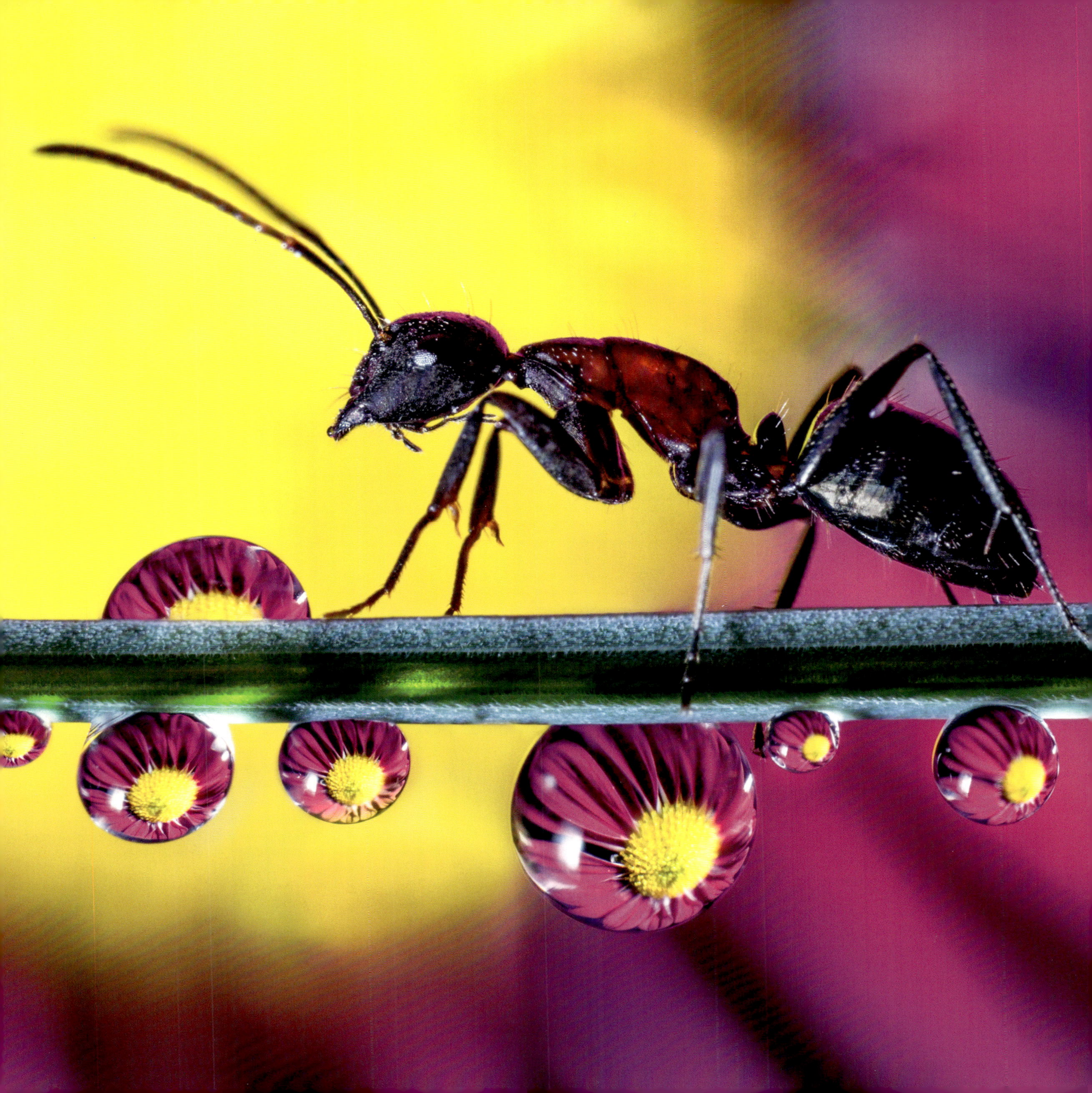

Jewels of Summer

Using "live actors" in macro photography can be a frustrating endeavour. This image represents my first attempt at wrangling an insect into the frame, and the concept evolved considerably through the day.

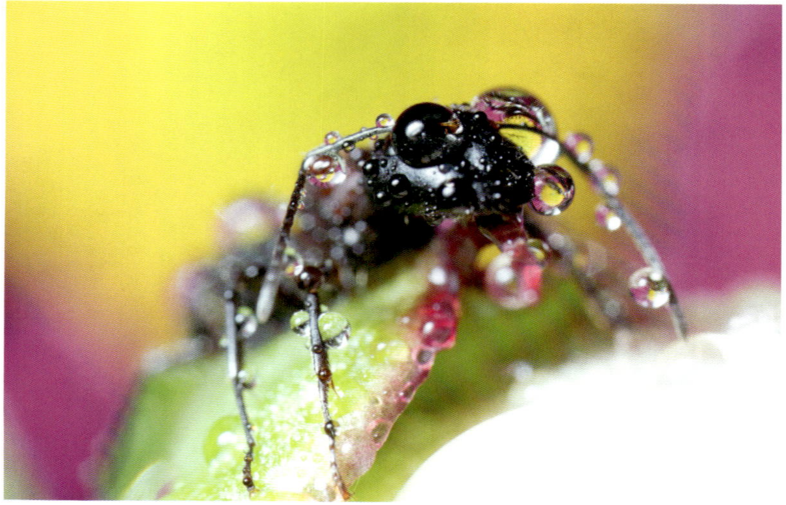

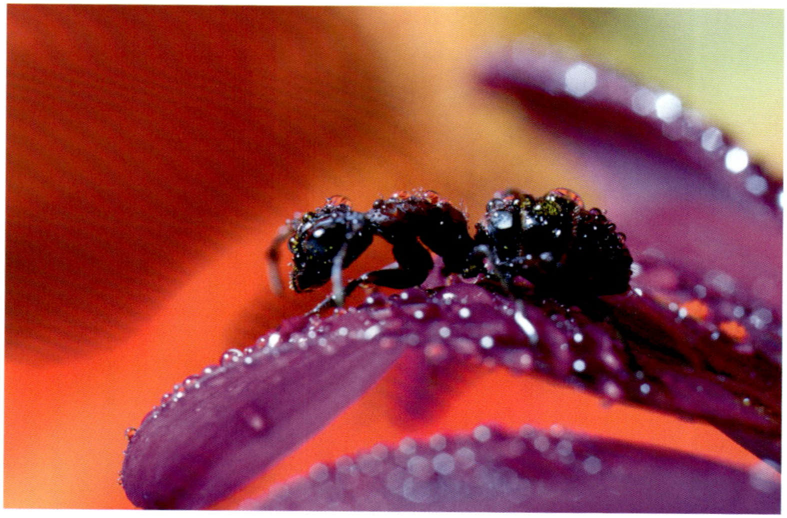

While working in the garden, I had noticed a number of ants collecting themselves on the soon-to-blossom Peony flowers in early summer. Peonies have a symbiotic relationship with ants that is often misunderstood. A common misconception is that the ants are helping the Peony flowers to bloom, whereas the real truth is slightly different: the ants are defending the flowers against predators. Peonies are a wonderful example of "extrafloral nectaries", plants that produce nectar outside of the flower itself. The ants seek out this treasure of sweet nectar for their own selfish consumption and will protect their constantly refreshing supply of nectar from any other insect. In so doing, they also protect the flower.

This provided a reliable supply of ants, all of which were moving slowly and staying in the same small area. What if I spray the ants with the "mist" setting on the garden hose? Could I get droplets to form on the ants themselves? The answer was a resounding "yes!", but that doesn't mean a successful image would result. Introducing a flower into the background for refraction purposes was going to be part of this process, but the off-white petals of the Peony blossoms were far brighter than anything else in the frame, and the water droplets wouldn't stand out. Depth of field was also an issue – how could I approach this differently?

Moving an ant to a more saturated flower petal was the next idea. Then a leaf, something darker and less saturated to give the background more impact.

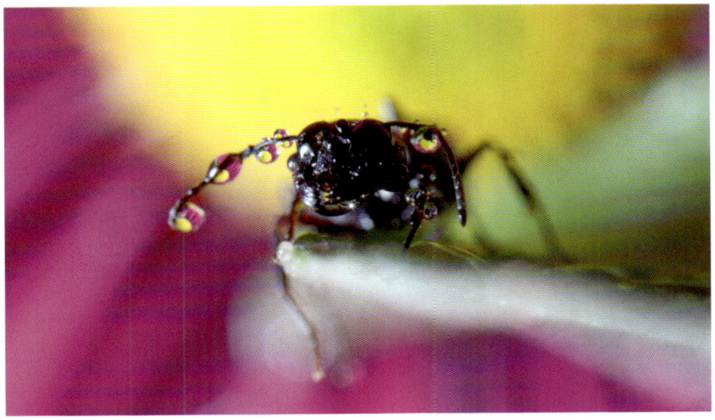

These ideas ultimately failed as well, in part because the ant felt inundated with droplets surrounding it and not providing the beauty associated with refracted flower imagery inside the droplets. Because the droplets were on the ant itself and the creature was not completely still, focus stacking would also be problematic. The ingredients could still work together, but how?

The droplets needed to be separated from the ant. If a stage could be created for the ant to be added to once attractive droplets had been established, it would be easier to predict the outcome of the image and frame things accordingly. A blade of Blue Fescue grass (*Festuca glauca*) would be perfectly suited with a Painted Daisy (*Tanacetum coccineum*) in the background. This was the idea – the theory – that would soon find its own hindrances.

The practical execution of this idea immediately presented me with a problem: the ants were oblivious to the water droplets. It might have been their frenzy to investigate a potential intruder to the realm of ever-flowing nectar, as the diminutive combatants plowed through the scene. In doing so, water droplets would glob up together, often sticking to the ant itself. Nothing quite like having a perfectly refracting water droplet hanging off of an ant's backside! Clearly, this wasn't the effect I was after – but I was so close!

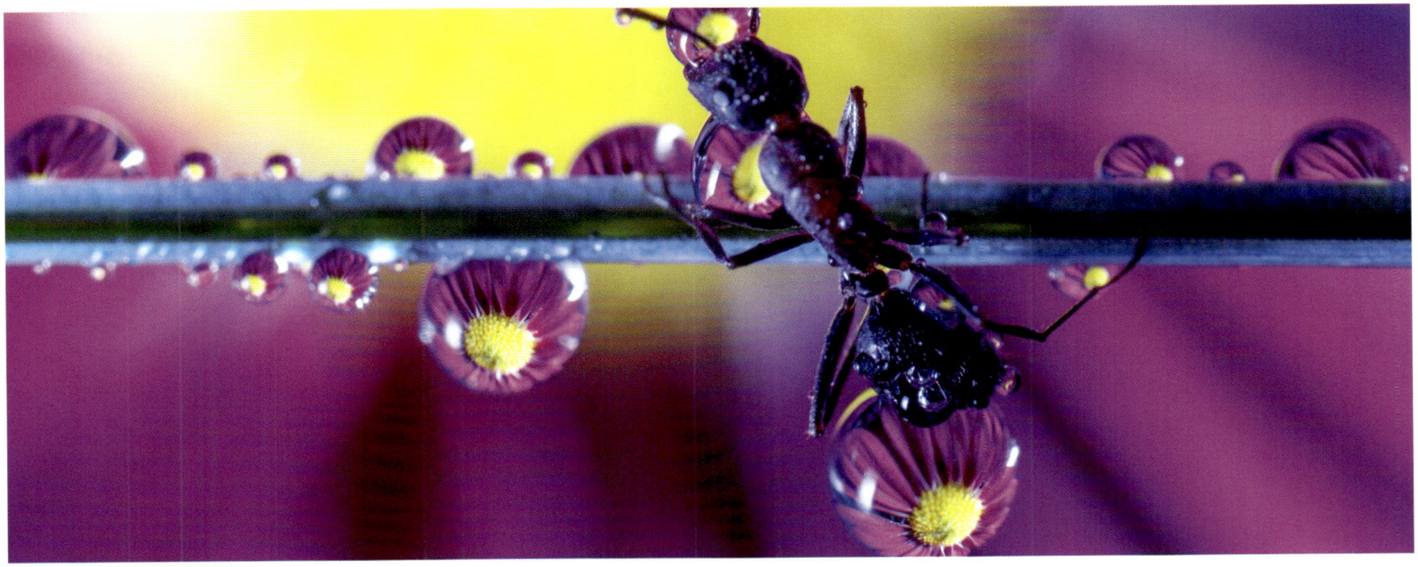

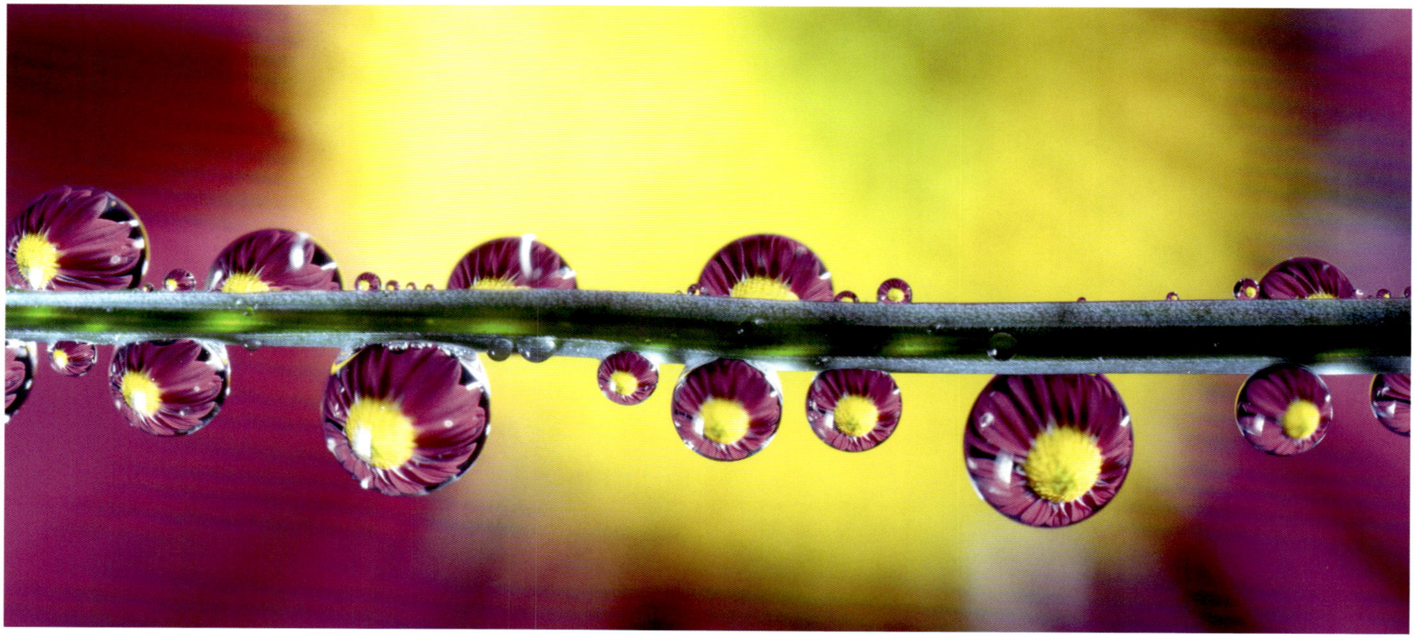

Ants are uncooperative actors. They would often walk in the wrong direction out of the frame, refuse to leave the "transfer twig" I had convinced them to climb onto, or would walk on the underside of the blade of grass; ants do not have the same relationship with gravity that we do.

The next play? Knowing that the stage will likely need to be reset multiple times when the actors make a wrong move, the goal was to limit the possibilities based on the placement of droplets. Offering an area on the top of the blade of grass with no droplets, it was my hope that the ant would stay stationary in this spot for a brief moment, just enough to fire off one shot. This did not happen immediately, and took five "stage resets" before I would get the ant in a favourable pose.

This all needs to be done handheld. Working quickly to adjust the framing and focus as the ant walked along the blade of grass, I knew that a tripod would be a limiting factor. Like many subjects from sublimating snowflakes to erratic insects, you never seem to have enough time. As the ant (likely a *Camponotus herculeanus* worker) moved through the frame, I moved the camera forward and back slightly to adjust the focal plane. This was a move to follow the ant as well as collect additional frames for focus stacking.

In total, eight frames were combined together to create the final image, allowing for extended focus across the blade of grass, all water droplets, and of course the actor. The problem? The ant was moving through the various frames. This meant that the content in each image would be drastically different, and no focus stacking algorithm would handle it well. Every automated solution was tried (Photoshop, ON1 Photo RAW, Zerene Stacker, Helicon Focus), but the input images simply generated garbage.

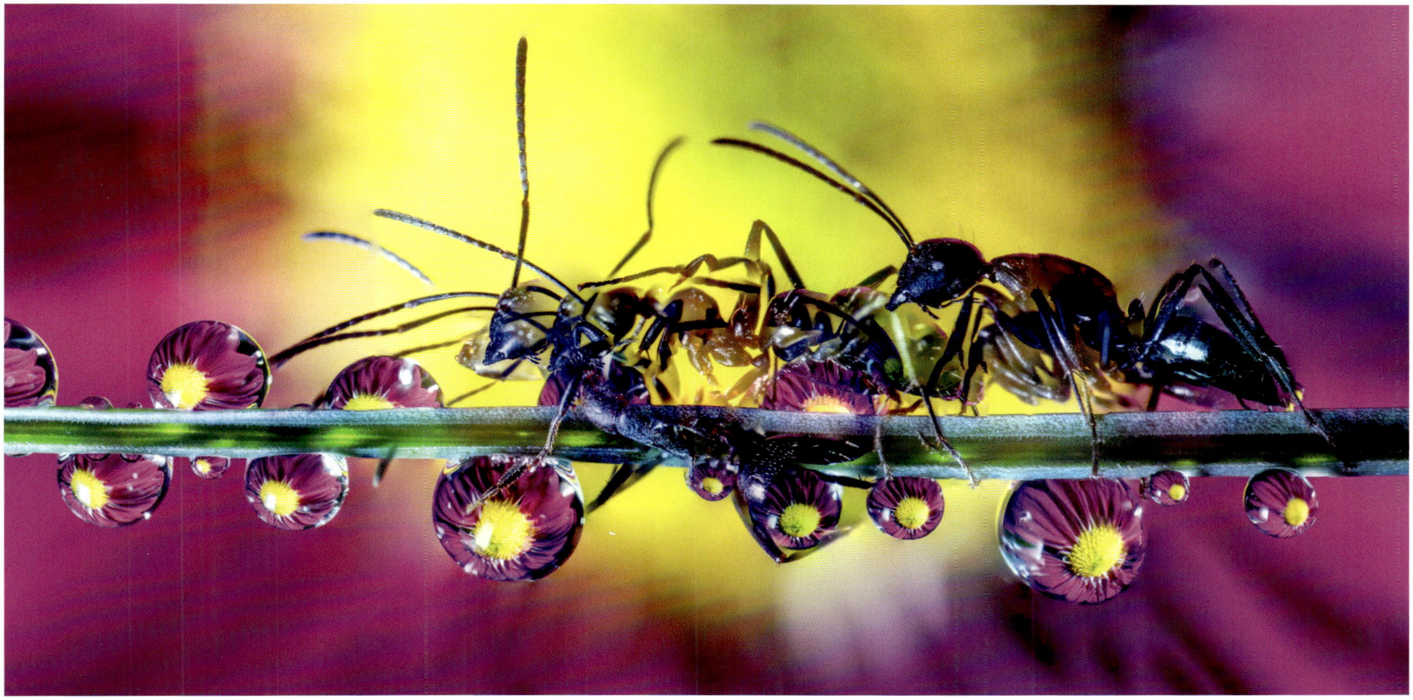

How about this for "results" (*above*)? Definitely a nightmare editing scenario to clean this up. After a brief attempt at sorting out the chaos, a better starting point was imagined: what if I cut out the ant from all of the frames except the one proper pose, and then stack the images with missing information in these areas?

Using the Lasso tool in Photoshop, the portion of the images that contain the ant in seven of the eight frames was outlined and deleted, and the stacking process was repeated. Watching that little green progress bar was never so spellbinding.

The results were vastly improved, but almost all stacking algorithms still take issue with hard edges at the border of the frame. These "hard edges" are now also present at the border of every cut-out within the frame, which generated artifacts such as duplicated information, hard transitions of colour and brightness, and generally misplaced pixels. All of these issues would be much easier to clean up than the above mess.

This approach of selectively removing components of a focus stack that would inherently not align well (the moving ant, in this case) will never find wide-spread use. It's rare that a moving subject can be stacked in any reasonable way unless the purpose is to extend the depth of field of static elements – in this case, the water droplets and grass. Understanding how to use tools in an unconventional way is paramount to the success of images like this. You'll also need more patience than you think you're capable of.

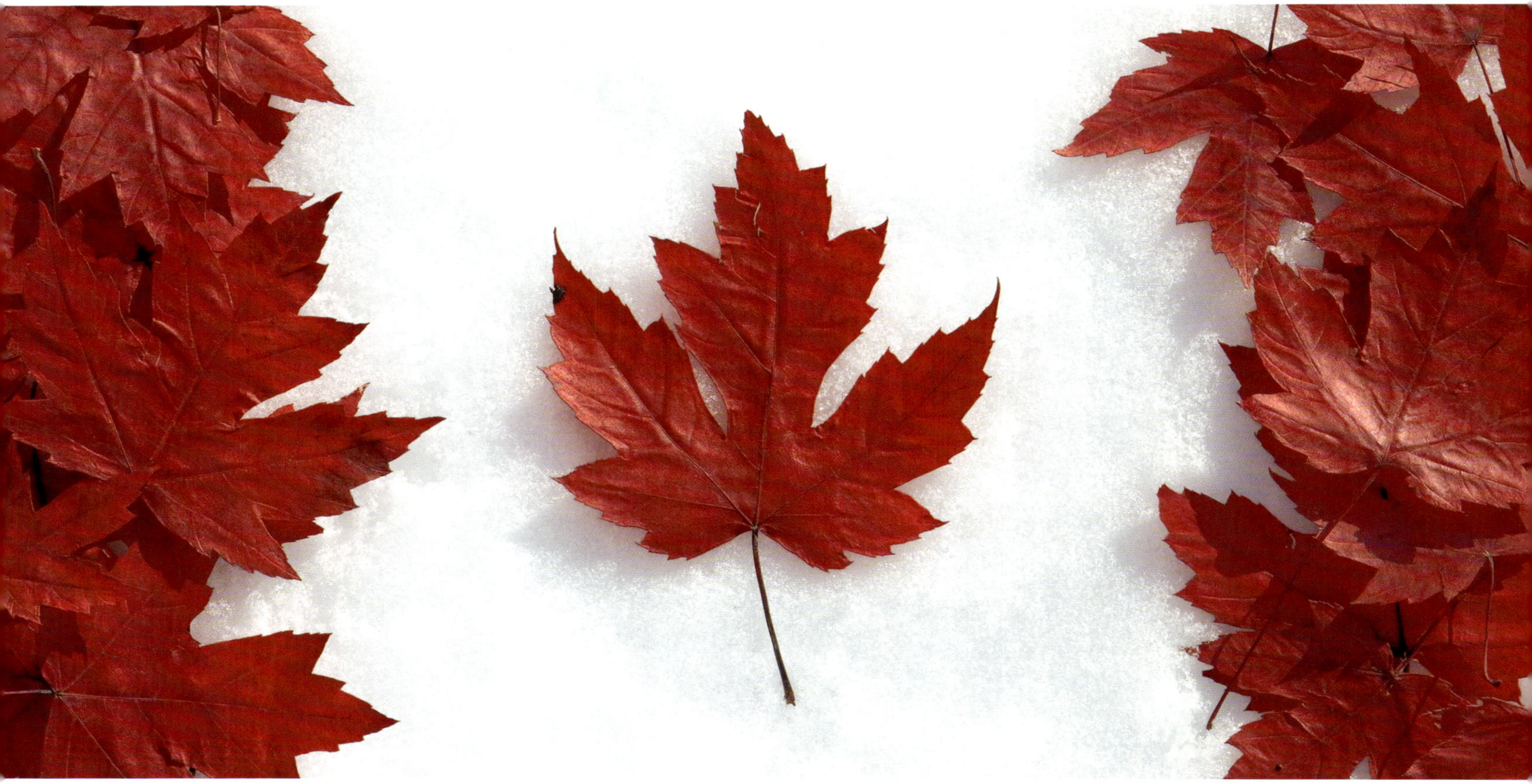

Canon 5D Mark II, Canon EF 24-105mm F/4L, F/16 ISO 100 1/125sec

Maple Leaf Flag

This image is an exception; it's not a macro photograph. It is, however, a perfect example of previsualizing and staging an image and it represents the start of my professional career in photography. Nothing is more iconically Canadian than red maple leaves on a bed of fresh snow arranged in the shape of the Canadian flag.

The concept was envisioned in the autumn of 2008, knowing that the height of fall colour is not likely to coincide with freshly falling snow. To compensate for this, I used my education dating all the way back to Kindergarten: ironing leaves between sheets of wax paper is a great way to preserve them. Collecting the best leaves from the trees in our neighbourhood – likely *Acer x freemanii* which is a hybrid of Silver and Red Maples – I set to work.

At this time, I was still living with my mother. Imagine her concern when she discovered me, at the age of 22, ironing leaves between wax paper for a "project". Simultaneously working towards an Advertising Diploma from Georgian College, no questions were presented to me. "It must be something school-related" I'm sure she thought, and let me carry on with the experiment.

Months passed while I waited for the right conditions: a morning with bright sunlight and freshly fallen snow. Impatiently grabbing the camera and my box of leaves, I headed to the back yard where my first attempt was made. After carefully placing a leaf on the snow, the tiniest whisper of wind hurled it into the air, impacting back onto the snow a second later and shattering to pieces. Lesson learned? Preserved leaves

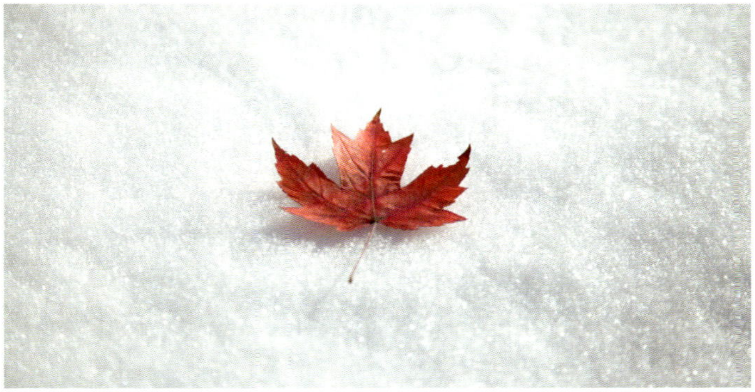

This first leaf placed on the snow was picked up by the wind and destroyed immediately after shooting this test frame.

are incredibly light and equally fragile. An additional criterion needed to be met to make this image, and I continued to wait for a day that had zero wind.

That day was January 11, 2009. The previsualized image was easy to construct with the precise placement of the leaves. Initial shots were taken from various angles, and revealed a problem I had not expected but wasn't surprised to encounter: the leaves were waxy, and the sunlight was reflecting off this wax and washing away the vibrant red colour. The fix for this was thankfully simple: use a polarizing filter.

Most photographers familiar with circular polarizing filters will attest to their usefulness in getting a deeper blue sky or to remove reflections off of the surface of water. While this is true, the effect is much broader. Polarizing filters will remove reflections off most non-metallic surfaces. This includes foliage, waxed or otherwise, and richer colours can be captured when shooting autumn landscapes using this technique. It also applies to this image, and beautifully cuts through the unwanted reflections.

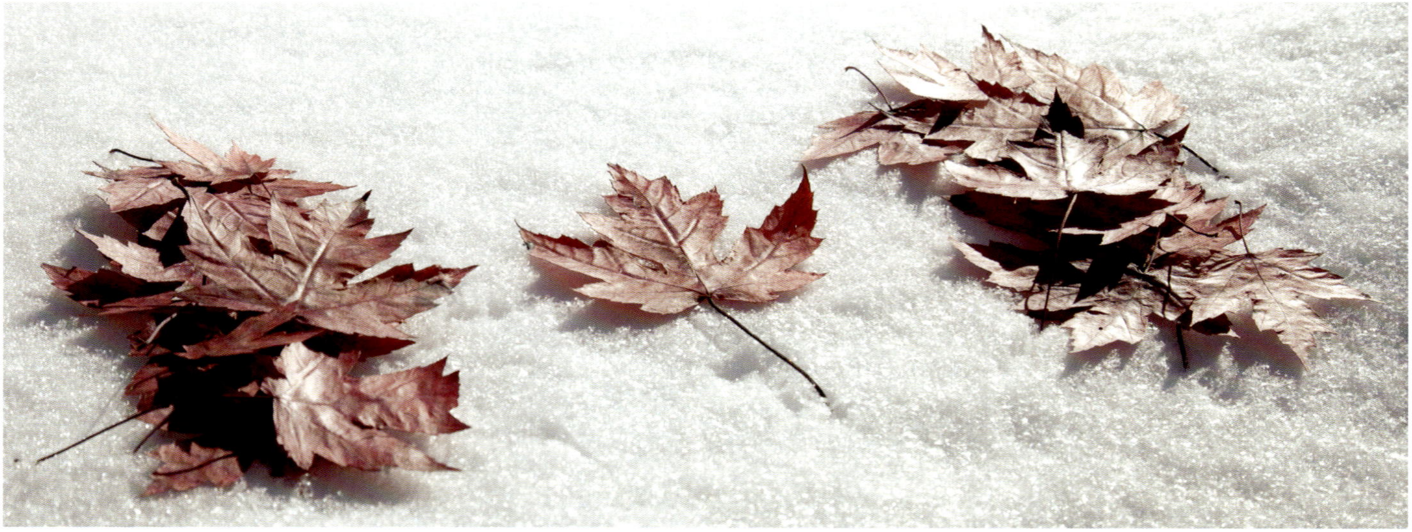

It's important to note that in the final image, the polarizing filter is not "dialed in" completely, allowing for a slight hint of reflection off the leaves to add an additional layer of depth. Coupled with the shadows on the snow, the intricacies of the visual ingredients give a three dimensional feel. It was better than I had imagined, but it wasn't perfect.

The stem of the central leaf was too long to mimic the design of the national flag of Canada. There was also a broken tip on a leaf that needed melting in post-processing. Both easy fixes with cloning tools in Photoshop, and once completed I was faced with a dilemma. Should I continue editing imperfections out of the image? Should it be perfect? I decided against

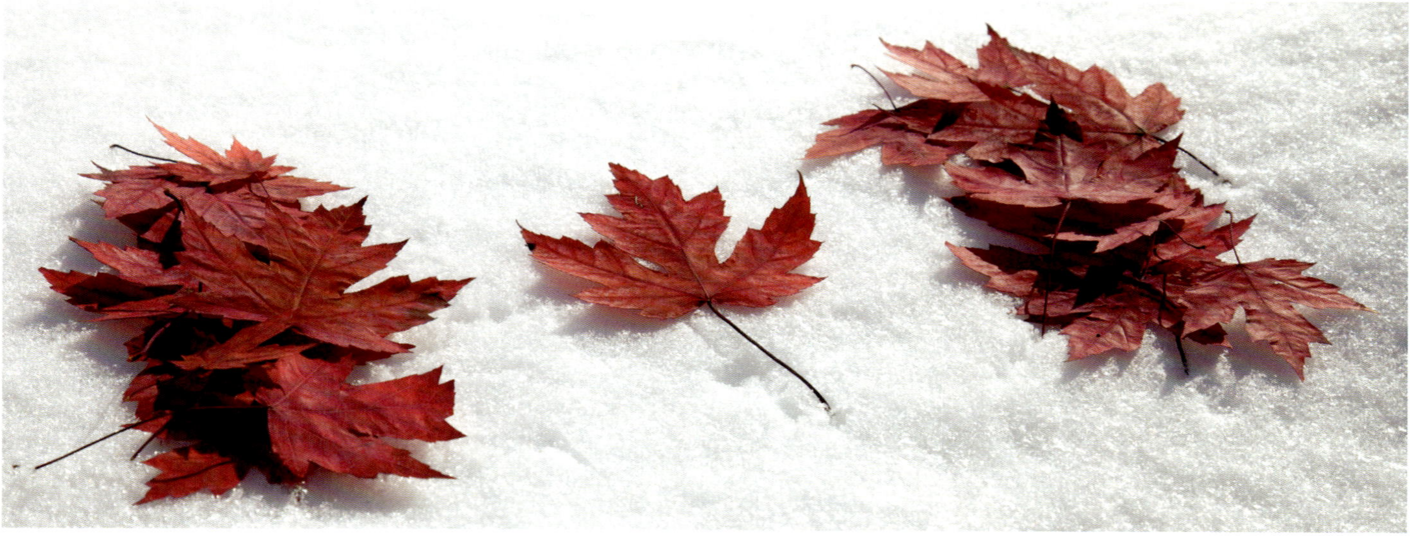

this, leaving a black spot and a crack on the main leaf as well as other imperfections in the surroundings.

The image represents Canada and my patriotism as a Canadian. While I love my country for countless reasons, it is not perfect. No nation is perfect, neither is any citizen of any nation. We all have our flaws, and this image needed to maintain a reflection of this truth.

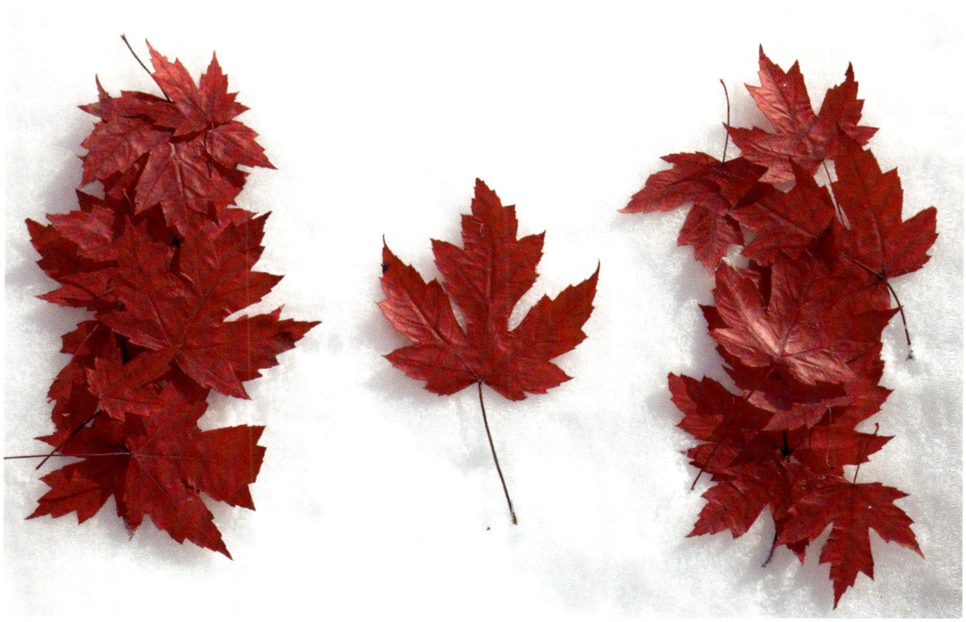

The day this image was successfully created is the day I feel I became a professional photographer. It started my career and impassioned me to follow the creative path I have been walking down for over a decade.

Copyright

Not only was this my first successful image, it is also sadly my most stolen one. You may have seen it floating around on the Internet around Canada Day or Remembrance Day / Veteran's Day without any attribution or permission. It has also been used in many product designs and commercial messaging, all without licensing the image. Because I don't want the image entangled with corporate or political interests, it's not an image I allow to be licensed at all for commercial use.

Defending one's copyright can be an exhausting and stressful endeavour. Other photographers have taken this same concept and shot their own image with different backgrounds and types of leaves, which I encourage! I cannot prove that I was the first person in history to come up with this idea, but many more followed after it was published.

What happened after the image was taken has further fueled my creativity. I didn't just pack up and head back inside even though I knew I got the shot; I continued to experiment.

What if I threw snow on the leaves themselves in an attempt to further integrate the visual ingredients? This didn't appeal to me, feeling like a layer of clutter in the frame that didn't add anything to the symbolism that had already been established. It was satisfying to explore these creative thoughts, however. You never know when a concept will excite you, or maybe even lead to new ideas for the future.

What if I arranged the leaves pseudo-randomly on the snow into an abstract pattern? Maybe this could be used as a background for something, a component in another project. Aside from appearing in this book, I haven't figured out if I'll use it for anything.

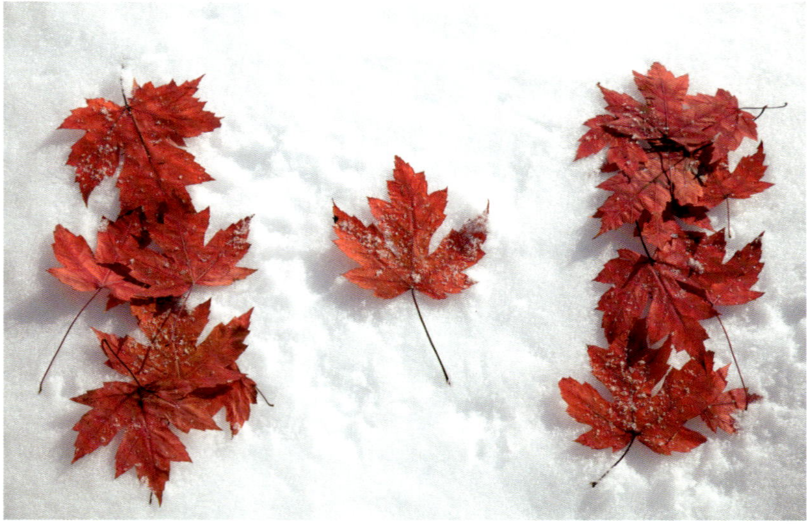

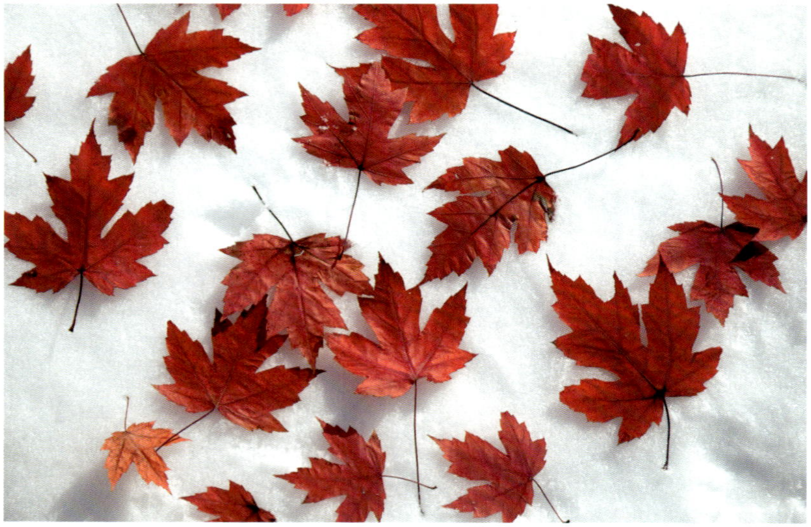

Your creative momentum shouldn't stop the moment you "get the shot". This is a more important moment than most beginner photographers realize: once you get what you came for, what comes next is unburdened from the desire to accomplish anything. You're free to experiment with no disappointment if it doesn't work out, and thereby much more likely to explore ideas that impulsively come to mind. Embrace those ideas as a sort of "victory lap" and exhaust your creativity. Even if you don't end up with anything useable as a result, you'll have gained more experience and likely new ideas for future images.

A similar line of thinking comes when you shoot the same subject numerous times – whether this is a waterfall or a water droplet, your initial images are almost always documenting the scene. I've been to a number of waterfalls in my area dozens of times, and only found my creative mojo after the fourth or fifth visit. All of the static, standard shots that immediately come to mind had been shot – so what next? Find inventive angles, try to tell stories, and explore compositions that are less likely to be successful. Spend the day trying to get one peculiar plan to be an artistic triumph, knowing that it might take more than a day to get things to work.

"Time you enjoy wasting is not time wasted."
– *Marthe Troly-Curtin, 1912*

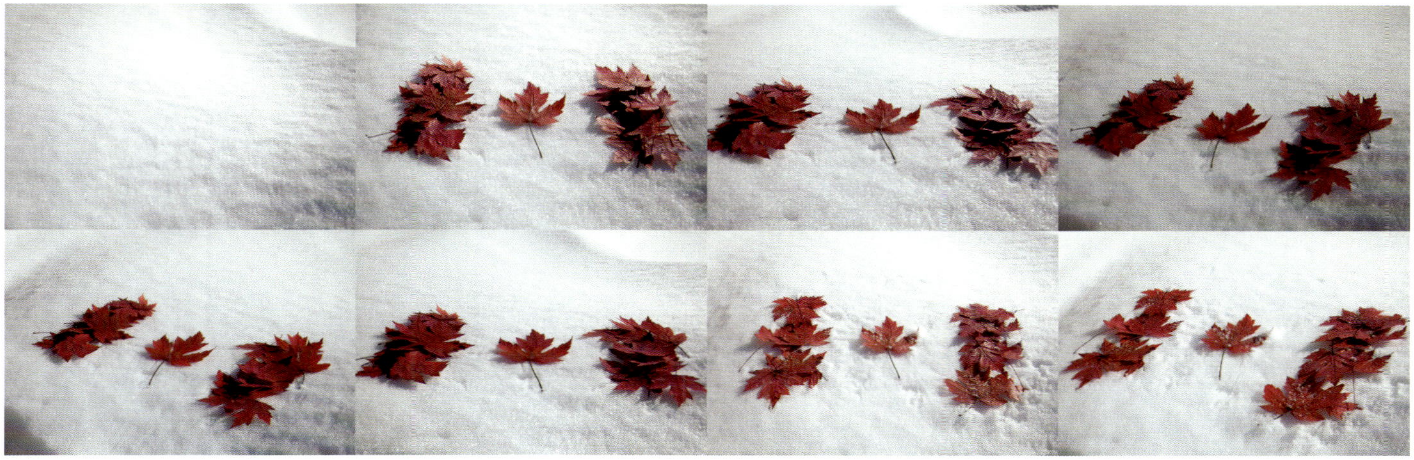

A selection of images from the shoot, which totalled 99 images that day. Many of them were multiples of the same frame to avoid any issues with motion blur, and there were numerous subtle variations on the same frame. The leaf positioning in the first frames differ slightly from the later ones. In hindsight, I should have put down the camera more often to make refinements to the subject itself.

My "keeper ratio" for macro photography work is roughly 100 images for every single frame that I love, and this shoot holds true to that. **Don't be afraid to take far more images than you think you need.**

THE SNOWFLAKE

"The Snowflake"

Photographing an individual snowflake takes patience and perseverance, technical skill and luck. It might be a difficult process, but most of these difficulties are related to techniques used to capture and edit the images. The images are documentary, with very little artistic involvement on the part of the photographer, especially when the same techniques are used repeatedly on different specimens.

Snowflake images are the ones most devoid of artistic influence. I have published nearly a thousand such images in the past decade, each of them unique. Acting on an impulse of curiosity, I wanted to see all of them in front of me at once: how many were there? At the time, there were roughly 450. Seeing them all at once was an impressive sight, but there was something bothersome about the collage: they weren't to scale with one another.

If I could find a way to calculate the exact size of each snowflake, I might be able to offer some artistic contribution to their placement together, building a narrative that added up to more than the sum of the parts. This synergistic reverie was more than just a fantasy; it could be made possible with some hidden data in each snowflake image.

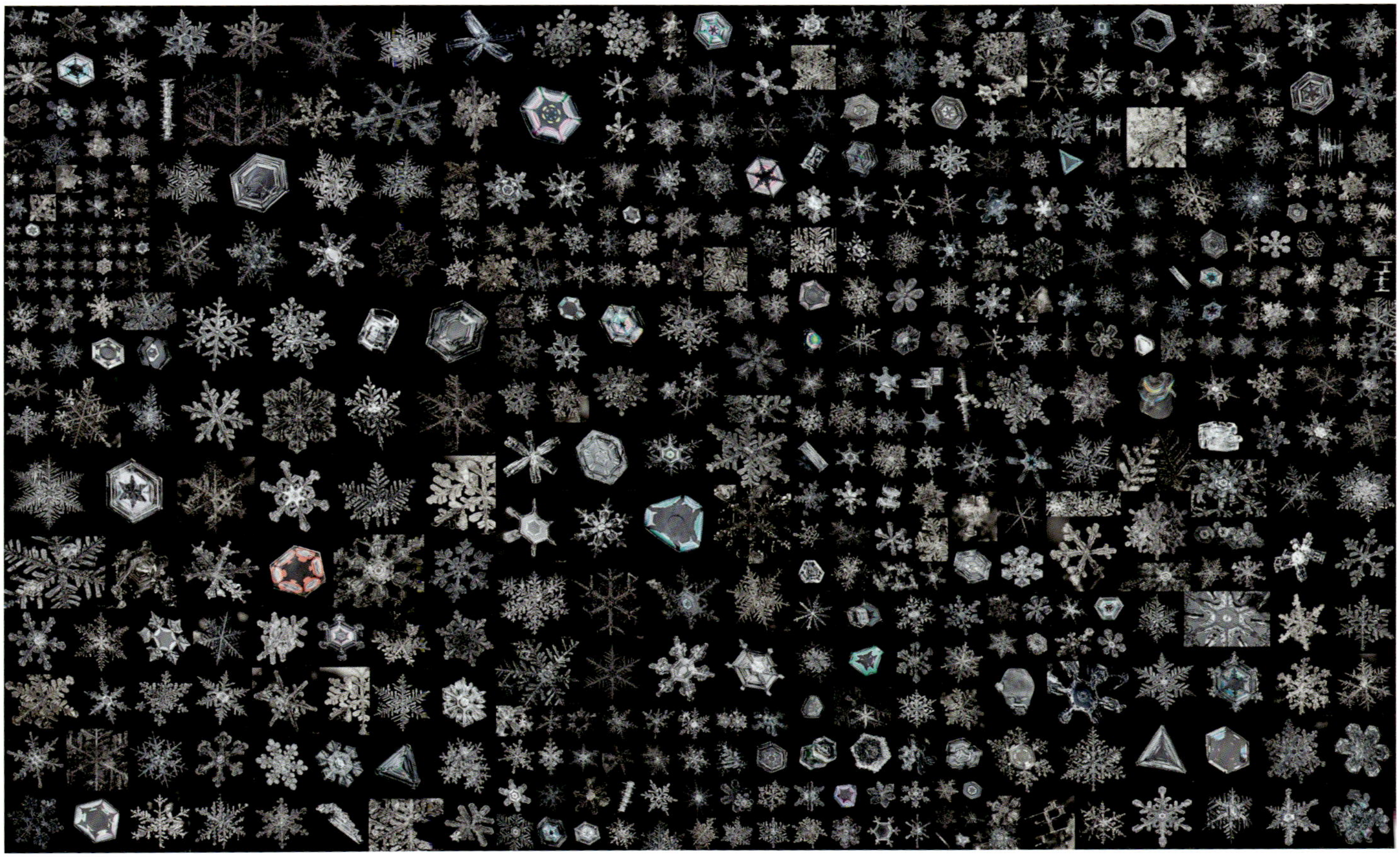

The Canon MP-E 65mm F/2.8 1x-5x Macro lens doesn't have a focusing or zoom ring of any kind, but rather a magnification ring that simultaneously increases the lens magnification while reducing the "working distance", the distance from the end of the lens to the subject. The lens reports the exact magnification factor back to the camera, and on capable camera bodies such as the 5D and 1D-series cameras, this gets recorded into every image.

The data is stored in an area of metadata called "Maker Notes". These are proprietary metrics that cannot fit into standard EXIF data and include things such as the "Picture Style" setting only found on Canon Cameras, since they do not fit into any predefined EXIF category and are used by only one manufacturer. The same is true for the Magnification Factor. This setting is buried deep within every RAW or in-camera JPG file created, and can be extracted with the proper tool.

EXIFTool, written and maintained by Phil Harvey, is the best tool I have seen to pull every bit of hidden information out of a RAW file, and decode it so it makes sense. The software is freely available at www.exiftool.org and is updated frequently.

"Send To EXIFTool"

For Windows users, there is a handy shortcut to use this program. If you place the stand-alone executable in the proper location, you can simply right-click on any RAW file and generate a text file with everything the file contains.

The process is simple:

Step 1: Open File Explorer and in the folder location at the top, simply type "**sendto**". This is a shortcut that will bring you to the SendTo folder on your computer – the longform of which is typically *C:\Users\[USER]\AppData\Roaming\Microsoft\Windows\SendTo* .

Step 2: In this folder, paste the EXIFTool executable and change the filename from exiftool(-k).exe to exiftool(-w txt).exe

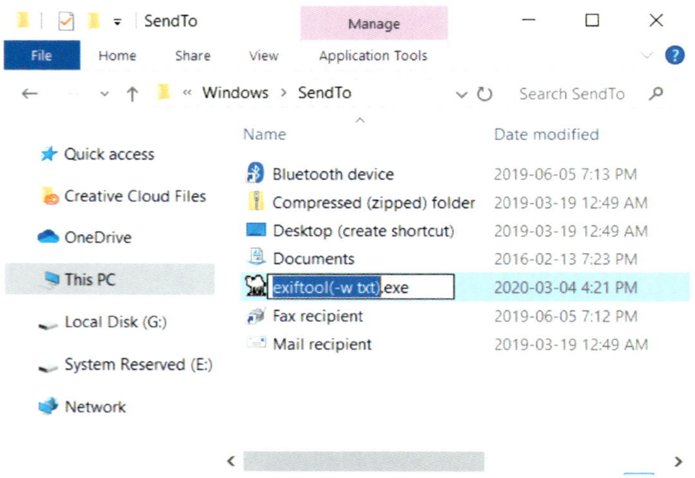

Step 3: Right-click on any image file, and Select EXIFTool from the "Send to" menu.

Step 4: EXIFTool generates a .txt file with the same filename as the image in the same folder. Open up that file and explore the details!

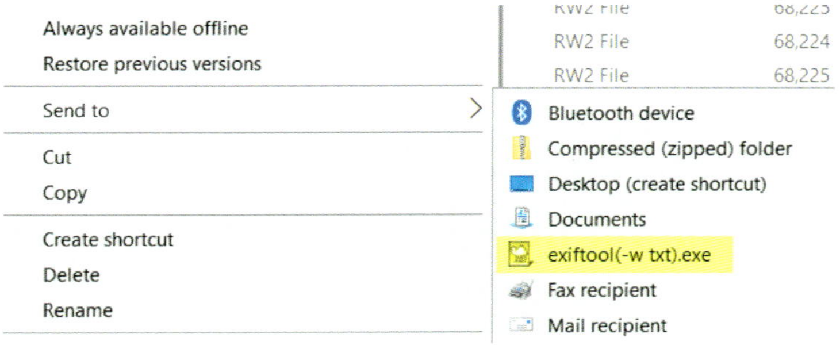

Note: If an image that has been processed, in almost every scenario you will lose the Maker Notes data. Software companies like Adobe will not re-save this information in any image resulting from a RAW file, nor will they maintain the data that would normally be presented in a JPG file created in-camera. You'll need to reference original data to get all the information you seek.

With this critical value for the magnification the camera was set to when an image was taken [C], it's a simple bit of algebra to calculate the size of a snowflake, if you know the physical size of the camera sensor [B] and the resolution in pixels [A], the latter two both in the horizontal direction:

A / (B / C) = number of pixels per millimeter

With that number, you can measure the number of pixels across opposing branches of a snowflake, and place them in scale to one another.

Right: Sample data from the text file generated by EXIFTool. Note the volume of information specific to the camera including the type of focusing screen used, microadjustments, serial number and more.

Among the chaos, we find "**Macro Magnification**"

```
Time Zone                                  : -04:00
Time Zone City                             : New York
Daylight Savings                           : On
Bracket Mode                               : Off
Bracket Value                              : 0
Bracket Shot Number                        : 0
Raw Jpg Size                               : Large
WB Bracket Mode                            : Off
WB Bracket Value AB                        : 0
WB Bracket Value GM                        : 0
Macro Magnification                        : 4.3x
Live View Shooting                         : Off
Focus Distance Upper                       : 0.28 m
Focus Distance Lower                       : 0.3 m
Flash Exposure Lock                        : Off
Internal Serial Number                     : X015483
Dust Removal Data                          : (Binary
data 1024 bytes, use -b option to extract)
Crop Left Margin                           : 0
Crop Right Margin                          : 0
Crop Top Margin                            : 0
Crop Bottom Margin                         : 0
Exposure Level Increments                  : 1/3-stop
set, 1/3-stop comp.
ISO Speed Increments                       : 1/3 Stop
AEB Auto Cancel                            : Off
AEB Sequence                               : -,0,+
AEB Shot Count                             : 7 shots
Spot Meter Link To AF Point                : Enable (use
active AF point)
Safety Shift                               : Disable
Usable Shooting Modes                      : Disable;
Flags 0x3f
Usable Metering Modes                      : Disable;
Flags 0xf0
Exposure Mode In Manual                    : Specified
metering mode
Shutter Speed Range                        : Disable; Hi
1/8192; Lo 32
Aperture Range                             : Disable;
Closed 91; Open 1
AE Microadjustment                         : Disable; 0;
8; 0
FE Microadjustment                         : Disable; 0;
8; 0
Focusing Screen                            : Ec-CV
View Info During Exposure                  : Disable
LCD Illumination During Bulb               : Off
WB Media Image Size Setting                : Rear LCD
panel
```

The math was simple, but there were a few pitfalls to avoid. The reported magnification factor did not change if extension tubes were used, which could throw off the scale of the smallest snowflakes. Thankfully, when using extension tubes with the Canon MP-E 65mm lens, I always used the same configuration and it always resulted in noticeable vignetting around the edges of the frame. If this was seen, the rule was to add one magnification factor to whatever the lens reported.

Furthermore, the use of the Canon Lifesize Converter EF was not reported in metadata. To account for this, all images that used this magnifying optic (much like a teleconverter but for macro purposes) were shot at F/2.8 whereas every other scenario was F/3.2 or smaller. This allows for a precise identification of what tools were used and I began to put the puzzle pieces together.

Gathering all the necessary information for each snowflake was frustratingly dreary. Once I had measured a number of snowflakes, I placed them on a canvas to see if this idea had any merit. It did, as my imagination filled in the empty space. I was on the right track, and patience was no longer necessary; I had a known amount of effort in front of me, and a well visualized final result.

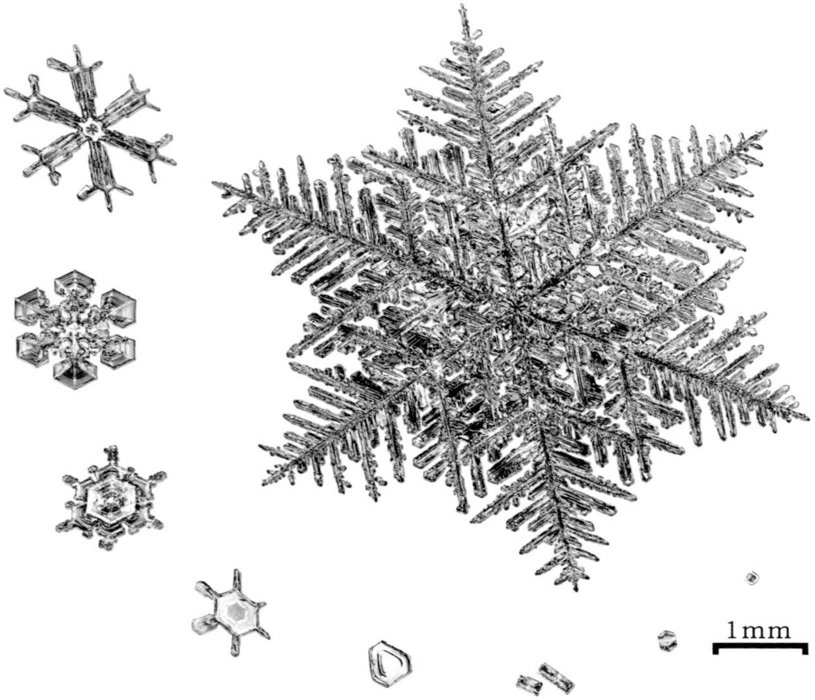

Above: Different types of snowflakes generally appear within specific size ranges. Fernlike Stellar Dendrites take the largest forms and column-type crystals are generally the smallest varieties able to be observed.

Adjacent Page: As more snowflakes were measured, they were placed on the canvas until all of the space was filled. This process alone took weeks of effort once fully arranged in the final composition.

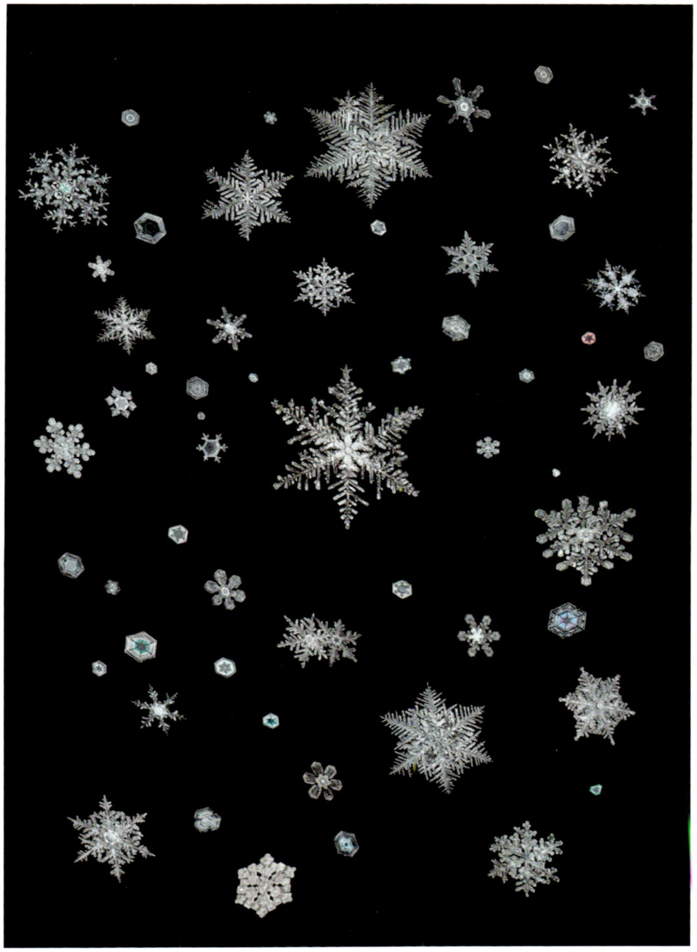

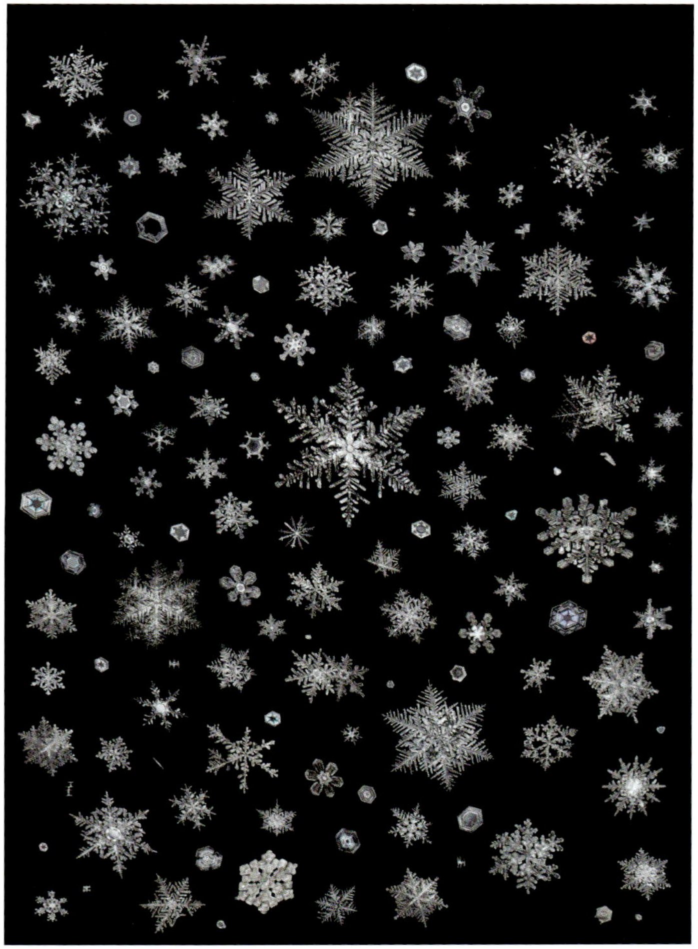

The smallest snowflakes measured 0.3 millimeters in diameter, with the largest one measuring 11 millimeters from tip to tip – featured in the center. The final arrangement of snowflakes would come once all of the individual crystals were measured and placed on the canvas. Because the individual images were themselves at a significant resolution, the final size of the composite image pushed well over one gigapixel in resolution. The largest that this has been printed is a staggering 5' 9" (3.6m) tall for a museum exhibition.

Collectively, including all of the time shooting and editing the individual snowflakes as well as the time it took to build the combined print, this was an incredibly time intensive project. 2500 hours across five years culminated in the artistic storytelling transformation of documentary puzzle pieces.

No two snowflakes are alike, the constantly changing design of a single snowflake is never repeated perfectly – just as identical twins still have individually unique fingerprints. That was the story I was looking to tell.

Handheld Microscope Snowflakes

The resolving power of most macro lenses, even with additional extension tubes and optics, has limits. In order to push past those limits you can use microscope objectives as discussed in this book, but this solution is tailored to studio and laboratory work. On a never-ending journey to capture as much detail as possible from the tiniest frozen sky crystals, I had a question: can I shoot with a microscope objective handheld?

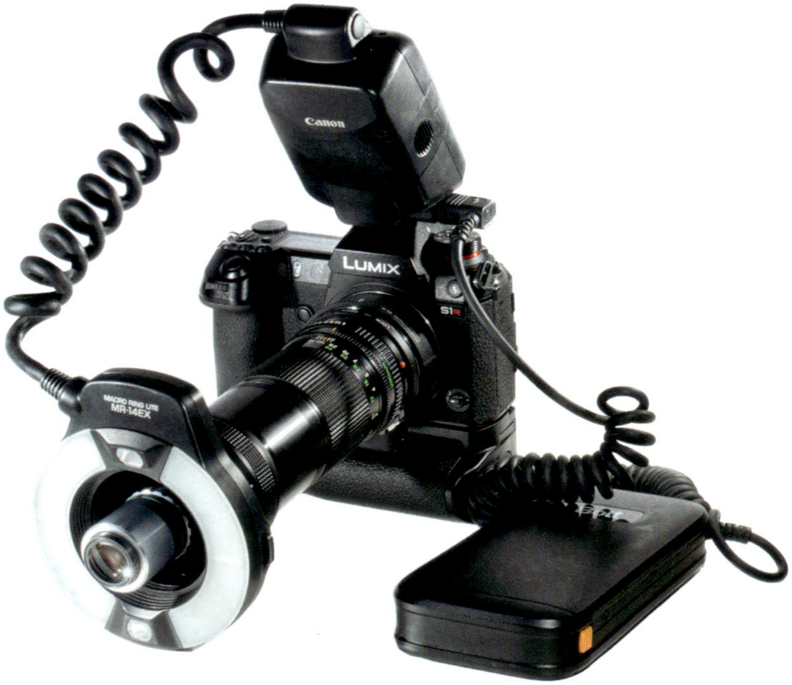

To be fair, microscope objectives are manufactured at magnifications as low as 1x. Having shot with the Canon MP-E 65mm F/2.8 1x-5x Macro lens, with additional bits and pieces, I was able to push my magnification as far as 12x; such efforts, however, were limited by diffraction. I couldn't gather any more detail simply by adding or extension tubes or by using a teleconverter in the optical path. The only solution to break this barrier would be attach a microscope objective to my camera and take it into the field using the same shooting techniques I had been accustomed to.

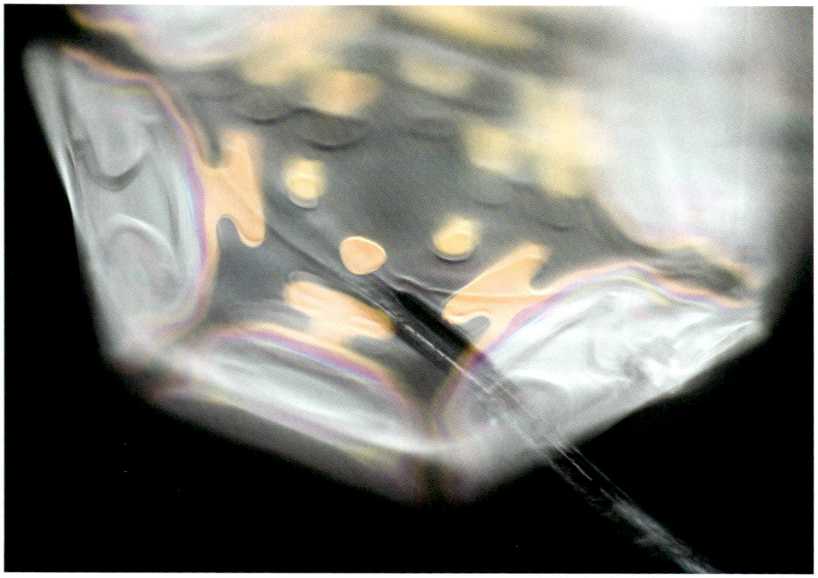

Surely if I had a good handle on 12x magnifications, 20x wouldn't be impossible. This would be my first foray into attaching a microscope objective to my camera. The process was simpler than I would have thought, described elsewhere in this book. Attaching the ring flash to the end of the microscope objective in a permanent and solid way proved to be the most difficult part.

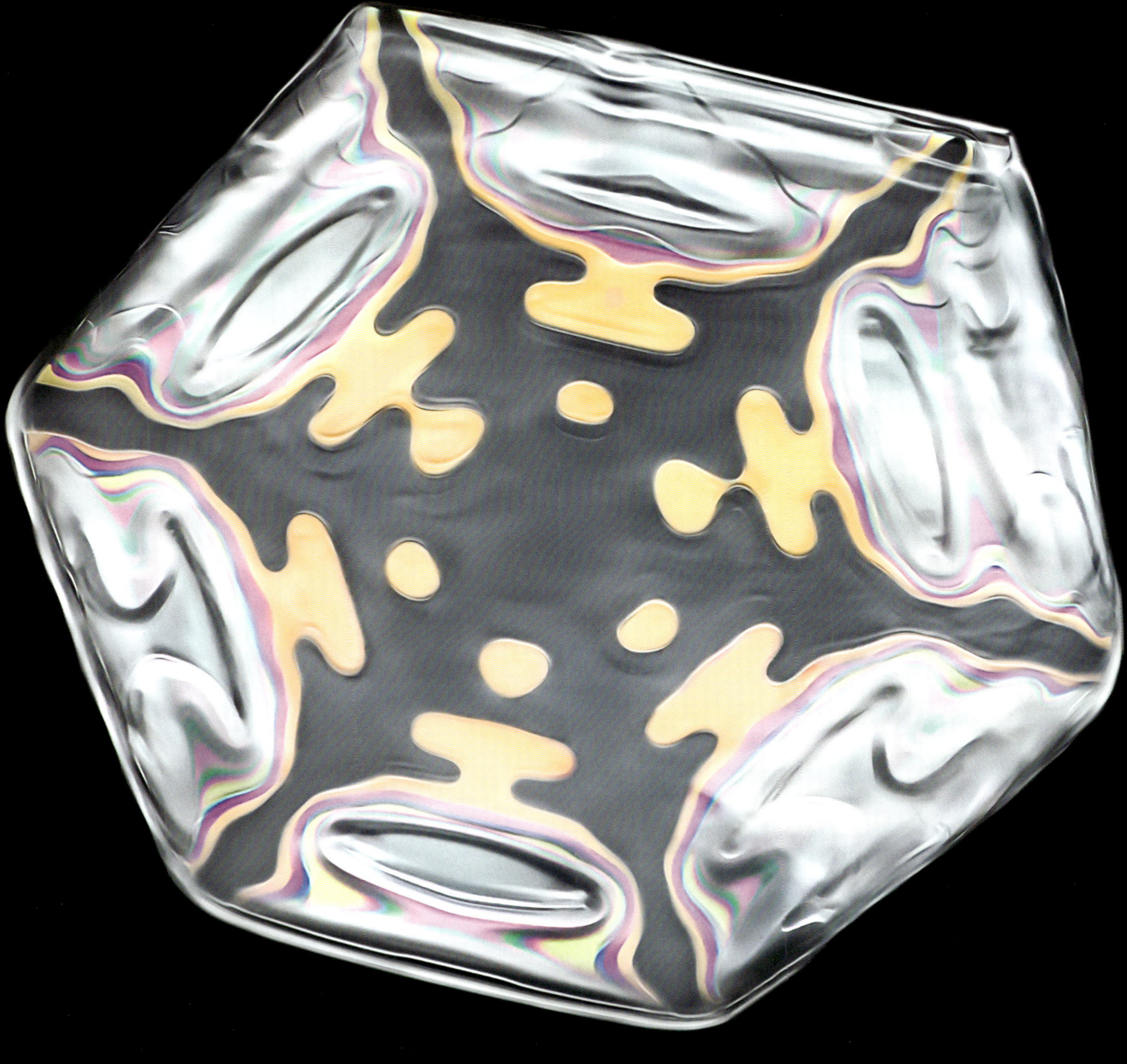

After significant pondering, the answer came in the form of the Canon MLA-DC1, an adapter that was designed to allow the use of Canon ring flashes on Canon G-series camera bodies.

This adapter has a proper mechanism for the Canon MR-14EX ring flash to clip on the end of it, and its length is perfect to allow for the microscope objective to protrude slightly beyond the flash. All that was needed was a little epoxy glue to firmly attach it to the filter thread adapter. We're ready to rock!

> *Side note:* The original Canon MR-14EX does not have anything to limit it from overheating. The successor, the MR-14EX II, has a thermal limiter but it is implemented in the worst possible way. To the best of my knowledge, the flash unit simply uses an internal counter that counts the number of flashes and approximates the heat that this would generate.

The working distance of the Mitutoyo Plan APO 20x object I am using is 2cm / 0.8". Not ideal, and it's the same reason why photographing snowflakes with the Mitakon 20mm F/2 4.5x-5x macro lens is a challenge – in addition to that lens also not having a proper ring flash mount. This means that the orientation of the snowflake to the camera has to be more precisely angled, as there is less room to rotate the camera around the subject. If the angle is less than optimal, reflected light becomes very difficult to achieve. Keep in mind the scale of these snowflakes: 0.25mm across. Positioning a snowflake of this size, wobbling on a coarse fiber of a black mitten, is a recipe for frustration.

From a technical perspective, these are the most difficult and challenging images I have created to date. The depth of field is so thin that missing a slice of focus is much more likely, and the number of frames required is far above other similarly simplistic hexagon crystals. 46 frames in total were required (*previous page*), roughly double what would have otherwise been expected for a tiny, flat crystal.

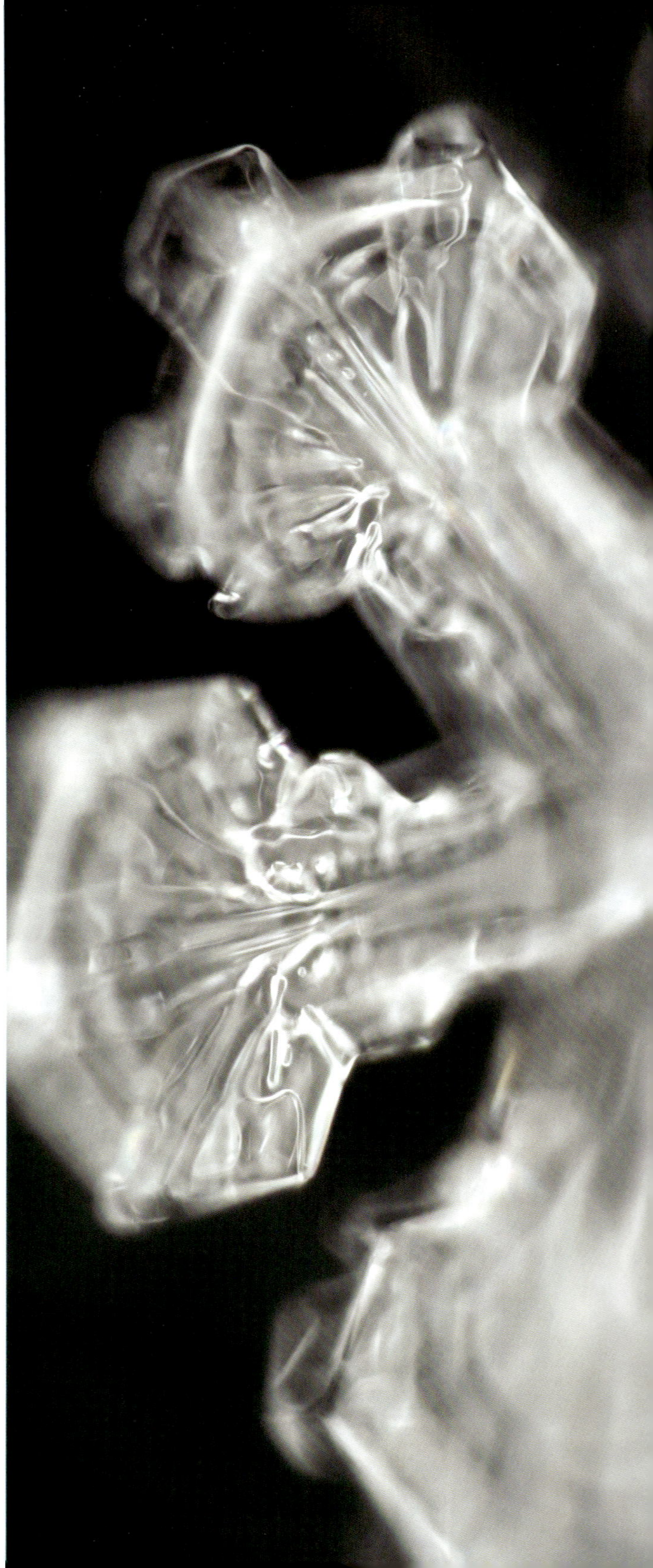

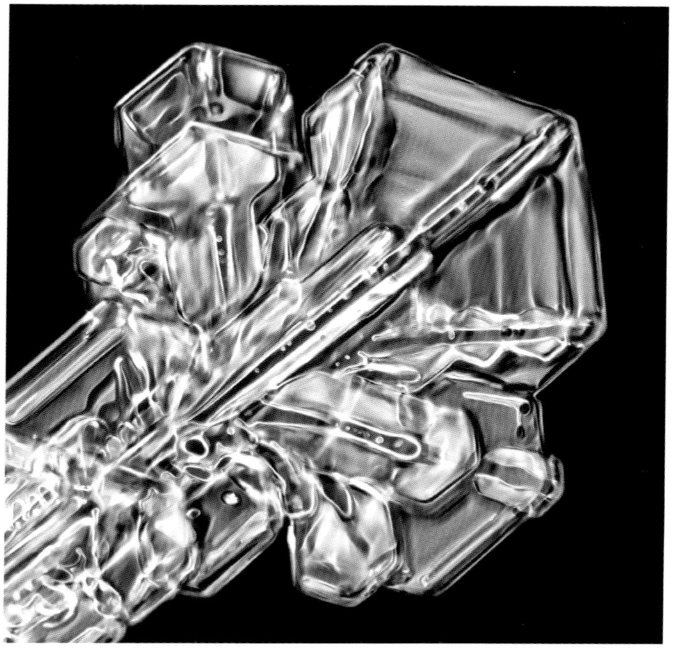

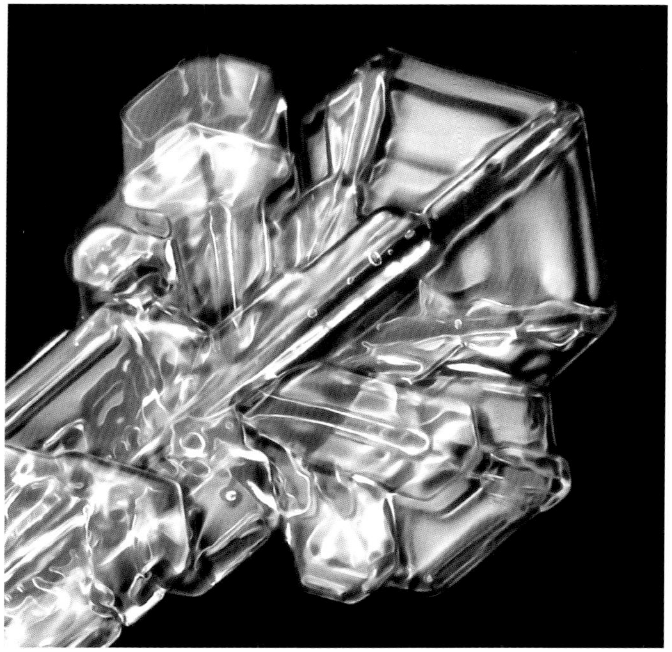

Putting those images together is also a challenge. It's the same process as any other snowflake, but because focus falls off so quickly (*facing page*) there are plenty of incorrect assumptions made by the focus stacking software, some failing outright to put the pieces together. Best handled in Photoshop with the "muscle memory" of previous snowflake edits, expect this to eat up half of your day for perfect results.

Is it worth it? I decided to compare the results with my previous ambitions at 12x magnification on the same snowflake (*left*). On the top, we have the branch of a snowflake photographed with the 20x Mitutoyo microscope objective, and at the bottom is the same portion of the same snowflake photographed with the Canon MP-E 65mm F/2.8 1x-5x Macro lens set to 5x, plus extension tubes and the Canon Lifesize Converter EF which totals 12x of magnification.

Not only is there less green and magenta colour fringing on the microscope objective, there is a noticeable increase in overall clarity and resolution. Only for the smallest details on the tiniest snowflakes would I attempt this, and only if I was feeling overly ambitious. Every part of the process is tedious and exasperating.

Was it worth the effort? Yes. Part of the answer rests not only in the resulting detail, but to prove that it was possible to handhold a high magnification microscope objective in a freezing and chaotic environment and successfully photograph a snowflake.

Don't try this at home.

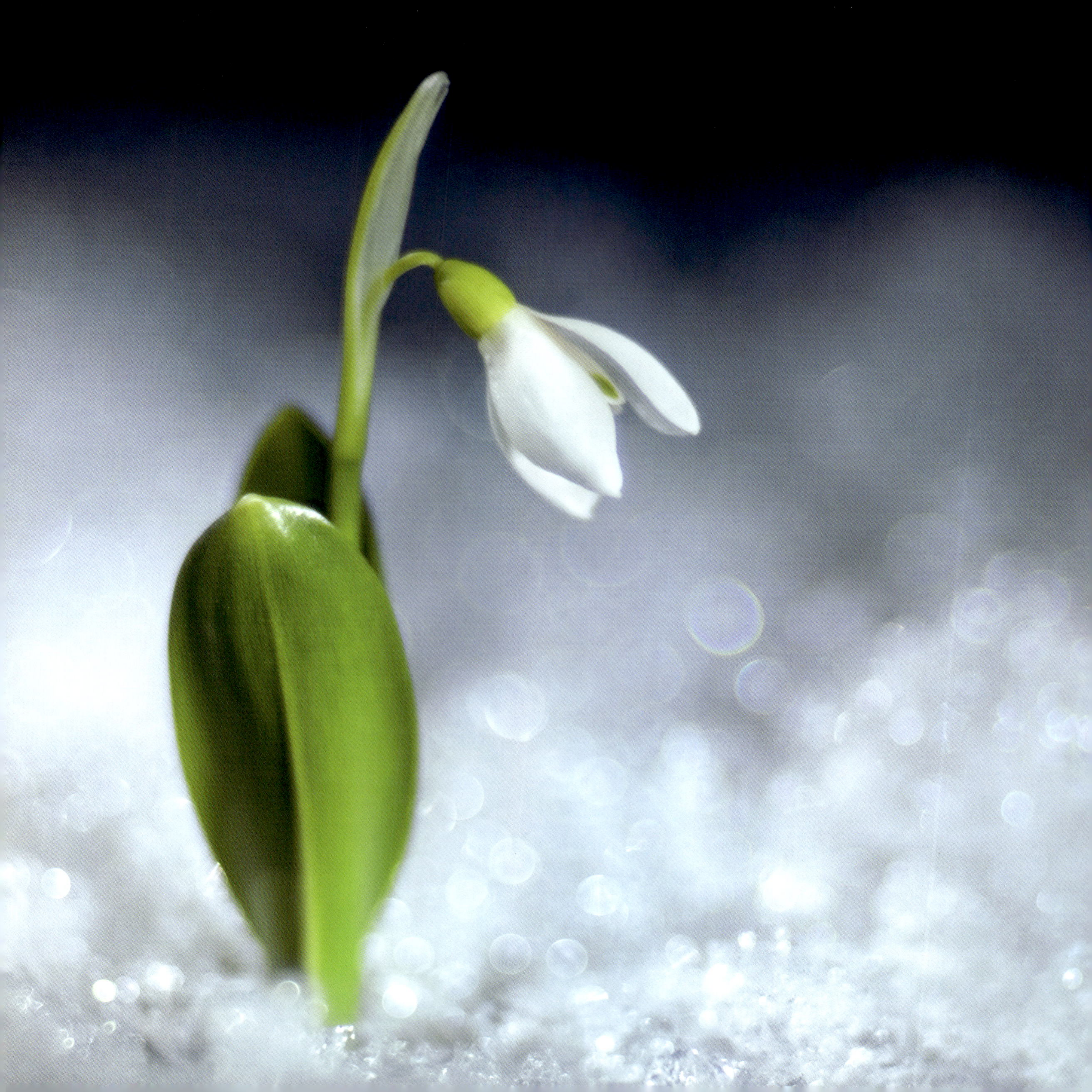

Snowdrop Sedulity

The creation of some images appear like simple, serene depictions of nature. The truth can be a little more deceitful.

In this image, the objective was to showcase a Snowdrop flower (genus Galanthus) in a powerfully beautiful way. These are one of the first flowers to bloom in early spring, often surrounded by the last seasonal snowfalls which do not harm the blooms. Like a sentinel of spring, these delicate flowers are unscathed by harsh conditions and stand strong.

We didn't have any late season snowfalls. We still had snow in the shade-covered portions of our gardens however, so a small amount was moved into position. The snow needed to sparkle, and that sparkle needed to feel as delicate as the flower. To achieve this, the Meyer Optik Trioplan 100 lens was used wide open at **F/2.8** to generate a subtle "soap bubble bokeh" effect, but initial test images were underwhelming.

The solution was simple: add a source of direct, harsh light to create additional points of specular highlights. When these points of light fall out of focus, they create the desired bokeh. Making minute adjustments to the angle of the camera would reveal different highlights in random locations. This meant I would shoot a series of images at slightly different perspectives to see what pattern of subtle circles would be most pleasing.

The background was still a problem. Dead grass, leaves and twigs were not appealing. I could have retrieved a shovel full of snow to place behind the flower to fill things in, but I had a different approach: fade to black. This would add to the contrast in the frame and also give a timeless feel to the composition, as if a snowdrop stays blooming through the night.

Creating this backdrop was as simple as placing an empty garbage bin behind the scene. Inventive effects can be incredibly simple.

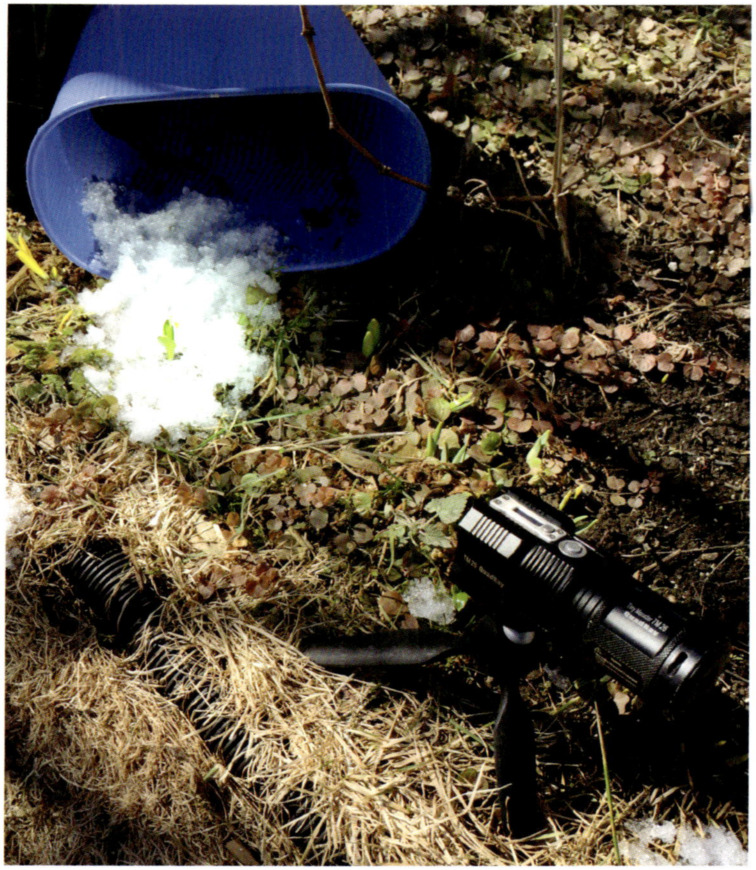

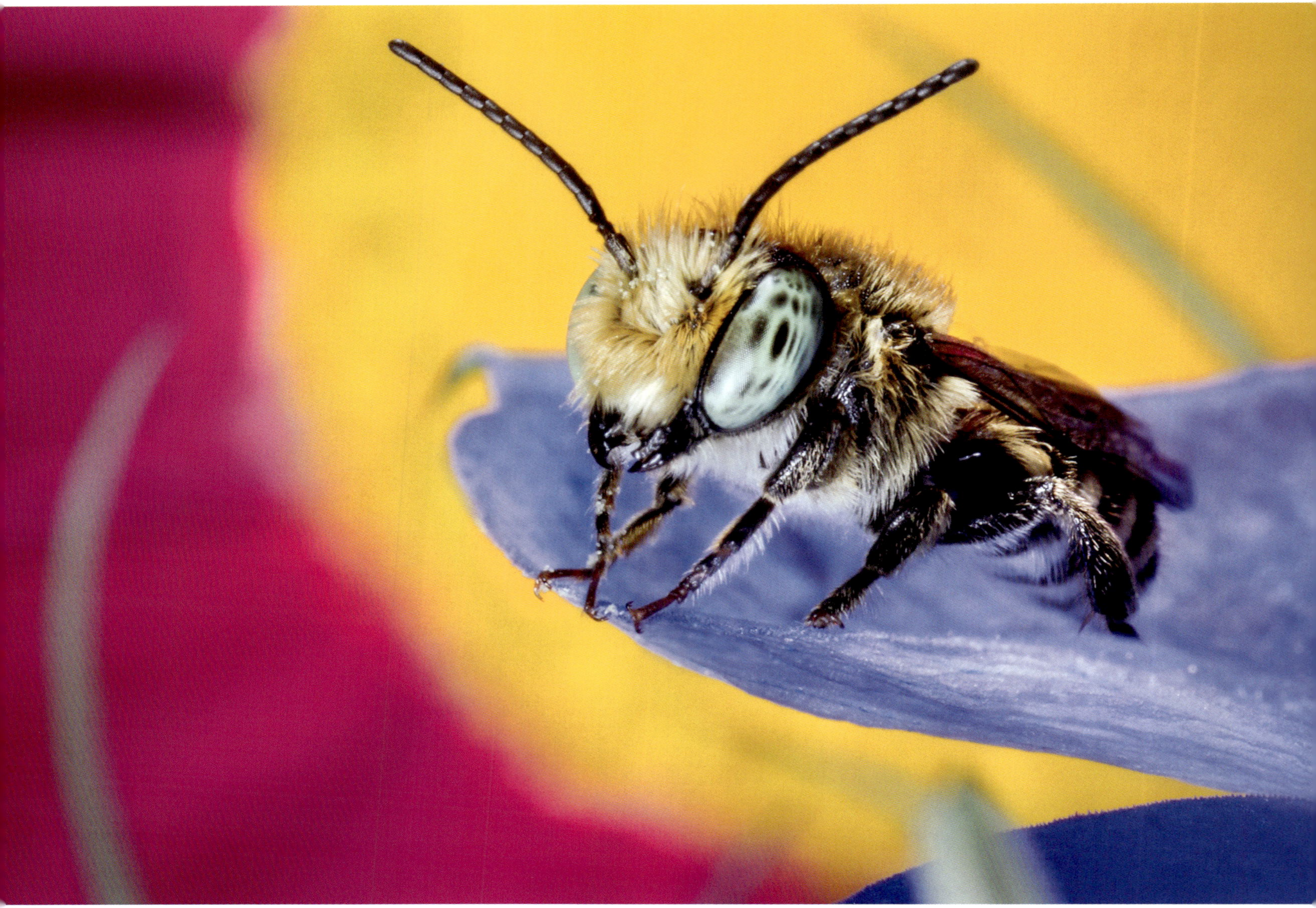

Canon 1DX Mark II, Canon MP-E 65mm F/2.8 1x-5x Macro,
F/16 ISO 250 1/250sec

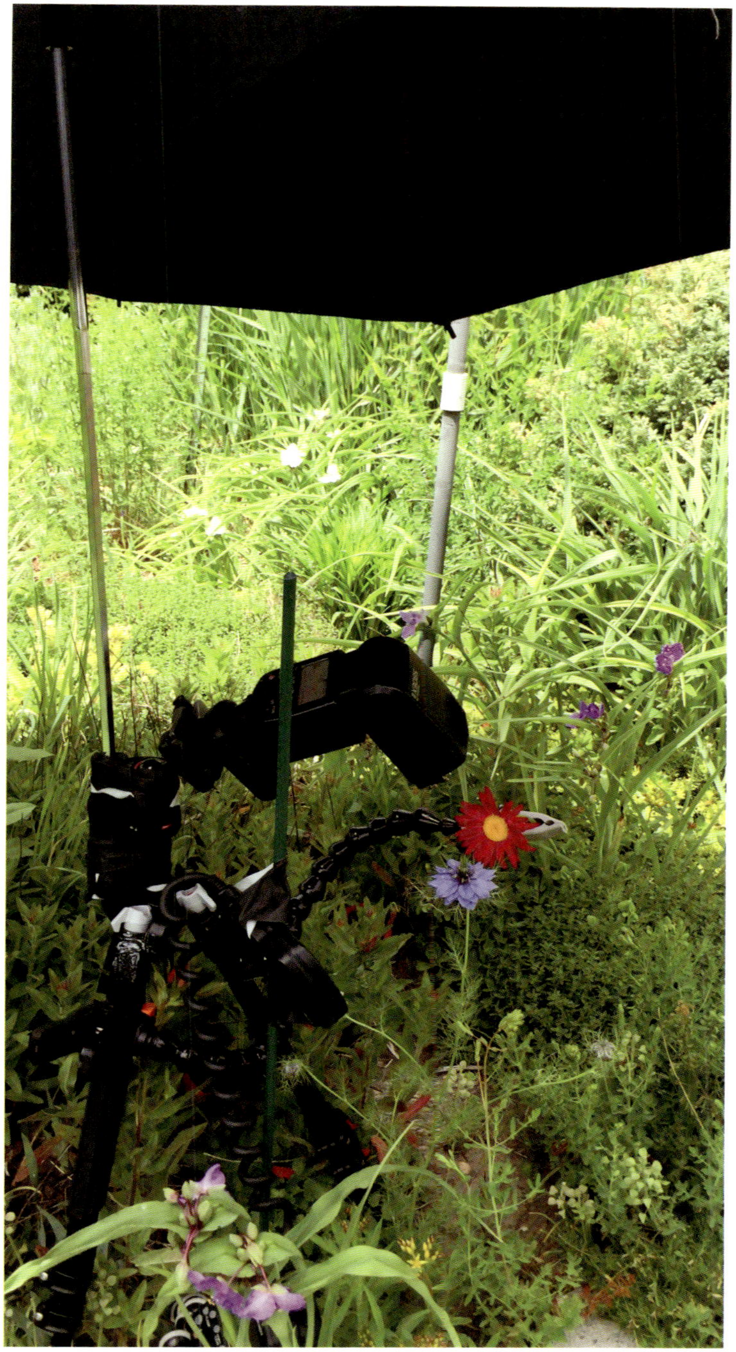

Bee Happy

The notion was simple: I wanted to take a staged portrait of a bee. Where to start? A quick walk around the garden gave me ideas for colour combinations; I wanted it vibrant. This image needed to be as saturated with colour from flowers as possible.

Nigella flowers (*Nigella damascene*), also called "Love-in-a-Mist", is a bright blue flower resembling a Passion Flower in some ways. These ornate petals would serve as the foreground, and a nearby stand of Painted Daisies (*Tanacetum coccineum*) would offer up the background, creating a charming palette for which to frame a bee.

The Painted Daisy was picked and placed behind the Nigella with a "Plamp", a wonderful tool with a solid clamp on one end (to hold onto a tripod or table) and delicate clamp on the other end to hold plant stems. The overall scene needed to be in open shade, which was accomplished by adding a black umbrella to a tripod. Lighting would be provided by two flashes: a speedlight and a ring flash, both off camera and controlled by a wireless trigger.

All of this staging was done well in advance of me procuring the actor for the scene. Everything would be tested to see how the exposure played out, how the lighting behaved, and where the bee might find a perfect perch. Knowing that a bee would not take direction to stand in a particular spot, the camera would not be locked down on a tripod. In order to achieve the best alignment between the foreground and background, the camera needed to be handheld to rotate around the foreground subject which would change the alignment with the background.

While all of this was being planned, the quest of "how will I get a bee to cooperate?" was ringing in my head. Based on previous experience, I had a secret weapon: my garden hose. I had noticed that bees would not fly away if their wings were wet. This could be caused by morning dew, or by droplets from a spray bottle or hose.

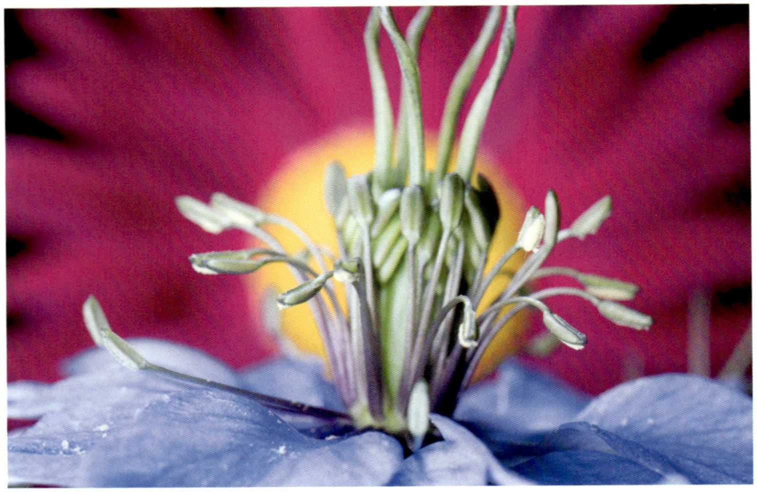

It would have been incredibly lucky to have a bee land exactly on the flower, pose for a moment and then carry on with its day. A more practical approach would be to pursue a bee actively foraging in other parts of the garden and give them some fresh mist to temporarily ground them. Once grounded, a bee will grab on to a twig placed in front of them, allowing them to be transported. Once placed on the Nigella flower, I had roughly a minute before the bee would fly away.

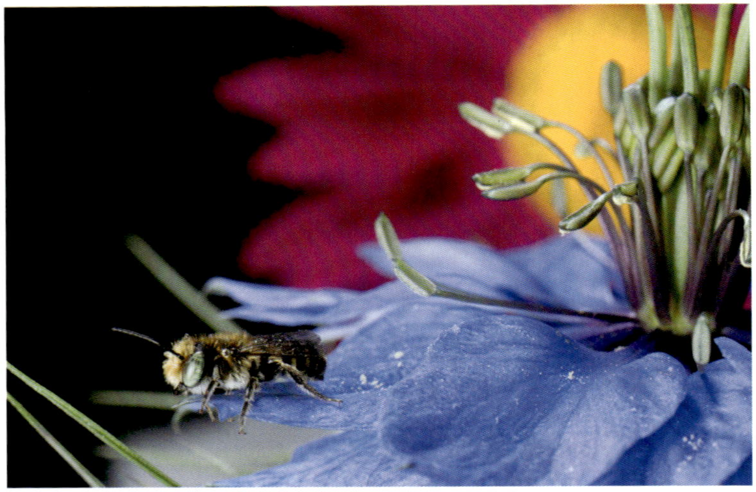

Above: Our actor here is an Alfalfa Leafcutting Bee *(Megachile rotundata).*

The bee did not stay where it was placed, and I had expected this. Originally situated on the right side of the flower, it moved to the edge of the left-most petal. I hastily repositioned the Painted Daisy in the background to be better framed behind this area of the flower, as no amount of simple repositioning of the camera would allow the background to be appropriately filled. The clock was ticking; the bee was drying off.

Reframing the shot was easy enough. Getting the bee framed behind the yellow center of the daisy with energetic magenta petals surround it was taking shape. The subject was too small in the frame, however. Thankfully this image was shot using the Canon MP-E 65mm F/2.8 1x-5x Macro lens, which allows for an immediate increase in magnification beyond 1:1 life size. Starting at 1x magnification, I quickly adjusted the lens to 1.5x. This magnification range can be accomplished with many lenses, including

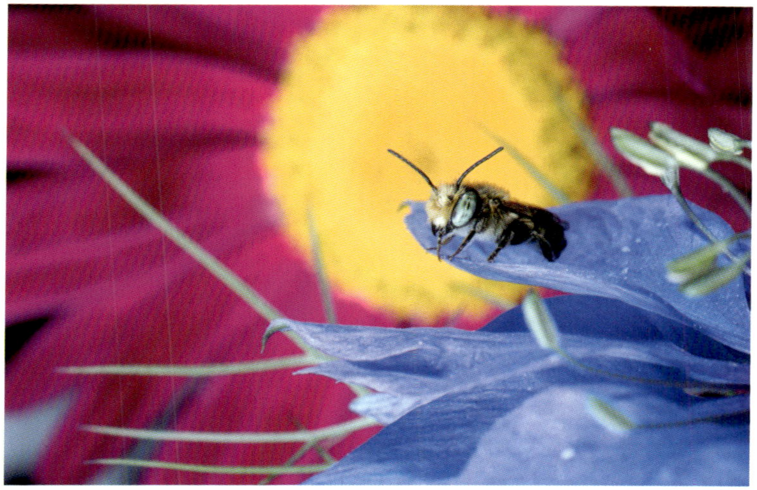

the Laowa 60mm F/2.8 and 100mm F/2.8 macro lenses from Venus Optics that can achieve 2x magnification without adding extension tubes or close-up filters. These lenses are very capable, and available in a variety of camera mounts.

With the bee filling the frame, I began shooting a continuous burst swaying slightly forward and back to vary my focal plane, just enough to ensure that one frame would have the eyes tack sharp. It was then I realized I had an equipment failure. The main light source, an off-camera speedlight, was firing intermittently due to low battery power.

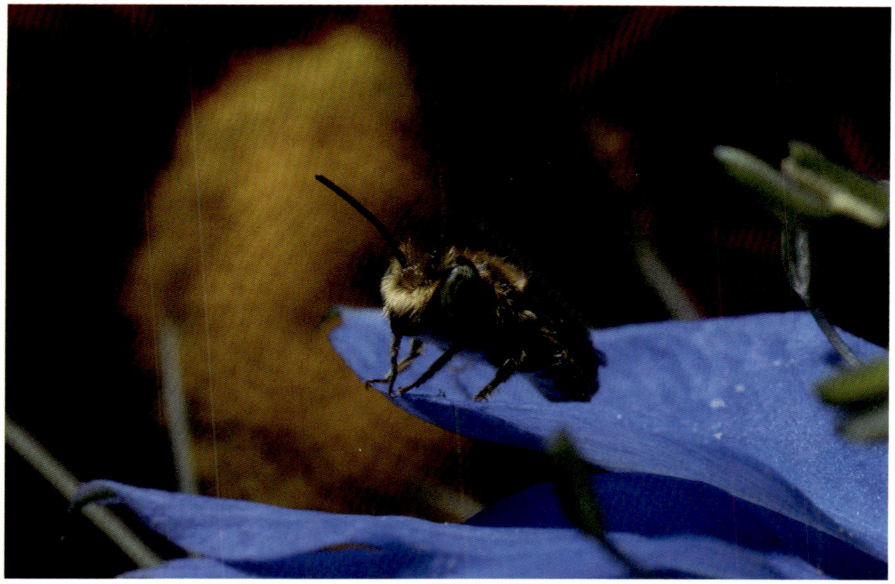

With no time to swap batteries, there was only one option: shoot slowly and deliberately, hoping to nail focus in a single frame. In one of four frames where both flashes fired, the bee's eyes (and knees) were sharp.

Aside from basic editing, there was one final trick. If I was going to these lengths to stage a shot, I shouldn't feel bad to bend reality slightly in post-processing. Using the Liquify Tool in Photoshop, I carefully adjusted the pointed green leaves of the Nigella flower into gently curving lines. The tip of the left leaf near the edge of the frame would have been cut off with the desired crop, but wrapping it back in to the shot helps guide a viewer's eye back toward the subject.

This may be going too far for some people, and even manipulating an insect to pose for a photo might cross the line for others. You'll only truly define where that line is for yourself by occasionally crossing it.

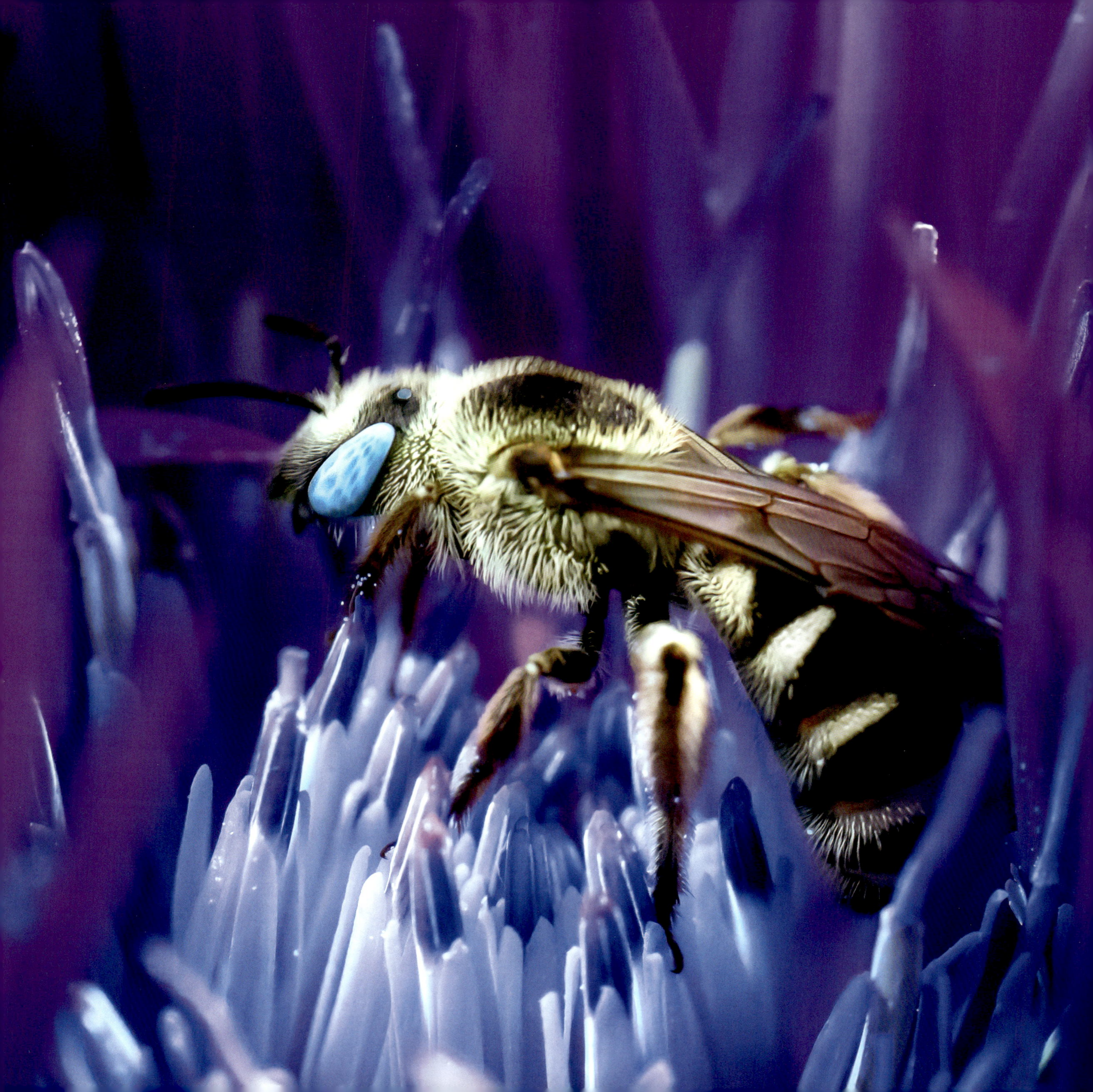

Fortress of Solitude

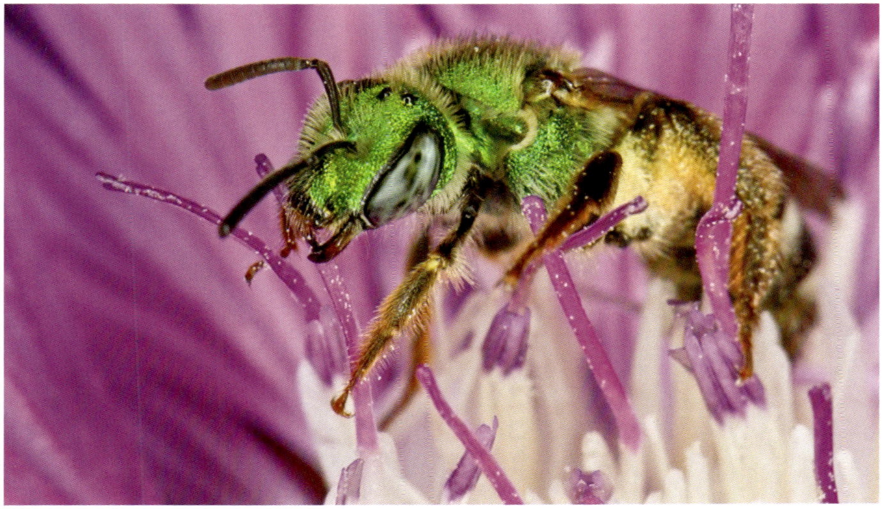

During warm sunny days through the summer, Metallic Green Sweat Bees (*Agapostemon virescens*) dance in the Pink Persian Cornflowers (*Psephellus dealbatus* 'Rosea') along the side of our house. They are a constant and predictable feature in our gardens, and beautiful to photograph.

One cold morning when the temperature dropped to 8C / 46F, I noticed that these bees were grounded; they were unable to fly due to the cold conditions. Some of them lay motionless inside the cornflowers. I had an idea. What if I could photograph these creatures in ultraviolet fluorescence? Normally this would be impossible, but I could bring my equipment outdoors and shroud the flower with a large sheet of black felt to create the proper scenario to make this work.

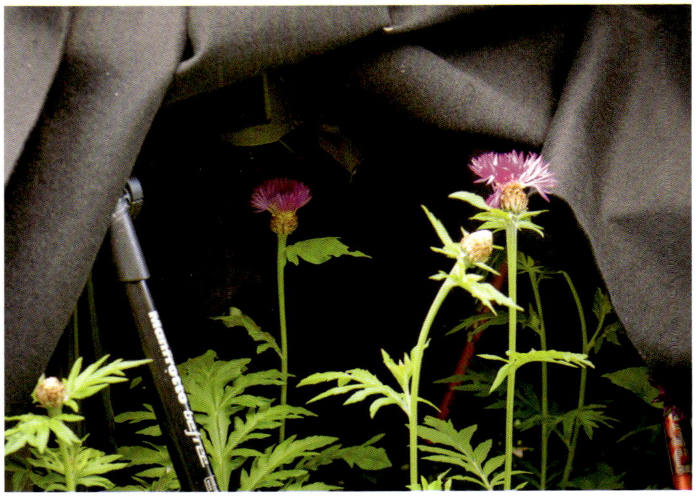

Near-complete darkness is required for this to work. The ultraviolet flashes, two modified Yongnuo YN-685 speedlights, emit no visible light. If the subject fluoresces, this is where the only source of visible light should come from, and any light from the environment would contaminate the image. Surrounded by darkness and cold, the bee quietly sleeps while the camera equipment is prepared.

The flashes are positioned as close to the subject as possible without ending up in the frame, and set to maximum output. Even with two powerful flashes in this configuration, the camera settings needed to be extreme. A number of test shots were taken to establish the best options here, starting with the easiest one: **1/160 second** shutter speed, which is the fastest flash sync speed on the Lumix GX9 used to make the image. **ISO 3200** is the highest I feel comfortable bringing the ISO sensitivity of this camera from previous experience, and I knew I'd need to push to that limit. With those two settings established, what aperture would provide

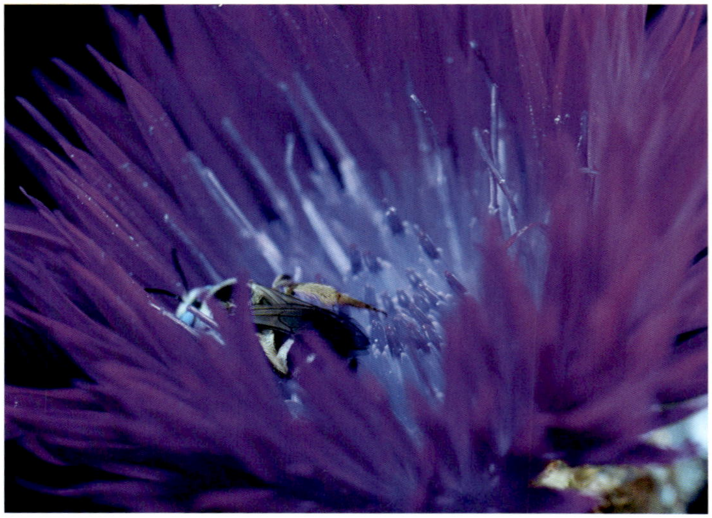

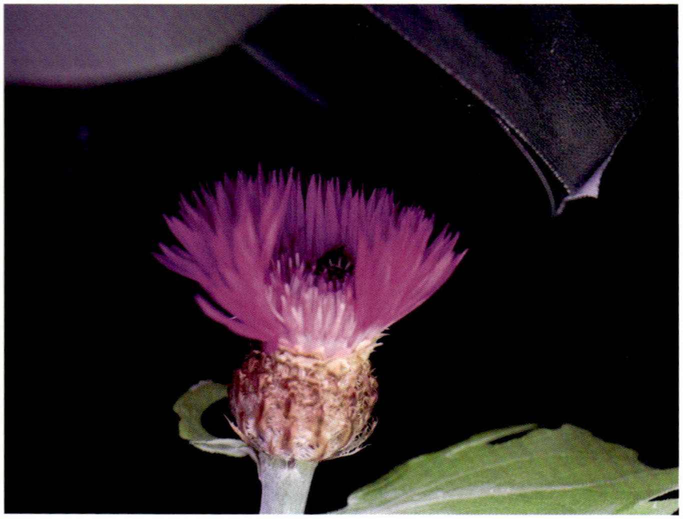

the proper exposure? **F/6.3** was all I could get. I would have liked greater depth by shooting at F/8 or F/11, but doing so would compromise on critical image quality by pushing the ISO setting too high. I had found the best settings possible, now to frame up the subject.

Problem: The cornflower petals rise into a vertical wall surrounding the subject, making it difficult to find a good angle to shoot into the subject.

Solution: Pluck petals to create the needed "window".

Yes, I am manipulating nature again for the benefit of a photograph. I suppose I could have bent them down and held them in place with an elastic band or a clamp, whatever you feel comfortable with to achieve the same results. Especially when shooting in my own gardens, it's well within my comfort zone to make these slight modifications. After all, I spend far more time pruning trees and picking weeds for the aesthetic impact on a much larger scale.

You're welcome to debate me on the ethics of this. I've had many intelligent conversations with people who possess different points of view, many of whom would also refuse to edit or manipulate an image after taking it. The prevailing argument is that modifying reality is something that should not be done to achieve an image. My answer to this is always the question "what do you define as reality?"

The camera always sees things differently than us. Human visions sees only one thing in an instant but possibly hundreds in a minute, whereas a camera captures everything at once. We can control shutter speed, focal length, magnification, resolution that all push beyond what humans see as "reality", and our reality is certainly different from this little Sweat Bee. Even more so when we shoot in naturally impossible light like pure ultraviolet, we bend reality to our creative efforts. We tell stories that inherently transform the world that we see with our own eyes, so what's the best way to tell these stories?

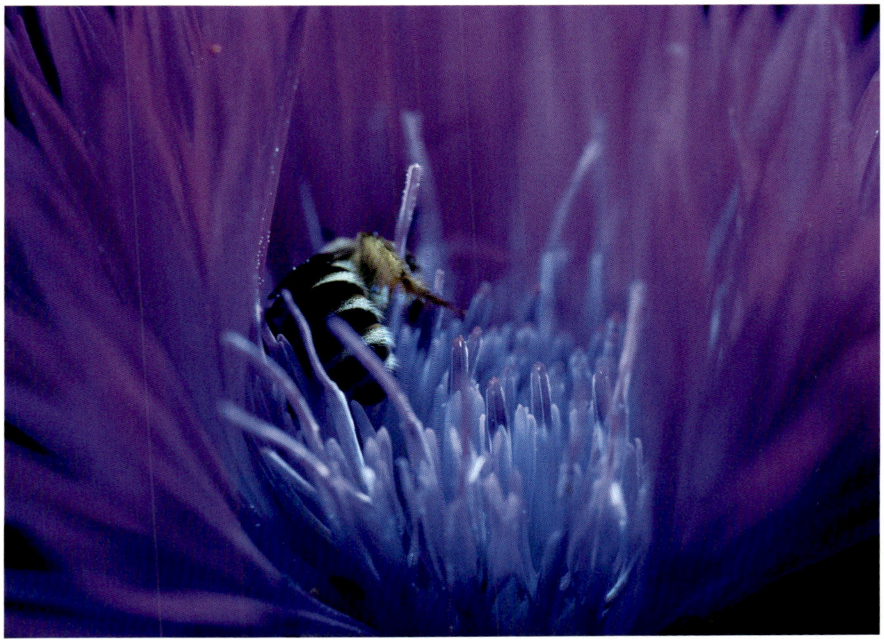

Now that we have a window into this unseen world, the image is starting to materialize. We have shades of purple and blue with structures not unlike some depictions of Superman's own Fortress of Solitude after which this image is named. The iridescent green colours on the bee are completely invisible in this new light, a darkness balanced with glowing blue eyes to offer a different sense of wonder.

However, I still have a problem. The bee is still cold, and therefore lethargic. The tiny creature was still capable of movement, but did not appear to be the lively actor I had hoped for. Just as the cold had slowed this bee to a crawl, warmth could revive it. Simply breathing on the bee was the answer here.

After a number of carefully directed gentle breaths of warm air, the insect began to rejuvenate. It made a circle from the back of the flower to the front before picking itself up strongly in the center of the flower. The proper pose was not held for long before the bee retreated back to the safety of the flower as it began to cool down in the cool ambient air.

Two hours later the bees were airborne once more.

A narrow window of time, and an idea that required me to drop what I was doing and discover new possibilities for already established photographic techniques. By the time I had all of my equipment outside I could have very easily been presented with an empty flower.

There are a lot of moving parts and in-situ problem solving required to create images like this. Even if it didn't result in a successful photograph, it would have been a valuable learning experience.

Could I have recreated this scene indoors by putting that bee in the freezer and picking the flower and bringing it into my studio? Sure. I've learned that this would personally cross my own boundaries and was thrilled for the opportunity to bring this image to life by other means.

"The more you know, the more luck you have."
– *The Burman: His Life and Notions, 1896*

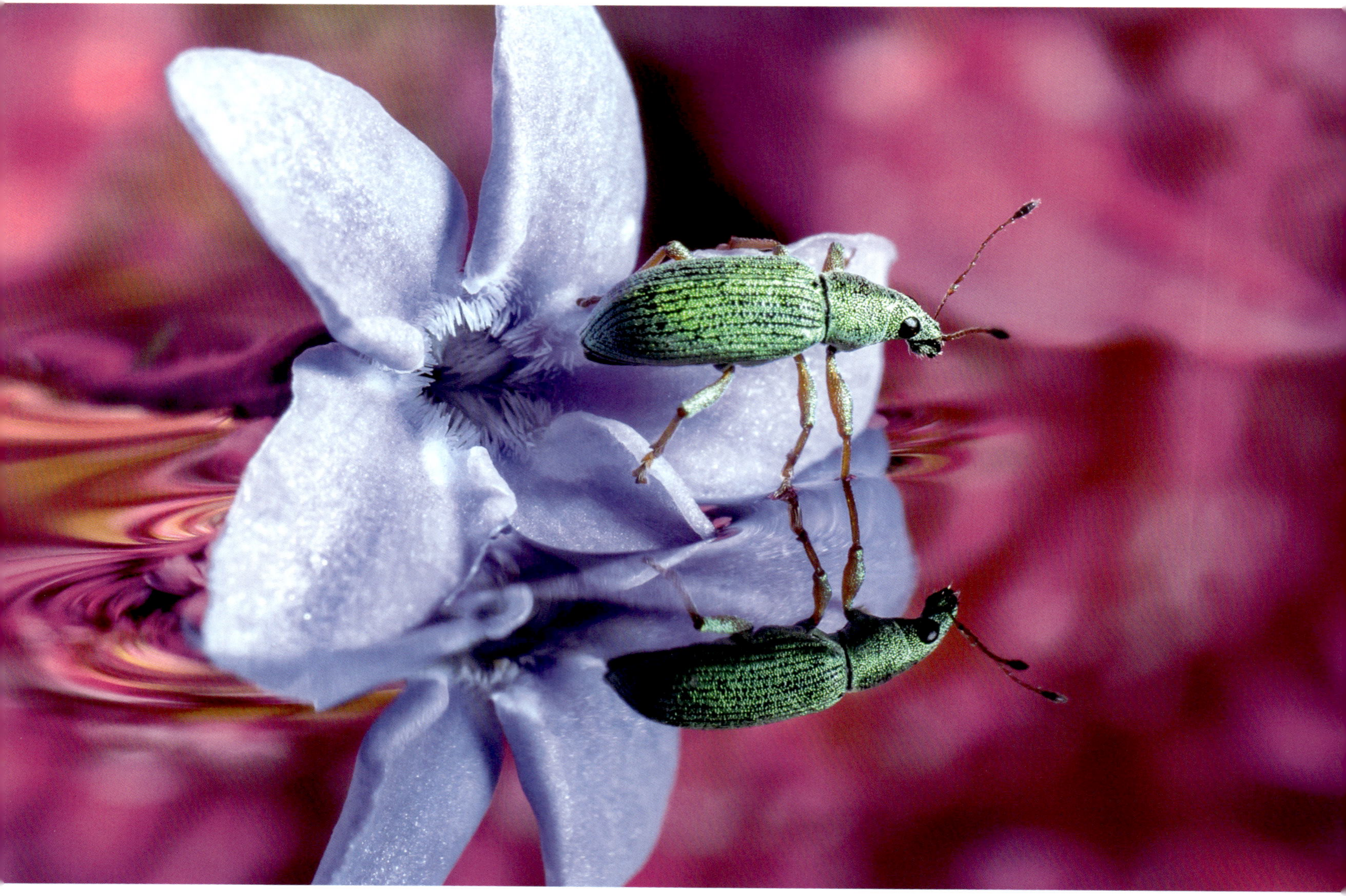

Canon 1DX Mark II, Meyer Optik Trioplan 100mm F/2.8, F/11 ISO 800 1/200sec

Gazing into Vibrancy

Sometimes a concept of the simplest ingredients can be more beautiful than one that takes weeks of technical and creative orchestration. Our ingredient list here is simple and effective:

- Small blue flower
- Large magenta-colour Gerbera Daisy
- Square bowl filled to the brim with water
- "Actor", in this case a Weevil
- Off-camera direct flash

The small flower is freely floating on the surface of the water. This could have been a fixed ingredient with a Third Hand Tool holding it in place, but it might have been difficult to find the perfect balance of angles, depth and composition. The floating flower bends the surface of the water around it slightly, which is where our background becomes much more dynamic.

The Gerbera Daisy is behind the subject at a distance of roughly 8 centimeters (3 inches). The distance is important, as the flower needs to be pleasantly out of focus while still filling the frame with colour. The flower is partially submerged under the surface of the water to ensure that it fills the background of the frame. Variations in colour from the yellow-green center appear, surrounding the blue flower. This is because the angle of reflection off the surface of the water changes as the surface is curved due to surface tension.

The reflection is as important as the background to complete this narrative. Stronger reflections are obtained by having the lens closer to the surface of the water with the water mostly perpendicular to the focal plane. The view is skimming across the surface of the water rather than looking down on it, which allows for an impressive mirror image. The same logic is true when shooting landscape images with a body of water in the foreground.

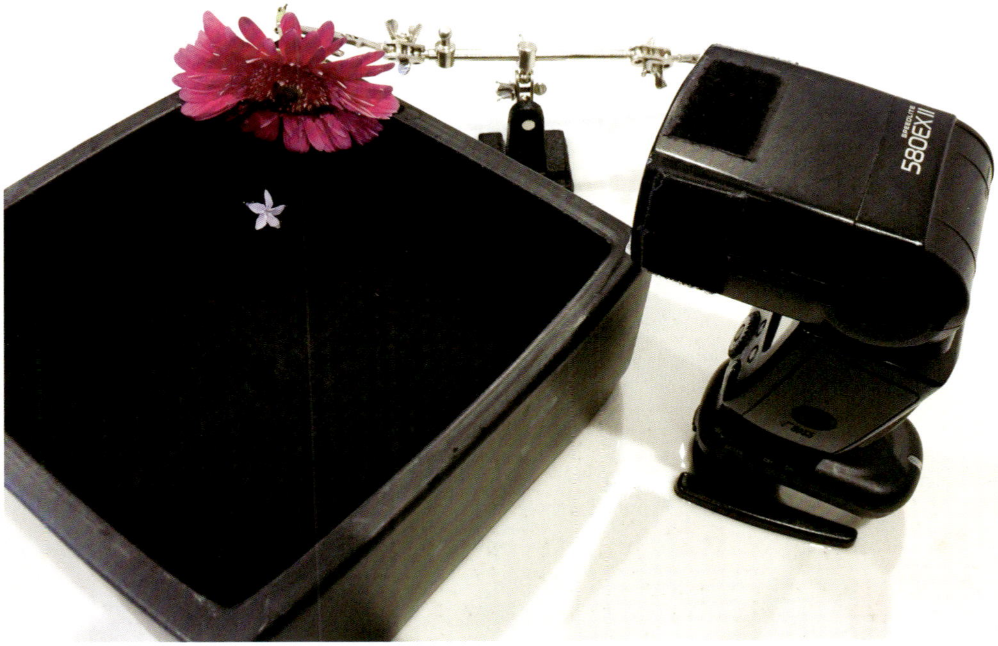

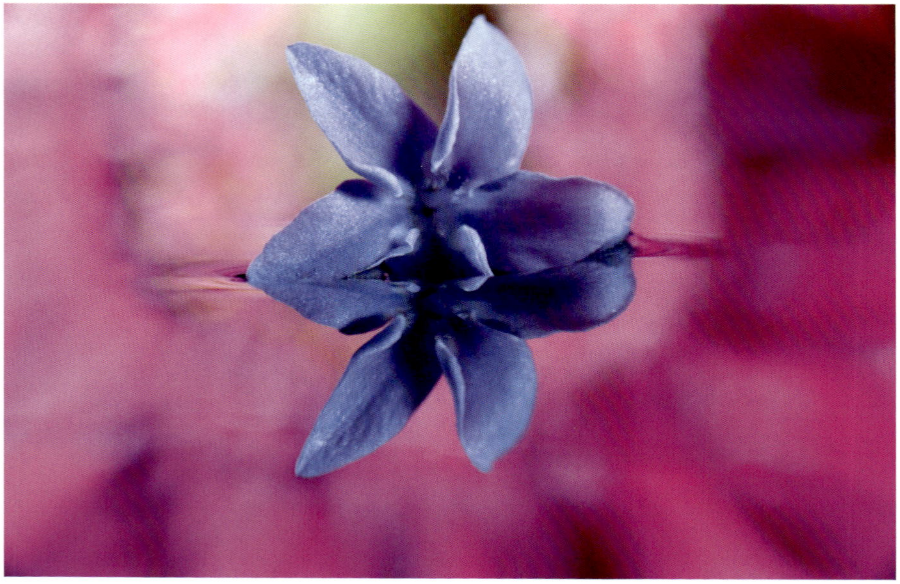

Above: Setting the stage for our weevil to play its role in the image, confirming first that the image has the proper look and feel.

Some larger lenses might have a hard time getting in close enough to the water's edge, depending on your setup. To get the proper angle, I used a lens with a relatively small barrel diameter, the Meyer Optik Trioplan 100 with a set of Kenko extension tubes attached to transform it into a macro lens. This lens is known for its "soap bubble bokeh" when wide open, but stopped down to **F/11**, the lens becomes very sharp for a simple triplet design. Many old lenses are very serviceable macro lenses with extension tubes, since images on a macro scale often use smaller apertures where the optical designs perform better. As many of these older lens designs have much smaller barrels, it could be just the ticket for an image like this!

Lighting this image is dead simple: a cheap wireless transmitter and the flash on manual power. Because the flash will need to recycle quickly for fast bursts of shooting, it would be ideal to set the flash at its lowest power setting and bring the ISO sensitivity up to a level where your exposure is appropriate. In this instance, it was **ISO 800** and a **1/200sec** shutter speed. That speed is the "sync speed" of the camera and flash, which varies by camera model.

Testing the exposure may take a few attempts at adjusting various settings; I like to do these tests without the "actor" present, just to solidify everything before adding additional chaos into the equation. With a proper magnification for filling the frame with the subject but still providing a little wiggle room, what does the background look like? Adjust the aperture to suit. Then move on to adjusting the ISO for proper exposure, or flash power if you have an external battery handy – you'll be taking many images in quick succession when you have everything dialed in.

Now the magic happens – or so you hope. There is such an element of luck in getting this to result in a successful image. The photograph is shot handheld in order to move the camera forward and backward to move the focal plane with the floating subject and reposition the camera such that the flower in the background is in a compositionally pleasing location. Even still, there were plenty of "near misses", and some adaptations to try and find the proper balance. If you

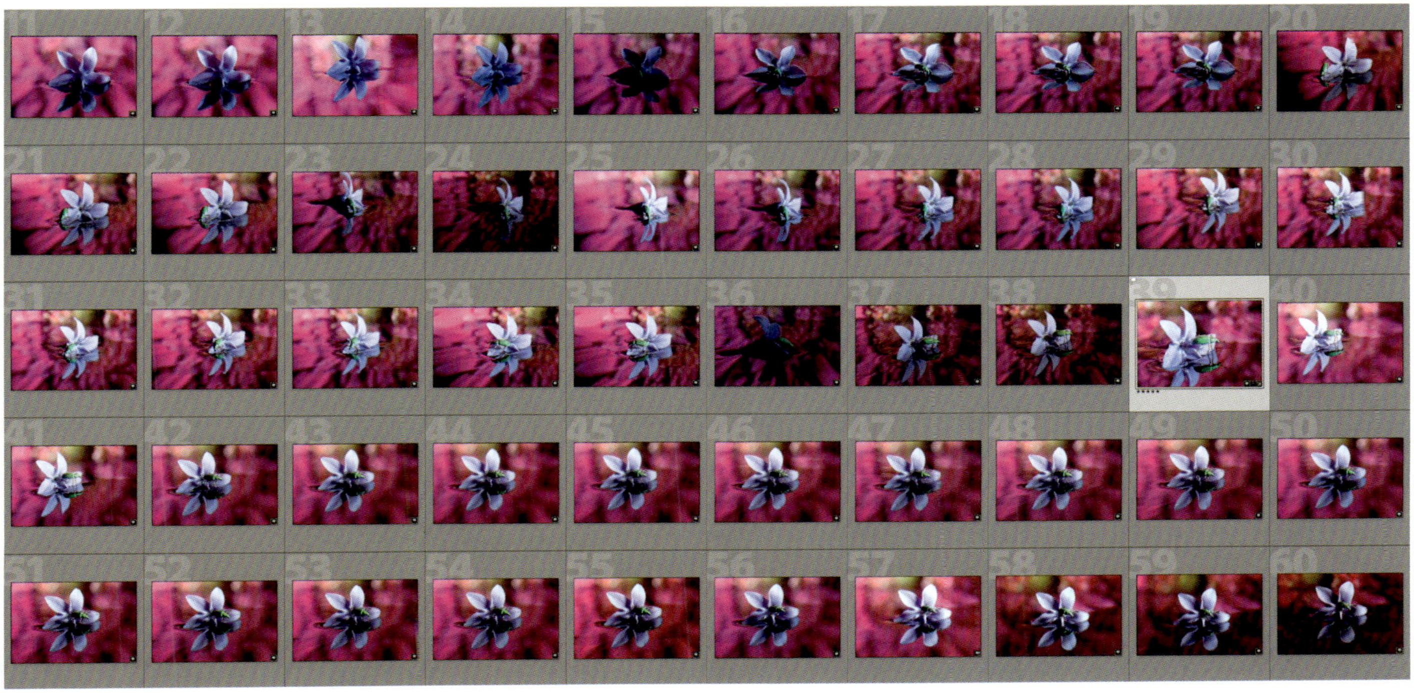

see the images in Adobe® Lightroom® Classic (*above*), you might notice a few clues to the tips I will provide next. First, the background varies by how much of it is in focus from some shots to others. This is not caused by changing my aperture between frames, but by the floating flower moving closer to the background, making it closer to the focal plane when the camera position is adjusted to keep the flower in focus. To overcome this, the flower needs to be constantly repositioned with a slight nudge from a toothpick.

The toothpick was truly critical here, not only to keep the floating flower from approaching the background but also to ensure that it would be facing the proper direction. With the flash in a fixed position and the lighting angle critical, the tiniest nudge of the flower can have a dramatic impact on the results.

You might also have noticed that the highlighted image, which ended up being the best of this set, is not the last photograph taken. Even if I think I may have gotten what I hoped for, I continue to shoot. You never know when a happy accident will happen. What if the weevil decided to open its wings and I snapped the perfect image just before it took flight? Sadly, this didn't happen. I'm still quite satisfied with the results.

"You could not direct the wind, but you could trim your sail so as to propel your vessel as you pleased, no matter which way the wind blew."
– *Cora L. V. Hatch, 1859*

Crystal Blossoms

Every few weeks during the summer months, I take time to explore my gardens – at night. Equipped with one of my ultraviolet flashlights, I explore every corner to see if something fluoresces in the darkness. Many times I re-enter the house with nothing but a mosquito bite. Occasionally, I hit the jackpot.

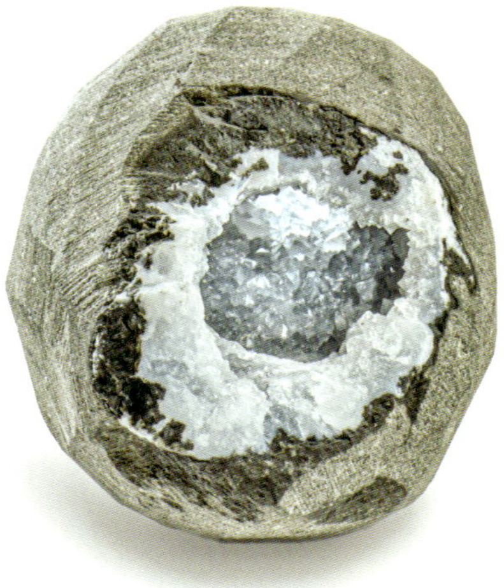

A somewhat invasive species, Gooseneck Loosestrife (*Lysimachia clethroides*) was quite excited to see me. The UV fluorescence was phenomenal, and the individual flowers were small. Small enough to fit inside a "tunnel geode" I had purchased a few years prior and was waiting for the perfect concept to explore with it.

What if I make it look like the flowers are growing out of the walls of a crystal cave? It would also be the perfect use for a lens I have been struggling to find viable subjects for: the Laowa 24mm F/14 2x Macro Probe lens from Venus Optics. Stick the probe lens in one side, angle an ultraviolet light source from the other end of the "tunnel", and the flowers would illuminate the crystalline cavern they would be carefully placed into. A solid plan for the beginning of a day-long session of experimenting and exploring.

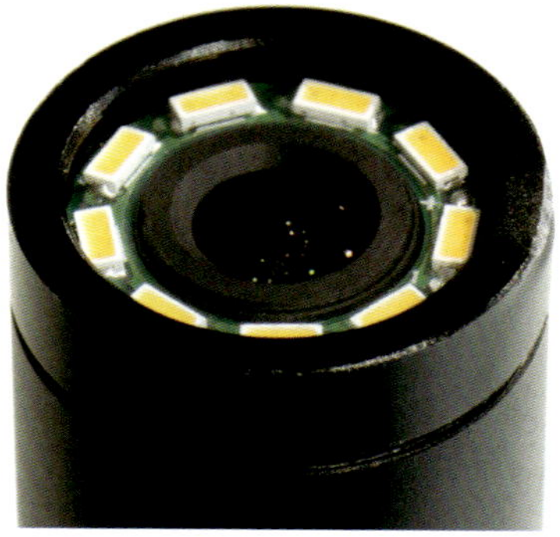

The first point on this journey of exploration was an unexpected discovery. The 24mm probe macro lens is uniquely equipped with a ring of LED lights around the end of the lens barrel, to provide light in tricky situations. White light LEDs commonly use a phosphor material which internally will translate a blue or UV LED into a broad-spectrum white light. Why is this little nugget of knowledge useful? Effectively, white LED lights use fluorescence to achieve their colour.

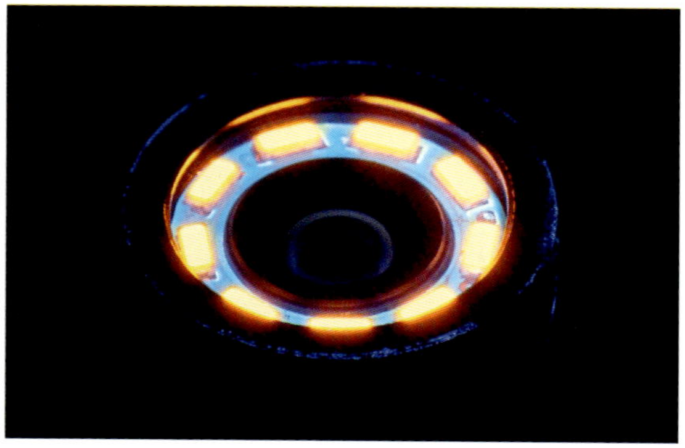

If I'm shining intense UV light towards the front of the lens, this light hits the small ring of diodes and they glow, not even being plugged in. Instead of the pale off-white light that they normally produce, they were fluorescing with saturated orange light (*right*).

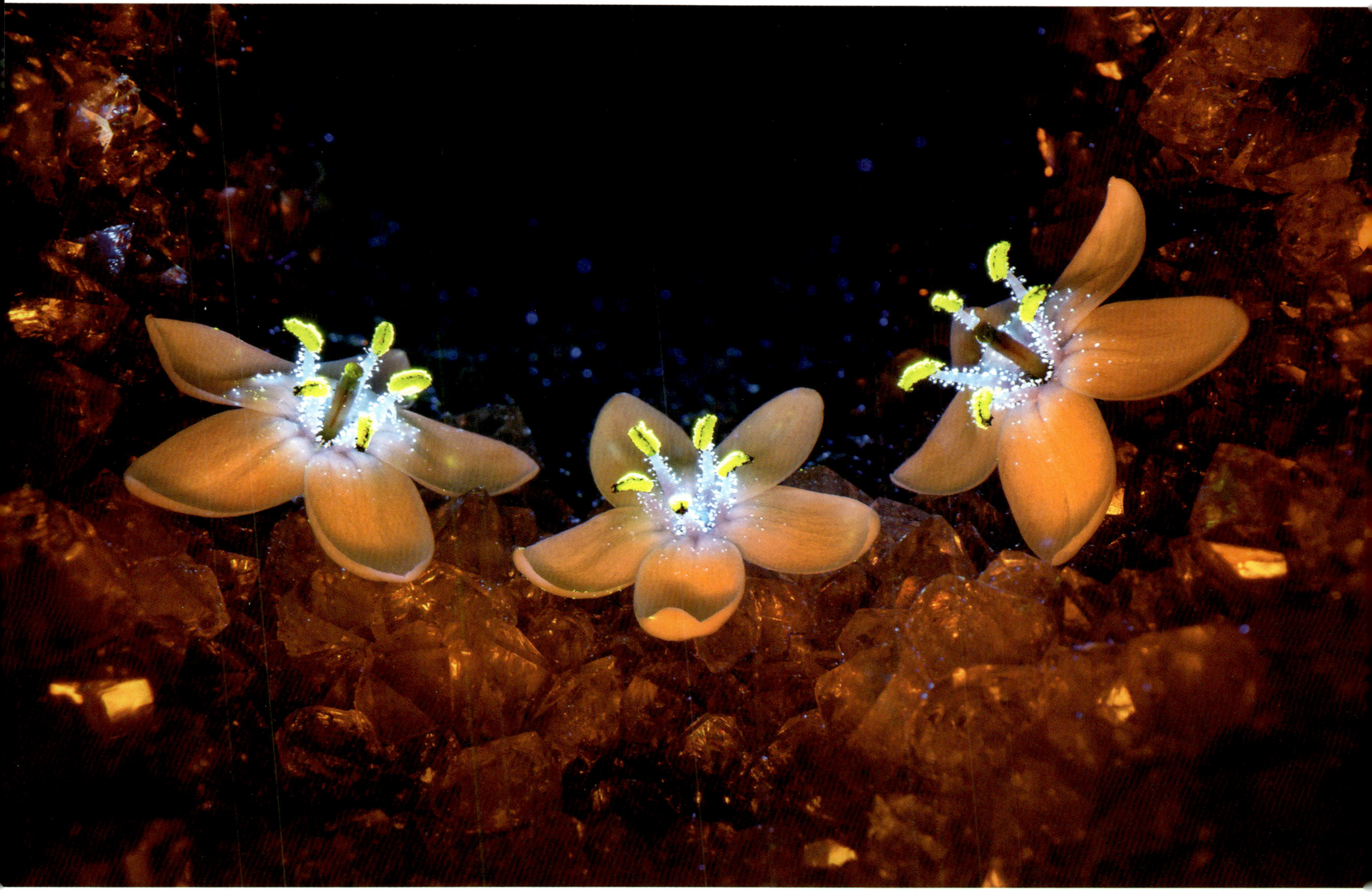

Lumix S1R, Laowa 24mm F/14 2x Macro Probe, F/20 ISO 100 20sec

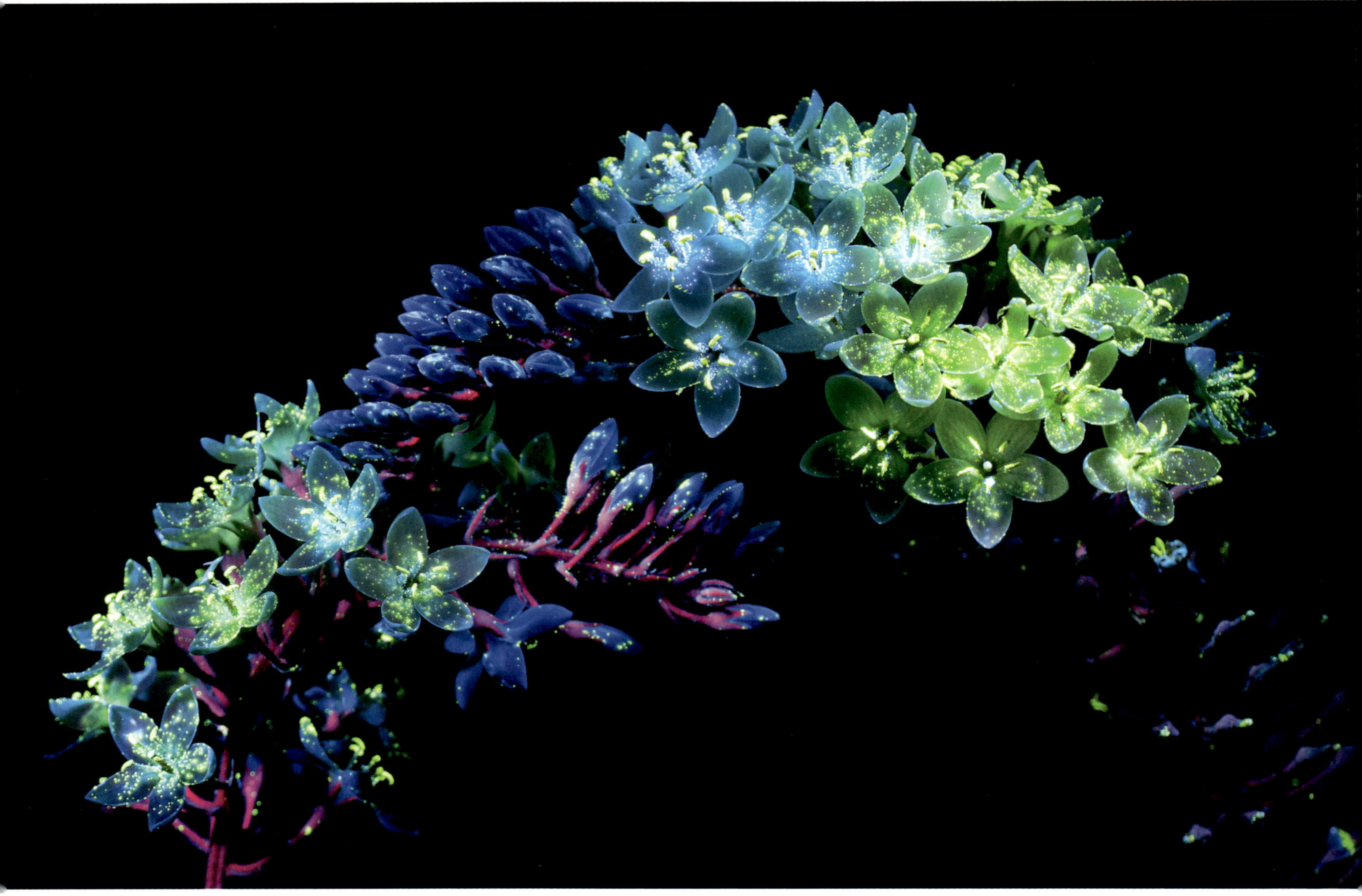

This was unexpected, and my previsualizations of the image concept didn't include this visual puzzle piece. Could I tape over the LED to block the light? Sure, but what if I embrace this warm tone and try to balance it with the rest of the image? I chose to embrace the accident and carry forward with building the image.

The flowers on their own (*above*) offered up a brilliant display not unlike trailing fireworks. I noticed a curiosity about the fluorescent behaviour, however; the more recently opened flowers appears to have a blue colour, whereas the more mature flowers favoured a green fluorescence. Choosing a few flowers in the

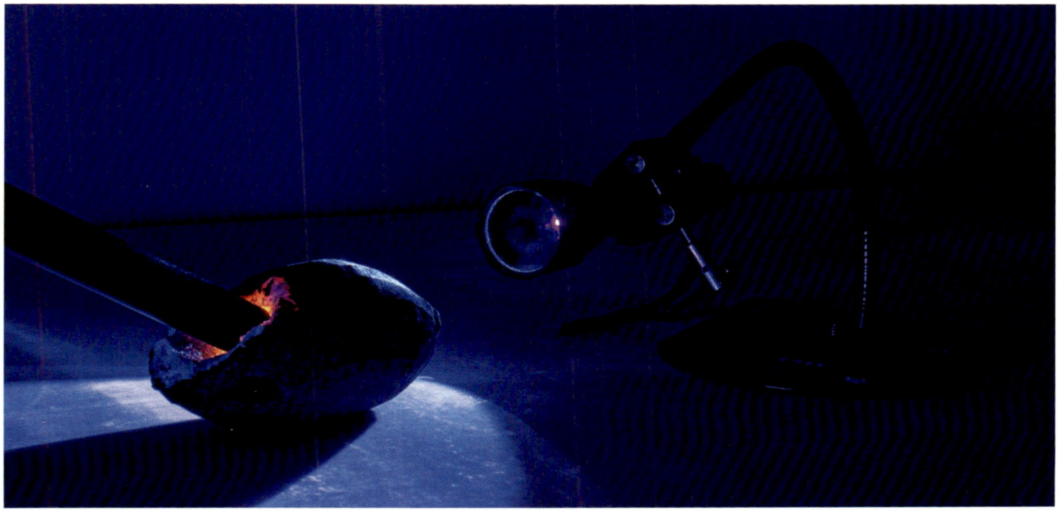

"blue range", these were carefully placed inside the crystal tunnel.

The placement of these flowers was critical. If one was a little too far forward or back, it would be out of focus. Getting all three flowers to be aligned on a flat surface is easy, but it became problematic on the pseudo-random edges of the crystals inside the geode. I shouldn't suggest that this was difficult – only time consuming with a half hour of slight adjustments until everything started to connect together.

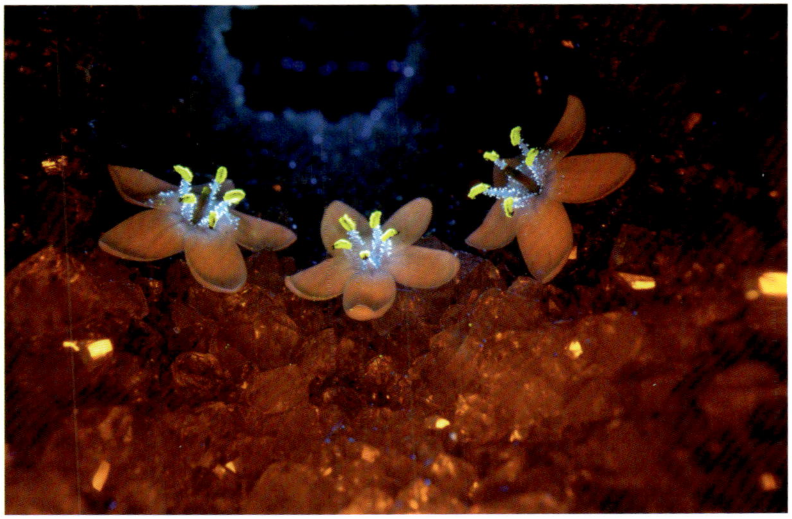

With the UV light on a Playpod Max with a gooseneck arm for the best amount of flexible positioning, the stage was set (*top right*). The flashlight could be easily maneuvered with minor adjustments so that the proper balance of blue and orange light was reached. The back of the geode where the light was entering was a considerable distraction however (right), which was modified in post processing for the final image to simply fade off into darkness.

Knowing that the flowers were relatively static, I opted for the highest quality image during a longer exposure of **20 seconds**. This allowed me to utilize **ISO 100** while the manual aperture was set to around **F/20** or so – just shy of F/22 on the clickless aperture ring on the 24mm probe lens.

The image straight out of camera (*above*) needed some extensive removal of dust specks that fluoresced blue, though some were left, especially in the out of focus background as they "sparkled" like out of focus crystal facets. You can also compare the "end of the tunnel" edit with the finished image on the previous pages.

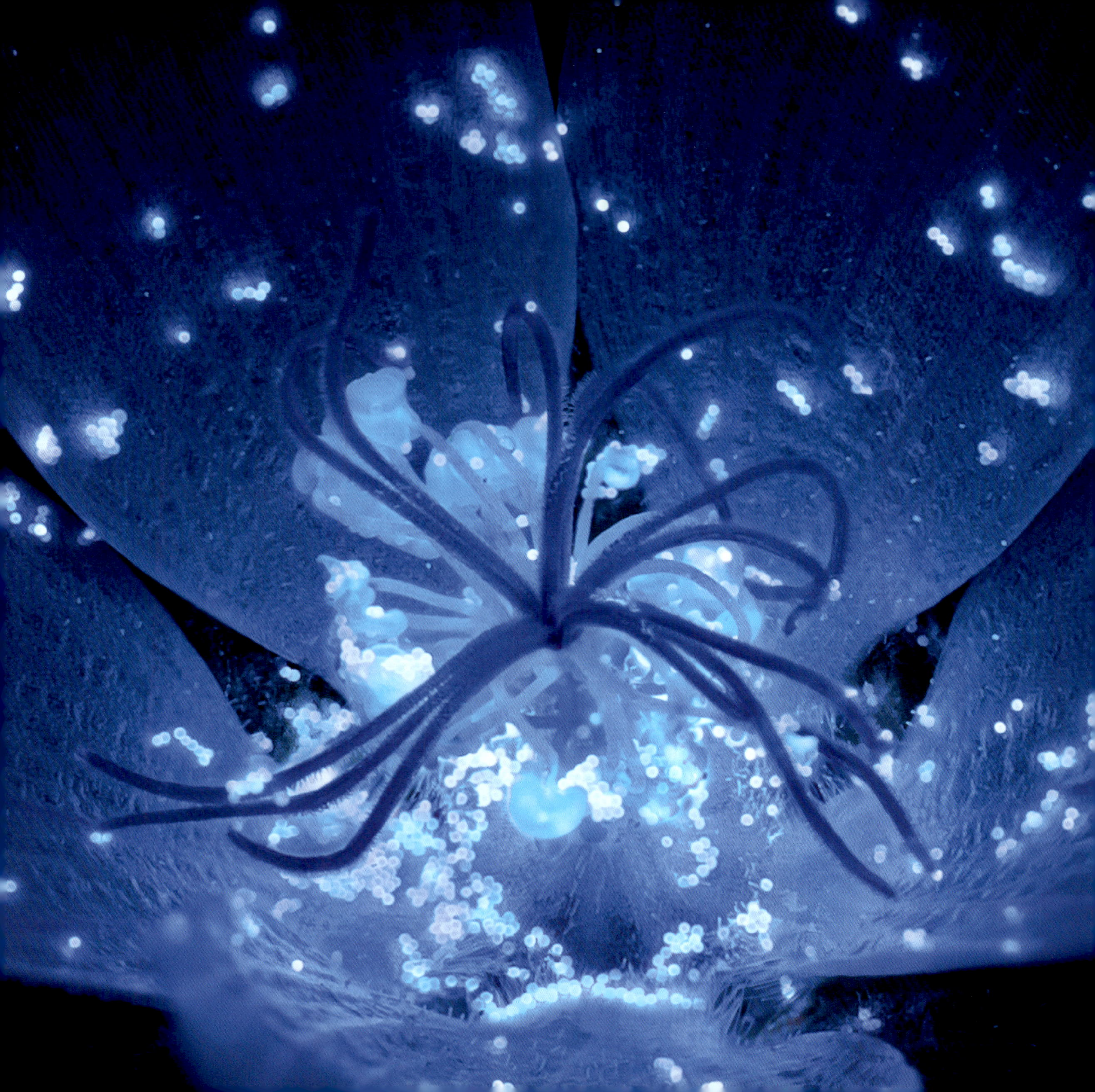

Editing Workflow

Almost every image needs "something" to complete it after the shutter is pressed on the camera. Sometimes it might be a simple crop and an adjustment of basic elements such as brightness or contrast. You might choose to work subtly and offer a multitude of slight enhancements that cohesively improve things. If an image is worth spending half a day shooting for, why would you stop there?

Some people associate image editing with trickery and falsehoods and not being true to the subject. Others embrace it far more than I do with multiple exposures and compositing. Everyone will arrive at a different point on the scale of how much editing is appropriate, though this portion of the book is based on my own beliefs. Simply put: edit an image to your heart's content, so long as you do not modify an image in a way that deceitfully presents something that would otherwise have "documentary value". You can choose to destroy the documentary value in an image – I take no issue with this; Just ensure that no one mistakes your creation for a version of reality. Even then, I've been on the other side of this coin, cloning in the broken tip of a snowflake branch.

Facing page: The result of subtle edits on a flower that was already magical to begin with straight out of camera (*right*).

Editing is supposed to enrich the magic that you already captured in camera. Take this image (*facing page*) as an example. Reality has been modified in camera by photographing this Dwarf Mallow flower (*Malva neglecta*) in ultraviolet light, causing it to fluoresce. This is so far from how I would see this flower with my own eyes, but it is still documentary.

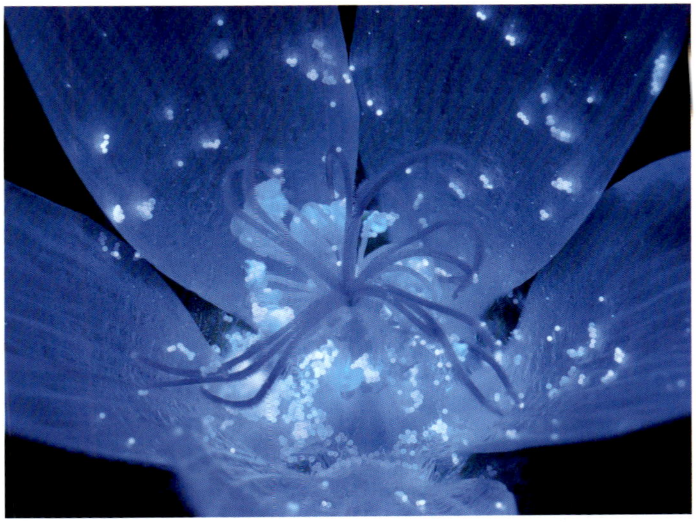

This mentality has been true since the beginning of commercial photography. You don't need to look any further than work we are all familiar with – Ansel Adams is a great example. He would spend hours in the darkroom working on a print, dodging and burning. We'll talk about the digital equivalent of those techniques, but in essence you can control the way you "read" an image. You can brighten, darken, or create contrasting lines that help guide your eyes through the frame. Enhancing many subtle things in an image can add up to a noteworthy improvement that any one adjustment would not accomplish.

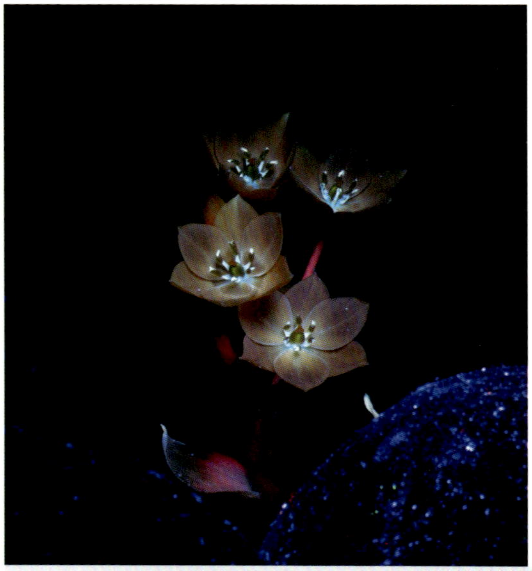

Take for example this Sun Star flower (*Ornithogalum dubium*). Straight out of the camera, you can tell it needs some work. The Ultraviolet lights were so close to the subject they nearly intersect it, covered in lint and dust that also fluoresces blue. The flowers themselves have some magic, but we can work through some basic edits globally to get an image where it "pops" and has the true impact we want others to appreciate.

Join the Process:
The image in this edit can be found at:
www.universeatourfeet.com/flower.zip

The editing process starts with the same order of adjustments:

- Global adjustments everywhere
- Focus stacking (if necessary)
- Local adjustments
- Fine tuning
- Cropping

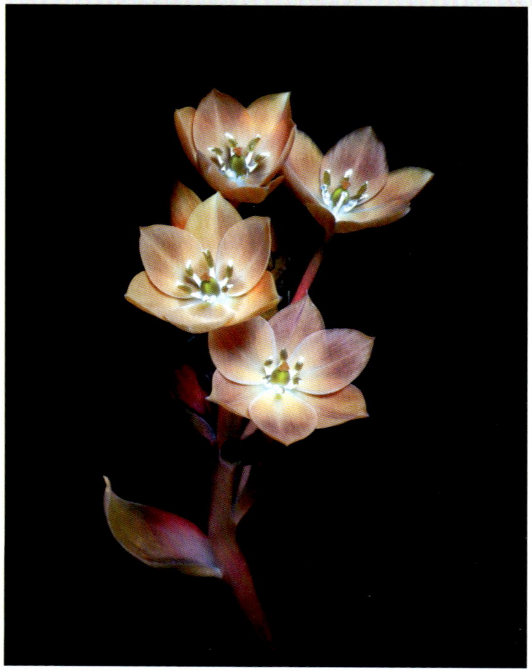

For this flower image, it was shot in a single frame and focus stacking is not a requirement. That technique will be covered shortly with additional examples. If we were to focus on global edits, what would you start with?

Know Your RAW Processor

In the past, the only completely reliable processor for your RAW files came from Adobe®. There were others, but they didn't offer up the same robust compatibility or features. Now, our choices are many – and the competition is a good thing! For this workflow we will predominantly be using Adobe® Lightroom® and Adobe® Photoshop® – but please do not feel the need to mimic this process perfectly. Many processing engines will have sliders with identical or similar names, and very similar functionality.

Think of this as a goals-based approach, as opposed to a tools-based approach. I will illustrate some tools that accomplish a specific result, but it's the result that needs the most attention – it can often be accomplished many different ways using different processing engines from a multitude of companies.

Brighten but Don't Over-expose

Especially early on within an edit, one of the first steps is often to establish how bright an image should be. The simple approach would be to increase the exposure, but by how much and what are the consequences? There's a simple tip to help you get a proper reference point: set the background surrounding the image to "white". This can be done in Lightroom by right-clicking on the background and selecting "white". In Photoshop, you can achieve a similar result by selecting "custom" from the list and selecting white.

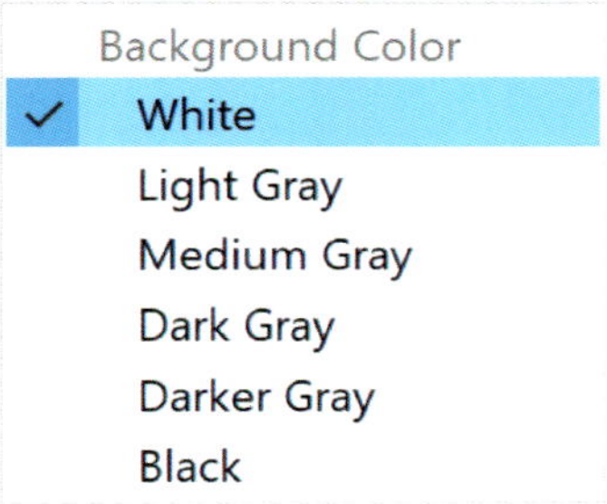

This gives you a solid baseline for what the image will look like against pure white. Many photographers don't realize that their monitors are too bright, and therefore edit images to what they perceive to be perfection. When sharing it with someone else or when printing the image, it's common to see the results far darker than originally intended. This white comparison helps alleviate this problem, though it is not a substitute for a properly calibrated display. I use X-Rite i1 calibrators for my displays and you can choose a target brightness – my personal favourite is a little darker than the default at 80cd/m2 (candela per square meter) in a room with no fluctuating window light.

If adjusting the brightness of an image using the "exposure" or the "whites" slider, you are likely going to over-expose your brightest areas of the image. Test this out: Decrease your exposure slider to a very low level and discover what details are available in the highlights. Subsequently, increase the exposure slider up to a level where the entire image is appropriately bright. What happened to those highlights? Very likely they have been "clipped", appearing as pure white with no detail present, even though the image file does have information in those areas.

There is no global setting to get things perfect, though you may have some luck by dropping the "highlights" slider down. As of version CC 2021 of Lightroom (process version 5), the highlights slider is too aggressive in bringing down the mid-tones in an image. It would be more advantageous to begin the journey into localized adjustments over portions of the image that need a specific tweak.

The Many Paths to Local Adjustments

When "Local Adjustments" in Lightroom allowed for the selective control of certain parts of a photograph with a non-destructive tool, I was elated. Non-destructive editing allows for you to undo or change anything that you have done to an image during the editing process, even if something you'd like to change was initially adjusted 100 steps prior. If you don't like the adjustment, it's easy to fix. In this example, We will brighten up the entire image, and then use the Local

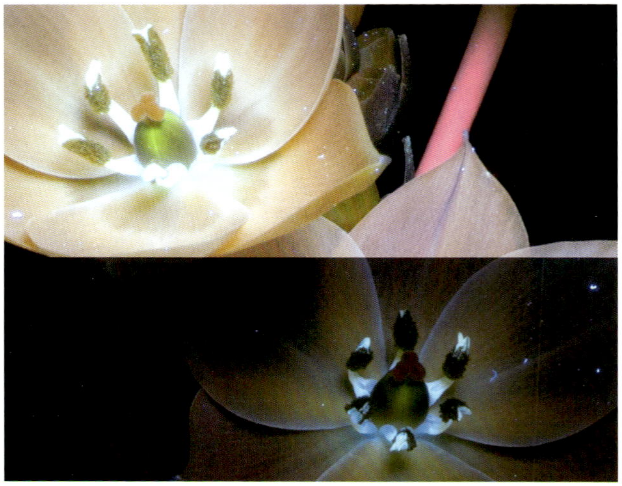

Above: Adjusting the exposure for the overall image can over-expose certain parts of the image like the stamens in the center of the flower, even though there is detail for this area when you under-expose it.

Below: Using a local adjustment, the overall brightness is maintained with the exposure in the center of the flower dropped back down to an appropriate level.

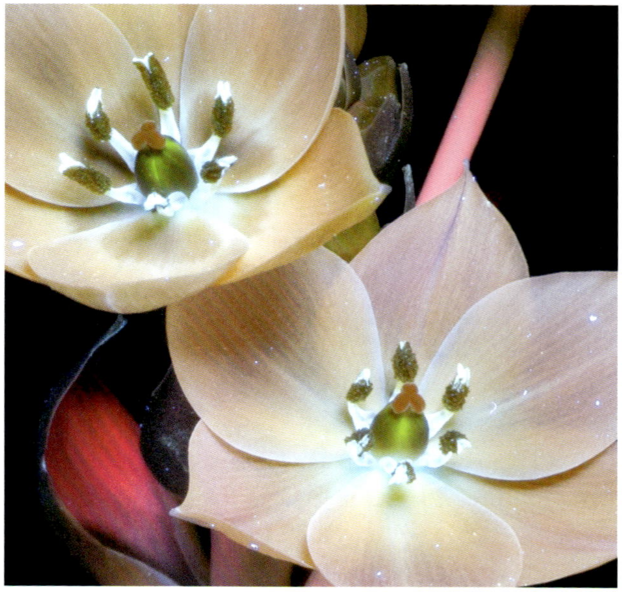

Adjustment Brush (*below*) to bring the centers of the flowers back down to a level that preserves detail in this region. You have plenty of adjustments that can be applied to the “brushed” areas.

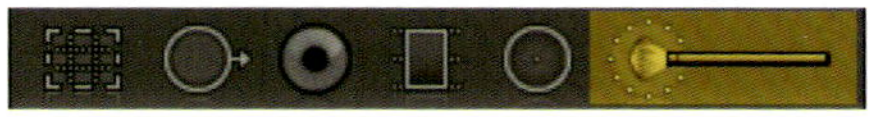

When dealing with the original RAW data, the information that we discovered inside the highlight is still present in the image data, and can be recovered. It’s important to remember that the adjustment should appear smooth, unnoticeable to anyone looking at the image. Setting the “feather” of the brush to its farthest setting ensures that the effect does not have any hard edges and the transition cannot be easily detected by a casual observer.

While these tools work well when you are still working from RAW data, they become less effective once you move your image into Photoshop, as any image data in over or under-exposed areas may be lost. Do as much as you can in your RAW processor first, before sending the image to another application or plugin for further editing efforts. As soon as an image leaves the RAW processor for any reason, it is now a rasterized TIF file.

The terms “dodging” and “burning” might be familiar to you, but if you haven’t experienced a darkroom printing workflow you might be unfamiliar with the origins of the terms. “Dodging” involves using a small circular disc attached to a ridged thin wire that can be placed above the photo-sensitive paper during the exposure. This blocks light over a small area, which prevents the paper from being fully darkened by the enlarger in this region: the area of the print dodged the light.

Conversely, “burning” involves holding up an opaque sheet with a hole in it, blocking all light except for in a certain area, which is “burned” with excess exposure to light. This excess light would make this portion of the print darker, as the photo-sensitive paper becomes darker as more light hits its surface. Materials with varying degrees of opacity and different shapes can be used to dial in the effect.

I hear the little voice inside your head: *Why am I learning about analogue print-making techniques in a modern photography book?* Were two paragraphs really needed for those descriptions? Yes. Photoshop has these tools, and now you know why their symbols are a circle with a stick (dodge) and a hand showing an opening in the middle (burn). While antiquated, I still use these tools on a regular basis.

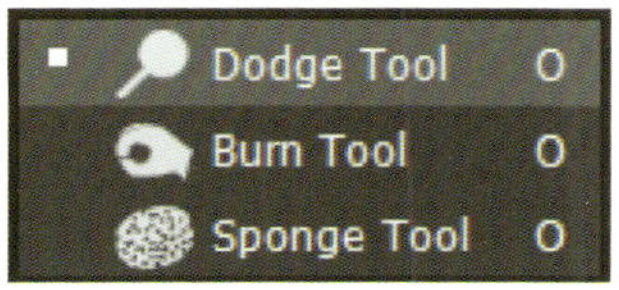

A perfect use case in this image would be to produce a perfectly black background. It looks mostly black, but it would be easy to get there by burning the shadows. Using the eyedropper tool I can see that the background isn't quite where I want it to be – solid black. Remember that it may appear brighter on some displays that have their brightness setting too high, so it's important to ensure that no unwanted details are lurking in the shadows of an image like this.

Remember that this is not a step for every time – it's only being taken because I have a particular goal in mind – the black background. Maybe different tools can be used to accomplish the same goal, and deciding what you want to do with an image can be the hardest part.

While the burn tool can darken certain areas, the dodge tool is equally useful in a "layered" approach to brightening parts of an image. Remember that each of these tools operate within a selectable range: shadows, midtones, and highlights. This means that if you choose to dodge (brighten) the midtones, they will get brighter. However, if you do so with a lower exposure value, they will only be raised slightly up. Herein lies the finesse: when you raise the midtones, they get slightly closer to the "highlight" range and the midtone dodging is less effective if you add another brush.

The effect of your adjustment becomes diminished the more you apply it within the same parameters. This helps prevent "run-away edits" where your attempt to subtly improve a part of an image becomes too extreme, too quickly. Equally useful is dodging the highlights on part of image that is largely midtones. The effect you create on the image will start almost unnoticeably, but as you slowly pull the pixels from midtones to highlights, the effect of the adjustment becomes more prominent with every brush. Every image that I create goes through this process of dodging and burning, bringing up certain parts of the image and dropping others down.

It is, however, destructive. Every brush you apply changes pixels, and the original pixels are no longer in existence. While Photoshop has a "history" buffer that remembers previous versions of an image, it only goes 20 steps back (by default) and this limit is quickly reached using these tools. To provide yourself a "safety net" of sorts, preserving the original image, there is a simple solution; Duplicate your image layer before you start working on it. This keeps a copy of the original to revert back to if required, and you're free to experiment. If you're new to the dodge and burn tools, it can take some time to get comfortable with them and there is no substitute for time spent experimenting.

Each brush stroke of brightening or darkening would have little appreciable impact, but collectively it begins to add depth and dimension to an image. Look at every part of your photo and ask yourself if some portion should be brighter, darker, or left alone.

The next part of this image is easy but tedious: cleaning it up. Those flash heads at the bottom of the frame have been annoying me through this edit and it's time for them to go. There is also a considerable amount of bright white specks on the flowers themselves – this is household dust that also fluoresces under UV light. Indoor plants are likely to be covered with dust that you normally wouldn't be able to see, but it makes a bold and bothersome entrance when illuminated by ultraviolet light.

The first of these issues, the larger unwanted objects in the frame, is almost always taken care of using the "content aware fill" tool. I could cheat here and just paint them all in black, since we have such a background conducive to that approach. Instead, we'll use the technique helpful in more than just this isolated scenario. This can be used for removing an unwanted twig in the frame, something distracting in the background,

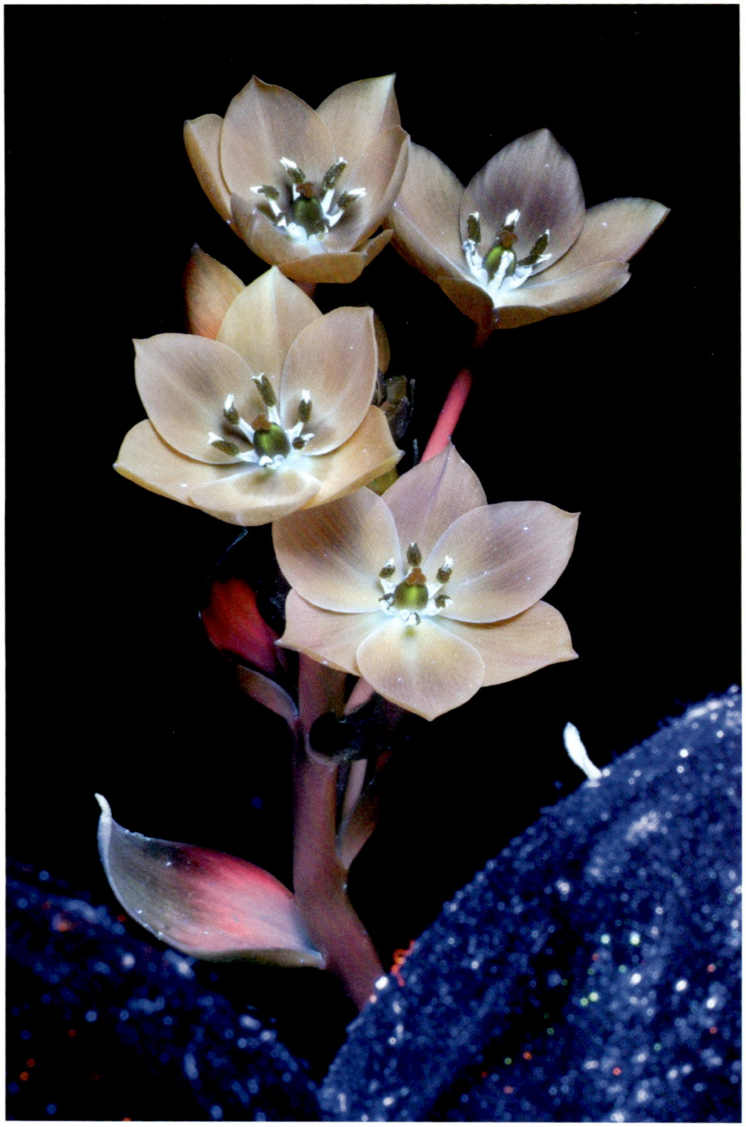

Above: Dodging and burning can give a little extra depth to an image. It's not the only tool available to achieve this type of effect, but it allows for progressive adjustments in a controlled manner.

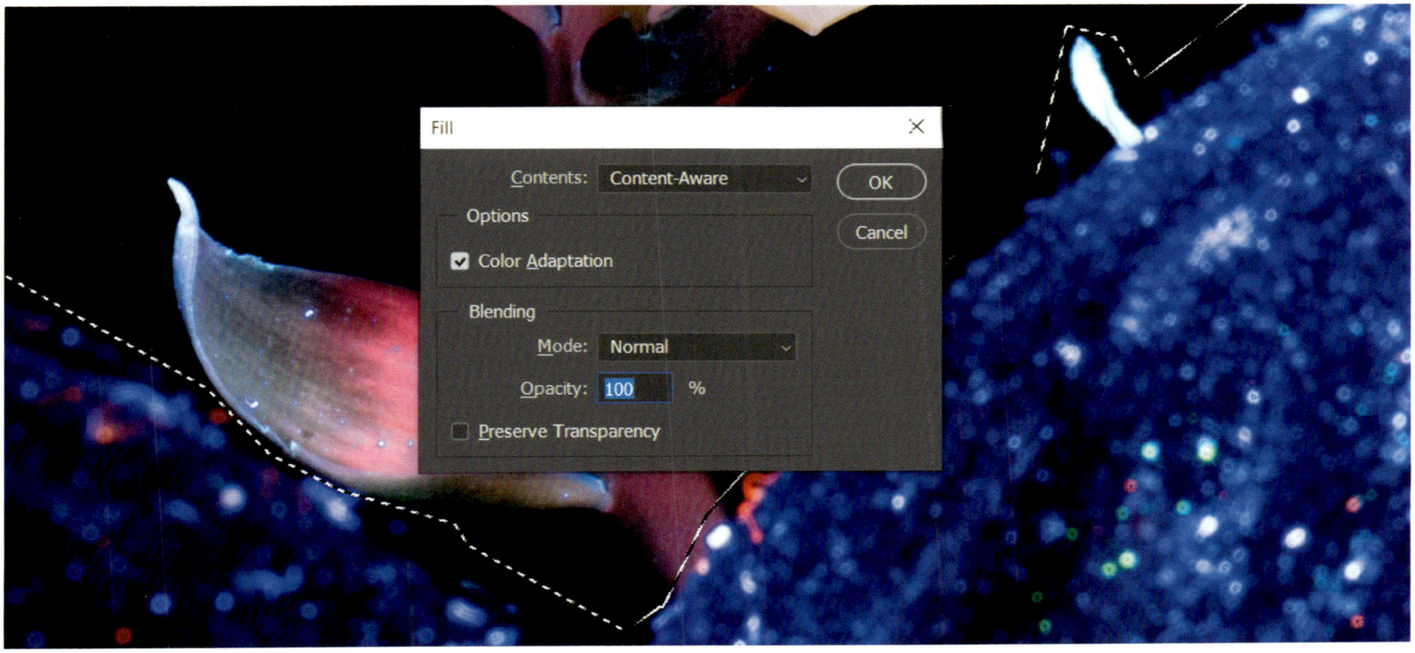

foreground, or anything you look at and think "this has got to go"!

The process is simple: use the lasso or polygonal lasso tool to select the object of your discontent. Be sure to leave a little extra space around it, not hugging too close to the edges to ensure that it will be completely removed. I prefer the lasso tools so that I can make my own wider selection than other automated tools would provide. Once selected, right-click on the image, choose "fill" and a dialogue box will be presented to you. This is how it appears by default, and this is how it should operate. Content-aware fill with Color Adaptation for best results.

"Best results" vary. In this case, there was too close of a connection between the left leaf and the flash head, and the software couldn't tell where the leaf was supposed to stop (*left*). Simultaneously, there's guesswork going on around the stem which ends abruptly and there is confusion about how to rebuild it.

This editing workflow chapter will not comprehensively describe every tool, but the next goal is clear: clean up the leftovers. If you're not friendly with the cloning tools in Photoshop, now's a great time to get acquainted!

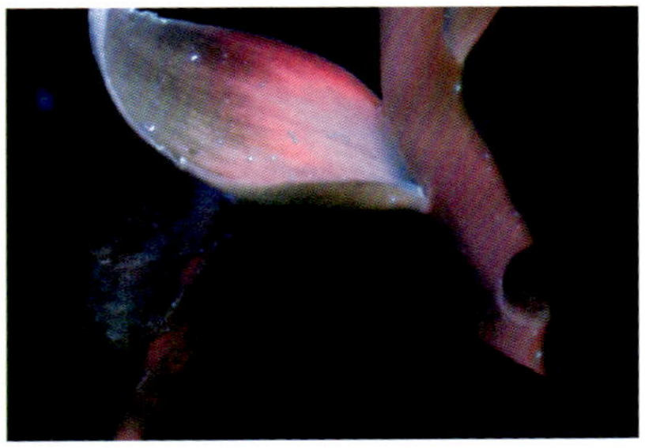

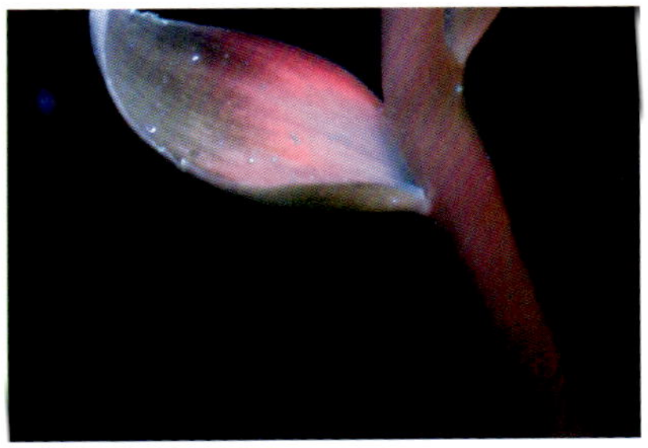

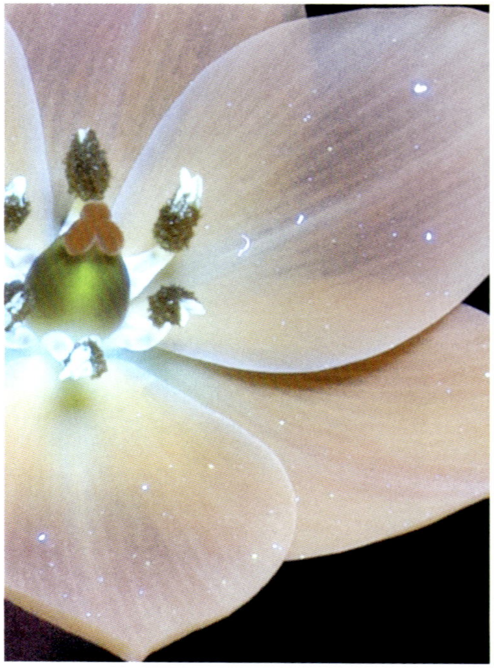

The clean-up continues into smaller places. While there is much work to do in massaging the colour and texture in the image, the focus should constantly be shifting to the next most obvious problem with a photograph. At this point, it's the abundantly sprinkled specks of dust. Clothes detergents and other optical whitening agents found in fabrics and paper will fluoresce a bright white/blue colour. The removal of most of these distractions is the sweeping and tedious use of the Spot Healing Brush.

Be aware that pollen can naturally fluoresce as well, so not all glowing spots are unwanted. In this flower, you can see the pollen appearing dark brown on the stamens which are intensely brighter than the pollen attached to it. Pollen could come from other flowers as well, so I generally leave anything that appears of natural origin but remove the artificially fluorescing annoyances. This includes the blue orbs in the background, which are out of focus specks of dust on a piece of black felt in the background.

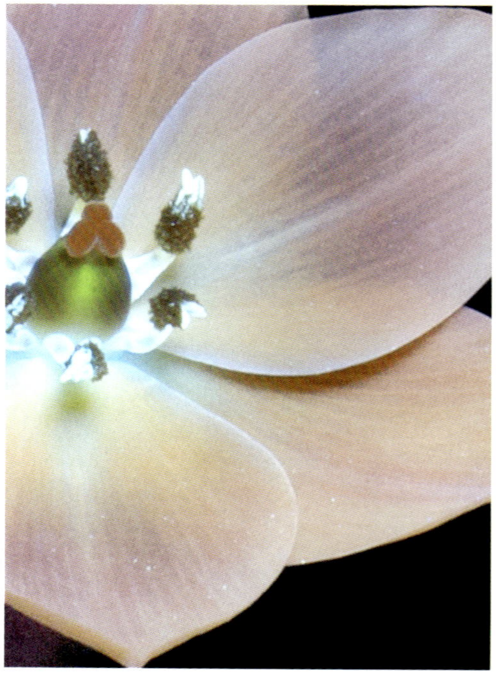

The Eye of the Beholder

Now that we have the framework of the image complete, we can work on enhancements to the colour. While this flower is already beautiful, I have found that there are subtle differences in how a camera renders certain images and how your own eyes perceive the same subject. Flowers of extremely saturated primary colours, for example, can appear washed out in images due to a single colour channel being over-exposed while the others are fine.

For a reason I have yet to completely identify, many images of fluorescence have slightly skewed colours. This could be for the aforementioned reason, it could be a white balance mistake, or it could be something more complex such as how our human vision and camera sensors interpret metamers differently. Metamerism is the ability for our eyes to combine multiple wavelengths of light together to see one distinct colour. A camera tries very hard to mimic these properties of human vision, with the best example being the colour magenta. It doesn't exist as a singular colour, it exists as a combination of red and purple being perceived simultaneously. There is a great deal of colour science that goes into making our cameras see the world in a similar way to us. In fringe scenarios, however, they can't be perfectly accurate.

This opens up a bit of creative license, especially since UV fluorescence is a phenomenon never found naturally in nature. How can we play with the colours in this image to attain the level of magic I remembered seeing it in person? This is a strategy that many photographers, from landscapes to portraits, apply to their editing workflow.

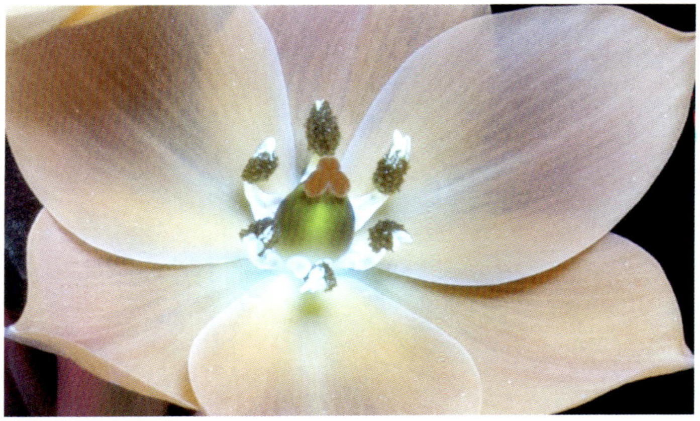

Above: Original *Below:* Vibrance Enhanced

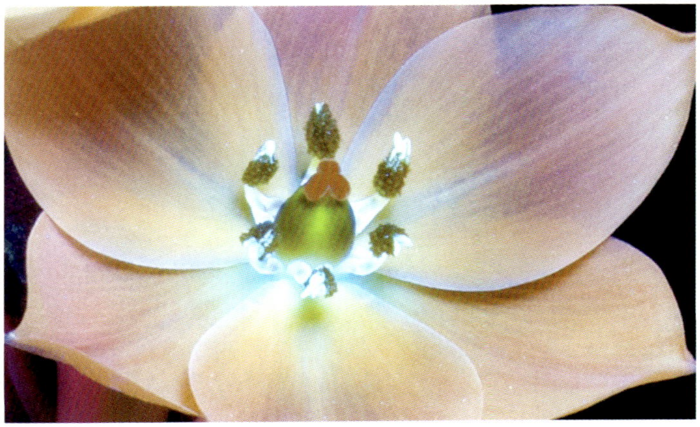

An easy way to get started with these colourful alterations is to use a number of adjustments layers in Photoshop. "Vibrance" tends to bring up colours that are less saturated, and leave already-saturated colours alone, often favouring an increase in blues while leaving skin tones alone. Because this flower is close enough to certain colours associated with skin tones, we get an increase in some of the hidden colours in the flower without being overly disruptive. This doesn't work in every case, and you can't be selective about what is happening aside from the intensity of it. How about a more controlled approach, then?

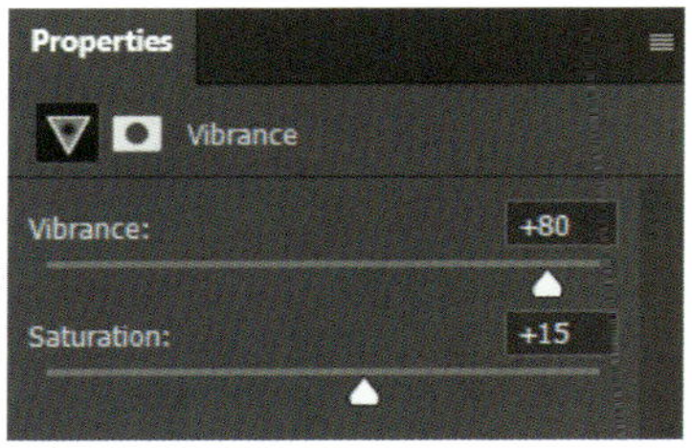

While the Hue/Saturation adjustments available in Photoshop are incredibly powerful, I find myself consistently returning to the Camera Raw via the Filter menu (*below*). The Hue / Saturation / Luminance sliders here are very fast and effective for nudging the colour values around in an image. These sliders have an excellent ability to make specific colours darker while still looking very natural, and I know I want to apply that to the red colour of the lower stem and leaf to prevent my eyes from lingering around this part of the image. When we look at an image, our eyes will often go to the most saturated part of the frame, even if that part of the image is of little importance.

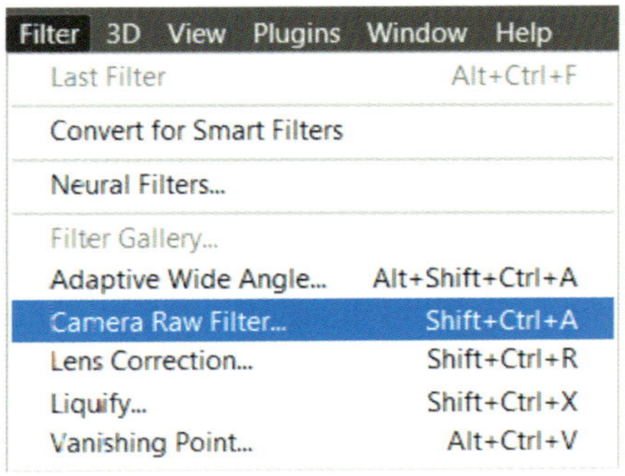

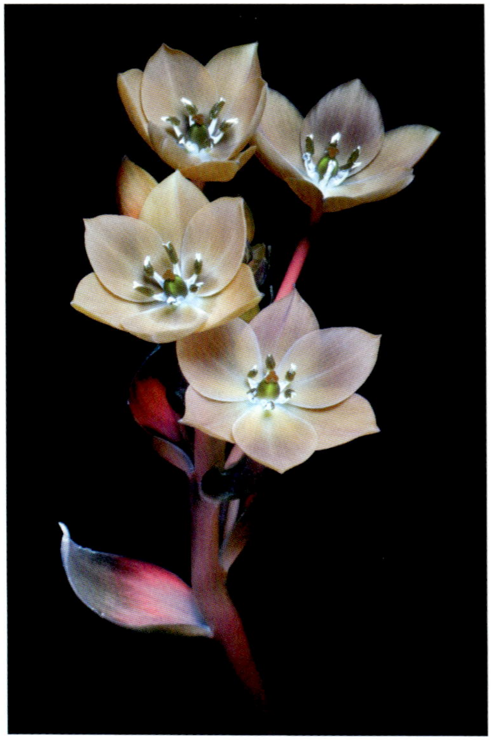

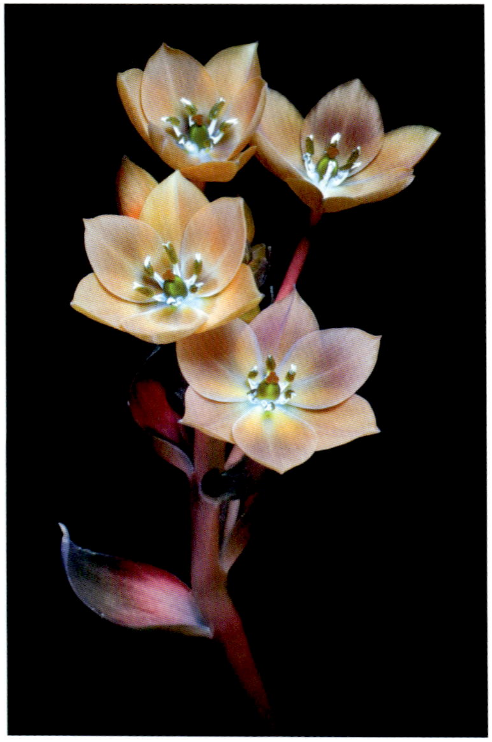

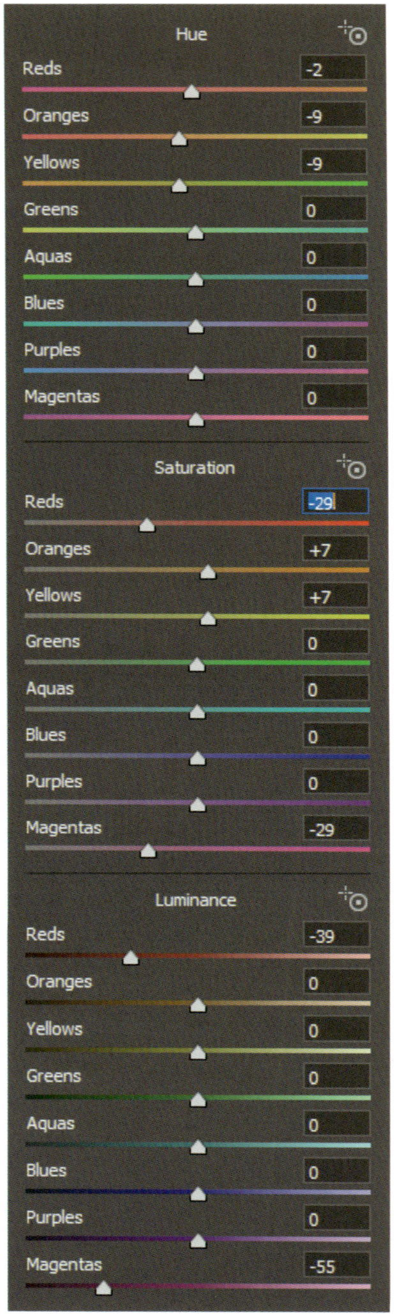

The settings in the H/S/L panel (*right*), combined with the Vibrance settings (*previous page*) offer up the colour transformation in the flowers. Remember that every image is different, and different tools can be used to achieve similar results. You never walk the same path twice when editing an image, though your goals are often the same.

The original image (*left*) is beautiful to me, and I enjoy the subtle tones. It has elements of red in the leaves that are too intense, which are darkened down with these latest adjustments. The resulting image (*middle*) packs a punch of vibrancy and a colour palette more closely mimicking my memory.

Still, the image is not complete. There are further enhancements to the texture, and finally sharpening and additional polish before I can call the image "whole".

Showcasing Structure

Plant leaves, flower petals, insect carapaces and compound eyes. There are many macro subjects that could use with a little extra depth and dimension, and had I been writing this book five years ago the options would have been limited. Today we have an overabundance of tools to achieve this goal, with my favourites being the "structure" slider in ON1 Photo RAW as well as the "texture" slider in Camera Raw. Each of these produce a similar effect, but we need to be selective about how they are applied.

Just like many of our other edits, a localized approach is important. To achieve this, I'll duplicate my layer before heading into the Camera Raw filter and use a layer mask to paint in the effect where I find it most helpful. The same is done when using ON1 Photo RAW through Photoshop, though it will duplicate the layer automatically and save you the step.

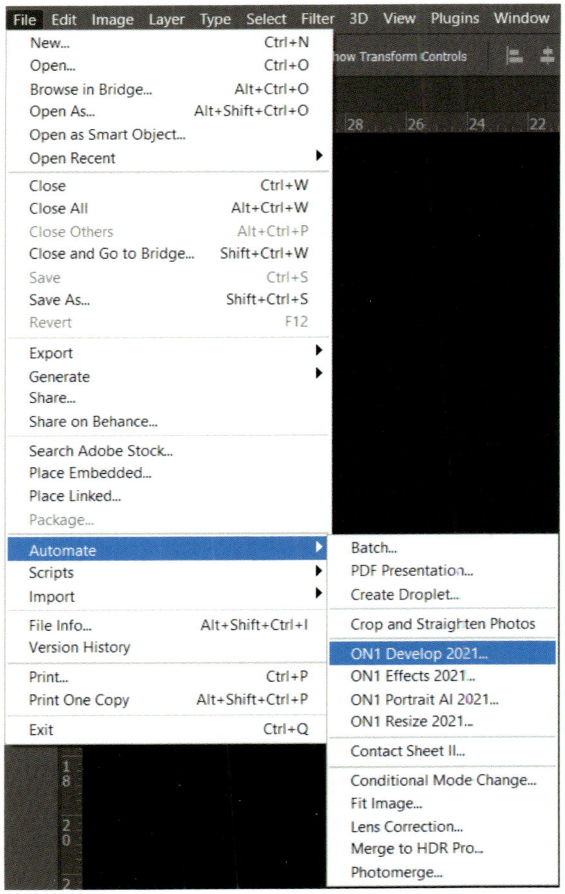

While there is no perfect setting for this structure slider, I find anything less than 50% has too minimal an impact and anything beyond 80% becomes too "grungy" for my tastes. In this example, to bring out the petal texture I found 75% to be the sweet spot. I feel the need to reiterate that the effect, on its own, is delicate.

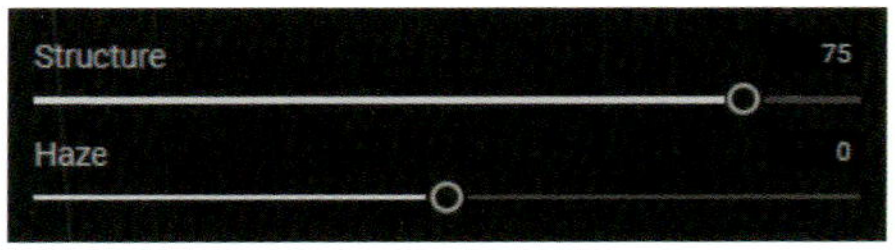

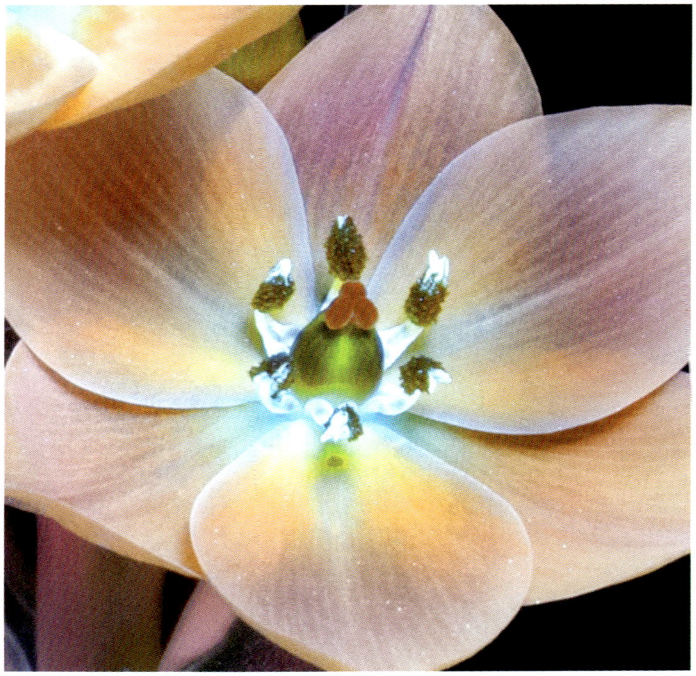

You may not be immediately aware of the impact, and using a layer mask it only gets applied to the petal textures and not the stems or other area of the image that have no need for this effect. If you apply it where it isn't needed, you'll bring attention to areas of the image that should stay unimportant.

Sharpened for Success

Just like the myriad of ways you can add additional texture and depth to an image, there are an incredible number of ways to sharpen. From the latest "AI"-branded algorithms to the obfuscated "output sharpening" in Lightroom Export dialogue, what should you explore for best results? This is something of a rolling target as technology advances, but I love an old technique with a modern twist: noise-reduced high-pass sharpening.

Start the process by duplicating your image to a new layer, and then selecting Filter > Other > High Pass... which will reveal to you a bizarre middle-grey version of your photograph. Anywhere there is detail in the image, some areas become brighter than middle-grey, and some darker. You want to dial in the effect to be subtle, as shown. The slider position is very much dependent on your cameras resolution and the detail in the image. For 20-24MP images I find a position between 2-3 works well (*lower right*), but that position changes with resolution. Experiment to see what works best for you. Aim for the same level of "fuzzy edges".

We're creating a "mask" for sharpening the image. Unfortunately, noise is also detected by this filter, particularly after all of our pixel pushing that can make noise more obvious! The last thing we want to do is sharpen the noise, so we take it a step farther into Camera Raw and push the noise reduction slider nearly to the limit (*facing page*).

This blurs out the sharpened noise, while still leaving smooth lines where the highest areas of contrasting edges in the image are found. Our mask is complete as soon as we hit the "OK" button,

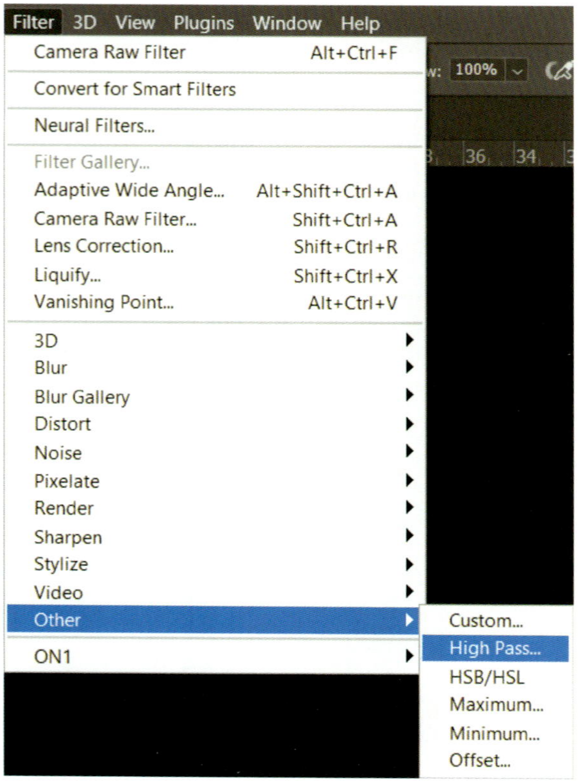

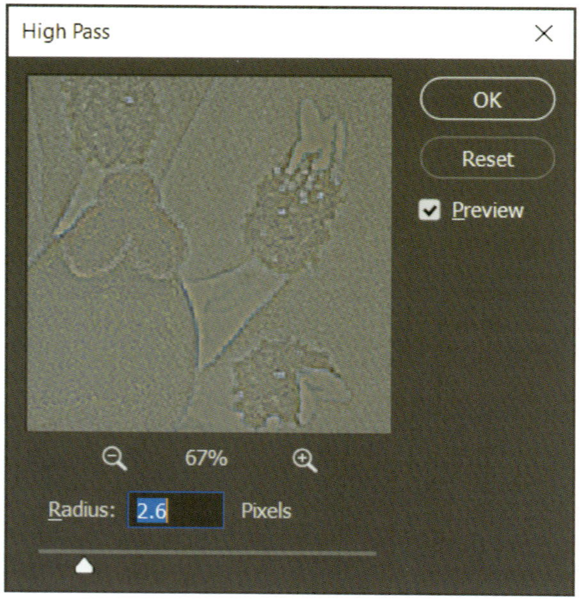

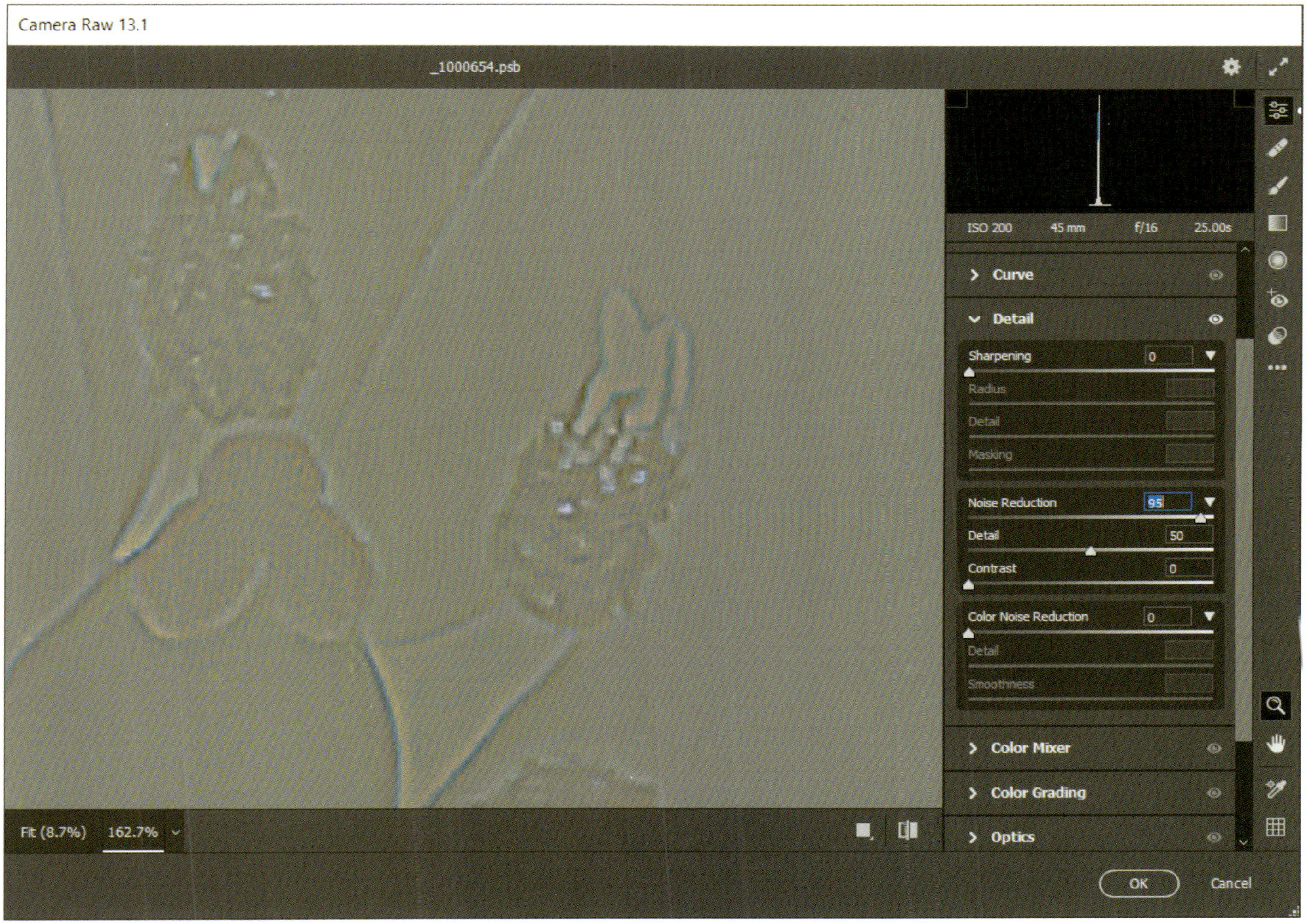

and return to Photoshop. At this point, it seems like a considerable amount of effort to create a "grey blob version" of our image that has absolutely zero appeal. And you'd be right, if it wasn't for the blending modes that Photoshop has available to us.

In the Layers panel (default location is the lower right corner of the Photoshop interface), you'll see a word there: Normal. This is the standard "blending mode", a way to combine (or blend) pixels of different layers in the image together. It can be used for adding a faded watermark to your image (soft light), or it can be used as an alignment aid to ensure two very similar photographs are aligned perfectly (difference). For our purposes, the best blending mode to use is **Overlay**.

The overlay blending mode does two things: for anything darker than middle grey, it "multiplies" the pixels, adding their values together to become darker. For anything above middle grey, it "screens" the pixels, adding their values in such a way that the image becomes brighter. **This creates sharpness.** Most sharpening tools and algorithms do exactly this: they brighten one side of an edge and darken the other, creating stronger contrast along those lines to make them stand out more. We are accomplishing the exact same goal here, but we're in control of the process every step of the way.

Cropping and Final Thoughts

While I may have cropped the image earlier in this workflow due to page space requirements, this is usually the final step for me. If I plan on printing a photograph on canvas, it's always better to have a little extra space to wrap around the edges of the canvas. Maybe I'll need a slightly different crop for a project, but if I commit to cropping the image early on, I'm stuck with that. There have been times where I have had to redo the entire editing process on an image because I cropped too early, so this was a lesson I had learned the hard way.

The workflow is fairly standard for every image I edit: start globally using edits that affect the entire image, transition to local adjustments that affect only portions of the frame, and finally move to the polishing phase. If you wonder why some images "pop" while others do not, it's because the camera is only the beginning of the image creation pipeline. I did not fundamentally change this image from its original reality; I've just brought it closer to my own reality rather than what the camera captured. The gap between human perception and what our cameras are able to capture is sometimes expansive. It is our prerogative as photographers that have any level of artistic interpretation of our subjects to attempt to close that gap.

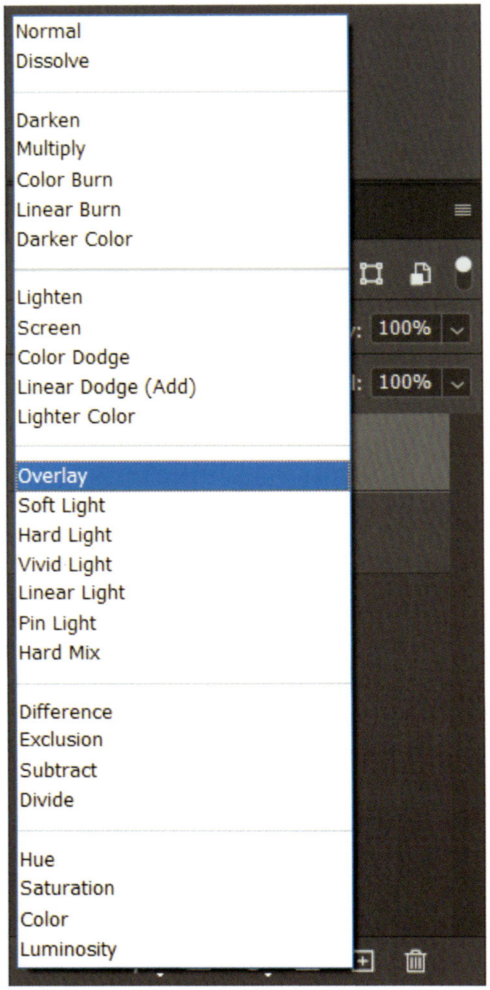

Every image has different goals. Some images need very little work, and I would consider this photograph an "easy" edit. That statement should not negate the effort in the process, but some steps were not required in this particular journey. A more intensive edit is required when the depth of field will not allow for the entirety of the subject to be photographed in focus in a single frame. "Focus stacking" is the solution there, where we attempt to overcome the limitations of physics by combining multiple images at different points of focus together. We'll tackle that next, along with the corrections required to achieve perfect results.

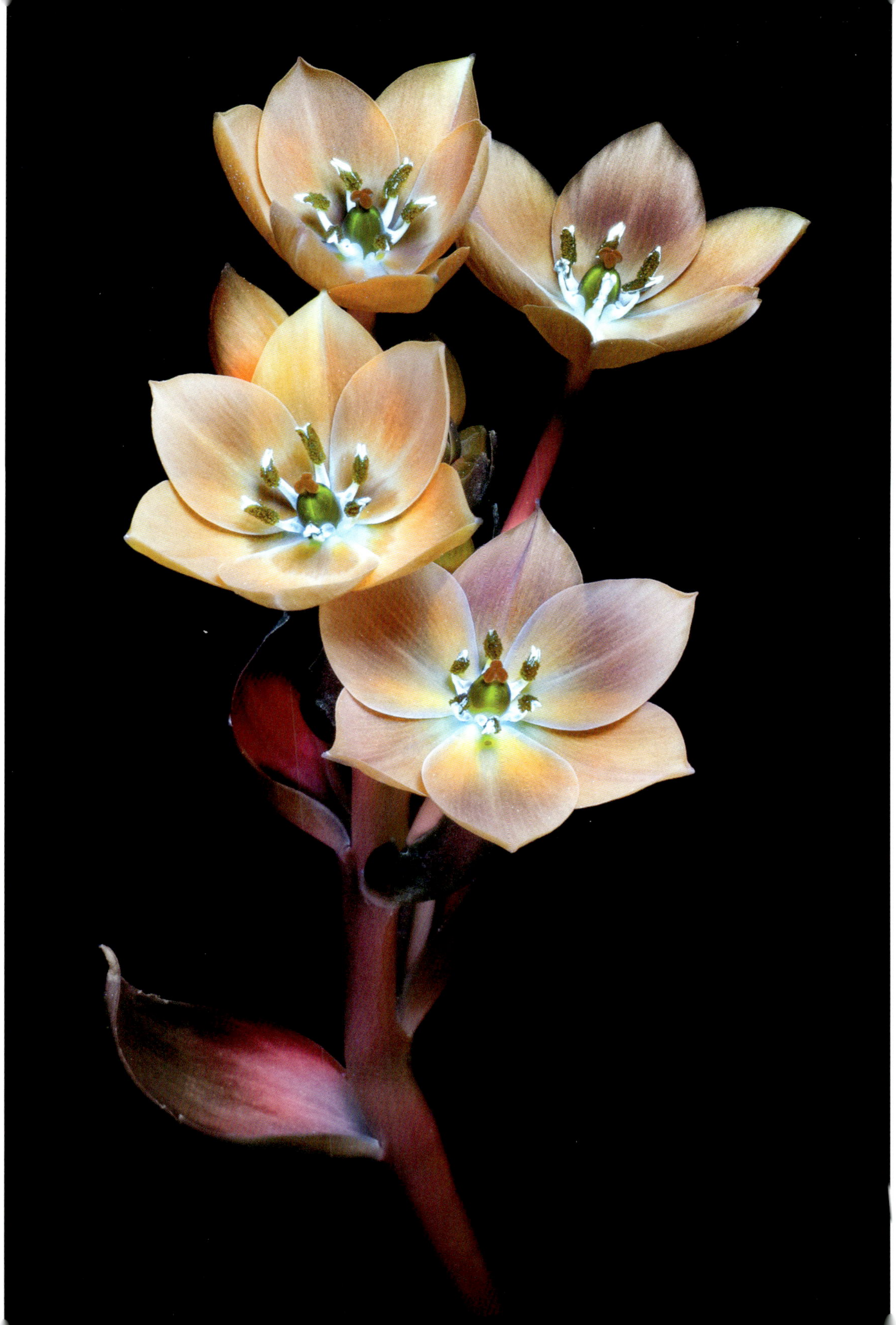

Lumix GX9, Leica DG Macro-Elmarit 45mm F/2.8, F/16 ISO 200 25sec

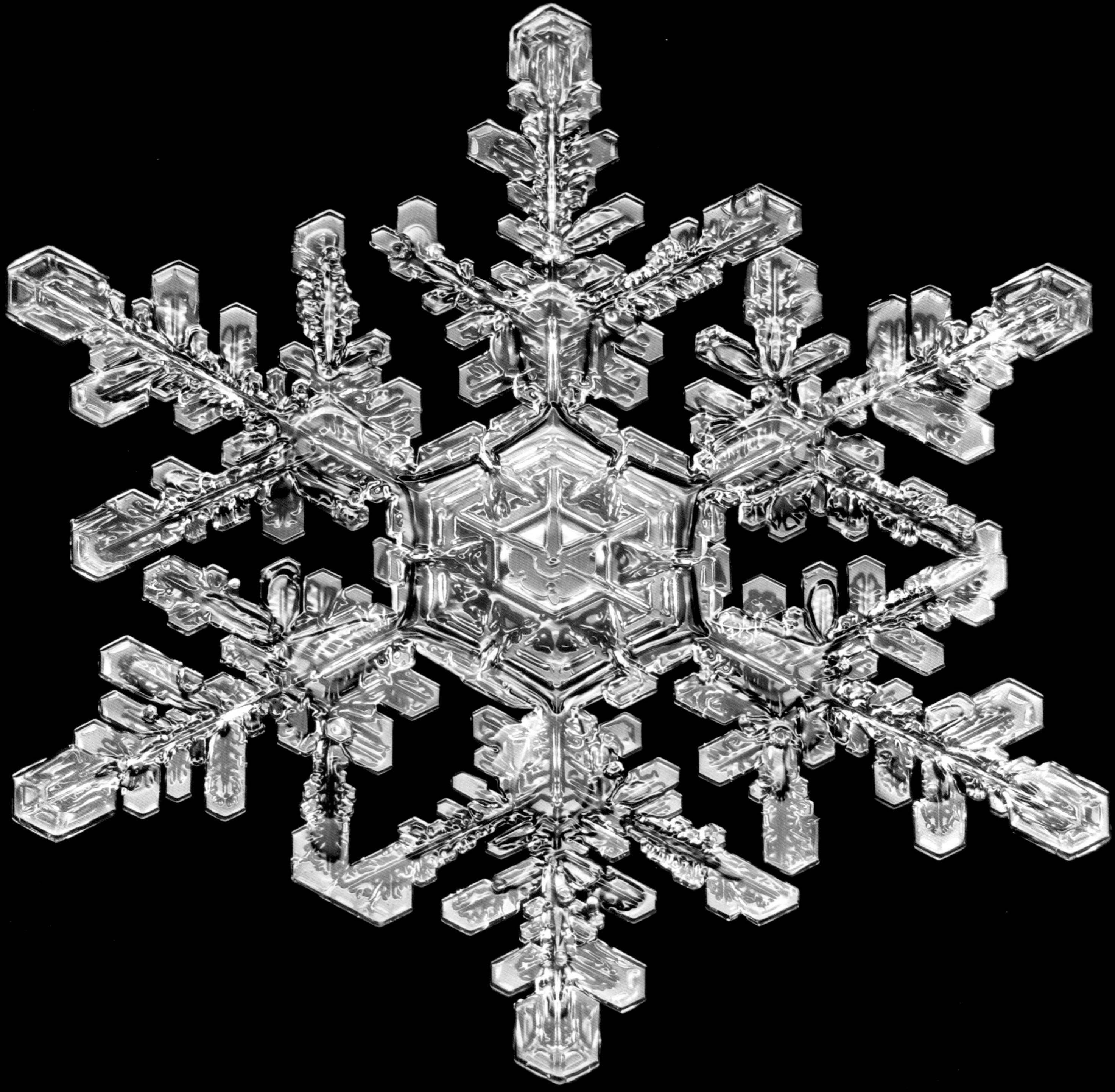

Snowflake Editing Workflow

Focus Stacking

Follow Along:
The files used in the snowflake edit can be found at:
www.universeatourfeet.com/snowflake.zip

Post-production of macro photographs becomes significantly more difficult when focus stacking is required – even more so when the images are shot handheld. A classic example is a snowflake: a seemingly simple subject, however a workflow that can take many additional steps.

As described in the snowflake photography section of the book, the goal is to capture as many focus "slices" as possible while shooting handheld. If you need 40 images to complete a snowflake, you cannot simply take 40 images – what if you needed 45? What if you missed an area of focus across the snowflake? It is a colossal frustration when you capture a beautifully symmetrical snowflake but have missed a large section of detail cutting straight through the middle. No matter how insistent I am that you should drastically overshoot to ensure that you have all the necessary slices, it seems nearly universal that the first time shooting, you'll encounter the annoyance of missing something. It is a lesson that needs to be learned the hard way. Prove me wrong!

For our example snowflake, 286 separate images were taken. In the end, only 45 were used. The last image used in this sequence was the 196th frame captured. Occasionally, it's the second-last frame that is used to complete the focus stacking "puzzle", and the elated feelings from this penultimate image are their own reward. It's quite common for 200-300 images to be taken of a single snowflake, just like this example, and then to sift through the necessary slices in your Digital Asset Manager of choice. For this workflow, we'll be using Adobe® Lightroom®.

The process begins by selecting a single snowflake with focus somewhere close to the center; anything that showcases the overall brightness and colour of the crystal will do. This will be our "starting point", and we can make some basic adjustments to the image that will eventually be copied-and-pasted (or synced) to all of the other focusing slices.

Our goal is to:

- Set a proper white balance
- Raise the brightness as much as possible without over-exposing the highlights
- Sharpen

White Balance
What is the colour of snow? In most cases, it is monochromatic. Grey. Colourless. However, we feel it as cold, often under moonlight that is cooler than sunshine. For this reason, I set my white balance just a bit cooler than neutral. Your preference may vary, and it can always be adjusted afterwards if it is close enough to where it should be. There is no "set value" for this, as it depends on your camera and your light source. That said, you'll find that you can often re-use this setting from one snowflake to another when using the same equipment.

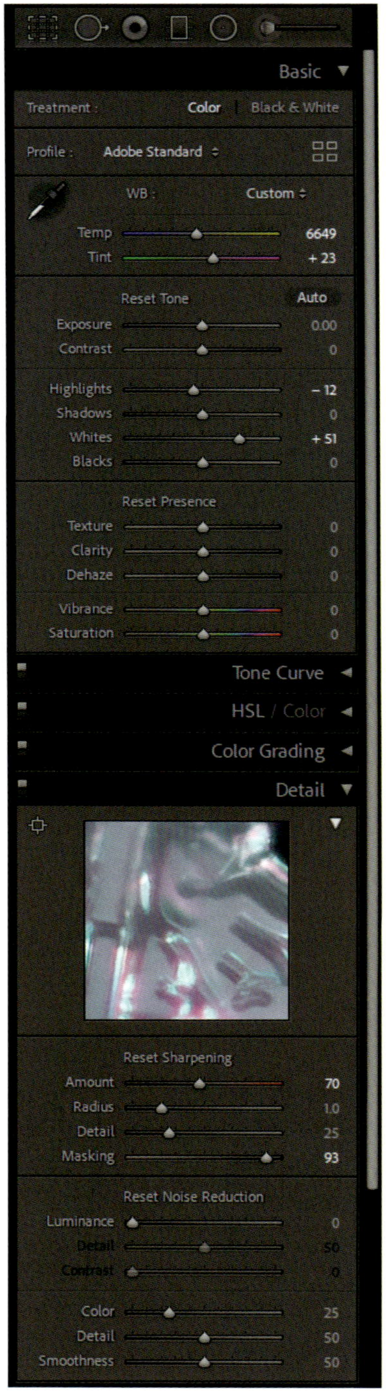

Adjust the Brightness
Most snowflakes are photographed slightly darker, so that there is better ability to recover the highlights. This means there is a two-fold adjustment for brightness: whites and highlights. The whites go up, the highlights come down a little to ensure that the brightest parts of the snowflake are not over-exposed. These areas can often include prism-like colours within the branches, and effort should be given to preserve this "magic".

Final brightness is established at the end of the editing process, but our goal here is simple: brighten the mid-tones without losing the highlights, while also leaving the near-black background dark.

Sharpen
There are countless ways to sharpen an image. I tend to apply a slight bit of sharpening during the RAW processing stage, and then again at the very end of the editing process. Near the beginning, I find that an extreme sharpening amount that is localized around key details is valuable.

A sharpening level of "70" is a great place to start, much higher than average. However, you'll need to take the "masking" slider all the way to 90+. This prevents the background and out-of-focus areas from being needlessly sharpened, which would increase the noise across the image. This type of sharpening adds a slight enhancement to the areas of detail that fall through the slice of focus, but nowhere else.

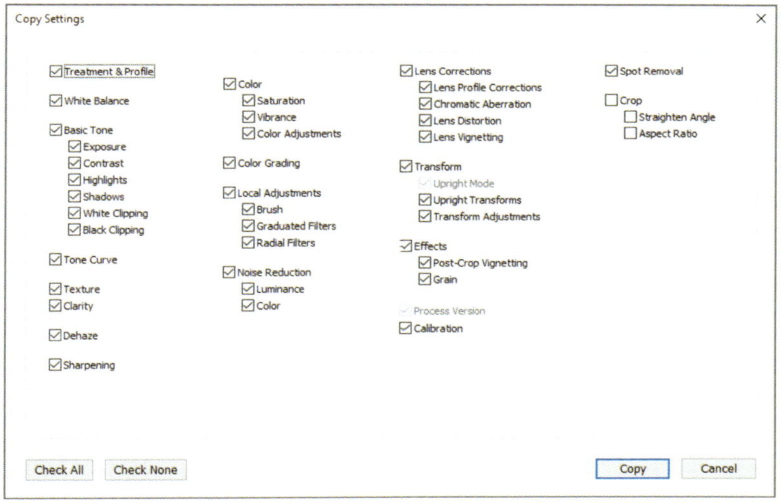

That's it!

You can always push and pull sliders around to your liking, but these are the basic, simple adjustments that happen to a snowflake before the image is sent to Photoshop for our focus stacking efforts. Many more adjustments can be made to put the polish on our image, but only after it is established as a single, completely sharp subject from tip to tip. Press **CTRL+SHIFT+C** (*PC*) or **CMD+SHIFT+C** (*Mac*) to copy your settings from this image. We will paste them to the others once they are selected.

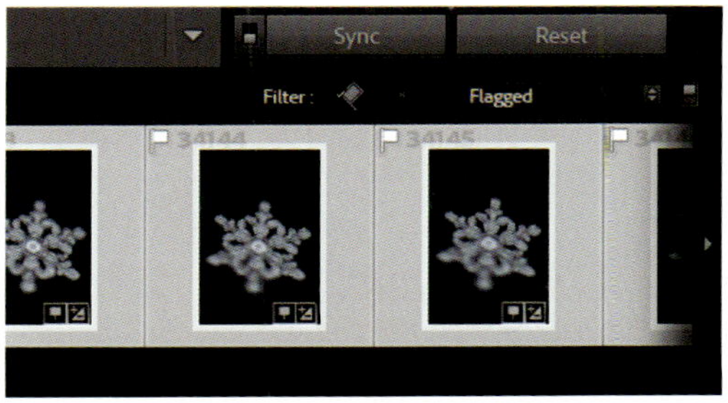

Selection of Slices

We've established adjustments that should work well for all focus slices, so now comes the monotonous task of selecting every slice that needs to be used. And you won't get every slice the first time by memory alone. Start somewhere near the middle, working your way through the images back to the "front" focused part of the snowflake. For every slice of focus you encounter that is not identical to a previous one, press the "**P**" key to flag it as a "pick". Once you've reached the end in one direction, work your way from the middle (your starting point) to the other side of the snowflake. "Pick" every slice of focus that you know you will need, but also remember that you are very unlikely to get every slice needed with this initial pass of selections.

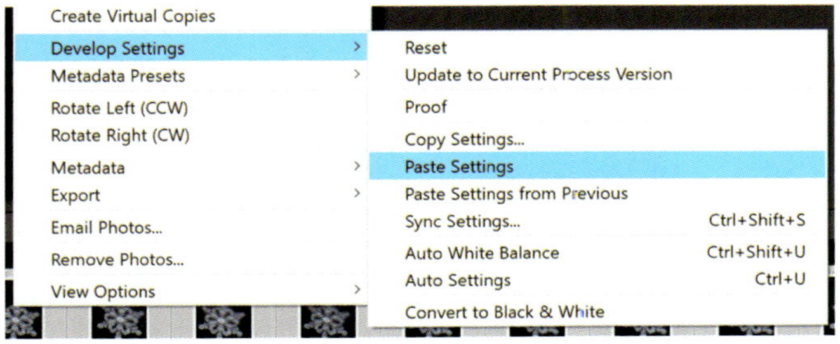

Paste Settings and Move to Photoshop

Once you have made an inexact pick of all needed slices of focus, we need to isolate just the flagged images. In the bottom right corner of the Lightroom interface, you can change the drop-down box from "**Filters Off**" to "**Flagged**" and you should see a set of exclusively the images you flagged with the Pick key. Note that any images flagged with the "**X**" key as rejected would also show up here, which is not part of the workflow.

Click on the first image in the set, hold down the shift key and click on the last image to select them all. Press **CTRL+SHIFT+V** (*PC*) or **CMD+SHIFT+V** (*Mac*) to paste your settings across all images. Sometimes this doesn't stick to all selected images – so the long-form method is to right-click on an image in the film strip, and choose "**Develop Settings > Paste Settings**".

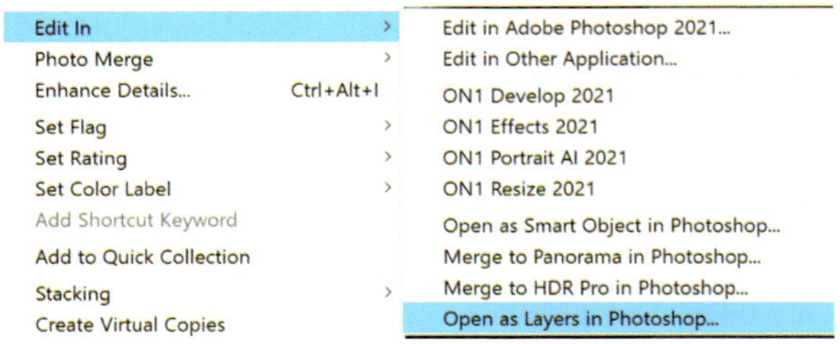

We are now ready to send out images to Photoshop for compositing as a focus stack. This process is equally simple. With all images still selected, right click on one image in the filmstrip and choose "**Edit In > Open as Layers in Photoshop...**". We now leave our experience in Lightroom, for the time being.

Align and Blend

The Focus Stacking process in Photoshop involves two stages:

- Auto-Align Layers
- Auto-Blend Layers

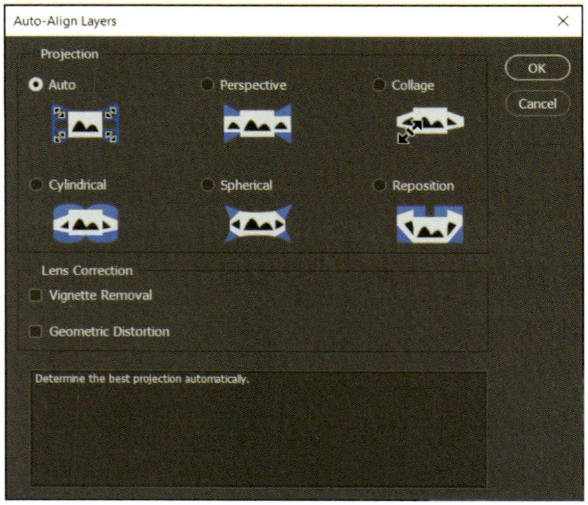

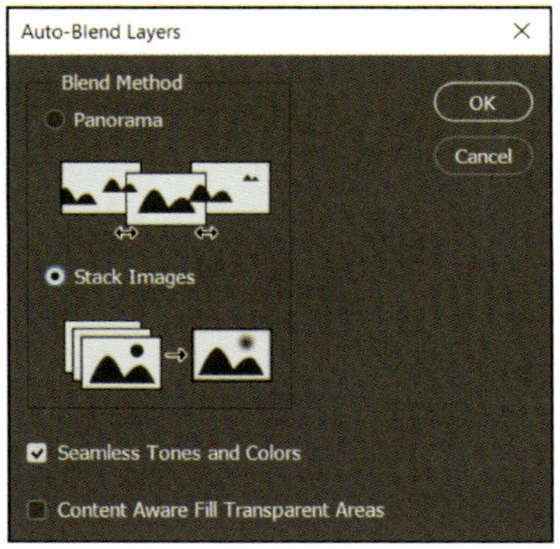

In this initial process, we will get a glimpse at our finished image. It's nearly certain that some slices will be missing, so this process is merely the creation of a map of sorts, to illustrate where the missing pieces will be. The tools can be found under the "Edit" Menu, as "**Edit > Auto-Align Layers...**" followed by "**Edit > Auto-Blend Layers...**"

Note: If you are following along with the sample images, you will not have any missing pieces. Everything is included.

Within both tools, you'll want to keep things as automatic as possible. Within "**Auto-Align Layers**", simply leave it on "**Auto**" with no checkboxes selected (*facing page*). This works well to correct for horizontal, vertical, rotational or perspective shifts that may have occurred between images in the sequence. Photoshop performs better than other focus stacking programs for handheld shooting due to its robust ability to correct for these deviations.

Once the layers have been aligned, we need to blend them together. "**Auto-Blend Layers**" is the tool for this (*facing page*). This feature can also create panoramas, so ensure that "**Stack Images**" is the selected option. As aperture blades in your lens might not be set to identical values between images or your flash power might fluctuate slightly, some of your images can be slightly brighter or darker than others. For this reason, we need the "**Seamless Tones and Colors**" checkbox selected. We do not, however, need to Content Aware Fill the outer transparent areas of the image; these portions of the image will be cropped away later.

Both of these tools can be resource intensive. They will consume a significant amount of computer memory and processing power to complete. The more RAM your computer has, and the faster the processor, the more quickly the progress bars will move. If your computer is older or your images are very high resolution, you might consider taking the dog for a walk while you wait.

When completed, you'll see a larger example of what is depicted (*below*). Almost all in focus! What next?

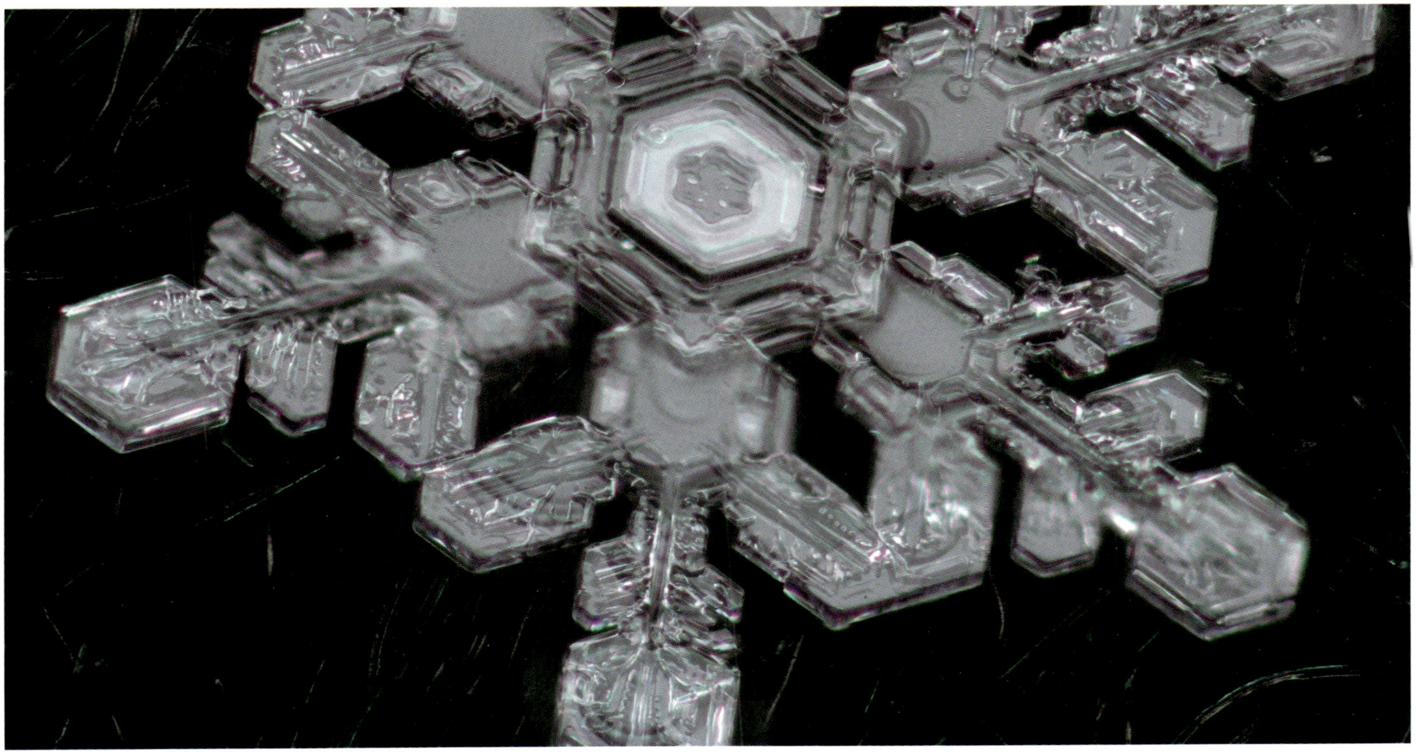

These results (*previous page*) are representative of a "first pass" selection of handheld focus stacking slices. You might get 80% of the needed slices, but some will always evade you. This version of the image is still critically helpful, however; it shows you exactly what slices you are missing.

Head back into Lightroom, and you can search through images taken later in the sequence from secondary "passes" across that particular crystal. Reset your filter to "Filters Off" in the lower right corner. Keep in mind the slices that you are missing, and ensure that there is enough overlap to cover the gaps appropriately. Assuming that you never closed Lightroom, you can simply press "**P**" to pick the missing slices and **CTRL+SHIFT+V** (*PC*) or **CMD+SHIFT+V** (*Mac*) to paste your settings. Do this for every missing slice of focus you encounter (*below*).

The process begins anew, with a slight modification to the progression:

- Select all images that are "flagged"
- Send to Photoshop as Layers
- Auto-Align Layers

Stop there! We need to interject an extra step in the process before we blend our layers for focus stacking.

Photoshop doesn't yield impeccable results. Certain parts of a snowflake, once aligned, don't connect perfectly. This could be due to a number of factors, including perspective corrections or overlapping details. No focus stacking algorithm is perfect, but in Photoshop we have an opportunity to fix the flaws. To do this, we'll need an extra step.

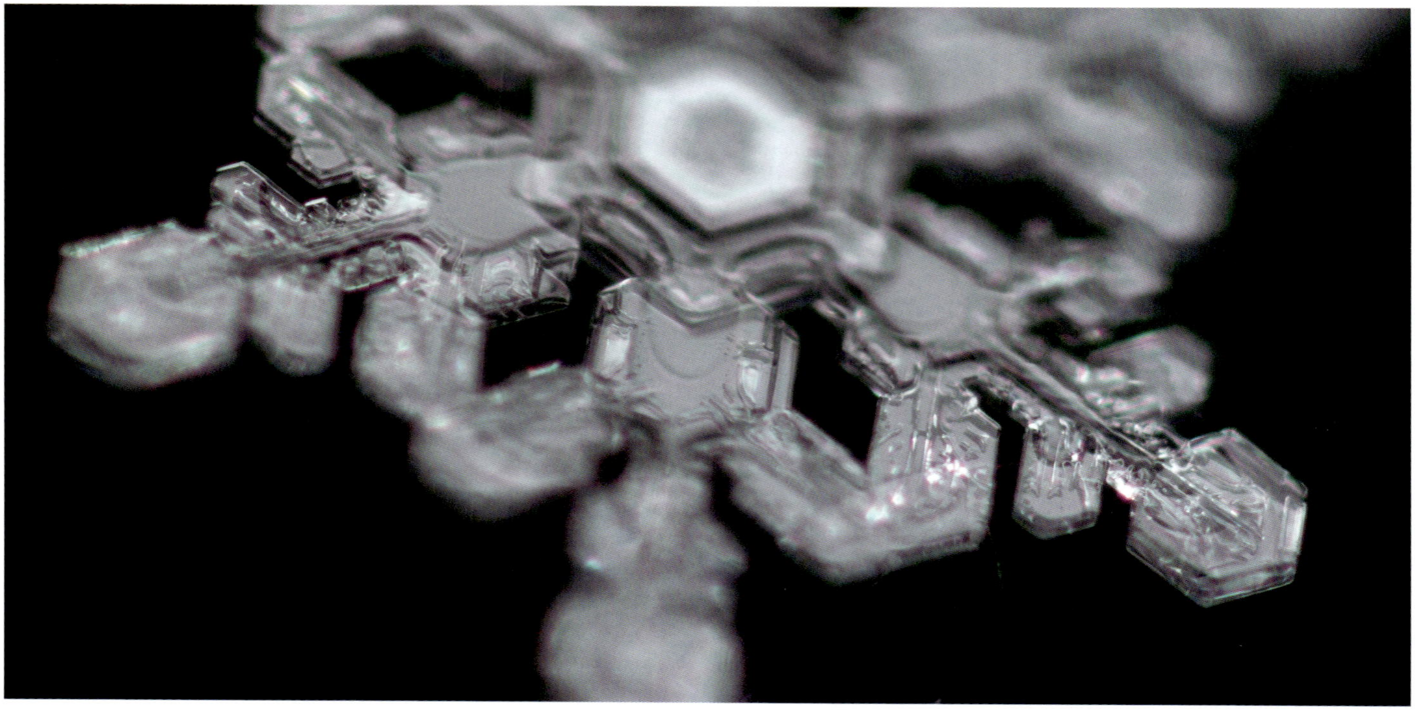

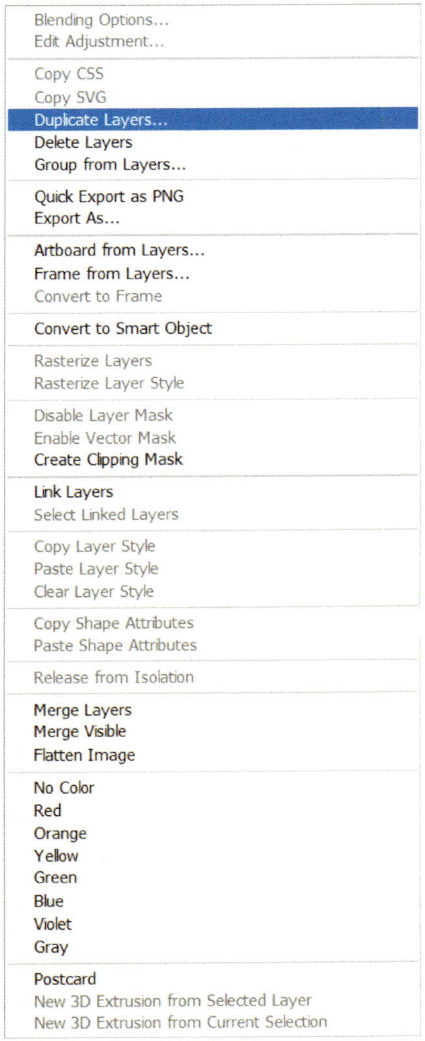

Facing page: This is the main missing slice of focus from the initial focus stacking attempt from memory alone. There may have been more, but this one was critical.

Duplicate Your Layer Stack

By right-clicking on your layers (we assume they are all still selected together after alignment), select "Duplicate Layers". If you had 45 layers previously, you now have 90 – and the duplicate set is selected. Now we continue with our regular routine for blending:

- Auto-blend Layers

Once this is completed, you should see a version of the snowflake with the missing slices of focus revealed. If there are still some areas missing, you might have to repeat this extended process with another trip to Lightroom to find the missing components. We can merge our duplicated stack of layers together, done by the keyboard shortcut **CTRL+E** (*PC*) / **CMD+E** (*Mac*).

This gives us what we need: Photoshop's imperfect attempt at blending all of the layers together, coupled with a completely aligned set of original focus slices. We can use these focus slices to "paint in" fixes using layer masks, allowing for the absolute best results possible.

This process begins by moving the already-blended layer to the very bottom of the layer stack, so that all of our individual slices are on top. Simply turn off the visibility to all of the slice layers so that the only layer visible is our blended image (*below*). This becomes the "foundation" layer that we apply all of our fixes to, working our way up the layer stack one slice at a time.

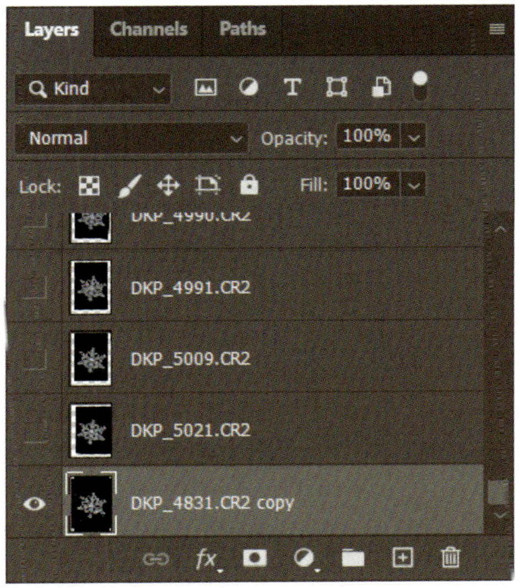

We systematically go through every layer, looking for areas on that particular slice of focus that looks better in the original data than in the Photoshop composite "foundation". To do, select the first layer (in this example, DKP_5021.CR2) and click on the small button at the bottom of the layers panel depicted by a dark circle with a larger brighter rectangle around it. This creates a layer mask, which will allow us to override parts of the foundational image with parts of the slice we care about.

It's important to remember one critical keyboard shortcut here: Invert. You can easily flip the layer mask from white to black to reveal or hide the layer, making it a bit of a game to easily see what parts of the image look better on what layer. This shortcut is **CTRL+I** (*PC*) / **CMD+I** (*Mac*). Get ready for a mental exercise in pattern comparisons:

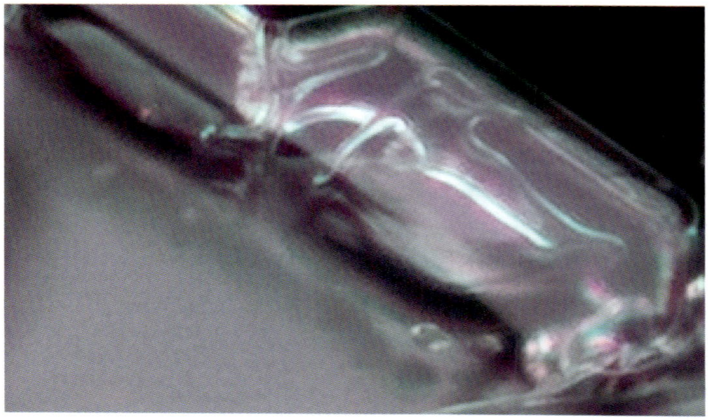

See the difference? In the Photoshop foundation layer (*above*), the reflections from bubbles in the ice are obscured. In our first layer (*below*), they are visible. Simply painting with a soft white brush on a black layer mask will reveal these features.

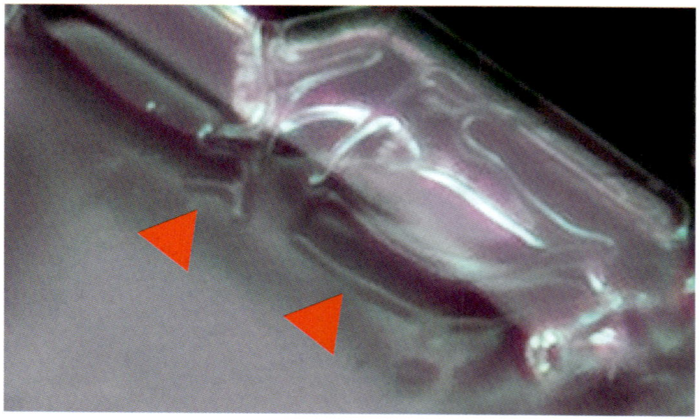

There will be subtle fixes on every layer. Move across the image to find areas to correct, clipping back and forth with the "invert" command to do a quick visual comparison. If you are unfamiliar with layer masks, you might want to study supplemental material for how they operate. If you are a novice with layer masks, this process is a fantastic way to solidify the skills surrounding the concept.

Some layers will have more drastic fixes required. Thankfully they are all mostly minimal on this snowflake. Near the edges you might encounter straight lines of blurriness that shouldn't be there (*above left*). This is caused by the Photoshop algorithm getting confused with the edge of one of the images during alignment. As with the missing reflections, misaligned edges and overlapping problems, you'll likely be able to find a "fix" on at least one layer. In this example, we would likely need a few layers to recover all of the detail in the vertical strip (*above right*). That's fine, since we're going through every layer anyway.

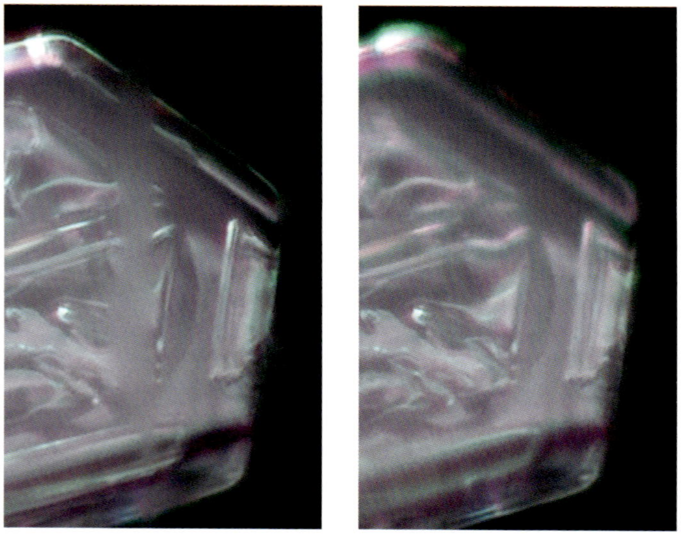

The Long, Boring Process.

Once you get the hang of this process of pattern / detail comparison, it slowly becomes muscle memory. You get accustomed to the process and can focus your mental attention elsewhere during the lengthy process. It usually takes me a few hours to comb over every detail and apply every fix for the average snowflake. During this time, I binge-watch dialogue-driven television shows, listen to podcasts and audio books, or simply chat on the phone. Like my grandmother who used to knit while watching The Price is Right, I too have found boring repetitive activity that eventually results in producing something useful!

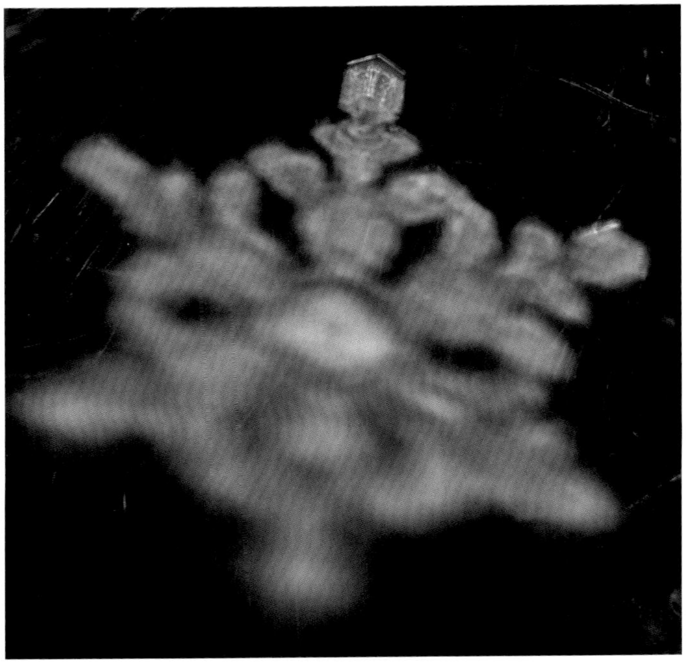

As you work your way through the layers, pay attention to the position of the snowflake, nestled into the fabric of the mitten. One side of the snowflake (in this stack, the top) will be embedded farther into the fabric than the other opposing side (*top*). The background of the focus stacked image, chaotic with mitten fibers, will be generated from the focus slices of the snowflake closest to them. Conversely, the portion of the snowflake farthest away from the background will have a softer, smoother background (*bottom*).

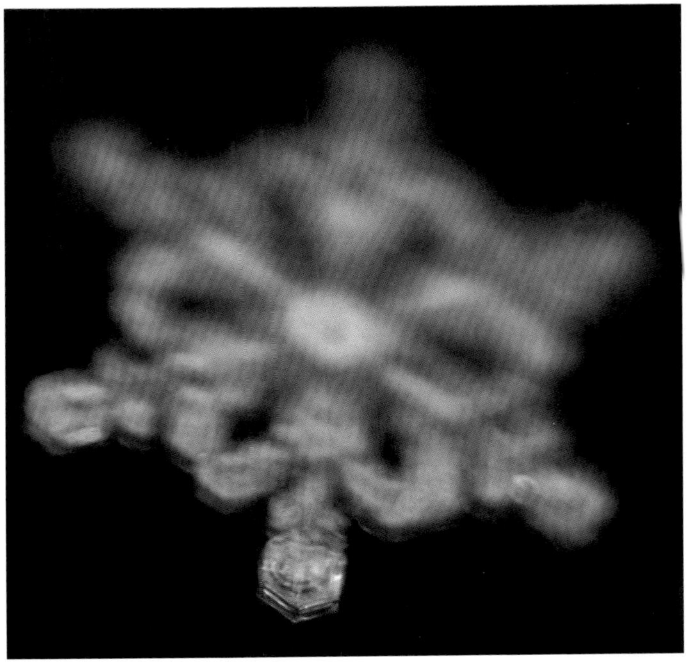

You might have assumed that you were going to need extensive utilization of your cloning and healing tools to achieve a soft background, but there it is! The majority of the black mitten surrounding the snowflake is a nice, soft, just-brighter-than-black blob. As you have been using the layer mask to paint in details of the crystal itself, once you land on the layer of focus furthest away from the background, go ahead and add this to the image.

You'll notice that if you get too close to the most out of focus elements of the snowflake that you cannot get perfect results – the snowflake is so out of focus that its brightness "bleeds" into the background; there's no such thing as a free lunch, at least not entirely. To clean up the persnickety details, you will have to clone them away for pristine results.

For now, however, we're still working through every layer until we reach the very top layer. It is a tedious process towards perfection, yielding a level of comprehensive detail and clarity that automated processes alone cannot yet replicate. How many adjustments are made? Hundreds. You can see a "map" of them (*facing page*) that is overlaid on the front-most layer, just as a visual reference. Once we arrive at the final layer, complete our adjustments, we have reached a milestone.

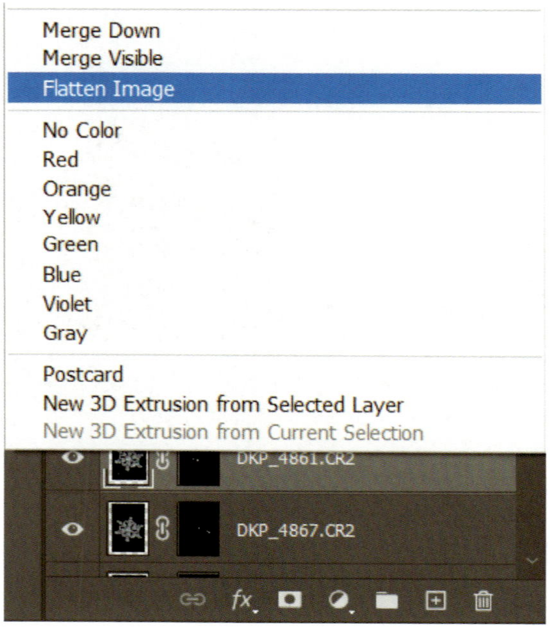

No longer do we need any of these layers as separate entities. Our focus stacking job is done, and this is the point of no return. It's time to flatten the image down to a single layer, and continue our editing with focus stacking no longer a part of the progression. Right-click on the name of any layer in the Layers panel, and select "**Flatten Image**" (*above*). You can breathe a sigh of relief, but it is not yet time to rest on our laurels.

Clean Up and Isolate

The next stage of the process will be critical to the success of the final image: background cleanup. There will still be bits of coarse fibers present in the image, as well as some "glow" of out-of-focus snowflake bits that interfered with our previous attempts to clean things up. The process isn't terribly difficult, just like the layer mask work, but it can be equally as tedious.

Inspect the image and see what remains to be corrected (*below*). You'll notice the elements that I've described, and we'll need to get acquainted with our cloning and healing tools at this stage.

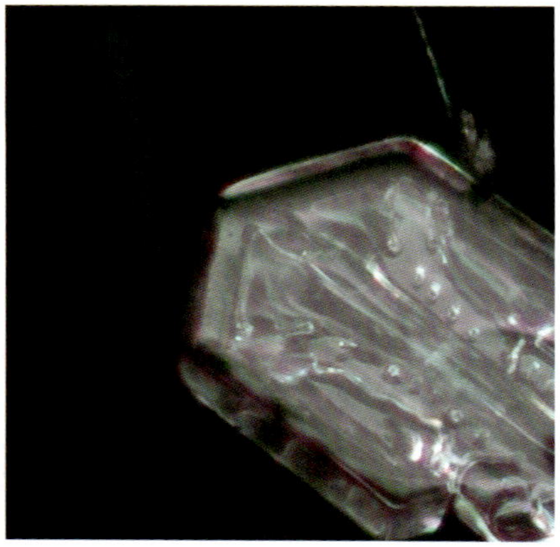

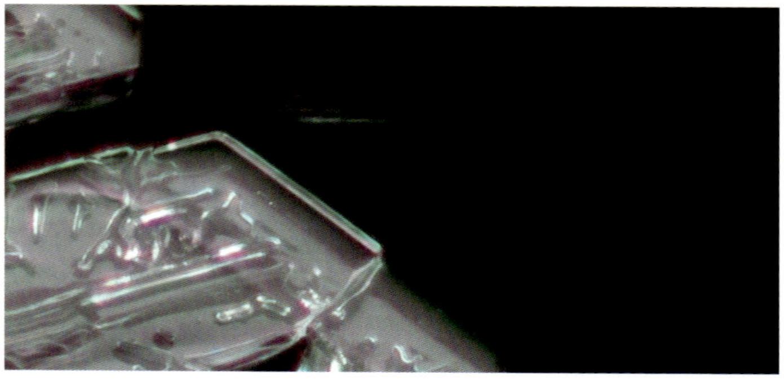

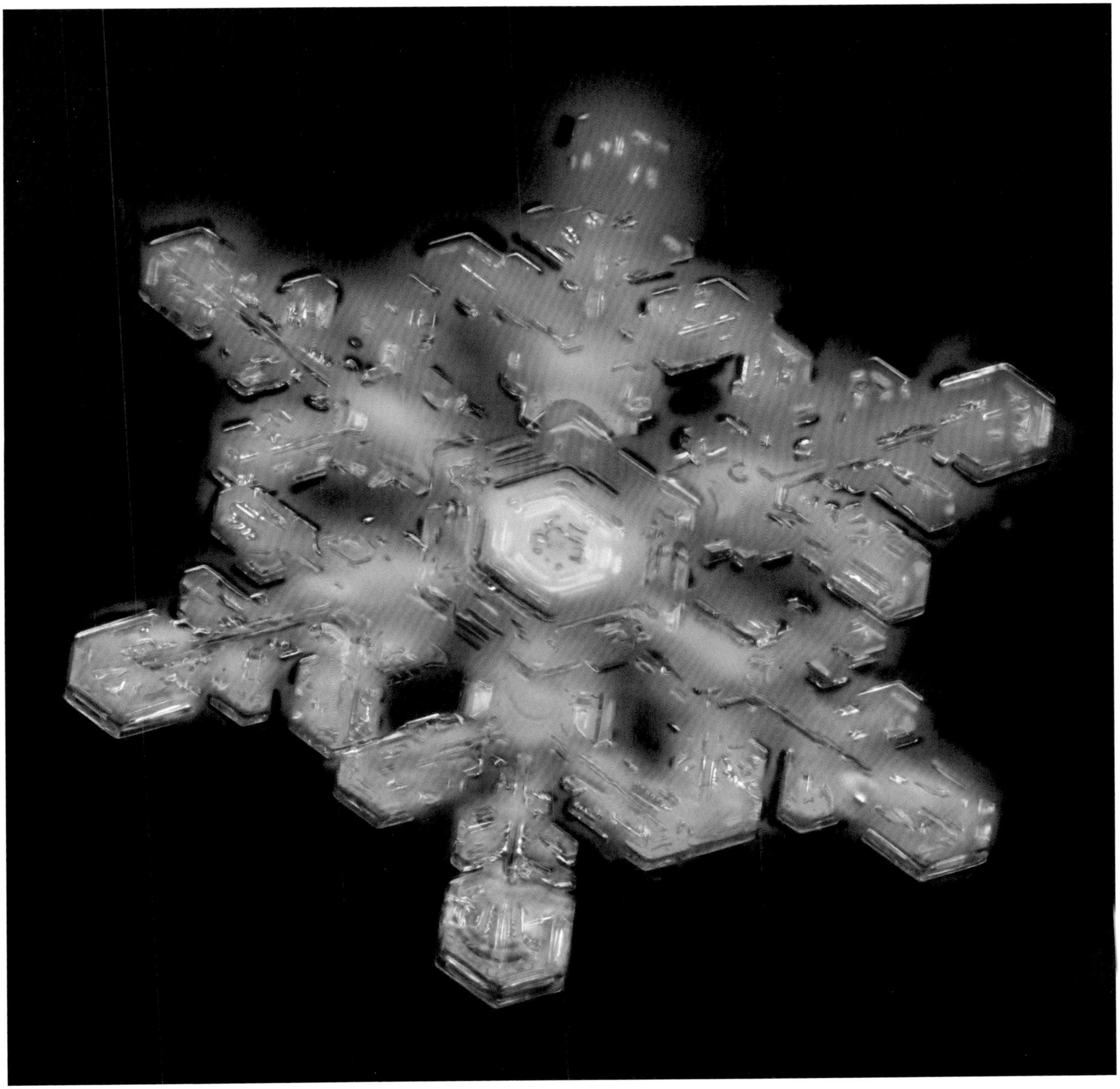

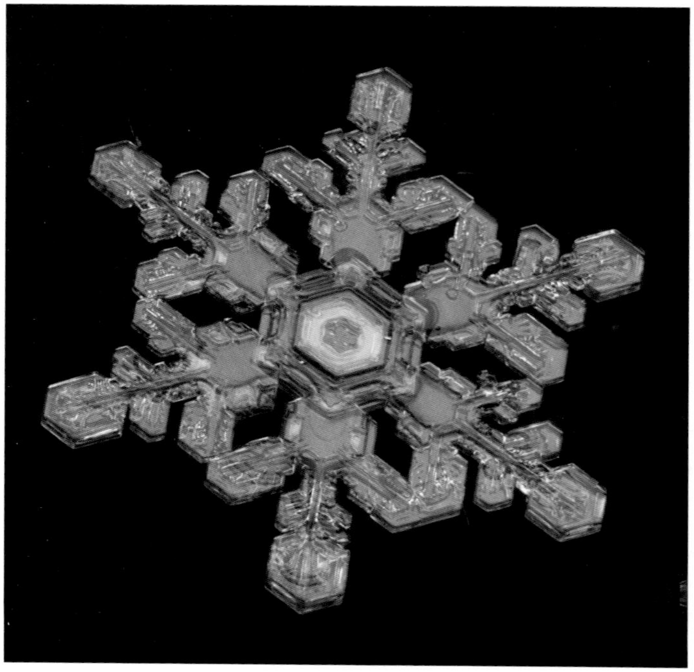

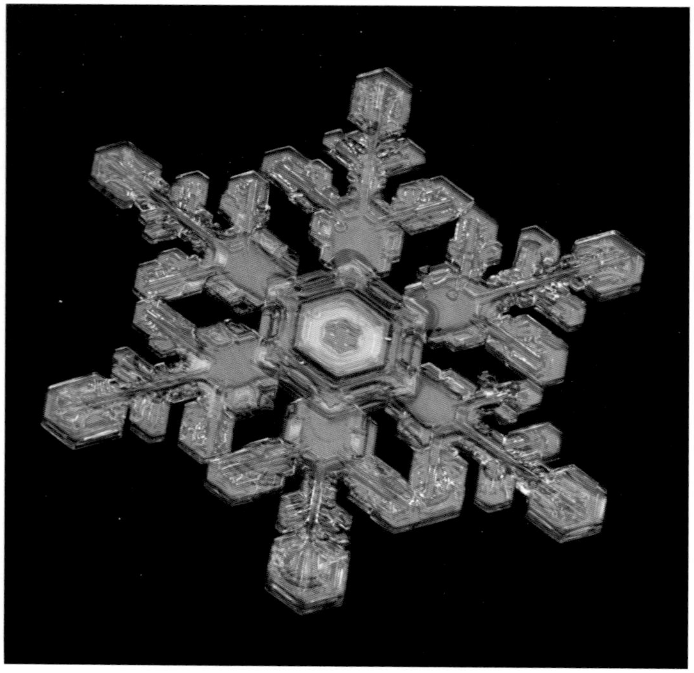

Using the **Healing Brush** tool, sample from one vaguely undetailed part of the background and cover up any elements you'd like to remove. Remember not to get too close to the edges of the snowflake with this tool, as its default configuration will cause a shift in brightness of the background when you get too close. For the fine detail work right close to the crystal, use the old fashioned **Clone Stamp** tool.

This tutorial cannot hope to cover the full exploration of these tools. Your mileage will vary based on your skills and past experience. At the very least, this becomes a fantastic sandbox of sorts to explore the ways you can clean a background of an image.

And yes, there are easier ways. You can just make the background solid black. Another technique would be to take an out-of-focus image of the mitten and just replace the background – something I have had to do on numerous occasions when there was not enough "clean" areas of the background in any one frame. You can even sample data from another snowflake image, or digitally generate it. That said, I try to be as genuine to the source material as possible.

In this example, the pixels are all from the original set of focus stacking slices, just massaged and moved where needed to make the background pristine.

The image (*left*) was the best that could be achieved with the layer masking from the original input material. It's not bad, but there are still a few areas that needed careful attention. The result (*right*) attends to that, and we've got an image cropped and fitted for the next challenges. They include colour correction, detail enhancement, and adjustments to brightness and contrast before we can say we're finished. We're now at the polishing stage, and the finish line is in sight.

Cleaning Up Colour

The Canon MP-E 65mm F/2.8 1x-5x Macro lens is a very sharp lens, but it begins to show its age when you notice the chromatic aberration presented in these snowflakes. Intense Cyan/Green and Magenta/Pink can be seen all across the contours of this crystal. Nearly every image editing program has tools to deal with colour fringing, but these colours are beyond fringes. They encompass the majority of the colour in the image. We cannot use conventional means, but that doesn't mean we cannot solve the problem.

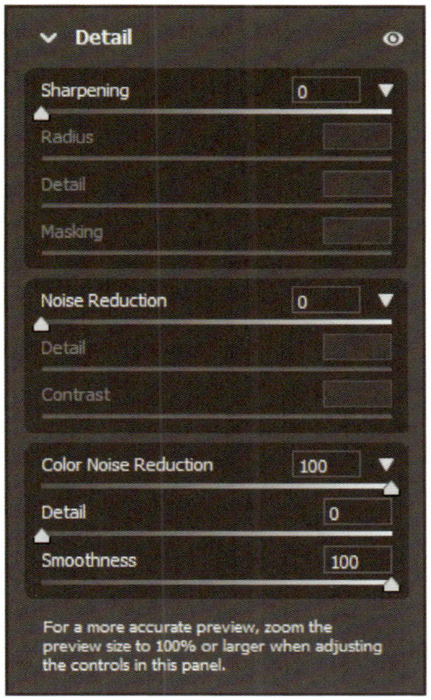

Duplicate your image to a new layer, then run the Camera Raw Filter. This can be easily found under "**Filters > Camera Raw Filter...**" or by pressing **CTRL+SHIFT+A** (*PC*) / **CMD+SHIFT+A** (*Mac*). Under the Detail panel, we have the ability to remove colour noise. Crank the settings to the maximum:

- Color Noise Reduction to 100
- Detail to 0
- Smoothness to 100

This will attempt to remove all colour from the image that deviates from the baseline of subtle blue-grey. And it works! You might even want to re-run the Camera Raw Filter by pressing **ALT+CTRL+F** (*PC*) / **CTRL+CMD+F** (*Mac*) for even "cleaner" results. The problem with this technique is that it will remove ALL colour from the snowflake, and some of it might be wanted. This is why we are working on a duplicate layer.

Create a layer mask for this new colourless layer. We are going to reduce the effect of it where we want some colour to still show through, giving a little bit of liveliness back to the crystal. This is especially true for areas that would have contained orange or blue colours, or areas around the brightest prismatic parts of the crystal. The approach here, however, is slightly unintuitive.

First, invert your layer mask with **CTRL+I** (*PC*) / **CMD+I** (*Mac*) so the mask is black – revealing your original colours. Paint with a white brush to hide any of the colours you eventually want to reveal. Once complete, invert the mask back! It can be difficult to see where the colours worth preserving are located if they have already disappeared, so this mask inverting technique allows for you to visualize things properly.

In the end, I still let some of the chromatic aberration back in by setting this layer to an opacity of roughly 75%. Otherwise, the results look too monochromatic. Dial this in at your preferred percentage. You can then press **CTRL+E** (*PC*) / **CMD+E** (*Mac*) to merge the layers together.

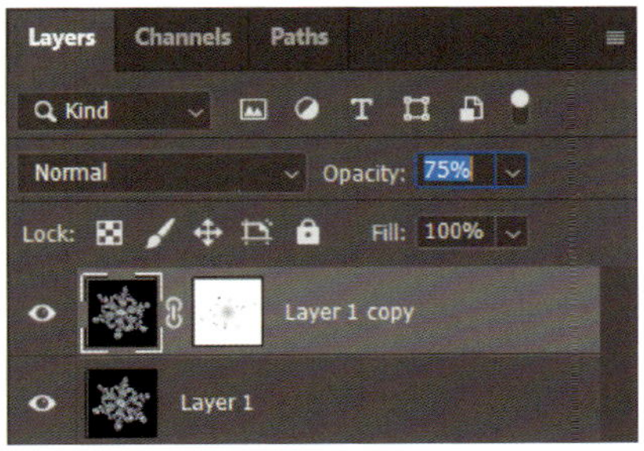

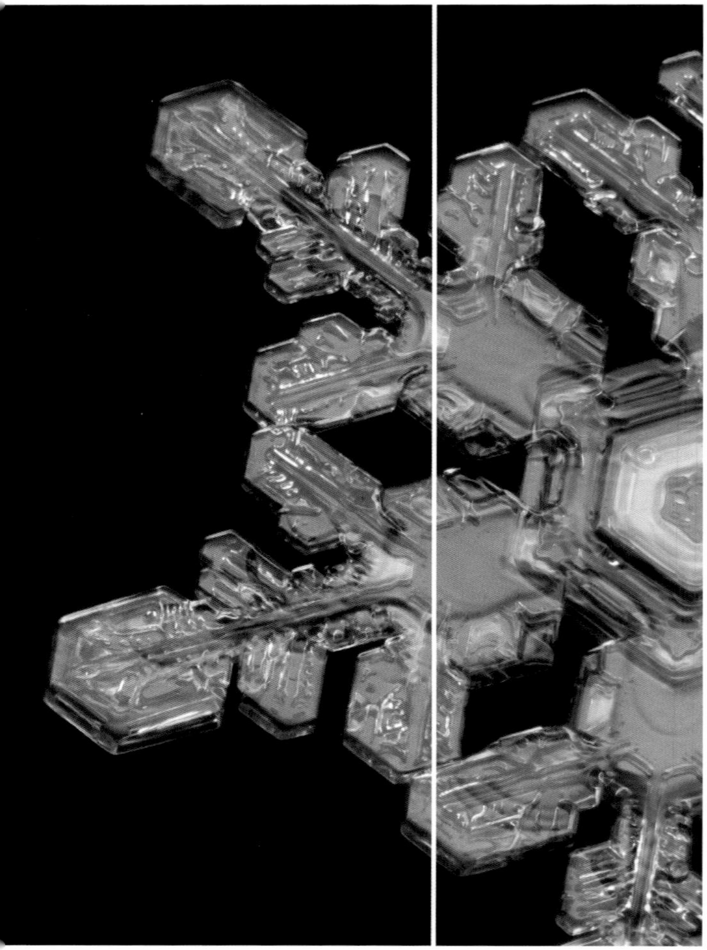

Above: A split-image of the edits on the previous pages. The left side depicts the snowflake with chromatic aberrations present. The right side has mitigated the unwanted colours.

Once we have the colour the way we want it on the snowflake, what about the background? Initial adjustments of the white balance would have also affected the background. As dark as it is, there is still some level of non-neutral colour present. It might be barely perceptible, but if you desaturate the background it will make the snowflake appear slightly "cooler" without actually changing its colour temperature.

Masking Out the Snowflake

Tools to isolate a subject from its background are improving at a rapid pace. By the time you read this, it might be even easier than it is when this book is published. Because this technology is evolving so quickly, let's take a simple, basic approach to separating the snowflake from the background.

First, we need to duplicate our layer again. On this duplicated layer, we need to convert it to black and white, and introduce an extreme levels adjustment to turn the image solid white and black – effectively creating a "mask".

Since we've been duplicating layers, it might be a helpful bonus to learn that keyboard shortcut as well: **CTRL+J** (*PC*) / **CMD+J** (*Mac*). I have no clue why the "J" key was chosen to "duplicate", but there you have it.

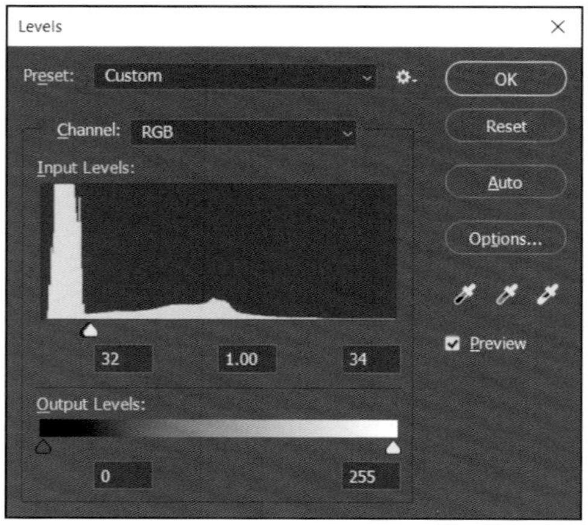

To make our new layer monochrome, use the tool found at "**Image > Adjustments > Black & White**". There isn't a need to play with these sliders much – it is just a temporary step. The real magic comes when you use the Levels adjustment: "**Image > Adjustments > Levels...**"

Here, we need to ride a thin line. We need to move the black out and white point right next to each-other, at precisely the ideal marker where the background is solid black but the majority of the snowflake is solid white. This varies for every image. There will always be some elements that spill over from one side to the other; for a simple crystal like this, we can fine tune the shape with a hard brush set to white or black.

Again, there are more modern ways to do this – but the old fashioned ways are easier to illustrate.

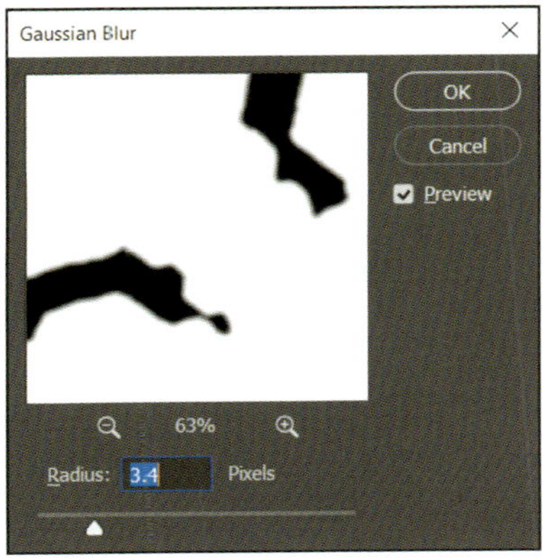

Once fully separated, we need to blur the edges slightly so that the application of this mask is less obvious. This is easily achieved with a "**Filter > Blur > Gaussian Blur...**" filter with a value set between 3 and 4.

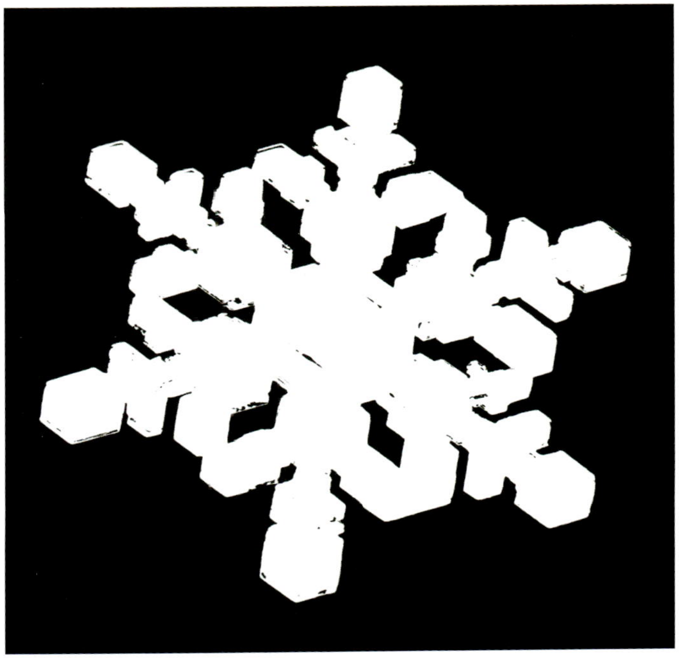

Above: Results of extreme levels adjustment.
Below: Completed mask, cleaned up and slightly blurred.

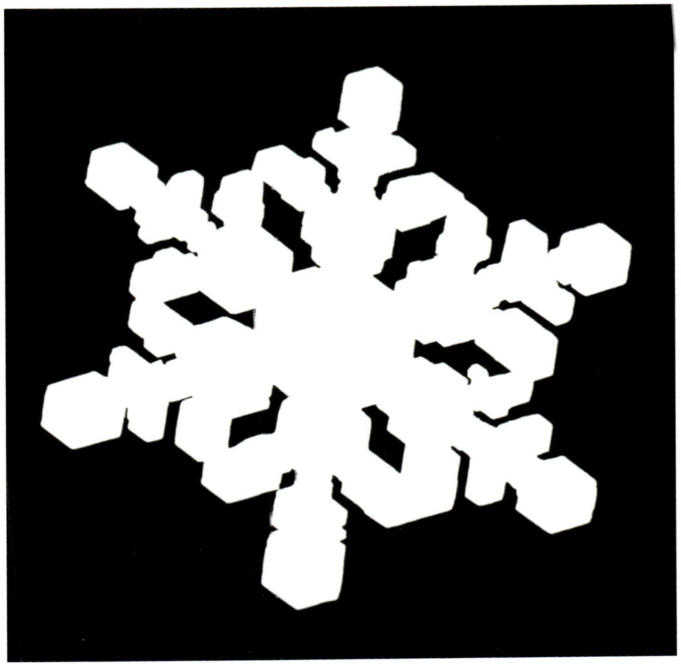

Monochromatic Background

This may seem like an intense amount of effort for just a monochrome background, but the mask will also be invaluable for more polishing edits. The first of which is the background clean-up: Create a **Hue / Saturation Adjustment Layer** in the Adjustments Panel, slide the saturation to -100, and copy/paste the mask onto the layer.

To do this, you'll need to have the mask layer selected, and press **CTRL+A** (*PC*) / **CMD+A** (*Mac*) to select the entire area of the image, then **CTRL+C** (*PC*) / **CMD+C** (*Mac*) to copy it. To paste into a layer mask, we need to first hold down the **ALT key** (*PC*) / **Option Key** (*Mac*) and then click on the mask. Then to paste, it's **CTRL+V** (*PC*) / **CMD+V** (*Mac*). Quite a bit of keyboard ballet, but the mask is in place.

But wait, it's inverted! The colour is being removed from the snowflake because it's white, while the background is black. To invert the mask, simply have it selected and press **CTRL+I** (*PC*) / **CMD+I** (*Mac*).

Mission accomplished.

Texture and Structure

Almost every snowflake needs enhancements to structure and texture. As with the fluorescing flower and with most images, I explore the "Structure" slider in ON1 Photo RAW, though the "Texture" slider in the Camera Raw Filter behaves in a similar fashion. Try both if you have ON1 Photo RAW available, or whatever future software you choose.

These adjustments are all to taste. Just remember that you'll want to make the adjustments on a duplicated layer so that you can apply the mask such that it will only apply to the snowflake and not the background. Far too many times I see the out-of-focus background over-processed and it detracts from the main subject. This applies to all macro images, no exclusivity to snowflakes.

Our goal here is to make the features of the snowflake stand out from the middle-grey tones that dominate the image: bubbles in the ice, shadows, surface features, multiple layers, edge details and more. This can be overdone. We're not looking for an artificial look, just a little enhancement of these features.

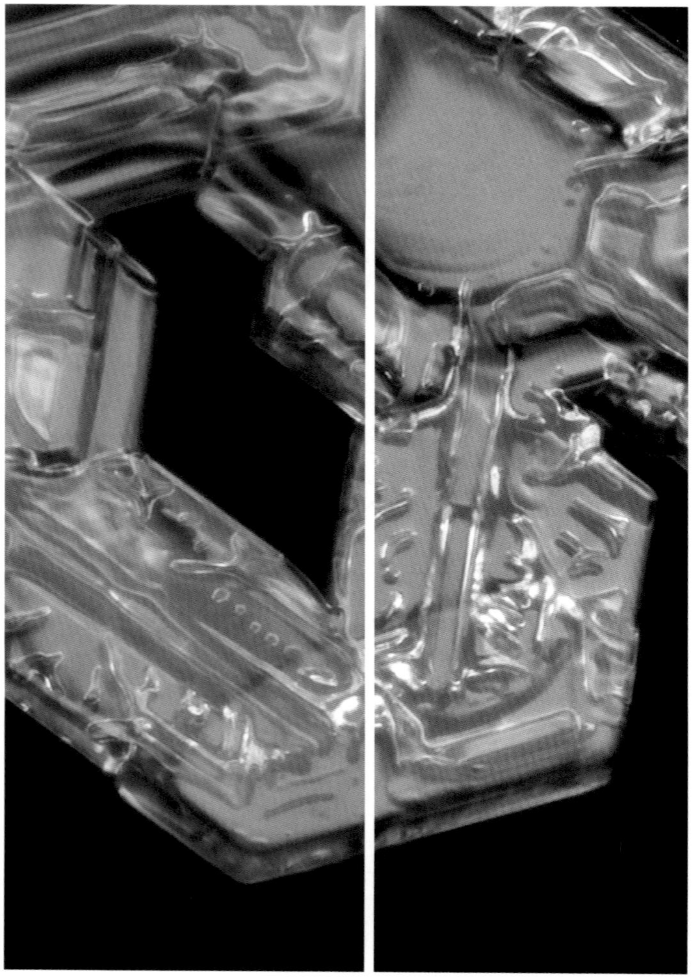

Original   Structure 75%

Ensure that you merge your enhancement down back to your original snowflake layer once completed. This step is necessary after each additional enhancement you want to make. Wer're very near the finish line - so close that you could call the image completed if you're happy with the results.

Crisping the Edges
Not a technique used with all snowflakes, but enhancing out the outer footprint of the crystal can sometimes help it appear to jump off the screen or the print. This is done with – you guessed it – a duplicate layer.

Run this duplicate layer through the Camera Raw Filter as previously described, this time with a grungy adjustment via the Clarity slider and a push on the highlights. You might also want to apply a small amount of noise reduction here, to calm things down:

- Highlights: +30
- Clarity: +70
- Noise Reduction: +25

Since this is done on a new layer, create a layer mask, invert it, and then apply it with a small brush narrowly around the edges of the snowflake. This gives a bit of extra "pop".

The Final Adjustments
For most purposes, we're done. However, there are a few things to consider before patting yourself on the back.

The brightness of the snowflake and of the background are always adjusted at the end. If you set the canvas surrounding the image in Photoshop to black, you can judge just how dark the background is. This is done by right-clicking anywhere outside of the image in Photoshop on the grey area beyond the edges of the frame, and choosing "Black" from the list. Use a Levels adjustment to pull the black point a few notches if desired. The same can be done by setting the canvas to white – we need to choose "Custom" from the list, after having set the custom colour to white. It's common that I will nudge the brightness up 5 or so points on a "Brightness and Contrast" adjustment.

You might revisit the colour and saturation across the snowflake. You might be finicky about the background if the background cloning needs to be fixed up. If you've spent enough time on a snowflake as I have, you give a good "once over".

As previously described in the fluorescing flower edit, a bit of sharpening that utilizes the high-pass filter is the icing on the cake. ***And voila!***

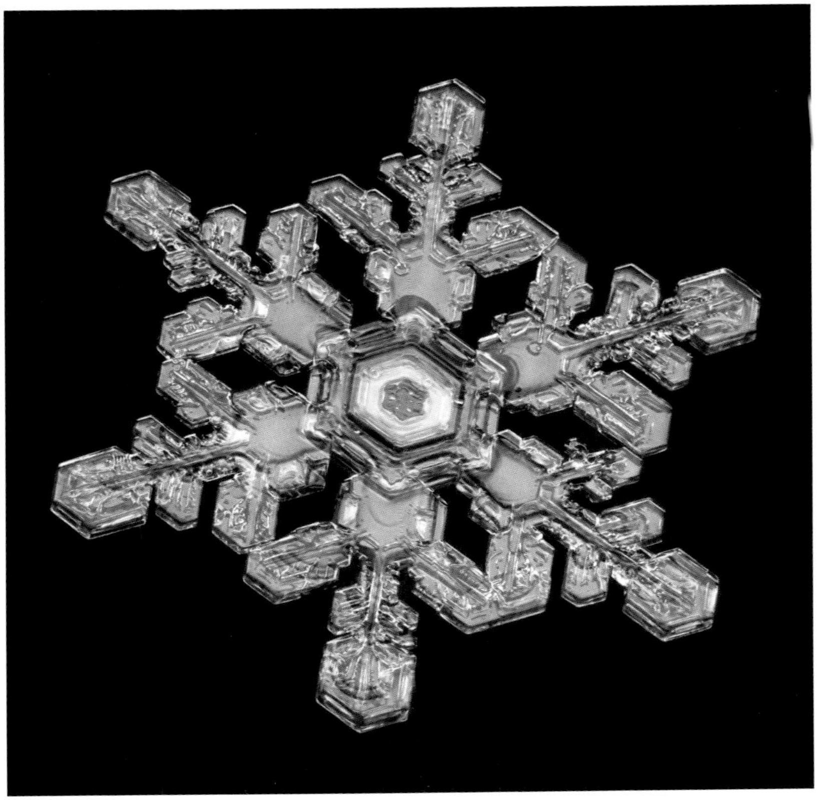

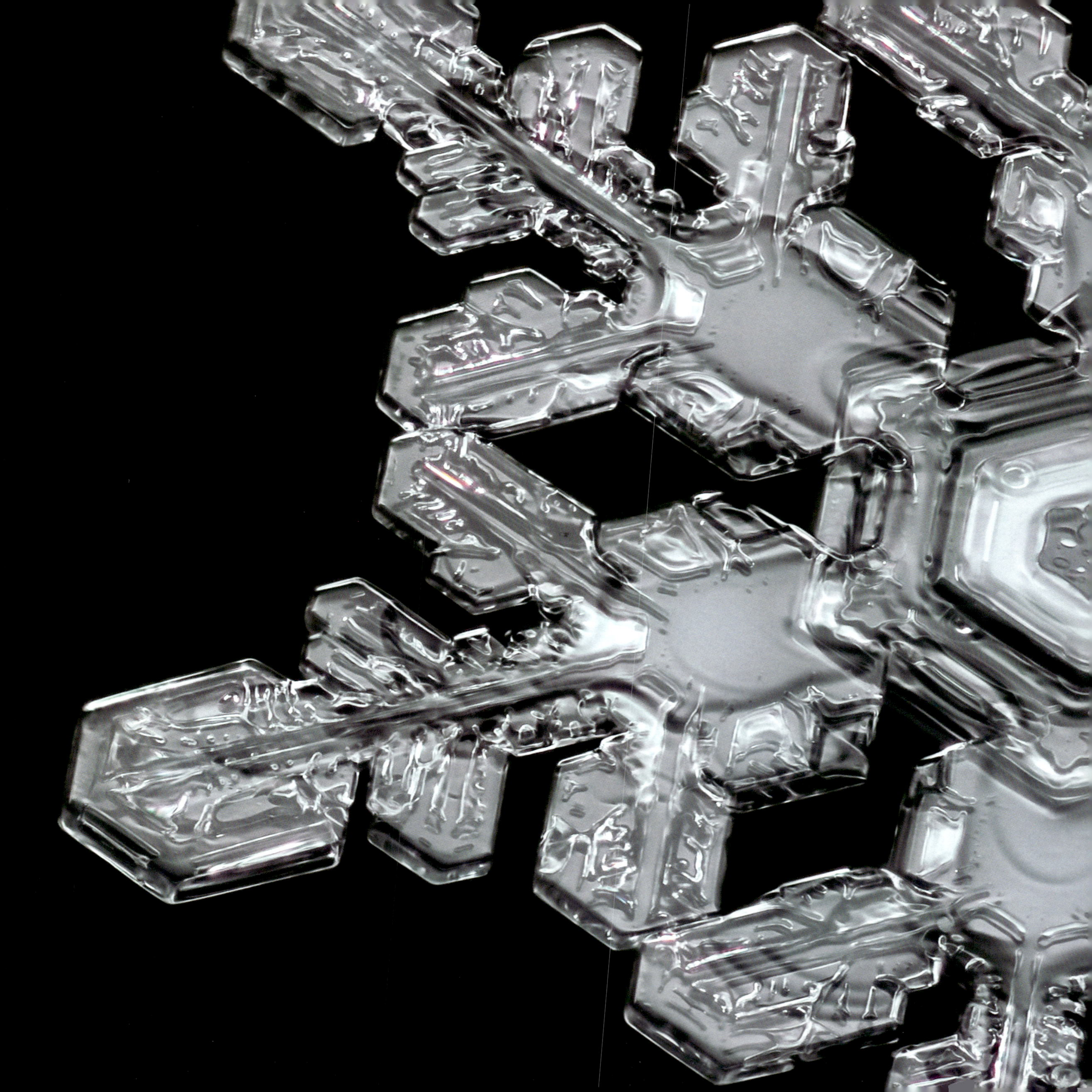

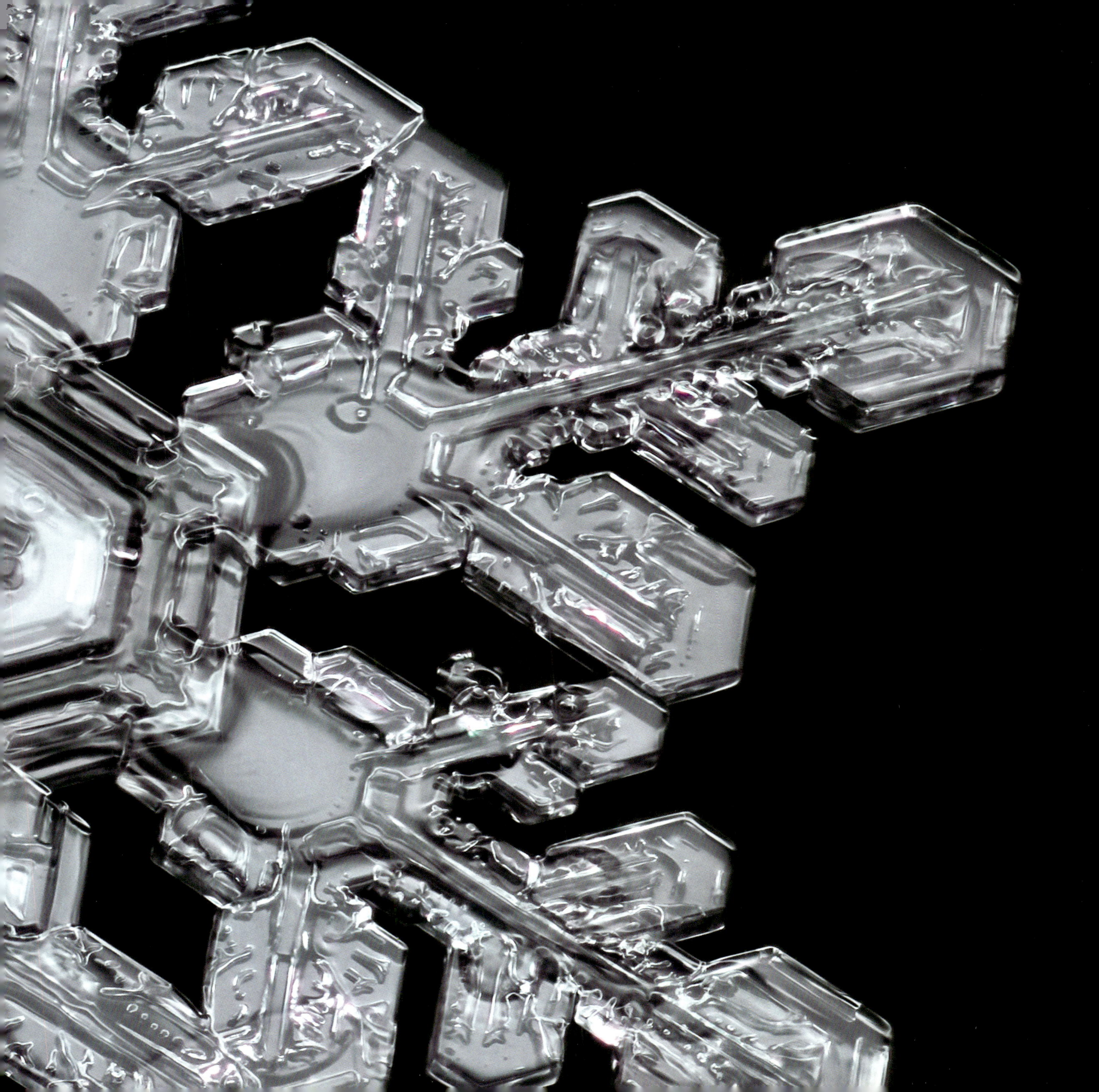

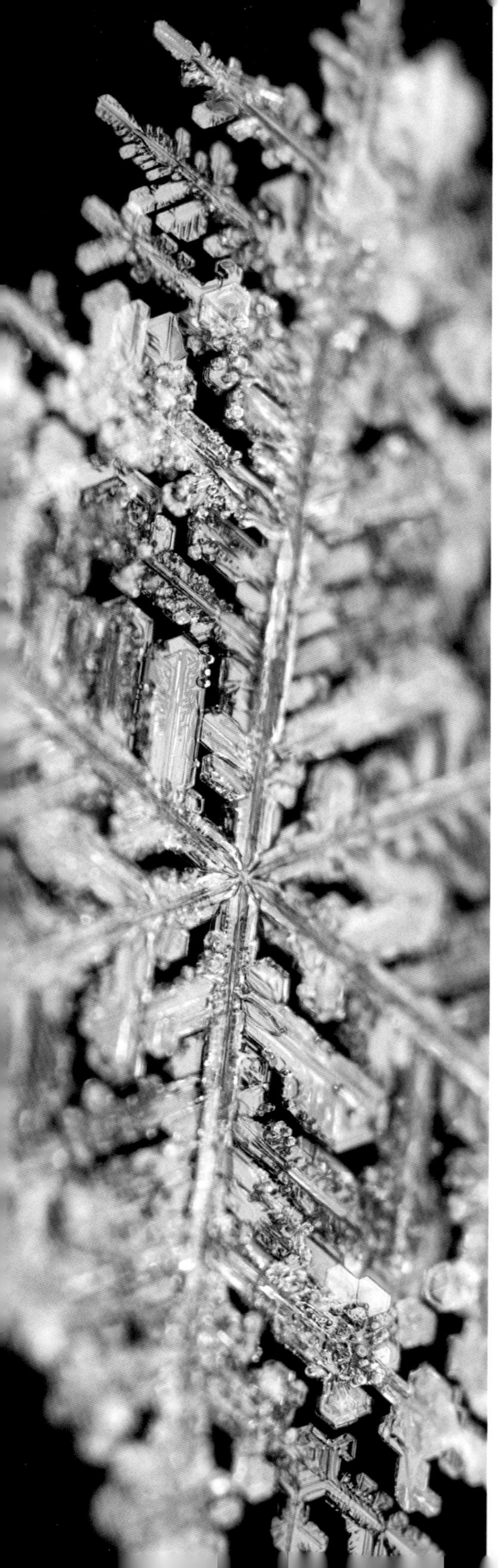

Summarizing a Snowflake
There it is – the entire process of editing a snowflake from raw focus slices to a final image. The average time to edit a snowflake, after having done hundreds of them, remains roughly four hours. There are plenty of steps involved, but it boils down to a few core components:

- Selecting all the relevant slices with the aid of a "map" of the missing pieces.
- Using Photoshop to create a "foundation" layer.
- Painting in fixes to that layer that are required.
- Background clean-up and enhancements.

Every snowflake is different. The crystal in this example workflow is an "easy" one, without any significant issues to deal with. There were no overlapping areas, everything aligned fairly well, and there were no fibers of the mitten that needed to be edited out from immediately underneath the crystal surface. In some images, the process is more akin to "snowflake surgery".

That said, there is still beauty in a single slice of focus from a snowflake (*left*). We don't need to go through this arduous progression of increasing depth and detail. We can just enjoy it for what it is: natural and fleeting beauty that we rarely see with our own eyes.

Glutton for Punishment
Was this snowflake too easy for you? Want to see what a truly challenging snowflake would present you with? This image (*facing page*) was nearly a disaster. The slices did not perfectly line up. There are multiple snowflakes overlapping, and even branches of the main snowflake that overlap the others. The background was a mess.

In addition to all that, it was photographed with a Panasonic Lumix S1R, yielding 47 megapixels images, and it's a stack of 56 images. I've occasionally joked that I've been losing my sanity one snowflake at a time; this image is the epitome of that statement.

Try for yourself! The files for this snowflake can be downloaded at:
www.universeatourfeet.com/complex.zip - but don't say I didn't warn you.

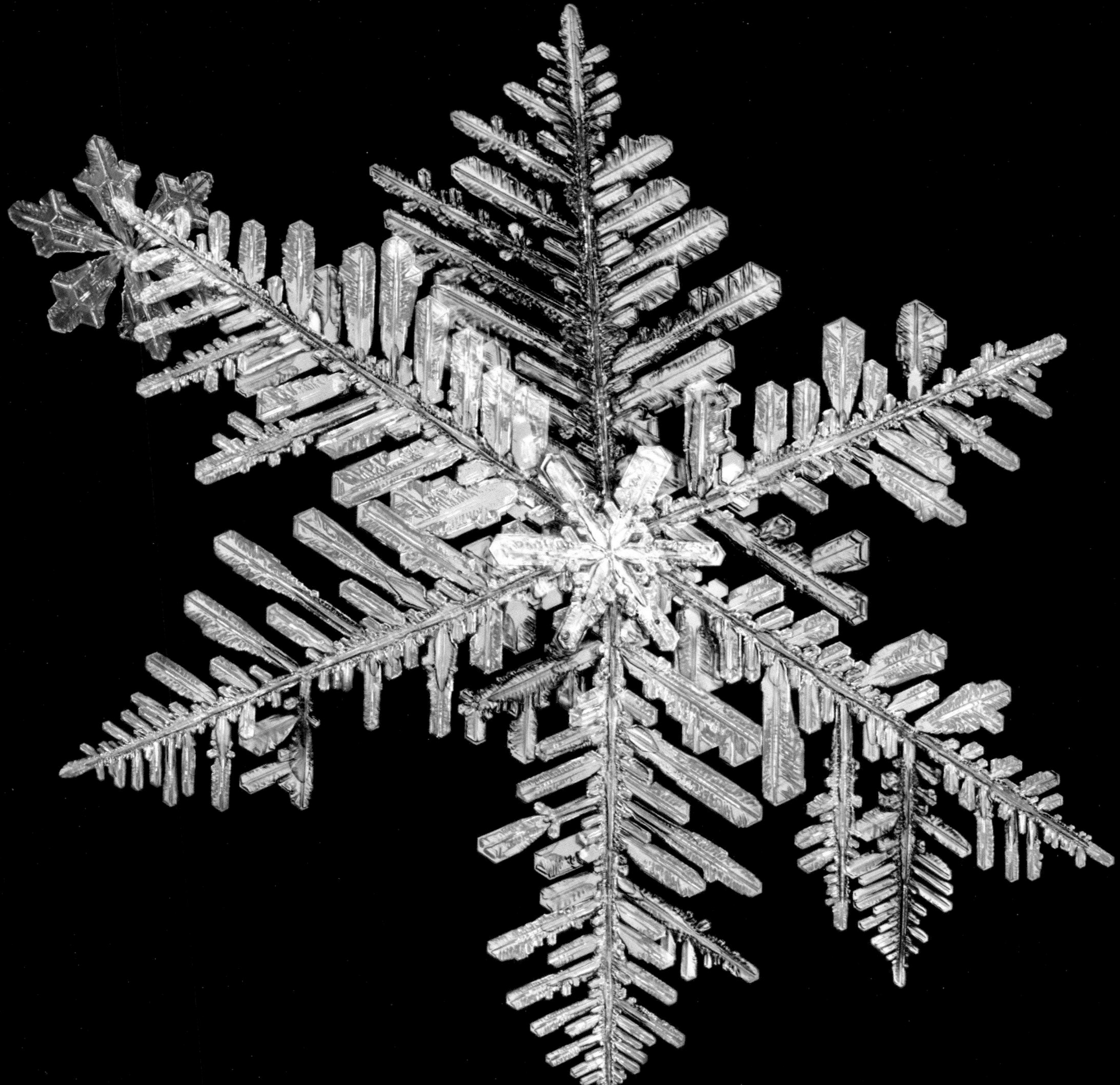

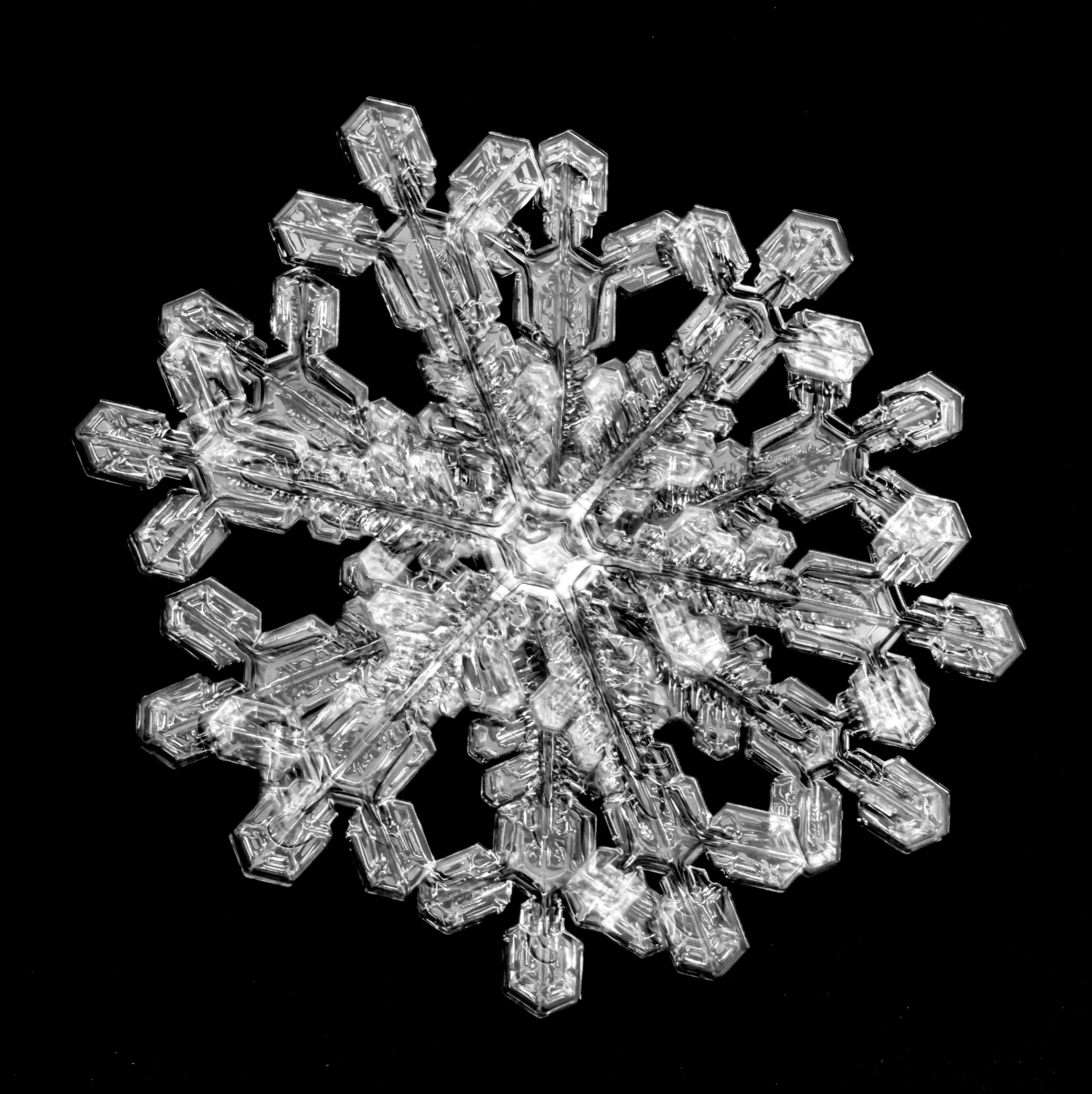

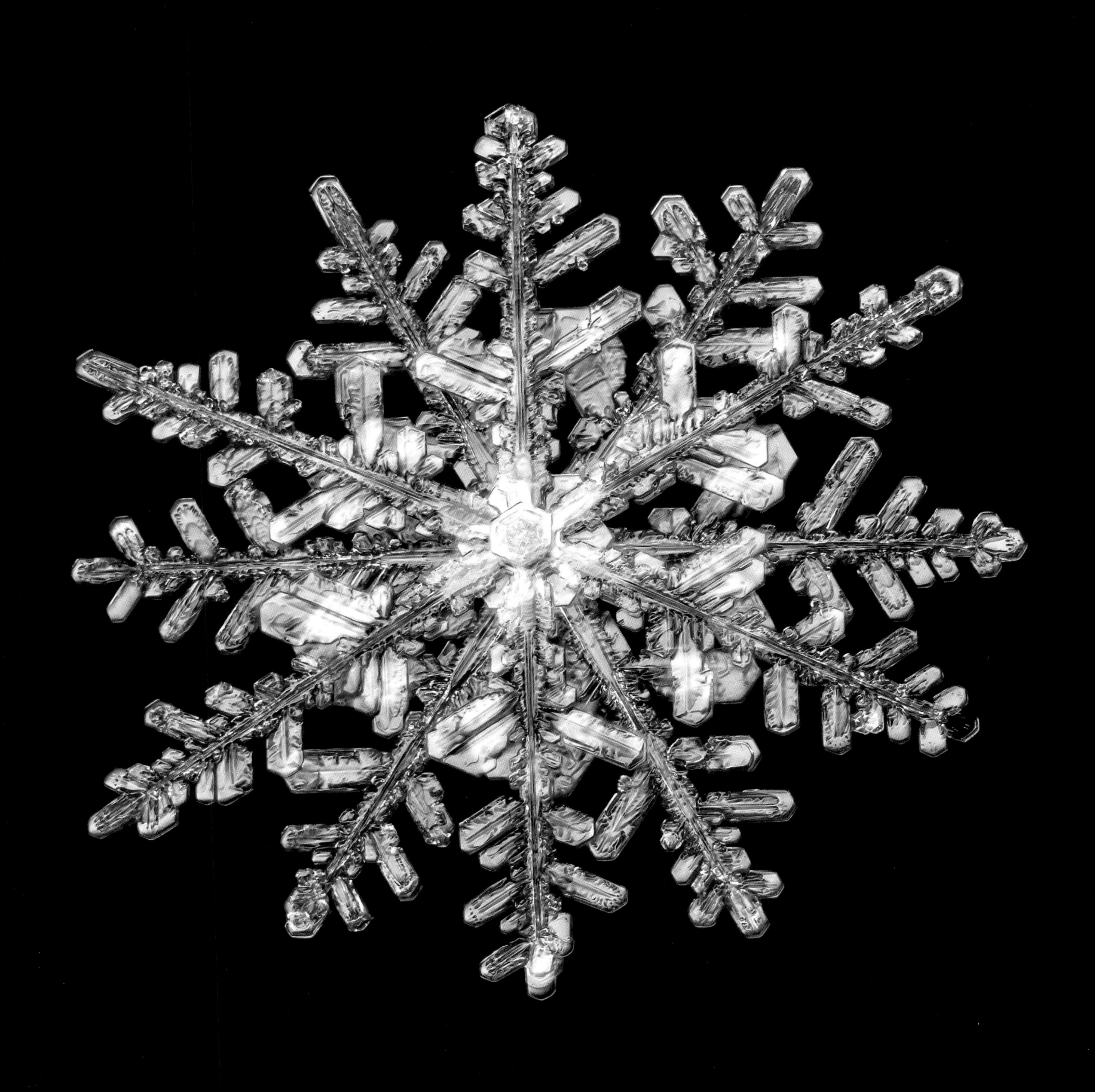

Water Droplet Workflow

Theoretically, editing a water droplet image is easier than a snowflake; there are fewer images required to stack together and rigid straight lines are much less common. In practice, however, we have more variables to deal with. The position of the background might change if you are hand-holding the camera, and the subject itself can be slightly animated. The "spokes" on this dandelion seed, as an example, might change their position from the first image to the last in a sequence. There is also the possibility for the water droplets to fall, merge, or evaporate slightly. This would change their outer "footprint" and result in focus stacking artifacts.

We also have to deal with a number of overlapping features. Focus stacking algorithms notoriously have a hard time dealing with overlaps, where there are resolvable details at different levels of depth but in the same two-dimensional space. This edit will showcase this, and it is part of the creative process to sort everything out.

During the RAW processing portion of these edits, we have a little more flexibility. What colour do you actually want the flower to be? This is open to interpretation and perception – the actual colour collected by the camera could easily be swayed by the colour of light hitting it, so why not use a little creative license? Should the flower be a little more yellow-green, or push further towards orange? Beyond that, much of the process is strikingly similar to a snowflake:

- Select your needed focus slices
- Send them to Photoshop as layers
- Auto-Align Layers
- Duplicate the layer stack
- Auto-Blend one set of layers
- Merge that down to a single "foundation" layer
- Place that layer at the bottom of the stack
- Turn off the visibility of all other layers
- Work your way up the layer stack with masks

Grab the files:
The files used in the droplet edit can be found at:
www.universeatourfeet.com/droplets.zip

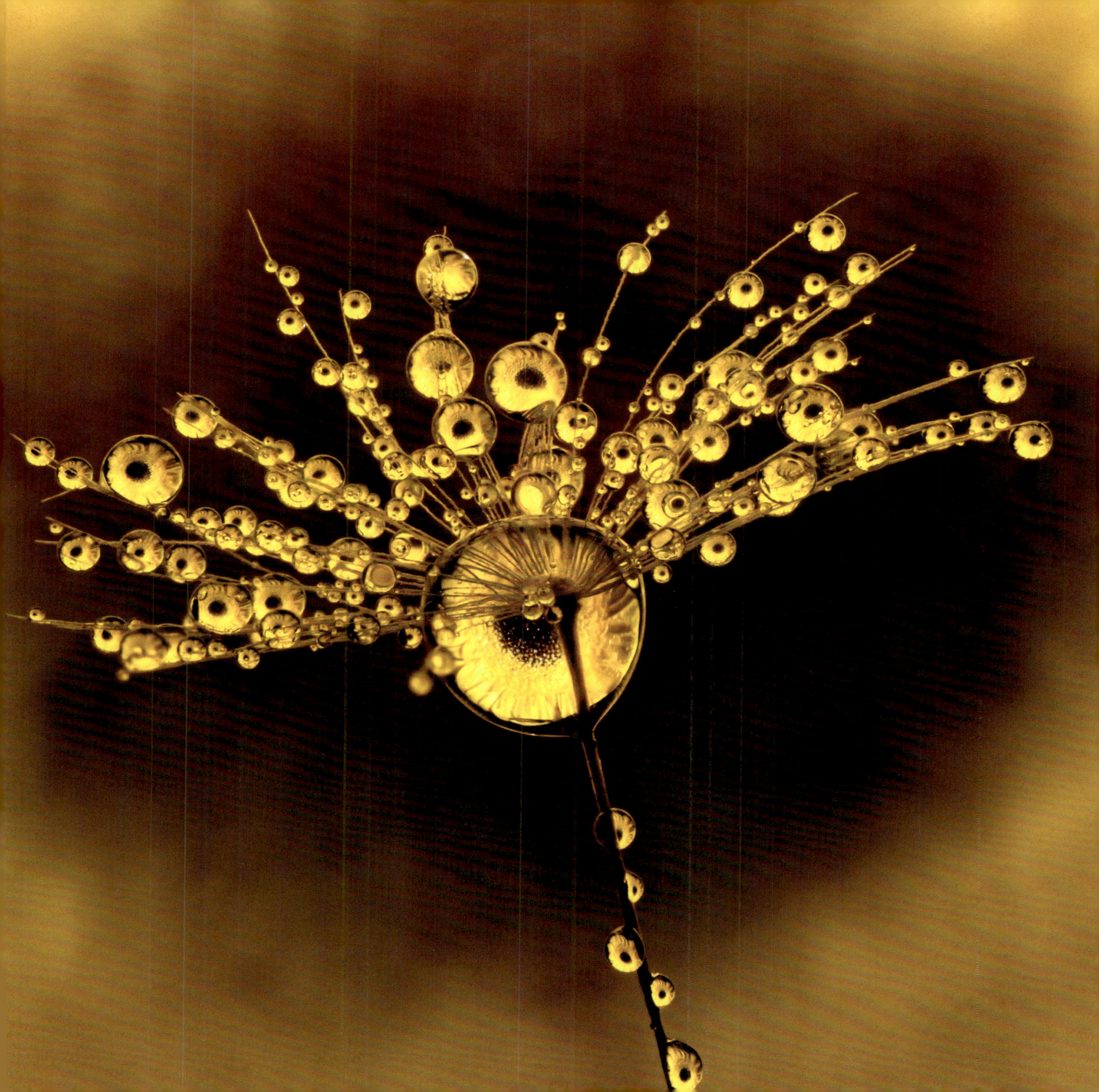

Devil the Details

After the procedural tasks outlined on the previous page, up to the **Auto-Blend Layers** point, there really isn't anything to do except press the right buttons. From a distance, when you see the stacked results, you'll be excited at how well it worked. As with any focus stack, the edges of the frame will all be a bit jagged and strange (*below*). This goes away with cropping to find your final composition near the end of the editing workflow. Keep yourself open to all options for the time being, and live with the cluttered edges of the frame. There's more important details to address, and errors to correct for.

The average focus stack for water droplet imagery can be anywhere for 5 to 20 images combined. This is far less than what we would expect from the average snowflake image, which in my experience is roughly 40 images. This means our computer doesn't take nearly as long crunching numbers, but the dynamic nature of the subject will translate into nearly as lengthy a corrective editing workflow. Thankfully, it's exactly the same process that we experienced in the snowflake edit. If you aren't yet familiar with layer masks, you will be soon.

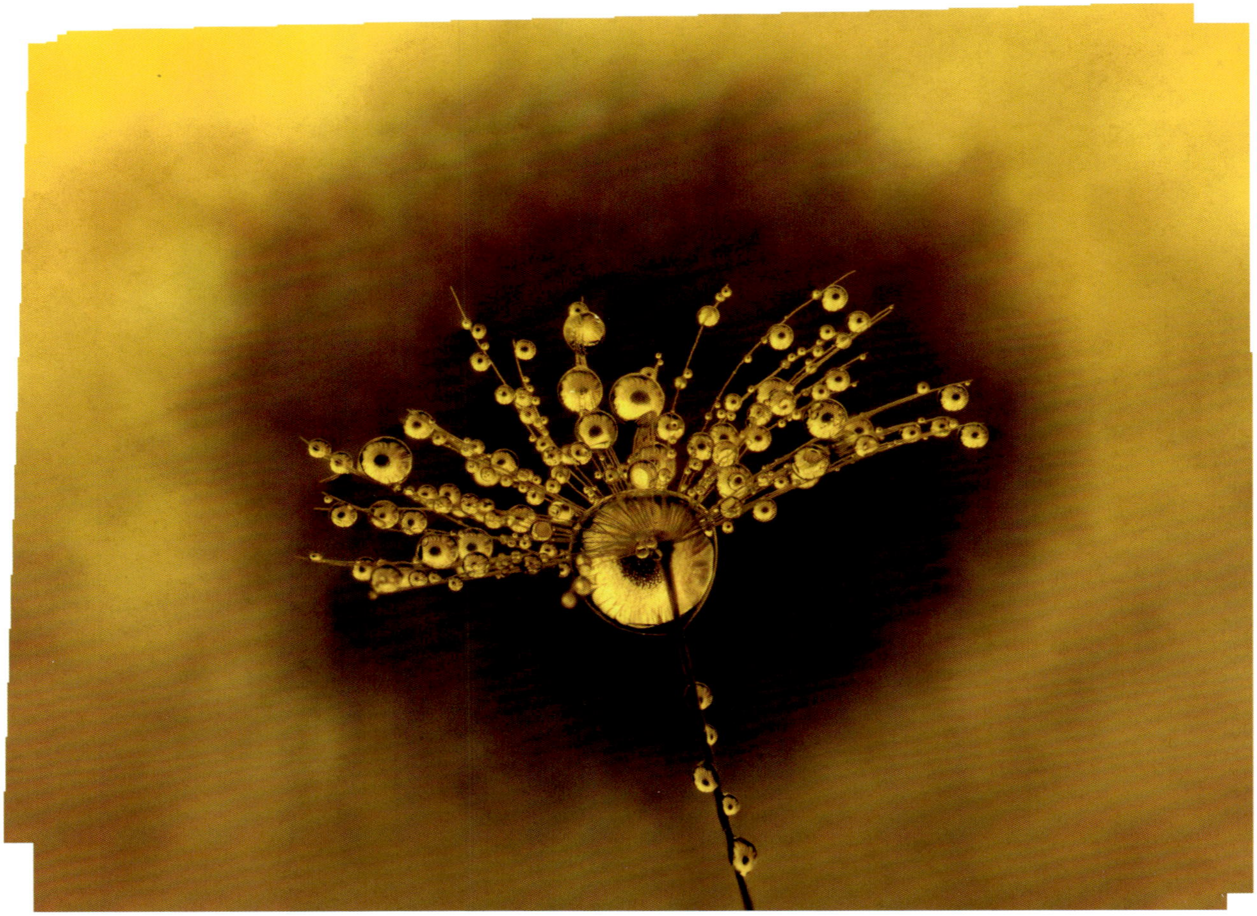

Working Through the Layers

These alignment issues are common (*right*). The closer you look, the more of them you will find. Some of the water droplets appear absolutely perfect, while others offer strange ghosted features that don't connect together properly.

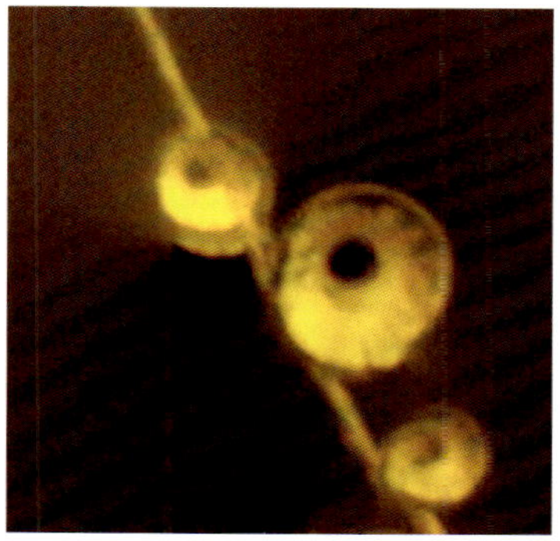

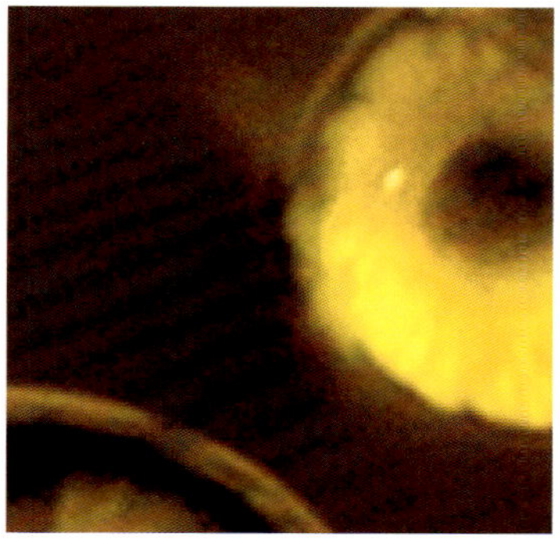

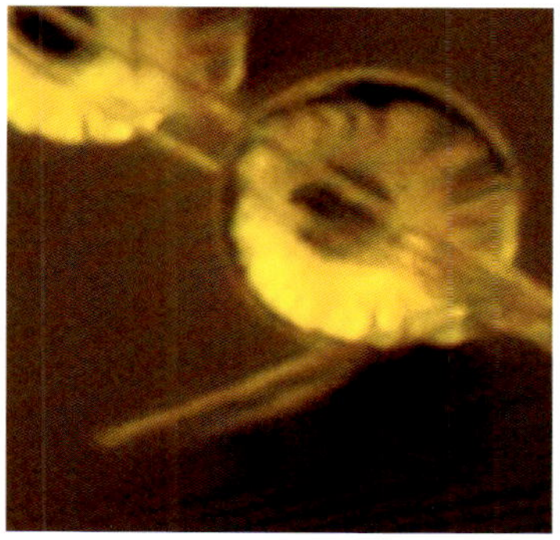

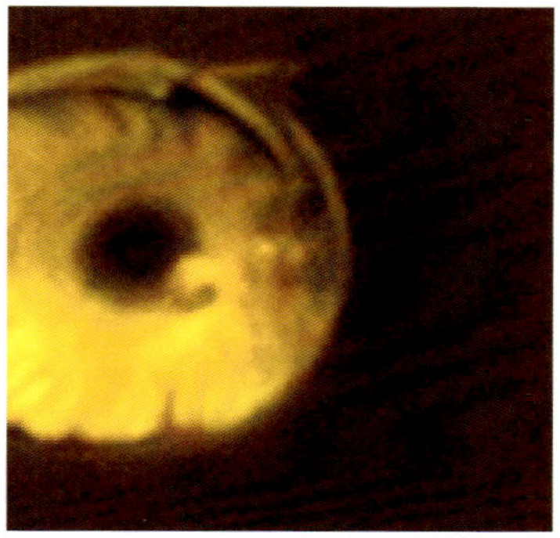

While some portions of the image align perfectly, we're assuming that nothing moves in the time that passes from the first image to the last image we use in a stacking sequence. That total time for these images is exactly five seconds. During this time, things change. As wildflower seeds get wet, they tend to move. Some change form dramatically – such as a clematis seed. Others, like a dandelion, will slowly droop under the weight of the water and eventually become conical as they absorb moisture. While it doesn't appear like much has changed, it's enough to drive a perfectionist to a mild level of frustration.

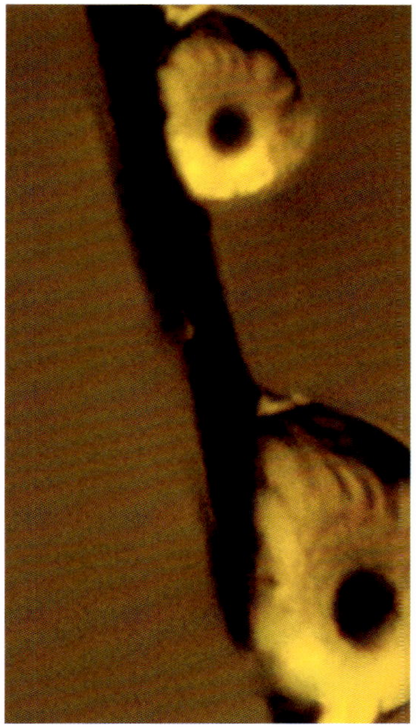

There are no shortcuts here, not if you want every pixel in the proper place. I am envious of people that can look at an image that is roughly 80% completed in my opinion and say "that's good enough for Instagram!" – and they're probably right. For my own sensibilities, the art is not in the automation, but rather in knowing an image is the best version of itself that it can be. How much time will you spend nudging pixels around? It's a rhetorical question where the answer changes with each image and your enthusiasm for it. There is no such thing as "perfect" in the art world, photography or any other artistic medium.

The process here ends the same way it does with the snowflake. Do you want to adjust the brightness? Do you want to adjust the colour? How is your final crop going to balance things out? You have the power of your own artistic intent at this point. Use it wisely, and find your final image.

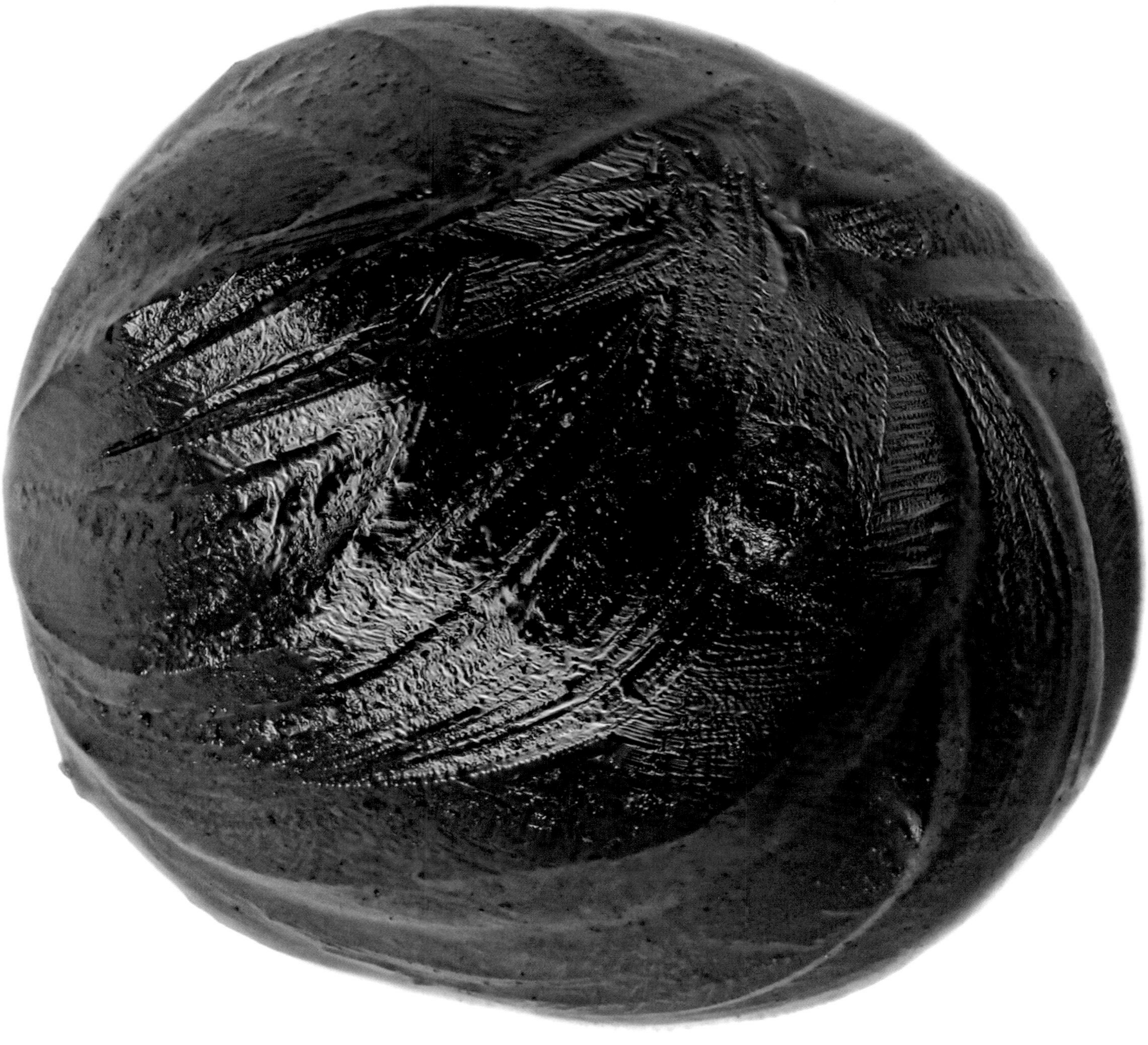

Automated / High Resolution Stacking

Manually correcting stacking efforts for a dozen images is tedious, but what if you added a zero to that number, then doubled it? Past a certain point, the ability to handhold the camera disappears. A focusing rail, and a static subject are required – and the entire focus stacking process opens up with additional options.

If you are in a controlled environment, and you can take all of your images sequentially on a focusing rail, there are a number of superb tools at your disposal beyond Photoshop. The two most commonly used are Helicon Focus and Zerene Stacker. It's important to remember, however, that no focus stacking algorithm is perfect and different algorithms work better for different subjects. For this reason and unlike Photoshop, there are multiple approaches to stacking in both programs.

Different modes are more effective for different subjects. When starting out down this path, I encourage you to try all modes and experience the differences. Yes, they can all be fine-tuned, but start with the default settings and see what the output is like. Here, we're working with a micrometeorite and a stack of 176 frames. The original sequence was 200 frames, but a bit was trimmed off either side that was just beyond the subject itself and not needed.

Try it Yourself:
The files used in this edit can be found at:
www.universeatourfeet.com/automated.zip

Why don't we use these tools for all focus stacking if they seem finely tuned to the task? Finely tuned is correct – and while there are some adjustments as to how far things can be aligned, they are designed with a narrow set of tolerances and subject matter in mind.

You can even see this for yourself! You've got the images from the snowflake editing workflow, what happens when you feed it into either program? Surely a simple crystal can be put together properly, right? Not if the perspective correction cannot be applied as well, and some algorithms expect the images to be in order from front to back.

The results (*following page*) leave a lot to be desired. Some stacking modes aren't awful, but fail to present the same level of detail as Photoshop. Others are a flat-out disaster no matter how you tweak the settings.

It's important to play each software to their strengths. Photoshop cannot handle large stacks of images, as

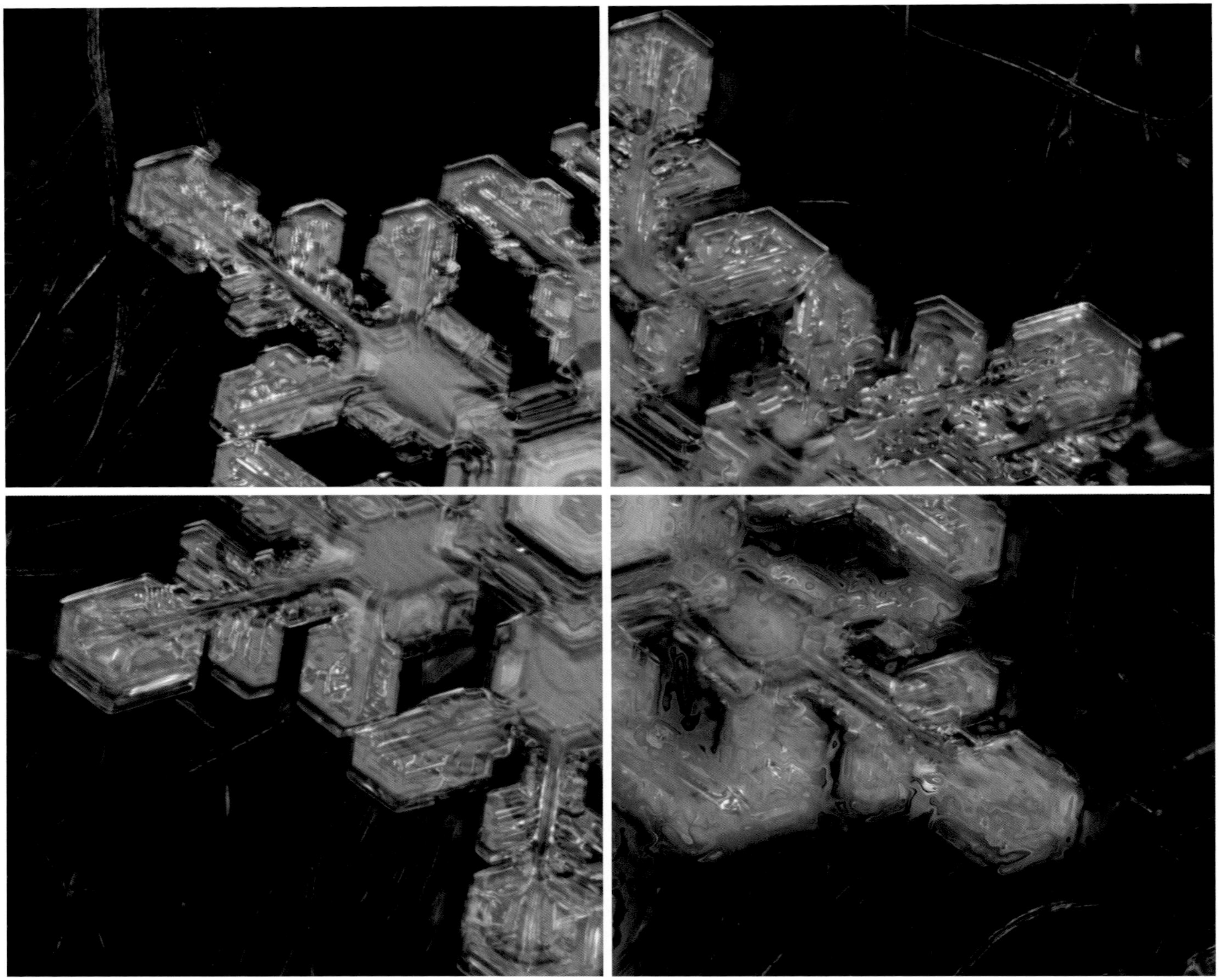

it keeps every image in active memory and outright fails to process the data past a certain point. While each software program has the ability to modify the stacking results with a masking feature for corrections, Photoshop features the most robust layer masking system. The right tool for the right job.

All the editing work will be done in Photoshop anyway, so I typically only use these other tools when the results are better than what Photoshop can generate. Our goal of using any focus stacking feature is not to end up with a perfect image, but to have all the necessary details in place.

Helicon Focus
Helicon Focus has three operating modes. Earlier in this book we reviewed these modes with a Madagascan Sunset Moth wing – but here we are with a micrometeorite. The moth example illustrated that Method B – Depth Map, yielded the best results. How do things change with an entirely different subject?

I encourage everyone to try all methods whenever you approach a new subject. They'll all behave a little differently, and aside from the processing time required, you have nothing to lose. Helicon Focus is currently the only focus stacking tool that utilizes your computer's graphics processing unit (GPU) for additional processing power.

Method A: Weighted Average (*top*)
This one rarely does the trick for me. In this example, we have acceptable detail in some regions but it seems to just "give up" when sorting out the edges of the micrometeorite beyond the face. There may be some acceptable scenarios to use this mode, but I haven't discovered them yet.

Method B: Depth Map (*middle*)
In this scenario, we cannot call this image victorious. It's slightly better in resolving detail on the face of the subject, but it also fails to produce the needed details as we look closer to the edges of the subject. This isn't ideal.

Method C: Pyramid (*bottom*)
Here, we have a great interpretation of the data along all of the edges, finally! However, the front-facing details are slightly muddy and less defined, with stronger flare on the direct light reflections.

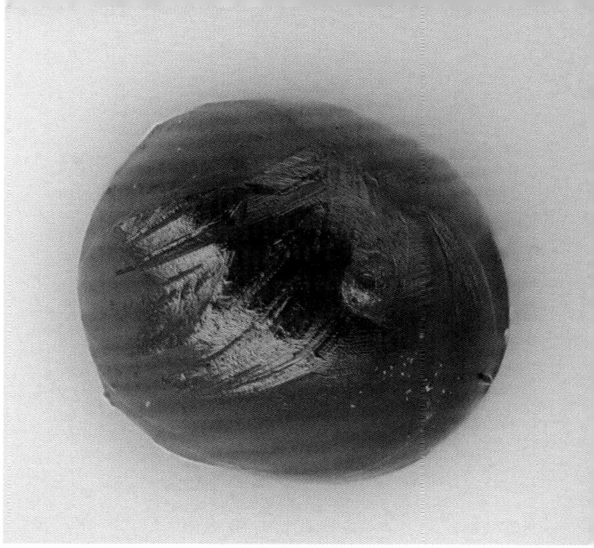

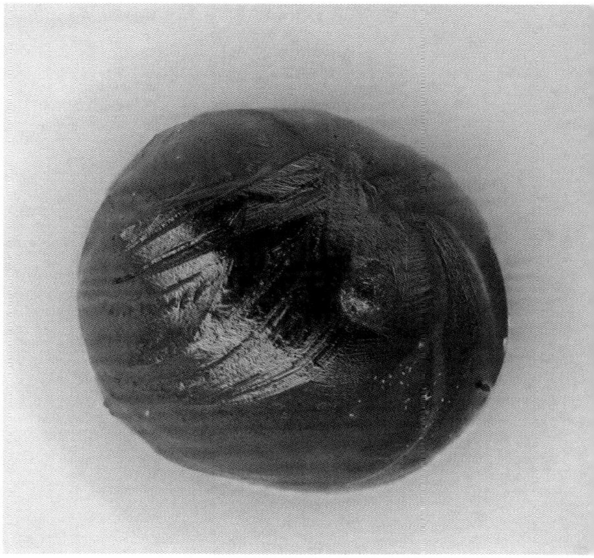

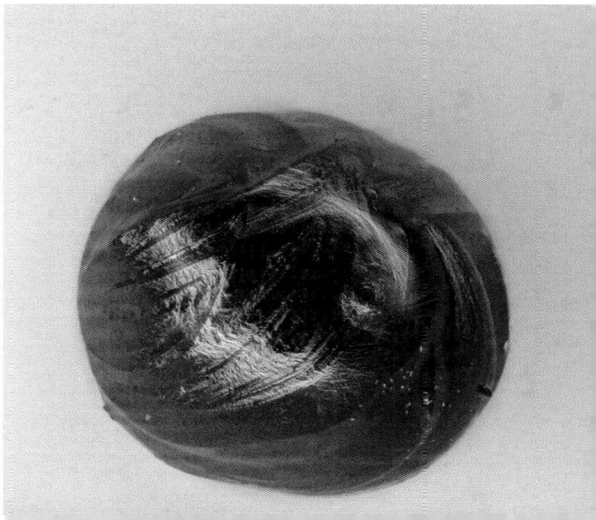

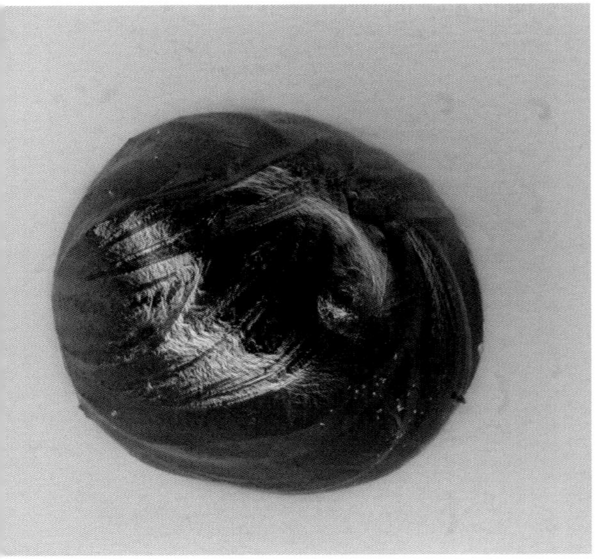

Zerene Stacker
Like Helicon Focus, Zerene Stacker has multiple options for stacking: PMax and DMap. They each offer a different approach to blending focus, as we can see here.

PMax (*top*)
PMax tends to give fairly decent results in many varied scenarios. It handles soft and subdued details with more careful consideration than almost every other algorithm, but it can be overwhelmed by flare and extreme contrast. The reflective areas on this micrometeorite aren't the best, but far from the worst.

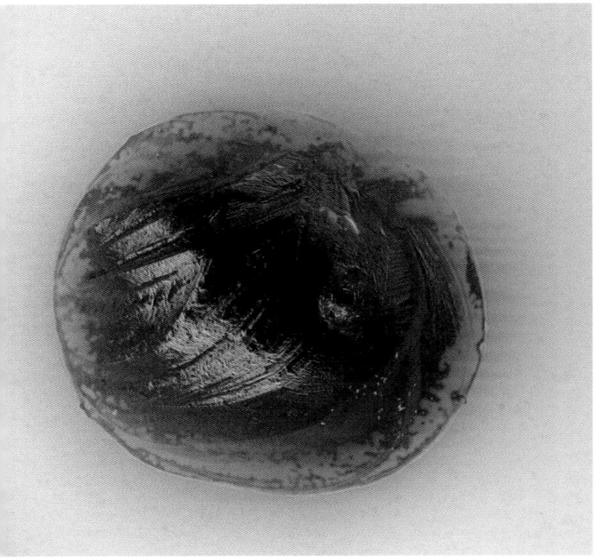

DMap (*middle*)
DMap is a tricky one. With its default settings, you'll be hard pressed to enjoy the results. The threshold needs to be set specifically for each image. If it is set incorrectly, for example as the initial default of 30, you'll get results like this. It is not completely unlike the blurry edges from Helicon Focus Method B: Depth Map. **Note:** your images cannot be randomly ordered!

DMap (*bottom*)
And in the same way that Helicon Focus can adjust the parameters for better results, so can the similar function in Zerene Stacker. With these example files, if we set the threshold to 74.5, it yields good results across the subject. This number, however, would vary with every subject and there is no easy way to preview exact results until you let the processing complete all the way.

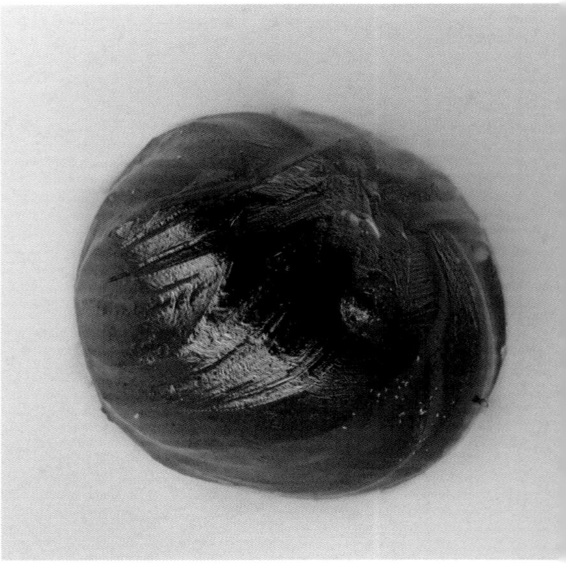

You can dive deep into the details of how all of these algorithms work for each program. To be candid, I never studied the inner workings with intense detail. I just tinkered and explored the results.

Multiple Paths Forward
You might look at all of these unpolished, "beginning stage" images before you take them into Photoshop for some touch-up work, and wonder: why are none of these the perfect starting point? Some are close, but nothing hits the mark perfectly. The answer is somewhere in between.

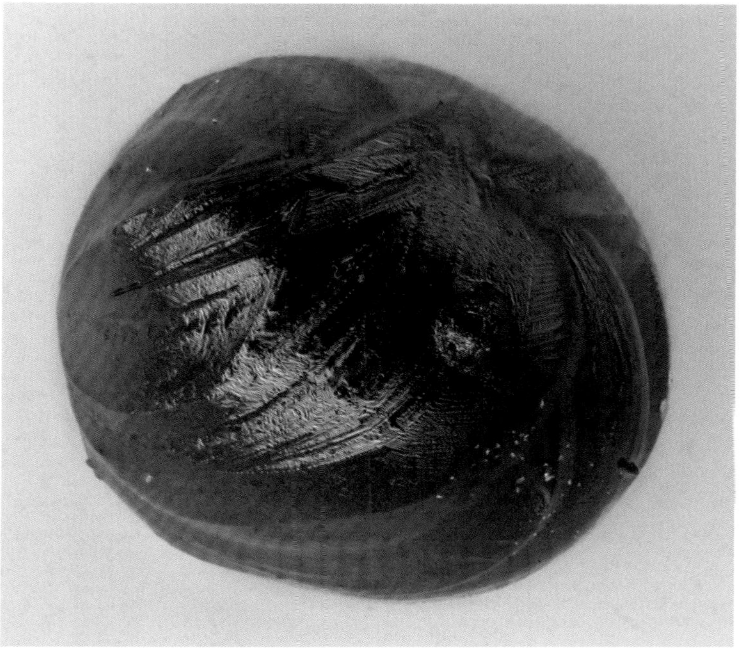

In a similar process to focus stacking, we can take our two favourite renditions of the data into Photoshop and choose the best elements of both. What's your favourite? Zerene Stacker DMap makes a good foundation, and Helicon Focus Method C (Pyramid) works well to set the outer edges better than anything else. Still, a bit of additional touch-up from Helicon Focus Method B (Depth Map) would fix a few flaws in the DMap foundation.

Do I recommend buying both programs? It's hard to say. You might be able to fine tune one to get perfect results. Just like all areas of education, I can provide you knowledge but I cannot provide you wisdom. In my experience, there's always some amount of additional work to present all critical details.

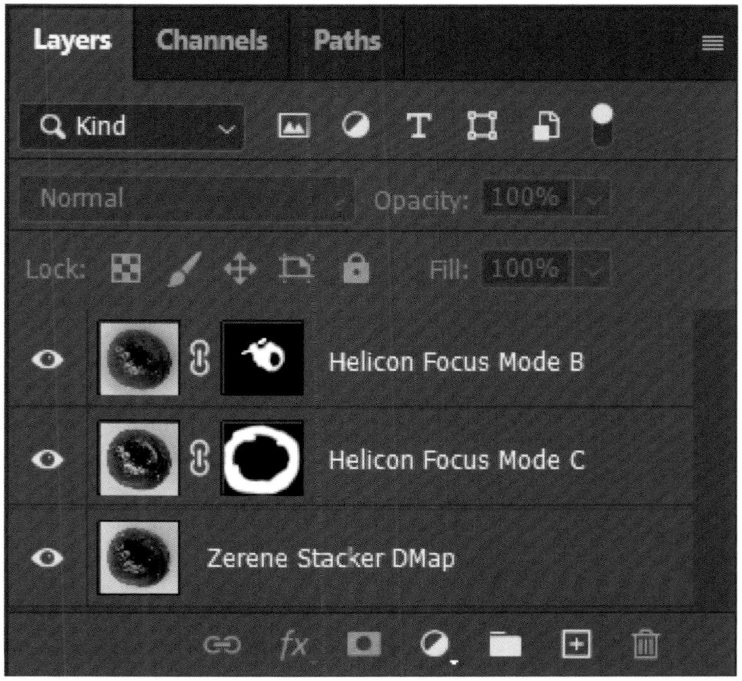

You can see in the screenshot of the Layers panel in Photoshop how the three chosen components fit together but looking at their masks (*bottom right*). The results (*top right*) are as good as it gets from a stacking standpoint. Like snowflakes and water droplets, however, focus stacking is only one component of the overall process. Let's continue on to make our image shine.

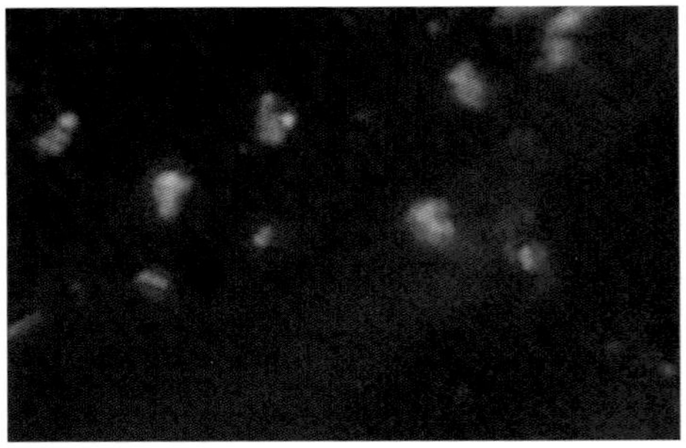

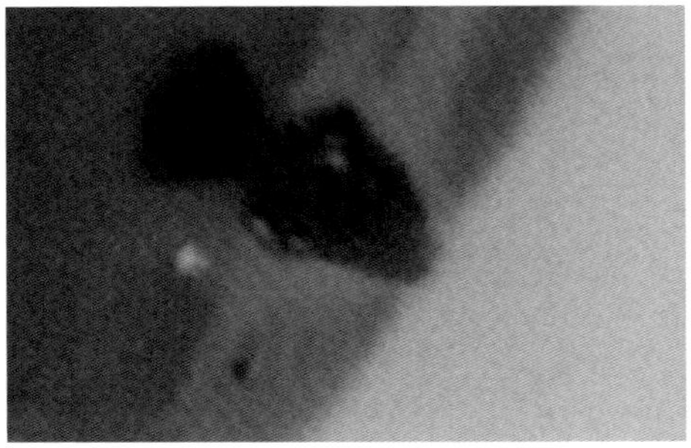

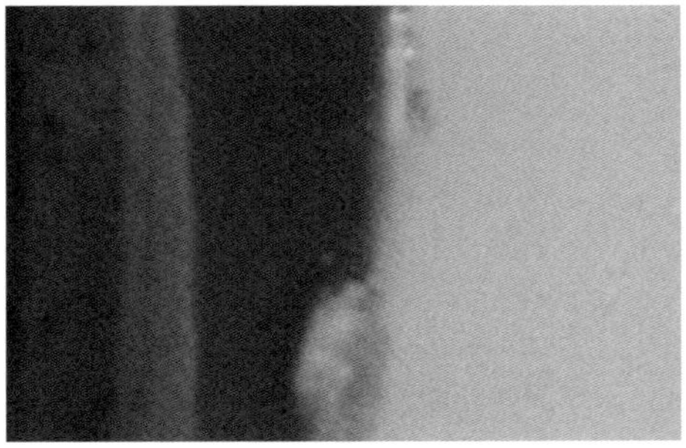

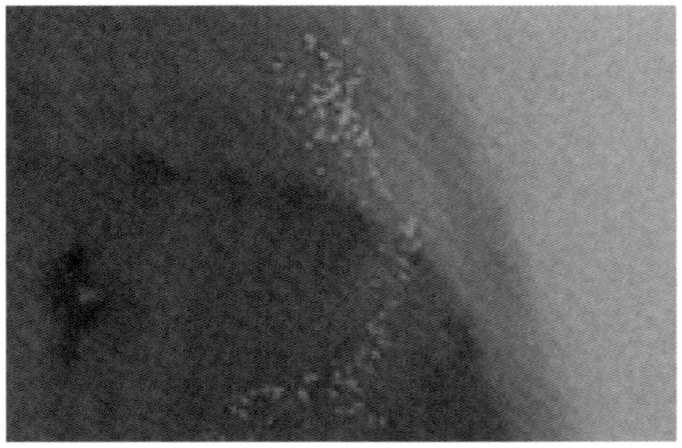

Dusting Stardust

These tiny space rocks can get dusty. Anything can, at this scale. Just like the annoyance of fluorescing dust on an indoor plant, we need to clean things up a bit. This isn't a difficult process, but it can be tedious and time consuming. For certain microscopic subjects, you might consider running them through an ultrasonic jewelry cleaner if they can stand getting wet, or have a bulb blower handy to get things started. If you can remove the dust before even taking the photographs, you'll have much less to deal with in post-production.

Since the individual layers used to create proper detail are no longer needed to be separate, feel free to "**Flatten Image**" by right-clicking on any layer name and select that from the menu. Before starting to remove the dust, it might be worthwhile to duplicate your new background layer – I do this in case I mess something up and don't realize it, since cloning is considered "destructive" editing. It can also be helpful to refer back to the original to see how far you've come as you continue to edit.

The primary tools here are the usual suspects: **Spot Healing Brush**, **Healing Brush**, and **Clone Stamp** tools. Take off everything you don't think belongs:

- The off-white tiny specks
- The bigger brown speck in the lower right
- Some larger dust on the periphery
- And even a "hot pixel" from the camera that jumped around a bit due to the aligning process of focus stacking.

If you're not sure if something is part of the specimen, leave it. An image like this should maintain as much integrity to the natural state of the subject as possible. That doesn't mean we can't enhance things, but part of the magic is knowing that this exists in nature the way we are presenting it. This last point might not be true of every subject, but usually if you are trying to capture such tiny details, it's because you want to showcase their natural wonder and not your own artificial constructs.

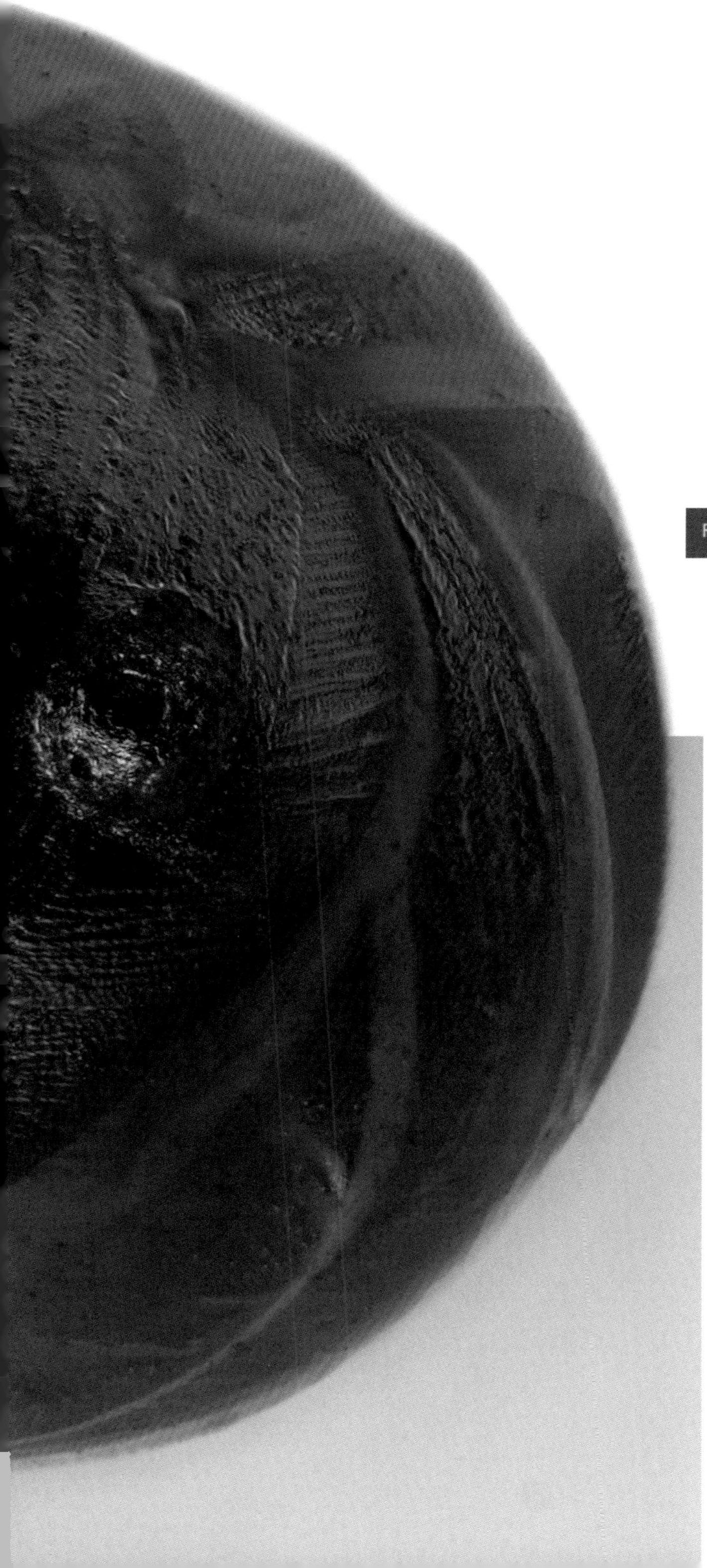

Background Cleanup

This part is deceptively easy. I'm sure the off-grey background of all of the previous versions of this edit have been somewhat annoying. It needs to disappear, but the time for such edits should not be given before we've gotten the most detail possible out of the focus stack. The process involves a few relatively simple steps, beginning with duplicating our image – the work we are about to perform is destructive, and we very likely will need the original image as part of the editing strategy. Always be protective of past efforts.

Dodge the Highlights. 100%. Just knock it out of existence.

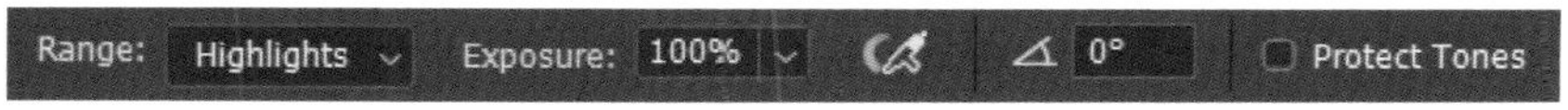

This will have a minimal impact on the outer edges of the micrometeorite, though it will lighten them slightly in the process of getting a good, clean outline. Thankfully, this is also easy to correct for, because we duplicated our layer containing the image. All that is needed is to create a layer mask on the layer with the white background, and paint with a soft black brush on the interior perimeter of the subject. This would successfully limit any brightening / fading of the details and maintain a nice contrasty edge.

Then, simply merge the two layers together when you are happy with the results.

You might be asking yourself, why am I learning how to knock the background out of a micrometeorite image? When the heck will I actually be photographing one of these myself? Maybe never. Even though there are likely micrometeorites in your eaves troughs or on your roof, they will stay in obscurity for the rest of their days. If you cannot find such space gems, fear not: controlling backgrounds and cleaning up images in many forms are useful skills there . Skills used on one subject might be translatable to another. The more experience, the better!

Extracting Maximum Details

I've always detested the scenes in crime dramas where the investigators task a computer technician to "enhance" the details of the evidence, and magically they can now read a license plate or make out someone's face. While there are newer artificial intelligence tools to "construct" additional details in certain images, these tools are usually tailored to subjects that an AI engine can be trained on. No one is going to train these tools on snowflakes, micrometeorites, or other niche subjects. Even if such tools could be effective, faking details is not the same as extracting the best details from the available data.

There are tools that we can use to produce the best possible results, however. There are three functions that I typically explore with every high-magnification image:

- Texture / Structure
- Clarity
- High-pass Sharpening

All of these tools have been discussed already in other post-processing workflows. The exact same process applies here as well: we can increase the contrast around the existing details for the perceived increase in detail. Overdo it, and things just turn into a grungy mess. The illusion of added detail is an easy one to break if you go too far.

Whether it's a grain of pollen, a micrometeorite, a speck of sand or a butterfly wing, the process is all largely the same. Different stacking algorithms might be preferred for different subjects or lighting conditions, but the work is largely procedural without significant artistic involvement. I suppose that's where the magic is: simply exploring and documenting the natural world on a scale that we could never hope to appreciate with our own senses.

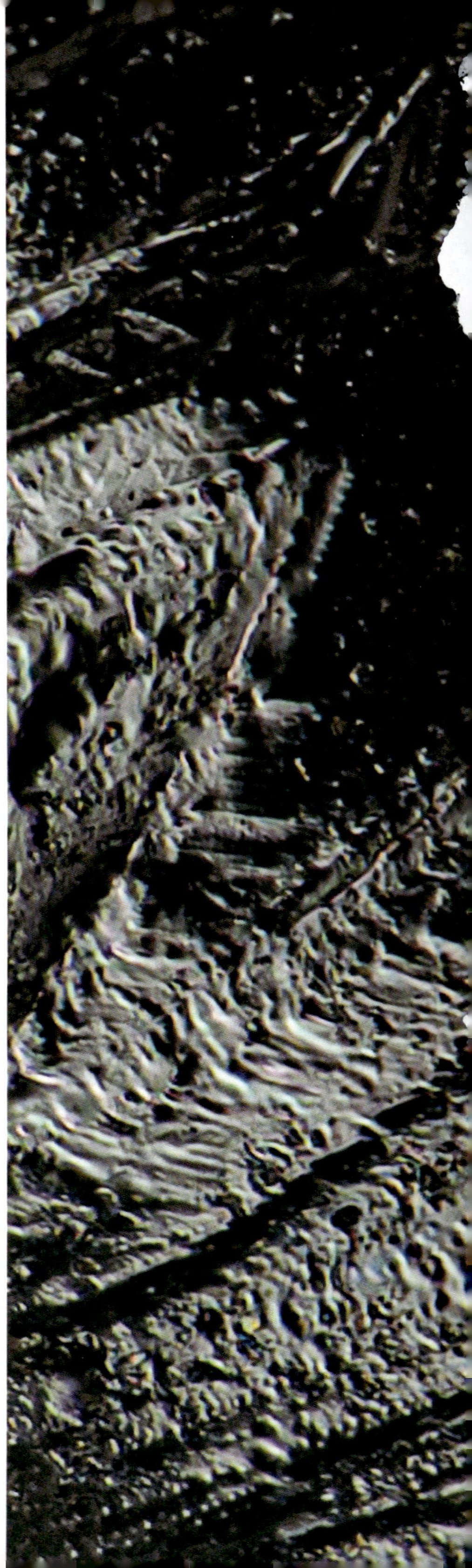

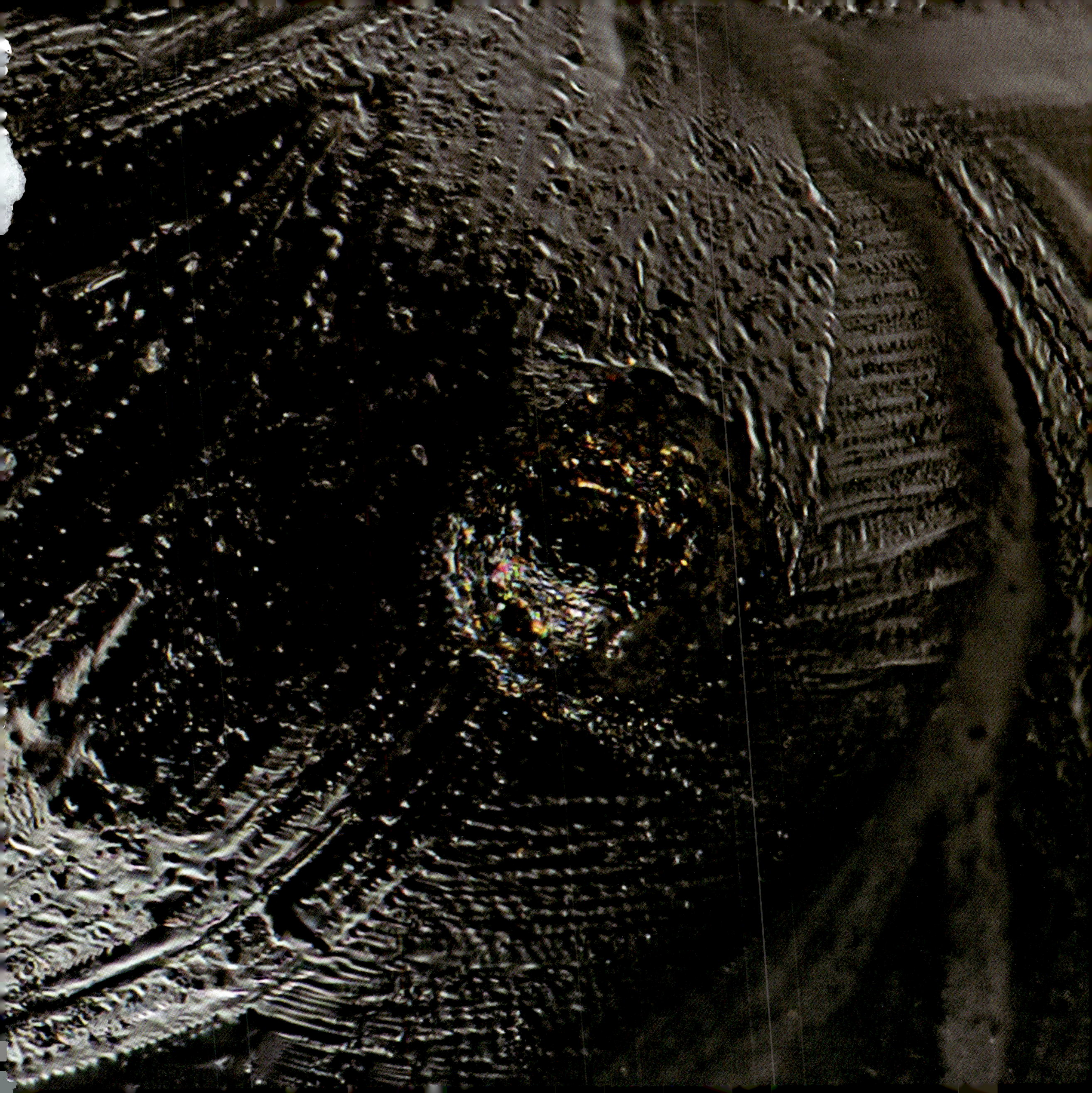

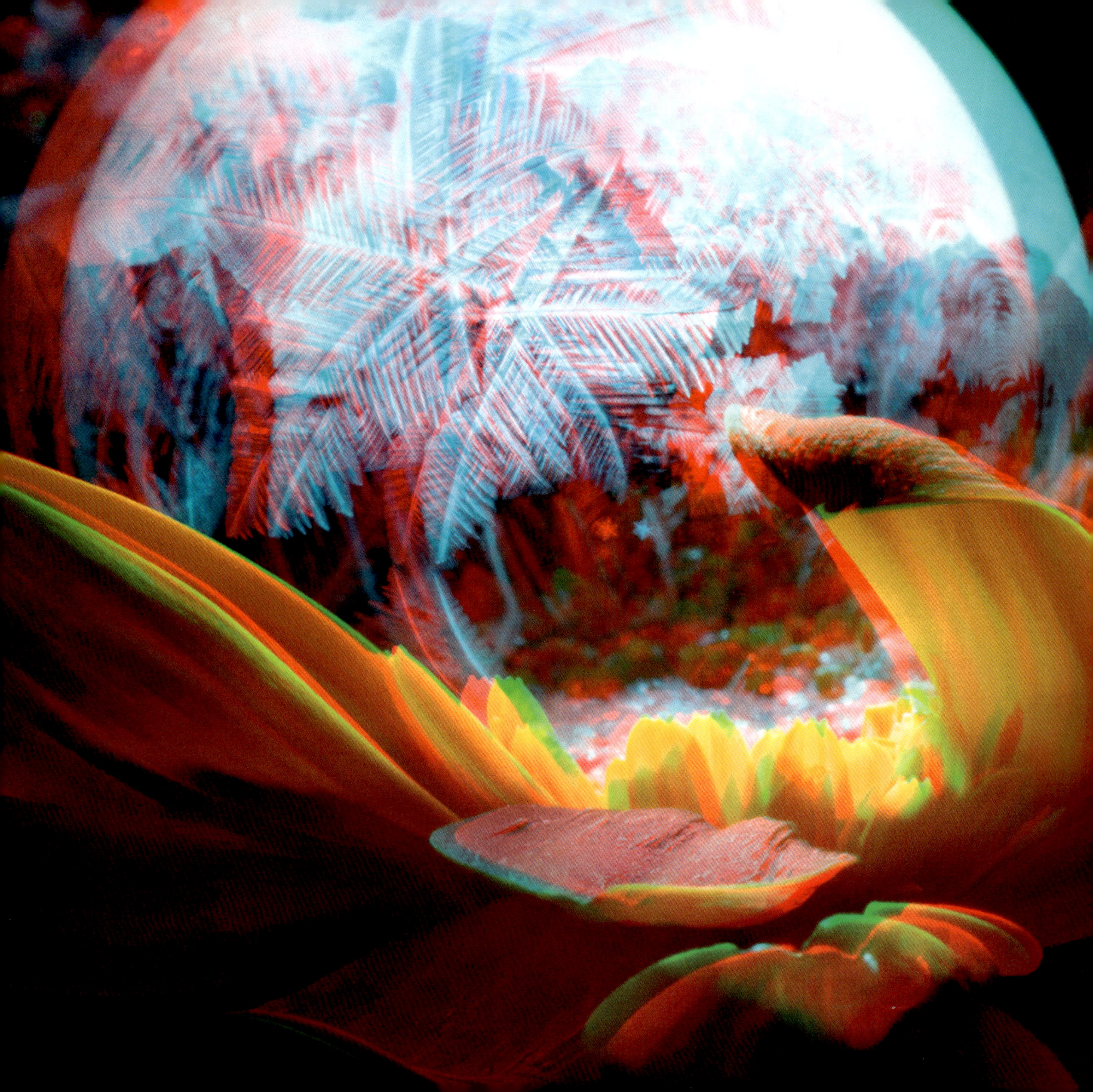

Stereoscopic 3D Macro

Stereoscopy pre-dates most photography, though one could say they were invented and evolved together. Louis-Jacques-Mandé Daguerre invented the Daguerreotype photographic process in 1839. It was seven years earlier that Charles Wheatstone first began experimenting with "stereoscopes", explored with drawings that had stereoscopic depth.

Why the history lesson? From the earliest days of photography, taking photos in 3D had fascinated the minds of intellectuals and royalty; a stereoscopic portrait of Queen Victoria was displayed at *The Great Exhibition* in 1851. The format offered a greater understanding of the world around us by being able to perceive depth and distance.

Those early stereoscopes were expensive, cumbersome and often proprietary. That all changed a decade later in 1861 when Oliver Wendell Holmes invented and intentionally did not patent the design for a less expensive device that spread across the world. The earliest such stereoscope I have been able to personally view images with was built in 1867 (*right*).

If you wanted to experience the world far from home, "stereoviews" were the best way to do it. The first news radio broadcast wouldn't be until 1920, and television wouldn't come along for several decades after that. Through all this time, stereo 3D photography was commonplace and enjoyed by many.

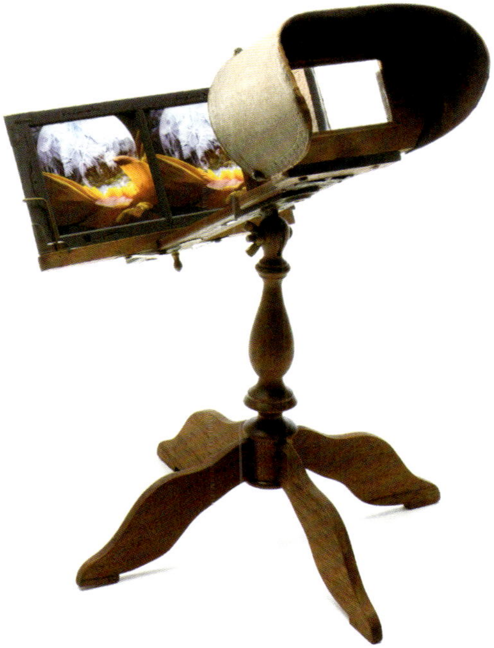

Above: A Bates stereoscope circa 1867 with a modern re-creation pedestal stand. The image being viewed in stereo is the same one being presented on the opposing page.

In the modern era, the closest you may have gotten to a stereoscope was a View-Master™ or a pair of red/blue anaglyph glasses from a novelty comic book as a child. Let's re-live that childhood and create our own 3D images – with the equipment you already have. It's far easier to do than you might expect, and you will be introduced to wondrously fascinating subjects at any scale or magnification.

For the purposes of ensuring that everyone gets in on the fun, the images in this book are printed to be viewed with anaglyph glasses. By filtering each eye with chromatically opposite colours – usually red and cyan – an image can be encoded with information visible to only one eye and not the other, allowing for a 3D effect to jump off the page. While this is accessible and easy for everyone to see, it isn't ideal. What if the image contained a significant amount of one of these colours? It would be difficult to see the full colour palette of the image. Other viewing options include:

Cross-View:
My favourite technique to view stereoscopic 3D images, but not everyone can perform this trick; it involves crossing your eyes. An object in front of you might appear as two objects if you cross your eyes, and this is where the magic begins. In stereo, you cross your eyes such that you get double vision, with the left and right images overlapping in the center. Focus on this central image and it will pop into focus. If you are having trouble, try moving the image closer or farther away from your eyes to fill your field of view differently.

Don't worry about the myth that crossing your eyes might cause harm, you'll quickly re-adjust. If you can't get this technique to work, you're not alone. Roughly half the people I have engaged to try this have failed, and some only succeeding after repeated tries.

In this orientation, the left image is on the right and the right image is on the left. The action of crossing your eyes corrects for this reversal.

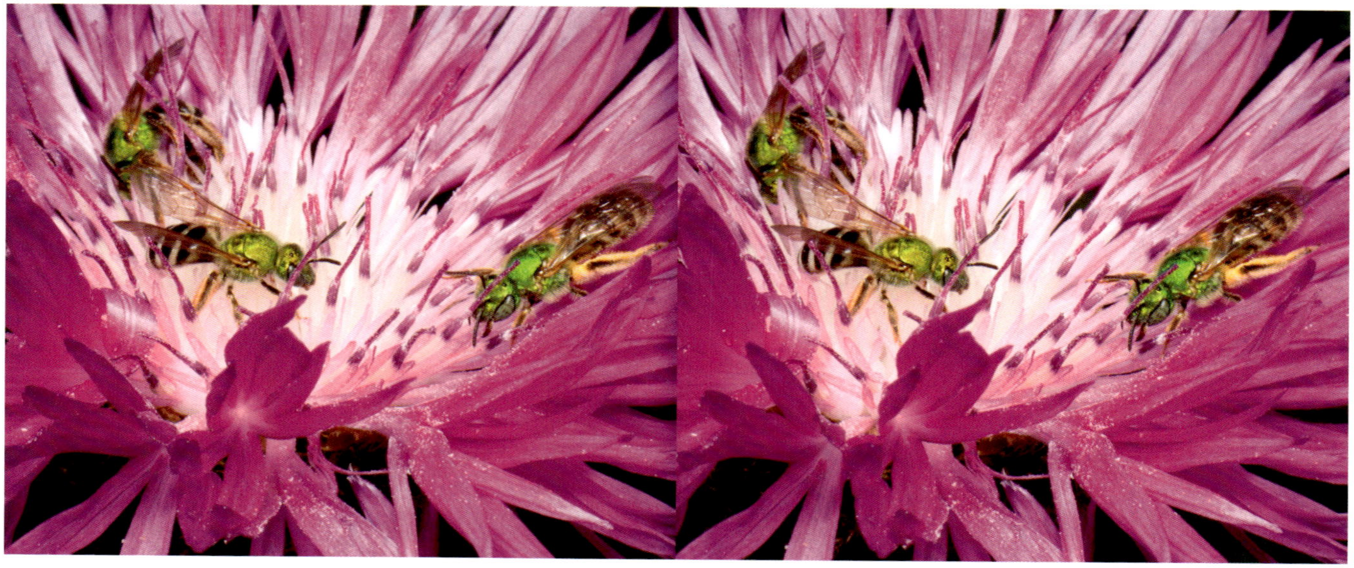

Side-by-Side:

Not just for antique stereo cards, you can easily load up a side-by-side image on your phone and view it with a simple and inexpensive device like a cardboard VR headset. Another popular viewer beyond a classic stereoscope is the OWL Viewer, pioneered by Dr. Brian May, more commonly known for his musical talent as the lead guitarist for the band Queen.

As a side note, this is how those Magic Eye® images worked. If you focused your vision to the far away while looking at something up close, from the right distance a 3D image would appear. I always found it easier to cross my eyes to see these images, but the resulting images were always inverted. The left image is on the left side, right on right.

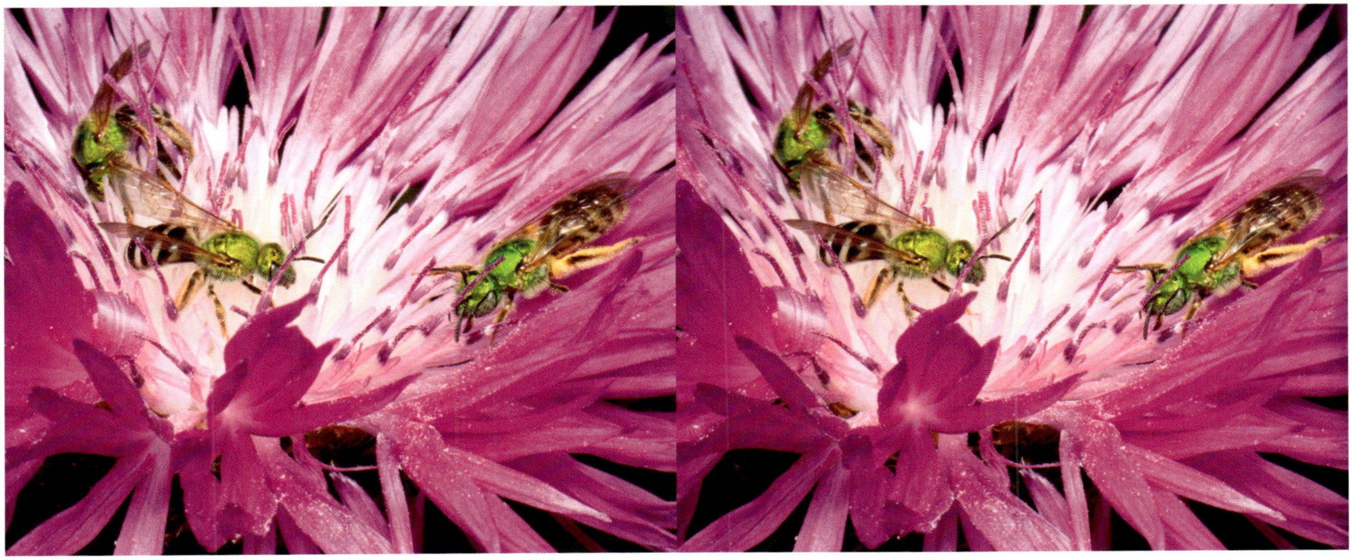

Facing page: A stereoscopic 3D image designed to be viewed with crossed eyes. The front of the cornflower will jump out in front of the sweat bees in the frame, with depth seen throughout.

Above: The same image configured for viewing with a stereoscope or 3D viewer. It is sized to 7" (17.8cm) to match the traditional width of stereo cards.

3D Television and more:

Polarized glasses, active shutter technology and others. There are so many ways to view 3D content, with many televisions compatible with the .MPO (Multi-Picture Object) file format. Who has such forgotten technology? Well, I have a stack of antique stereoscopes so I'm not the best person to ask. Many televisions can support the loading of a USB stick directly on the device with the images – if you have a 3D TV collecting dust.

Side-by-Side, Crossview, and .MPO files of the images in this chapter can be downloaded at **universeatourfeet.com/3D**

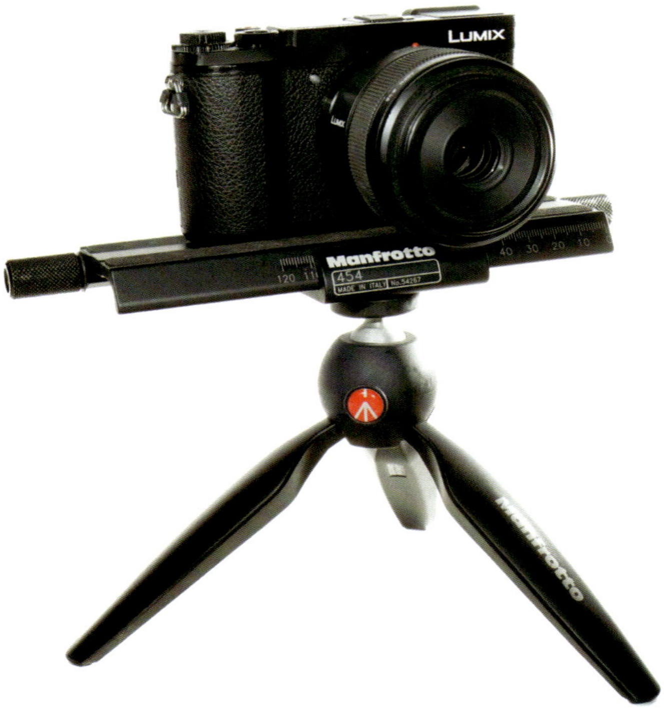

Shooting in 3D with Your Current Equipment

Now that we know how to properly perceive three dimensional imagery, it's time to create our own. One of the simplest configurations includes the macro equipment you already own, but operated with a different purpose. If you own a focusing rail to aid in focusing as well as focus stacking techniques, you've got everything you need. Instead of mounting the camera to move forward and back in a linear movement, position the camera sideways on the rail, which would allow for a left/right movement.

Take a photo in one position, and move the camera to the right by adjusting the rail. Make sure that in both images, the subject remains within the frame. There is some level of experimenting here, and taking multiple images at different points is encouraged. This technique requires a static subject, but it's a great way to start.

If you don't have anything but a camera and a lens, you can even just shift the camera on the surface of a table left and right, so long as the angle to the subject doesn't change.

This technique was used to photograph a passionflower (*Passiflora caerulea*) blossom in ultraviolet fluorescence. The lighting, exposure, and focus between the two frames are identical, and when properly processed will reveal the beautiful depth and structure of the flower.

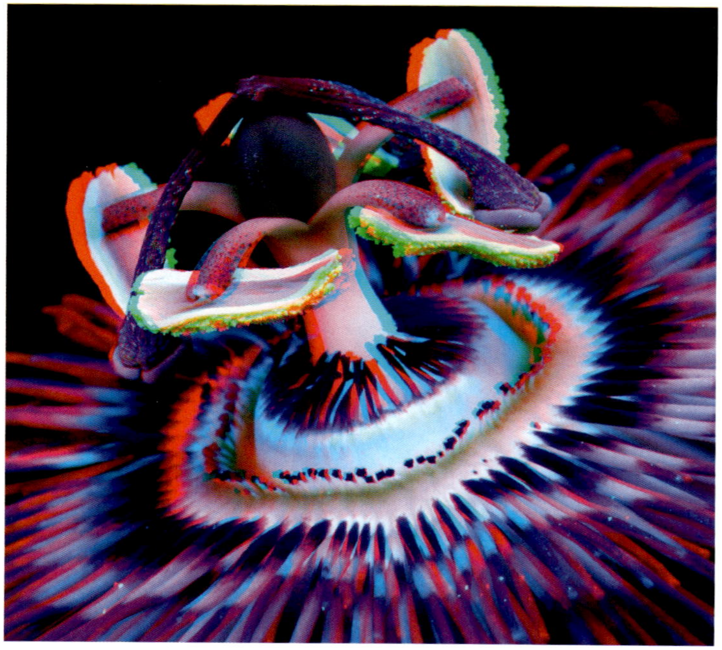

Lumix GX9, Leica DG Macro-Elmarit 45mm F/2.8, F/14 ISO 200 15sec x2

Creating 3D Images with Dedicated Optics

My preferred way to shoot stereoscopic 3D macro images is with dedicated lenses. These lenses often contain two sets of optics, one intended to create the image for each eye. The resulting image capture divides your image frame in two, half for each eye. Some of them can be very expensive and impossible to find, while others are incredibly common and inexpensive. What are your options here and what can you expect?

Panasonic Lumix G 3D 12.5mm F/12 lens

This little gem seriously underperformed as a "regular" 3D lens, with no significant 3D effect due to the small distance between the two sets of optics. It was released for the Micro Four Thirds system in September 2010. To photograph people and larger objects, it would be ideal to have the spacing between the lenses to match closely to human pupillary distances which average about 64mm, or just beyond 2.5 inches. This lens has fixed focus, with a hyperfocal distance of 0.6 meters / 2 feet to infinity, where the stereo impact is lacking. So, why is this a "little gem" of a lens? It can be modified easily.

The modification is simple: remove the three screws from the back of the lens mount and insert a small washer in this space before replacing the screws. 0.5mm through 1.5mm worth of washers will give the best results and turn this lens into a very capable 3D macro lens. Why the washers? That's enough of a distance to function as an extension tube! Extension tubes, normally a stand-alone addition to shift a non-macro lens into the close-up realm, would be too much for this much-maligned lens. The washers do the trick.

The lens is still detected by most Micro Four Thirds cameras for metadata purposes, but the lens itself is inert. It cannot change its focus and it has a fixed F/12 aperture that cannot change. Some cameras forbid the use of shooting in video modes with this lens, but by simply taping over the electrical contacts you can overcome this limitation. It's a fun and accessible piece of equipment, and as of the publication of this book can be found for under USD$150 on marketplace websites like eBay. A washer kit for conversion to macro is also available for $10.

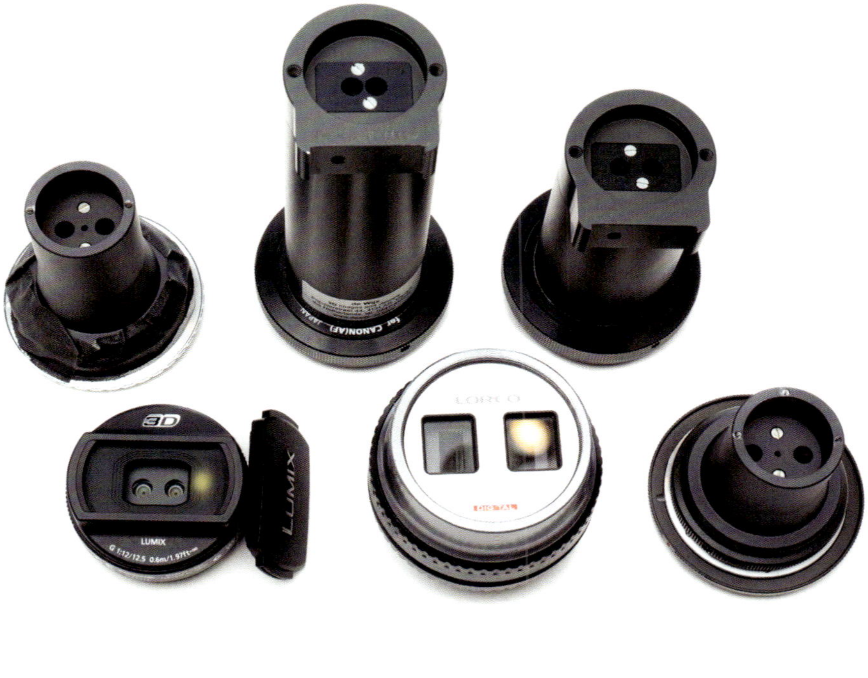

Loreo 3D Macro Beamsplitter Model 9006

Everything about this lens is plastic – including the 2-element optical design. It uses a "beamsplitter" principal that makes use of first surface mirrors to shift the incoming light farther away from the center of the lens, providing a similar effect to two distinct optical systems. It's one of the only 3D macro lenses still being sold by the manufacturer, at the time of publication of this book, for USD$120. If "all plastic" gave it away, the quality here leaves a lot to be desired, but it's available in Pentax, Nikon, Canon and Sony A mount, designed for APS-C sized camera sensors.

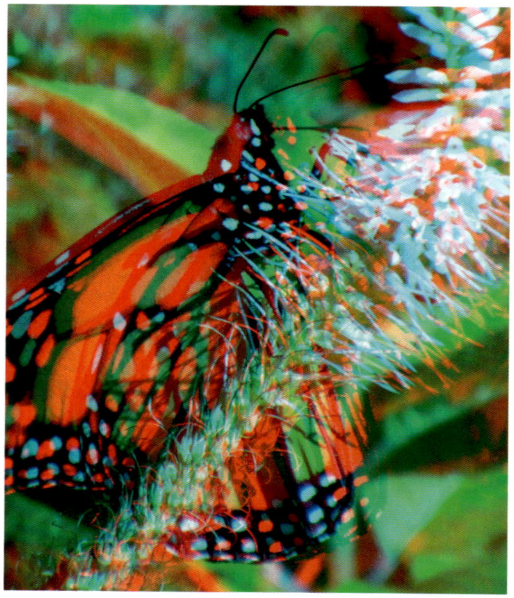

As an out-of-the-box solution that can be used with full-frame cameras and a bit of cropping, it is still worth experimenting with despite its cheap design. Adjustable focus and aperture, what more could you ask for? My personal experience with the lens hasn't been fantastic, but this is likely due to being spoiled with other high-quality options.

deWijs 3D Macro Lenses

These are the best little lenses for stereoscopic 3D macro, and they're also as rare as hens' teeth. My personal collection of four lenses has taken over five years to accumulate since they are no longer being manufactured and few were made. The optics are simple but effective, and they are designed around different magnifications.

The highest magnifications achieve a subject size filling the frame of 10mm x 14mm. If placed on a full-frame camera sensor (measuring 36mm x 24mm) the magnification factor is nearly 2:1 in stereo 3D. Diffraction eats away at the resolution with modern cameras, keeping in mind these were all designed to be attached to film-era cameras.

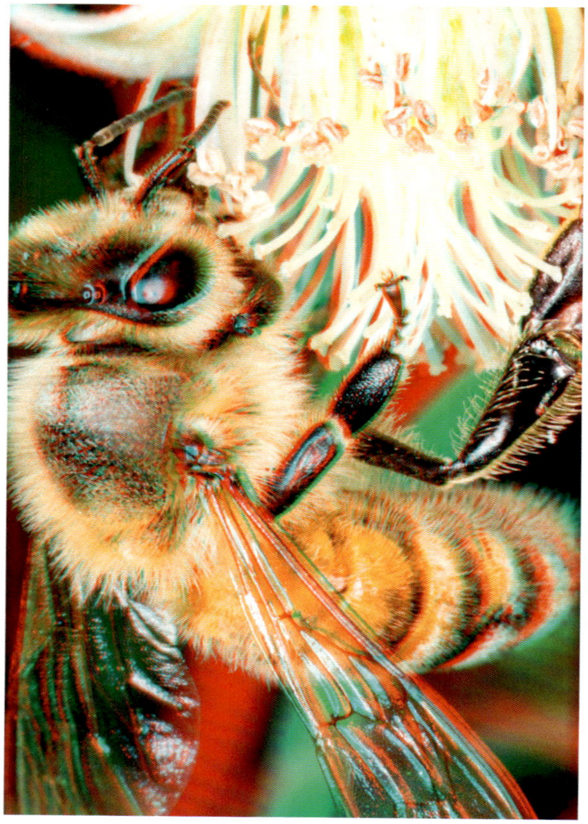

Lenses in this series with lesser magnification perform much better on modern digital cameras. Subjects as large as freezing soap bubbles can be easily shot with them, as well as flowers, insects and more.

Inclusive for all lenses described thus far, the image on the sensor is two separate views of the same subject divided down the middle of the frame. This information likely needs to be interpreted in software for best results, which we will discuss in the 3D editing section of this book.

RED Hydrogen Smartphone

Here's a novel idea – a smartphone capable of taking 3D images – AND displaying them without the need for glasses. RED usually manufactures high end cinema cameras, but this adventure into the smartphone realm was a financial disaster for them and it never met its full potential. Still, for about the price of a Loreo plastic lens, you can get an entire camera system in the second-hand market. It generates two full 12MP images with a landscape orientation that can be useful for many subjects, though it wasn't designed for macro.

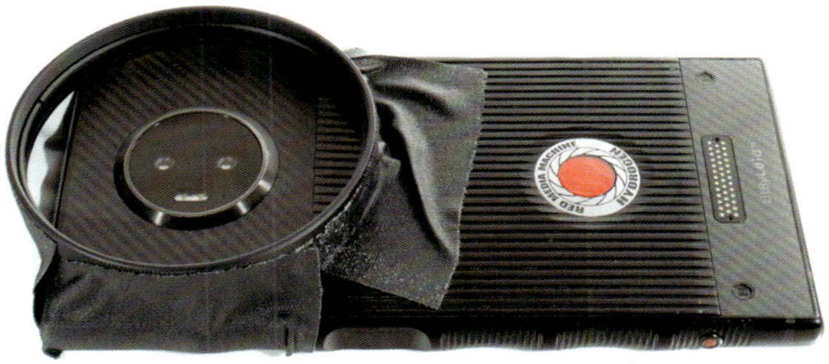

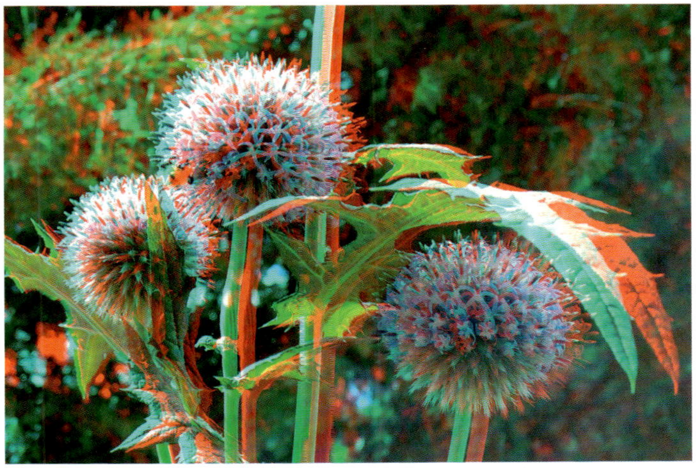

Facing page, left: Image shot with a Loreo 3D Macro lens model 9006. Image was taken at F/22.

Facing page, right: Image taken with the deWijs 3D macro lens model 07-14-F10x14. This lens has a fixed aperture of F/80.

Above right: Image taken with a RED Hydrogen smartphone with the attachment of the Canon 500D close-up filter (*above left*).

Experiment time: can it shoot macro? I decided to tape a Canon 500D close-up filter on the back of it and take it for a spin in the garden. It worked, though not ideal. It's very nice to see the 3D effect as you shoot, though the screen is difficult to see in bright sunlight. Devices like this are a missed opportunity, and like many products made for stereoscopic photography, disappear quickly.

Composing in Three Dimensions

Potentially the hardest element of stereoscopic 3D photography on any scale is how to compose an image with an extra dimension present. Where your subjects intersect with the edge of the frame becomes less important, and depth perception through the frame becomes the overriding principal. Not all subjects are suited for stereoscopic work either; a great example would be snowflakes:

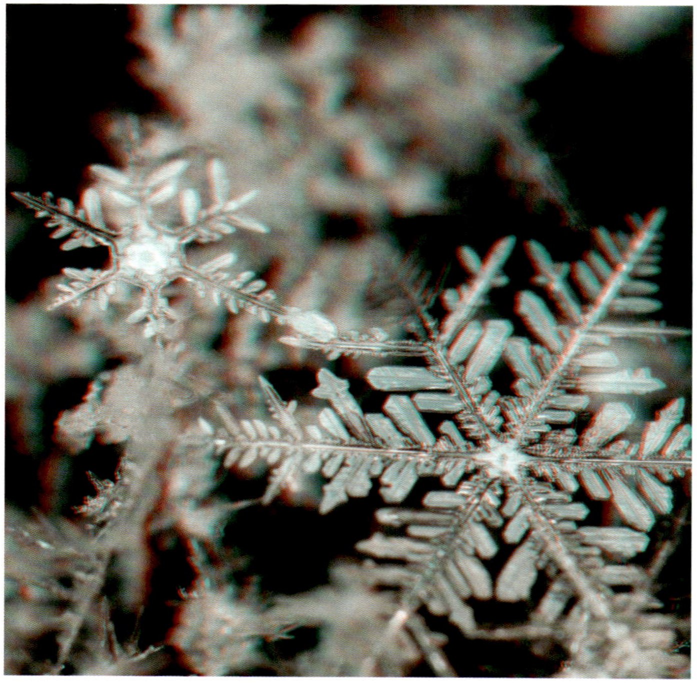

There is some separation between the foreground and the background, but the overall feel is still "flat". And rightfully so – snowflakes are very two dimensional subjects. While endlessly captivating in two dimensions, they don't make the transition to 3D very well. This doesn't stop my own experimentation, and neither should it stop yours. There's bound to be a way to make this work but it hasn't struck me yet. I foresee many additional experiments and mistakes in my future with every possible macro subject. Closely linked to snowflakes would be freezing soap bubbles, which excel when depth information is added:

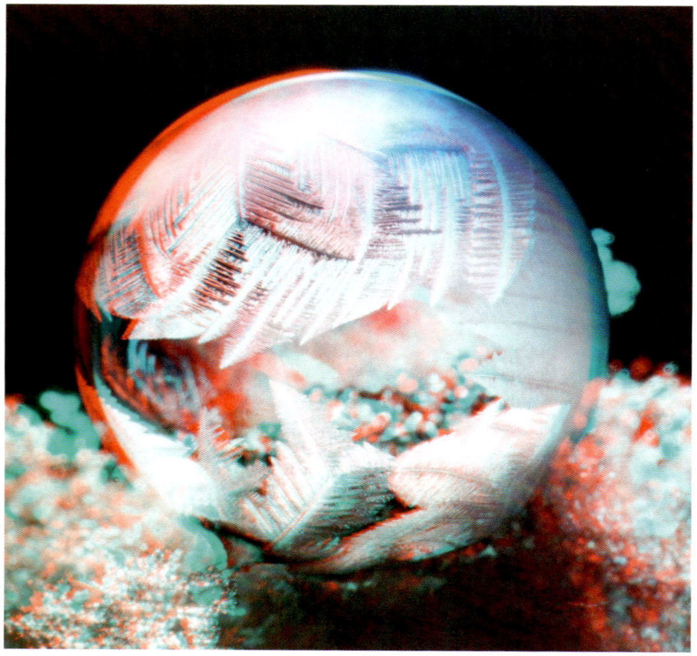

Because the subject has multiple planes of detail through the scene, especially visible in the unfrozen gaps in the bubble, it works well. Elements of an image can lead you through the frame without interacting with the edges. There is a significant amount of trial and error required to build your skills in composing in 3D – similar to when you first started exploring 2D macro photography. Many of the same rules apply in terms of lines, shapes and colours, but lines and shapes that might be completely hidden in a 2D composition now become dominant features.

A great example of this is a photography of an ant tending aphids. The subject is hard to visually isolate in a 2D image, and it seems like certain elements are overlapping and "cluttered". That changes with the addition of a stereoscopic image pair.

The location and position of depth in a 3D composition is paramount to the success of the image. The challenge then becomes previsualizing this with any level of accuracy.

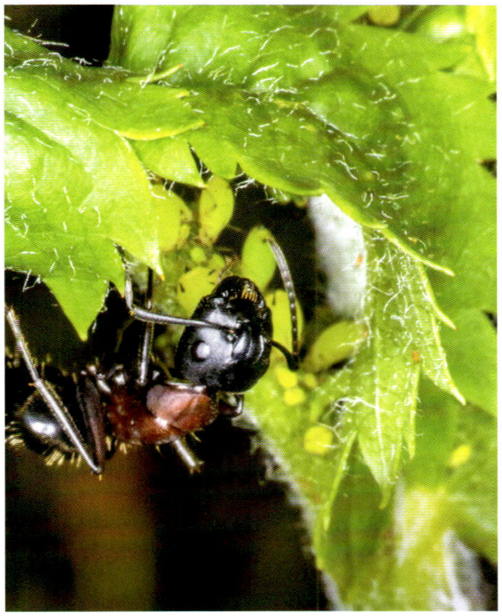

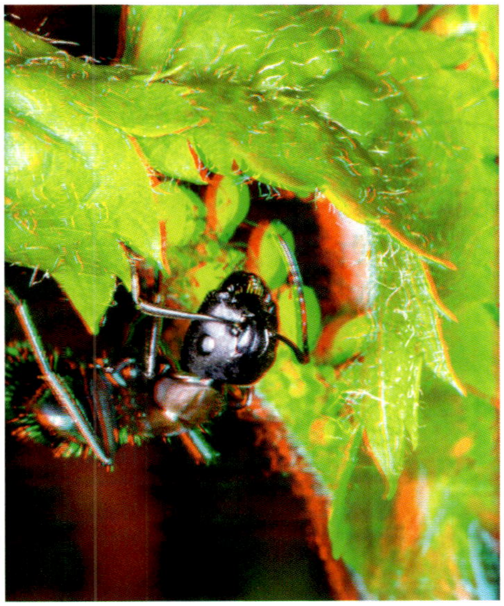

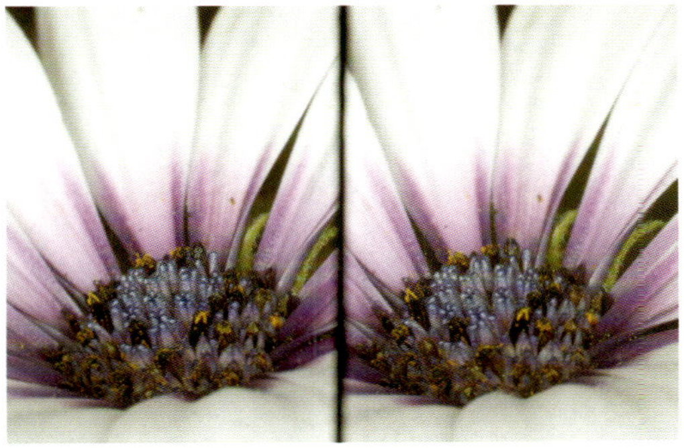

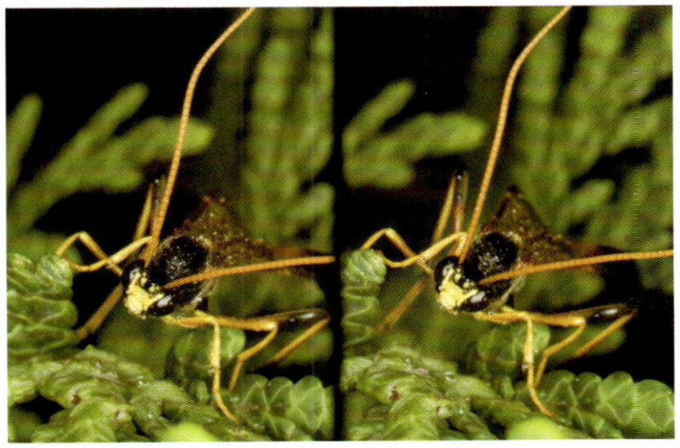

Above: Images on the rear camera screen can be viewed in 3D by crossing your eyes.

Strategy: Crossview Your Rear Screen

Here's a fun tip if you have the ability to "crossview" 3D images by crossing your eyes. Lenses refract light, and when light refracts it "flips". You might not have realized this, but every camera collects light upside down, and software in the camera flips it around for us. A prism viewfinder in a traditional DSLR also flips things back so that we see things in the proper orientation.

Any lens that uses two distinct sets of optics such as the deWijs lenses or the Lumix G 3D 12.5mm lens independently flip the images inside each image circle, and the software on the camera flips the pair of them together. This means that these lenses present an inverted image pair on your LCD screen: the left-eye image is on the right, and the right-eye image is on the left.

While working in the field, potentially even looking at the screen before pressing the shutter button, you can cross your eyes to see the depth of your composition as you're setting up the image. In practicality this is difficult due to glare on the screen, but it is very easy to check your results by moving to a shaded area or draping a sheet over you and your camera.

3D Framing, Focus and Lighting

Photographers encounter a few hurdles when shooting with 3D lenses. When looking through the viewfinder, you'll be seeing two images! Which one do you focus on? I developed a simple strategy: focus on the left image, but give more space around your subject before it hits the left edge of the frame. This advice is inverted if you're using a beamsplitter: focus on the right image, giving more space around the right edge of the frame for the subject.

Each lens has a slightly different view of the subject, and countless times I framed things up perfectly for one eye but missed some part of the subject that was clipped out of frame for the other eye. In general, just give yourself some extra "breathing room" and don't frame too tightly. If you're missing part of your subject, this will come back to haunt you when processing the image and setting the "stereo window".

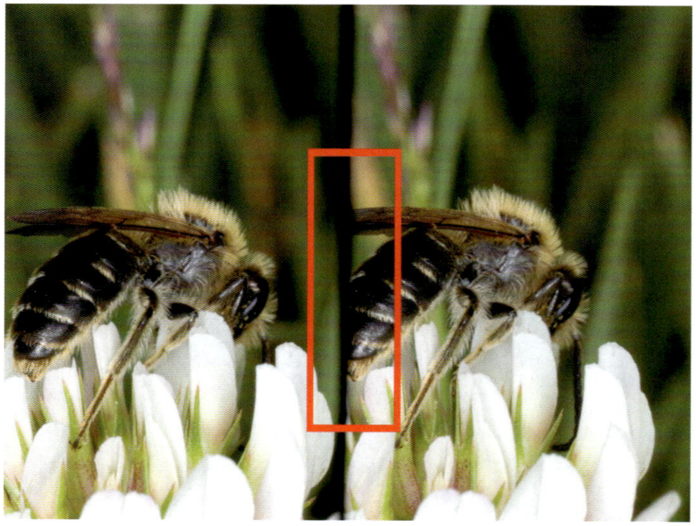

Focusing Techniques

All of these lenses have fixed or manual apertures, with very small openings being commonplace. This maximizes the depth of field so that your eyes can wander around the frame and "refocus" anywhere needed. This is extremely important in stereoscopic imaging. Because these apertures stay small when shooting, it brings up some issues with finding that perfect slice of focus.

Similar techniques to standard macro photography apply: sway back and forth through your desired focus and keep shooting. The trouble here is that your apertures remain very small while shooting, extending your depth and potentially adding diffraction now seen through your viewfinder. It becomes a frustrating guessing game with more misses than hits.

Mirrorless cameras with "focus peaking" are a huge benefit here. The camera will shift some pixels on digital screens (electronic viewfinders and rear LCDs) to a solid colour such as red or blue when they reach their peak focus point. Once activated. this feature more than doubled my hit rate for focus compared to shooting with a traditional DSLR, as you can focus more "by the numbers" without being distracted.

Left: Oops! The subject is being clipped in the view to be seen by your left eye (appearing on the right side of the frame).

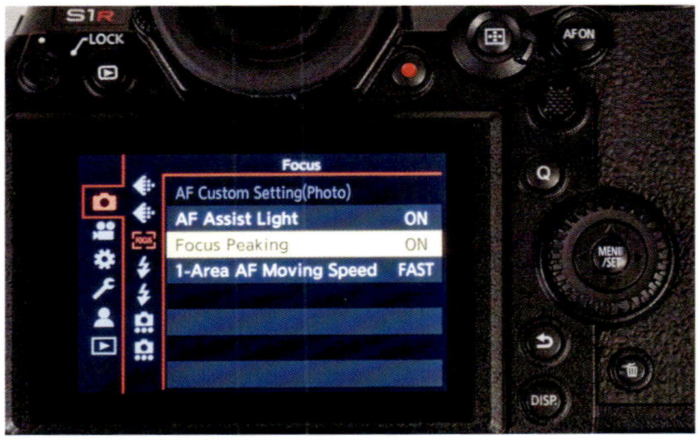

The deWijs 3D lenses were originally constructed with an outstretched physical "window" designed to help you frame and focus on your subject, but they're usefulness on modern cameras is limited. Such a window would have scared off the honeybee that has jumped into the frame (*right*), and focus peaking would only help you vaguely in such a scenario.

No matter what tools you have available and how advanced your technology is, there is a stronger element of luck required here. You'll have far more "near misses" which can be frustrating, but even in those images there is a sense of enjoyment when you see the stereoscopic component; enough to motivate you to keep trying.

Top Left: Focus peaking menu option on a Lumix S1R.

Top Right: Getting a bee in focus, flying into a flower is challenging enough. Try it in 3D to really pull out some hair!

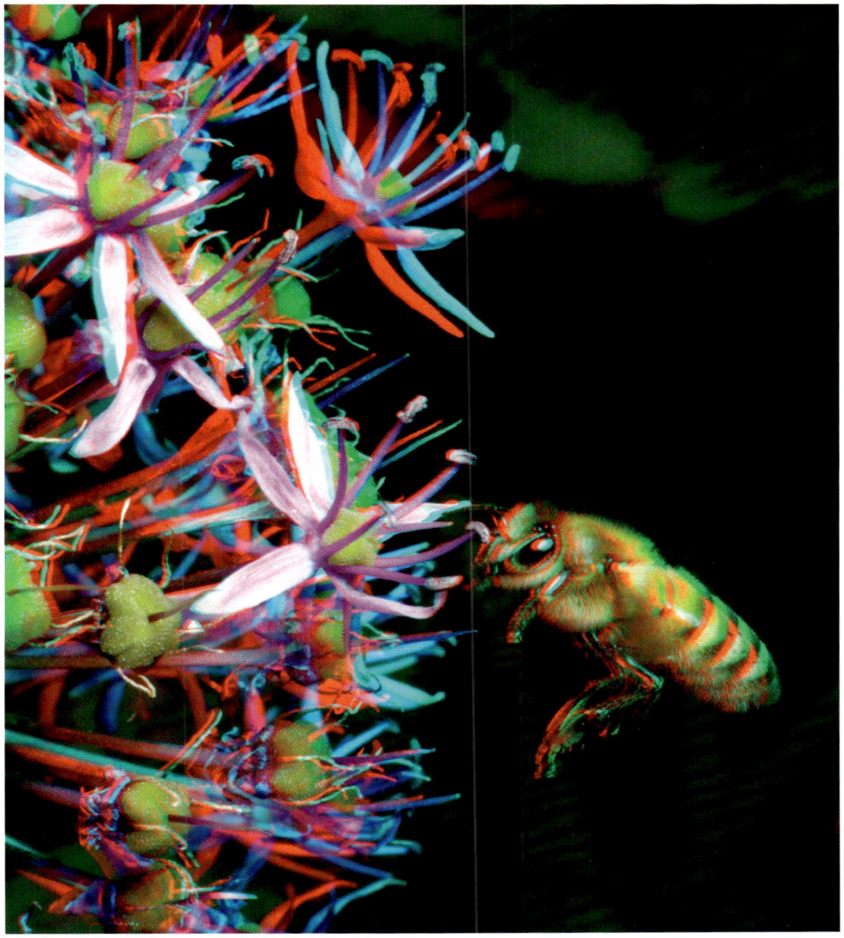

Lighting for 3D (and small apertures)

In order to maintain maximum depth for a better stereoscopic experience, many 3D lenses are designed around small apertures. The deWijs lenses are designed around apertures of F/40 through F/80, and the Loreo lens performs best at F/22. If you want to freeze action or simply to reduce motion blur, you need to be thinking about using a flash.

All of the insect images in this chapter have been shot with a ring flash. The trouble is that only the Loreo lens has a filter thread to mount it properly. I've overcome worse hardships with the use of Gaffer's tape, and this situation is no different.

The instantaneous light from any xenon-based ring flash is a great action stopper, but because of the smaller apertures and desire to shoot for longer continuous bursts, an external battery pack is recommended to keep the flash recycling fast enough to be ready for the next frame. Lithium Ion packs exist, but I find that a Bolt P12 that has 12 additional AA batteries works nicely. A good set of Eneloop rechargeable batteries and you're set to shoot.

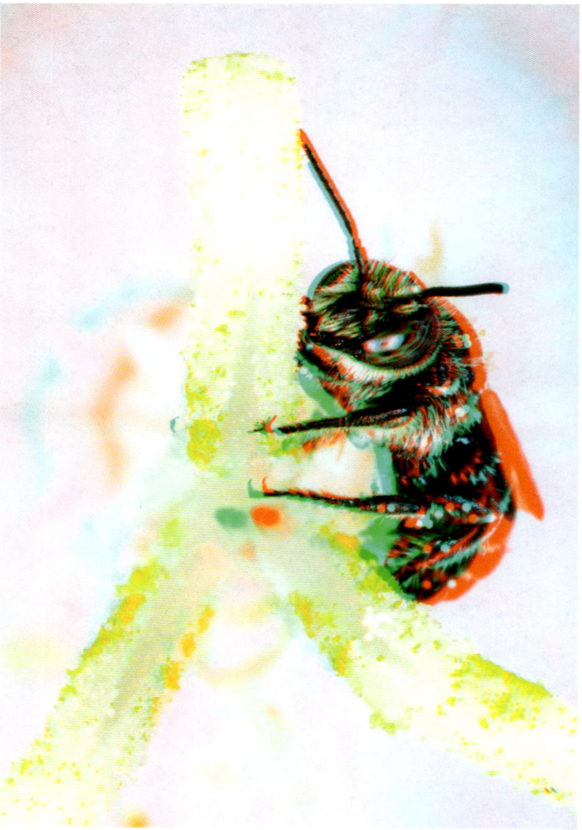

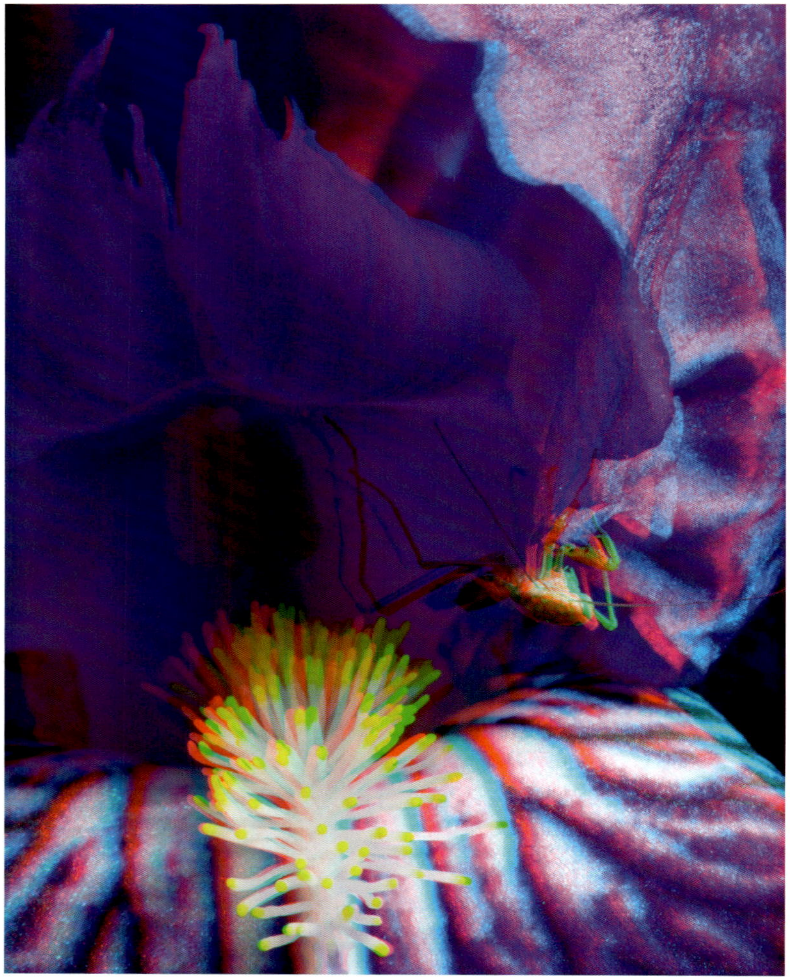

The bees (*left*) and Praying Mantis nymphs (*above*) didn't seem to mind the repeated flashes, though it annoyed some beetles enough to take flight. Lesson learned: to minimize the impact on your subject, bring your ISO up a few notches and use a black umbrella to cast shade into the area. You'll be able to decrease the amount of ambient light and prevent the motion blur it would cause, while also decreasing your flash output. These 3D images survive noise reduction exceptionally well, since you'll be overlapping information in the end anyhow, adding detail in the process.

Off-camera Flash

Just like a ring flash, using a flash off-camera can offer up some significant advantages over ambient light. The same rule applies: using an instantaneous light source results in crisp details with no motion blur.

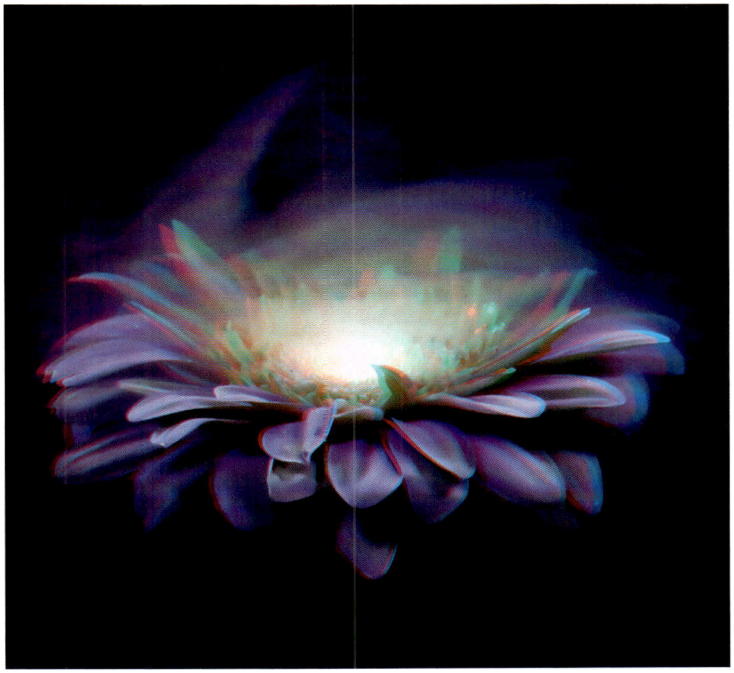

This image (*top*) was created using specially modified ultraviolet flashes and showcases a Gerbera Daisy with a droplet of invisible ink in the center. The ink fluoresces intensely blue, which lights up the center of the flower. To add dimension to this image, a fog machine was activated just prior to the shutter being pressed. The illumination from the fluorescence thereby extends into the fog.

This glowing daisy is a great example of an image taken with the Panasonic Lumix G 3D 12.5mm F/12 lens on a Lumix GX9. It can be more difficult to work with than the extremely rare deWijs lenses, but it has proven itself capable.

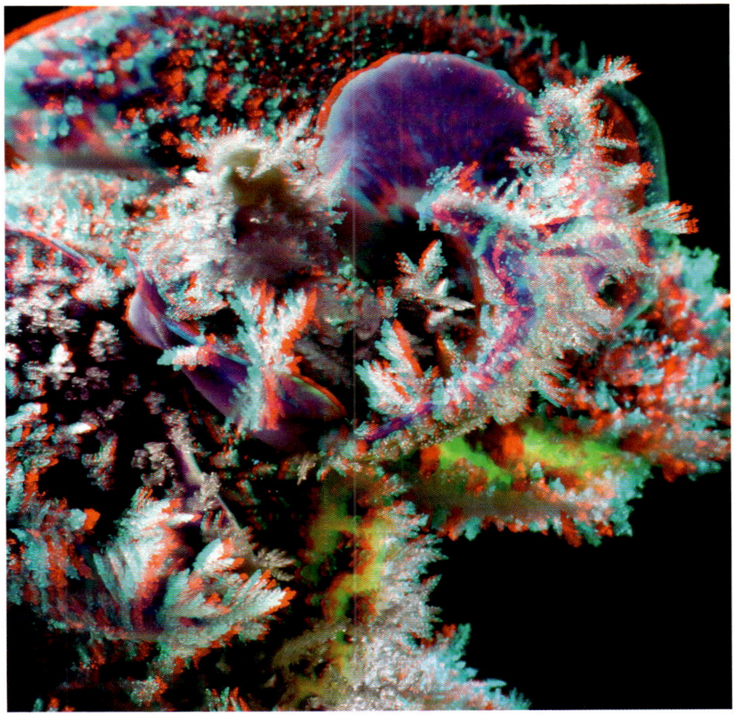

The next image (*bottom*) was an exercise in curiosity: what happens if I leave a miniature orchid flower outside on one of the coldest winter nights? Specifically, what happens when I place it over a heated dog water bowl? The electric coil under the bowl keeps the water from freezing, so it can freely evaporate. It quickly drops back below the freezing point in the air, coalescing into icy formations on the first surface it encounters.

As a 2D image, it's cluttered chaos. In 3D, it takes on a beautifully defined form. Shot with a deWijs lens and an off-camera flash, though I would easily have been able to create an identical image with the focus rail technique described earlier.

3D Image Preparation and Editing

Creating the image in camera is only half the battle. We need to ensure that the two frames align properly and that no important elements of the composition are missing from one side or the other. While there are many ways to accomplish this, the easiest solution is a free software program called StereoPhoto Maker (SPM), created and actively maintained by Masuji Suto. While the software has many robust features, the intention is to illustrate the core concepts.

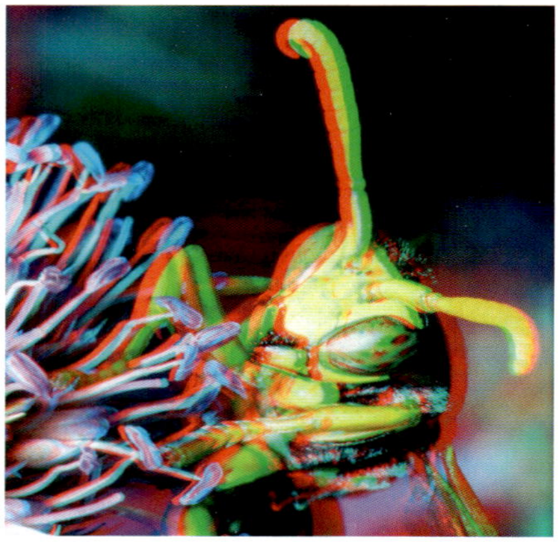

Opening Your Image

While this would seem fairly straightforward, there is one element that you might overlook. First, we need to decide how you took the image: as two separate photographs on a rail, or as a single frame. These options are self-explanatory under the file menu.

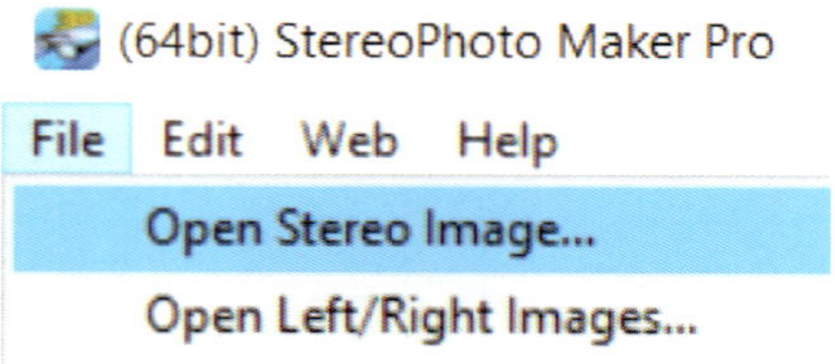

When opening an image taken with a Lumix 3D lens, deWijs lens, or other lens that has two distinct sets of optics, you need to remember that the image pair is inverted. There is a checkbox at the bottom of the window that allows you to swap the left/right images in order for the software to properly interpret them. If you are using a beamsplitter device, including the Loreo 3D lens, this checkbox needs to be left unselected.

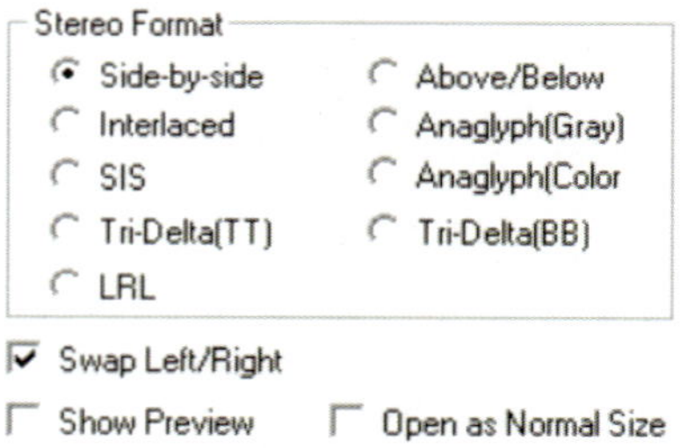

For this tutorial, we will be using a high magnification image of a Bee Balm (*Monarda didyma* L.) flower. The image was taken with a deWijs model 07-14-F10x14 lens, which means that "Swap Left/Right" option needs to be checked. To use the same image to work through this tutorial step-by-step, it can be downloaded here:

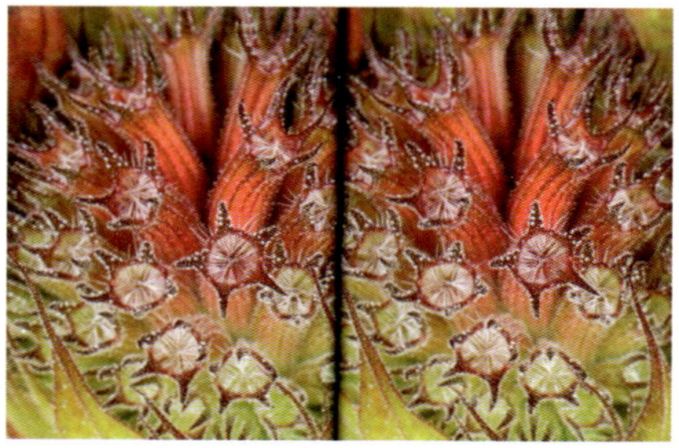

universeatourfeet.com/3d-tutorial.jpg

Aligning Images

No alignment is perfect right from the camera. The horizontal dividing line created by the "septum" inside the lens isn't perfectly straight in this example. The septum is a piece of metal that extends down the barrel of the lens to prevent the light from one set of optics from interfering with the other. It is perfectly straight inside the barrel, so if it appears slightly off? The lens might be rotated by a fraction of a degree off center.

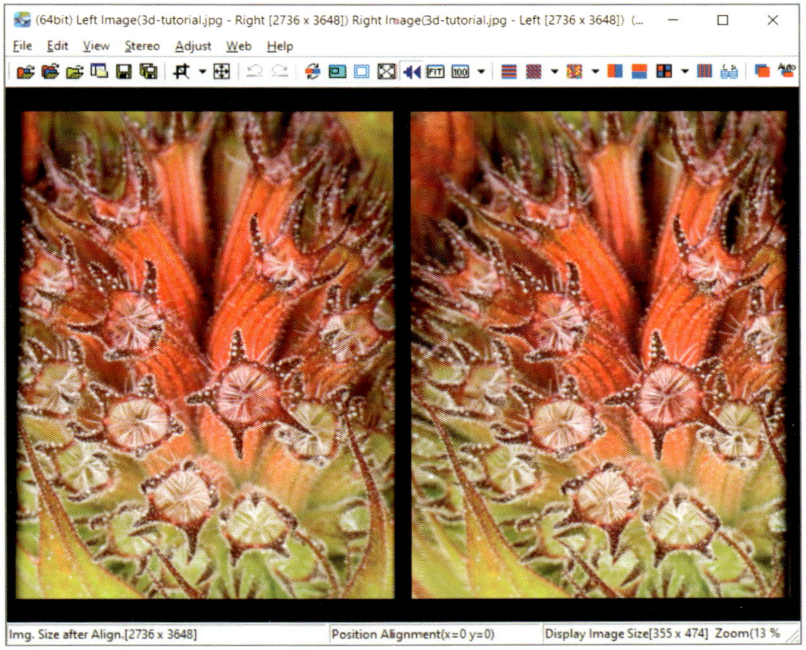

There will likely be rotational, vertical, or horizontal shifts required to bring everything to a good starting point. Thankfully, StereoPhoto Maker has a very good tool to handle this all automatically. Under the "Adjust" Menu, we find an option called "Auto Alignment". This handles the heavy lifting for us in most cases, such as this image. It will display an output of what it has calculated and adjusted.

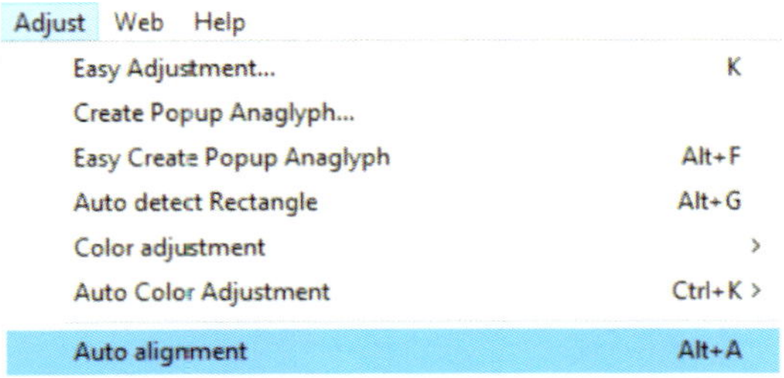

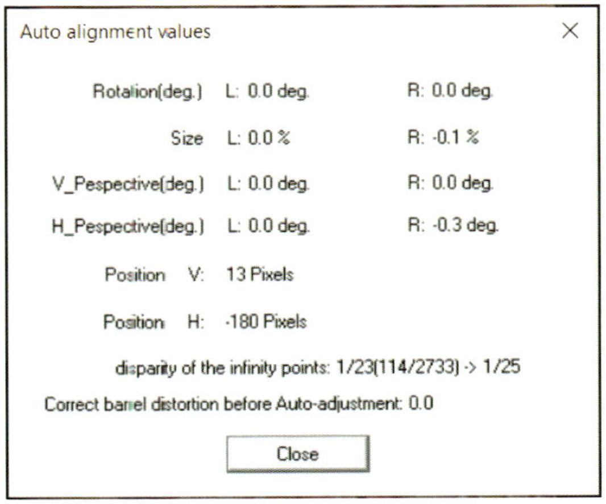

This is where we begin our editing journey. Just like focus stacking in Photoshop which offers an automated initial output, we can fine tune the results. Also under the "Adjust" menu we find the "Easy Adjustment" tool. If the Automatic alignment fails or it isn't perfectly accurate, we can take control of the results to our liking.

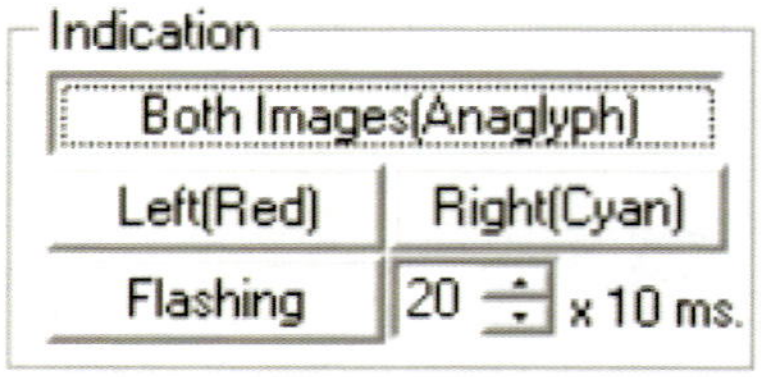

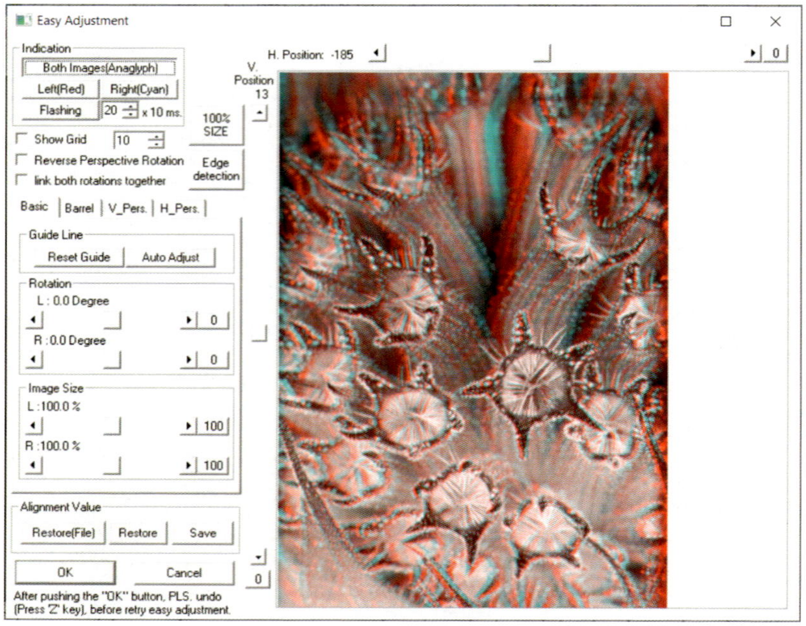

We can take control of all of the adjustments that the automatic process made with sliders. Pay special attention to the "Indication" options at the top, which allow you to view either the left or right eyes independently, and flip between them to see the image "wiggle". Here, we're looking for signs that some element of the image near the edge of the frame needs to be aligned better. This is effectively setting the "Stereo Window".

Setting the Stereo Window

The center of a stereo image is usually well enough aligned to generate a 3D effect, but what about the edges? If they don't line up properly, you could have objects in your image appear to one eye, but have no corresponding information for the other eye to perceive in 3D. This creates visual artifacts that cause portions of the image to appear flat. This can be jarring, especially if you have an element of the image with prominent stereoscopic depth that suddenly drops back down to 2D with no depth information.

Thankfully, this image doesn't need much tweaking. This is not always the case, especially when taking images on a rail or with a modified Lumix 3D lens. Let's take a look at an image requiring an extreme adjustment when we're finished with this image.

The Stereo Window is also defined by cropping, so that the elements that actually appear at the edges are properly represented. This tool automatically crops when the H. Position slider is moved. Experiment with this – move that slider left and right while wearing anaglyph glasses. The crop will be adjusted as the amount of overlapping information decreases. Past a certain point, you'll notice that your eyes can no longer perceive the stereoscopic effect.

Final Output

You can choose to create a Side-by-Side image, anaglyph and others. Since you've got your anaglyph glasses handy, click through the colour and gray menus to see the differences in how the two images can be interwoven together. Some images appear to have a stronger 3D effect when set to a monochromatic anaglyph, but all of the colour is lost.

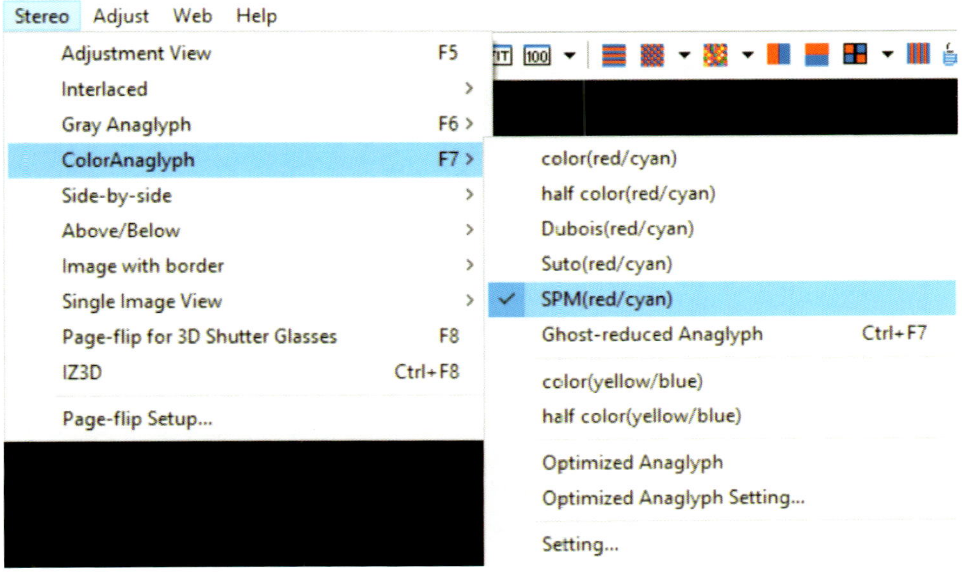

Much of the colour information doesn't survive this process anyhow. I ended up liking the results of the "SPM" algorithm the best, and while you can see the red tones of the original image without the glasses, this gets obscured when seen in 3D. As mentioned earlier, the anaglyph format is very accessible but it has drawbacks. Attempting to overlay the same information in the same space with coloured filters will inherently lead to a loss of information, traded for depth.

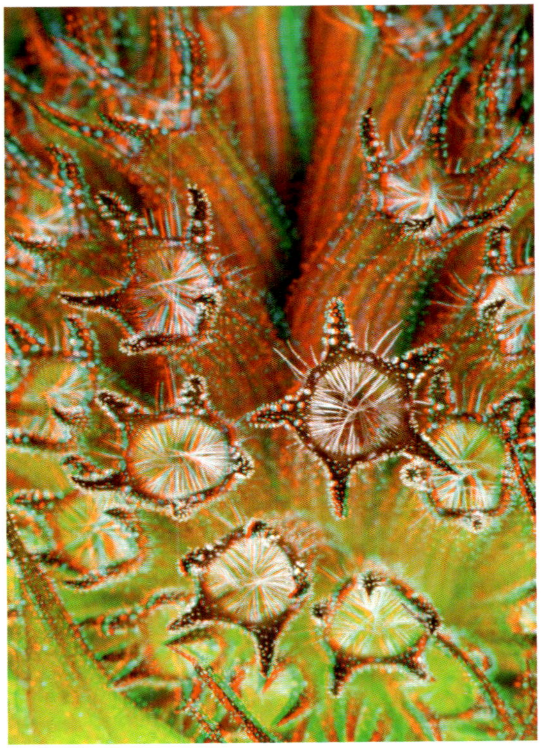

Saving Your Image

Regardless of how you're currently viewing the image, you can save it in any format you'd like: Side-by-Side, anaglyph, .MPO files for 3D TVs and even as an animated GIF that wiggles back and forth. It's all under the file menu.

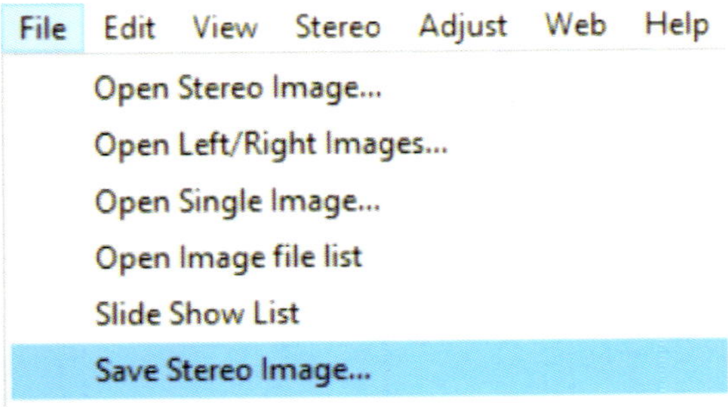

Challenging Stereo Windows

Not all stereo windows align so well. A perfect example is images taken with a modified Lumix 3D lens, where an increasing number of washers will shift the focus closer and closer forward. In its original design, there is a very good overlap of the resulting left and right images. The further you shift the focus forward, the further out of alignment they will become.

The best example I have of this is a photograph of a bee taken in a village in rural Bulgaria. When you travel, why not bring a 3D lens along? This was modified with 1.5mm of washers for a very strong 3D macro feel, but that also introduces frustrations. It was this image that finally taught me what a stereo window really should be defined as.

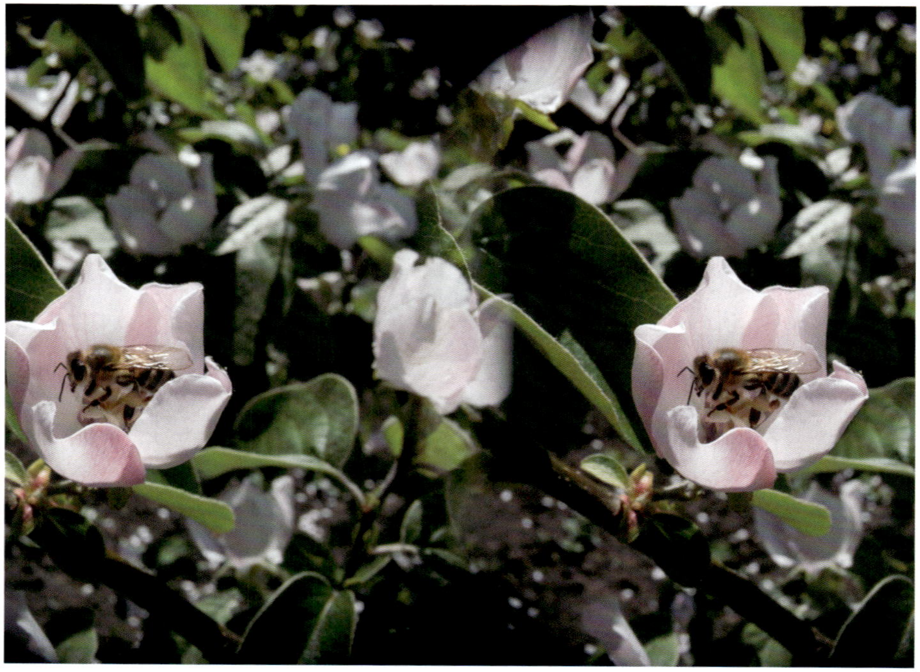

First, look at the image as it appears straight out of camera. We have a bee frolicking in a flower! Notice how the right image is centered nicely, but the left image has the flower pushed all the way to the edge of the frame, clipping part of the flower. **This will be problematic.**

When this image is loaded into StereoPhoto Maker, the auto alignment feature does not go far enough. We'll need to push farther using the "Easy Adjustment" tool. The problem arises because of the disparity in the background vs. the foreground. If I were to force the foreground to be aligned on the edge of the flower, this would push the background so far out of alignment that it wouldn't have any perceivable depth – just some random cluttered colours that our eyes can't recombine into recognizable objects.

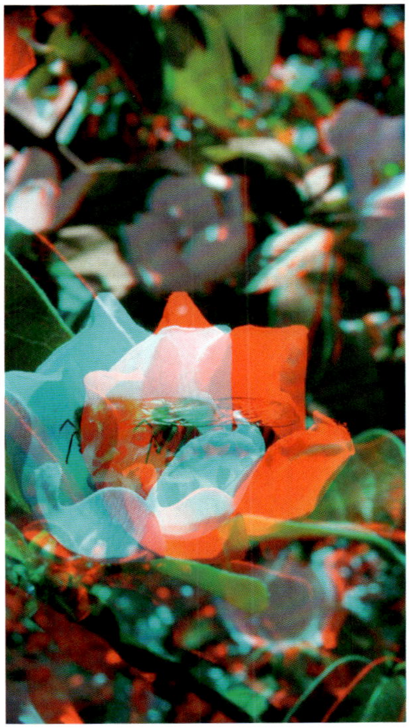

Left Side: The results from "Auto alignment". Notice how it favours the background to be aligned and the foreground to be greatly separated. Especially when looking at the left edge of the flower in 3D, I see a very strong "invisible line" hitting the edge of the frame. The window is misaligned.

Right side: This version has been realigned using the Easy alignment tool. Notice that the flower is very much aligned at the left edge of the frame, but the separation of the background is extreme. Partly because the background is less in focus and due to the separation, it's difficult for my eyes to reconcile the depth. Not an impossible task, but it takes effort.

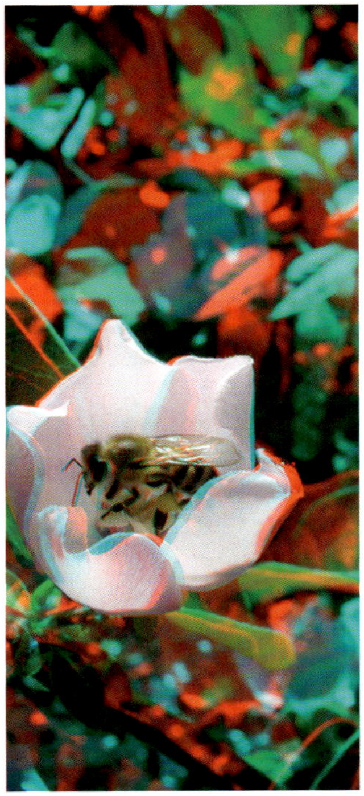

Thankfully, the answer here can be simple. Keep cropping. Just because the stereo window doesn't overlap to any great extent doesn't mean you cannot make a useable image. If you were to crop down to just the flower, much of the background "interference" would be eliminated. We can take this even further.

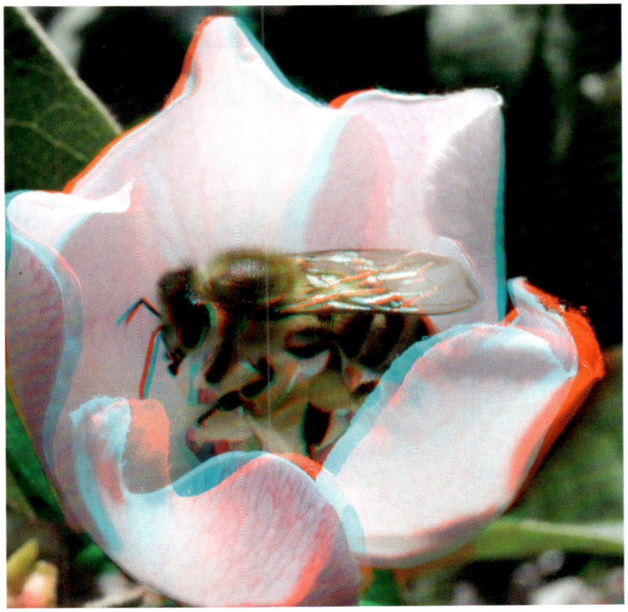

What if you were to overlay one of the original images in Photoshop, and create a layer mask to paint in the elements surrounding the flower? Those parts of the image would thereby have no perceptible stereoscopic effect. Care must be taken not to intersect with the anaglyph red/cyan information, so always double-check your work by putting the glasses on to see if anything looks unusual.

The image was shot on a Lumix GH5, which offers up 20MP of resolution. In the end, we're down to just under two megapixels. Remember that the depth information from one image is overlayed onto another, allowing us to perceive more detail. This is also why high magnification images such as the Bee Balm example, which suffer greatly from diffraction, will appear dramatic when fully processed.

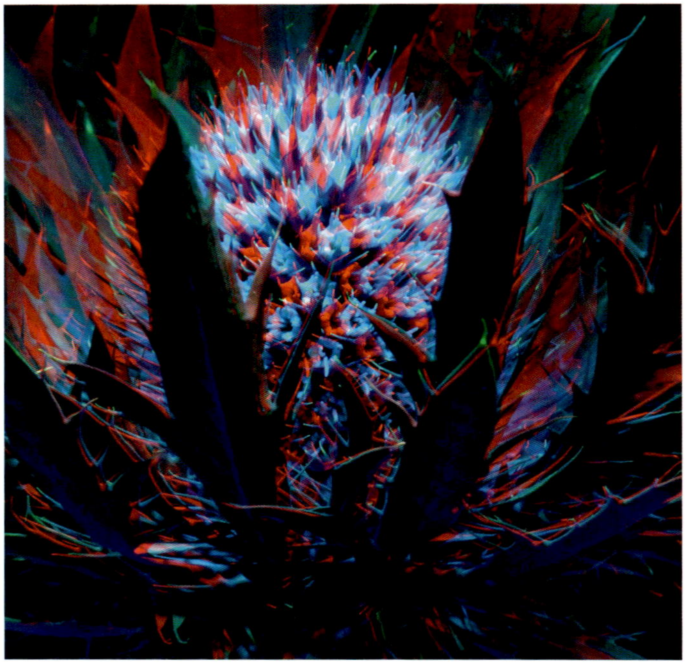

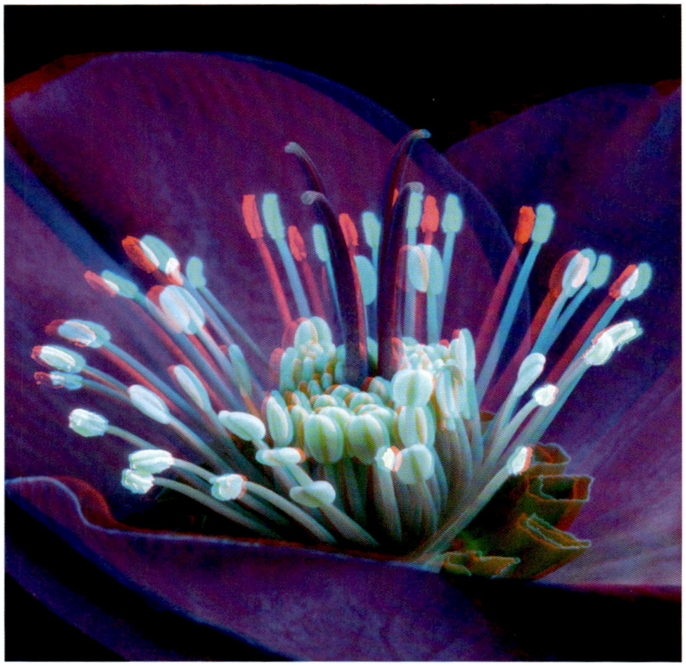

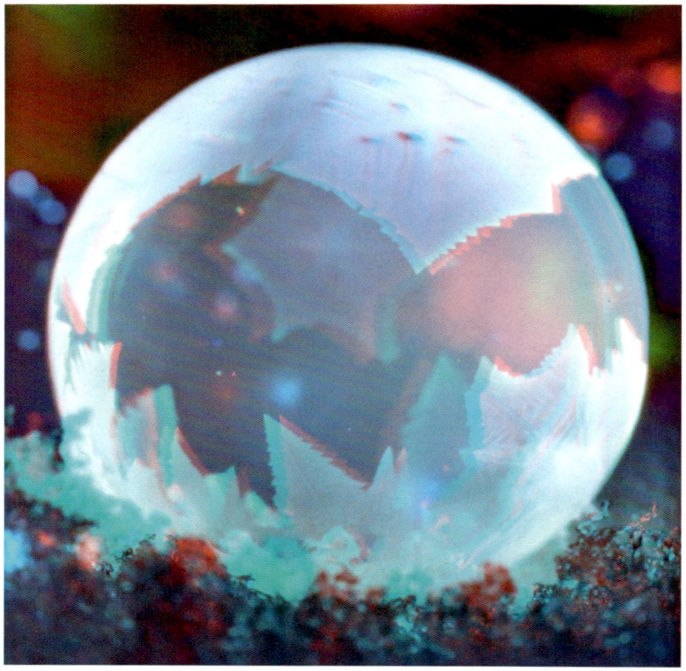

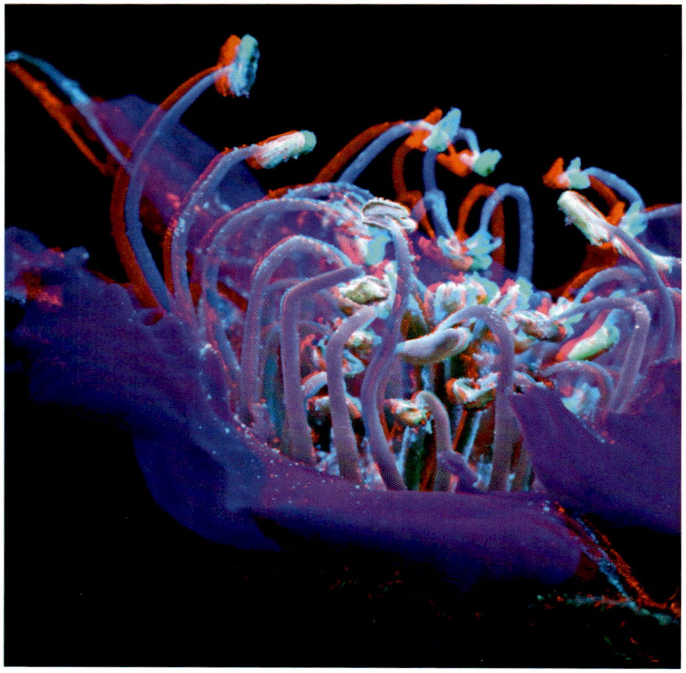

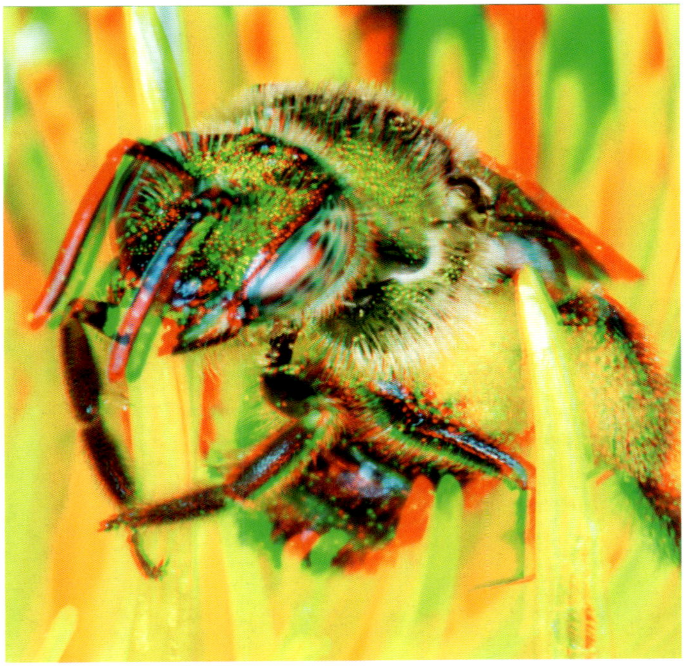

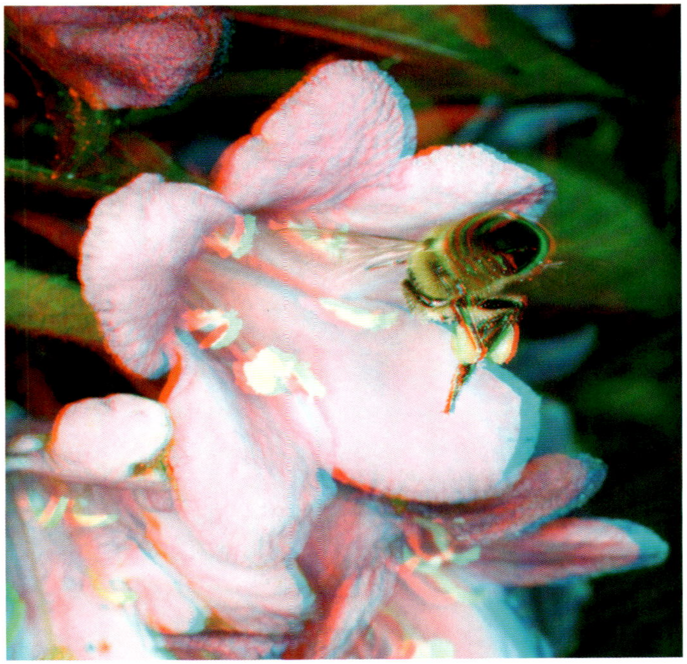

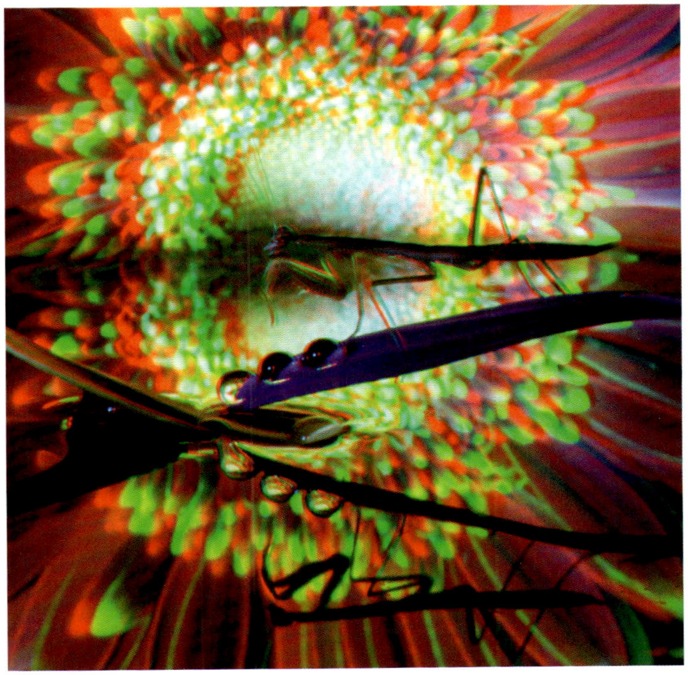

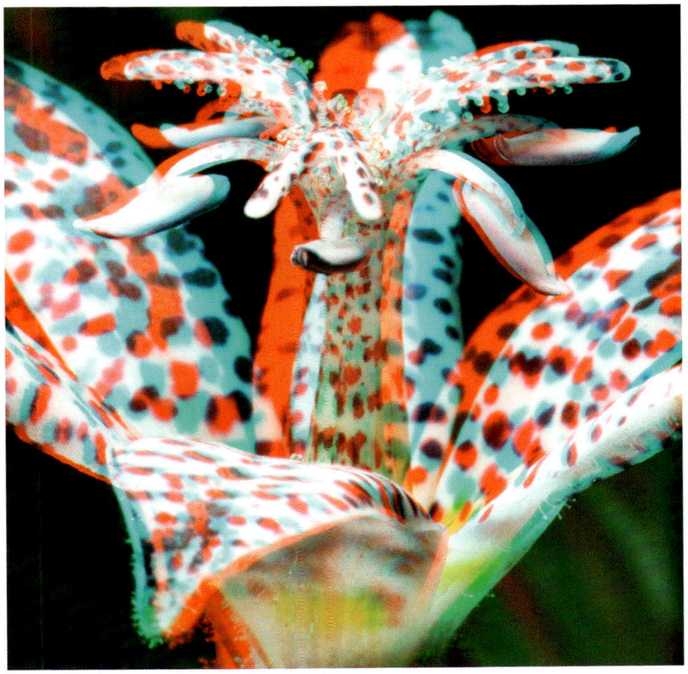

Taking 3D Further

Stereoscopic 3D photography is a passion project for me. I doubt it will ever return to the era when a large portion of the population enjoyed stereoviews daily. There might come a day when "no glasses required" 3D viewing is ubiquitous on all our digital screens, but the technology isn't there yet. Even if it was, a concerted effort would be required from all photographers to start thinking about compositions with depth. Just because an image is beautiful in 2D doesn't mean adding a third dimension will improve it. A boring snapshot in 2D would not be magically transformed when viewed in 3D. This makes the results feel gimmicky if not properly understood and executed.

Still, there is a community of stereoscopic enthusiasts globally. Currently there are two publications, *Stereo World Magazine* published by the National Stereoscopic Association and *Stereoscopy*, published by the International Stereoscopic Union.

I strongly encourage you to experiment in this niche of macro photography, and stereoscopic photography in general. Like seeing a magical transformation when a flower fluoresces, adding depth to your imagery can ignite your curiosity and imagination. It's not for everyone, and your friends and family will think you've lost a few marbles if you ask them to cross their eyes or put on anaglyph glasses.

The further you go down this particular rabbit hole, the more you'll discover. Unfortunately, you'll also find fewer people with whom you can share and enjoy your creations.

To make the barrier of enjoyment fade away, you can have your images turned into lenticular prints. View-Master™ compatible reels can also be made to bring you right back to your childhood, now with your own images. Imagine the delight of handing such a gift to a child today to spark their imagination.

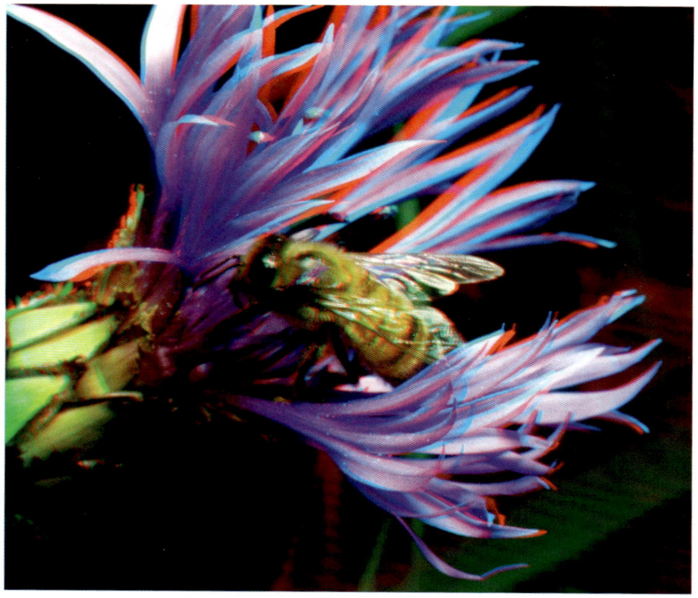

Above: Honey bee in a Bachelor's Button flower (*Centaurea cyanus*).

Facing page: A freezing soap bubble nestled in a frozen orchid.

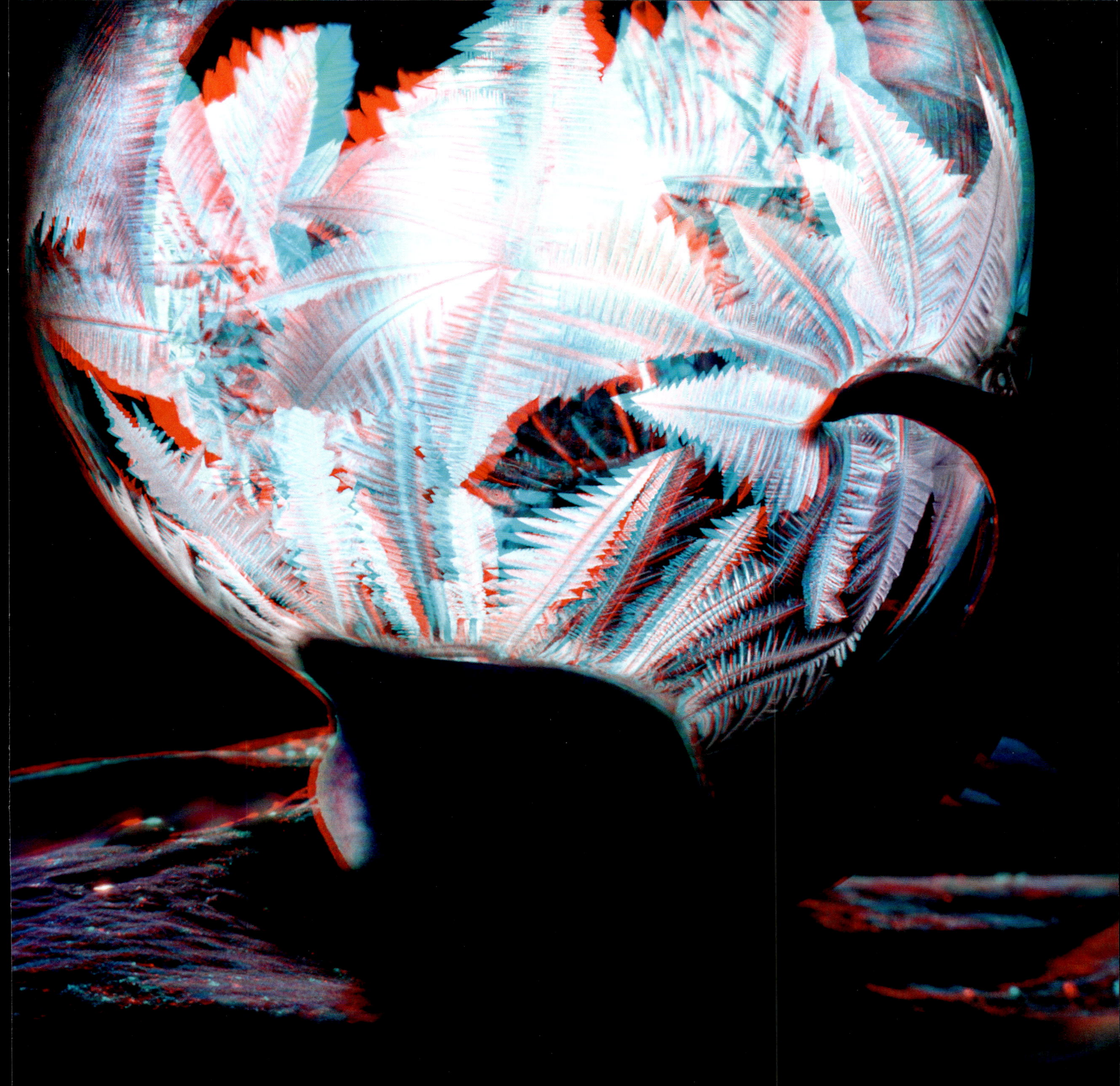

Epilogue

The beginning of this project was full of lighthearted excitement to create a book that both educated and entertained, combining over a decade of work and many thousands of hours. The book lives up to that goal, but to cross the finish line, it wasn't easy. Some experts will tell you that the final 10% takes 90% of the effort. A similar aphorism is the "Ninety-ninety rule", humorously written by Tom Cargill in 1985 at Bell Labs and relates to computer programming: "*The first 90 percent of the code accounts for the first 90 percent of the development time. The remaining 10 percent of the code accounts for the other 90 percent of the development time.*"

Indeed, this book has taken considerably more development time than originally intended. I hope that it shows through the detailed descriptions and fine-tuned page layouts, but there's more to this story. While the book was originally delayed to add additional content, productivity came to a grinding halt due to the COVID-19 pandemic. The best work done on this project was when I would have 6-8 hours in complete isolation. This was replaced with a different kind of isolation, with my wife and daughter being home 24/7, later replaced with many "Daddy Daycare" moments and ultimately transforming me into a teacher's assistant for my daughter's virtual kindergarten class. Such an immediate pivot!

As you've read the book, you no doubt understand me to be a detail-oriented, fact loving science geek as much as I am a photographer. This spills over into other areas of life including interests in biology, space exploration and computer science. With plenty of fear and bleak unknowns, I found myself "doomscrolling" news and social media in search of answers which only served to keep my body's "fight or flight" response engaged. All the while, my primary focus was on family. There were periods of time when this book was not a part of my daily workflow anymore.

Compounded by people close to me receiving cancer diagnoses as well as some contracting COVID-19, there were many elements involved in derailing this project and delaying its release. "Life" became an obstruction. Finding a creative spark became increasingly difficult.

While family and friends offered the support structure needed to be happy, this did not equate to professional motivations; I rarely picked up my cameras in 2020.

It's not all bad. I learned to cook! I discovered the science of indoor and greenhouse gardening. This tendril (*right*) is from a cucumber vine, with parthenocarpic properties, which means that the flowers do not require pollination to produce fruit, and unpollinated flowers will produce fruit without seeds. The things you learn in a pandemic, right? This was photographed in April 2020, during an initial push for a greater degree of self-sustainability. At the time, I was hopeful that we'd be on the other side of this global crisis by mid-summer. As I write the final words of this book, it is now January 2021.

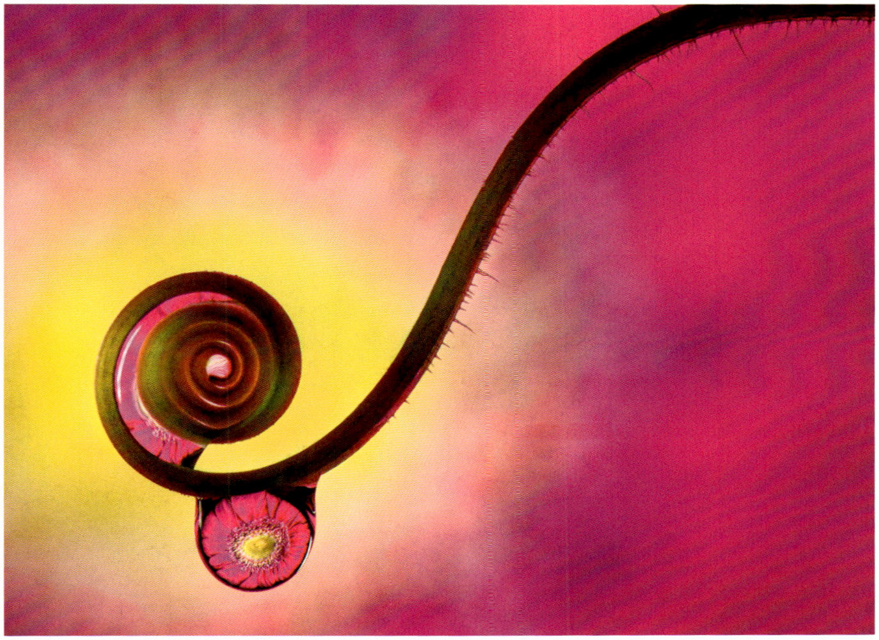

If you're reading this in print, then mission accomplished. This has been by far the largest project I have ever embarked on and is now complete. While my sanity was ruffled during the final year of production, seeing this project in its completed form gives me inspiration to pick up my camera again. There have been many photographic ideas stored away in the back of my mind while I waited for that creative energy to re-emerge. With the beginning of 2021, that energy is back.

I owe it to the people who supported this project from the very beginning. Thank you to everyone who has been patient and understanding through all of the delays and would simply say "I can't wait for the book, whenever I get it". This, combined with encouragement from my family and friends, and especially my wife. As I write this, she and my daughter are chasing each-other around upstairs while laughing, filling this home with elation and contentedness.

This epilogue may read differently a few years from now, as I have no idea what 2021 will truly bring for my own creativity as well as the global shift to whatever we'll call "normal" in the future. The world is still very much in flux, while my intent was to create this book as a timeless publication that should be equally relevant a decade or more beyond its publication date. You be the judge if I have succeeded.

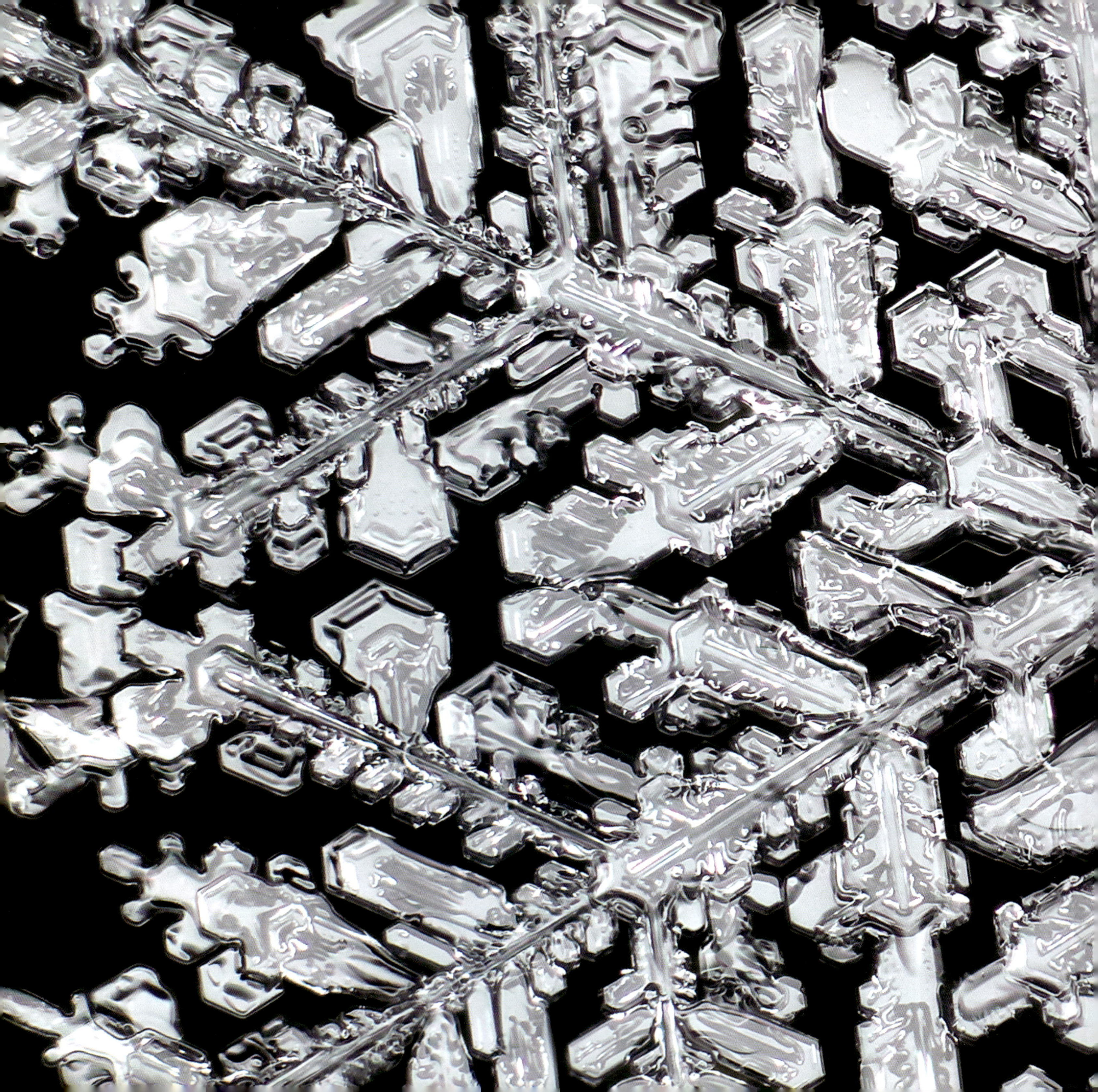

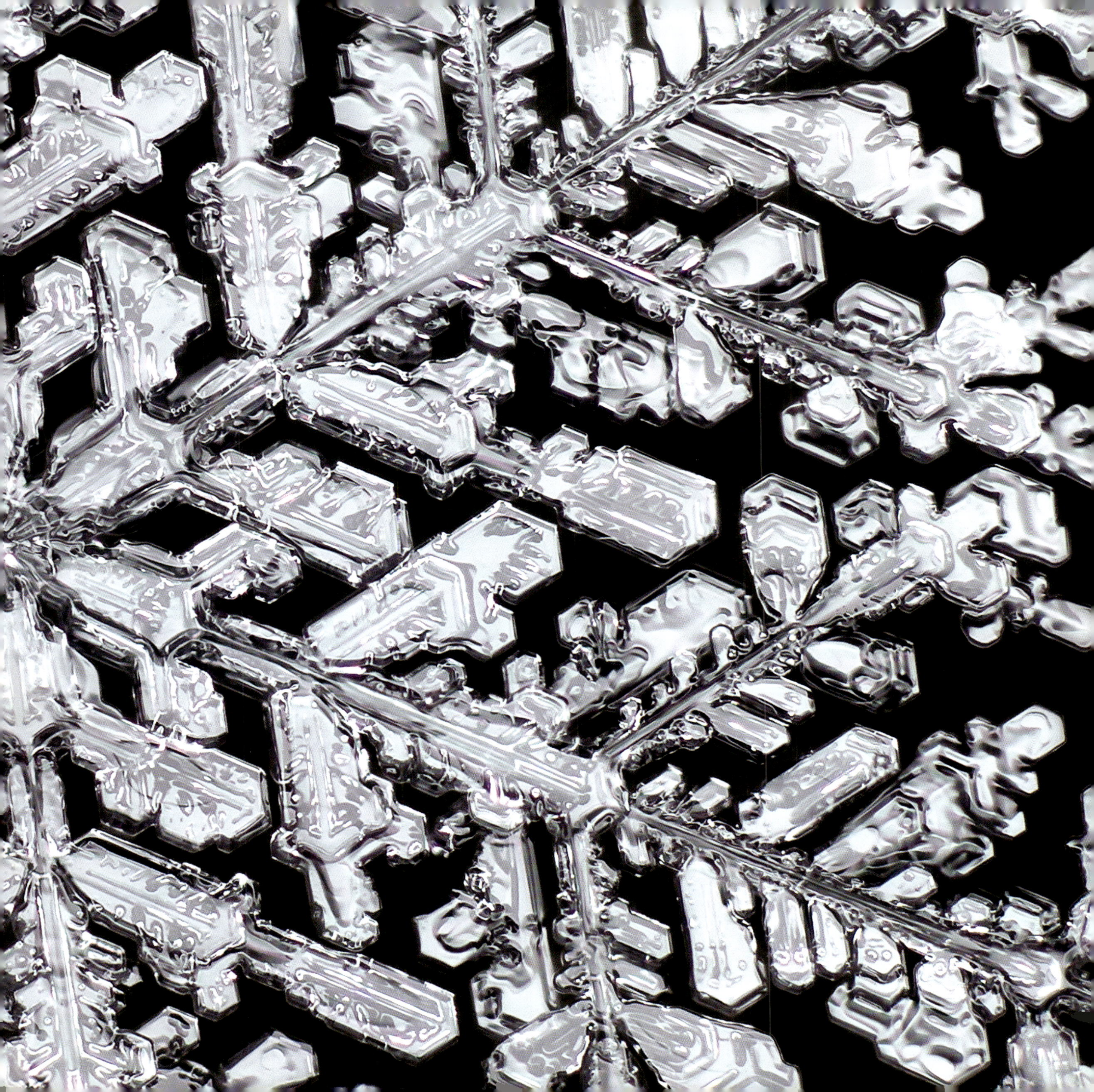

About the Author

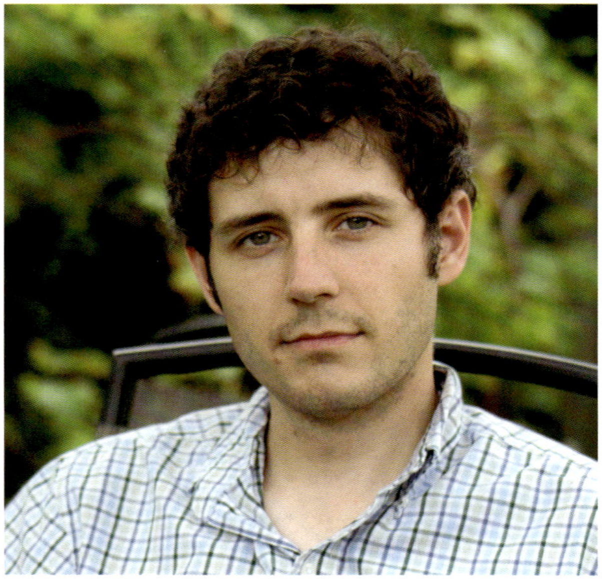

Photo Credit: Sean Galbraith

Don Komarechka is a nature, macro and landscape photographer located in Barrie, Ontario, Canada. From auroras to pollen, insects to infrared, much of Don's photographic adventures reveal a deeper understanding of how the universe works. Exploring the world that we cannot see with our own eyes has been a common thread in Don's career as a professional photographer.

Always science-minded but never formally trained, Don uses photography as a way to explore and understand the world around him. Photographing something unusual or unknown is the perfect excuse to learn something new. Don's work often pushes up against the technical limitations of modern camera equipment and the physical limitations of light itself.

More of Don's photography, books and workshops can be found at his website, **www.donkom.ca**

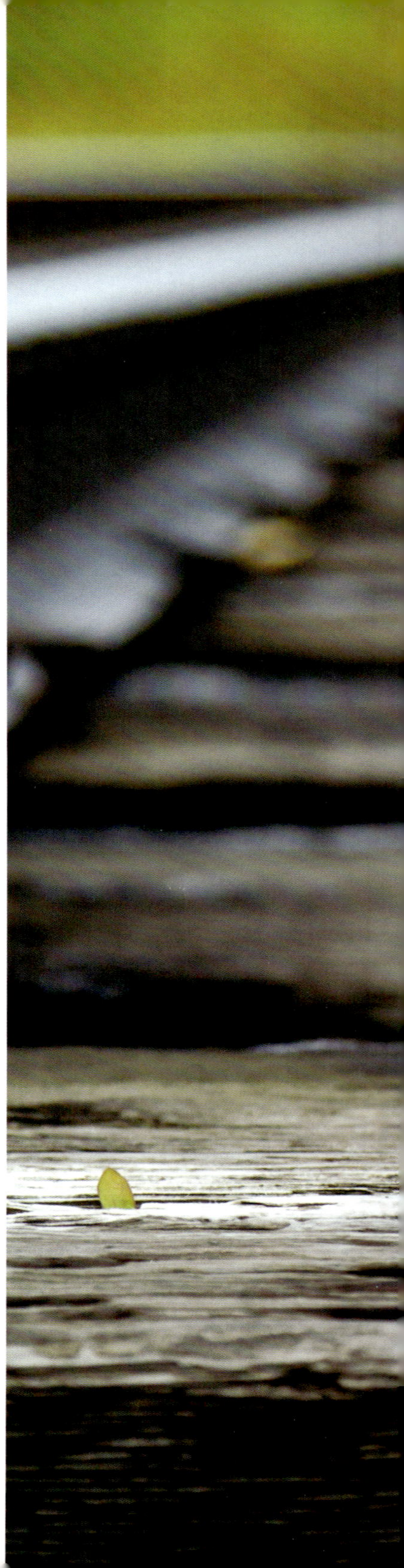

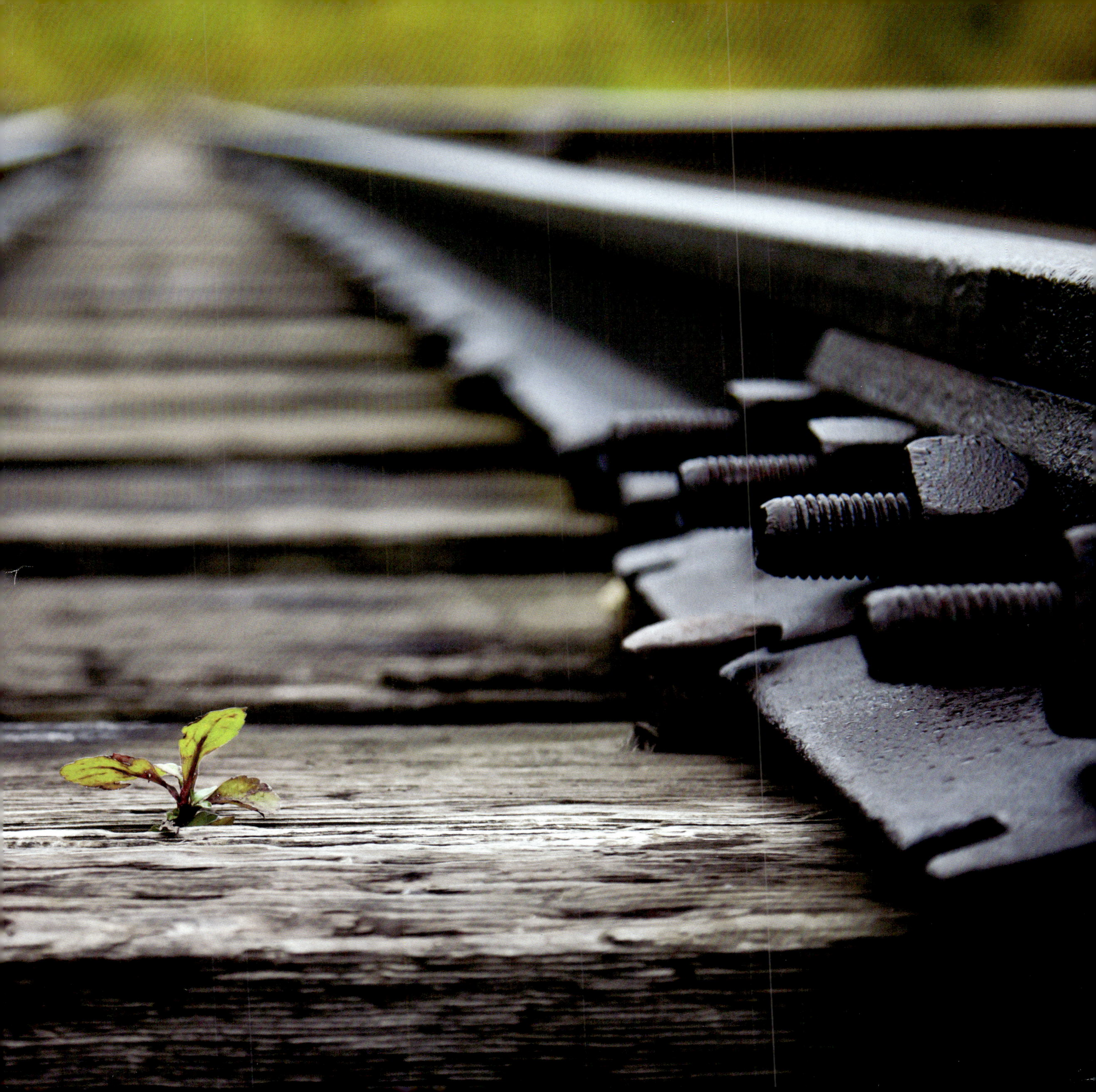

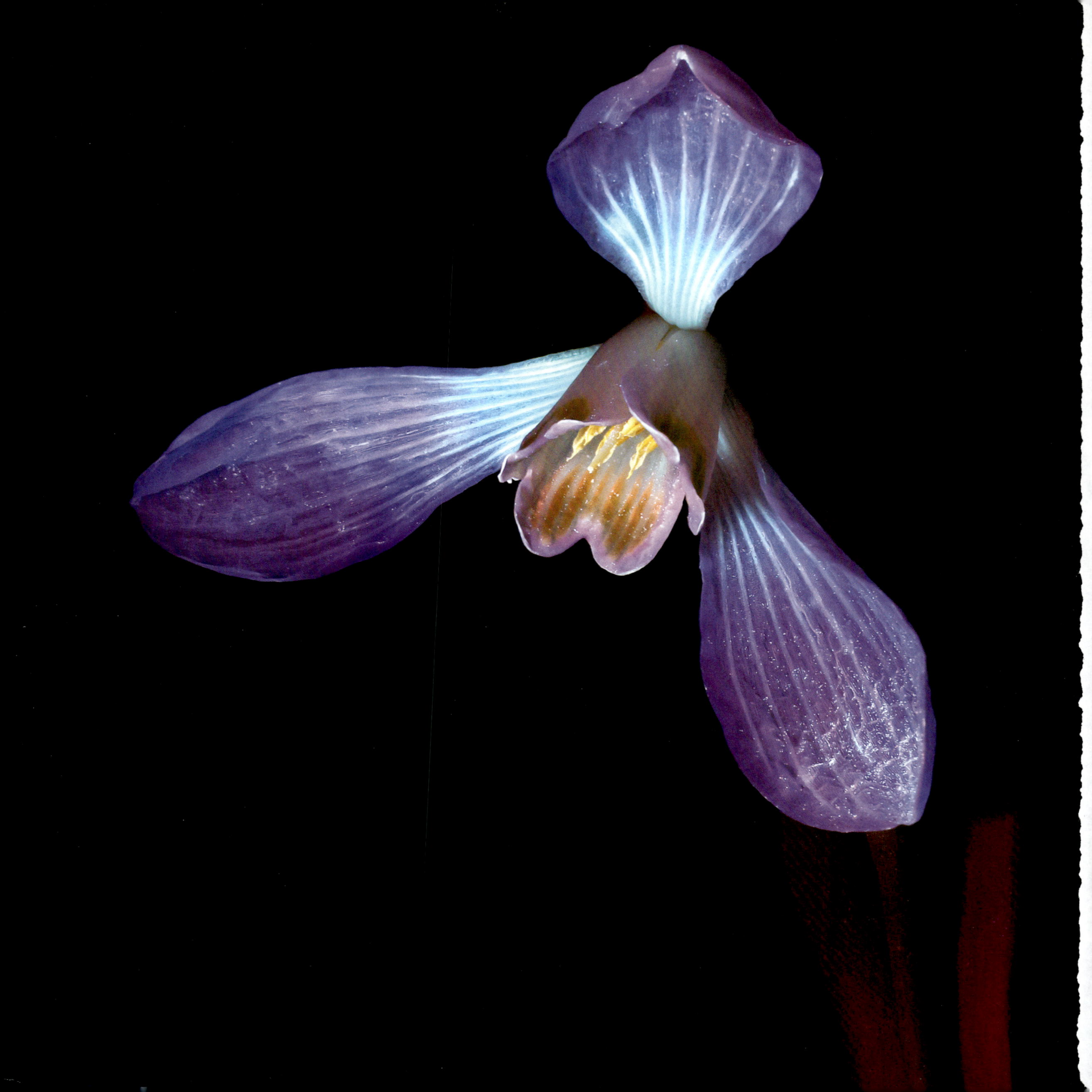